U0591250

出版说明

　　人类历史的发展过程也是思想文化不断积累和沉淀的过程。在几千年的人类历史发展长河中，先贤们或在人文社科领域，或在科学技术领域创作出了无数经典名著。这些著作所蕴藏的思想财富和学术价值，早已为世人所熟知，它们无不体现了作者所处的特定时代的思想和文化。通过这些经典名著，读者不仅可以欣赏到流畅的文笔、生动的描述和详细的刻画、深邃的思想，更可以领悟它们各自独特的历史与文化内涵。可以说，这些作品深深地影响了世世代代的读者，也引导着当今的学人以此来充实和丰富自己的头脑。有鉴于此，我们邀请了专门研究世界历史文化的专家学者，精心挑选代表世界历史文化不同领域的经典作品，采取英汉双语对照的形式出版，一方面为读者提供原汁原味的世界经典名著，让读者自由地阅读，在此过程中逐渐提升自己的英语水平；另一方面通过这种阅读，以达到对世界历史文化的整体了解，开阔自己的视野，打开通往世界的心灵之窗，同时又获得思想文化、个人修养、伦理道德等多方面的提升。

　　我们衷心期待这套书成为大家学习道路上不可或缺的好伙伴！如果您在阅读中发现有疑问或错误之处，请不吝指正，以便我们更加完善这套书。

英国语文 ⑥

（英汉双语）

［英］托马斯-尼尔森公司⊙编　季　翊⊙译

THE ROYAL READERS

北京工业大学出版社

图书在版编目（CIP）数据

英国语文.6：英汉对照 / 英国托马斯–尼尔森公司
编；季翊译. — 北京：北京工业大学出版社，2017.7
ISBN 978–7–5639–5266–3

Ⅰ.①英…　Ⅱ.①英…②季…　Ⅲ.①英语 – 教材
Ⅳ.①H31

中国版本图书馆CIP数据核字（2017）第060380号

英国语文 6（英汉双语）

编　　者：〔英〕托马斯–尼尔森公司

译　　者：季　翊

责任编辑：王　喆

封面设计：同人阁 文化传媒 · 书装设计

出版发行：北京工业大学出版社

　　　　　（北京市朝阳区平乐园100号　邮编：100124）

　　　　　010–67391722（传真）bgdcbs@sina.com

出 版 人：郝　勇

经销单位：全国各地新华书店

承印单位：大厂回族自治县正兴印务有限公司

开　　本：787毫米×1092毫米　1/16

印　　张：29

字　　数：473千字

版　　次：2017年7月第1版

印　　次：2017年7月第1次印刷

标准书号：ISBN 978–7–5639–5266–3

定　　价：58.00元

译者前言

　　《英国语文》原名《皇家读本》（The Royal Readers），是20世纪前后由英国著名的教材出版公司托马斯—尼尔森公司编写出版的一套小学语文教材。这套教材共分为六册，分别对应西方英语国家小学一至六年级的语文教学。这套书出版后，在西方英语国家的学校被广泛使用。根据这套书原编者的初衷，是为了引导孩子们对他们所阅读的作品产生真正的兴趣，并通过阅读提升他们的能力，最终将阅读所获得的能力运用到生活实践中去。可以说，这是一套以兴趣为引导、学以致用的教材。

　　这套书的编写体例非常严谨，一至四册教材的每篇文章后面基本都有课后提问、拼读训练、书写练习等内容，从第五册开始，又增加了单词解释，使学生通过阅读增加词汇量，进一步巩固和加深对文章的印象。

　　在选文内容上，这套书由浅入深，每一册对应不同年龄段的读者，选文也从简单的儿歌、短文、常用句型开始，逐渐提升为篇幅稍长的作品，再进阶到中长篇的经典著作。从难易程度来看，这套书前三册内容简单浅显，文字朴素简洁，比较适合国内中低年级小学生阅读；后三部分的内容相对繁复深奥，开始有侧重性，有的笔法精妙、描写细腻，有的文风犀利、寓意深刻，比较适合高年级小学生和中学生阅读。总之，这套书的选文内容丰富，从其所选文章涉及的体裁来看，包括了故事、童话、传记、诗歌等；题材涉及旅游、历险、历史、自然、科学等。这些选文体现了英国丰富的历史文化知识和西方国家的道德价值观念，让小读者们在提高文学修养的同时，也可以开阔自己的视野。

　　这套书的最大特色在于它所包含的内容非常贴近生活，能让小读者们觉得书中讲述的事情就发生在他们身边。而且，这套书所选的文章除了颂扬真、善、美之外，并没有回避生活中的艰难与困苦，突出了困境之下个人的坚守与成长。这样的文章往往更容易引起心灵的共鸣，也将对小读者们的人生观起到正面积极的作用。

我们衷心希望通过这套书的出版，让中国的读者朋友学习地道标准的英语，打开通往世界的心灵之窗；同时还能获得文学知识、个人修养、伦理道德等多方面的提升。

如果您在阅读中发现有疑问或错误之处，请不吝指正，以便我们更加完善这套书的编写。

目录
Contents

Lesson 1　THE GREAT SIEGE OF GIBRALTAR／第一课　直布罗陀大围攻… 1

Lesson 2　BATTLE OF CORUNNA AND DEATH OF MOORE

第二课　拉科鲁尼亚之战和莫尔爵士之死 ……………… 9

Lesson 3　THE BURIAL OF SIR JOHN MOORE

第三课　约翰·莫尔爵士的葬礼 …………………………14

Lesson 4　THE BED OF THE ATLANTIC／第四课　大西洋的海床 ………17

Lesson 5　BINGEN ON THE RHINE／第五课　莱茵河畔的宾根 ………22

Lesson 6　THE CLOUD／第六课　云　朵 ………………………………26

Lesson 7　THE TRIAL BY COMBAT（Ⅰ）／第七课　决斗裁判（一）………32

Lesson 8　THE TRIAL BY COMBAT（Ⅱ）／第八课　决斗裁判（二） ……37

Lesson 9　DAMASCUS AND LONDON（Ⅰ）

第九课　大马士革和伦敦（一）…………………………45

Lesson 10　DAMASCUS AND LONDON（Ⅱ）

第十课　大马士革和伦敦（二）…………………………52

Lesson 11　BATTLE OF TRAFALGAR, AND DEATH OF NELSON（Ⅰ）

第十一课　特拉法加海战和纳尔逊之死（一）…………59

Lesson 12　BATTLE OF TRAFALGAR, AND DEATH OF NELSON（Ⅱ）

第十二课　特拉法加海战和纳尔逊之死（二）…………66

Lesson 13　ROUND THE WORLD／第十三课　环球航行 ………………74

Lesson 14　NATURE／第十四课　自　然 ………………………………85

Lesson 15　THE TROPICAL WORLD（Ⅰ）／第十五课　热带世界（一）…87

Lesson 16　MAN AND THE INDUSTRIAL ARTS

第十六课　人类和工业艺术 ………………………………97

Lesson 17 SOMEBODY'S DARLING／第十七课　某人的亲爱的人 ······ 103

Lesson 18 THE TROPICAL WORLD（II）／第十八课　热带世界（二）··· 106

Lesson 19 THE SONG OF THE SHIRT／第十九课　衬衫之歌 ············ 117

Lesson 20 LAND AND SEA BREEZES／第二十课　陆地风与海洋风······ 120

Lesson 21 THE RELIEF OF LEYDEN／第二十一课　莱顿市的救援 ······ 124

Lesson 22 THE GLOVE AND THE LIONS／第二十二课　手套与狮子 ··· 130

Lesson 23 THE POLAR WORLD（I）／第二十三课　极地世界（一）··· 132

Lesson 24 THE BELLS／第二十四课　钟　声 ························ 138

Lesson 25 THE POLAR WORLD（II）／第二十五课　极地世界（二）··· 141

Lesson 26 THE BURNING OF MOSCOW

第二十六课　莫斯科的大火 ···························· 147

Lesson 27 THE RETREAT OF THE FRENCH ARMY FROM MOSCOW

第二十七课　法国军队从莫斯科撤退···················· 155

Lesson 28 THE TEMPERATE REGIONS／第二十八课　温带地区 ········ 161

Lesson 29 THE OVERLAND ROUTE／第二十九课　陆　路 ············ 170

Lesson 30 CAIRO AND THE PYRAMIDS／第三十课　开罗和金字塔 ··· 180

Lesson 31 FAMILY WORSHIP／第三十一课　家庭敬拜 ··············· 185

Lesson 32 THE VALLEY OF THE NILE／第三十二课　尼罗河流域 ······ 189

Lesson 33 PANEGYRIC ON MARIE ANTOINETTE

第三十三课　玛丽·安托瓦内特的颂歌···················· 197

Lesson 34 CRUELTY TO ANIMALS／第三十四课　对动物的残忍行为 ··· 199

Lesson 35 THE DELUGE／第三十五课　大洪水 ···················· 202

Lesson 36 WHAT IS WAR?／第三十六课　战争是什么 ············· 205

Lesson 37 COLONIAL LOYALTY／第三十七课　殖民地的忠诚········· 208

Lesson 38 JERUSALEM FROM THE MOUNT OF OLIVES

第三十八课　橄榄山上的耶路撒冷···················· 210

Lesson 39 THE SIEGE OF JERUSALEM／第三十九课　公元70年 ······· 216

Lesson 40 LEBANON／第四十课　黎巴嫩 ························ 224

Lesson 41 GREAT OCEAN ROUTES／第四十一课　大洋航线 ········· 230

Lesson 42　THE LLANOS OF SOUTH AMERICA
第四十二课　南美大草原··················239

Lesson 43　THE DEATH OF NAPOLEON AT ST. HELENA
第四十三课　拿破仑死于圣海伦娜··················244

Lesson 44　HYMN BEFORE SUNRISE, IN THE VALE OF CHAMOUNI
第四十四课　日出之前的赞歌，于沙莫尼山谷··········247

Lesson 45　"WITH BRAINS, SIR" ／第四十五课　"先生，用脑子"··· 252

Lesson 46　LIFE IN SAXON ENGLAND（Ⅰ）
第四十六课　撒克森时期英国的生活（一）··········257

Lesson 47　LIFE IN SAXON ENGLAND（Ⅱ）
第四十七课　撒克森时期英国的生活（二）··········265

Lesson 48　THE RELIEF OF LUCKNOW ／第四十八课　勒克瑙的救援··· 270

Lesson 49　THE BALACLAVA CHARGE
第四十九课　巴拉克拉瓦冲锋··················275

Lesson 50　THE CHARGE OF THE LIGHT BRIGADE
第五十课　轻骑兵进击··················280

Lesson 51　THE DISCOVERY OF THE SEA ROUTE TO INDIA
第五十一课　通往印度海上航线的发现··········283

Lesson 52　GREECE ／第五十二课　希　腊··················288

Lesson 53　THERMOPYLÆ ／第五十三课　塞莫皮莱　··········293

Lesson 54　PAUL AT ATHENS ／第五十四课　保罗在雅典··········296

Lesson 55　EVIDENCES OF DESIGN IN CREATION
第五十五课　世界中设计的证据··················301

Lesson 56　THE STORY OF HORATIUS ／第五十六课　贺雷修斯的故事··· 308

Lesson 57　ROMAN GIRL'S SONG ／第五十七课　罗马女孩之歌　········319

Lesson 58　REGULUS BEFORE THE ROMAN SENATE
第五十八课　雷古拉斯在罗马元老院前··········322

Lesson 59　THE SAHARA ／第五十九课　撒哈拉沙漠　··········329

Lesson 60　THE LIGHT-HOUSE ／第六十课　灯　塔··········337

Lesson 61   THE LAST FIGHT IN THE COLISÆUM

第六十一课   竞技场最后的战斗……………………………… 341

Lesson 62   THE DESTRUCTION OF POMPEII

第六十二课   庞贝的毁灭……………………………………… 350

Lesson 63   THE SOUTH-WEST MONSOON IN CEYLON

第六十三课   锡兰的西南季风………………………………… 357

Lesson 64   THE SEVEN AGES OF MAN / 第六十四课   人生七阶 ……… 361

Lesson 65   LIFE IN NORMAN ENGLAND

第六十五课   诺曼时代的英国生活…………………………… 363

Lesson 66   SIR ROGER DE COVERLET

第六十六课   罗杰·德·克里夫爵士…………………………… 371

Lesson 67   OLD ENGLISH AND NORMAN-FRENCH

第六十七课   古英语与诺曼法语……………………………… 376

Lesson 68   VENICE / 第六十八课   威尼斯 ……………………… 383

Lesson 69   THE CIRCULATION OF WATER / 第六十九课   水循环 …… 390

Lesson 70   GINEVRA / 第七十课   吉内乌拉 ………………………… 394

Lesson 71   THE DIGNITY OF LABOUR / 第七十一课   劳动的尊严 …… 399

Lesson 72   THE PROBLEM OF CREATION / 第七十二课   宇宙的问题 … 403

Lesson 73   EDUCATION AND THE STATE / 第七十三课   教育与国家 … 406

Lesson 74   ENGLISH SELF-ESTEEM / 第七十四课   英国的自尊 ……… 411

Lesson 75   PLEASURES OF KNOWLEDGE / 第七十五课   知识的快乐 … 414

Lesson 76   THE BRITISH CONSTITUTIONAL SYSTEM OF CANADA

第七十六课   加拿大的英国宪法制度………………………… 418

Lesson 77   THE SCHOOLMASTER AND THE CONQUEROR

第七十七课   教师与征服者…………………………………… 421

Lesson 78   BRITISH COLONIAL AND NAVAL POWER

第七十八课   英国殖民和海军的力量………………………… 424

Lesson 79   KING JOHN / 第七十九课   约翰王 ……………………… 429

Lesson 1
THE GREAT SIEGE OF GIBRALTAR
第一课　直布罗陀大围攻

1779-1782

Gibraltar fell into the hands of the English in 1704, during the War of the Spanish Succession—the war in which Marlborough gained so much glory for the English arms. Admiral Sir George Rooke had been sent to the Mediterranean, to watch the French and Spanish fleets. For a long time he was unable to accomplish anything of importance; but, learning that Gibraltar was very poorly garrisoned, he suddenly attacked and captured it, and hoisted the English flag on its Signal Station.

That flag is the only one that has ever floated there since the 23rd of July 1704. Time after time have the Spaniards tried to recover this "key of the Mediterranean;" but every effort has been repulsed most gallantly, and often with tremendous loss to the enemy.

The last attempt they made was the most gigantic and determined of all; and its successful resistance by the English garrison forms one of the most heroic incidents in the annals of modem warfare. It occurred during the struggle which severed from England her North American colonies. France recognized the United States as an independent power in 1778, and a war with England was the consequence. In the following year Spain joined France, and Gibraltar was immediately blockaded.

The siege which followed lasted three years. Every appliance which experience could suggest, or skill could devise, was brought into requisition. Never before had such tremendous armaments, by sea and by land, been brought against any fortress. Yet the garrison held out bravely; and twice their friends outside—once by Admiral Darby, and once by Rodney—succeeded in sending them reinforcements and supplies.

Early in 1781, there was a terrific bombardment of the place; but so effectual was the shelter afforded by the casemates, or bomb-proof vaults, that the garrison lost only seventy men. In November of the same year, General Elliot, who conducted the defence, headed a midnight sortie, which annihilated the entire line of the enemy's works. Their floating batteries were at the same time destroyed with red-hot balls. That one night cost the Spaniards two millions sterling!

But the final effort was made in 1782, when the Duke de Crillon, flushed with his success in capturing Minorca, took the command of the besiegers. He had under him upwards of 30,000 of the best troops of France and Spain, and his heavy guns amounted to the then unprecedented number of one hundred and seventy. The combined fleets numbered forty-seven sail of the line, with ten great floating batteries—the contrivance of a French engineer, and deemed invincible,—and frigates, gun-boats, mortar-boats and small craft without number. The besieged numbered only 7000 men with eighty guns.

The siege attracted the interest of the whole civilized world. Two French princes joined the besiegers' camp, to witness the fall of the place. "Is it taken?" was the first question asked each morning by the King of Spain. "Not yet; but it will be soon," said his courtiers: and still Elliot's guns thundered defiance from the Rock.

At length, on the morning of the 13th of September, the grand and decisive attack commenced. The ten battering-ships bore down in admirable order to their several stations. The Admiral, in a two-decker, moored about nine hundred yards off the King's Bastion. The other vessels took their places in a masterly manner, the most distant being eleven hundred or twelve hundred yards from the garrison. Under shelter of the walls, furnaces for heating shot had been lighted; and, from the instant the ships dropped into position, a continuous fire of red-hot balls was directed upon them by the garrison.

In little more than ten minutes, continues Drinkwater, the enemy were completely moored, and their cannonade then became tremendous. The showers of shot and shell which were directed from their land-batteries and battering-ships, on the one band, and, on the other, the incessant fire from the various works of the garrison, exhibited a scene of which neither the pen nor the pencil can furnish a competent idea. It is sufficient to say that upwards of four hundred pieces of the heaviest artillery were playing at the same moment—a power of ordnance which up till that time had scarcely been employed in any siege since the invention of those wonderful engines of destruction.

After some hours' cannonade, the battering-ships were found to be no less formidable than they had been represented. Our heaviest shells often rebounded from their tops, whilst the thirty-two pound shot seemed incapable of making any visible impression upon their hulls. Frequently we flattered ourselves that they were on fire; but no sooner did any smoke appear, than, with the most persevering intrepidity, men were observed applying water from their engines within, to those places whence the smoke issued.

View of Gibraltar

Though vexatiously annoyed from the isthmus, our artillery directed their sole attention to the battering-ships, the furious and spirited opposition of which served to excite our people to more animated exertions. A fire more tremendous, if possible, than ever, was therefore directed upon them from the garrison. Incessant showers of hot balls, carcasses, and shells of every species, flew from all quarters; yet, for some hours, the attack and defence were so equally maintained as scarcely to indicate any appearance of superiority on either side. The wonderful construction of the ships seemed to bid defiance to the powers of the heaviest ordnance.

In the afternoon, however, the face of things began to change considerably. The smoke which had been observed to issue from the upper part of the flag-ship appeared to prevail, notwithstanding the constant application of water; and the Admiral's second was perceived to be in the same condition.

As night came on, the flames fairly gained the ascendant. The confusion which reigned on board of these vessels soon communicated itself to the whole line. The fire of the battering-ships gradually slackened: that of the garrison, on the contrary, seemed to become more animated and tremendous.

It was kept up during the entire night. At one in the morning, two of the ships were entirely a prey to the flames. It was not long before the others also caught fire, either from the operation of the red-hot balls, or, as the Spaniards afterwards alleged, because they set them on fire themselves, when they had lost all hope of saving them. It was then that trouble and despair broke out in all their violence. Every moment the Spaniards made signals of distress, and fired off rockets to implore assistance.

All their boats were immediately sent off, and surrounded the floating gun-ships, in order to save their crews—an operation executed with extreme intrepidity, in spite of perils of every sort. Not only was it necessary for the men to brave the artillery of the besieged: they had also to expose themselves to almost inevitable burning in approaching the flaming vessels. Never, perhaps, did a spectacle more horrible—more deplorable—present itself to the eyes of men. The profound darkness that covered— the earth and the sea intensified, by contrast, the lurid flames; and the shrieks of the victims were distinctly heard by the garrison, in the intervals of their cannonade.

A fresh incident arose to interrupt the succour carried to them, and to redouble the terror and confusion. Captain Curtis, a sailor as daring as he was skilful, suddenly advanced with his gun-boats, which had been constructed to confront those of the Spaniards, and each of which carried in front an eighteen or twenty-four pounder. Their fire at water-level rendered them exceedingly formidable; and they were disposed by Captain Curtis so as to take the line of floating batteries in flank.

From that moment the position of the Spaniards became terribly critical. The boats no longer dared to approach them, but were constrained to abandon those enormous machines, so lately the objects of their admiration, to the flames, and their companions in arms to the mercy of an enraged enemy. Several of them were seen to founder. Others only escaped by forced rowing. A few sought shelter by the land during the night; but, on the appearance of daylight, they were easily captured by the English.

Then was witnessed, in all its horrors, a scene, the most harrowing features of which had hitherto remained concealed. In the midst of the flames appeared unhappy

Subterranean Gallery, Excavated out of the Solid Rock

wretches, who, with loud shrieks, implored compassion, or precipitated themselves into the waves. Some, on the point of drowning, clung with weakened grasp to the sides of the burning vessels, or floated at hazard on fragments which they chanced to encounter, and, in the agony of desperation, convulsively implored the compassion of their victors.

Touched by this deplorable spectacle, the English listened to humanity alone, and ceased their fire, to occupy themselves solely with the rescue of their enemies; a proceeding the more generous on their part, as they thereby exposed themselves to the most imminent hazard. Captain Curtis, in particular, covered himself with glory, by prodigally risking his own life to save those of his fellow-creatures. Some of his own men were wounded in this honourable enterprise; others were killed; and he himself narrowly escaped from partaking the fate of a ship which blew up at the moment when he was about to board her. More than four hundred of the enemy's troops were rescued by this intrepid sailor from certain death!

The greater number of the famous battering-ships were either blown up or burnt. The Spanish Admiral quitted his flag-ship a little before midnight, as did also D'Arcon, the French engineer, that on board of which he had embarked to witness the triumph of his contrivances.

Meanwhile, the most intense anxiety as to the fate of Gibraltar prevailed in England. Admiral Howe had sailed from Portsmouth with a convoy containing fresh troops and provisions, and a fleet of thirty-four sail of the line. Relieved by the news of Elliot's brilliant victory, which he received off the coast of Portugal, he steered direct for the Straits, and succeeded in bringing the whole of his transports to their destination, even in presence of the enemy's fleets. Thus Gibraltar was saved, and the continuance of the blockade till the peace (Jan. 20, 1783) was little more than a form.

Words

accomplish, *perform.*

annihilated, *destroyed.*

anxiety, *solicitude.*
appliance, *contrivance.*
armaments, *forces.*
blockaded, *invested.*
brilliant, *splendid.*
cannonade, *sustained fire.*
capturing, *seizing.*
competent, *adequate.*
continuance, *prolongation.*
contrivances, *inventions.*
convulsively, *spasmodically.*
decisive, *final.*
defiance, *contempt for an enemy.*
destination, *haven.*
destruction, *devastation.*
enterprise, *exploit.*
executed, *performed.*
formidable, *dangerous.*
gigantic, *stupendous.*
imminent, *threatening.*

importance, *moment.*
incapable, *unable.*
incessant, *ceaseless.*
inevitable, *unavoidable,*
intensified, *made greater.*
interrupt, *hinder.*
intrepidity, *daring.*
invincible, *invulnerable.*
ordnance, *cannon.*
precipitated, *cast.*
prodigally, *generously.*
recognized, *acknowledged.*
reinforcements, *fresh troops.*
repulsed, *driven back.*
requisition, *operation.*
resistance, *defeat.*
slackened, *declined.*
sortie, *sally.*
tremendous, *overwhelming.*
unprecedented, *unparalleled.*

Questions

When and how did Gibraltar fall into the hands of the English? When did the Spaniards make the most determined effort to recover it? How long did the siege last? How often during that time was the garrison succoured? What was done in 1781? When was the final effort made? Who took the command of the besiegers? How many men had he? To what did the combined fleets amount? What was the strength of the garrison in men and in guns? What is the date of the decisive attack? Upon what had the besiegers placed most reliance? What proved the great strength of these ships? How were they at length destroyed? What movement compelled the Spaniards to abandon them? What humane service did Curtis afterwards render? Who brought fresh troops and provisions from England to the garrison? When did the blockade finally terminate?

1779—1782

直布罗陀于1704年在马博罗为英国军队赢得众多荣誉的西班牙王位继承战争中，落入英国人手中。海军司令乔治·鲁克爵士被派往地中海，以监视法国和西班牙联合舰队。很长一段时间，他都毫无建树；但在得知直布罗陀驻防力量薄弱之后，他突袭并占领了那里，并在信号站上升起了英国国旗。

这是唯一一面自1704年7月23日后在那里飘扬的旗帜。西班牙人曾一次又一次试图恢复这一"地中海要塞"，但每一次努力都被极其有力地击退了，并经常伴有敌人巨大的损失。

他们做了最后一次巨大并带有决定性意义的尝试，而英国驻军的成功抵抗则成为现代战争史上最英勇的事件之一，此次战争发生在英国北美殖民地的斗争恶化之后。法国于1778年承认美国的独立权，结果便是与英国交战。在接下来的一年，西班牙加入法国，而直布罗陀立即遭到封锁。

接下来的围攻战持续了三年。每次之前根据经验能够考虑到的装备，或者可以设想出的技能，都被派上了用场。之前无论是海上还是陆上，都从未有过如此巨大的武器装备来进攻堡垒。然而，驻军进行了勇敢的抵抗；而他们的朋友也两次从外围不断地向他们运送增援和补给——一次是海军上将达比，另一次是罗德尼。

1781年初，此地经历了一次可怕的轰炸，但炮塔和防空洞提供了很有效的避难所，驻军只损失了70人。同年11月，指挥此次防御的埃略特将军领导了一次午夜突围，毁灭了敌人工程的整条防御线，他们的浮动炮台同时也被炮弹破坏。西班牙人当晚损失了200万英镑！

最后的努力是在1782年。因成功攻占了米诺卡而得意扬扬的德克里伦公爵取得了围攻部队的指挥权，他手下拥有超过3万的法国和西班牙最精锐的部队，而他的重机枪多达前所未有的170架。联合舰队帆的编号为47，拥有由法国工程师设计并被公认为无敌的十大浮动炮台，另外还有无数的护卫舰、炮艇、迫击炮船和小艇。而遭到他们围困的，不过是拥有80条枪的7 000人。

本次围攻激发了整个文明世界的兴趣。两个法国王子为见证这个地方的沦陷，进入了围攻者的营地。每天早上西班牙国王问的第一个问题是："占领了吗？""还没有，但很快了。"他的侍臣会这样回答。不变的是，埃略特的枪弹轰鸣地从堡垒后反抗着。

最终，在9月13日清晨，决定性的大进攻开始了。十艘炮船在最高统帅的命令下，朝向几处全力进发。海军上将所在的双甲船，停泊在国王堡垒的大约900码之外。其他船只熟练地到达各自的位置，最远的距离守军有1 100～1 200码。在城墙的庇护下，如熔炉一般火热的炮弹稍微温凉了一些；当这些船只到达相应位置，守军就会立即用炮弹对准它们进行连续射击。

德林克沃特继续说道，在不到十分钟的时间内，敌人完全停滞住了，自此之后，他们的连续炮击也继而变得更加猛烈。一方面，他们的枪林弹雨从他们的地面炮台和浮动炮台上对准了这里；另一方面，从驻军的各项工事中发出的持续火力，也展现出了一种人类的笔墨无法描绘的场景。可以说，超过400发最重的炮弹，在同一时刻打在一个地方——到那时为止，自从这种无与伦比的毁灭性武器被发明出来之后，这样的炮击方式就几乎没有在攻城战斗中使用过。

在几小时的炮轰之后，炮舰已经不像当初表现那么强大了。我们最重的炮弹经常可以从顶端弹跳，但这种32磅重的炮弹却不能有任何客观的表现。我们经常得意于它们着火了，但一旦出现了烟雾，人们就会从内部的引擎到起火的地方用水来灭火。

虽然我们的军队为如何穿越地峡伤透了脑筋，但他们仍拼尽全力瞄准敌方的炮舰，而敌方狂暴激烈的抵抗则引发了我方将士更加激励的攻击。因此在我方驻地的堡垒上，将士们遭到了敌方发起的比以往都更加猛烈的炮轰。炮弹、尸体、各种物品的碎片，不停地从各个部分被砍劈下来。然而几个小时过去了，进攻方和防守方如此势均力敌，几乎看不出哪一方占了上风。舰船绝佳的结构似乎对如此猛烈的炮击力量发起了挑战。

然而在下午，局面开始发生显著的变化。之前从旗舰上部升起的烟雾，尽管不停地用水浇，但此时开始扩散。海军司令的指令也面临同样的不利局面。

当夜晚来临时，火势完全占据了优势。笼罩着舰船的困惑感很快在整个进攻线上蔓延开来，敌方炮船上的火力逐渐变弱，相反，驻防要塞的火力似乎开始更加猛烈。

火力整晚都很猛烈。在凌晨1点钟，敌方的两艘舰船完全成为火焰的猎物。没过多久，其他的船也都完全着起了火，有的是因为炮弹的袭击，有些正如后来西班牙人宣称的，因为他们完全放弃补救的希望时，自己放了火。也就是在那时，绝望在整个进攻线上爆发。西班牙人不停地放出危难的信号，并发射火箭来恳请支援。

他们所有的船只都立即出发，包围住浮动炮台来拯救他们的船员。这是一种即使面临着各种危险，也必须采取的极端大胆的行为。这些人不仅要勇敢面临我方被围攻部队的将士，而且还要将自己置身于在靠近着火船只时几乎是必然会引发的火焰。从未有过一种景象比如今更可怕、更可悲地展现在人们眼前。深深的黑暗笼罩着大地，相反，海面映衬着可怕的血红色的火焰。在炮轰的间歇，防守要塞的将士们清晰地听到牺牲者的尖叫声。

另一件事情的发生，打断了对他们的救助，同时也大大增加了他们的恐惧和困惑。柯蒂斯船长——一个既勇敢又熟练的船员——突然带领他的炮舰前进，来直面西班牙人的炮舰。每一艘柯蒂斯船长的炮船，都发射出18或24磅的炮弹，在水面高度上的火力让它们变得极其可怕。柯蒂斯船长命舰船排列出一种阵势，可以从侧翼攻击敌方的浮动炮台。

从这一刻开始，西班牙人的处境变得特别危险。船只不再敢靠近他们，在火中，他们被迫放弃了那些巨型器械和他们所赞美的装备，而在暴怒的敌人的怜悯中放弃他们配有武装的同伴。有人看到其中一些人被海水淹没了，其他人依靠划船得以逃脱，个别人趁夜里在陆地上找到了避难所，但当黎明来临，英国人又轻易地抓获了他们。

接下来人们极其恐惧地目睹了一幅场景，而它最悲惨的特性迄今为止一直隐藏着。在火光之中，这些可怜的人大声尖叫，乞求着同情，或者一头栽到水里。他们中的某些人，在被淹没的当口，紧抓住破败的燃烧着的船只边缘；或者在危急中，漂浮在他们恰巧碰到的碎片上，在绝望的挣扎中，不由自主地向看到他们的人恳求怜悯。

被这种可悲的景象所震撼，英国人听从于自己的人性，停止了开火，而仅仅专注于营救他们的敌人。由此在这一仁慈的过程中，他们也将自己置身于最紧迫的危险中。特别是柯蒂斯船长，因此为自己带来了无限荣光。因为他慷慨地冒着生命危险，救助了这些虽是敌人的他的同类。他的部下，其中一些人在这一光荣的事业中也受了伤，其他人甚至牺牲了。而他本人在与一艘敌船上的敌人决一死战的过程中，勉强脱逃。当时他刚要登上这艘船，船只就爆炸了。敌军中的400多人，被这一勇敢的水手从死亡边缘营救了出来。

更多的著名炮舰爆炸或烧毁了。西班牙海军司令在午夜之前放弃了他的旗舰。而登上自己发明的战舰的法国工程师德阿尔孔也一样，他本想目睹自己发明的船只的胜利。

同时，对直布罗陀命运的最强烈的不安笼罩着英格兰。豪司令率领装有另外一些部队和储备的护航舰，还带有一支拥有34艘船只的舰队，从朴次茅斯出发。听到艾略特将军伟大胜利的消息后，他径直前往海峡，并成功地在敌方联合舰队面前，将他全部的运输船运往了目的地。而艾略特将军的胜利已经蔓延至葡萄牙海岸。因此直布罗陀保住了，直到和平结束（1783年1月20日）之前的持续封锁，也只等同于一种形式而已。

Lesson 2
BATTLE OF CORUNNA AND DEATH OF MOORE
第二课 拉科鲁尼亚之战和莫尔爵士之死

January 17, 1809.

As the troops approached Corunna, the General's looks were directed towards the harbour; but an open expanse of water painfully convinced him that to Fortune, at least, he was no way beholden: contrary winds still detained the fleet at Vigo, and the last consuming exertion made by the army was rendered fruitless! The men were put into quarters, and their leader awaited the progress of events.

Three divisions occupied the town and suburbs of Corunna, and the reserve was posted near the neighbouring village of El Burgo. For twelve days these hardy soldiers had covered the retreat; during which time they had traversed eighty miles of road in two marches, passed several nights under arms in the snow of the mountains, and been seven times engaged with the enemy. They now assembled at the outposts, having fewer men missing from the ranks than any other division in the army.

The town of Corunna, although sufficiently strong to oblige an enemy to break ground before it, was weakly fortified, and to the southward was commanded by some heights close to the walls. Sir John Moore therefore caused the land front to be strengthened, and occupied the citadel, but disarmed the sea face of the works.

The late arrival of the transports, the increasing force of the enemy, and the disadvantageous nature of the ground, had greatly augmented the difficulty and danger of the embarkation; and several general officers now proposed to the commander-in-chief that he should negotiate for leave to retire to his ships upon terms. Moore's high spirit and clear judgment revolted at the idea, and he rejected the degrading advice without hesitation.

All the encumbrances of the army were shipped in the night of the 15th and morning of the 16th, and everything was prepared to withdraw the fighting men as soon as the darkness would permit them to move without being perceived. The precautions taken would, without doubt, have insured the success of that difficult operation; but a more glorious event was destined to give a melancholy but graceful termination to the campaign. About two o'clock in the afternoon a general movement along the French line gave notice of an approaching battle...

Sir John Moore, while earnestly watching the result of the fight, was struck on the left breast by a cannon shot. The shock threw him from his horse with violence; but he rose again in a sitting posture, his countenance unchanged, and his steadfast eye still fixed upon the regiments engaged in his front, no sigh betraying a sensation of pain. In a few moments, when he was satisfied that the troops were gaining ground, his countenance brightened, and he suffered himself to be taken to the rear.

Then was seen the dreadful nature of his hurt. The shoulder was shattered to pieces; the arm was hanging by a piece of skin; the ribs over the heart were broken and bared of flesh; and the muscles of the breast were torn into long strips, which were interlaced by their recoil from the dragging of the shot, As the soldiers placed him in a blanket, his sword got entangled, and the hilt entered the wound. Captain Hardinge, a staff officer who was near, attempted to take it off; but the dying man stopped him, saying, "*It is as well as it is. I had rather it should go out of the field with me*;"—and in that manner, so becoming to a soldier, Moore was borne from the fight.

Sir John Hope, upon whom the command of the army now devolved, resolved to pursue the original plan of embarking during the night. This operation was effected without delay. The arrangements were so complete that neither confusion nor difficulty occurred. The piquets, kindling a number of fires, covered the retreat of the columns; and being themselves withdrawn at daybreak, were embarked under the protection of General Hill's brigade, which was posted near the ramparts of the town. This done, Hill's brigade embarked from the citadel; while General Beresford, with a rear guard, kept possession of that work until the 18th, when, the wounded being all put on board, his troops likewise embarked. The inhabitants faithfully maintained the town against the French, and the fleet sailed for England.

From the spot where he fell, Sir John Moore had been carried to the town by a party of soldiers. His blood flowed fast, and the torture of his wound was great; yet such was the unshaken firmness of his mind, that those about him, judging from the resolution of his countenance that his hurt was not mortal, expressed a hope of his recovery. Hearing this, he looked steadfastly at the injury for a moment, and then said, "*No; I feel that to be impossible.*" Several times he caused his attendants to stop and turn him round, that he might behold the field of battle; and when the firing indicated the advance of the British, he discovered his satisfaction, and permitted the bearers to proceed.

Being brought to his lodging, the surgeons examined his wound; but there was no hope. The pain increased, and he spoke with great difficulty. At intervals he asked if the French were beaten; and addressing his old friend, Colonel Anderson, he said, "*You know that I always wished to die this way.*" Again he asked if the enemy were defeated; and, being told that they were, observed, "*It is a great satisfaction to me to know that we have beaten the French.*" His countenance continued firm and his thoughts clear. Once only, when he spoke of his mother, he became agitated; but he often inquired after the safety of his friends and the officers of his staff; and he did not, even in that moment, forget to recommend those whose merit had given them claims to promotion.

His strength failed fast, and life was nearly extinct, when, with an almost un-subdued spirit, he exclaimed, "*I hope the people of England will be satisfied! I hope my country will do me justice!*" A few minutes afterwards he died; and his corpse, wrapped in a military cloak, was interred by the officers of his staff in the citadel of Corunna, The guns of the enemy paid his funeral honours; and Soult, with a noble feeling of respect for his valour, raised a monument to his memory.

Thus ended the career of Sir John Moore, a man whose uncommon capacity was sustained by the purest virtue, and governed by a disinterested patriotism, more in keeping with the primitive than with the luxurious age of a great nation. He maintained the right with a vehemence bordering upon fierceness; and every important transaction in which he was engaged increased his reputation for talent, and confirmed his character as a stern enemy to vice, a steadfast friend to merit—a just and faithful servant of his country.

—Sir W. Napier

Words

agitated, *moved.*
approached, *neared.*
attempted, *endeavoured.*
augmented, *increased.*
capacity, *ability.*
citadel, *fortress.*
consuming, *exhausting.*
convinced, *satisfied.*
defeated, *beaten.*
devolved, *fell*
disadvantageous, *unfavourable.*
discovered, *exhibited.*
disinterested, *unselfish.*
embarking, *going aboard.*
encumbrances, *baggage.*

interlaced, *entangled.*
interred, *buried.*
melancholy, *sad.*
precautions, *measures.*
promotion, *advancement.*
protection, *cover.*
reputation, *fame.*
resolution, *firmness.*
resolved, *determined.*
steadfast, *firm.*
sufficiently, *adequately.*
transaction, *business.*
traversed, *crossed.*
violence, *force.*

Questions

When was the Battle of Corunna fought? Who was the British commander-in-chief? Why was it necessary to fight the battle? What proposal of some of his officers did he reject? How was he wounded? What was the result of the engagement? When did the embarkation take place? In whom did Moore show much interest in his later moments? What were his last words? What was his character?

1809年1月17日

部队渐渐接近拉科鲁尼亚，将军径直望向海港。眼前苍茫的海水痛苦地提醒着他，至少，他是没有责任的。舰队被大风滞留在比戈，上一次敌军猛烈的阻击毫无建树。部队已经驻扎在此，他们的首领正等待着事态有所进展。

三个师的部队已经占领了拉科鲁尼亚的城镇和郊野，储备也放置在邻近的埃尔武尔戈村。过去的12天中，这些勇敢的将士们分为两队行军，撤退了128公里。期间，他们带着武器翻越了众多雪山，并且七次与敌人相遇。他们如今聚集在前哨，比其他部队的队列都更好地保存了兵力。

拉科鲁尼亚镇虽然足够抵抗敌军在它前方开辟阵地，但防守相对薄弱。约翰·莫尔爵士因此加强了陆上的防守，占领了要塞，但解除了靠海方面的工事。

运送物资抵达的推迟，敌军火力的增强，此地的自然缺陷，都大大增强了登船的困难与危险。众多主要将领都向他们的主将提议，他应该同大家商议，以撤回船只。但莫尔爵士的进取心和清晰判断力使他坚决反对并拒绝了这一提议。

所有部队的装备都在15日夜里和16日凌晨装运上船。为了能让战士们趁敌人察觉不到而尽快在黑暗中撤离，一切都准备好了。毋庸置疑，为了保证这一困难行动的成功，预防措施也已做好。但另一件更光荣的事件注定会让这一行动终止。大约下午2点钟，法国沿岸的一次行动带来了一场战斗。

在焦虑地观看战事结果时，约翰·莫尔爵士的左胸被炮弹射中。他从马背上猛地摔了下来。但他立即又恢复了坐立的姿势，表情丝毫未变，眼神刚毅地盯着他前方的战场，甚至没有一声因为疼痛而发出的叹息。当最终满意地得知他的部队占领了阵地时，他的表情又一次明朗起来，他才允许将自己抬到后方。

接下来人们看到了他的伤势有多可怕。肩膀已经碎裂，胳膊只由一层皮肤连接着悬挂在那里，心脏上方的肋骨已经断了，甚至都露出了肉，胸部的肌肉被撕裂成一条一条，因为炮弹的袭击而相互交错。战士们用毯子裹住了他，他的剑已经缠绕弯曲，甚至插进了他的伤口。一位在附近的军官——哈丁格上尉试图将碎片取出，但奄奄一息的莫尔爵士阻止了他："就这样待着吧。我宁愿它们随我从战场上一起出去。"一位亲历这一刻的战士说道："莫尔爵士在战斗中获得了重生！"

约翰·霍普爵士如今掌管了部队的指挥权。他决定坚持夜间出发的最初计划，行动立即得以执行。事先的安排如此完备，没有任何困难发生。部队的撤退，由哨兵点燃的大火掩护完成。这支部队在黎明完成撤退，其间驻扎在镇中要塞的希尔将军的军团提供了保护。这一步之后，希尔将军的军团也从要塞出发。同时，贝雷斯福德将军在后方部队的掩护下，占据了这一要塞，直到18日。在所有伤员都成功登船之后，他的部队也同样出发了。舰队出发前往英格兰，当地居民信誓旦旦地要从法国人手中保住镇子。

从他受伤的地方出发，莫尔爵士被一队战士拉到了镇子上。他血流不止，伤口疼痛难忍。但他的意志依旧坚忍，从他坚定的表情可以判断，这个伤口可能不是致命的。大家都盼望着他能够康复。他坚定地看了伤口一会儿，说道："不，我觉得不可能。"他好多次让随从停下来，把他抬回去，这样他能看到战场。当获悉英国部队又前进了，他才满意地允许战士们继续前进。

把莫尔爵士抬到他的屋子之后，军医检查了他的伤口，希望全无。疼痛在滋长，他说话都费力了。他不停地询问，法国是否已经战败。他对他的老朋友安德森上校说："你了解，我一直想这样死去。"然后他又一次问敌军是否已战败。当得知结果时，他说："得知我们战胜了法国，我很满足。"他的表情依旧坚定，思维依旧清晰。只有一次，当他说到自己的母亲时，他变得异常激动。他还经常询问他的朋友、部下是否安全。此时此刻，他甚至没有忘记推荐让几个因优秀品质而著名的将士得到提拔。

他的力气消退得很快，生命也几乎停止。当他的神智几乎紊乱时，他说道："我希望英格兰人民能够满意，我希望我的祖国充满正义。"几分钟之后，他去世了。战士们将他的尸体包裹在一件军大衣里，埋葬在拉科鲁尼亚的要塞。敌人的枪支为他的葬礼带来了荣光。带着对他的勇敢的崇敬，人们为他树起了一座纪念碑。

约翰·莫尔爵士的事业就此终结，他的纯净美德支撑着他的超凡能力。他无私的爱国情谊在一个伟大国家的初始阶段，甚至超过了在它的繁盛时期。在严厉的反对声中，他能够坚定地坚持正确的决定。这增加了他天才的声誉。他的名字，对于他凶残的敌人，意味着让人痛恨的罪恶；而对他坚定的朋友，则意味着值得称颂的美德。因此，他可谓他的祖国最忠诚的仆人。

——W·内皮尔爵士

Lesson 3
THE BURIAL OF SIR JOHN MOORE
第三课　约翰·莫尔爵士的葬礼

Not a drum was heard, not a funeral note,
　　As his corpse to the ramparts we hurried;
Not a soldier discharged his farewell shot
　　O'er the grave where our hero we buried.

We buried him darkly at dead of night,
　　The sods with our bayonets turning;
By the struggling moonbeam's misty light,
　　And the lantern dimly burning.

No useless coffin enclosed his breast,
　　Not in sheet nor in shroud we wound him;
But he lay like a warrior taking his rest
　　With his martial cloak around him.

Few and short were the prayers we said,
　　And we spoke not a word of sorrow
But we steadfastly gazed on the face that was dead,
　　And we bitterly thought of the morrow.

We thought, as we hollowed his narrow bed,
　　And smoothed down his lonely pillow,
That the foe and the stranger would tread o'er his head,
　　And we far away on the billow!

Lightly they'll talk of the spirit that's gone,
　　And o'er his cold ashes upbraid him;
But little he'll reck if they let him sleep on
　　In the grave where a Briton has laid him!

But half of our heavy task was done
　　When the clock struck the hour for retiring;
And we heard the distant and random gun

That the foe was sullenly firing.

Slowly and sadly we laid him down,
　　From the field of his fame fresh and gory:
We carved not a line, and we raised not a stone—
　　But we left him alone with his glory.

　　　　　　　　　　　—Charles Wolfe (1791−1823).

☆ ☆ ☆ ☆ ☆ ☆ ☆ ☆ ☆ ☆ ☆ ☆ ☆ ☆ ☆ ☆ ☆ ☆ ☆

没有打鼓，也没有哀乐，
当我们把它的尸体运到城堡，
在我们的英雄埋葬者的墓上，
也没有一名士兵鸣放礼炮。

我们埋葬他在悄悄的夜晚，
使用我们的刺刀在土中翻；
靠着雾中露出的朦胧月光，
还有些闪着光的暗淡灯火。

包藏它的胸坎没有无用的棺，
也没有寿衣寿布把他裹缠；
但他躺着正如一名战士，
穿着他的军服和衣而眠。

祈祷的话语人少而语短，
我们所说的没有一句哀婉；
我们坚定凝视着死者的面庞，
只沉痛地在想到明天。

当我们掘着他狭窄的墓坑，
我们把他头上的土块放平，
我们想到未知的敌人回来蹂躏他的头颅，
而我们已经在海上航行！

敌兵会轻蔑这阵亡了的将军，
会在他的尸骸上议论纵横；
但只要他们让他安睡在墓中，
所埋葬的英国人，他会泰然不问。

但我们的埋葬工作只到一半，
时钟已报道着撤退的时间；
我们也听到远远的散乱炮声，
敌人在向我们乱放子弹。

悲伤地让他徐徐躺下，
浑身还带着荣誉阵地的血花；
我们没写一行字，没立一块碑，
但只让他的光荣永远伴着他。

——查尔斯·沃尔夫（1791—1823）

Lesson 4   THE BED OF THE ATLANTIC
第四课   大西洋的海床

(To be read before a Map.)

If the waters of the Atlantic could be drawn off, so as to expose to view the great trough which separates the Old World from the New, a scene would present itself of the grandest and most imposing character. The very ribs of the solid Earth, and the foundations of the hills, destitute of the garniture of vegetation, would be brought to light. We should have unrolled before us a vast panorama of mountains and valleys, of tablelands and plains, of deep gorges and lofty peaks, rivalling in grandeur and in variety the continents of the upper world.

Comparatively little is yet known of the bed of the South Atlantic; but the basin of the North Atlantic has been extensively surveyed by the English and American Navies. Let us suppose this vast basin to be emptied of its waters; and, with the aid of the charts which have been constructed, let us in imagination traverse these deep places of the Earth and learn what we can of their secrets. Remembering that what we have to explore is really a vast system of table-lands, mountains, and valleys, let us first endeavour to grasp its broad outstanding features.

In the northern part of the basin there stretches across the Atlantic from Newfoundland to Ireland a great submarine plain, known in recent years as Telegraph Plateau. About one hundred miles from the coast of Ireland this plateau, rising as a broad terrace, reaches to within a hundred fathoms of the surface of the ocean. On this terrace stand the British Islands, the climate of which is materially affected by their being thus removed from the influence of the colder waters in the depths of the Atlantic. About midway between these islands and Iceland, it has been found that icy cold water is constantly flowing towards the Equator, at a considerable depth beneath the surface, to supply the place of the warm surface-water moving northward from the Equator. At the depth of three-quarters of a mile, the temperature of this great polar current is two degrees below the freezing point. The British terrace raises these isles out of this cold stream, and thus none but the warmer upper waters flow around the British coasts.

From the middle of Telegraph Plateau an immense submarine continent, nearly as extensive as South America, stretches first southward and then towards the west, occupying the whole central area of the North Atlantic basin.

On either side of this central continent there is a broad and deep valley. These valleys converge as they go southward, and meet in mid-ocean between the Cape Verd and the West India Islands. Of these valleys, the western is much deeper than the eastern. Its deepest parts are found midway between the Bermudas and the Azores, and off the island of Porto Rico, where the sounding-line has been carried deeper than anywhere else in the ocean. It is the deepest part of the Atlantic.

Could we transport ourselves to that point, we should stand on what is perhaps the very lowest part of the Earth's crust. We should be at least five miles below the ordinary level of the sea, surrounded on all sides by great mountains. On the north the Bermudas would be seen as lofty mountain-peaks, rising half as high again as the summits of the Alps or the Andes. On the north-east we should see the Azores as the culminating points of the central continent. Pico, their highest point, would appear, from the general level, as a mountain 400 feet higher than Mont Blanc; but from our imaginary standpoint in the lowest depths of the Atlantic, it would be six and a half miles in height—a mile higher than the highest peak of the Himalaya, the loftiest mountain on the globe.

Each of these great ocean valleys rises in a series of terraces to the sides of the Old and New Worlds respectively. The course of the western valley, which lies off the United States and the West India Islands, has been traced as far south as to the Equator. The terraces of the eastern valley rise from the depths of the ocean to the western coasts of Europe and Africa. Off the coast of Africa they rise into a series of lofty and rugged summits, which we call Madeira, the Cape Verd, and the Canary Isles; and the whole system culminates in the Peak of Teneriffe in the last-named group. That peak is two miles and one-third above the level of the sea. The lowest point yet sounded in the bed of the Atlantic is five miles and a third below that level. The whole mountain system of the Atlantic basin, therefore, extends to upwards of seven miles in vertical height, or higher than any of the mountains of the globe are above the level of the sea.

By bringing up specimens from the depth of the Atlantic, and studying them under the microscope, it has been ascertained that the bed of the ocean is covered with very minute shells, which lie on the bottom as lightly as gossamer. The microscope has not detected a single particle of sand or gravel among these little mites of shells. This fact proves that quiet reigns in the depths of the sea: that as in the air ocean there is a region of perpetual calm, "above the clouds;" so in the ocean of waters there is a region where perpetual calm prevails, beneath the troubled waves. There is not motion enough to abrade these very delicate organisms, nor current enough to sweep them about, or to mix with them a grain of the finest sand.

It may be that the myriads of animalcules which make the sea glow with life are secreting from it solid matter which is destined to fill up the cavities below. They furnish the atoms of which mountains are formed and plains are spread out. Our marl-beds, the clay in our river-bottoms, large portions of many of the great basins of the Earth, even flinty rocks, are composed of the remains of just such minute animals as those which have been fished up from a depth of three miles below the sea-level. These creatures, therefore, when living, may have been preparing the ingredients for the fruitful soil of a land that some earthquake or upheaval, in ages far away in the future, may yet raise up from the bottom of the sea for the use of man.

Words

ascertained, *found.*
cavities, *hollow places.*
converge, *draw near to each other.*
culminating, *crowning.*
destined, *appointed.*
detected, *discovered.*
garniture, *embellishment.*
gossamer, *cobweb.*
ingredients, *elements.*

organisms, *structures.*
panorama, *comprehensive view.*
perpetual, *constant.*
separates, *keeps apart.*
submarine, *under the sea.*
summits, *peaks.*
surveyed, *examined.*
temperature, *degree of heat.*
transport, *convey.*

Questions

Of what does the bed of the ocean consist? What part of the Atlantic has been surveyed? By whom? What plain stretches across the northern part of the basin? On what do the British Isles stand? What effect has this on their climate? Why? What extends southward from the middle of Telegraph Plateau? What is there on either side of the central continent? Where is the deepest part of the Atlantic? If we could stand there, how far should we be below the sea-level? By what should we be surrounded? What would the Bermudas appear to be? And the Azores? Where does the whole Atlantic mountain system culminate? What is its extent in vertical height? With what is the bed of the ocean covered? What shows that quiet reigns in the depths of the sea? Of what are the animalcules found in the bed of the ocean the elements?

（请参照地图阅读此文）

　　如果大西洋的水可以被抽干，来显现出分隔开新世界与旧世界的一条巨大海槽，一幅宏伟壮观的景象会展现在我们面前。坚硬地球的山脊、山脉的形成、植被装饰的贫乏，会被一一发现。在我们面前展现出的是一幅巨大的关于山脉和山谷、高原和平原、深邃峡谷和巍峨山峰的全景，竞相展现着它们的宏伟和上层世界的多样性。

　　相比之下，人们对南大西洋的海床知之甚少。但英国和美国海军已经对北大西洋盆地进行了广泛勘测。我们可以假设这片广阔的盆地没有水，在已经构制的航海图的帮助下，我们的想象可以穿越这片地球上最深的海域，去了解我们可以得知的秘密。须谨记我们要探索的的确是一片广阔的高原、山脉和山谷，我们首先可以尝试的是，掌握它们众多的显著特征。

在这片盆地的北部区域，横跨大西洋，从纽芬兰岛到爱尔兰岛，绵延着一片宽广的海底盆地，近年来被称作"电报高原"。在距爱尔兰海岸大约100英里处，这片高原如一片宽广的梯田升起，一直到达距海面不足100英寸之内。不列颠群岛矗立其上，而不列颠群岛的气候深受这些梯田的影响，而免受大西洋底部冰冷海水的影响。大约在这些岛屿和冰岛的正中，人们发现寒冷的冰水在海面以下极深的深度，不停地向北流向赤道，供给这片区域温暖的海面水，向北部的赤道流淌。在大约四分之三英里的深度，水的温度低于冰点两度。不列颠梯田因为寒流升高影响到这些小岛，以至于只有这种温暖的上层水流围绕不列颠海岸流淌。

一片几乎和南美洲一样广阔的巨大的海底陆地，从电报高原的中央首先向南延伸，之后向西，占据了北大西洋盆地的整个中心地区。

在中央陆地的周围，有宽广且深邃的山谷，它们向南部延伸时同时汇聚集，在佛得角和西印度群岛中央处聚于一处。这些山谷的东部比西部深得多，它最深的地方位于百慕大和亚速尔群岛之间，而在波多黎各岛的外围，攀升至比海洋中其他任何地方都更深的部位，这就是大西洋最深的地方。

如果我们能够到达这一点，我们即将位于地壳最低点，也就是在平均海洋高度下至少5英里处，且四周都包围着高山。在北部，百慕大是一片巍峨的山峰，高至如阿尔卑斯和安第斯山制高点一半的高度。在东北部，我们会看到亚速尔群岛是整个中央陆地的最高点。从海洋的一般高度出发，最高点皮科，相当于比勃朗峰还要高400英寸的山。而从我们想象中的站立点出发，在大西洋的最深处，它会有6.5英里高。这比全球最巍峨的山峰——喜马拉雅山的最高峰——还要高出一英里。

这些广阔的海洋山谷都沿梯田状分别攀升至新旧世界的边缘。西部山谷的攀升轨迹沿着美国和西印度群岛的外围，一直向南延伸至赤道。东部山谷的梯田从海底攀升，一直到欧洲和非洲的西海岸。在非洲海岸边缘，它们形成了巍峨崎岖的制高点，也就是马德拉、佛得角和加那利群岛。而这整个一片山谷达到特内里费峰这一最高点时，位于海平面的英里之上。而大西洋海床的最低点，在海平面之下英里处。因此大西洋盆地的整个山区在垂直高度向上延伸了7英里。或者可以说，这比地球上海平面之上的所有山峰都要高。

通过从大西洋底部采取的样本，并在显微镜下对它们进行的研究，我们能确定大西洋海床遍布了微小的贝壳。它们像游丝一样微小，停留在海洋底部。显微镜没有在这些贝壳中发现任何颗粒物或者砾石。由此可以得知，宁静统治了整个海洋底部，这里是一片如云端之上由宁静统治的区域。海水中，在汹涌的波涛之下，四处都笼罩着这种永久的宁静。没有任何动态能够腐蚀这些微妙的微生物，也没有任何波涛让它们随波逐流，或者任何细沙能够将它们混杂。

也许正是这无数的微生物使海洋变得生机盎然，而它们隐匿于那些注定要充斥着海底空洞的坚硬物质，它们提供了构成山脉和延展平原的原子。正是这些在海平面之下3英里处可以找到的微生物，构成了我们海床的泥灰、河流的黏土，还有地球广阔盆地的绝大份额，甚至是坚硬的岩石。因此当这些生物还有生命时，就已经做好了准备成为地球肥沃土壤的成分，在将来的许多年之后，甚至会引发地震或者地壳隆起。也正是它们，可能会从海洋底部升起，为人类所用。

Lesson 5   BINGEN ON THE RHINE
第五课   莱茵河畔的宾根

A soldier of the Legion lay dying in Algiers;
There was lack of woman's nursing, there was dearth of woman's tears;
But a comrade stood beside him, while his life-blood ebbed away,
And bent, with pitying glances, to hear what he might say.
The dying soldier faltered, as he took that comrade's hand,
And he said: "I never more shall see my own, my native land:
Take a message and a token to some distant friends of mine;
For I was born at Bingen—at Bingen on the Rhine.

"Tell my brothers and companions, when they meet and crowd around,
To hear my mournful story, in the pleasant vineyard ground,
That we fought the battle bravely; and when the day was done,
Full many a corse lay ghastly pale beneath the setting sun.
And amidst the dead and dying were some grown old in wars—
The death-wound on their gallant breasts, the last of many scars;
But some were young, and suddenly beheld life's morn decline;
And one had come from Bingen—fair Bingen on the Rhine.

"Tell my mother that her other sons shall comfort her old age,
And I was aye a truant bird, that thought his home a cage;
For my father was a soldier, and, even as a child,
My heart leaped forth to hear him tell of struggles fierce and wild;
And when he died, and left us to divide his scanty hoard,
I let them take whate'er they would, but kept my father's sword;
And with boyish love I hung it where the bright light used to shine,
On the cottage-wall at Bingen—calm Bingen on the Rhine!

Tell my sister not to weep for me, and sob with drooping head,
When the troops are marching home again, with glad and gallant tread;
But to look upon them proudly, with a calm and steadfast eye,
For her brother was a soldier too, and not afraid to die.
And if a comrade seek her love, then ask her in my name
To listen to him kindly, without regret or shame;
And to hang the old sword in its place (my father's sword and mine),
For the honour of old Bingen—dear Bingen on the Rhine!

"There's another—not a sister: in the happy days gone by,
You'd have known her by the merriment that sparkled in her eye;
Too innocent for coquetry—too fond for idle scorning!—
O friend, I fear the lightest heart makes sometimes heaviest mourning!
Tell her the last night of my life (for ere this moon be risen
My body will be out of pain—my soul be out of prison
I dreamed I stood with her, and saw the yellow sunlight shine
On the vine-clad hills of Bingen—fair Bingen on the Rhine

"I saw the blue Rhine sweep along; I heard, or seemed to hear,
The German songs we used to sing in chorus sweet and clear;
And down the pleasant river, and up the slanting hill,
That echoing chorus sounded, through the evening calm and still;
And her glad blue eyes were on me, as we passed with friendly talk
Down many a path beloved of yore, and well-remembered walk;
And her little hand lay lightly, confidingly in mine;—
But we'll meet no more at Bingen—loved Bingen on the Rhine!"

His voice grew faint and hoarser; his grasp was childish weak;
His eyes put on a dying look; he sighed, and ceased to speak:
His comrade bent to lift him, but the spark of life had fled;
The soldier of the Legion in a foreign laud—was dead!
And the soft moon rose up slowly, and calmly she looked down
On the red sand of the battle-field, with bloody corses strown;
Yea, calmly on that dreadful scene her pale light seemed to shine,
As it shone on distant Bingen—fair Bingen on the Rhine!

—Caroline Norton.

Words

comfort, *soothe*.	foreign, *distant*.
comrade, *companion*.	merriment, *happiness*.
confidingly, *trustfully*.	mournful, *sad*.
coquetry, *flirtation*.	scanty, *meager*.
decline, *fall away*.	steadfast, *unwavering*.
faltered, *trembled*.	truant, *wandering*.

☆ ☆

军团中一名战士在阿尔及尔奄奄一息，

没有女性的护理，也没有女人为他流下眼泪；

当他的生命迹象在衰退，只有一名战友站在他身旁，
他俯下身，怜惜地凝望，听他说话。
奄奄一息的战士颤抖着，握住战友的手，
他说："我再也见不到我自己的祖国，
请向我远方的朋友们带去我的信息，
因为我出生在宾根——莱茵河畔的宾根。

"告诉我的兄弟和同伴，当他们聚于一处，
在欢愉的葡萄园中，聆听我哀伤的过往；
我们勇猛地战斗，日子就这样过去，
众多尸体沉寂在落日之下。
在已死与将死的人们之中，一些人在战争中老去，
他们身上的最后一处伤痕，是死亡刻在他们勇敢的胸膛；
另一些人如此年轻，但在生命的黎明时分凋零，
其中一人便来自于宾根——莱茵河畔美丽的宾根。

"告诉我的母亲，我的兄弟们会代替我照顾年迈的她，
我就像一支逃脱牢笼的小鸟；
父亲是名军人，当我还是个孩子，
我的心沉浸于他讲的故事里，那些激烈的战斗；
当他去世，让我们兄弟分割他的所剩积蓄，
他们拿走了其他所有，但我留下了父亲的剑；
怀着少年的情怀，我将它挂在曾熠熠生辉的高墙，
在那宾根的茅舍里的高墙——莱茵河畔安详的宾根！

"告诉我的姐妹不要为我哭泣，也不要垂下头呜咽，
当部队再次踏着欢愉的步伐来到我们的家乡；
她只要骄傲地望着他们，用平静、坚定的眼神，
因为他的兄弟也是一名战士，对于死亡毫不畏惧；
若一名士官追求她，并向她追问起我的姓名，
让她认真倾听，不要悲伤或者羞愧；
让她将父亲与我共有的那柄剑挂在原处，
为了宾根的荣耀——莱茵河畔的宾根！

"还有另外一个重要的人，但并非也是我的姐妹，
在那些逝去的日子里，你会看到她眼睛里欢快的光亮；
她如此单纯乐观，不会卖弄风情，也不会蔑视懒惰！
朋友，我真害怕些许沉重的哀伤会伤害她的心灵！
告诉她在我生命的最后一天，在月亮升起之前，
我的身躯再也不会感受到疼痛，我的灵魂再不会受到羁绊。
我梦想着站在她的身旁，看着金黄的阳光，
照耀在宾根藤蔓覆盖的山上——莱茵河畔的美丽宾根。

"我看到蔚蓝的莱茵河流淌着，我听到了，似乎能够听到，
我们过去愉快地合唱着德国之歌，如此悦耳清晰；
沿着欢愉的河流，在倾斜的山顶，
歌声在这里回荡，回荡在静谧的夜里；
她幽兰色的眼睛愉快地望着我，友好的交谈就这样过去，
我们过去爱在一条幽径漫步，每一次都让我难以忘记；
她的小手轻轻地放在我的手里，饱含着对我的信任；
然而我们将不会重逢在宾根——莱茵河畔我挚爱的宾根。"

他的声音逐渐微弱、沙哑，他抓住同伴的手也开始变得无力，
他的眼神涣散着死亡的无神，他叹息着，不再说话；
战友俯下身子去扶他，但他的生命之光却在逐渐消退；
这个年轻的战士死在了他乡！
温柔的月亮缓缓升起，平静地照耀着大地，
照亮了战场血红的地面，这里布满了战士们的血肉之躯；
他苍白的目光变得平静，洒在这片死亡之地，
如它照耀在遥远的宾根——莱茵河畔美丽的宾根！

——卡洛琳·诺顿

Lesson 6 THE CLOUD
第六课 云 朵

I bring fresh showers for the thirsting flowers,
    From the seas and the streams;
I bear light shade for the leaves when laid
    In their noonday dreams.
From my wings are shaken the dews that waken
    The sweet buds every one,
When rocked to rest on their Mother's breast,
    As she dances about the Sun.
I wield the flail of the lashing hail,
    And whiten the green plains under;
And then again I dissolve it in rain,
    And laugh as I pass in thunder.

I sift the snow on the mountains below,
    And their great pines groan aghast;
And all the night 'tis my pillow white,
    While I sleep in the arms of the blast
Sublime on the towers of my skiey bowers
    Lightning my pilot sits;
In a cavern under is fettered the Thunder—
    It struggles and howls at fits:
Over earth and ocean, with gentle motion,
    This pilot is guiding me,
Lured by the love of the Genii that move
    In the depths of the purple sea;
Over the rills, and the crags, and the hills.
    Over the lakes and the plains,
Wherever he dream, under mountain or stream.
    The Spirit he loves remains;
And I all the while bask in heaven's blue smile,
    Whilst he is dissolving in rains.

The sanguine Sunrise, with his meteor eyes.
    And his burning plumes outspread,
Leaps on the back of my sailing rack,
    When the morning-star shines dead,—

As on the jag of a mountain crag,
  Which an earthquake rocks and swings.
An eagle alit one moment may sit
  In the light of its golden wings.
And when Sunset may breathe, from the lit sea beneath,
  Its ardours of rest and of love,
And the crimson pall of eve may fall
  From the depth of heaven above,—
With wings folded I rest, on mine airy nest,
  As still as a brooding dove.

That orbed maiden with white fire laden,
  Whom mortals call the Moon,
Glides glimmering o'er my fleece-like floor,
  By the midnight breezes strewn;
And wherever the beat of her unseen feet,
  Which only the angels hear,
May have broken the woof of my tent's thin roof,
  The stars peep behind her and peer;
And I laugh to see them whirl and flee,
  Like a swarm of golden bees,
When I widen the rent in my wind-built tent,—
  Till the calm rivers, lakes, and seas,
Like strips of the sky fallen through me on high,
  Are each paved with the moon and these.

I bind the Sun's throne with a burning zone,
  And the Moon's with a girdle of pearl;
The volcanoes are dim, and the stars reel and swim,
  When the Whirlwinds my banner unfurl.
From cape to cape, with a bridge-like shape,
  Over a torrent sea,
Sunbeam-proof, I hang like a roof;
  The mountains its columns be.
The triumphal arch through which I march
  With hurricane, fire, and snow,
When the Powers of the air are chained to my chair,
  Is the million-coloured bow;
The Sphere-fire above, its soft colours wove,
  While the moist Earth was laughing below.

I am the daughter of Earth and Water,

And the nursling of the Sky:
　I pass through the pores of the ocean and shores;
　　I change, but I cannot die.
For after the rain—when with never a stain
　　The pavilion of heaven is bare,
And the winds and sunbeams', with their convex gleams,
　　Build up the blue dome of air—
I silently laugh at my own cenotaph,
　　And out of the caverns of rain,
Like a child from the womb, like a ghost from the tomb,
　　I arise and unbuild it again.

—P. B. Shelley

Words

ardours, *fervours*.
dissolve, *melt*.
earthquake, *a convulsion of the earth*.
glimmering, *flickering*.
guiding, *conducting*.
hurricane, *tempest*.
lashing, *scourging*.
meteor, *flashing*.

mortals, *human beings*.
nursling, *child*.
pavilion, *canopy*.
sublime, *imposing*.
thirsting, *parched*.
unfurl, *unfold*.
volcanoes, *burning mountains*.
whirlwinds, *violent blasts*.

☆ ☆

我为焦灼的花木，洒下清新的雨露——
我来自江河湖海；
当梦境在晌午恍恍惚惚——
我为绿叶提供阴凉的庇护。
我让清香簇拥，蓓蕾复苏——
我抖落叶瓣上的露珠，
在慈母的胸膛，我感觉温暖的爱抚，
当她围绕太阳翩翩起舞。
我挥舞连枷，像冰雹在击打，
我将绿野铺满皑皑的冰花，
哗哗的雨水之中，我再将其溶化，
我边走边笑，任雷电交加。

我将绒绒雪花，撒向群山，
葱郁的松林，发出骇人的呻吟；
在狂风的怀中，我睡意蒙胧，
夜晚，我头枕白雪，沉入梦境。
我的塔楼天穹，雄伟高耸，
我的向导，端坐其中，
雷声轰鸣，幽囚于地洞，
忽然之间，发出阵阵狂嚎；
缓缓飞临大地与碧浪之上，
那向导将我引领，
用爱慕之情，将其引诱，
游弋在紫色大海深处的精灵。
在山涧、险崖和山峦之上游弋，
越过湖泊和平原，
无论梦在山峦，或在河川，
他钟爱的精灵依旧不变；
天空蔚蓝的微笑，始终赐给我温暖，
虽然在雨中，他会渐渐消散。

红艳的朝霞，他流星一般的眼睛，
展露他火红色的翎羽，
当晨星渐渐幻灭，
跃上我浮云的脊背飞行；
当嶙峋的山崖，凹凸有致，
摇摆晃动、天崩地裂，
刚飞落的雄鹰，如愿栖身于此——
在它们金光闪闪的羽翎之间。
在明亮的海底水域之上，斜阳在怯怯低语，
休眠的热切，挚爱的情趣，
绯红的夜幕，会渐渐
降临在高深、浩瀚的苍穹之上，
我在云层的巢穴中，合翅休憩，
似正在孵卵的母鸽般静谧。

圆润的女郎，泛起盈盈的白光，
尘世之间，将其称为月亮，
飞掠的微光，恰似羊毛覆盖在大地之上，
任凭午夜的微风，送来阵阵清凉；
无论隐形的玉足在哪里停留，
只有天使才能感悟其中，
他们会踩破我的帐篷，顶部的薄纱，
群星在她背后窥探、凝望；
我笑看他们似旋风般奔逃，
宛若一群金色的蜜蜂，
当我在飓风的天篷，撑开裂缝，
直到江河湖海风平浪静，
就像来自我头顶的苍穹一般的条纹，
每一片都镶嵌着月亮和这些繁星。

我缠住太阳的宝座，用火红的绫罗绸缎，
珍珠腰带包裹住月亮的宝座；
火山隐隐闪烁，星星飘忽颠簸，
我的旗帜在旋风中飘过。
从一处海角到另一处，似拱桥的形状，
在奔流不息的大海之上，
我像悬空的穹顶，遮挡住阳光，
崇山峻岭是我的柱廊。
我途经凯旋之门，
裹挟着火焰、雪片和飓风，
当空中的神灵，被我的马车拘禁，
五彩缤纷，姹紫嫣红；
天上的火星，柔和的色彩交织一起，
湿润的大地之上，泛起笑语声声。

我是来自天庭的圣婴，
是大地、水域的千金之女；
我穿梭于海洋与海岸的隙缝之间；

我时刻变换，绝不消停。
雨后天晴，没有一点痕迹——
天国的帐篷此时毫无遮掩，
和风与日光显出莹莹凹面，
勾画出蔚蓝的大气穹顶，
我在自己的墓冢之中暗暗嘲讽，
而洞穴之外，却是烟雨蒙蒙，
似来自荒冢的幽灵，出自子宫的婴儿，
我会将其夷平，继而再度升空。

——P.B·雪莱

Lesson 7　THE TRIAL BY COMBAT (I)
第七课　决斗裁判（一）

Rebecca the Jewess, when condemned to death for sorcery by the Grand Master of the Order of Knights Templars, challenged the privilege of " Trial by Combat," in proof of her innocence. Her challenge was accepted, and Sir Brian, a valiant Templar, was named the champion of the holy Order.

Rebecca had difficulty in finding a messenger who would undertake to carry a letter to her father, Isaac of York; at last Higg, the son of Snell, a poor cripple whom she had befriended, volunteered his services.

"I am but a maimed man," he said, "but that I can at all stir is owing to her charitable aid.—I will do thine errand," he added, turning to Rebecca, "as well as a crippled object can.—Alas! when I boasted of thy charity, I little thought that I was leading thee into danger."

"God," said Rebecca, "is the Disposer of all. He can turn back the captivity of Judah even by the weakest instrument. Seek out Isaac of York—here is that will pay for horse and man—let him have this scroll. Farewell!—Life and death are in thy haste."

Within a quarter of a mile from the gate of the Preceptory the peasant met two riders, whom, by their dress and yellow caps, he knew to be Jews; and, on approaching more nearly, he discovered that one of them was his ancient employer, Isaac of York. The other was the Rabbi Ben Samuel; and both had approached as near to the Preceptory as they dared, on hearing that the Grand Master had summoned a chapter, or meeting of the Order, for the trial of a sorceress. -

" How now, brother?" said Ben Samuel, interrupting his harangue to look towards Isaac, who had but glanced at the scroll which Higg offered, when, uttering a deep groan, he fell from his mule like a dying man, and lay for a minute insensible.

The Rabbi now dismounted in great alarm, and hastily applied the remedies which his art suggested for the recovery of his companion. He had even taken from his pocket a cupping apparatus, and was about to use it, when the object of his solicitude suddenly revived; but it was to dash his cap from his head, and to throw dust on his gray hairs. The physician was at first inclined to ascribe this sudden and violent emotion to the effects of insanity; and, adhering to his original purpose, began once again to handle his implements. But Isaac soon convinced him of his error.

"Child of my sorrow," he said, "well shouldst thou be called Benoni, instead of Rebecca! Why should thy death bring down my gray hairs to the grave?"

"Brother," said the Rabbi, in great surprise, "I trust that the child of thy house yet liveth?"

"She liveth," answered Isaac, "but she is captive unto those men of Be'lial, and they will wreak their cruelty upon her, sparing her neither for her youth nor her comely favour. Oh, she was as a crown of green palms to my gray locks; and she must wither in a night, like the gourd of Jonah! Child of my love! child of my old age!—O Rebecca, daughter of Rachel, the darkness of the shadow of death hath encompassed thee."

"Yet read the scroll," said the Rabbi; "peradventure it may be that we may yet find out a way of deliverance."

"Do thou read, brother," answered Isaac, "for mine eyes are as fountains of water."

The physician read, but in their native language, the following Words:—

"To Isaac, the son of Adoni'kam, whom the Gentiles call Isaac of York, peace and the blessing of the promise be multiplied unto thee.

"My father, I am as one doomed to die for that which my soul knoweth not —even for the crime of witchcraft. My father, if a strong man can be found to do battle for my cause with sword and spear, according to the custom of the Nazarenes, and that within the lists of Tem'plestowe, on the third day from this time, peradventure our fathers' God will give him strength to defend the innocent, and her who hath none to help her. But if this may not be, let the virgins of our people mourn for me as for one cast off, and for the hart that is stricken by the hunter, and for the flower which is cut down by the scythe of the mower. Wherefore, look now what thou doest, and whether there be any rescue.

"One Nazarene warrior might, indeed, bear arms in my behalf, even Wilfred, son of Ced'ric, whom the Gentiles call I'vanhoe. But he may not yet endure the weight of his armour. Nevertheless, send the tidings unto him, my father; for he hath favour among the strong men of his people, and as he was our companion in the house of bondage, he may find some one to do battle for my sake. And say unto him, even unto him, even unto Wilfred, the son of Cedric, that if Rebecca live, or if Rebecca die, she liveth or dieth wholly free of the guilt she is charged withal.

"And if it be the will of God that thou shalt be deprived of thy daughter, do not thou tarry, old man, in this land of bloodshed and cruelty; but betake thyself to Cordo'va, where thy brother liveth in safety, under the shadow of the throne, even of the throne of Boab'dil the Sar'acen: for less cruel are the cruelties of the Moors unto the race of Jacob than the cruelties of the Nazarenes of England."

Isaac listened with tolerable composure while Ben Samuel read the letter, and then again resumed the gestures and exclamations of Oriental sorrow, tearing his garments, besprinkling his head with dust, and ejaculating, "My daughter! my daughter!"

"Yet," said the Rabbi, "take courage, for this grief availeth nothing. Seek out this Wilfred, the son of Cedric. It may be he will help thee with counsel or with strength; for the youth hath favour in the eyes of Richard, called of the Nazarenes the Lion-Heart, and the tidings that he hath returned are constant in the land. It may be that he may obtain his letter, and his signet, commanding these men of blood, who take their name from the Temple, to the dishonour thereof, that they proceed not in their purposed wickedness."

"I will seek him out," said Isaac; "for he is a good youth, and hath compassion for the exile of Jacob. But he cannot bear his armour, and what other Christian shall do battle for the oppressed of Zion?"

—Sir W. Scott

Words

availeth, *profiteth*.	harangue, *speech*.
bondage, *slavery*.	implements, *apparatus*.
challenged, *claimed*.	insanity, *delirium*.
companion, *associate*.	insensible, *unconscious*.
compassion, *pity*.	multiplied, *increased*.
cruelties, *atrocities*.	peradventure, *perchance*.
deliverance, *release*.	physician, *healer*.
deprived, *bereft*.	privilege, *right*.
discovered, *found*.	remedies, *restoratives*.
dishonour, *shame*.	solicitude, *anxiety*.
ejaculating, *exclaiming*.	sorcery, *witchcraft*.
employer, *master*.	summoned, *called*.
encompassed, *surrounded*.	volunteered, *offered freely*.
gestures, *actions*.	

Questions

What privilege did Rebecca claim when she had been condemned? Who was named the champion of the Temple? Who at last volunteered to carry her letter? Where did he meet Isaac? What effect had the perusal of Rebecca's letter upon the latter? Who accompanied him? Whose help did Rebecca ask him to obtain?

犹太女人丽贝卡，当被骑士团团长因其使用巫术而判处死刑时，挑战决斗裁判的特权，以证明自己的清白。兵团接收了她的挑战，布莱恩爵士——一位英勇的圣殿骑士，被任命为维护神圣秩序的战士。

丽贝卡在万难之中，终于找到一个人，愿意帮她把信带给她的父亲艾萨克·约克，最终，她认识的一个可怜的跛子——斯奈尔的孩子海格，自愿完成这项任务。

"我只是一个残疾人，"他说道，"但是我的所有行动都归功于你对我仁慈的帮助。我将做你吩咐的事，"他转身面向丽贝卡补充道，"像我这样的残疾人，虽然我赞美你的仁慈，但是我不认为我会把你带入危险之中。"

丽贝卡说道："上帝是处置一切的人。他甚至可以用最无理的手段，把犹大给带走。找到艾萨克·约克，让他看看这个卷轴。这是用来支付你需要的马匹和人手的钱。再见了！我的生死全取决于你的速度了。"

在离开圣殿骑士的大门四分之一英里远的时候，这个农民遇到了两个骑士。从他们的衣着和那显眼的黄帽子上，他可以看出他们是犹太人。他们慢慢地走近了，他发现其中一个是他原来的雇主艾萨克·约克，另一个是拉比本·赛弥尔，他们两人冒险接近圣骑士的领地。他们能够听见骑士团长在宣布一件大事，要对一个女巫进行审判。

"怎么样了，兄弟？"本·赛弥尔打断了他的长篇大论，看向艾萨克。艾萨克只瞥了一眼海格给他的卷轴，然后闷哼了一声。他像一个奄奄一息的人一样，从驴子上掉了下来，一分钟之内都毫无知觉地躺着。

拉比惊恐地下了马，马上对他的同伴实施急救。他甚至从他的口袋里拿出了一个火罐，想要用它。当他关心的同伴突然苏醒过来时，他只能匆忙将他头上戴的帽子拿下来，拂去他苍白的脸颊上的灰烬。起初，这个医生更偏向于将这种突然而强烈的情感归因于精神错乱的影响，而他还是坚持自己原来的打算，开始再一次使用他的工具来治疗他，但艾萨克马上让他相信他弄错了。

"孩子，你受苦了，"他说道，"你应该叫作贝诺尼而不是丽贝卡！为什么你的死亡，会将我的生命也带进坟墓之中？"

"兄弟，"拉比异常惊讶地说道，"我相信你家的孩子还活着。"

"她还活着，"艾萨克说道，"但她被贝利奥的人俘房了，他们会用尽残忍的手段来虐待她，她的年轻和美丽的容貌都不可能使她得到偏袒。她就像我头上棕榈叶做成的花冠一样。但她一定会在晚上枯萎，像犹大的葫芦一样！我亲爱的孩子啊，我长大的孩子啊，哦，丽贝卡，瑞秋的女儿，死亡的黑暗阴影正笼罩着你！"

"读读卷轴吧，"拉比说道，"如果可能，我们也许会找到一个解救她的办法。"

"你看吧，兄弟，"艾萨克回答道，"因为我的眼睛已经泪如泉涌了。"

医生读着卷轴。卷轴用他们的母语写成，写了如下一段话：

"致艾萨克，安东尼·凯姆的儿子，人们都称其为艾森克·约克。和平和承诺将给你祝福。

"我的父亲，我是注定要死去的，虽然我的灵魂不这么想，我是因为巫术而犯下了罪。我的父亲，如果能够找到一个健壮的人，为了赢得我的官司，根据拿撒勒派的习俗和他们列表里的内容，从现在开始的第三天，用剑和矛为我战斗。也许我们的列祖列宗将赐予他力量，让他去保卫那些无辜的人，去保卫那个没有人可以帮助的她。但如果这些都没有发生，就让我们的人民为我哀悼，因为我得到了解脱。让他们同样为了猎人伤害的驯鹿，为了那些被大镰刀砍掉的花朵而哀悼。因此，看看是否还有什么营救我的方法。

"事实上，一个拿撒勒派的勇士可能会代表我拿起武器，可能是塞德里克的儿子威尔弗雷德。但他也许无法承受他沉重的武器。然而，发一条信息给他，我的父亲。因为他偏袒了他的人民之中的那些强壮之人，因为作为我们的朋友，他同样受到了奴役。他可能会找到一个愿意为我战斗的人。告诉他，甚至告诉塞德里克的儿子威尔弗雷德，就说，不管丽贝卡是活着还是死了，她都完全没有犯下她被判决的这些罪行。"

"如果这是上帝的旨意，要夺走你女儿的性命，那么，我的老父亲，绝对不要逗留！不要逗留在这片血腥而残酷的大地之上。你要尽快去卡多瓦，你的兄弟在那里安全地生活着，生活在王位的庇护之下。因为摩尔人对于雅各的族人，比起英国人来，没有那么残忍。"

艾萨克从容淡定地听完了本·赛弥尔读完这封信，接着，他再一次变成了那个姿势，大声地呼喊着，双手扯裂了自己的上衣，披散着头发，仰天大喊道："我的女儿！我的女儿！"

"但是，"拉比说道，"鼓起你的勇气，现在我们需要的不是悲伤。找到塞德里克的儿子威尔弗雷德。或许他会给你一些建议和力量。在理查德的眼中，这个青年受到了青睐，被称为拿撒勒的狮心王。他一定会回到这片土地。也许他可以得到他的信和印章，继而命令那些好战的人们，那些从神庙中得到自己名字的人们，他们因此不应该向着邪恶前行。"

"我会找到他的，"艾萨克说，"他是一个好青年，他对于雅各族人的流亡表示同情。但是如果他不能拿起他的武器，而其他的基督徒，会为了锡安族人的受压迫而参与到斗争中来吗？"

——沃尔特·司各特爵士

Lesson 8　THE TRIAL BY COMBAT (II)
第八课　决斗裁判（二）

Our scene now returns to the exterior of the Castle, or Precep'tory, of Tem'plestowe, about the hour when the bloody die was to be cast for the life or death of Rebecca. A throne was erected for the Grand Master at the east end of the tilt-yard, surrounded with seats of distinction for the Preceptors and Knights of the Order.

At the opposite end of the lists was a pile of fagots, so arranged around a stake, deeply fixed in the ground, as to leave a space for the victim whom they were destined to consume, to enter within the fatal circle in order to be chained to the stake by the fetters which hung ready for the purpose.

The unfortunate Rebecca was conducted to a black chair placed near the pile. On her first glance at the terrible spot where preparations were making for a death alike dismaying to the mind and painful to the body, she was observed to shudder and shut her eyes—praying internally, doubtless, for her lips moved though no speech was heard. In the space of a minute she opened her eyes, looked fixedly on the pile, as if to familiarize her mind with the object, and then slowly and naturally turned away her head.

It was the general belief that no one could or would appear for a Jewess accused of sorcery; and the knights whispered to each other that it was time to declare the pledge of Rebecca forfeited. At that instant a knight, urging his horse to speed, appeared on the plain advancing towards the lists. A hundred voices exclaimed, "A champion! a champion!" And despite the prejudices of the multitude, they shouted unanimously as the knight rode into the tilt-yard.

The second glance, however, served to destroy the hope that his timely arrival had excited. His horse, urged for many miles to its utmost speed, appeared to reel from fatigue; and the rider, however undauntedly he presented himself in the lists, either from weakness, from weariness, or from both combined, seemed scarce able to support himself in the saddle.

To the summons of the herald, who demanded his rank, his name and purpose, the stranger knight answered readily and boldly, "I am a good knight and noble, come hither to uphold with lance and sword the just and lawful quarrel of this damsel, Rebecca, daughter of Isaac of York; to maintain the doom pronounced against her to be false and truthless, and to defy Sir Brian the Templar as a traitor, murderer, and liar; as I will prove in this field with my body against his, by the aid of God, and of Saint George, the good knight."

"The stranger must first show," said a Templar, "that he is a good knight, and of honourable lineage. The Temple sendeth not forth her champions against nameless men."

TILT—YARD

"My name," said the knight, raising his helmet, "is better known, my lineage more pure, than thine own. I am Wilfred of Ivanhoe."

"I will not fight with thee at present," said the Templar, in a changed and hollow voice. " Get thy wounds healed, purvey thee a better horse, and it may be I will hold it worth my while to scourge out of thee this boyish spirit of bravado."

"Ha! proud Templar," said Ivanhoe, "hast thou forgotten that twice thou didst fall before this lance? Remember the lists at A'cre—remember the passage of arms at Ash'by—remember thy proud vaunt in the halls of Roth'erwood, and the gage of your gold chain against my reliquary, that thou wouldst do battle with Wilfred of Ivanhoe, and recover the honour thou hadst lost! By that reliquary, and the holy relic it contains, I will proclaim thee, Templar, a coward in every Court in Europe—unless thou do battle without further delay."

Sir Brian turned his countenance irresolutely towards Rebecca, and then exclaimed, looking fiercely at Ivanhoe, "Dog of a Saxon! take thy lance, and prepare for the death thou hast drawn upon thee!"

"Does the Grand Master allow me the combat?" said Ivanhoe.

"I may not deny what thou hast challenged," said the Grand Master, "provided the maiden accept thee as her champion. Yet I would thou wert in better plight to do battle. An enemy of our Order hast thou ever been, yet would I have thee honourably met withal."

"Thus—thus as I am, and not otherwise," said Ivanhoe; "it is the judgment of God—to his keeping I commend myself.—Rebecca," said he, riding up to the fatal chair, "dost thou accept of me for thy champion? "

"I do," she said, "I do,"—fluttered by an emotion which the fear of death had been unable to produce—"I do accept thee as the champion whom Heaven hath sent me. Yet, no—no; thy wounds are uncured. Meet not that proud man—why shouldst thou perish also?"

But Ivanhoe was already at his post; he had closed his visor and assumed his lance. Sir Brian did the same; and his esquire remarked, as he clasped his visor, that his face—which had, notwithstanding the variety of emotions by which he had been agitated, continued during the whole morning of an ashy paleness—had now become suddenly very much flushed.

The Grand Master, who held in his hand the gage of battle, Rebecca's glove, now threw it into the lists. The trumpets sounded, and the knights charged each other in full career. The weary horse of Ivanhoe, and its no less exhausted rider, went down, as all had expected, before the well-aimed lance and vigorous steed of the Templar. This issue of the combat all had foreseen; but although the spear of Ivanhoe, in comparison, did but touch the shield of Sir Brian, that champion, to the astonishment of all who beheld it, reeled in his saddle, lost his stirrup, and fell in the lists!

Ivanhoe, extricating himself from his fallen horse, was soon on foot, hastening to mend his fortune with his sword; but his antagonist arose not. Wilfred, placing his foot on his breast, and the sword's point to his throat, commanded him to yield him, or die on the spot. The Templar returned no answer.

"Slay him not, Sir Knight," cried the Grand Master "unshriven and unabsolved—kill not body and soul! We acknowledge him vanquished."

He descended into the lists, and commanded them to unhelm the conquered champion. His eyes were closed—the dark red flush was still on his brow. As they looked on him in astonishment, the eyes opened—but they were fixed and glazed.

The flush passed from his brow, and gave way to the pallid hue of death. Unscathed by the lance of his enemy, he had died a victim to the violence of his own contending passions.

"This is indeed the judgment of God," said the Grand Master, looking upwards—"Fiat voluntas tua!"

When the first moments of surprise were over, Wilfred of Ivanhoe demanded of the Grand Master, as judge of the field, if he had manfully and rightfully done his duty in the combat?

"Manfully and rightfully hath it been done," said the Grand Master; "I pronounce the maiden free and guiltless. The arms and the body of the deceased knight are at the will of the victor."

"I will not despoil him of his weapons," said the Knight of Ivanhoe, "nor condemn his corpse to shame. God's arm, no human hand, hath this day struck him down. But let his obsequies be private, as becomes those of a man who died in an unjust quarrel.—And for the maiden —"

He was interrupted by the clatter of horses' feet, advancing in such numbers, and so rapidly, as to shake the ground before them; and the Black Knight galloped into the lists. He was followed by a numerous band of men-at-arms, and several knights in complete armour.

"I am too late," he said, looking around him. "I had doomed Sir Brian for mine own property.—Ivanhoe, was this well, to take on thee such a venture, and thou scarce able to keep thy saddle?"

"Heaven, my liege," answered Ivanhoe, "hath taken this proud man for its victim. He was not to be honoured in dying as your will had designed."

"Peace be with him," said Richard, looking steadfastly on the corpse, "if it may be so—he was a gallant knight, and has died in his steel harness full knightly."

During the tumult Rebecca saw and heard nothing: she was locked in the arms of her aged father, giddy, and almost senseless, with the rapid change of circumstances around her. But one word from Isaac at length recalled her scattered feelings.

"Let us go," he said, "my dear daughter, my recovered treasure—let us go to throw ourselves at the feet of the good youth."

"Not so," said Rebecca; "oh no—no—no;—I must not at this moment dare to speak to him. Alas! I should say more than—No, my father; let us instantly leave this evil place."

Isaac, yielding to her entreaties, then conducted her from the lists, and by means of a horse which he had provided, transported her safely to the house of the Rabbi Nathan.

—Sir Walter Scott

Words

antagonist, *opponent.*
astonishment, *surprise.*
bravado, *boastfulness.*
champion, *defender.*
commend, *intrust.*
consume, *destroy.*
demanded, *asked.*
designed, *intended.*
destined, *appointed.*
dismaying, *appalling.*
distinction, *honour.*
entreaties, *solicitations.*
exhausted, *wearied.*
extricating, *disengaging.*
familiarize, *accustom.*
fluttered, *agitated.*
forfeited, *sacrificed.*
honourably, *worthily.*
internally, *mentally.*

interrupted, *checked.*
irresolutely, *unsteadily.*
lineage, *descent.*
notwithstanding, *in spite of.*
obsequies, *funeral rites.*
prejudices, *predilections.*
proclaim, *denounce.*
pronounced, *proclaimed.*
purvey, *provide.*
transported, *conveyed.*
unabsolved, *unpardoned.*
unanimously, *with one accord.*
undauntedly, *valiantly.*
unfortunate, *luckless.*
unscathed, *uninsured.*
unshriven, *not confessed.*
vanquished, *defeated.*
venture, *hazard.*
vigorous, *powerful.*

Questions

Where was the combat to take place? Where was the Grand Master position? What was at the opposite end of the lists? What was the general belief? Who at last appeared? Why did the Templar at first decline to fight with him? What fear did Rebecca express? What was the result of the encounter of the knights? What befell the Templar immediately afterwards? What had killed him? What verdict did the Grand Master now give regarding Rebecca? Who presently arrived on the scene? Why was the Black Knight disappointed? Who was this Black Knight? Who had embraced Rebecca? What did he ask her to do? What did she reply?

现在，让我们将场景返回到城堡的外墙，也就是坦普尔斯托的领地。大约就在这时，丽贝卡将在血腥的死亡之后被判决生或死。在决斗场的最东边，已经专门为骑士团团长准备好了一张座椅，而周围也有为教区校长和骑士们准备的不同的座位。

在比武场的另一头，放着一堆柴火，围在一根木桩的四周。木桩已经深深地固定在地面之上，为接下来他们注定要审判的受害者留下空间，能够让这个人进入到这个最终处决他的圆圈之中。在那里，她将被已经为这个目的而拴在桩上的链子勒死。

不幸的丽贝卡被关押在靠近木桩的一个黑色的椅子之上。她朝着这可怕的、会令精神沮丧、令身体痛苦的即将来临的死亡的地方看了一眼，人们可以观察到她禁不住的颤抖和紧闭上的双眼——她的内心在祈祷，毫无疑问，因为她的嘴唇微微地动着，但却没有人能听到任何声音。在短短一分钟之后，她睁开了眼睛，目不转睛地盯着木桩，仿佛要让她的头脑熟悉它一样，然后慢慢地、自然地将头转开了。

当时的人们普遍相信，不可能会出现一个人，为一个被指控实施了巫术的犹太女人而决斗；骑士们小声地互相说话，到了宣布对丽贝卡的指控的时候了。就在那一瞬间，一个骑士策马疾驰，出现在这片平地之上，来到在座的人群面前。许多人大声喊道："骑士！一个骑士！"尽管众人对他充满了偏见，当这位骑士冲进比武的院子里时，他们还是一致地喊出声来。

然而，再看第二眼时，就摧毁了他的及时到来所引发的希望。这个人已经敦促他的马，用最快的速度飞奔了许多英里，此时它似乎正忍受着疲劳，这个骑马的人，虽然无畏地出现在众人面前，也同样显得虚弱和疲惫。而这两者的组合，似乎使他都不能让自己坐稳在马鞍上。

传令官呼唤这位陌生的骑士，要求说出他的头衔、他的名字与来此的目的。那位骑士立即勇敢地回答道："我是一个优秀的骑士和贵族，带着我的枪和剑来到这里，来参与这场公正、合法的对于丽贝卡的审判，她是艾森克·约克的女儿；我来维护对她而言明显是虚假的、不真实的控告，来控告圣殿骑士布瑞恩爵士是一名叛徒、杀人犯和骗子；我将在这个地方与他相抗衡，用我的身体，在上帝和圣乔治的帮助之下，证明我是好骑士。"

"这个陌生人必须首先证明，"一个圣殿武士说道，"他是一个很好的骑士，拥有尊贵的血统。圣殿骑士从不和无名的人进行战斗。"

"我的名字，"骑士举起了他的头盔，说道，"非常著名，我的血统也比你自己的更加纯正，我是艾文荷的威尔弗雷德。"

"目前我还不想与你战斗，"圣殿骑士用一种和刚才不一样的空灵的声音说道。"等你的伤口愈合，找到一匹更好的马。这段时间，对我来说很有价值，可以灭掉你这虚张声势的孩子气的气焰。"

"哈！骄傲的圣殿武士，"艾文荷说，"你忘了你曾经两次倒在这杆枪之下吗？记得那次决斗吗？记住那次在阿什比，记得另一次你在罗舍伍德的大厅骄傲地吹牛，你的黄金链还有我的圣物作为赌注，你要同艾文荷的威尔弗雷德决斗，来恢复你已经失去的荣誉！这个圣物，和它承载的神圣遗物，圣殿武士，会在欧洲的各个宫廷之中宣布你的懦弱——除非你毫不迟疑地与我决斗。"

布瑞恩爵士迟疑不决地转向了丽贝卡，然后严厉地望着艾文荷，大声喊道："撒克森人的走狗！拿起你的枪，准备迎接死亡吧！"

"骑士团团长允许我战斗了吗？"艾文荷说道。

"我不否认你所挑战的，"骑士团团长说着，"因为这个少女接受你作为替她决斗的骑士。然而，我却希望你在更好的情况下进行决斗。你曾经是我们的敌人，但是我会让你成就你的荣耀。"

"因此是我，而不是其他人，"艾文荷说，"这是上帝的审判——我接收了他的旨意。丽贝卡，"他说着，走到她坐着的死亡之椅旁，"你接受我做你的骑士吗？"

"我接受，"她说，"我接受，"她被一种能够抑制对死亡的恐惧的情绪所激励，"我接受你来做我的骑士，你是上天派给我的。然而，现在不能——不能，因为你的伤口还没有痊愈。不要去和那个骄傲的人决斗，你为什么要自取灭亡呢？"

但艾文荷已经站在他的位置上；他已经戴上了他的面罩，拿好了他的枪。布瑞恩爵士也一样；他的扈从说，他将自己的面罩戴上时，他的脸——尽管他整个早上一直由于多种情绪而变得烦躁，他的脸也因此变得苍白——现在，他的脸却突然变得绯红。

骑士团团长手里拿着决斗的权杖，还有丽贝卡的手套，现在他把它扔到决斗场里。喇叭吹响了，双方的骑士全速骑马飞奔向对方。正如所有人预料的一样，艾文荷疲惫的马以及马上这个也同样劳累的骑士，在圣殿骑士瞄准的枪和生机勃勃的骏马面前跌落了下来。人们都已经预见到了这场决斗的结果，尽管艾文荷的枪也触碰到了布瑞恩的盾牌，但相比之下，让所有在场观看决斗的人都惊讶的是，这个骑士在他的马鞍上却没有踩住他的马镫，跌落在了决斗场上！

艾文荷从他倒下的马上将自己解脱出来，迅速站起来，急忙拿起他的剑重新进入决斗中，但他的敌手却没有过来。威尔弗雷德迅速踢了一脚他的胸膛，并把剑指向他的喉咙，命令他要么认输，要么当场死去。圣殿骑士没有回答。

"不要杀他，骑士先生，"骑士团团长喊道，"赦免他，不要杀死他的身体和灵魂！我们承认他已经被征服了。"

他倒在了决斗场上，并吩咐他们除去被征服的骑士的头盔。他闭上了眼睛，暗红色的鲜血仍然在他的额头上流淌。当人们惊讶地看着他，他睁开了眼睛，但他的眼睛此时却目不转睛、炯炯有神。鲜血在他的额头慢慢褪去，取而代之的是死亡的苍白色调。没有死在敌人的枪下，他却成为死在自己暴力决斗的激情之下的受害者。

"这真是上帝的审判，"骑士团团长说。他抬头向上看着，说道，"我们将遵照您的旨意！"

当惊喜的第一时刻已经过去，艾文荷的威尔弗雷德向作为该判决的法官的骑士团团长询问，他是否已经勇敢地、公平地完成了决斗。

"你进行的决斗非常英勇，也很公平，"骑士团团长说道，"我宣布这名少女自由、无罪。得到战败骑士的武器和身体，是胜利者的意志。""我不会抢占他的武器，"骑士艾文荷说，"也不会谴责他的身体的耻辱。今天，是上帝的手，而不是人类的手将他打败。但让他的葬礼秘密进行吧，假装他是在一次不公正的决斗中被杀害。而对这个少女……"

他被一阵马蹄声打断，众多的马匹迅速地在他们面前震撼着地面，黑骑士疾驰到决斗场之中。他身后跟着一队手持武器的士兵，还有几个全副武装的骑士。

"我来晚了，"他望向他的周围说道，"我已经认定布瑞恩爵士是我自己的财产。艾文荷，你冒这样的风险，而几乎不能够停留在自己的马鞍之上，这样好吗？"

"天啊，上帝，"艾文荷回答道，"这个骄傲的人已经被判作了这场决斗的失败者。他不会按照您设计的方式光荣地死去了。"

"和平将与他同在，"理查德说，目光坚定地望着地上的尸体，"如果是这样，他是一位勇敢的骑士，而他充满骑士精神的全副武装而死。"

在一片喧哗声中，丽贝卡什么也看不到、听不到了。在她年迈的父亲的臂膀之中，她几乎被定格住了，目光晕眩，几乎毫无知觉，因为她周围的环境是如此快速地发生了变化。但艾萨克的话，终于让她从散乱的感觉中苏醒了过来。

"我们走吧，"他说，"我亲爱的女儿，我失而复得的宝贝，让我们走到这个好青年的面前。""不，"丽贝卡说；"哦不——不——不——在这一刻，我不敢和他说话。唉！我本应该多说点什么——不，父亲，让我们立即离开这个邪恶的地方吧。"艾萨克听从了她的恳求，把她从这个决斗场带走了，并把她放在一匹马上，安全地带到了拉比的家中。

——沃尔特·司各特爵士

Lesson 9　DAMASCUS AND LONDON (I)
第九课　大马士革和伦敦（一）

Damascus is one of the greatest and most truly oriental cities in the world; let us, therefore, for our amusement and instruction, *compare it in its general external features with London*. In this way we may, perhaps, be able to get a clear idea of an oriental city.

From the dome of St. Paul's you behold London lying around, like a wide, waving, endless sea of slates, tiles, houses, churches, spires and monuments of all kinds. The eye is relieved with the heights and the hollows, the great and the little, the lowly lanes and the heaven-pointing spires.

In Damascus the scene is very different: there is much less variety; no spires, but multitudes of domes upon the mosques, and baths surmounted by little minarets. The houses are all flat-roofed, and the hue of the whole is a dim ash colour. A stillness like that of the dead reigns over the whole scene; and the city, surrounded with its celebrated evergreen gardens, suggests the idea of a ship sailing away through an ocean of verdure. Dun walls, flat roofs, domes and minarets, the stillness of death and the verdure of paradise, make up the elements of this most charming oriental scene. Tradition tells that Moham'med refused to enter the city, saying, "As there is only one paradise allotted to man, I shall reserve mine for the future world."

London and most large western cities are very often surmounted by clouds of smoke, owing to the coldness of the climate and the great consumption of coal. The sky over Damascus appears as bright and serene as elsewhere. For the greater part of the year the climate renders little or no fire necessary; and the little that is used is not from coal, but from wood or charcoal. The rooms have neither chimneys nor fire-places, and, except for the preparation of the supper, fire is rarely required during the course of the day. Hence the oriental city is not encircled with a graceful wreath of smoke, to remind you either of an ungenial clime or of the progress of mechanical genius.

But approach the city. All seems very still and quiet. Is it an enchanted capital, whose inhabitants have been turned into stone or brass? No; but the streets are not paved; there are no wheel-carriages of any kind; the shoes, more like foot-gloves than shoes, have no nails; no cotton-mills lift up their voice in the streets;—all those noisy triumphs of mechanical genius, in the way of forging, spinning, weaving, beetling, which are so frequent among us, are unknown in Damascus. The Easterns hold on their old course steadily, and yield to no seductions of novelty: the water-pump was invented in Alexandria, but the Alexandrians still prefer the ancient well and bucket.

But if the ear is not saluted with the roar and turbulence of mills, forges, and mechanical operations, Damascus has its own peculiar sounds, not less various and interesting in their way. The streets are filled with innumerable dogs, lean, lazy, and hungry-like; mules, donkeys, camels, dromedaries, meet and mingle in those narrow streets, and impress both the eye and the ear of the traveller with a pure and perfect idea of Orientalism.

British cities spread out, as it were indefinitely, into the country, in the way of parks, gardens, summer-houses, gentlemen's seats, and smiling villages. It is not so in the East. The city is within the walls, and all without is garden as at Damascus, or desert as at Jerusalem. Single houses are, in any country, the proof of the supremacy of law as well as of the respectability and independence of labour. Life and property have not attained perfect security in the East: a pistol, or rather a musket, was presented at my breast, within half a mile of Damascus, in broad daylight!

These noble gardens have no inhabitants; nor do any fine cottages, tasteful houses, or princely palaces, adorn this fertile region. Within the city you are safe;—without are dogs, insecurity of property, and the liability of being shot. The whole population, therefore, live either in cities or in villages, except in such regions as Beirout, where European influence and power prevail. There, you have gardens and single houses, much after the English fashion.

But place a Damascene at Charing Cross, or at Cheapside, and what do you think would amaze him most? The number of vehicles, undoubtedly. He would say, "When will this stream of cars, cabs, coaches, carriages, omnibuses of every shape and size, have an end? Are the people mad? Can they not take their time?"

But had the oriental nations of antiquity no wheel-carriages? They had; the Jews and the Egyptians had them, the Greeks and the Romans had them, and perhaps they may exist in some parts of the East to the present time. Here in Damascus there are none. The streets are not formed for them. The horses are trained only for riding. There are no common, levelled, and well-ordered public roads. Our fathers used no coaches; they preferred the more manly exercise of horsemanship, and yielded the soft, effeminate luxury of the coach to the ladies. But in London there are now about nine hundred omnibuses, each of which takes about £1000 annually. Such is the present state of coaching with us. How different is Damascus! and how different must the aspect of the streets appear!

With us, the city is laid out in streets, squares, crescents, royal circuses, and similar devices of beauty and regularity. This is the case particularly in the "west-ends" and newer parts of our cities and towns. There is nothing of this in Damascus, or in any of the eastern cities that I have seen: squares, crescents, and circuses are unknown. The streets are extremely irregular, crooked, winding, and narrow; which seems to arise out of the anxiety to find a protection from the sun.

In the narrower streets, where the houses are high, the sun's rays are effectually excluded; and in the wider ones, where this is not attainable, the numerous windings and angles afford salient points where the passenger may for a moment of two enjoy the shade. This may appear trifling, but I have often found the heat of the solar rays so intense and unendurable that even the sun-burnt Bedouins, the children of the desert, were glad of the least passing shade, the least momentary shelter, from the intolerable heat.

In the bazaars of Damascus, on the contrary, the streets or avenues are laid out with the greatest regularity, and are as straight as possible. In the heat of the day these are nearly deserted; business is at a stand; the merchant is reclining with pipe in mouth, in a state of semi-somnolence, in which the influence of opium or the odour of the redolent weed has carried the fertile imagination into the regions of celestial ease.

In an eastern city you have no prospect. With us you can see a considerable way along the streets. In Damascus you feel absolutely isolated; the streets are so narrow and crooked that at the most you can rarely see a perch before you, and nothing that does meet the eye in the way of buildings has the least attraction. Irregularity in style and clumsiness of execution, combined with the absence of fine doors, all windows, everything in the shape of fronts, railings, ornaments, &c., make the impression in that respect very disagreeable.

In our streets, we are pleased with large houses, fine rows of large windows, tastefully arranged doors and entrances;—everything seems to convey the idea of order, attention, cleanliness combined with the possession of wealth and the consciousness that it is our own. We conceal nothing, for we have no motive for concealment. Our house is our palace, and though the winds may thistle whorugh our dilapidated halls, the Queen herself dare not enter without our permission. Freedom has increased our property, and our wealth has enhanced the value of our freedom. Our temptation is not to concealment, but to ostentation and unnecessary display.

This tendency or temptation among us stands in connection with our character as a highly civilized and commercial nation. Great transactions cannot be carried on without credit, and credit is necessarily based on the belief of wealth; so that very often, where there may be little real property, it may be most desirable that there should be the appearance of it......

The mean, low door in Damascus, tells you of tyranny, concealment, and the want of confidence in public justice. Misery without and splendour within, is a principle which befits a land where paper is just paper, whatever name it bears; where gold is the only circulating medium; where a man's own house is his bank; and where the suspicion of being rich may make him a prey to the rapacity of the government.

On the contrary, the noble streets, squares, crescents, &c., of our modem cities, are clear indications, not only of great wealth and power, but also of something far dearer and nobler—namely, that *confidence in one another*, formed by myriads of concurring circumstances, of which Christianity is one of the mightiest, and out of which flow most of the blessings of European civilization and free political institutions.

But what is the use of that stone by the door-post? These stones are the steps from which ladies mount their donkeys, mules, and horses. Nor should you think this strange. In the fourteenth and fifteenth centuries, Paris presented these mounting-stones at all the angles of the streets, and at other convenient places. At Frankfort on the Main, there was a certain gate at which these conveniences were prepared for the emperor and the magnates of the German Diet; and I have no doubt that, in the days of feudalism and knightly glory, London was not behind its neighbours in this respect.

—Rev. Dr. Graham

Words

absolutely, *wholly*.	isolated, *alone*.
allotted, *assigned*.	levelled, *smoothed*.
attainable, *procurable*.	liability, *danger*.
celebrated, *renowned*.	momentary, *temporary*.
celestial, *heavenly*.	myriads, *hosts*.
circumstances, *events*.	oriental, *eastern*.
concealment; *secrecy*.	preparation, *cooking*.
concurring, *agreeing*.	protection, *covering*.
confidence, *trust*.	reclining, *resting*.
consciousness, *knowledge*.	redolent, *fragrant*.
consumption, *employment*.	relieved, *gratified*.
disagreeable, *unpleasant*.	respectability, *estimation*.
effectually, *successfully*.	seductions, *allurement*.
effeminate, *womanish*.	semi-somnolence, *being half-asleep*.
enchanted, *bewitched*.	supremacy, *authority*.
encircled, *encompassed*.	suspicion, *surmise*.
enhanced, *increased*.	tendency, *inclination*.
external, *outward*.	turbulence, *tumult*.
extremely, *very*.	vehicles, *carriages*.
indefinitely, *without bounds*.	verdure, *greenness*.
intolerable, *insufferable*.	

Questions

What contrast to London does Damascus present, in respect of its buildings? What, in respect of its atmosphere? What is the cause of the great stillness in the eastern city? Why are there no country-houses around Damascus? What are these the proof of in any country? What would most strike a Damascene in the streets of London? Why are the streets in eastern cities made narrow and crooked? What effect has this upon the prospect? What are fine houses and streets proof of in a commercial nation? What do the mean low doors in Damascus indicate? For what purpose are stones set up at the door-posts?

　　大马士革是世界上最伟大和最真实的东方城市之一。因此，为了自我娱乐和学习，我们可以将其一般性的外部特征与伦敦进行比较。这样我们也许能得到一个东方城市的清晰的概念。

　　从圣保罗大教堂的圆顶上，你可以俯瞰伦敦横亘于此，就像一片广阔、飘动、无尽的石板、瓷砖、房屋、教堂、尖顶和各种纪念碑的海洋。眼前会布满各种建筑，高耸的和凹陷的，伟大的与渺小的，卑微的小巷和指向天际的尖顶。

　　在大马士革，人们看到的场面则十分不同：建筑的多样性不像伦敦；这里没有尖顶，而是众多清真寺的圆顶，和占据整个城市的小尖塔。这些房子都是平顶的，而整体的色调是暗淡的灰色。这样死亡一般的寂静统治着整个场景，周围布满著名的常青花园的城市，让人想到一艘轮船漂洋过翠绿海洋的场面。盾墙、平顶、圆顶和尖塔、死亡的寂静和天堂的翠绿，构成了这最迷人的东方场景的各种元素。传说中讲道，穆罕默德拒绝进入这座城市，他说：“由于人间只能有一个这样属于人类的天堂，我将保留我的天堂，直到未来世界。”

　　由于气候的寒冷和对煤炭的巨大消耗，伦敦和大多数西方大都市都经常笼罩在烟雾中。大马士革的上空则呈现出如其他地方一样的明亮而宁静的天际。一年中的大部分时间，这里都很少或根本没有烟火；而那很少的烟火也不是由燃煤引起的，而是源自木材或木炭。这里的房子既没有烟囱也没有火炉，并且除了准备晚餐，火在一天的生活中都很少需要。所以，东方的城市从未环绕着烟雾的曼妙晕圈——这些会提醒你恶劣的气候或者工业的进步。

　　但接近城市之后，你会发现一切似乎都很宁静安详。这里难道是一座被施了魔法的都城，这里的居民已经变成了石头或黄铜吗？当然不是，但街道没有铺砌；这里也没有任何带车轮的车辆；鞋子，更像脚套而不是鞋子，没有任何鞋跟；没有棉厂在街道上喧嚣它们的声音——所有这些属于机械的灵光的那些嘈杂的胜利，比如锻造、纺纱、织布、锤木，这些在我们的城市中如此频繁活动，在大马士革都似乎是未知的。东方人保持稳步推进他们的进步，从不屈服于新颖的诱惑。水泵是在亚历山大发明的，但亚历山大的人们还是喜欢古井和水桶。

　　但耳朵即使没有充斥着这种磨坊、熔炉和机械操作的吼声和湍流，大马士革也有其自身特有的声音，而其自身特有的方式也同样多样、有趣。街道上到处都是瘦弱懒惰、饥肠辘辘的狗；骡子、驴、骆驼、干草，在那些狭窄的街道上交汇、嘈杂，给旅行者的耳朵和眼睛留下深刻印象，让你清楚地明白这就是东方。

　　英国的城市向外扩散，正如它无限地延伸到乡村之中。公园、花园、避暑的凉亭、绅士的座椅和微笑的村庄，则是城市的模样。但在东方，却不是这般状况。城市都是在围墙之内，其外部都是像大马士革的花园，或是耶路撒冷的沙漠一样的地带。在任何国家，单独一座房子都是法律至高无上的证明，和对劳动的尊重和独立。生命和财富，在东方世界从未拥有过完全的安全。一支手枪或是滑膛枪，在大马士革之外的半英里内，在光天化日之下，就能穿透我的胸膛！

这些尊贵的花园里没有人居住，也没有美好的别墅、雅致的房子或王族的宫殿来装饰这片肥沃的土地。在城市之内你是安全的——在城市外面，会有狗，财产没有安全，而且可能会被击毙。因此，所有人都生活在城市或村镇中，除了贝鲁特——欧洲的影响和权力在这里盛行。在那里，你有花园和独栋的房子，这与英国的风景是一致的。

但如果把一个大马士革人放在十字广场，或在齐普赛，你觉得什么最容易让他感到惊奇？毫无疑问，是车辆的数目。他会说："如此大流量的汽车、出租车、大马车、货车、巴士，什么时候是个尽头啊？人们疯了吗？他们不可以放松心情，慢慢来吗？"

但古代的东方国家就没有四轮马车吗？他们有；犹太人和埃及人有四轮马车，希腊人和罗马人也有，或许如今，它们仍可能存在于东方世界的某些地方。在这里，在大马士革，却没有。街道并不是为四轮马车而铺就的。马匹只被训练来骑行。这里也没有共用的、平坦而秩序井然的公共道路。我们的父辈没有用大马车，他们更喜欢更有男人味的马术练习，并将柔软、柔弱的马车的奢侈赋予了女士们。但如今在伦敦，有大约九百辆公共机车，每辆车大约每年会花费一千英镑。这就是我们现在使用的大马车。但大马士革却是如此不同！街道呈现出来的不同也是如此明显！

这座城市给我们展现出来的是街道、广场、新月形建筑、王室马戏团、美容院和常规性的类似设施。这种情况特别出现在"最西方的世界"和我们崭新的城市和城镇之中。但这在大马士革是不存在的，或者在任何我见过的东方的城市也是一样，广场、新月形建筑和马戏在这些地方是不存在的。街道都极不规则、弯曲、卷绕而狭窄。这似乎让人产生了焦虑感，想要赶快找寻太阳的保护。

在更为较窄的街道上，那里的房子都很高，太阳的光芒被有效地遮挡在外；而在更广阔的街道上，如果太阳不是被高耸的房屋挡住，众多的拐角和角度也能使走过这里的路人享受到片刻的阴凉。这有时可能会显得微不足道，但我经常会觉得太阳光线的热量如此炙热和让人难以忍受，即使是习惯于太阳灼烤的游牧民族，沙漠中的子民，也会从酷暑难耐的内心深处因为哪怕一点点的阴影和片刻的遮蔽而感到欢愉。

相反，在大马士革的集市上，街道的布局则呈现出最大的规律性，并极端笔直。在热天，这些地方几近冷清，所有店铺都处于待业状态，商贩们都斜倚在某处，嘴里吹着口哨，打着瞌睡，这时鸦片或香草散发出来的气味，已经影响人们产生丰富的想象力，仿佛有了天国的安逸。

在一个东方的城市，你找不到前方的路。在我们的城市，你可以沿着街道看到一条大路。在大马士革，你会感觉到彻底的隔离。街道是如此的狭窄、弯曲，即使你看到最远处，你也看不到一个休息的地方，也没有什么样式的建筑物能够吸引人们的一点点关注。风格的不规则和制作的笨拙难看，加上没有漂亮的大门，所有的窗口看着像前门，栏杆、装饰物等东西，都使得这里的建筑给人留下极其不好的印象。

在我们的街道，我们很高兴能见到大房子，精妙排列的大窗户，布置高雅的大门和入口——似乎这一切事物都在传达着这些理念的互相结合。秩序、关注、清洁的理念，对财富的占有，这些都属于我们自己的意识。我们什么也不隐瞒，因为我们没有隐瞒的动机。我们的房子是我们的宫殿，虽然风可以吹拂我们破旧的厅堂，但就连女王陛下本人也不敢未经我们许可就进入我们的房间。自由增加了我们的财产，我们的财富增强了我们自由的价值。诱惑我们的并不是不隐瞒，而是排场和不必要的炫耀。

我们中间的倾向或诱惑在于将我们的性格和一个高度文明和商业化的国家相连接。伟大的交易无法在无信用的前提下进行，信用一定是基于财富的信念而建立起来的，所以很多时候，在那些可能不会有什么真正财富的地方，可能最需要财富的外观呈现……

大马士革的破败、低矮的大门，显示出这里统治的暴虐性和隐蔽性以及公共司法信念的意图。外在的苦难和内在的辉煌，是这里的一个原则，而此原则恰可以使这个任何事物的本质都不会随意改变的地方受益。在这里，黄金是唯一的循环介质；在这里，一个人的房子就是他的财产储存地；而他富有的任何显露都可能使他成为贪婪政府的猎物。

相反，我们的现代城市里高贵的街道、广场、新月形建筑，等等，不仅是巨大的财富和权力的明显的标志，同时也彰显了一些更美好和更高贵的事物——也就是，在无数相同的情况下，人与人之间的相互信任；其中，基督教就是最强大的一种情况。除此之外，充满对欧洲文明和自由的政治制度的祝福。

但是，门柱旁边那块石头是做什么用的？某个叫朱利的人为他的驴、骡子和马装上鞍子的时候，这些石头是他站着的垫脚石。你不要觉得这很奇怪。在14和15世纪，巴黎提出在所有街道的拐角处，或者在其他方便的地方，安装这样的垫脚石。在法兰克福，某种这样的大门也为皇帝和德国国会的富豪们准备了这种便利。我对此毫不怀疑，在封建社会和骑士荣耀的日子里，在这方面，伦敦也一定与它的这些邻居一样。

——雷夫·格雷厄姆

Lesson 10
DAMASCUS AND LONDON (II)
第十课　大马士革和伦敦（二）

Our cities are filled and ornamented with hotels, coffee-houses, hospitals, work-houses, prisons, and similar conspicuous buildings. Generally speaking, there are none of these in the East. Hospitals and institutions for the sick and the poor were the offspring of Christianity, and are, I am inclined to think, peculiar to Christian lands.

There are few prisons in the East, and these are very wretched. Imprisonment as a *punishment* is little practiced, and is altogether unsuited to the Mohammedan law and mode of thinking. Life is not so sacred as with us. It is urged that if a man deserves to be confined as a dangerous member of society, he deserves to die; society will never miss him, and some expense will be spared: "Off with his head;—so much for Buckingham."

Hence in Damascus, and in the East generally, people are not liable to the reproach which is sometimes brought against us—that the best house in the county is the jail. Besides, in the East, punishment follows crime instantaneously. The judge, the mufti, the prisoner, and the executioner, are all in the court at the same time. As soon as the sentence is delivered, the back is made bare, the donkey is ready (for perjury, in Damascus, the man rides through the city with his face to the tail), or the head falls, according to the crime, in the presence of all the people. Awful severity, and the rapidity of lightning, are the principles of their laws; nor do they deem it necessary to make the exact and minute distinctions of crime that we do. The object is to prevent crime, and this is most effectually done by the principle of terror and the certainty of immediate punishment.

A certain baker in Constantinople used false weights in selling his bread: the Sultan ordered him to be roasted alive in his own oven, and afterwards boasted that this one act of severity had effectually prevented all similar crimes. Here you see the principle of government in the East;—it is nothing but terror and religious fanaticism.

As to coffee-houses, there are plenty of them in Damascus; but they can hardly be called houses, much less palaces: they are open courts with fountains of water, sheltered from the sun; and in many cases they have little stools, some six inches high, on which, if you do not prefer the ground, you can rest while you enjoy your sherbet, coffee, and tobacco. Pipes, nargilies, ices, eau sucre, sherbet, and fruits of all kinds, are in abundance, and of the lowest possible price.

These cafes are very quiet: there is no excitement, no reading of newspapers, no discussion of politics and religion; no fiery demagogue or popular orator to mislead the people; no Attic wit provokes a smile, and no bold repartee calls forth applauding laughter on the other side. But yet they have their own amusements, and they play earnestly at games both of chance and of skill. The traveller tells his escapes and dangers to an admiring little circle; the story-teller repeats one of the "Thousand and One Nights" to a wondering audience; and if memory fails, the imagination, fertile as an oriental spring, supplies its boundless stores.

We have in the East great khans, but they bear little relation to our hotels. *Ring, eat, and pay*, is not the law in the East. They have no bells in Damascus, nor even the silver call or whistle which our grandmothers used in England. Bells in churches and in houses are alike an abomination to the Moslems; and the Maronites alone, by permission of the Government, have a right to use them.

The Khan in Damascus is a large circular building surmounted by a noble dome, in which the great merchants have their goods and wares of all kinds; and in which the traveller can find a resting-place for himself and his camels, and be supplied with water from the central fountain;—but there are no tables spread for the travellers, and no beds ready made for the weary pilgrims: you must find your dinner as you best can, make your own bed, and when you rise, take it up, and walk. The Khan is, however, a very noble building, and excites not a little astonishment among the Orientals.

In European cities your attention is arrested by book-shops, pictures, placards, caricatures, &c.; now in Damascus we have nothing of the sort. Among the Jews you may find a few miserable stalls, from which you may pick up a copy of the Talmud, or some old rabbinical prayer-book. The sheikh who sold me the Koran, laid his hand upon his neck, and told me to be silent, for were it known that he had done so, he might lose his head. In the schools they are taught only to read the Koran, and to master the simplest elements of arithmetic and writing.

Men of letters there are at present none, and the highest of their sciences is the knowledge of grammar. When I lived in Damascus, some wit (the first thing of the kind known) uttered a pun or squib reflecting on the corpulency of the pasha, and he was banished for it! The old observation of the caliph, as he fired the Alexandrian library, holds true in the East still—"If the books agree with the Koran, they are useless; if they oppose it, they are pernicious; and in both cases they are unnecessary."

"But has not Damascus one hundred thousand inhabitants?" says the traveller. "Where are their newspapers, spreading light and knowledge through a portion of the sixty millions who use the noble Arabic language? Take me to the office of some Oriental *Sun*, *Times*, Globe, *or Morning Chronicle*."

There is no such thing. Even in Constantinople there is only one newspaper, and the one half of it is in Turkish, and the other in French! Tyranny and superstition, like two monstrous mill-stones, rest upon and compress the energies of the oriental nations; even Greece, the fountain of science and literary and mental activity, was for a time blotted from the rank of nations, and the inquisitive character of its people all but annihilated by the stern rule of the Turks.......

But there is another great difference between the general appearance of London and of Damascus, namely, in the eastern city you see not the bright, joyous countenance of woman—she is deeply veiled. In Egypt she is enveloped from head to foot in a dark, and in Syria in a white sheet, which effectually obliterates all traces of shape, absolutely equalizes to the eye all ranks, ages, and conditions, and suggests to the beholder the idea of a company of ghosts......

Conceive now how ludicrous the streets of London would appear, if green, white, black, and gray turbans moved indiscriminately, instead of the present hats; and if all the ladies, walking or on donkeys, instead of the present varieties of showy dress, beautiful bonnets, and smiling faces, presented only the appearance of headless ghosts clothed in white!

As to the *general motion and life*, the difference is immense between Damascus and a western city. Let us glance for a moment at two streets, and compare them:—

1. In Damascus there is more *openness and publicity*. The tradesmen of every kind work in the open bazaars; many of the merchants and artisans dine in public—that is, eat their bread and oil, bread and honey, or bread and grapes, in the street where they work. All are smoking, without exception, in the intervals of business. Some are engaged in reading the Koran, swinging their bodies to and fro in the most earnest and violent manner. Some are sleeping calmly, with the long pipe in their mouth! There a butcher is killing a sheep, surrounded by a circle of hungry, expectant dogs. Yonder is a company engaged at a game of skill. Everything is done in the open air, and nothing seems to be concealed but the ladies.

2. In the eastern city there is much more quiet. Their manners are sober, formal, and stately; arising partly, I believe, from the famous and universal dogma of obedience. There is, indeed, hardly any other law. The subject, the wife, the son, the slave obeys: to hear is to obey. This principle of unhesitating, unquestioning obedience leads to quiet. There is no contradiction. There is nothing to talk about. There is nothing like politics. There is no public opinion, of course; for that is upon private opinion, and determined, resolute will. This extraordinary quiet and solemnity of demeanour may rise partly, also, from a sense of danger. Every man has arms, and has the right both of wearing and of using them: and no man makes a journey, be it only to a neighbouring village, without sword and pistols. Now this tends to quiet, earnest, solemn manners. If a scuffle takes place, it is not a black eye or a bloody face that is the result, but the certain death of some of the parties; and hence they are taught the principle of self-restraint and moral control......

3. The Arabs, and Orientals in general, sit much more than we do. The tradesmen all sit at their work: the smith, the carpenter, and the merchant, the butcher, the joiner, and the spice-monger, sit quietly and transact their business. They sit as tailors do, cross-legged, but with their feet doubled in beneath them. They sit on their feet, and maintain that such is the most natural and easy position! They seem to have no pleasure in motion: no man goes out to take a walk; no man moves for the sake of exercise. They go out, as they say, to s*mell the air*, by some spreading tree or fountain of water. And yet they are capable of enduring great and long-continued labour. Abu Mausur travelled with us nearly forty days, during which we rode at the rate of from

six to eighteen hours a day; and yet, though never upon a horse, he was always with us at the requisite time and place. He performed the journey on foot, and was rarely far behind.

Take, then, these things together, and you will easily perceive that in the city of Damascus everything is still and calm as the unclouded sky and the balmy air. The hoof of the camel falls noiselessly on the unpaved street; the sheep-skin foot-gloves of the Damascenes make no sound; and all the movements, both of men and of animals, are slow and solemn.

—Rev. Dr. Graham

Words

abomination, *object of disgust.*
amusements, *entertainments.*
annihilated, *extinguished.*
applauding, *approving.*
astonishment, *wonder.*
corpulency, *fatness.*
demean our, *deportment.*
distinction, *discrimination.*
dogma, *Maxim, law.*
effectually, *thoroughly.*
enduring, *undergoing.*
engaged, *occupied.*
excitement, *stir.*
expectant, *waiting.*
hospitals, *infirmaries.*
inclined , *disposed.*
indiscriminately, *confusedly.*

inquisitive, *prying.*
instantaneously, *immediately.*
ludicrous, *ridiculous.*
obliterates, *destroys.*
perjury, *false swearing.*
permission, *sanction.*
pernicious, *mischievous.*
principle, *rule.*
reflecting, *animadverting.*
reproach, *censure.*
sheltered, *protected.*
similar, *of the same na.*
solemnity, *gravity ture.*
superstition, *fanaticism.*
transact, *discharge.*
unsuited, *inappropriate.*

Questions

Of what public buildings are eastern cities generally destitute? Why are there few prisons in the East? What is the object of their penal system? How do they attain it? Describe the appearance of a Damascus coffee-house. What is a khan? What are the children taught in the schools? How is the absence of newspapers to be explained? How do women go about in Damascus? In comparing two streets, one in London, the other in Damascus, what three points of difference would be most noticeable?

在我们的城市里，遍布酒店、咖啡屋、医院、工厂、监狱和类似显眼的建筑，它们同时也装饰了我们的城市。一般来说，这些在东方世界都是不存在的。医院及为病人和穷人而设置的机构是基督教的产物，我倾向于认为，这些是基督教国家所特有的。

在东方，很少有监狱，即使有也都几乎形同虚设。作为惩罚的监禁在东方很少执行，并且是完全不适应伊斯兰教法和思维方式的。他们的生活并不像我们这样。人们都认为，一个危险的社会成员应该受到限制，应该被处死；社会永远不会怀念他，有些代价也将不能幸免，"砍掉他的头——在白金汉宫是这样的。"

因此，在大马士革和普遍的东方世界一样，人们有时不应因为对我们提出的羞辱而负责，一个国家最好的房子就是监狱。此外，在东方，处罚和犯罪几乎同时进行。法官、法学家、囚犯和刽子手，都同时出现在法庭上。判决一旦交付，囚犯的后背会被脱光，驴子也会准备好（在大马士革，犯伪证罪的人，会被罚脸面对着驴子的尾巴，骑行穿城而过，或依据他所犯的罪行，在所有人面前被砍头示众。）可怕的严重程度以及闪电般的快速决断，是他们的法律原则；他们也不认为有必要确定犯罪之间精确和微小的区别，就像我们一样。他们这样做的目的是通过最有效的恐惧和惩罚的确定性原则，来防止犯罪。

某个面包师在君士坦丁堡以虚假的重量销售他的面包，皇帝就会下令，他将在他自己的烤箱中被活活烤死，事后再吹嘘这一行为的严重性。这样可以有效地阻止所有类似的罪行。通过这件事情，你可以看到在东方国家，政府的运行原则，仅在于恐怖和宗教狂热。

至于咖啡屋，在大马士革有很多；但它们也很难被称为房子，更不用说是宫殿了。他们是带有流水喷泉的开放庭院，处在太阳光线的隐蔽处，而且在许多咖啡屋里几乎没有凳子，如果你不喜欢坐在地上，你可以休息在大约六英寸高的地方，享受你的果子露、咖啡和烟草。烟斗、水烟斗、冰块、淡苏克雷、果子露，还有各种水果，在这里都十分充足，价格也极其低廉。

这些咖啡馆都非常安静，没有令人兴奋的事件，没有人读报，没有人讨论政治和宗教，没有狂热的煽动者或流行的演说者在这里误导民众，没有智者的话语挑逗其他人大笑，也没有大胆的辩论者让对方鼓掌欢呼。但是，他们有自己特有的娱乐方式，他们认真地玩游戏，机遇和技巧是他们的两大法宝。一名旅客会对着一小圈围在他周围显露出崇拜目光的听众，讲述他的逃逸和危险的故事。说书人对着许多好奇的听众一遍一遍地重复着"一千零一夜"的故事。如果他的记忆力减退，想象力却如东方的春天一样蓬勃，他就会无穷无尽地讲述他的故事。

在东方，我们会见到很多小客栈，但它们与我们这里的酒店似乎没有多大关系。摇铃、吃饭、付钱，这不是东方世界的规矩。在大马士革，你根本听不到铃声，甚至也没有银勺子敲击的声音或口哨声，就像我们英国的祖母做的那样。在教堂和房间里，钟声意味着对穆斯林的憎恶，只有马龙派教徒在政府的许可之下，有权使用它们。

大马士革的客栈是一个巨大的圆形建筑，最上方是一个壮观的圆顶，其中放置着许多商家自己的各种商品和器皿，而旅客可以在这里找到一个安身之处，中央喷泉可以为他和他的骆驼提供水源。但这里没有供旅客休息驻足的桌子，也没有为疲惫的朝圣者准备床铺，你必须自己准备晚餐，自己铺床，当你起床后，要将床支起，然后离开。然而，客栈是一种非常尊贵的建筑，对于东方人来说，它引起的不仅仅是一点兴奋的感受。

在欧洲的城市里，你的注意力可能会被书店、图片、标语、漫画等事物所吸引。然而，在大马士革，根本不是这回事。在犹太人中间，你可能会发现一些惨淡的摊位，从中你可以挑出一本犹太法典的副本，或者一些古老的犹太教的祈祷书。卖给我一本《古兰经》的酋长，把他的手放在他的脖子上，告诉我不要作声，因为如果有人知道他这样做，他可能会被砍头杀死。在他们的学校里，人们接受教育只能读《古兰经》，并掌握最简单的元素，那就是算术和写作。

迄今为止，那里还没有能读书识字的人。而那里，最高深的科学是语法知识。当我住在大马士革时，一些智者（类似事件的第一件）说出一个关于帕夏的肥胖病的双关语、嘲讽的话，很快他就被驱逐了！老国王焚烧了亚历山大图书馆，而他在东方拥有真正的权威。他说："如果这些书与《可兰经》表达的意见相同，它们就是无用的；如果它们胆敢反对，它们就是有害的，而在这两种情况下，它们都是不必要的。"

"但大马士革不是拥有十万居民吗？"旅客会问，"哪里有他们的报纸，可以在这六千万高贵的阿拉伯语使用者中的一部分人群中，传播光明和知识？谁能带我找到东方的《太阳报》《泰晤士报》《环球时报》或《纪事晨报》？"

我没有见到这样的事情。即使在君士坦丁堡，也只有一种报纸，而它的一半是在土耳其，另一半在法国！专制和迷信，就像两个怪异磨石，倚靠和压缩着东方国家的能源，甚至希腊这个科学、文学和心理活动的源泉，也有一段时间从国家的排名中被抹去，而它的人民所特有的好学的特性，也因土耳其人的规则而彻底泯灭了……

在大马士革和伦敦的普遍外观之间，还存在另一个巨大的区别，那就是，在东方的城市中，你看不到女人明亮、快乐的面容——她们的脸庞都深藏在面纱之下。在埃及，她们甚至从头到脚都包裹在深色的面纱之中。在叙利亚，女性则包裹在白色的蔓布之中，这有效地抹杀了任何她们身材的痕迹，而且让人们看到了绝对相同的阶层、年龄和生活条件……

设想一下，如果这样的街道出现在伦敦；如果绿色、白色、黑色和灰色的头巾到处移动，而不是现在我们这样的帽子；如果所有的女士，无论是走路或是骑在驴子上，不穿着多姿多彩的绚丽礼服，戴着美丽的头巾，显露出面带微笑的面孔，而是呈现出白色纱幔下无头的幽魂，这些场景，会是多么可笑！

至于一般化的运动和生命，大马士革和西方城市之间的不同也是巨大的。我们可以花片刻的时间瞥一眼两座城市的两条街道，并加以比较：

（1）在大马士革有着更多的开放性和公众性。经营各种物品的商人都在露天集市做买卖，很多商人和工匠都在公共场合吃饭。也就是说，他们在他们工作的街道上吃面包和黄油、面包和蜂蜜，或者面包和葡萄。没有例外，所有人都在生意的间隔时间内吸烟。一些人会平静地睡着，口哨就在他们的嘴里含着！一个屠夫在杀一只羊，四周就会围着一圈饥肠辘辘、充满期待的狗。在街道的那边，一群人正在探讨游戏的技巧。这一切都是在户外进行，除了女士们，似乎没有什么是隐藏着的。

（2）东方的城市安静得多。当地人的举止清醒、正式、庄重。我相信，这种现象的一部分原因是对著名的和普遍教条的服从。事实上，这里几乎不存在任何其他律法。归属物、妻子、儿子、奴隶都服从于此，听到便要服从。毫不犹豫的、无条件地服从，就会带来这样的安静。这里不存在矛盾。没有什么可谈论的，不存在政治。当然也不存在公众舆论，因为公众舆论是基于私人的意见而存在的，而且是坚决的、坚定的意志。这非凡的安静，庄严的神态可能一部分也来自于危险感。每个人都拥有武器，并有权佩戴、使用它们，没有人不佩戴着剑和手枪去旅行，即使只是去一个邻近的村子。如今，这些都带来了安静的、认真的、严肃的举止。如果混战发生，黑眼圈或血肉模糊的脸并不会是混战的结果，而一定是某些当事人的死亡，因此，他们学会了自我约束和道德控制的原则……

（3）阿拉伯人和一般的东方人一样，比我们坐着的时候要多得多。商贩在工作的时候都是坐着的，铁匠、木匠、商人、屠夫、木匠和香料贩子，都静静地坐着，做着他们的生意。他们的坐姿像极了裁缝，盘着双腿，双脚重叠着放在双腿之下。他们坐在自己的脚上，认为这是最自然和简单的姿势。他们似乎在运动中没有什么乐趣，没有人出去散步，没有人为了锻炼而活动。他们走出去，正如他们所说的，在一些青翠的树下或喷泉周围去"呼吸空气"。然而，他们能够承受巨大的和长期持续的劳动。阿布·毛瑟与我们一起行进了近40天，在此期间，我们以每天6至18个小时的速度骑行，然而，他虽然从未骑过马，他总是在必要的时间和地点跟得上我们。他一直是徒步前进，并很少落后于我们。

那么，将所有这些混杂在一起思考，你会很容易察觉到，在大马士革，一切都像万里无云的天空和温暖的空气一样安详、平静。骆驼的蹄子无声地落在了尚未铺砌的街道之上，大马士革人做成的绵羊皮脚套也完全不会发出任何声音，所有动物和人类的动作，都是如此的缓慢而庄重。

——雷夫·格雷厄姆

Lesson 11
BATTLE OF TRAFALGAR,
AND DEATH OF NELSON (I)

第十一课　特拉法加海战和纳尔逊之死（一）

October 21, 1805.

Early on the morning of September 14th, Nelson reached Portsmouth, and having dispatched his business on shore, endeavoured to elude the populace by taking a by-way to the beach; but a crowd collected in his train, pressing forward to obtain a sight of his face. Many were in tears, and many knelt before him and blessed him as he passed.

England has had many heroes, but never one who so entirely possessed the love of his fellow-countrymen as Nelson. All men knew that his heart was as humane as it was fearless; that there was not in his nature the slightest alloy of selfishness or cupidity, but that, with perfect and entire devotion, he served his country with all his heart, and with all his soul, and with all his strength: and therefore they loved him as truly and as fervently as he loved England.

They pressed upon the parapet to gaze after him when his barge pushed off; and he returned their cheers by waving his hat. The sentinels, who endeavoured to prevent them from trespassing upon this ground, were wedged among the crowd; and an officer, who (not very prudently, upon such an occasion) ordered them to drive the people down with their bayonets, was compelled speedily to retreat; for the people would not be debarred from gazing till the last moment upon the hero—the darling hero of England!......

At daybreak, the combined fleets were distinctly seen from the Victory's deck, formed in a close line of battle ahead, on the starboard tack, about twelve miles to leeward, and standing to the south. Our fleet consisted of twenty-seven sail of the line and four frigates; theirs, of thirty-three and seven large frigates. Their superiority was greater in size and weight of metal than in numbers. They had four thousand troops on board; and the best riflemen that could be procured, many of them Tyrolese, were dispersed over the ships.

Soon after daylight Nelson came upon deck. The 21st of October was a festival in his family, because on that day his uncle, Captain Suckling, in the *Dreadnought*, with two other line-of-battle ships, had beaten off a French squadron of four sail of the line and three frigates. Nelson, with that sort of superstition from which few persons are entirely exempt, had more than once expressed his persuasion that this was to be the day of his battle also; and he was well pleased at seeing his prediction about to be verified.

The wind was now from the west,—light breezes, with a long, heavy swell. Signal was made to bear down upon the enemy in two lines; and the fleet set all sail. Collingwood, in the *Royal Sovereign*, led the lee line of thirteen ships; the *Victory* led the weather line of fourteen. Having seen that all was as it should be, Nelson retired to his cabin, and wrote the following prayer:—

"May the great God, whom I worship, grant to my country, and for the benefit of Europe in general, a great and glorious victory; and may no misconduct in any one tarnish it; and may humanity after victory be the predominant feature in the British fleet! For myself individually, I commit my life to Him that made me; and may His blessing alight on my endeavours for serving my country faithfully. To Him I resign myself, and the just cause which is entrusted to me to defend. Amen, amen, amen."

Blackwood went on board the *Victory* about six. Nelson, certain of a triumphant issue to the day, asked him what he should consider as a victory. The officer answered, that, considering the handsome way in which battle was offered by the enemy, their apparent determination for a fair trial of strength, and the situation of the land, he thought it would be a glorious result if fourteen were captured. He replied, "I shall not be satisfied with fewer than twenty!"

Soon afterwards he asked him if he did not think there was a signal wanting. Captain Blackwood made answer, that he thought the whole fleet seemed very clearly to understand what they were about. These Words were scarcely spoken before that signal was made which will be remembered as long as the language, or even the memory of England, shall endure—Nelson's last signal: "ENGLAND EXPECTS EVERY MAN TO DO HIS DUTY!" It was received throughout the fleet with a shout of answering acclamation, made sublime by the spirit which it breathed and the feeling which it expressed. "Now," said Lord Nelson, "I can do no more. We must trust to the Great Disposer of all events, and the justice of our cause. I thank God for this great opportunity of doing my duty."

He wrote that day, as usual, his admiral's frock-coat, bearing on the left breast four stars of the different orders with which he was invested. Ornaments which rendered him so conspicuous a mark for the enemy, were beheld with ominous apprehensions by his officers. It was known that there were riflemen on board the French ships, and it could not be doubted that his life would be particularly aimed at.

They communicated their fears to each other; and the surgeon, Mr. Beatty, spoke to the chaplain, Dr. Scott, and to Mr. Scott the public secretary, desiring that some person would entreat him to change his dress, or cover the stars; but they knew that such a request would highly displease him. "In honour I gained them," he had said when such a thing had been hinted to him formerly, "and in honour I will die with them."

Nelson's column was steered about two points more to the north than Collingwood's, in order to cut off the enemy's escape into Cadiz; the lee line, therefore, was first engaged. "See!" cried Nelson, pointing to the *Royal Sovereign*, as she steered right for the centre of the enemy's line, cut through it astern of the *Santa*

Anna three-decker, and engaged her at the muzzle of her guns on the starboard side, "see how that noble fellow, Collingwood, carries his ship into action!" Collingwood, delighted at being first in the heat of the fire, and knowing the feelings of his commander and old friend, turned to his captain and exclaimed, "Rotherham, what would Nelson give to be here!"

The enemy continued to fire one gun at a time at the *Victory*, till they saw that a shot had passed through her main-top-gallant sail; then they opened their broadsides, aiming chiefly at her rigging, in the hope of disabling her before she could close with them. Nelson, as usual, had hoisted several flags, lest one should be shot away. The enemy showed no colours till late in the action, when they began to feel the necessity of having them to strike! For this reason the Santissima Trinidad, Nelson's old acquaintance, as he used to call her, was distinguishable only by her four decks; and to the bow of this opponent he ordered the Victory to be steered.

Meantime an incessant raking fire was kept up upon the Victory. The Admiral's secretary was one of the first who fell: he was killed by a cannon-shot while conversing with Hardy. Captain Adair of the marines, with the help of a sailor, endeavoured to remove the body from Nelson's sight, who had a great regard for Mr. Scott; but he anxiously asked, "Is that poor Scott that's gone?" and being informed that it was indeed so, exclaimed, "Poor fellow!" Presently a double-headed shot struck a party of marines, who were drawn up on the poop, and killed eight of them; upon which Nelson immediately desired Captain Adair to disperse his men round the ship, that they might not suffer so much from being together.

A few minutes afterwards, a shot struck the fore-brace bits on the quarter-deck, and passed between Nelson and Hardy, a splinter from the bit tearing off Hardy's buckle and bruising his foot. Both stopped, and looked anxiously at each other; each supposed the other to be wounded. Nelson then smiled and said, "This is too warm work, Hardy, to last long."

The *Victory* had not yet returned a single gun; fifty of her men had been by this time killed or wounded, and her main-top-mast shot away, with all her studding-sails and her booms. Nelson declared that in all his battles he had seen nothing which surpassed the cool courage of his crew on this occasion. At four minutes after twelve she opened her fire from both sides of her deck.

It was not possible to break the enemy's line without running on board one of their ships. Hardy informed him of this, and asked him which he would prefer. Nelson replied, "Take your choice, Hardy; it does not signify much." The master was ordered to put the helm to port, and the Victory ran on board the *Redoubtable*, just as her tiller-ropes were shot away. The French ship received her with a broadside, then instantly let down her lower deck ports, for fear of being boarded through them, and never afterwards tired a great gun during the action.

—Southey

Words

anxiously, *concernedly,*
apprehensions, *fears.*
bayonets, *spears or swords fixed on guns.*
communicated, *conveyed.*
conspicuous, *prominent.*
declared, *asserted.*
despatched, *conceded.*
determination, *resolution.*
dispersed, *scattered.*
distinguishable, *recognizable.*
engaged, *in action.*
entirely, *completely.*
entreat, *beseech.*
exempt, *free.*
fervently, *warmly.*

humane, *merciful.*
incessant, *unceasing.*
invested, *decorated.*
necessity, *need.*
ominous, *boding evil.*
persuasion, *conviction.*
prediction, *prophecy.*
predominant, *over-ruling.*
prudently, *discreetly.*
splinter, *chip.*
superiority, *ascendency.*
surpassed, *excelled.*
tarnish, *sully.*
triumphant, *victorious.*
understand, *comprehend.*

Questions

What was peculiar in the feeling of Englishmen towards Nelson? How was this shown at his last departure? What presentiment had Nelson regarding the day of the battle? Who commanded the lee line? What did Nelson do when all was ready? What was his last signal? How did Nelson make himself conspicuous? Why did none of his officers request him to avoid this? Who began the attack? To what vessel did Nelson order the *Victory* to be steered? How had she suffered before she opened her guns? Why was the *Redoubtable* attacked? With what effect?

1805年10月21日

9月14日清晨，纳尔逊到达朴次茅斯，并把他的部队派遣到岸上，试图以绕道去海滩的方式躲避开大众的视线，但是在他乘坐的那次列车上，人群拥挤过来，人们急切地想看到他的脸，一直向前推压。许多人都流下了眼泪，在他走过去的时候，还有许多人跪在他面前为他祝福。

英格兰有很多英雄，但是没有一个人像纳尔逊这样拥有自己同胞所有的爱。所有人都知道他的心是如此慈善和无畏，他的本性，甚至不掺杂一丝一毫的自私贪心。他服务于他的国家时，会付出他全部的心灵、所有的灵魂和他所有的力量，全心全意地献身其中，因此人们爱他，正如他如此真挚而热烈地爱着英格兰一样。

人群压在护墙上注视着他，他勇敢地推开他们，挥舞着他的帽子，回敬他们的欢呼。那些试图去阻止人群侵犯纳尔逊的哨兵们，却被挤在了人群之中；一个军官命令哨兵用他们的刺刀驱赶人群（在这样一个场合，这样做不是很谨慎），人们被迫迅速退去，因为他们不想让人群直到他生命的最后一刻还凝视着这位英雄——英格兰亲爱的英雄。

天亮时，人们可以从胜利号的甲板上清楚地看到联合舰队的踪迹，形成之前的战斗将要结束的阵势。在右舷，约下风口的12英里处，这些舰船面朝南方待命。我们的舰队包括27艘帆船和4艘护卫舰，敌方则拥有33艘帆船和7艘大型护卫舰。然而他们在尺寸和载重量方面的优势，甚至比数量上的优势更大。他们有4 000人的部队驻扎在船上；还有当时世界上最好的步兵，其中不乏许多提洛尔人也分散在船上。

天刚亮不久，纳尔逊来到甲板上。10月21日是他家族的一个节日，因为在这一天，他的叔叔萨克灵上校在无畏战舰上，与其他两艘舰船一起，打败了法国的四支帆船中队和三支护卫舰中队。纳尔逊具有某种迷信的思想（然而，很少有人是完全不相信这种迷信的），他曾不止一次表达了他的意愿，这一天也可能会成为他战斗胜利的一天，而且他兴奋地等待着事实来验证他的预言。

现在海风从西方吹来，掀起一片持续的大浪。信号冲向了敌人的两条战线，舰队扬起了所有的帆。皇家君主号舰上的科林伍德率领13艘舰船，胜利号率领十四艘舰船。看到一切都在按部就班地进行，纳尔逊回到自己的小屋，写下了以下的祷告："愿我所崇拜的伟大的神，为了整个欧洲的利益，赐予我的国家一次伟大的、光荣的胜利，并保佑没有任何一个不当行为可以玷污它；将胜利赐予英国舰队！至于我个人，让我将我的生命托付给创造我的主，愿他祝福我为了服务于我的国家而进行的忠诚的努力。我愿服从于他，愿服从于我有责任去为之努力的正义事业。阿门，阿门，阿门。"

布莱克伍德于大约6点登上了胜利号。纳尔逊坚信这一天他会有所建树，就问他什么才是胜利。这名士官回答说，考虑到敌军如此漂亮的战斗方法以及他们对双方力量获得公平对抗和占领这片土地的明显决心，他认为，如果击毁敌人的14艘船，这将是一个光荣的结果。他回答说："少于20艘，我都不会满意！"

不久之后，纳尔逊问他，是否觉得现在的希望还不明显。布莱克伍德上校回答说，他认为整个舰队似乎非常清楚地了解他们将要做什么。他刚说完这些话，纳尔逊就发出了最后一个信号："英格兰期待每个人各尽其责！"只要语言和英格兰的记忆一直存在，这些话都将被人们永远铭记。接受这一信号，整个舰队的将士们都欢呼喝彩，因为它传达出来的精神和表达出来的感情是如此崇高。"现在，"纳尔逊爵士说，"我能做的只有这些了。我们必须相信所有事件的巨大推助力，还有我们事业的正义性。感谢上帝，给我这么好的机会，让我完成我的责任。"

在他写下这些话的那一天，像往常一样，他穿着海军上将的外套，在左胸位置上佩戴着的四颗星承载着他不同阶段的责任。一个敌军标记的饰品使他显得如此引人注目，看见它的军官们都会产生一种不祥的忧虑。众所周知，在法国的舰船上有众多步兵，而毫无疑问的是，他们会特别瞄准纳尔逊。

他们把他们的担心互相告知，外科医生比提先生告诉纳尔逊的秘书斯科特博士，希望有人能劝他脱掉他的衣服，或遮盖住那些显示出军衔的星星，但他们知道，这样的要求会使他特别不高兴。"为了纪念我获得它们，"当有人暗示他脱掉衣服或遮盖住徽章时，他这样说道，"我会以死来纪念它们"。

为了切断敌人通往加的斯的退路，纳尔逊的纵队转向比科林伍德的舰队更向北两度，因此，舰队的背线第一次参与到其中。这时，皇家君主号瞄准敌人的战线，并转向右方，切断了圣安娜号尾部的三层甲板，并将枪口对准敌舰的右舷。纳尔逊指着皇家君主号喊道："看！看我们的同伴多么英勇！科林伍德带领他的战士们行动起来了！"

科林伍德在第一次开火后显得格外兴奋，他也知道他的指挥官和老朋友纳尔逊正在试探，他转向他的队长喊道："罗瑟汉姆，你看看纳尔逊会干些什么！"

敌人继续向胜利号瞄准射击，直到他们的一次射击穿过了位于胜利号顶端的一根桅杆。然后他们打开全部的舷侧炮，瞄准胜利号最重要的绳索，希望她无法靠近自己。像往常一样，纳尔逊的身上悬挂了几个标志，他害怕其中任何一个会被敌人射击掉。在战斗中敌人一直没能给英国的舰队造成威胁，因此后来他们开始觉得有必要放弃进攻！为此，纳尔逊很早就熟悉的一艘舰船特立尼达号，正如他曾经描述她的那样，只有四层甲板是比较显眼的；继而，他命令胜利号掉头转向敌船的船首部位。

同时，敌军也不断向胜利号扫射。将军的秘书斯科特是最早倒下的人之一，他是在与哈代的交谈中被炮弹击中身亡的。在一个水手的帮助下，海军陆战队队长阿代尔努力把尸体从纳尔逊的视线中移开。斯科特曾非常敬重纳尔逊。纳尔逊不断焦急地问："那可怜的斯科特牺牲了吗？"在被告知事实如此时，他叫道："可怜的家伙！"此时，双头枪的炮弹击中了海军陆战队的队员，并夺去了他们之中八个人的性命。基于此，纳尔逊命令阿代尔上校立即将他的战士分散在船上的不同位置，这样他们可能就不会遭受如此惨重的人员伤亡。

几分钟之后，一发子弹穿过纳尔逊和哈代之间，打在了甲板前部的支撑位置上。碎片一下子把哈代的搭扣撕了下来并且擦伤了他的脚。两个人都停了下来，神情焦急地看着对方，担心对方受伤。然后纳尔逊笑着说："这激烈的战斗，哈代会持续很长时间。"

胜利号没有做出任何回击。到目前为止，船上有五十人在这次战斗中死的死伤的伤。船的中桅连同船的所有帆桁全被射中。纳尔逊宣布，在他一生所经历的所有战斗中，他从未看到过哪一次的将士们拥有超过今天他的船员们这般的勇气。12点零4分，胜利号开始从它的甲板两侧对准敌军开火。

如果不登上敌人的一艘舰船，就根本不可能突破敌人的防线。哈代告诉纳尔逊这一点，问他倾向于怎样进行下一步行动。纳尔逊说："你自己选择，哈代；这并不重要。"船长下令驶向港口，当它的分蘖绳索被打掉时，胜利号的船员们登上了敬畏号。英军的将士们全部登上了这艘法国舰船，然后由于害怕敌人再次从这里登船，他们立即放下了它的下甲板。而在整场战斗中，他们从未尝试向后方射击。

——骚塞

Lesson 12
BATTLE OF TRAFALGAR,
AND DEATH OF NELSON (II)
第十二课　特拉法加海战和纳尔逊之死（二）

It had been part of Nelson's prayer that the British fleet might be distinguished by humanity in the victory which he expected. Setting an example himself, he twice gave orders to cease firing on the *Redoubtable*, supposing that she had struck because her guns were silent; for, as she carried no flag, there was no means of instantly ascertaining the fact. From this ship, which he had thus twice spared, he received his death. A ball fired from her mizzen-top, which, in the then situation of the two vessels, was not more than fifteen yards from that part of the deck where he was standing, struck the epaulet on his left shoulder, about a quarter after one, just in the heat of the action. He fell upon his face on the spot which was covered with his poor secretary's blood.

Hardy, who was a few steps from him, turning round, saw three men raising him up. "They have done for me at last, Hardy," said he. "I hope not," cried Hardy. "Yes," he replied; "my back-bone is shot through." Yet even now, not for a moment losing his presence of mind, he observed, as they were carrying him down the ladder, that the tiller-ropes, which had been shot away, were not yet replaced, and ordered that new ones should be rove immediately; then, that he might not be seen by the crew, he took out his handkerchief and covered his face and his stars! Had he but concealed those badges of honour from the enemy, England, perhaps, would not have had cause to receive with sorrow the news of the Battle of Trafalgar.

The cockpit was crowded with wounded and dying men, over whose bodies he was with some difficulty conveyed, and laid upon a pallet in the midshipmen's berth. It was soon perceived, upon examination, that the wound was mortal. This, however, was concealed from all except Captain Hardy, the chaplain, and the medical attendants. He himself being certain, from the sensation in his back, and the gush of blood he felt momently within his breast, that no human care could avail him, insisted that the surgeon should leave him and attend to those to whom he might be useful; "for," said he, "you can do nothing for me." All that could be done was to fan him with paper, and frequently to give him lemonade to alleviate his intense thirst.

He was in great pain, and expressed much anxiety for the event of the action, which now began to declare itself. As often as a ship struck, the crew of the Victory hurrahed; and at each hurrah a visible expression of joy gleamed in the eyes and marked the countenance of the dying hero. But he became impatient to see Hardy; and as that officer, though often sent for. could not leave the deck, Nelson feared that some fatal cause prevented him, and repeatedly cried, "Will no one bring Hardy to me? He must be killed! he is surely dead!"

An hour and ten minutes elapsed from the time when Nelson received his wound, before Hardy could come to him. They shook hands in silence, Hardy in vain struggling to suppress the feelings of that most painful and yet sublime moment. "Well, Hardy," said Nelson, "how goes the day with us?" "Very well," replied Hardy: "ten ships have struck; but five of the van have tacked, and show an intention to bear down upon the *Victory*. I have called two or three of our fresh ships round, and have no doubt of giving them a drubbing."—"I hope," said Nelson, "none of our ships have struck?" Hardy answered, "There is no fear of that."

Then, and not till then, Nelson spoke of himself. "I am a dead man, Hardy," said he. "I am going fast; it will be all over with me soon." Hardy observed that he hoped Mr. Beatty could yet hold out some prospect of life. "Oh, no," he replied; "it is impossible. My back is shot through. Beatty will tell you so." Hardy then once more shook hands with him, and with a heart almost bursting, "hastened upon deck."

By this time all feeling below the breast was gone, and Nelson having made the surgeon ascertain this, said to him, "You know I am gone. I know it. I feel something rising in my breast," putting his hand on his left side, "which tells me so." When Beatty inquired whether his pain was very great, he replied, "So great, that I wish I were dead. Yet," he added, in a lower voice, "one would like to live a little longer too!"

Captain Hardy, some fifty minutes after he had left the cockpit, returned, and again taking the hand of his dying friend and commander, congratulated him on having gained a complete victory. How many of the enemy were taken he did not know, as it was impossible to perceive them distinctly, but fourteen or fifteen at least. "That's well," said Nelson; "but I bargained for twenty." And then, in a stronger voice, he said, "Anchor, Hardy, anchor." Hardy thereupon hinted that Admiral Collingwood would take upon himself the direction of affairs. "Not while I live, Hardy," said the dying Nelson, ineffectually endeavoring to raise himself from the bed; "do you anchor." His previous orders for preparing to anchor had shown how clearly he foresaw the necessity of this.

Presently calling Hardy back, he said to him in a low voice, "Don't throw me overboard;" and he desired that he might be buried beside his parents, unless it should please the King to order otherwise. Then reverting to private feelings,—"Kiss me, Hardy," said he. Hardy knelt down and kissed his cheek; and Nelson said, "Now I am satisfied. Thank God, I have done my duty!" Hardy stood over him in silence for a moment or two, then knelt again and kissed his forehead. "Who is that?" said Nelson; and being informed, he replied, "God bless you, Hardy." And Hardy then left him for ever.

Nelson now desired to be turned upon his right side, and said, "I wish I had not left the deck, for I shall soon be gone." Death was, indeed, rapidly approaching. His articulation became difficult, but he was distinctly heard to say, "Thank God, I have done my duty! " These words he repeatedly pronounced, and they were the last words which he uttered. He expired at thirty minutes after four, three hours and a quarter after he had received his wound.

Within quarter of an hour after Nelson was wounded, above fifty of the *Victory's* men fell by the enemy's musketry. They, however, on their part were not idle; and it was not long before there were only two Frenchmen left alive in the mizzen-top of the *Redoubtable*. One of them was the man who had given the fatal wound. He did not live to boast of what he had done. An old quartermaster had seen him fire, and easily recognized him, because he wore a glazed cocked hat and a white frock. This quartermaster and two midshipmen, Mr. Collingwood and Mr. Pollard, were the only persons left in the *Victory's* poop. The two midshipmen kept firing at the top, and he supplied them with cartridges.

One of the Frenchmen, attempting to make his escape down the rigging, was shot by Mr. Pollard, and fell on the poop. But the old quartermaster, as he called out, " That's he—that's he," and pointed to the other, who was coming forward to fire again, received a shot in his mouth, and fell dead. Both the midshipmen then fired at the same time, and the fellow dropped in the top. When they took possession of the prize, they went into the mizzen-top and found him dead, with one ball through his head and another through his breast.

The total British loss in the Battle of Trafalgar amounted to one thousand five hundred and eighty-seven men. Twenty of the enemy's ships struck, but it was not possible to anchor the fleet, as Nelson had enjoined. A gale came on from the southwest: some of the prizes went down, some went on shore; one affected its escape into Cadiz, others were destroyed; four only were saved, and those by the greatest exertions.

The death of Nelson was felt in England as something more than a public calamity: men started at the intelligence, and turned pale, as if they had heard of the loss of a dear friend. An object of our admiration and affection, of our pride and of our hopes, was suddenly taken from us; and it seemed as if we had never till then known how deeply we loved and reverenced him. What the country had lost in its great naval hero—the greatest of our own and of all former times—was scarcely taken into the account of grief.

So perfectly, indeed, had he performed his part, that the maritime war, after the Battle of Trafalgar, was considered at an end. The fleets of the enemy were not merely defeated—they were destroyed: new navies must be built, and a new race of seamen reared for them, before the possibility of their invading our shores could again be contemplated.

It was not, therefore, from any selfish reflection upon the magnitude of our loss that we mourned for him: the general sorrow was of a higher character. The people of England grieved that funeral ceremonies, and public monuments, and posthumous rewards, were all that they could now bestow upon him whom the King, the Legislature, and the Nation would have alike delighted to honour; whom every tongue would have blessed—whose presence in every village through which he might have passed would have awakened the church bells, have given schoolboys a holiday, have drawn children from their sports to gaze upon him, and "old men from the chimney corner" to look upon Nelson ere they died.

The victory of Trafalgar was celebrated, indeed, with the usual forms of rejoicing, but they were without joy; for such already was the glory of the British Navy, through Nelson's surpassing genius, that it scarcely seemed to receive any addition from the most signal victory that ever was achieved upon the seas. The destruction of this mighty fleet, by which all the maritime schemes of France were totally frustrated, hardly appeared to add to our security or strength; for while Nelson was alive to watch the combined squadrons of the enemy, we felt ourselves as secure as now when they were no longer in existence.

The most triumphant death is that of the martyr; the most awful, that of the martyred patriot; the most splendid, that of the hero in the hour of victory; and if the chariot and the horses of fire had been vouchsafed for Nelson's translation, he could scarcely have departed in a brighter blaze of glory. He has left us, not, indeed, a mantle of inspiration, but a name and an example which are at this hour inspiring thousands of the youth of England—a name which is our pride, and an example which will continue to be our shield and our strength. Thus it is that the spirits of the great and the wise continue to live and to act after them.

—Southey

Words

achieved, *gained.*
alleviate, *assuage.*
articulation, *utterance.*
ascertaining, *determining.*
calamity, *disaster.*
celebrated, *signalized.*
congratulated, *complimented.*
contemplated, *meditated.*
conveyed, *carried.*
distinguished, *characterized.*
elapsed, *transpired.*
enjoined, *advised.*
epaulet, *shoulder-badge.*
expected, *anticipated.*
frustrated, *baffled.*
hand-kerchief, *a cloth of silk or linen.*
hastened, *hurried.*

impatient, *eager.*
ineffectually, *unsuccessfully.*
inspiration, *divine influence.*
intelligence, *news.*
legislature, *parliament.*
momently, *continually.*
musketry, *small guns.*
prevented, *detained.*
prospect, *hope.*
recognized, *identified.*
replaced , *renewed.*
reverenced, *revered.*
reverting, *returning.*
satisfied, *contented.*
sublime, *grand.*
vouchsafed, *granted.*

Questions

How did Nelson give an example of humanity? How was this ill requited? Where was Nelson struck? Why did he tell the surgeon to attend to the others in the cockpit? Whom did he become impatient to see? What news of the battle did Hardy bring him? What wishes did he express regarding his burial? What were his last Words? What was the fate of the man who had shot him? How many of the enemy's ships struck? What was the great result of the victory? Why was It celebrated without joy?

☆ ☆

英国舰队会因为他所希望的胜利而留名于青史，这已经成为纳尔逊祷告的一部分。他自己树立了一个榜样，考虑到敬畏号可能会因为没有足够枪支炮弹进行射击而沉没，他曾经两次下令停止对它射击。因为它没有悬挂任何旗帜，纳尔逊没有任何办法可以即刻查明事实。在这艘他曾两次幸免于难的船上，他最终还是迎来了死亡。一发子弹从船的后桅顶部射过来，从两艘船当时的情形看，子弹是从甲板上他站着的地方不超过15码的距离射过来的。子弹打在他的左肩肩章上，此时大约是1点15分，正值战斗最白热化的时候。他身体的热量开始慢慢流失，他的脸转向了他可怜的秘书牺牲的地方，那里落满了血迹。

哈代站在离纳尔逊几步远的地方，他转过身来，看见三个人抬着纳尔逊走过。"哈代，他们还是射中了我，"纳尔逊说。哈代哭着说："我希望这不是真的。""是真的，"纳尔逊回答道，"我的背骨被射穿了。"但即使是这个时候，他都没有片刻的意识不清。当他们把他从梯子上放下来时，他注意到分蘖绳已被敌人的炮击打掉了，而没有人将其更换。于是他下令立即更换成新的，然后，等船员们可能看不见他时，他掏出手帕蒙住自己的脸和他的徽章。如果他早早地就隐藏起那些代表战胜敌人的荣誉徽章，也许英格兰就不会如此悲伤地收到这样一则来自特拉法加海战的噩耗。

驾驶舱里挤满了伤员和奄奄一息的士兵，在这些战士的身躯之上将他运递出去是有一定难度的。战士们将他的身体放在一个草垫子上，经检查，很快得出结论，这个伤口是致命的。然而，除了哈代上校、牧师和医疗人员，没有其他人得知这一消息。但纳尔逊自己非常确定，从他背部的感觉和血涌出的那一刻起，他心里就能感到没有人能救得了他。纳尔逊坚持医生应该离开他去救那些可能还能救活的人。纳尔逊说："因为我，你什么也不能做了。"医生可以做的一切，就是用纸做的扇子为他扇风，并经常给他柠檬水，以减轻他强烈的口渴。

他处于巨大的痛苦中，但仍然表达出对战斗过程的焦虑。这份焦虑现在已经很明显地展现在他的表情里。由于经常有敌船被击溃，每次胜利号发出的欢呼声和每个船员欢呼喜悦的表情，都能让这位垂死的英雄眼神重新闪闪发光，这形成了他此刻最主要的表情。但他开始变得不耐烦起来，想看到哈代；作为官员，哈代虽然经常过来照看纳尔逊，但却不应该离开甲板。纳尔逊担心，是死亡阻止了他过来见自己，所以反复喊道："怎么没有人把哈代给我带来？他一定是被杀死了！他肯定是牺牲了！"

在纳尔逊受伤一小时十分钟之后，哈代来看望他。他们沉默地握了握手，在这庄严的时刻，哈代徒劳地努力抑制住痛苦。"好了，哈代，"纳尔逊说，"战斗进行得怎么样？""很好，"哈代回答，"我们已经击溃了敌方十艘船了；还有五艘已经调转了航向，胜利号看来都承受下来了。我又调来了两三艘我们的舰船，毫无疑问也将给他们以痛击。"纳尔逊说："我希望我们的船一艘也不要沉！"哈代回答道："不用担心。"

然后，也是直到此时，纳尔逊才说到自己。"我是一个死人，哈代，"他说，"我马上就快死了，很快我的一切都会结束。"哈代说他希望比提先生还可以对他的生命前景有所期望。"噢，不，"他回答，"这是不可能的。我的背部被子弹射穿了。比提会告诉你。"哈代再次与他握手，心脏几乎快爆炸了，他赶紧跑到甲板上。

到现在，他感觉到胸口的心跳慢慢停止了，纳尔逊让医生确认一下，并说道："你知道我要走了。我很清楚。我感觉到我的胸部有东西在上升，"他把医生的手放在他的左边胸口，说道，"这里告诉了我。"当比提医生问他是不是伤口极其痛苦时，他回答说："太疼了，我希望我已经死了。然而，"他用较低的声音补充道，"但我还是想再活得长一点呢！"

在离开驾驶舱大约五十分钟之后，哈代上校又回到了这里，并再次和他垂死的指挥官朋友握手，向他祝贺战斗取得了完全的胜利。他不知道有多少敌船被击败，因为不可能清楚地计算出来，但至少14或15艘。"很好，"纳尔逊说，"但我希望是20艘。"然后，他用一个更强大的声音说道："抛锚，哈代，抛锚。"哈代随即暗示海军上将科林伍德立即接管一切事务。"不要在我还活着的时候，哈代。"垂死的纳尔逊徒劳地努力在床上提高自己的声音说："你做你的事去。"他之前下令准备抛锚，已经清楚地表明他预见到这样做的必要性。

不久纳尔逊又叫哈代回来，低声对他说："不要把我扔到船外。"他希望自己能埋在他的父母旁边，除非国王下令把他葬在他处。然后他又说到个人的感情："吻我，哈代。"哈代跪下来亲吻了他的脸颊；纳尔逊说："我现在很满足。感谢上帝，我已经完成了我的任务！"哈代站在他身边沉默了片刻，然后再跪下来在他的前额上吻了一下。"那是谁？"纳尔逊说，"上帝保佑你，哈代。"然后哈代永远离开了他。

纳尔逊现在想要转向他的右侧，说，"我希望我没有离开我的甲板，虽然我很快就要离开了。"事实上，死亡正迅速接近。他连发出声音都变得很难，但人们清楚地听到了他说："感谢上帝，我已经完成了我的任务！"他反复说着这些话，这也是他最后的话。他逝世于4点30分，在他受伤三小时一刻钟之后。

在纳尔逊受伤一刻钟之后，胜利号上的50个人在敌人的射击中倒下。然而，他们也没有闲着；不久，在敬畏号的后桅顶部，只有两个法国人还活着，其中一个人受了致命的伤。他不会还能活下来吹嘘他做过什么。一名老舵手看到他们进攻，很容易认出了他们，因为他们戴着釉面的三角帽，穿着白色的工装。这名舵手以及两个名叫科林伍德和波拉德的实习船员，是仅剩在胜利号船尾的人。这两个实习船员在顶端一直射击，老舵手为他们提供弹药筒。

一个法国人试图逃脱束缚他的索具，但被波拉德一枪击中，倒在了船尾。那个老舵手喊道："是他，就是他！"他指给其他人看，并上前向他的嘴里又开了一枪，继而证实他彻底死了。两个实习船员同时开枪，他们射击的那个人应声倒地。当他们走到后桅上收缴战利品时，发现他已经死了。一发子弹穿过他的头部，另一发穿过了他的胸膛。

在特拉法加海战中，英国的总损失达1 587人。他们击溃敌人的20艘舰船，但舰队没有办法服从纳尔逊的命令在此抛锚。来自西南的一场大风即将到来，一些战利品只好被英国人丢掉，另一些则运上了岸；一艘逃往加的斯的敌船受到了狂风的影响，其他的都被摧毁，只有四艘法国人的船被努力保留下来。

对于英格兰来说，纳尔逊的死亡是比其他任何事情都要严重的公共灾难，人们开始颤抖，脸色发白，仿佛听到他们失去了一位亲爱的朋友。他是我们钦佩和喜爱的对象，是我们的骄傲，我们的希望，却突然离开了我们；而我们似乎从来没有意识到，我们是如此深深地爱戴和尊敬着他。人们几乎不用考虑什么是悲伤的理由。这个国家已经失去了她在现在和所有以前时代里最伟大的海军英雄。

的确，他已经如此完美地执行了他的一部分任务。海上战争，在这场特拉法加战役之后，被认为从此终结。

敌人的舰队被击败了——他们被摧毁了。新的海军必须建立，一群新的海员需要培育，在他们入侵我们的海岸之前，这些都值得我们深思细想。

因此，我们对失去纳尔逊的哀悼和对这一巨大损失的思考，不是出自任何自私的初衷，而是对一个崇高民族的哀痛。英国人非常痛心，他们举行葬礼仪式，竖立公共纪念碑，对他进行死后的奖励，这些是他们现在能够赐予他的全部，也是国王、立法机关和国会同样甘愿赐予他的荣誉；每个人都在为他祝福，他可能已经穿过了每一个村庄，唤醒了教堂的钟声。小学生也放假了，孩子们从各种运动中停下来去关注他。当"在烟囱角落的老人"死去，他也会仰望纳尔逊。

实际上，人们以平常的欢乐形式庆祝着特拉法加海战的胜利，但他们却高兴不起来，因为通过纳尔逊超人的天赋，英国海军获得了无上的荣耀。他似乎无须获得任何其他功劳，他已经取得了海洋历史上最伟大的胜利。法国强大的舰队毁灭了，因而她所有的海运方案完全受挫，几乎不会再给我们的安全或军队带来威胁。当纳尔逊活着的时候，他看着敌人的联合舰队。现在我们感到自己如此安全，就像它们已经不复存在。

烈士的牺牲是最成功的死亡方式，爱国者的牺牲是最糟糕的殉道，转瞬即逝的胜利来自最光荣的英雄；正如战车和马匹被册封给纳尔逊，他的名字从此都与荣耀的明亮光芒紧紧相连。他已经离开了我们——不，事实上，他灵感的衣钵却成为一个名字和榜样，在这个时刻激励着成千上万的英国青年。一个无名的英雄，这是我们的骄傲，他是一个榜样，将继续成为我们的盾牌和我们的力量。因此，他的精神和智慧会一直存在，用行为影响着后来的人。

——骚塞

Lesson 13 ROUND THE WORLD
第十三课　环球航行

To be read before a Map of the World.

A voyage round the world can be made only through the Southern Seas; for though there exists a north-west passage between the Atlantic and Pacific Oceans, it is so obstructed with ice as to be practically useless. Vessels leaving the coast of Nova Scotia or New Brunswick sail south-eastward to the Cape of Good Hope, cross the Indian Ocean to Australia and New Zealand, and continue their course through successive groups of sunny isles till they reach Cape Horn and re-enter the Atlantic, and sail homeward to some Canadian port. The reverse course may be followed. A vessel from Halifax or St. John may sail down past the West Indies and the South American coast, double Cape Horn, and thence cross the Pacific to China, Ceylon, the Cape of Good Hope, and homeward through the Atlantic. Such ocean voyages are tedious, being liable to long delays on account of calms and storms.

The tourist who wishes in these days to make the tour of the world under the most advantageous circumstances usually starts from London, the throbbing centre not of the British Empire only, but of the whole world; the largest, the wealthiest, the most influential of cities. The route is partly by sea, partly by land. Swift steamers, and swifter railway trains, contribute to make the journey rapid, safe, and delightful. Early in the nineteenth century, vessels sailing between England and Canada often had to battle with waves and winds for fifty or sixty days; to-day, by the Canadian Pacific route, the traveller can go round the world in sixty days.

In a few hours after the tourist has left London by rail he will arrive at Liverpool, one of the greatest seaports in the world. Its population exceeds three-quarters of a million. Its docks cover six hundred acres, and its wharfs extend nearly forty miles. Steamers of every size, and from every land, arrive here with their cargoes, and carry afar the products of British industry.

Swift Canadian "liners" are ready to bear the traveller in winter to Halifax, in summer to Halifax or Quebec. Halifax, the capital of Nova Scotia, is a city of nearly 60,000 inhabitants. It is beautifully situated on the west side of the harbour, and is so strongly fortified as to merit the name of the "Gibraltar of America." The harbour is one of the finest in the world—safe whatever wind blows, accessible to steamers of the largest tonnage at all states of the tides. Halifax harbour, and the sheltered "basin" which extends landward beyond it, would easily afford safe anchorage to all the ships of the British navy.

From Halifax the tourist may proceed to Montreal by the Canadian Pacific Railway route by way of St. John, or he may proceed by the Intercolonial Railway to Quebec and thence to Montreal. The route from Halifax to St. John affords interesting glimpses of the Bay of Fundy, whose tides are among the wonders of the world, alternately rising and falling from sixty to seventy feet. The railway crosses extensive "marshes," and skirts "dike-lands" which, in the eighteenth century, were owned by the French "Acadians."

St. John is the commercial capital of New Brunswick, and is a thriving, well-built city of 47,000 inhabitants. In its immediate vicinity the St John River pours its waters into the Bay of Fundy. At low tide the noble river rushes through a narrow gorge and leaps into the bay with a fall of perhaps thirty feet. When the tide returns full and strong the fall is reversed: the Bay of Fundy pours its turbid waters into the basin of the river. From St. John to Montreal the route lies largely through an uncultivated country.

By taking the Intercolonial Railway from Halifax to Quebec, the tourist sees such progressive towns as Truro and Amherst in Nova Scotia, and Moncton and Campbellton in New Brunswick. Scenery of the most delightful description will be enjoyed along the Baie Chaleur, the Restigouche River, the Metapedia valley, and at length along the majestic St. Lawrence. In the province of Quebec he sees hamlets and towns reminding him of France as it was in the seventeenth century.

The city of Quebec presents peculiar attractions—new and old, French and English, past and present gracefully blending together. No city in America is more picturesquely situated, or presents a greater variety of natural and historic attractions. Cape Diamond is seen from afar as it frowns upon the low-lying portion of the city between it and the great river. The St. Lawrence as it sweeps past the Cape abates its swiftness and expands into a placid harbour, guarded by the Isle of Orleans. The city now extends from the river brink away up beyond the old walls to the famous Plains of Abraham, where Wolfe and Montcalm fought the battle which placed Canada under the British flag. The old walls and gates of the city are in as good repair as in the days of struggle and war happily long gone by.

Views of singular beauty may be enjoyed from Dufferin Terrace and other points in Quebec. The Falls of Montmorenci may be seen eight miles below the city—unquestionably the most beautiful falls in America. From this port enormous quantities of lumber and timber are shipped every season to Great Britain and other countries.

The tourist may proceed from Quebec to Montreal, a distance of 172 miles, by one of the great St. Lawrence steamers, or by either of two railways.

Montreal lies outspread between the river and the towering heights of "Mount Royal." From this "mountain" behind the city the tourist may enjoy one of the finest views imaginable. At his feet, on the flanks of the hill, are stately palaces, the residences of the merchant princes of Montreal. The fair city extends for miles before him. In the distance he sees the spreading river spanned by Victoria Bridge, over two miles in length. A few miles above is the airy modern structure of the Lachine

Bridge, which also spans the river. The foreground is occupied by churches, colleges, convents, the tall chimneys of factories and grain elevators, long streets of handsome dwellings, quays and wharfs crowded with steamers, railway trains and canal boats bringing from the west the products of the wheat-fields of Manitoba and Ontario, huge warehouses filled with merchandise for whole provinces.

The country traversed abounds with scenes of deep historic interest, covering a period of more than two centuries. Here planned and struggled Jacques Cartier, Champlain, Wolfe, and Montcalm, and many others, and here are the battlefields of two great and gallant nations who strove during a hundred years for the possession of a continent. There are also traces of a more recent struggle, when Canadians sprang to arms to repel invaders from the powerful Republic to the south of them. Happily "Peace hath her victories no Less renowned than war," and the people of Canada have conquered for themselves and for the travel and traffic of two continents a highway from the Atlantic to the Pacific. In this magnificent achievement, the building of the Canadian Pacific Railway, p' inestimable boon was conferred on those who desire a safe, rapid, and comfortable journey "round the world."

The pioneers who explored Canada thought the St. Lawrence would lead them to China, and that the river above Montreal was the gateway of that country. Hence the name "La Chine." The forecast of those men was in a sense realized, the shortest route to China being by Montreal and "La Chine."

The Ottawa pours its dark waters into the clear flood of the St. Lawrence, partly above the city and partly below it. Montreal is thus built upon an island; and near the centre of the island rises the "mountain" which lends to the fair city so much of its loveliness. A journey of three or four hours takes the traveller from Montreal to Ottawa, the capital of the Canadian Dominion. Here the Chaudiere. Falls will attract attention and admiration. A group of elegant and substantial public buildings adorns the city, and indicates where the legislature of the Dominion sits, and where the Executive Government transacts the public business of the country.

From Ottawa westward the route lies through a famous "timber" country, with no charms for the farmer, but rich in lakes and streams, and abounding with fish and game. At the head of Lake Nipissing is North Bay Junction, where passengers from Toronto join the transcontinental trains. At Sudbury and other points along the line, very valuable mineral deposits have been discovered. Nickel has been found in quantities unequalled in any other part of the world. Iron, silver, and other minerals are also abundant.

For two hundred miles the road skirts the north shore of Lake Superior, that vast fresh-water sea whose cool breezes refresh the traveller in the hottest days of summer. It required skill, courage, and ample financial resources to build a railway through a territory so rocky, so mountainous, so barren. The mineral wealth of this belt will, it is hoped, amply repay the country for the cost and risk it has incurred. Besides, a railway connecting the western provinces with the older portion of the Dominion is essential to its national existence.

Thunder Bay, at the head of Lake Superior, presents very bold and beautiful scenery. Fort William and Port Arthur, in the vicinity, are the headquarters of an important lake traffic energetically prosecuted during the summer. Immense elevators receive millions of bushels of grain to be transferred to steamers and borne down the lakes, the canals, the St. Lawrence, and at last perhaps across the Atlantic to supply the markets of the British Isles.

A little over four hundred miles westward from Port Arthur stands the young and handsome prairie city Winnipeg, the capital of Manitoba, and the chief centre of trade for the great Canadian West. In 1871 Fort Garry, a trading-post of the Hudson's Bay Company, and the humble dwellings of a score of half-breeds, occupied the site of this busy and well-governed city of 180,000 inhabitants. Here the Assiniboine and the Red River of the north unite their turbid waters and hasten through the fertile plain to Lake Winnipeg.

We are now in the prairie-land, seemingly level and boundless as a sea. In summer it is richly clad in verdure, brightened with the gayest wild flowers. In winter it is covered with snow, but not to such depth as to prevent herds of buffaloes and cattle in the ranches from feeding on the frozen grasses. Only in the coldest weather do the herds on the ranches require to be sheltered or fed in barn or storehouse.

The settler's plough has transformed many a league of North-West prairie into the finest wheat-fields in the world. The process of settlement is going on with increasing rapidity. Hamlets, villages, and towns are rising where the conditions are favourable. The church and the school-house, unfailing signs of religion and civilization, appear at frequent intervals. There are many "junctions" where branch railways start from the main line, in order to render available for settlement millions of acres, fertile, well-watered, richly wooded, inviting the husbandman with the promise of abundant harvests.

A railway ride through nine hundred miles of prairie enables the tourist to see towns like Brandon, Regina, and Calgary, and many smaller ones, which have rapidly become important as centres of commerce, and the growth of which indicates the steady development of the surrounding country. Calgary is the centre of vast "ranching" enterprises, the place of the vanished buffalo being taken by immense herds of cattle intended for far-distant markets. The westward horizon seems closed against further advance, guarded by the snow-crested bastions of the Rocky Mountains. But the swift-flowing Bow River furnishes a key to the very heart of the mountains. The railway track keeps close to the river, which in fact digged out for it this "gap" and the whole pass long ages ago. We glance at the Kananaskis Falls, which are a prelude of wonders to come. Banff National Park has numerous attractions to induce the tourist to take a few days for the study of these majestic mountains at close quarters. As you fill eye, mind, heart, and imagination with these mountain forms and mountain masses, you feel overwhelmed with their grandeur. The six hundred miles from Calgary to Vancouver form beyond comparison the most striking and wonderful railway ride that can be enjoyed going round the world—rushing torrents, silvery cascades falling thousands of feet down steep mountain sides; mighty rivers hurrying to the sea; slumbering lakes reflecting snowy summits; deep and dark gorges torn by raving waterfalls; beetling precipices; forests of stately pines in quiet valleys; mountain sides ploughed and scarred by avalanches; leagues of slumbering glaciers slowly grinding their way down the rocky slopes; four vast ranges to be crossed— the Rockies, the Selkirks, the Gold and the Coast ranges, each with peculiar features of grandeur and beauty, of loveliness and terror. The road follows the Fraser River along its wild cañon for several hours. Nowhere else is such a sight or such a series of sights to be witnessed—the mighty river rushing with headlong haste, and bearing on its seething bosom all the wreckage borne by the swollen torrents from the impending cliffs overhead; the train winding its way into tunnels, out of tunnels, along the face of the solid rock, over bridges that span nameless cataracts. Even in midsummer the Fraser is full-flooded, angry, furious; and it seems a wonderful achievement of human science to wrest from its banks a safe highway for the "iron horse."

The terminus on the Pacific Coast is Vancouver City, which sprang into existence in consequence of the building of the railway. Its population is now nearly 120,000, and is growing rapidly. Here the tourist embarks on one of the splendid steamers provided by the Canadian Pacific Railway for travel and trade across the Pacific Ocean. The steamers call at Victoria, the handsome capital of British Columbia. This city, of over 80,000 inhabitants, is on Vancouver Island, and is sixty miles distant from Vancouver City. Near Victoria is the town of Esquimalt, where there is a large dry dock, and where the British Pacific squadron usually makes its headquarters. From Vancouver to Yokohama, the chief commercial city of Japan, it is now a sail of ten days. From Japan to Shanghai, in China, a distance of 1,047 miles, is the next stage of the journey. From this port the steamer proceeds to Hong-Kong, where the Canadian Pacific Company hand over their tourists to the Peninsular and Oriental Company. The next stage in the voyage is Singapore, about five days from Hong-Kong. Then come Penang and Ceylon, Calcutta and Bombay. The Arabian Sea is crossed to Aden, through the Red Sea, through the Suez Canal, across the Mediterranean to Brindisi or Trieste, overland through Italy and France, and across the Strait of Dover to England; or by water through the Strait of Gibraltar, and up through the Atlantic to some British port. The tour may, of course, be prolonged indefinitely for rest, for pleasure, for business, or for study. Attractions abound on every hand. Happily, the modern "grand tour" is becoming more popular and more practicable every passing year.

Words

accessible, *can be approached.*
achievement, *exploit.*
advantageous, *profitable.*
alternately, *by turns.*

avalanches, *falling masses of snow and ice.*
canon (canyon), *deep gorge made by a rapid river.*

cataract, *waterfall.*

circumstances, *surroundings.*

commercial, *trading.*

contribute, *aid.*

double, *sail round.*

dry dock, *artificial basin in which ships are repaired.*

elevators, *buildings for storage of grain.*

energetically, *actively.*

enormous, *vast.*

essential, *necessary.*

financial, *relating to money.*

glaziers, *fields of ice on mountains; ice rivers.*

half - breeds, *descendants from white fathers and Indian mothers.*

husbandman, *farmer.*

imagination, *fancy.*

industry, *labour.*

inestimable, *very valuable.*

junctions, *points where railways meet.*

majestic, *grand.*

obstructed, *hindered.*

picturesquely, *strikingly.*

precipices, *steep declivities.*

prosecuted, *followed.*

rapidity, *swiftness.*

residences, *dwellings.*

reversed, *turned back.*

substantial, *firm*; *strong*

tonnage, *capacity.*

transcontinental, *crossing the continent.*

transferred, *passed.*

transformed, *changed.*

turbid, *muddy.*

vicinity, *neighbourhood.*

Questions

How must a voyage round the world be made? How long does it usually occupy? By what route may the journey be made in sixty days of continuous travel? Where does the tourist begin his journey? At what city in Canada does he arrive in winter? What city is first reached by the St. Lawrence route in summer? Arriving at Halifax, what is the next maritime city reached? How far is Montreal from Halifax? From St. John? What rivers surround Montreal? On what river is the city of Ottawa built? What notable buildings are in Ottawa? What metals are found in large quantity along the railway route from Ottawa to Lake Superior? What towns are built near Thunder Bay? What business gives chief employment to the railway and to steamers at this point? What is the chief city in Manitoba? What rivers unite their waters here? What is the principal industry in the province of Manitoba and in the North-West? Through what mountain range does the railway pass? What famous cañon does the road traverse? At what city does the tourist take a steamer in order to cross the Pacific? Name the ports the tourist must visit before arriving at London. Give the principal distances.

（请参照世界地图阅读此文）

在世界各地航行可以只通过南部海域，因为在此，存在着太平洋和大西洋之间的西北通道，也是因为冰的阻碍，实际上几乎是不可通行的。船只离开新斯科舍和新布伦瑞克的海岸，驶向东南部的好望角，穿越印度洋，到达澳大利亚和新西兰，并通过阳光群岛，直到它们到达合恩角，并由此进入大西洋，继续它们的航程，然后在加拿大的一些港口原路返航。

一艘来自哈里法克斯或者圣约翰的船只，越过西印度群岛和南美洲的海岸，折返于合恩角，在那里穿越太平洋，到达中国、锡兰、好望角，并穿越大西洋返航。海上的平静或风暴容易长时间地拖延航行，以致这样的海洋航行是乏味的。

如今，许多游客们希望周游世界，在最有利的情况下，他们通常会从伦敦出发。伦敦不但是大英帝国活力的中心，而且是世界最大、最富有、最有影响力的城市。这条航线一部分在海上，一部分在陆地上。快速的轮船和火车，有助于让旅行变得快速、安全、令人愉快。在19世纪早期，船只在英格兰和加拿大之间航行的50或60天中，经常不得不与海浪和风速进行战斗。然而如今，在加拿大至太平洋的路线中，旅行者在60天里就可以环游世界。

游客乘火车离开伦敦后，在几个小时之内，将会抵达世界上最大的海港之一——利物浦。它的人口超过75万。这里的船坞占600英亩，码头延展近40英里。各种规模的轮船从各地载着货物到达这里，或者载着英国的工业产品驶向远方。

快速的加拿大"班轮"已经准备好承载旅行者在冬天去哈里法克斯，而在夏天，则从哈里法克斯到魁北克。哈里法克斯是新斯科舍的首府，是一个拥有近6万居民的城市。美丽的哈里法克斯位于港口西岸，它拥有一个非常突出的名字，彰显了它的优势——"美国的直布罗陀"。这里是世界上最好的港口之一——即使海风吹拂也很安全，在任何潮汐状况下，即使最大吨位的轮船也可以在此靠泊。哈里法克斯港，连同它向内陆伸展的庇护"盆地"，都将轻易地向所有英国海军的船只提供安全的锚地。

从哈里法克斯，游客们可以继续通过加拿大太平洋铁路路线，途经圣约翰，到达蒙特利尔。或者他们也可以继续沿着洲际铁路向魁北克前行，继而到达蒙特利尔。从哈里法克斯到圣约翰的路线中，可以瞥见一处有趣的名为芬迪湾的景象。这里的潮汐堪称世界奇迹之一，可以交替上升和下降直至60~70英尺。铁路跨越广阔的"沼泽"地带和裙带的"壕沟地带"，在18世纪，这里是属于法国"阿卡迪亚人"的。

圣约翰是新不伦瑞克的商业之都，是一个繁荣、发展迅猛的城市，拥有47 000名居民。它紧邻的圣约翰河，将河水倾泻到芬迪湾之内。在退潮时，这条壮阔的河流，会冲过一条狭窄的水道，汹涌跃到大概30英尺的高度，奔涌到海湾之中。当潮水涨满时，水的倾泻会变得相反，芬迪湾浑浊的水注入圣约翰河的河床之中。从圣约翰河到蒙特利尔的路线，主要穿过一片未开化的乡村。

通过洲际铁路，从哈利法克斯到魁北克，旅行者可以陆续看到一些城镇，比如特鲁罗、阿默斯特和新斯科舍，还有在新布伦瑞克的蒙克顿和坎贝尔顿。沿着沙乐海湾、雷斯蒂古什河和麦特皮迪亚山谷到雄伟的圣劳伦斯河，人们会享受到令人愉快的风景。在魁北克省，人们会看到一些村庄和城镇，似乎在告诉着他们这是在17世纪的法国。

魁北克市呈现出一种独特的吸引力——崭新的与古老的，法国的和英国的，过去的和现在的，都优雅地结合在一起。在美洲，没有其他任何一座城市比魁北克更加风景秀丽，更独特地展现出各种各样的自然和历史景观。从远处看，钻石角是一片位于城市和大河之间的不起眼的低洼地带。圣劳伦斯河在冲刷过钻石角之后，减缓了流速，舒展开来，形成了一个平静的港湾，奥尔良岛环绕在它四周。在这里，魁北克沿着河流边缘延伸，越过了旧墙，一直到著名的亚伯拉罕平原。也就是在这里，沃尔夫和蒙卡姆赢得了战斗胜利，将加拿大置于英国的管辖之下。冲突和战争的日子一去不复返了，城市的老墙和大门却完好地保留了下来。

在特勒斯的达幅和魁北克的其他地方，人们都可以享受到独特的美景。人们可以在低于城市8英里的地方，看到蒙特默伦西瀑布——毫无疑问，它是美洲最美丽的瀑布。从这个港口，每个季节都会有大量的木材运往英国和其他国家。

旅客们可以从魁北克继续前行，到达蒙特利尔。其间有172英里的距离，旅客们可以乘坐圣劳伦斯大轮船，或两条铁路中的任意一条。

蒙特利尔在圣劳伦斯河和高耸巍峨的"皇家山"之间延展开来。从这座城市背后的山上，游客们可以享受到他们能想象到的最美丽的景色之一。在山脚之下和山的侧翼，是一片庄严的宫殿，这里是蒙特利尔富商们的府邸。在这座山后面，平坦的城市延伸数英里。人们可以看到远方的维多利亚桥，跨越河流，有两英里长。几英里以上，是现代结构的拉钦桥，它也跨越了整条河流。山的前麓布满了众多教堂、学校、修道院、工厂和谷仓的高大烟囱，美丽住宅区长长的街道，挤满了轮船的渡口和码头，从西部马尼托巴省和安大略省的小麦产地运载产品的铁路列车和运河船只，还有来自于整个省的装满商品的巨大仓库。

延展开的乡村遍布历史古迹，贯穿了两个多世纪的漫长时期。雅克·卡地亚、尚普兰、沃尔夫、蒙卡姆，还有许多其他人，都曾在这里抗争和战斗。在这片战场上，曾经有两个伟大、英勇的国家在一百年的时间内，为争夺一个大陆的统治权而进行过战斗，更近的战斗的痕迹是加拿大人为击退入侵共和国南部的侵略者而突然发起的进攻。"和平胜利的著名程度不亚于战争，加拿大人民为自己实现了征服，也为从大西洋到太平洋以及两大洲之间的旅游和交通实现了征服"。在这辉煌的成就里，加拿大太平洋铁路的修建，给予了那些渴望一个安全、快速、舒适的"周游世界"旅程的人们无价的恩惠。

早期探索加拿大的先锋者们认为，圣劳伦斯河将带领他们到达中国。而流经蒙特利尔的水域则是通向那个国家的关卡，因此得名"中国河"。那些人的预测在某种意义上是真实的，从这里去中国的最短路线，确实是通过蒙特利尔和"中国河"。

渥太华河将其浑浊的河水注入清澈的圣劳伦斯河之中。一部分在城市中的地面之上，一部分在地面之下。蒙特利尔因此建立在一个岛屿之上，在这个岛的中心附近，突起了一片山地，让这座平坦的城市显得尤其可爱。三到四个小时的旅程，会将旅客们从蒙特利尔带往加拿大的首都渥太华。在这里，超迪乐瀑布吸引了人们的注意力和赞赏。众多优雅、巨大的公共建筑装扮着这座城市，并展示出这个国家的立法机关以及政府是如何从事国家的公共事务。

从渥太华向西，通过一个著名的"木材"之城，虽然对农民没有什么魅力，但充满了丰富的湖泊和溪流，还有大量的鱼虾和游戏。在尼比斯英湖的湖口处是北海湾，在这里，从多伦多驶来的乘客们，加入到横贯整片大陆的火车航程中。在萨德伯里和这条线路上的其他地点，人们发现了许多非常有价值的矿藏。此处发现镍的产量远远超过世界上的其他任何地方。另外，铁、银和其他矿物质也相当丰富。

这条铁路围绕苏必利尔湖北岸，延绵200英里。这是一片巨大的淡水湖，在夏天最热的日子里，它凉爽的微风，能给旅行者带来清凉。在如此崎岖、多山、贫瘠的区域修建一条铁路，需要技巧、勇气和充足的财力。人们希望，这条铁路带上的矿产财富，能够充分偿还国家修造这条铁路所花费的成本和所承担的风险。此外，这条铁路能够通往到古老的西部省份，对国家来说也是十分必要的。

位于苏必利尔湖河头的桑德角，展现出壮阔而美丽的风景。附近的威廉堡和阿瑟港是重要的湖区交通枢纽，在夏天尤为活跃。巨大的升降机接收着数以百万计的大量谷物，它们从这里被转移到轮船上，越过湖泊、运河、圣劳伦斯河，最后跨越大西洋，供应不列颠群岛的市场。

阿瑟港向西400英里多一点的距离之外，有一座年轻而美丽的草原城市温尼伯。它是马尼托巴省的首府和加拿大西部主要的贸易中心。1871年，哈得孙湾公司的一个交易站加里堡，还有一些混血儿的定居住所，占据了这个繁忙的、拥有18万居民的城市。在这里，阿希尼伯因河和红河的北段浑浊、湍急的水流，穿越过其间肥沃的平原，最终注入温尼伯湖之中。

现在，我们处于一片大平原之上，就像一片平静而无限的海洋。夏天，草原穿披翠绿，布满华美的野花。冬天，这里覆盖着积雪，但积雪也不是很厚，但足以防止牧场里成群的水牛和野牛啃食雪下的冻草。只有当天气最冷时，牧场上的牛群才需要庇护在谷仓或仓库里进行喂养。

定居者们用犁改变了许多北部联盟的面貌——西部的大草原变成世界上最好的小麦田。部落、村庄、城镇，只要条件允许，就不停地增加扩大。教堂和学校，作为经久不衰的宗教和文明的标志，以一定的时间为间隔不停地出现。有许多"接口处"，铁路从主线在这里分出支线。以便向定居者提供数百万英亩的土地，这里土壤肥沃，水分充足，有丰富的森林，能够保证农民有丰富的收成。

穿越大草原900英里的铁路航行，游客们能够看到许多城镇，比如布兰登、雷吉娜、卡尔加里，当然还有许多较小的城镇，但它们也已迅速成为重要的商业中心，其迅速发展也表明周围地区的稳定进步。卡尔加里是一片巨大"牧场"企业的中心，这里的水牛已然消失，取而代之的是饲养牛群来满足远方市场。西方的地平线在很远的地方逐渐消逝，积雪覆盖的落基山脉像一座堡垒一样守卫着这里。

但快速流动的河流为落基山的中心提供了一个关卡。铁路轨道继续靠近河边，实际上，在很多年之前，这条沟壑是为它专门挖掘出来的。卡纳纳斯基斯瀑布就像是奇迹的序幕。班夫国家公园有许多景点，旅行者要在这里花费几天的时间，以便近距离地研究这些雄伟的高山。当你的眼睛、意识、心灵、想象力，都充斥着这些山峦，它们的宏伟会让你深深陶醉。在这次周游世界的旅程中，从卡尔加里向温哥华行进的600英里，人们可以享受到声音与景致形成的无与伦比的美景——湍急的激流；从陡峭的山壁下降数千英尺、奔流而下的银色的瀑布；奔向大海的壮丽河流；沉睡的湖泊表面反射出的山峰；奔流的瀑布割裂的深邃、黑暗的峡谷；割裂开的悬崖；宁静的山谷里庄严的松树林；被雪崩割裂得伤痕累累的山涧；沉睡的冰川慢慢打磨的岩石斜坡。其间列车驶过四大山峦：落基山脉，塞尔扣克山脉，黄金山脉和海岸山脉。它们形状各异，因此宏伟而美丽，可爱而令人畏惧。道路沿着弗雷泽河蜿蜒几个小时。在其他任何地方，人们很难看到这样一系列的景象——壮丽的河流卷着泥沙，匆忙地奔涌，激流从头顶的悬崖夹杂着各种物体的残骸而来。火车蜿蜒着进入了隧道，继而又驶出隧道，途经坚硬的岩石和跨过众多无名河流之上的桥梁。即使在仲夏时节，弗雷泽河河水涨满，愤怒地咆哮，人们在河岸之上建造了一条如此安全的，称为"铁马"的高速铁路，印证了人类科学的精彩成就！

太平洋海岸航线上的终点站是温哥华市，它的存在是铁路建设的结果。这座城市的人口如今接近12万，并且还在迅速增长。从这里开始，游客们可以享受由加拿大太平洋铁路提供的壮观轮船，在太平洋上进行旅行和贸易。轮船会停靠在不列颠哥伦比亚省的美丽首府维多利亚。这个处于温哥华岛上的城市，拥有超过8万居民，距离温哥华市有60英里远。在维多利亚附近，有一个埃斯吉摩镇，那里是一个大型的干船坞，英国的太平洋舰队通常将这里作为他们的总部。从温哥华到日本的主要商业城市横滨，现在需要10天的航程。然后从日本到中国的上海，距离1 047英里。再从这个港口出发，轮船继续前行至香港，在那里，加拿大太平洋公司会将他们的游客转送给半岛公司和东方公司。旅程的下一个阶段是新加坡，从香港出发，需要大约5天到达。然后来到槟城和锡兰、加尔各答和孟买。轮船穿越阿拉伯海，开往亚丁湾，穿过红海，通过苏伊士运河，穿过整个地中海，到达布林迪西或的里雅斯特，再通过陆路穿越意大利和法国，穿过多佛海峡到达对岸的英格兰；或通过水路，穿越直布罗陀海峡，到达英国在大西洋沿岸的一些港口。当然，这一旅程可能会因为休息、游乐、业务或研究，被无限期地延长。但其景点比比皆是。幸运的是，现代的"环球旅游"一年比一年变得更受欢迎，也更加可行。

Lesson 14　NATURE
第十四课　自　然

Beautiful are the heralds
That stand at Nature's door,
Crying, "O traveller, enter in,
And taste the Master's store!"

美丽的使者，
站在自然的门外，
里面有人喊道："哦！旅行者，进来吧！
来欣赏主人的宝藏！"

"Enter," they cry,
"to a kingly feast,
Where all may venture near;—
A million beauties for the eye,
And music for the ear:

"进来，"他们呼喊，
"来品尝这高贵的盛宴！"
所有人都会冒险靠近，
靠近眼前的万千风情，
靠近耳边的绝美乐章。

"Only, before thou enterest in,
Upon the threshold fall,
And pay the tribute of thy praise
To Him who gives thee all.'"

"不过，在你进门之前，
请走到门槛旁，
赞美那个人，
那个将这些礼物赠送于你的人。"

So some kneel down, and enter
With reverent step and slow;
And calm airs fraught with precious scent
Breathe round them as they go:

有些人跪下了，进门，
内心虔诚，脚步缓慢，
当走进时，他们嗅到，
宁静的空气洋溢沁人的清香。

Gently they pass 'mid sight and sound
And the sunshine round them sleeping,
To where the angels Faith and Love
The inner gates are keeping.

在光影与声响中，他们轻轻地走近，
阳光在他们周围徜徉，
走近天使信仰与热爱的地方，
里面的大门在此紧紧闭上。

Then backward rolls the wondrous screen
That hides the secret place,
Where the God of Nature veils himself

背后奇妙的屏障翻滚，
遮蔽了这一神秘之地，
自然之神隐匿在这里，

In the brighter realms of Grace: 在明亮的优雅之邦。

But they who have not bent the knee 然而那些没有跪下的人们，
Will smile at this my story; 会嘲笑我的这个故事；
For, though they enter the temple gates, 因为他们虽然走进了庙宇大门，
They know not the inner glory. 却发现里面没有光芒。

—W. E. Littlewood ——利特尔伍德

Words

fraught, *laden*.
heralds, *proclaimers*.
realms, *regions; kingdoms*.
reverent, *humble*.
screen, *curtain*.

threshold, *entrance*.
tribute, *meed; homage*.
venture, *dare to come*.
wondrous, *wonderful*.

Lesson 15 THE TROPICAL WORLD (I)
第十五课 热带世界（一）

THE WESTERN HEMISPHERE

The tropical regions, more than any other part of the world, are suggestive of magnificence—of luxuriant vegetation and diversified animal life; yet they embrace but a small portion comparatively of the land of the globe. While the greater part of the North Temperate Zone is occupied by land, the floods of ocean roll over much the larger portion of the equatorial regions; for both torrid America and Africa appear as mere islands in a vast expanse of sea. This superabundance of water is one of the great provisions which Nature has made for mitigating the heat of the vertical sun. To this cause the Tropics are indebted for those copious rains and periodic winds and constant ocean currents, which endow them with such an amazing variety of climate. The Indian Archipelago, the Peninsula of Malacca, the Antilles, and Central America, are all undoubtedly indebted to the waters which bathe their coasts for a more temperate climate than they would have had if they had been grouped together in one vast continent.

Another cause of the varieties of tropical climate is to be found in varied elevation of surface. Thus the high situation of many tropical lands moderates the effects of equatorial heat, and endows them with a climate similar to that of the temperate, or even of the cold regions of the globe. The Andes and the Himalaya, the most stupendous mountain-chains of the world,, raise their snow-clad summits either within the tropics or immediately beyond their verge, and must be considered as ordained by Providence to counteract the effects of the vertical sunbeams over a vast extent of land. In Western Tropical America, in Asia, and in Africa, there are immense countries rising like terraces thousands of feet above the level of the ocean, and reminding the European traveller of his distant northern home by their productions and their cool temperature. Thus, by means of a few simple physical and geological causes acting and reacting upon each other on a magnificent scale, Nature has bestowed a wonderful variety of climate upon the tropical regions, producing a no less wonderful diversity of plants and of animals.

Embracing the broad base of South America, the tropical regions bring before us the wide-spreading llanos of Venezue'la and New Grana'da; the majestic Andes, rising through every zone of vegetation to an Arctic region of perpetual snow; and the high table-lands of Peru and Bolivia, where the llama, the alpaca, and the vicuna have their home. The frosts of winter and an eternal spring are nowhere found in closer proximity than in the Peruvian highlands: for deep valleys cleave the windy *Puna*, as these lofty table-lands are called; and when the traveller, benumbed by the cold blasts of the mountain-plains, descends into the sheltered gorges, he almost suddenly finds himself transported from a northern climate to a terrestrial paradise.

Situated at a height where the "enervating power of the tropical sun is not felt, and where at the same time the air is not too rarefied, these pleasant mountain vales, protected by their rocky walls against the gusts of the *puna*, enjoy all the advantages of a genial sky. Here the astonished European sees himself surrounded by the rich corn-fields, the green lucern-meadows, and the well-known fruit trees of his distant home; so that he might almost fancy that some friendly enchanter had transported him to his native country, but for the cactuses and the agaves on the mountain-slopes by day, and the constellations of another hemisphere in the heavens by night.

There are regions in this remarkable country where the traveller may leave the snow-roofed puna hut in the morning, and before sunset pluck pine-apples and bananas on the cultivated margin of the primeval forest; where in the morning the stunted grasses and arid lichens of the naked plain remind him of the Arctic regions, and where he may repose at night under the fronds of gigantic palms.

Descending to the Pacific sea-bord, we come upon the desolate Peruvian sand-coast, where the eye seldom sees anything but fine drift-sand and sterile heaps of stone; and where for miles and miles the traveller meets no traces of vegetation, nor finds one drop of water. But when we pass to the other side of the Andes, how marvellous the contrast! On the one side, an arid, waterless, treeless waste; on the other, the luxuriant valley of the Amazon, the giant of rivers, which has made a broad course for itself through vast savannas and stupendous forests!

The Amazon has its cradle high up among the peaks of the Andes, where the condor, the vulture of America, builds its nest. So vast is the basin of that great river, that all Western Europe could be placed in it without touching its boundaries! It is entirely situated in the Tropics, on both sides of the Equator, and receives over its whole extent the most abundant rains.

The swelling of the river, after the rainy season, is gigantic as itself. In some parts the water rises above forty feet; and travellers have even seen trees whose trunks bore marks of the previous inundation fifty feet above the height of the stream during the dry season. Then for miles and miles the swelling giant inundates his low banks, and, majestic at all times, becomes terrible in his grandeur when rolling his angry torrents through the wilderness. The largest forest-trees tremble under the pressure of the waters. Huge trunks, uprooted and carried away by the stream, bear witness to its power. Fishes and alligators now swim where a short while ago the jaguar lay in wait for its prey; and only a few birds, perching on the highest tree-tops, remain to witness the tumult which disturbs the silence of the woods.

When at length the river retires within its usual limits, new islands have been formed in its bed, while others have been swept away; and in many places the banks, undermined by the floods, threaten to crush the passing boat by their fall,— a misfortune which not seldom happens, particularly when, along with the loosened banks, high trees fall headlong into the river.

The magical beauty of tropical vegetation reveals itself in all its glory to the traveller who steers his boat through the solitary mazes of the Amazon. Here the forest forms a canopy over his head; there it opens, allowing the sunshine to disclose the secrets of the wilderness; while on either side the eye penetrates through beautiful vistas into the depths of the woods. Sometimes, on a higher spot of ground, a clump of trees forms an island worthy of Eden. A chaos of bush-ropes and creepers flings its garlands of gay flowers over the forest, and fills the air with the sweetest odors. Numerous birds, rivalling in beauty of colour the flowers of these hanging gardens, animate the banks of the lagoon; gaudy macaws perch on the loftiest trees; humming-birds dart with lightning speed from flower to flower—now hovering for an instant before you, as if to allow you to admire their surpassing beauty—now

Vegetation in the Tropics

vanishing again with the rapidity of thought. But, as if to remind on that death is not banished from this scene of Paradise, a dark-robed vulture screeches through the woods; or an alligator, like a black log of wood or a sombre rock, rests on the dormant waters.

In these boundless forests the monkeys form much the greater part of the mammalian inhabitants; for each species, though often confined within narrow limits, generally consists of a large number of individuals. The various arboreous fruits which the savage population of these immeasurable wilds is unable to turn to advantage, fall chiefly to their share; many of them also live upon insects. They are never seen in the open savannas, as they never touch the ground unless compelled by the greatest necessity. The trees of the forests furnish them with all the food they require; it is only in the woods that they feel "at home," and secure against the attacks of mightier animals: why then should they quit them for less congenial haunts?

For their perpetual wanderings from branch to branch, Nature has bountifully endowed many of them, not only with robust and muscular limbs and large hands, whose moist palms facilitate the seizure of a bough, but in many cases also with a prehensile tail, which may deservedly be called a fifth hand, and is hardly less wonderful in its structure than the proboscis of the elephant Covered with short hair, and completely bare underneath towards the end, this admirable organ rolls around the boughs as though it were a supple finger, and is at the same time so muscular that the monkey frequently swings by it from a branch, like the pendulum of a clock. Scarce has he grasped a bough with his long arms, when immediately coiling his fifth hand round the branch, he springs on to the next; and secure from a fall, he hurries so rapidly through the crowns of the highest trees that the sportsman's bullet has scarce time to reach him in his flight.

Of the beasts of prey that frequent these vast woods, the jaguar is the most formidable, resembling the panther by his spotted skin, but almost equaling the Bengal tiger in size and power. He roams about at all times of the day, swims over broad rivers, and even in the water proves a most dangerous foe; for when driven to extremities he frequently turns against the boat which contains his assailants, and forces them to seek their safety by jumping overboard. Many an Indian, while wandering through thinly peopled districts, where swampy thickets alternate with open grass plains, has been torn to pieces by the jaguar; and in many a lonely plantation the inhabitants hardly venture to leave their enclosures after sunset, for fear of his attacks. Far from being afraid of man, this ferocious animal springs upon him when alone; and when pressed by hunger he will even venture during the day-time into the mountain villages to seek his prey.

The dreadful storms which burst suddenly over the Amazon recall to memory the tornadoes of the ocean. The howlings of the monkeys, the shrill tones of the mews, and the visible terror of all animals, first announce the approaching conflict of the elements. The crowns of the palms rustle and bend, while as yet no breeze is perceptible on the surface of the stream; but a hollow murmur in the air precedes the black clouds ascending from the horizon, like grim warriors ready for battle.

And now the old forest groans under the shock of the hurricane; a night-like darkness veils the face of nature; and, while torrents of rain descend amid uninterrupted sheets of lightning and terrific peals of thunder, the river rises and falls in waves of a dangerous height. Then it requires great skill to preserve the boat from sinking; but the Indian pilots steer with so masterly a hand, and understand so well the first symptoms of the storm, that it seldom takes them by surprise, or renders them victims of its fury.

A majestic uniformity is the character of European woods, which often consist of only one species of tree; but in the tropical forests an immense variety of families strive for existence, and even in a small space one tree scarcely ever resembles its neighbour. Even at a distance this difference becomes apparent in the irregular outlines of the forest, as here a dome-shaped crown, there a pointed pyramid, rises above the broad flat masses of green, in ever-varying succession. On approaching, differences of colour are added to irregularities of form; for while our forests are destitute of the ornament of flowers, many tropical trees have large blossoms, mixing in thick bunches with the leaves, and often entirely overpowering the verdure of the foliage by their gaudy tints. Thus splendid white, yellow, and red-coloured crowns are mingled with those of darker or more humble hue. When at length, on entering the forest, the single leaves become distinguishable, even the last traces of harmony disappear. Here they are delicately feathered, there lobed: here narrow, there broad: here pointed, there obtuse: here lustrous and fleshy, as if in the full luxuriance of youth; there dark and arid, as if decayed with age. As the wind plays with the foliage, it appears now silvery, now dark green—now of a lively, now of a sombre hue.

Variety of vegetation is characteristic of all tropical countries, but nowhere are the varieties so wonderfully brought together as on the Mexican plateaux. There the vegetation rises in successive zones from the base of the mountains to heights unparalleled in any other part of the world. It is literally true that the inhabitants, without leaving their native land, may view the vegetable forms of every country on the globe, and pluck nearly every fruit that is found between the Equator and the Arctic Circle.

Words

appears, *produced on trees*.
assailants, *pursuers*.
astonished, *surprised*.
benumbed, *stupefied*.
congenial, *suitable*.
constellations, *star*.
desolate, *barren groups*.
distinguishable, *recognizable*.
diversified, *varied*.
dormant, *sleeping*.
elevation, *altitude*.
enervating, *weakening*.
facilitate, *make easy*.
ferocious, *fierce*.
formidable, *terrible*.
gigantic, *colossal*.
inundation, *flood*.
irregularities, *diversities*.
lobed, *having rounded divisions*.
lustrous, *shining*.
luxuriant, *abundant*.
magnificent, *grand*.
majestic, *grand*.

mammalian, *of the order of suck-givers*.
marvelous, *wonderful*.
misfortune, *accident*.
mitigating, *moderating*.
obtuse, *having a broad point*.
penetrates, *pierces*.
perceptible, *apparent*.
perpetual, *everlasting*.
prehensile, *adapted for seizing*.
primeval, *original*.
proboscis, *trunk*.
proximity, *nearness*.
rivaling, *emulating*.
savannas, *meadows*.
solitary, *lonely*.
stupendous, *enormous*.
superabundance, *excess*.
tumult, *commotion*.
undoubtedly, *certainly*.
uniformity, *sameness*.
verdure, *greenness*.
uninterrupted, *unbroken*.

Questions

Of what are the tropical regions suggestive? Wherein do they differ from the north temperate zone? What effect has this on their climate? Mention another cause of the varieties of tropical climate. Give examples of its operation? In what do these diversities produce corresponding variety? What are the great physical features of tropical America? What constitute the Puna? For what are these regions chiefly remarkable? What is the nature of the Peruvian sea-bord? What contrast do the two sides of the Andes present? To what is this due? To what height does the Amazon rise after the rainy season? What changes are observed after it has fallen again? Where is the beauty of tropical vegetation seen to greatest advantage? Mention birds that are seen there. What mammals are most numerous in these forests? What is the monkey's fifth hand? What does it enable him to do? What is the most formidable beast of prey in the Brazilian forests? What do the storms of the Amazon recall to memory? Mention some of their striking features. Wherein do tropical woods chiefly differ from European ones? What produces their differences colour? Where is variety of vegetation most strikingly exhibited? How is this variety illustrated?

西 半 球

热带地区比世界上的其他任何地方都更加富丽堂皇——它拥有繁茂的植被和多样化的生物，然而它们簇拥着的仅仅是地球上相对较小的一部分土地。北温带的大部分区域都由陆地占据，海洋则滚动在赤道地区的更大一部分。无论是热带的美洲还是非洲，都作为一个单纯的岛屿出现在浩瀚无垠的大海之上。水的过剩是大自然为减轻太阳的垂直热量而做出的伟大规定之一，因为这个缘故，热带地区的人们非常感激那些丰富的降水和周期性的季风以及恒定的洋流，这些都赋予了他们这样一种惊人而多样的气候。印度群岛、马六甲半岛、安的列斯群岛以及中美洲，都无疑相当感激那些将它们环绕在内的海域，正是这些海域，彼此将它们连接在一片广阔的大陆里，给了它们一种更温和的气候。

热带气候多样的另一个原因在于地表的不同海拔。因此，许多热带地区的较高海拔缓和了赤道的热量效应，并赋予了它们类似于温带的气候，甚至与地球上寒冷的地区相似。安第斯山脉和喜马拉雅山脉，是世界上最巍峨的山脉，将它们积雪覆盖的顶峰提升在热带地区或是刚刚超越了热带边缘的区域。它们一定是受上帝指派，来抵消垂直的阳光效果的辽阔土地。在热带美洲的西部、亚洲和非洲，许多幅员辽阔的国家如梯田一般崛起，超越到海平面的数千英尺以上，并通过它们的产品和凉爽的气温，提醒来自于欧洲的旅客，遥远的北方才是他们的家。因此，通过一些对热带地区精彩、多样的气候产生影响并且相互影响的简单的物理和地质成因，产生了这里同样精彩、多样的植物和动物群族。

环抱着南美洲广阔的地域，热带地区把委内瑞拉和新格拉纳达广阔的大草原呈现在我们面前；还有雄伟的安第斯山脉，在海拔上升的过程中展现出每一个植被带，直到一个永久积雪的北极地区；而秘鲁和玻利维亚的高原给了骆驼、羊驼和骆马一个家园；没有其他地方像秘鲁高原这般，拥有如此接近的冬天的严寒和永恒的春天，因为深邃的山谷劈裂了这片多风的秘鲁高原，也正是因此，这片巍峨的高原才被叫作"秘鲁"（它的本意是"寒冷贫瘠的高地"）。当旅行者快要被高山平原冻僵的时候，他会到达海拔较低的有所庇护的峡谷。这时，他会突然发现自己从北方气候区域来到了大陆上的天堂。

坐落在这样一个高度，在那里，热带太阳的使人衰弱的力量难以感觉得到，同时那里的空气也不是太稀薄。这里有众多令人愉快的山谷，保护它们的岩石墙壁对抗着贫瘠高地的狂风，享受着和煦阳光下所有的美好气候。在这里，惊讶的欧洲人会发现在自己的周围，布满富饶的麦田、绿色的苜蓿草地和本应只生长在他远方家乡的著名的果树。这让他几乎会想象到，一些友好的魔法师已经将他带回到他的祖国。但白天，他会看到山坡上的仙人掌和龙舌兰，夜晚，还有属于另一个半球天空中的星座。

在这个非凡国度的一些地区，游客可能在清晨离开冷风吹过屋顶的小屋，而在日落之前，却能在原始森林已开化的边际采摘菠萝和香蕉；早上，发育迟缓的草地和赤裸平原的干旱地衣可能会提醒他这里是北极地区，而到了夜间，他就可能静卧在巨型棕榈树的树荫之下了。

来到太平洋沿岸，我们会看到荒凉、沙质的秘鲁海岸。在这里，除了细细的流沙和成堆的干瘪石头之外，我们什么都不会见到，前行数英里，旅客都不会看到任何植被的痕迹，也不会发现一滴水。但是，当我们来到安第斯山脉的另一边，对比确是如此神奇！山的一面是干旱、缺水、寸草不生的荒芜；山的另一面，却是亚马孙平原繁茂的山谷和澎湃的河流。而在茫茫的大草原和广阔的森林之中，河流已经为自己开辟了一条宽阔的流经之地！

亚马孙平原的摇篮高耸在安第斯山脉之间，那里的秃鹰和美国秃鹫建立了自己的巢穴。如此宽广的大河流域，甚至可以将整个西欧安置其中，而不触及它的边界！它完全坐落在热带地区，在赤道两侧，并在其整个范围内接收了最丰富的降雨。

雨季过后，河流的膨胀像其本身一样巨大。在一些地方，河水甚至高于40英尺，游客甚至看到树木的树干上，有比之前旱季时候的浸水线高出50英尺的标志。然后绵延数英里的宽广河流，淹没了它的低矮河岸，时刻都如此雄伟，而当它翻滚着愤怒洪流经过无边的旷野时，它又变得如此可怕。森林中最高大的树木也在水的压力下颤抖。水流将巨大的树干连根拔起，证明了它的力量。鱼类和短吻鳄现在游泳的地方，不久之前还是美洲虎躺着等待猎物的角落；只有少数鸟类栖息在树梢的最高处，仍然可以见证这骚动扰乱了寂静的树林。

当长河在其通常的极限处退却，新的岛屿已经在它的河床上形成，而另一些却被一扫而空，很多地方的河岸都已经被洪水破坏。它们的落下可能会击碎路经此地的渔船。这种不幸在这里时有发生，特别是随着河岸的松动，高耸的树木也会掉下来扎进河里。

当一名旅客驾驶着他的船舶通过亚马孙河孤独的迷宫中时，热带植物的神奇之美会向他揭示出它们本身所有的荣耀。这里的森林形成一个树冠，遮盖了他的头顶，有时它也会被打开，让阳光透露旷野的秘密，而两边的目光穿过美丽的景观，进入树林的深处。有时候，在地面较高的地方，树丛会形成一个堪比伊甸园的小岛。一个混乱的灌木绳索和藤蔓攀缘在一个姹紫嫣红的花环之上，遍布整个森林，散发出融融的甜蜜香气。众多的鸟类可以与空中花园的鲜艳的花朵媲美，使河岸边的小小湖泊生机勃勃；色彩艳丽的金刚鹦鹉栖息在高耸的树上；蜂鸟以闪电般的速度在花间飞快移动，一会儿在你面前盘旋片刻，仿佛让你赞叹它们无与伦比的美丽，一会儿又像敏捷的思想一般快速消失。但是，一只黑袍秃鹫的尖叫声穿过森林，仿佛为了提醒你死亡并没有从这一幕天堂般的盛景中被驱逐；或者一条鳄鱼，像黑色的木柴或阴暗的岩石一般，停留在安静的水域之中。

在这片广阔的森林里，猴子是这里最重要的哺乳动物居民。每一个物种，虽然经常局限在狭小的范围内，通常都由大量的个体组成。在这片无法估量的野外，许多种不同树木的果实，都是这些原始的居民所无法利用的，它们其中还有许多要靠昆虫来维持生命。人们从来没有在开放的热带草原见到过它们，因为除非迫于需要，它们从来不会接触地面。森林中的树木为它们提供了所有所需的食物，也只有在树林之中，它们才能有家的感觉，并确保能对抗强大动物的攻击，所以为什么它们应该离开这里，而到一个不适宜的栖息地呢？

因为它们永远在树枝与树枝之间漫游，大自然也慷慨地赋予了它们很多。它们不仅拥有具有强大肌肉的四肢和巨大的手掌，它们湿润的手心也非常便于扣住树枝。而在许多情况下，它们也会长出卷尾，这可以当之无愧地被称为第五只手，并且其结构的精彩之处，几乎不亚于大象的长鼻子。它们的毛发很短，并且在体表的最里面几乎完全裸露。这一令人钦佩的器官可以卷在树枝上，仿佛是一个柔软的手指。与此同时，猴子通过摆动它的肌肉，可以在树枝之间摇摆，就像一个钟摆。它很少用它长长的手臂去抓住一根树枝，当它马上要将它的第五只手盘绕着树枝，它就会弹到另一个树枝，然后安全地降落；它如此迅速地穿梭在最高树木的树冠之间，运动员射出的子弹，也很少能够在它跳跃的过程中追得上它。

在频繁出现在这些巨大森林内部猎取猎物的野兽之中，美洲虎是最强大、最可怕的。它带斑点的皮肤与猎豹相似，但它的大小和力量几乎相当于孟加拉虎。在一天中的任何时候，它都咆哮着出没，在宽阔的河流之中游泳，甚至在水里，它也是最危险的敌人。当它认定一艘船上有会攻击它的人类，它会倾其所能地发动攻击，并迫使他们为寻求安全而弃船跳水。许多印第安人，当在沼泽和灌木丛交替存在的人口稀少的地域漫步时，可能会被美洲狮撕成碎片，在许多孤立的种植园里，因为担心受到美洲狮的攻击，居民们很少冒险在日落之后离开他们的围场。美洲狮对人类的恐惧则少得多，这种凶猛的动物会在人类孤单一个出现时，跳跃到他的身上，而迫于饥饿，它甚至会冒险在白天到山村里去寻找它的猎物。

亚马孙平原上突然袭来可怕的暴风雨，会让人想到海洋上的龙卷风。猴子来回平稳跳跃，马厩里刺耳的音调，还有所有动物脸上的惊恐表情，都首先宣布着一场灾难的即将到来。棕榈树的树冠沙沙作响，有所弯曲，而这时地面上还没有感受到明显的风力，但空中一阵低沉的声音，会在乌云从地平线上升之前来到，像一个严肃的战士已经准备好了投入战斗。

如今，原始森林在突然爆发的可怕风暴之下呻吟。如夜晚一般的黑暗笼罩了这里的整个大自然。当漂泊的大雨不停地在电闪雷鸣中落下，河流的水浪上升、下降到一种可怕的高度。这时，想保持船舶不沉需要很高的技巧。但是印第安舵手拥有一双如此娴熟的掌舵的手，他们也十分清楚地了解暴风雨的第一个预兆。因此，暴风雨很少会让他们感到震惊，或者给他们造成伤亡。

雄伟的一致性是欧洲森林的特点，通常它只由一种树种构成，但在热带森林之中，各种各样的种族争奇斗艳，甚至在一个狭小的空间之内，树木都很少会与周围的树木相似。即使离得稍远一些，这种差异也会因不规则的森林轮廓而变得更加明显。这里是一个圆顶的树冠，而那边是一棵如金字塔尖般的高树，用不同的持续性，跃于绿色的宽阔树丛之上。接近它们，颜色的不同会添加在形状的不规则之上，因为虽然我们的森林缺乏花朵的点缀，许多热带的树木却长满绚丽的花朵，混杂在它们厚重的树丛之间，经常彻底压倒了翠绿的树叶花哨的颜色。因此灿烂的白色、黄色和红色的树冠，会夹杂在森林中黯淡或更谦虚的色调之中。最后，当你进入森林之中，会发现单一的叶子变得稀少，甚至最后的和谐也消失了它的踪迹。这里的树木被绚烂的色彩装扮着；这里的树窄，那里的树宽；这里的树叶尖，那里的树叶是钝形的；这里的树木拥有光泽的肉质，好像青春的华美；那里的树木则黯淡、干瘪，仿佛随着年龄的增长而衰老。随着微风吹拂着树叶，它一会儿显出银色的吸引力，一会儿又是深绿色的，一会儿生机盎然，一会儿又色泽黯淡。

　　植被的丰富多样是所有热带国家的特点，但没有什么地方如墨西哥高原一样，能如此精彩地将这些多样性结合在一处。在这里，植被从山脚开始，连续上升到一个世界上其他地方都无可比拟的高度。绝对真实的一点是，这里的居民不用离开自己的故土，就可能看到来自于地球上每一个国家的蔬菜，采摘几乎在赤道和北极之间可以发现的所有水果。

Lesson 16
MAN AND THE INDUSTRIAL ARTS
第十六课　人类和工业艺术

As industrial creatures, we often look like wretched copyists of animals far beneath us in the scale of organization; and we seem to confess as much by the names which we give them. The mason-wasp, the carpenter-bee, the mining caterpillars, the quarrying sea-slugs, execute their work in a way which we cannot rival or excel the bird is an exquisite architect; the beaver a most skilful bridge-builder; the silk-worm the most beautiful of weavers; the spider the best of net-makers. Each is a perfect craftsman, and each has his tools always at hand.

Those wise creatures, I believe, have minds like our own, to the extent that they have minds, and are not mere living machines, swayed by a blind instinct; but their most wonderful works imply neither invention, contrivance, nor volition, but only a placid, pleasant, easily rendered obedience to instincts which reign without rivals, and justify their despotic rule by the infallible happiness which they secure. It has cost none of these ingenious artists any intellectual effort to learn its craft, for God gave it to each perfect in the beginning; and, within the circle to which they apply, the rules which guide their work are infallible, and know no variation.

To those creatures, however, the Author of all has given, not only infallible rules for their work, but unfaltering faith in them. Labour is for them not a doubt, but a certainty. Duty is the same thing as happiness. They never grow weary of life, and death never surprises them; and they are less to be likened to us than to perfect self-repairing machines, which swiftly raise our admiration from themselves to Him who made and who sustains them.

We are industrial for other reasons, and in a different way. Our working instincts are very few; our faith in them still more feeble; and our physical wants far greater than those of any other creature. Indeed, the one half of the Industrial Arts are the result of our being born without clothes; the other half, of our being born without tools.

I do not propose to offer you a catalogue of the arts which our unclothedness compels us to foster. The shivering savage in the colder countries robs the seal and the bear, the buffalo and the deer, of the one mantle which Nature has given them. The wild huntsman, by a swift but simple transmutation, becomes the clothier, the tailor, the tanner, the currier, the leather-dresser, the glover, the saddler, the shoemaker, the tent-maker. And the tent-maker, the arch-architect of one of the great schools of architecture, becomes quickly a house-builder, building with snow where better material is not to be had; and a ship-builder, constructing, out of a few wooden ribs and stretched animal skins, canoes which, as sad experience has shown, may survive where English ships of oak have gone to destruction.

Again: the unchilled savage of the warmer regions seeks a covering, not from the cold, but from the sun which smites him by day, and the moon which smites him by night. The palm, the banana, the soft-barked trees, the broad-leaved sedges and long-fibred grasses are spoiled by him, as the beasts of the field are by his colder brother. He becomes a sower, a reaper, a spinner, a weaver, a baker, a brewer, a distiller, a dyer, a carpenter; and whilst he is these, he bends the pliant stems of his tropical forests into roof-trees and rafters, and clothes them with leaves, and makes for himself a tabernacle of boughs, and so is the arch-architect of a second great school of architecture; and, by-and-by, his twisted branches and interlaced leaves grow into Grecian columns with Corinthian acanthus capitals, and Gothic pillars, with petrified plants and stony flowers gracefully curling round them.

Once more: in those temperate regions where large animals and trees do not greatly abound, turfs, or mud, or clay, or stones, or all together, can be fashioned into that outermost garment which we call a house, and which we most familiarly connect with the notion of architecture.

It is not, however, his cultivation either of the arts which have been named, or of others, that makes man peculiar as an industrial animal;—it is the mode in which he practices them. The first step he takes towards remedying his nakedness and helplessness, is in a direction in which no other creature has led the way, and none has followed his example. He lays hold of that most powerful of all weapons of peace or war, *Fire*, from which every other animal, unless when fortified by man's presence, flees in terror; and with it alone not only clothes himself, but lays the foundation of a hundred arts.

Man may be defined as the only animal that can strike a light,—the solitary creature that knows how to kindle a fire. This is a very fragmentary definition of the "Paragon of animals," but it is enough to make him the conqueror of all the rest. The most degraded savage has discovered how to rub two sticks together, or whirl the point of one in a socket in the other till the wood is kindled. And civilized man, as much as his savage brother, is a fire-worshipper in his practical doings. The great conquering peoples of the world have been those who knew best how to deal with fire. The most wealthy of the active nations are those which dwell in countries richly provided with fuel. No inventions have changed the entire world more than steam and gunpowder. We are what we are, largely because we are the ministers and masters of Fire.

Clothe-less creatures by birth, we are also tool-less ones. Every other animal is by nature fully equipped and caparisoned for its work; its tools are ready for use, and it is ready to use them. We have first to invent our tools, then to fashion them, and then to learn how to handle them. Two-thirds at least of our industrial doings are thus preliminary. Before two rags can be sewed together, we require a needle, which embodies the inventiveness of a hundred ingenious brains; and a hand, which only a hundred botching and failures have, in the lapse of years, taught to use the instrument with skill.

It is so with all the crafts, and they are inseparably dependent one on another. The mason waits on the carpenter for his mallet, and the carpenter on the smith for his saw; the smith on the smelter for his iron, and the smelter on the miner for his ore. Each, moreover, needs the help of all the others;—the carpenter the smith, as much as the smith the carpenter; and both the mason, as much as the mason both. This helplessness of the single craftsman is altogether peculiar to the human artist. The lower animals are all poly artists, amongst whom there are no degrees of skill; and they have never heard of such a doctrine as that of the division of labour.

The industrialness, then, of man, is carried out in a way quite peculiar to himself, and singularly illustrative of his combined weakness and greatness. The most helpless, physically, of animals, and yet the one with the greatest number of pressing appetites and desires, he has no working instincts (at least after infancy) to secure the gratification of his most pressing wants, and no tools which such instincts can work by. He is compelled, therefore, to fall back upon the powers of his reason and understanding, and make his intellect serve him instead of a crowd of instinctive impulses, and his intellect-guided hand instead of an apparatus of tools. Before that hand, armed with the tools which it has fashioned, and that intellect, which marks man as made in the image of God, the instincts and weapons of the entire animal creation are as nothing. He reigns, by right of conquest, as indisputably as by right of inheritance, the king of this world.

—George Wilson

Words

apparatus, *collection.*
caparisoned, *harnessed.*
catalogue, *list.*
constructing, *fashioning.*
craftsman, *skilled worker.*
defined, *described.*
despotic, *tyrannical.*
execute, *perform.*
fragmentary, *imperfect.*
gracefully, *elegantly.*
gratification, *indulgence.*
illustrative, *expository.*
indisputably, *unquestionably.*
industrial, *manufacturing.*

infallible, *incapable of error.*
inheritance, *descent.*
inseparably, *indissolubly.*
inventiveness, *ingenuity.*
organization, *animal life.*
preliminary, *preparatory.*
provided, *supplied.*
remedying, *correcting*
sustains. *supports,*
tabernacle, *dwelling-place.*
temperate, *mild.*
transmutation, *alteration.*
unfaltering, *unhesitating.*
volition, *exercise of will.*

Questions

What is the great difference between man and the lower animals, as industrial workers? Of what two deficiencies are man's industrial arts the result? What arts result from his unclothedness? What is it, more than the arts themselves, that makes man peculiar as an industrial animal? How, in this respect, may man be defined? Show how two-thirds of all our industrial doings are preliminary. Show how the crafts are thus inseparably dependent on one another. How does man's industrialness illustrate his combined weakness and greatness?

☆ ☆

作为工业的产物，我们经常看起来就像自然界里那些远不如我们高级的动物一样可怜，并且我们似乎承认了我们给它起的名字。像瓦工黄蜂、木匠蜜蜂、采矿的毛虫，它们以自己独有的方式执行着我们做不到或者不能与之媲美的职责。鸟儿是精妙的建筑师，海狸是最具技巧的桥梁筑造者，蚕宝宝是最美丽的织工，蜘蛛呢，则能编织精美的网。这些动物都是大自然中完美并且天赋异禀的工匠，并且它们的工具时常是信手拈来的。

我相信，这些聪明的生物就像我们人类一样，也拥有自己的想法。从这个层面来说，它们不仅仅是有生命、受盲目的直觉支配的机器，它们绝伦的作品揭示了这些并不是发明创造也不是意志力。而仅仅是平静的愉悦的，很容易体现的不服从于竞争者的本能，并且凭借它们所维护的不可动摇的幸福衡量判断它们残暴专横的规则。这些大自然中完美的工匠，无须花费一丝一毫的精力去获得这些独特的技能，因为这是在它们出生的时候上天已然赋予它们的。并且，在自然界的循环中，这些指引它们工作的规则是毫无谬误并且是不会产生变化的。

对于这些生物来说，这不仅仅保证了它们的工作绝不会出现差错，还有它们坚定的信仰，奋力前行是毫无疑问的，责任等同于幸福和快乐。它们不知疲倦，就连死亡也不会令它们吃惊，并且它们是可以完美地自我修复的机器，这一点就像我们人类本身，这让我们对它们的崇敬很快提升到了创造它们并供养它们的造物主身上。

我们之所以是属于工业的，从不同的角度来说，还有其他一些原因。我们的工作直觉是很有限的，我们的信仰仍然比较无力、虚弱，然而我们的物欲却比其他生物强烈很多很多。实际上，工业的产生，一方面是因为我们衣不覆体，另一方面是因为我们没有生产工具。

我并不想列出一个目录去说明我们的衣不覆体迫使我们去发展工业。在寒冷的国度，未开化的人类掠夺海豹和熊，水牛和鹿，这些生活在地球表面的生物。野生动物的狩猎者们，以敏捷并且便于演变的进程，成为裁缝、制革工人、制革匠、皮裙制造者、手套贩制者、马具商、制鞋者、帐篷制造者，并且经过对建筑更深的认知和学习，这些帐篷的制造者们，作为建筑这一广泛流派中的伟大建筑师之一，很快成为房屋建造者。在得不到好的建筑材料的地方，他们用雪来筑造房屋。船舶制造商呢，在像我们之前提到过的那些窘迫的环境中，在缺乏木材与可伸展的动物皮做架构的情况下，也可能在英国橡木船已经一去不返的地方存活下去。

再者，生活在温暖地区的未开化的人们寻找遮盖物，并不是为了抵御严寒，而是为了避免白天太阳对他们的侵袭以及夜晚月亮对他们的干扰。棕榈树、香蕉、软树皮、阔叶以及长纤维的草地被人们破坏，正如在寒冷地带人类杀戮野兽一样。

他成为一个播种者，收割者，一个纺纱工人，一个织布者，一个面包师，一个啤酒制造者，一个蒸馏酒者，一个染色工，一个木匠；当他们做这些工作时，他到热带树林里将树顶和橡木上易弯曲的茎折了下来，他们用树叶做成衣服，还为自己用大树枝做了临时帐篷，这是建筑中的第二大流派了；而且在将来，他扭曲的树枝和交错的树叶变成了具有希腊式的圆柱还有科林斯艺术风格叶形装饰的柱顶，这种用石头做成的花优雅地卷曲着围绕着他们，令人称奇。

从另一角度说，在温带地区生长的大型动物和树木并不是很丰富，草皮、泥浆、黏土或石头，全部混杂在一起，可以形成我们称之为一个房子的外形，这是我们最熟悉的可以与建筑这一概念相联系的物体。

然而并不是人类对其他工艺形式或任何其他方式的培育，都是由此而得名的。这使得人类成为一种特殊的工业动物，这是他们实践工业的模式。第一步是他需要对他无能为力的状态进行弥补，没有其他的人来指引方向，并且没有人以他为榜样来追随他。他展示了通往和平或战争道路上最强大的武器，这就是火。在人类出现之前，其他任何动物都会恐惧地逃离大火。人类用火为自己披上了外衣，并且为众多工艺奠定了基础。

人们可能被定义为唯一可以点火的动物——唯一一种知道该如何使用火的生物。"万物之灵"是一个非常不完全的解说，但这足以使他征服所有的依赖。最低级的野蛮人已经发现如何摩擦两根棍子，或者在一个窝点一直旋转直到木头点燃为止。一个文明人正如他原始的先人一样，在他的实际行为中也是一个火的崇拜者，世界上最伟大的征服者已经知道如何更好地处理火了。活跃国家中最富有的国家，居住在那些能够提供丰富燃料的地域。没有任何发明能够如蒸汽和火药一般，可以更多地改变世界。我们变成现在这样，很大程度上是因为我们是火的主人。

生来衣不蔽体，我们同时也是生来工具贫乏的。其他的生物为了它们的工作，天生就充分地做好装备并且盛装打扮；它的工具可以使用了，并且它也准备使用它们。首先我们必须发明工具，然后去改变它们，再学习如何使用它们。因此我们的工业至少有三分之二是原始而初级的。在将两块破布缝在一起之前，我们需要一根针，这使众多聪明的大脑体现了它们的创造性，一只手在无数次笨拙的修补和失败之后，在岁月的流逝中，才学会了使用工具的技能。

所有的工艺都是如此，它们也是紧密地相互联系着。泥瓦匠正等着木匠和他的木槌，木匠在铁匠铺等着他的锯，铁匠在熔炉中将他的矿石冶炼。此外，每一个人都需要另一个人的帮助——木匠需要铁匠，铁匠也一样需要木匠；同时还有泥瓦匠，也需要木匠和铁匠的帮助，反之亦然。对于人类来说，无助的单一的工匠是相当怪异的。低级动物都是独立的工匠，它们之间没有技能的等级区分；它们之间也从未有过这样一种社会分工的原则。

人类的工业，在对他自己来说的某种程度上，是以相当特殊的方式发展起来的，这也特别说明了他是弱点和伟大的结合。最无助的动物，还有一个最迫切的需求和心愿，他没有工作的本能（至少在初期）来确保满足他最迫切的希望，并且在没有工具的情况下依然可以工作。因此他被迫去依靠推理和理解的力量，并使他的智慧为他服务，而不是出自本能的冲动，还有他非凡才智指引的双手可以代替工具的装置。在人类装备了工具的双手和让人类有了上帝形象的智慧面前，所有动物创造的本能和武器，似乎都不算什么了。他通过征服，毫无疑问也同样通过继承，来统治世界，成为这个世界的王者。

——乔治·威尔逊

Lesson 17　SOMEBODY'S DARLING
第十七课　某人的亲爱的人

Into a ward of the white-washed halls,
　　Where the dead and dying lay,
Wounded by bayonets, shells, and balls,
　　Somebody's Darling was borne one day—
Somebody's Darling, so young and so brave,
　　Wearing yet on his pale sweet face,
Soon to be hid by the dust of the grave,
　　The lingering light of his boyhood's grace,

Matted and damp are the curls of gold.
　　Kissing the snow of that fair young brow;
Pale are the lips of delicate mould—
　　Somebody's Darling is dying now.
Back from his beautiful blue-veined brow
　　Brush all the wandering waves of gold;
Cross his hands on his bosom now—
　　Somebody's Darling is still and cold.

Kiss him once for Somebody's sake,
　　Murmur a prayer soft and low;
One bright curl from its fair mates take—
　　They were Somebody's pride, you know;
Somebody's hand had rested there;
　　Was it a mother's, soft and white?
And have the lips of a sister fair
　　Been baptized in the waves of light?

God knows best. He has Somebody's love;
　　Somebody's heart enshrined him there;
Somebody wafted his name above
　　Night and morn on the wings of prayer.
Somebody wept when lie marched away,
　　Looking so handsome, brave, and grand;
Somebody's kiss on his forehead lay,
　　Somebody clung to his parting hand.

Somebody's waiting and watching for him—
   Yearning to hold him again to her heart;
And there lie lies, with his blue eyes dim,
   And the smiling, childlike lips apart.
Tenderly bury the fair young dead,
   Pausing to drop on his grave a tear;
Carve on the wooden slab at his head,—
   "Somebody's Darling slumbers here."

—Mrs. Lacoste

Words

delicate, *refined.*
enshrined, *cherished.*
handsome, *graceful.*
lingering, *lagging.*
matted, *twisted together.*
murmur, *whisper.*

pausing, *waiting.*
slumbers, *sleeps.*
tenderly, *gently.*
wafted, *floated.*
wandering, *straggling.*
yearning, *longing.*

☆ ☆

在一间四面白墙的病房里，
躺着已逝和奄奄一息的人，
他们被刺刀、炮弹、子弹所伤，
某一天某人亲爱的人出生，
他如此年轻，如此英勇，
灰暗的脸庞布满甜蜜，
他还拥有男孩的优雅面容，
不久就要埋葬于墓穴之中。

他金色的卷发如今无光、消沉，
亲吻着他娇好的年轻面容，
细嫩的嘴唇已变成灰色，
某人亲爱的人如今奄奄一息。
从他的美好面容中看得到血管，
被所有金色卷发的波涛拂过；

他的手臂交叉在胸口，
如今却已静止冰冷。

为了爱他的人而亲吻他，
轻轻地低语着祷告；
他浅色的卷发曾被他的爱人抚摸，
他们是某些人的骄傲；
深爱他的人的手曾经放置在此，
可能是他的妈妈，温柔又纯净；
他的姐妹的唇也曾亲吻过他，
在光影中接受了洗礼。

上帝会了解，他是某个人的爱人；
某个人的心里深刻着他，
某个人曾在黑夜和清晨的祷告中，
将他的名字蕴藏在内。
当谎言散去，某个人曾因此哭泣，
如此英俊、勇猛、容光焕发；
某个人曾亲吻他的前额，
某个人曾紧抓着他要离别的双手。

某个人在等待着盼望着他，
期盼着能够再次拥他进自己怀中；
此刻他躺在这，蓝色的眼睛已经黯淡，
他微笑着，孩童般的嘴唇张开着，
温柔地埋葬这个美好的年轻人，
暂停一下，为他留下一滴眼泪；
在他头顶的平板上刻字：
　"某人亲爱的人在此长眠。"

——拉科斯特夫人

Lesson 18　THE TROPICAL WORLD (II)
第十八课　热带世界（二）

THE EASTERN HEMISPHERE

Owing to the absence of inlets, gulfs, and great estuaries, Africa has been the last of the continents to yield to the advances of civilization. Its interior is therefore less known than any other part of the tropical world, excepting perhaps the centre of Australia; but what is known of it shows that it is not destitute of those grand and varied features which characterize the western tropics. Tropical Africa extends from the middle of the Sahara in the north to the plains of the Bushmen in the south. Chief among the natural features of this wide area are the great lakes lying across the Equator, which most probably constitute the highest sources of the Nile. The Nile itself, which rivals the Amazon in the length of its course, is a tropical river; and it is one of the wonders of the world. Three other great rivers belong to tropical Africa;— the Niger in the north; the Congo in the west; and in the south the Zambeze, on which is the highest waterfall in the world.

The interior of Africa—so far from being a desolate waste, as was at one time supposed—is a well watered and fertile region, and is remarkable for the extraordinary dimensions both of its vegetable and of its animal life. The chief of its vegetable wonders is the baobab-tree, which has been well called the elephant of the vegetable world. One baobab has been seen whose trunk was thirty feet in diameter and ninety-five in circumference. As these trees are generally hollow, they are frequently made use of as dwellings or stables; and Dr. Livingstone mentions one in which twenty or thirty men could lie down and sleep as in a hut! There are also gigantic sycamores, under whose branches the negroes pitch their huts; while picturesque-looking mangroves are found fringing the shores of the sea and the mouths of rivers.

To the presence of mangrove trees must be attributed, in part at least,

The Mangrove

the unhealthy character of the estuaries of African rivers. From the roots, when left bare by the tide, a sickly odour arises; and the vicinity of a mangrove forest is always exposed to the deadly malaria. "The shore," says Kingsley, describing a mangrove forest, "sank suddenly into a low line of mangrove wood, backed by primeval forest. The loathsome floor of liquid mud lay bare beneath. Upon the endless web of inter-arching roots great purple crabs were crawling up and down. The black bank of dingy leathern leaves above; the endless labyrinth of stones and withes (for every bough had lowered its own living cord, to take fresh hold of the foul soil below); the web of roots, which stretched far away inland;—all seemed one horrid, complicated trap for the voyager: there was no opening, no relief—nothing but the dark ring of mangroves, and here and there an isolated group of large and small, parents and children, bending and spreading, as if in hideous haste to choke out air and sky. Wailing sadly, sad-coloured mangrove-hens ran off across the mud into the dreary dark. The hoarse night-raven, hid among the roots, startled the voyager with a sudden shout, and then all was again silent as the grave."

In the rivers of Africa the terrible crocodile takes the place held by the alligator in America. There also we encounter the hippopotamus and the still more frightful rhinoceros. Herds of elephants may be seen winding through the open plains, swimming across the rivers in majestic lines and with elevated trunks, or bathing in the shallow lakes for coolness or protection against insects. The antelope (of which Africa is the special nursery), the giraffe, the buffalo, the zebra, are all found in abundance in the plains of southern and central Africa, from Orange river in the south to the Senegal and Nubia in the north.

The African desert produces only a few plants and animals; but it stamps them all with its own peculiar mark. From the tawny Bedouin to the worm scarcely distinguishable in the sand, it gives all its creatures the same dress—the same colour, which might justly be called the colour of the desert. It is the pale grayish-yellow tint which belongs as well to the gazelle as to the small lark of the sandy wastes. Among the birds there are no doubt many modifications of this general rule, and the deviations increase as the desert gradually merges into the more fertile steppes, but even here its characteristic mark is not to be mistaken.

When we consider the scanty vegetation of the Sahara, we cannot wonder that animal life is but sparingly scattered over its surface. The lion, so frequently misnamed "The king of the desert," only shows himself on its borders. As lions cannot exist without flesh and water, they avoid the sandy desert. In fact, they never leave the wooded mountains of the Atlas, or the fruitful plains of the Soudan, to wander far into the Sahara, There snakes and scorpions are the only dangerous animals to be met with.

According to the seasons, animal life fluctuates in the Sahara from north to south. In winter and spring, when heavy rains, falling on its northern borders, provide wide districts, thoroughly parched by the summer heat, with the water and pasturage needed for the herds, the nomadic tribes wander farther into the desert with their camels, horses, sheep, and goats, and retreat again to the coast-lands as the sun gains power. At that time of the year the wild animals—the lion, the gazelle, and the antelope— also wander farther to the south, which then provides them, each according to its taste, with the nourishment which the dry summer is unable to bestow. The ostrich, too, which during the summer ranged farther to the north, then retreats to the south; for hot and sandy plains are the paradise in which this singular bird delights to roam.

Though Arabia possesses some districts of remarkable fertility, which enjoy almost perpetual verdure, yet the greater part of that vast peninsula consists of burning deserts lying under a sky rarely traversed by a cloud, and stretching into boundless plains, where the eye meets nothing but the uniform horizon of a wild and dreary waste. These naked deserts are encircled, and sometimes intersected, by barren mountains, which run in almost continuous ridges and in different directions from the borders of Palestine to the shores of the Indian Ocean. Their summits tower up into lugged and insulated peaks, but their flinty bosoms supply no humidity to nourish the soil; they concentrate no clouds to screen the parched earth from the withering influence of a tropical sky.

Were it not for the wadys—verdant valleys lying here and there among the hills— and the various wells or watering stations supplied by periodical rains, the greater portion of Arabia must have remained unpeopled, and uninhabitable. In a country like this, where whole years occasionally pass away without a refreshing shower, the possession of a spring is not unfrequently the most valuable property of a tribe. There are large tracts, however, where the luxury of water, as it may well be called, is unknown, and where the desert extends for many a day's journey without affording the traveller the welcome sight of a single well.

Although the high steppes of central Asia are probably the genuine and original country of the horse, yet in Arabia that generous animal attains the highest degree of spirit and swiftness. The tender familiarity with which the horses are treated trains them to habits of gentleness and attachment. When not employed in war or in travelling they loiter about the tents, often going over numbers of children lying on the ground, and carefully picking their steps lest they should hurt them. They are accustomed only to walk and to gallop. Their sensations are not blunted by the incessant abuse of the spur and the whip. Their powers are reserved for the movement of flight and pursuit, and no sooner do they feel the touch of the hand and the stirrup than they dart away with the swiftness of the wind; but if their friend be dismounted in the rapid career, they instantly stop till he has recovered his seat.

In the sands of Arabia the camel is a sacred and precious gift. That strong and patient beast of burden not only supplies the wandering Arab with the greater part of his simple wants: it serves also to secure his immemorial independence by placing the desert between the enemy and himself. Thus the Bedouin has ever been indomitable; and while in other parts of the world we find that the possession of an animal— the sable, the sea-otter—has entailed the curse of slavery upon whole nations, the dromedary in Arabia appears as the instrument of lasting freedom.

As the lion reigns in Africa, so the tiger is lord and master of the Indian jungles. He is a splendid animal—elegantly striped with black on a white and golden ground; graceful in every movement—but of a most sanguinary and cruel nature. The lengthened body resting on short legs, lacks the proud bearing of the lion; while the miked head, the wildly rolling eye, the scarlet tongue constantly lolling from the jaws, and the whole expression of the tiger's physiognomy, indicate an insatiable thirst for blood, a pitiless ferocity, which he wreaks indiscriminately on every living thing that comes within his grasp. In the bamboo jungle on the banks of pools and rivers, he waits for the approaching herd; there he seeks his prey, or rather multiplies his murders, for he often leaves the nylghau still writhing in the agony of death, to throw himself upon new victims, whose bodies he rends with his claws, and then plunges his head into the gaping wound, to absorb in deep and luxurious draughts the blood whose fountains he has just laid open.

Nothing can be more delightful than the aspect of a Javanese savanna, to which clumps of noble trees, planted by Nature's hand, impart a park-like character; yet, even during the daytime, the traveller rarely ventures to cross these beautiful wilds without being accompanied by a numerous retinue. The horses frequently stand still, trembling all over, when their road leads them along some denser patch of the jungle, rising like an island from the grassy plain; for their acute scent informs them that a tiger lies concealed in the thicket but a few paces from their path.

Both the panther and the leopard are widely diffused through the tropical regions of the Old World, being natives of Africa, Persia, China, India, and many of the Indian islands; so that they have a much more extensive range than either the tiger or the lion the manner in which they seize their prey, lurking near the sides of woods, and darting forward with a sudden spring, resembles that of the tiger; and the chase of the panther is said to be more dangerous than that of the lion, as it easily climbs the trees and pursues its enemy upon the branches.

On turning to the wilds of northern Australia, new aspects of savage life rise before our view. With new plants and new animals, a new variety of the human race makes its appearance, differing from the Malayan in figure, in physiognomy, in language, and in many of its customs and manners. Though this nice occupies one of the lowest grades in the scale of humanity, it still offers many points of interest to the observer, and claims our attention both by its qualities and its defects.

When hunting the kangaroo, the native Australian rivals in energy and perseverance, in skill and keenness of eye, the Red Indian tracking the wild animals of the Brazilian forest. His glance roves from side to side, in a vigilant, uneasy manner. As soon as he sees a kangaroo, he checks his pace and stands immovable, like one transfixed; while his wives, who are at some distance behind him, fall to the ground as if they had been shot. Looking about a hundred yards to the right of the native, you will see a kangaroo erect upon its hind legs and supported by its tail; it is reared to its utmost height, so that its head is between five and six feet above the ground; its short fore-paws hang by its sides, its ears are pointed: it is listening as carefully as the native; and you see a little head peering out from the pouch, to inquire what has alarmed its mother. The native moves not: you cannot tell whether it is a human being or the charred trunk of a burned tree which is before you, and for several minutes the whole group preserve their relative position. At length the kangaroo becomes reassured, drops upon its fore-paws, gives an awkward leap or two, and goes on feeding.

Meantime the native advances stealthily and by slow stages, with his arm raised in the attitude of throwing his spear, until he is within reach of his prey. At last the whistling spear penetrates the devoted animal: then the wood rings with shouts; women and children all join pell-mell in the chase. After a time the exhausted animal turns on its pursuers, places its back against a tree, and prepares to seize and rend any one who may approach too near. The wily native keeps clear of its murderous embrace, and kills it by throwing spears into its breast from the distance of a few yards.

As the land within the tropics is remarkable for the greatness of its physical aspects, so the tropical oceans are preeminent for the violence of their storms. In the Indian and Chinese Seas these convulsions of nature generally take place at the change of the monsoons; in the West Indies, at the beginning and at the end of the rainy seasons. The tornado which devastated the Island of Guadeloupe in July 1846, blew down buildings constructed of solid stone, and tore the guns of a battery from their carriages. Another, which raged some years ago in the Mauritius, demolished a church and drove thirty-two vessels on the strand. A few days later, a fleet of crippled vessels, the victims of the recent hurricane, might have been seen making their way into the harbour of Port Louis—some dismasted, others kept afloat with difficulty, firing guns of distress or giving other signs of their helpless condition.

Such are the terrible effects of the tornadoes and cyclones of the Atlantic and the Indian Oceans; but the storms of the misnamed Pacific are no less furious, and frequently overwhelm the coral islands and palm-groves of Polynesia with destruction. A hurricane which, in April 1845, burst over Pitcairn Island, washed all the fertile mould from the rocks, and, uprooting three hundred cocoa-nut trees, cast them into the sea. Every fishing-boat on the island was destroyed, and thousands of fruit-bearing bananas were swept away.

Though the tropical storms are thus frequently a scourge, they are often productive of no less signal benefits. Many a murderous epidemic has suddenly ceased after one of these natural convulsions; and myriads of insects, the destroyers of the planter's hopes, are swept away by the fierce tornado. Besides, if the equatorial hurricanes are much more furious than our storms, a more luxurious vegetation effaces their vestiges in a shorter time. Thus Nature teaches us that a preponderance of good is frequently concealed behind the paroxysms of her apparently unbridled rage.

—Adapted from Hartwig

Words

antelope, *a ruminant animal.*
awkward, *clumsy.*
characterize, *distinguish.*
circumference, *measurement around.*
complicated, *involved.*
concentrate, *attract.*
constitute, *form.*
cyclones, *rotatory storms,*
devastated, *desolated,*
diameter, *measurement through,*
dismounted, *unhorsed,*
distinguishable, *discernible,*
elevated, *held aloft.*
encounter, *meet with,*
epidemic, *infectious disease.*
estuaries, *river-mouths.*
exhausted, *tired-out.*
familiarity, *friendliness.*
fertility, *fruitfulness.*
fluctuates, *moves about.*
gazelle, *a kind of antelope.*
humanity, *the human race.*
hurricane, *violent storm.*

immemorial, *long-established.*
indomitable, *not to be subdued.*
insulated, *solitary.*
intersected, *traversed.*
luxury, *dainty.*
malaria, *poisonous air.*
modifications, *limitations.*
myriads, *immense numbers.*
nomadic, *wandering.*
nourishment, *sustenance.*
paroxysms, *convulsions.*
penetrates, *pierces.*
perpetual, *unbroken.*
perseverance, *persistence.*
physiognomy, *cast of countenance.*
preponderance, *excess.*
retinue, *convoy.*
sanguinary, *blood-thirsty.*
sensations, *feelings.*
steppes, *plains.*
tornadoes, *whirling tempests.*
transfixed, *pierced through.*
writhing, *making contortions.*

Questions

Why is so little known of the interior of Africa? What are the limits of tropical Africa? What are its chief natural features? Name its four great rivers. What great waterfall is on the Zambeze? What is the chief vegetable wonder of tropical Africa? For what are these trees sometimes used? Name the chief animals found in that region. What is remarkable about the plants and animals of the desert? Where has the lion his home? What are the only dangerous animals met with in the Sahara? What causes animal life to fluctuate in the desert? What is the character of most of Arabia? What alone saves it from being uninhabitable? What two animals do we associate with Arabia? What is the original country of the horse? How does the camel secure the freedom of the Arab tribes? What animal is lord of the Indian jungles? How does the tiger multiply his murders? Where are the panther and the leopard found? Wherein do these animals differ? What animal is characteristic of Australia? How do the natives hunt it? For what are the tropical oceans remarkable? What are the circular storms in the Atlantic and Indian Oceans called? Mention Instances of great storms in the different oceans. In what way are these storms often beneficial?

东 半 球

由于没有入口、海湾和较大的河口，非洲一直是最后屈服于人类文明进步的大陆。因此，它的内部比起其他的热带世界，更不为人们所知，或许澳大利亚中部除外。但它已知的部分却表明，它并不缺少那些宏伟多样的、刻画了西部热带地区的特点。热带非洲从北部的撒哈拉沙漠中间地带延伸到南部的布须曼平原。这片宽广的区域最主要的自然特征就是拥有一些大面积的湖泊横跨赤道，而它们极有可能构成了凯尔河的最主要水源。尼罗河本身可以与亚马孙河的流经长度相媲美，它是一条热带河流，也是世界奇观之一。其他三大河流——北部的尼日尔河，西部的刚果河，南部的赞比西河，属于热带非洲而世界上最高的瀑布就位于赞比西河之上。

非洲内部一直以来都被人们认为是一片荒凉的荒野之地，但它却是多水而富饶的地区，并因其内部非凡地存活着多种植物和动物而特征显著。其中最主要的植物——猴面包树，是一个奇迹，它被称为世界植物的巨人。一棵猴面包树一般拥有直径30英尺、周长95英尺的树干。这些树通常是空心的，所以它们经常被用来作住宅或马厩，还可以用来建造利文斯通博士提到的，一个二三十人可以躺下来睡觉的小屋！这里还有巨大的梧桐树，在其树枝的荫蔽之下，当地黑人可以建起他们的小屋；而在海岸边缘和河口处，人们还会看到风景如画的红树林。

红树林的存在必须归因于——至少部分归因于——非洲河流入海口的不良特性。从河流的源头，当潮流退下，源头处干涸裸露，一种奇怪的气味就会产生，而红树林的附近总会出现致命的疟疾。金斯利在描述一片红树林时说："海岸会突然陷入原始森林变干之后形成的红树林之下。泥泞的污泥形成的可恶的河床，则裸露在红树林之下。在无尽的树根盘根错节形成的网络之中，巨大的紫色的蟹爬上爬下。黑色河岸上面布满暗色、皮一样的叶子，石头和树枝形成了无尽的迷宫（每棵大树枝都向下延展，把新鲜的部分置于土壤下面），网状的树根向着遥远的内陆延伸——所有这一切，对于航行者来说，似乎是一个可怕的、复杂的陷阱，这里没有出口，没有救援，只有红树林形成的暗环，随处可见的是一个个孤立的或大或小，或弯曲或伸展的红树林，仿佛在可怕的匆忙阻塞着大气和天空。如此色彩斑斓的红树林伤心地哭泣着，穿过泥土，进入了一片沉闷的黑暗之中。叫声沙哑难听的乌鸦藏在红树林根部，用突然的一声啼叫使航行于此的人受到惊吓，然后又是死一般的寂静。

在非洲的河流里，可怕的鳄鱼替代了生长在美洲的短吻鳄。在这里，我们还会遇到河马和更可怕的犀牛。人们还会看到成群的大象在开阔的平原蜿蜒前行，游过雄伟的河流，其中会有升高到水面之上的树干。或者，它们还会为了抵御酷热或昆虫，沐浴在清凉的浅红树林湖泊之中。非洲羚羊（非洲是它们特殊的栖息地）、长颈鹿、水牛、斑马，都大量地生长在非洲南部和中部的平原之中，从南部的奥兰治河一直到北部的塞内加尔和努比亚。

非洲沙漠只孕育了很少的植物和动物，但它却将自己特有的标志印在了这些动植物的身体上。从茶色的贝都因人，到几乎在沙地上很难被辨识出来的昆虫，它给这里所有的生物穿上了同样的衣服、同样的颜色，这被称为沙漠的颜色。羚羊和沙漠荒野中的小云雀，都同样拥有浅灰黄色的色调。毫无疑问，这里的鸟类对这个一般的规则有了许多修改，随着沙漠逐渐合并到较肥沃的草原地带，这种偏差会逐渐增加。但即使是在这里，非洲的特性标记也不会被弄错。

当我们考虑到撒哈拉大沙漠的稀少植被，就不会怀疑为什么动物的生命会如此稀少地分散在其表面之上了。狮子如此经常地被名不副实地称作"沙漠之王"，仅出现在沙漠的边界地带。狮子存活离不开肉和水，因此它们不会出现在沙质的荒漠之中。事实上，它们永远不会离开阿特拉斯的山林或苏丹物产富饶的平原，而漫步在遥远的撒哈拉沙漠之中。在那里，只有蛇和蝎子是人们可能看见的危险的动物。

根据季节，动物在撒哈拉沙漠上从北向南迁移。在冬季和春季，当大雨落在沙漠的北部边界，它向已经被夏天的酷暑彻底烤透的广泛地区，提供了牛群所需的水和牧草。游牧部落带着他们的骆驼、马、羊，向沙漠内部游荡到更远的地方，而当太阳再次获得能量之时，他们会再次撤退到海岸周围。一年中的这个时间，野生动物们——狮子、瞪羚和羚羊还会向更远的南部徘徊。这些区域会按照它们各自的口味，提供给它们干燥的夏季无法赐予的营养食物。鸵鸟也一样，它在夏季会停留在更远的北方，这时就会撤退到南部，炎热、沙质的平原，是这种奇异鸟儿愉悦漫游的天堂。

虽然阿拉伯地区的部分区域拥有让人惊羡的肥沃土地，这些地方几乎享受着永远的翠绿，但这个庞大半岛的大部分地区，也一样蔓延着燃烧的沙漠，躺在云朵很少出现的天空之下，并延伸到无边的平原之中。在那里，人们看到的无非是单一的地平线，上面是野性和沉闷的一片荒野。这些赤裸的沙漠被荒山包围着，它们有时也会交织在一起。这些荒山形成了几乎连续的山脊，从四面八方一直延伸到巴勒斯坦的边界和印度洋沿岸。它们的顶峰会高耸成巍峨、孤立的山峰，但它们的坚硬山峰却不会提供任何水分，来滋润这片土壤；在干燥的热带天空的影响之下，这些山脉也不能聚拢起片片云朵来笼罩住焦渴的大地。

如果不是因为有一些山谷——这些青翠的山谷位于四处的山脉之间和各种水井或者周期性降雨所形成的水道，阿拉伯的较大部分一定还会保持着无人居住，也没有任何生命体。在这样的一个国家足足两年的时间里，只会有偶尔的降水，一口泉眼就会很自然地成为一个部落之中最宝贵的财产。然而，在大片大片的区域，正如他们所说的，奢侈的水是当地人根本就未知的。在这些地方，沙漠会延伸到很遥远的地方，让在此的旅客几天之内也见不到一口井水来欢迎他们。

虽然中亚的高地草原是马真正原始的故乡，然而在阿拉伯，这种慷慨的动物才达到了它精神和敏捷度的最高点。当地人对这种动物的温柔对待，训练了它们亲切和服从的习性。当不用于战争和旅行之中时，它们会在人类的帐篷周围闲晃，这期间，会有很多孩童躺在地上玩耍，马就会小心翼翼地选择它们蹄子的落脚点，以免伤害他们。它们已经习惯于走或者驰骋。它们的感觉不会因为持续不断的马刺和马鞭的滥用而变得迟钝。它们的力量都为了飞驰和追逐的时刻而保留了下来，只要感觉到手的触摸和马刺的刺激，它们就会以飞镖与风的速度疾驰前行，但如果它们的朋友在快速的奔跑中栽下了马背，它们会立即停止，直到他回到马背上坐好。

在阿拉伯的沙漠之中，骆驼是一种神圣并珍贵的礼物。这种强壮而耐心的能够承重的动物，不仅向阿拉伯人简单的四方游荡的欲望提供了更大的可能，它也同时可以通过在敌人和他们本族之间的沙漠之间定位，以确保阿拉伯人的独立性。因此，贝都因人过去任何时候都不屈不挠，虽然在世界上的其他地方，我们发现一种更巨大的动物紫貂，在整个国家引发了对奴隶制的诅咒，而阿拉伯地区的单峰驼成为一种保持持久自由的工具。

如果说狮子统治了非洲，那么老虎就是印度丛林中的贵族和王者。它是一种出色的动物——在白色和金色的毛皮之上，拥有优雅的黑色条纹；它的每一个动作都如此优美，但同时又拥有最血腥和残忍的本性。极长的身躯，搁在非常短的腿上，没有狮子一样的骄傲举止；它疯狂滚动的眼睛，猩红的舌头不断懒洋洋地舔舐着爪子。老虎展现出的所有体貌，都表示出一种对鲜血的贪婪渴求和一种无情的凶猛，当它握住任何鲜活的生物时，都会十分严重地给它们致命的一击。在水塘和河流两岸的竹林之中，它等待着即将到来的兽群；在那里，它寻找它的猎物，或者更确切地说，它不断进行残暴的行为，因为它经常会丢下那些仍然在死亡的痛苦之中挣扎扭动的动物，而向自己下一个新的受害者发起攻击。它会用爪子撕开它们的躯体，然后将头伸进敞开的伤口之中，在它刚刚打开的伤口之中，深深地吮吸如泉水一般喷涌出来的鲜血。

没有什么能比爪哇稀树草原的景象更让人愉快的了。大自然的手将高贵的树木丛栽种在这里，给人一种公园般的奇观；然而，即使是在白天，旅客如果不伴随着众多的随从，也很少敢冒险跨越进这些美丽的荒野之中。当前方的路径，将他们沿着一片片密集的丛林带向前方，马经常会站在原地浑身发抖，而这些丛林就像从草原之中升起的一个个小岛，因为有一种刺鼻的气味会告诉它们，在灌木丛的后面，离它们将通过的小路只有几步远的地方，隐藏着一只老虎。

无论是黑豹还是美洲豹，都广泛地分布在古老的热带地区，成为非洲、波斯、中国、印度和印度群岛许多地区的"土著居民"，比起老虎或狮子，它们有一些更丰富的捕获猎物的手段。它们会潜伏在附近树林的两侧，并采用突然弹跳出来，向前疾飞的方式，类似于老虎；而黑豹对猎物的追逐，据说比狮子更危险，因为它很容易爬上树，并在树枝间追逐它的敌人。

再转回到澳大利亚北部的荒野之中，我们眼前会呈现出野蛮生活的另一些新的景象。伴随着其他植物和动物，另一种人类的种族会出现在这里。在外貌、语言和习俗、礼仪等方面，他们都与马来人有所不同。虽然这个漂亮的种族是人类发展之中的最低等级，他们仍然向观察者提供了许多兴趣点，而且他们的优点和缺陷都一样值得我们注意。

当狩猎袋鼠的时候，在力量和毅力、技能和眼睛的敏锐程度上，澳大利亚的土著居民都可以与在巴西森林中追踪野生动物的红种印第安人相媲美。他目光警惕，不安地从一边向另一边移动。当他看到一只袋鼠，他审视它的步伐，并站在原地一动不动，呆若木鸡，而他的妻子就站在他身后一段距离之外，倒在地上，犹如被射伤了一般。向他们右侧大约一百码的地方望去，你会看到一只袋鼠靠它的后腿直立着，而它的尾巴做着支撑；它成长的最大高度是头部达到地面以上的五六英尺之间；它的爪子挂在身躯的两侧，耳朵突出来。此时，它就像那两个土著人一样，在仔细地倾听；此时，你还会看到一个小脑袋从袋子里探出来窥视，询问是什么惊动了它的母亲。土著人一动也不动，你甚至不能区分，在你面前的，到底是一个人，还是一株被烧焦的树干。整整几分钟之内，整个这个团队，都保持着它们的相对位置。最后，袋鼠变得放心，将它的前爪放下，进行了一下、两下笨拙的跳跃，继续喂养它的幼崽。

与此同时，土著人会用缓慢的节奏悄悄前进，他的手臂会保持随时能够投掷出矛的姿势，直到他的猎物到达他的射程范围之内。最后呼啸而过的矛，会穿透这种忠厚的动物，然后是木环呼啸而过；妇女和儿童们，也都全部加入进这混乱的追逐之中。经过一段时间之后，这只动物的体能耗尽，最终向它的追逐者屈服，它会背对着一棵树，并准备抓住并撕裂任何一个可能靠得太近的人。老谋深算的土著人，依然保持清晰的思路进行他的进攻，并从几码的距离之外，向它的胸部投掷长矛来杀死它。

由于热带地区的土地拥有极其显著的伟大景象，所以热带海洋的风暴也异常凶猛。在印度洋和中国海，大自然的这种惊厥，一般发生在季风变化时分；在西印度群岛，则发生在雨季开始或结束的时候。1846年7月，毁灭了瓜德罗普岛的龙卷风，吹倒了坚实的石头建造的建筑物，并撕毁了当地堡垒的火力。另外一次龙卷风，几年前曾在毛里求斯肆掠，它拆毁了教堂，并打翻了32艘海岸边的船只。几天后，这次飓风的受害者，一艘残缺船队的船只找到了返回到路易港的路——其中一些桅杆已经折断，其他一些则艰难地保持漂浮。在这种无助的状态下，它们绝望地发射着枪弹，或者发出了一些其他的求救信号。

这是大西洋和印度洋的龙卷风和飓风所带来的可怕后果，但太平洋名不副实的风暴，其狂暴程度也毫不逊色，会经常毁灭波利尼西亚的珊瑚岛和棕榈园。其中，1845年4月的一场飓风在皮特克恩岛突然出现，冲刷掉了岩石上方的所有肥沃土壤，并将三百棵坚果树连根拔起，扔进了海里。而岛上，每一艘捕鱼船都被彻底摧毁，还有数千棵长满了香蕉的香蕉树，也都被洪水冲走了。

尽管热带地区的风暴经常如洪水猛兽一般带来破坏，但它们也往往为生产力带来一些好处。许多流行性疾病会在这些大自然的抽搐之后突然停止，而种植者希望毁灭的无数昆虫，也会由激烈的龙卷风一扫而空。此外，如果赤道地区的飓风比我们的暴风雨更猖狂，在较短的时间之内，更繁茂的植被就会抹去自己的痕迹。因此，大自然教会了我们，在它表面肆无忌惮愤怒的发作背后，其实经常隐藏着一些会带来益处的优势。

——哈特维希

Lesson 19 THE SONG OF THE SHIRT
第十九课　衬衫之歌

With fingers weary and worn, with eyelids heavy and red, a woman sat in unwomanly rags, plying her needle and thread—Stitch! stitch! stitch! in poverty, hunger, and dirt; and still with a voice of dolorous pitch she sang the "Song of the Shirt!"

"Work! work! work! while the cock is crowing aloof! and work! work! work! till the stars shine through the roof! It's oh, to be a slave along with the barbarous Turk, where woman has never a soul to save, if this is Christian work!

"Work! work! work! till the brain begins to swim; work! work! work! till the eyes are heavy and dim! Seam, and gusset, and band; band, and gusset, and seam; till over the buttons I fall asleep, and sew them on in a dream. O men, with sisters dear! O men, with mothers and wives! it is not linen you're wearing out, but human creatures' lives. Stitch! stitch! stitch! in poverty, hunger, and dirt; sewing at once, with a double thread, a shroud as well as a shirt.

"But why do I talk of Death? that phantom of grisly bone; I hardly fear his terrible shape, it seems so like my own. It seems so like my own, because of the fasts I keep; O God, that bread should be so dear, and flesh and blood so cheap!

"Work! work! work! My labour never flags; and what are its wages? A bed of straw, a crust of bread—and rags. That shattered roof and this naked floor, a table, a broken chair, and a wall so blank, my shadow I thank for sometimes falling there.

"Work! work! work! from weary chime to chime; work! work! work! as prisoners work for crime. Band, and gusset, and seam; seam, and gusset, and band; till the heart is sick, and the brain benumbed, as well as the weary hand.

"Work! work! work! in the dull December light; and work! work! work! when the weather is warm and bright, while underneath the eaves the brooding swallows cling, as if to show their sunny backs, and twit me with the spring.

"Oh, but to breathe the breath of the cowslip and primrose sweet, with the sky above my head, and the grass beneath my feet; for only one short hour to feel as I used to feel, before I knew the woes of want, and the walk that costs a meal! Oh, but for one short hour! a respite however brief! No blessed leisure for love or hope, but only time for grief! A little weeping would ease my heart; but in their briny bed my tears must stop, for every drop hinders needle and thread."

With fingers weary and worn, with eyelids heavy and red, a woman sat in unwomanly rags, plying her needle and thread—Stitch! stitch! stitch! in poverty, hunger, and dirt; and still with a voice of dolorous pitch—would that its tone could reach the rich!—she sang this " Song of the Shirt!"

—Thomas Hood

Words

barbarous, *uncivilized.*
benumbed, *stupefied.*
brooding, *rearing young.*
dolorous, *sorrowful.*
gusset, *insertion.*
hunger, *craving for food.*
labour, *work.*
leisure, *spare time.*

phantom, *spectre.*
plying, *working busily.*
poverty, *indigence.*
respite, *pause,*
shadow. *reflection,*
shattered, *broken.*
terrible, *horrible.*

☆ ☆

　　拖着疲惫、困乏的手指，睁着沉重、血红的眼睛，一个女人穿着褴褛破衣，不停地穿针引线。针！针！针！在贫困、饥饿和污垢中穿梭。她仍然用忧伤的声音唱着：衬衫之歌！

　　"工作！工作！工作！当公鸡刚刚在黎明啼叫！工作！工作！工作！直到星星在屋顶发光！是啊，作一个陪伴着野蛮的土耳其人的奴隶，女人从来不能在这里拯救她的灵魂，虽然这是基督徒的工作！"

　　"工作！工作！工作！直到脑子变得混沌；工作！工作！工作！直到眼睛睁不开变得模糊。缝补，上袖，镶边；镶边，上袖，再缝补；直到我拿着纽扣睡着，而在梦里把它们缝上。人啊，有亲爱的姐妹！哦人啊，有母亲和妻子！你缝出来的不只是亚麻布料，而是人的性命。针！针！针！在贫困、饥饿和污垢中穿梭。用一股双线缝上，有时候是寿衣，有时候是衬衫。"

　　"但为什么我谈论死亡，可怕骨头的幻影；我几乎从不担心它可怕的形状，看起来就像我自己的。这看起来就像我自己的，因为我几乎天天没有饭吃。上帝啊，面包如此珍贵，但人的血肉之躯却是这样卑贱！"

　　"工作！工作！工作！我的劳力从不保留；但我的工资在哪里？一张稻草床，一片面包，一块破布。破败的房顶，光溜的地板，一张桌子，一把破了的椅子，光秃秃的墙壁，我自己的影子，有时会落在这面墙上。"

　　"工作！工作！工作！一刻也不停歇；工作！工作！工作！就像犯人在赎罪。缝补，上袖，镶边；镶边，上袖，再缝补；直到心都沉了，脑子也开始发木，疲惫的手也一样。"

　　"工作！工作！工作！在阴沉的十一月的微光里；工作！工作！工作！当天气

变得温暖明亮。一窝燕子在屋檐下面搭窝，好像它们也要展现自己晒在太阳下面的背羽，嘲笑我的春天过得如此苦闷。"

"我呼吸着九轮草淡甜的气息。天空在我的头顶，草地在我脚下。短短的一个小时，我感受到了曾经的感觉。在我知道我想要什么之前，在吃完一顿饭的时间里！哦，只有短短的一个小时！一个如此短暂的喘息之机！没有爱情或者希望带来的开怀，而只有悲伤的时间！一点哭泣就会缓解我的心；但在针线的床前，我必须停止我的眼泪，因为每一滴眼泪都会阻碍我针和线的工作。"

拖着疲惫、困乏的手指，睁着沉重、血红的眼睛，一个女人穿着褴褛破衣，不停地穿针引线，仍然用忧伤的声音唱着："针！针！针！在贫困、饥饿和污垢中穿梭。衬衫之歌！"声音如此之高，富人也能听到。

——托马斯·胡德

Lesson 20   LAND AND SEA BREEZES
第二十课   陆地风与海洋风

The inhabitants of the sea-shore in tropical countries wait every morning which impatience for the coming of the sea breeze. It usually sets in about ten o'clock. Then the sultry heat of the oppressive morning is dissipated, and there is a delightful freshness in the air, winch seems to give new life to all for their daily labours. About sunset there is again another calm. The sea breeze is now over, and in a short time the land breeze sets in. This alternation of the land and sea breezes—a wind from the sea by day, and from the land by night—is so regular, in tropical countries, that it is looked for by the people with as much confidence as the rising and setting of the sun.

In extra-tropical countries, especially those on the polar side of the trade-winds, these breezes blow only in summer and autumn; for then only is the heat of the sun sufficiently intense to produce the requisite degree of atmospherical rarefaction over the land. This depends in a measure, also, on the character of the land upon which the sea breeze blows; for when the surface is arid, and the soil barren, the heating power of the sun is exerted with most effect. In such cases the sea breeze amounts to a gale of wind.

In the summer of the southern hemisphere the sea breeze is more powerfully developed at Valparaiso than at any other place to which my services afloat have led me. Here regularly in the afternoon, at this season, the sea breeze blows furiously: pebbles are torn up from the walks and whirled about the streets; people seek shelter; business is interrupted, and all communication from the shipping to the shore is cut off. Suddenly the winds and the sea, as if they had again heard the voice of rebuke, are hushed, and there is a great calm.

The lull that follows is delightful. The sky is without a cloud; the atmosphere is transparency itself; the Andes seem to draw near; the climate, always mild and soft, becomes now doubly sweet by the contrast. The evening invites abroad, and the population sally forth—the ladies in ball costume, for now there is not wind enough to disarrange the lightest curl.

In the southern summer this change takes place day after day with the utmost regularity; and yet the calm always seems to surprise one, and to come before one has had time to realize that the furious sea wind could so soon be hushed-Presently the stars begin to peep out; timidly at first, as if to see whether the elements here below have ceased their strife, and whether the scene on Earth be such as they, from their bright spheres aloft, may shed their sweet influences upon.

Alone in the night-watch, after the sea breeze had sunk to rest, I have stood on the deck under those beautiful skies, gazing, admiring, rapt. I have seen there, above the horizon at the same time, and shining with a splendor unknown to northern latitudes, every star of the first magnitude—save only six—that is contained in the catalogue of the one hundred principal fixed stars of astronomers. There lies the city on the sea-shore, wrapped in sleep. The sky looks solid, like a vault of steel set with diamonds! The stillness below is in harmony with the silence above; and one almost fears to speak, lest the harsh sound of the human voice, reverberating through those vaulted "chambers of the south," should wake up echo, and drown the music that fills the soul.

Within the tropics the land and sea breezes are more gentle; and though the night scenes there are not so suggestive as those just described, yet they are exceedingly delightful, and altogether lovely. The oppressive heat of the sun is mitigated, and the climate of the sea-shore is made both refreshing and healthful, by the alternation of those winds, which invariably come from the cooler place;—from the sea, which is the cooler by day; and from the land, which is the cooler by night.

About ten in the morning the heat of the sun has played upon the land with sufficient intensity to raise its temperature above that of the water. A portion of this heat being imparted to the air above it, causes it to rise; when the air, first from the beach, then from the sea, to the distance of several miles, begins to flow in with a most delightful and invigorating freshness.

When a fire is kindled on the hearth, we may see, if we observe the motes floating in the room, that those nearest to the chimney are the first to feel the draught and to obey it—they are drawn into the blaze. The circle of inflowing air is gradually enlarged, until it is scarcely perceived in the remote parts of the room. Now, the land is the hearth; the rays of the sun the fire; and the sea, with its cool and calm air, the room: and thus have we at our firesides the sea breeze in miniature.

When the sun goes down the fire ceases; then the dry land commences to give off its surplus heat by radiation, so that by dew-fall it and the air above it are cooled below the sea temperature. The atmosphere on the land thus becomes heavier than that on the sea, and, consequently, there is a wind sea-ward, which we call the land breeze.

—Maury

Words

alternation, *interchange; succession.*
]atmosphere, *air.*
catalogue, *list; enumeration.*
character, *nature.*
commences, *begins.*
communication, *intercourse.*
delightful, *delicious.*
developed, *exhibited.*
disarrange, *ruffle.*
dissipated, *driven off.*

furiously, *violently; vehemently.*
impatience, *eagerness.*
intensity, *power.*
interrupted, *suspended.*
invariably, *uniformly.*
invigorating, *strengthening.*
mitigated, *softened.*
oppressive, *overpowering.*
population, *inhabitants.*
regularity, *punctuality.*

requisite, *necessary*.
reverberating, *echoing; resounding*.
splendour, *magnificence*.

suggestive, *significant; expressive*.
transparency, *clearness*.

Questions

Where do the sea and the land breezes blow with the greatest regularity? When does the sea breeze set in? When does the land breeze? When do these breezes blow in extra-tropical countries? Where has the writer seen the sea breeze most powerfully developed? By what is it followed there? What is the character of these breezes within the tropics? What is their effect upon the climate? What is the cause of their alternation? Illustrate this by a fire on a hearth.

☆ ☆

　　每天早上，住在热带国家海边的居民们都极不耐烦地等待海洋风的到来。它一般在10点钟到达，然后沉闷清晨的湿热空气会慢慢消散，取而代之的是空气中令人愉悦的新鲜，似乎能给他们的劳作带来全新的生命力。大约在日落时，会有另一阵平静。这时海洋风停止，很短时间内陆地风就会到来。住在热带国家的人们非常自信地像认定日出日落一般，认定这种陆地风和海洋风的变化。早上从海洋吹来，夜间从陆地吹来，它们是如此的富有规律。

　　在热带之外的国家，尤其在信风带的极地边缘，这种陆地风和海洋风只在夏秋两季吹拂。因为只有这时，太阳的热量才足够强烈，从而足够产生陆地上方必要程度的稀薄空气。这同样也取决于海洋风吹拂其上的陆地的特性。因为当陆地的表面干燥、土壤贫瘠时，太阳的热量就会施展它的最大影响力。而在这种情况下，海洋风会形成暴风。

　　在南半球的夏天，海洋风在瓦尔帕莱索形成最强烈的大风，比起我在航海生涯中去过的所有其他地方，这里的风最为强烈。一般在这个季节的下午，在这儿，海洋风会狂暴地刮起。地面上的卵石会被刮起，在大街上旋转。人们寻找避难所，各种生意停止，到达岸边的船运也会中断。忽然之间，海洋风和大海仿佛像又一次听到了人类的指责，忽然安静下来。宁静又一次回归了。

　　随之而来的宁静令人愉悦。天空万里无云，空气也透明纯净，安第斯山仿佛就在眼前。相比之下，温和的气候变得让人倍加舒适。夜晚邀请人们出门，大家也都迸发出热情。女士们都穿着狂欢的衣着，因为这时没有大风弄乱她们的卷发。

　　在南半球的夏天，这种变化极其规律地日复一日地重复着。而这种宁静也时常会令人惊讶，在一个人能够有时间意识到海洋风如此迅速地平静下来之前，就戛然而止。不久，星星就会从隐蔽处出现，开始时很害羞，像要观察下面的地球是否已经停止了争斗，或者是否地球上的景象像它们一样，从高空中明亮的球体上洒下甜蜜的光芒。

在海洋风沉寂下来之后，我独自站在甲板上仰望星空，在这美丽的星空下，充满敬意地着迷地凝望。在那儿，同时在地平线之上，我看到了在未知的北纬度上方，每颗星星都异常明亮地闪耀着光辉。这也被天文学家记载在他们一百颗重要星球的目录之中。天空像是实体的钢铁穹顶，布满了钻石。天空下方的宁静与它完全和谐。这时一个人几乎害怕讲话，唯恐人类刺耳的声音会在拱顶的"南方密室"里产生回响，而淹没了这充入灵魂的乐章。

在热带地区之内，海洋风和陆地风比较温和。虽然在这儿，夜间的景象没有如我刚刚描述的那般引人入胜，然而它们也特别令人愉悦，同时也极其可爱。此时太阳沉闷的热浪已经缓和下来，海边的气候也因为始终从更凉爽地带吹来的风的交替，而变得既新鲜又健康。这股风白天从海洋，而夜间从陆地吹来。

大约早上10点时，太阳的热量开始足够强烈，使陆地的温度高于海洋。这股热量的一部分被传送到之上的大气中，引发它上升。开始时从海岸，后来从海洋吹来的空气，在蔓延数英里之后，就带着一股令人愉悦又生机勃勃的新鲜感吹拂起来。

如果我们观察房间里浮动的尘埃，我们会看到当炉灶生起火时，离烟囱最近的尘埃会首先感受到气流并跟随它浮动，然后它们会形成风。流动空气的中心会慢慢扩大，直到在房间里最边缘的角落也可以感觉到风的浮动。现在的大地就是炉灶，而太阳的射线就是火，而海洋像房屋一样，拥有凉爽宁静的空气，因此我们能够在我们的炉灶边感受到这种微缩的海洋风。

当太阳落山时，火就熄灭了。干燥的陆地通过释放射线，散发它过剩的热量。到露降时，陆地上空的温度比海洋上的温度更低，陆地上空的大气也更沉重，也因此会有一股风吹向海洋，我们称其为陆地风。

——莫里

Lesson 21   THE RELIEF OF LEYDEN
第二十一课　莱顿市的救援

A. D. 1574.

The besieged city was at its last gasp. The burghers had been in a state of uncertainty for many days; being aware that the fleet had set forth for their relief, but knowing full well the thousand obstacles which it had to surmount. They had guessed its progress by the illumination from the blazing villages; they had heard its salvos of artillery on its arrival at North Aa; but since then all had been dark and mournful again, hope and fear, in sickening alternation, distracting every breast. They knew that the wind was unfavourable, and at the dawn of each day every eye was turned wistfully to the vanes of the steeples. So long as the easterly breeze prevailed, they felt, as they anxiously stood on towers and house-tops, that they must look in vain for the welcome ocean.

Yet, while thus patiently waiting, they were literally starving; for even the misery endured at Haar'lem had not reached that depth and intensity of agony to which Leyden was now reduced. Bread, malt-cake, horse-flesh, had entirely disappeared; dogs, cats, rats and other vermin, were esteemed luxuries. A small number of cows, kept as long as possible for their milk, still remained; but a few were killed from day to day, and distributed in minute portions, hardly sufficient to support life, among the famishing population. Starving wretches swarmed daily around the shambles where these cattle were slaughtered, contending for any morsel which might fall, and lapping eagerly the blood as it ran along the pavement; while the hides, chopped and boiled, were greedily devoured.

Women and children, all day long, were seen searching gutters and dunghills for morsels of food, which they disputed fiercely with the famishing dogs. The green leaves were stripped from the trees, every living herb was converted into human food; but these expedients could not avert starvation. The daily mortality was frightful. Infants starved to death on the maternal breasts which famine had parched and withered; mothers dropped dead in the streets, with their dead children in their arms.

In many a house the watchmen, in their rounds, found a whole family of corpses— father, mother, children—side by side; for a disorder called " the Plague," naturally engendered of hardship and famine, now came, as if in kindness, to abridge the agony of the people. Pestilence stalked at noonday through the city, and the doomed inhabitants fell like grass beneath his scythe. From six thousand to eight thousand human beings sank before this scourge alone; yet the people resolutely held out, women and men mutually encouraging each other to resist the entrance of their foreign foe—an evil more horrible than pest or famine.

Leyden was sublime in its despair. A few murmurs were, however, occasionally heard at the steadfastness of the magistrates; and a dead body was placed at the door of the burgomaster, as a silent witness against his inflexibility. A party of the more faint-hearted even assailed the heroic Adrian Vander Werf with threats and reproaches as lie passed along the streets. A crowd had gathered around him as he reached a triangular place in the centre of the town, into which many of the principal streets emptied themselves, and upon one side of which stood the church of St. Pancras.

There stood the burgomaster, a tall, haggard, imposing figure, with dark visage and a tranquil but commanding eye. He waved his broad-leaved felt hat for silence, and then exclaimed, in language which has been almost literally preserved, "What would ye? my friends? Why do ye murmur that we do not break our vows and surrender the city to the Spaniards?—a fate more horrible than the agony which she now endures. I tell you I have made an oath to hold the city; and may God give me strength to keep my oath! I can die but once, whether by your hands, the enemy's, or by the hand of God. My own fate is indifferent to me; not so that of the city in trusted to my care. I know that we shall starve if not soon relieved; but starvation is preferable to the dishonoured death which is the only alternative. Your menaces move me not. My life is at your disposal. Here is my sword; plunge it into my breast, and divide my flesh among you. Take my body to appease your hunger, but expect no surrender so long as I remain alive.".......

On the 28th of September a dove flew into the city, bringing a letter from Admiral Boisot. In this despatch the position of the fleet at North Aa was described in encouraging terms, and the inhabitants were assured that, in a very few days at furthest, the long-expected relief would enter their gates.

The tempest came to their relief. A violent equinoctial gale, on the night of the 1st and 2nd of October, came storming from the north-west, shifting after a few hours fully eight points, and then blowing still more violently from the south-west. The waters of the North Sea were piled in vast masses upon the southern coast of Holland, and then dashed furiously landward, the ocean rising over the earth and sweeping with unrestrained power across the ruined dikes. In the course of twenty-four hours the fleet at North Aa, instead of nine inches, had more than two feet of water......

On it went, sweeping over the broad waters. As they approached some shallows which led into the great Mere, the Zeelanders dashed into the sea, and with sheer strength shouldered every vessel through!

It was resolved that a sortie, in conjunction with the operations of Boisot, should be made against Lam'men with the earliest dawn. Night descended upon the scene— a pitch-dark night, full of anxiety to the Spaniards, to the Arma'da, to Leyden. Strange sights and sounds occurred at different moments to bewilder the anxious sentinels. A long procession of lights issuing from the fort was seen to flit across the black face of the waters, in the dead of night; and the whole of the city wall between the Cowgate and the town of Burgundy fell with a loud crash. The horror-struck citizens thought that the Spaniards were upon them at last; the Spaniards imagined the noise to indicate a desperate sortie of the citizens. Everything was vague and mysterious.

Day dawned at length after the feverish night, and the admiral prepared for the assault. Within the fortress reigned a death-like stillness, which inspired a sickening suspicion. Had the city indeed been carried in the night? had the massacre already commenced? had all this labour and audacity been expended in vain?

Suddenly a man was descried wading breast-high through the water from Lammen towards the fleet, while at the same time one solitary boy was seen to wave his cap from the summit of the fort. After a moment of doubt, the happy mystery was solved. The Spaniards had fled panic-struck during the darkness. Their position would still have enabled them, with firmness, to frustrate the enterprise of the patriots; but the hand of God, which had sent the ocean and the tempest to the deliverance of Leyden, had struck her enemies with terror likewise.

The lights which had been seen moving during the night were the lanterns of the retreating Spaniards; and the boy who was now waving his triumphant signal from the battlements had alone witnessed the spectacle. So confident was he in the conclusion to which it led him, that he had volunteered at daybreak to go thither alone.

The magistrates, fearing a trap, hesitated for a moment to believe the truth, which soon, however, became quite evident. Val'dez, flying himself from Ley'derdorp, had ordered Colonel Borgia to retire with all his troops from Lammen.

Thus the Spaniards had retreated at the very moment that an extraordinary accident had laid bare a whole side of the city for their entrance! The noise of the wall as it fell only inspired them with fresh alarm; for they believed that the citizens had sallied forth in the darkness to aid the advancing flood in the work of destruction.

All obstacles being now removed, the fleet of Boisot swept by Lammen, and entered the city on the morning of the 3rd of October. Leyden was relieved!

—J. L. Motley

Words

appease, *satisfy*.	imagined, *fancied*.
audacity, *daring*.	indifferent, *immaterial*.
bewilder, *perplex*.	inflexibility, *pertinacity*.
conjunction, *combination*.	inspired, *suggested*.
deliverance, *relief*.	intensity, *extremity*.
disputed, *contended for*.	massacre, *butchery*.
distracting, *tormenting*.	mortality, *death-rate*.
distributed, *dispensed*.	mysterious, *incomprehensible*.
engendered, *produced*.	obstacles, *hindrances*.
extraordinary, *remarkable*.	occurred, *happened*.
furiously, *violently*.	panic-struck, *terrified*.

preferable, *more to be wished.*　　　　tranquil, *calm.*
spectacle, *sight.*　　　　　　　　　　uncertainty, *doubt.*
summit, *highest point.*　　　　　　　unrestrained, *unchecked.*
surmount, *overcome.*　　　　　　　　wistfully, *longingly.*

Questions

What means did the burghers of Leyden know were being taken to relieve them? What was unfavourable to the advance of the fleet? In what condition were the citizens at this time? What added its horrors to those of famine? Whom did some of the faint-hearted assail? How did he address the people? What news arrived on the 28th of September? What at last came to their relief? What did the citizens resolve upon, on the night of the 2nd October? What strange sight occurred during the night? What strange sound was heard? By what was it caused? What had the Spaniards supposed it to be? What were the lights which had been seen moving? Who was the only occupant of Lammen visible in the morning? When was Leyden relieved?

公元1574年

到了被围困的最后一刻，这个城市的市民们已多日处于心神不宁的状态中。虽然知道舰队已出发救援，但他们也清楚地意识到舰队所必须战胜的千难万阻。他们从村庄那里的熊熊火光与舰队到达北部地区时舰炮齐射的轰响声中，猜到了舰队的进展。但是之后，一切又再次陷入黑暗与沉痛中，希望与担忧在恐慌的人群中更替，涣散着每一个人的内心。风向对救援十分不利，市民们都清楚这一点。在每个黎明的开始时分，所有的目光都充满希望地盯向塔尖上的风向标。只要从东方稍稍吹来一小阵风，站在塔顶与屋顶上焦急的市民们就能感受到，他们这次的迎接又将是徒劳的。

然而，在耐心等待的同时，他们实在是太饿了。即使在哈莱姆地区，人们也不必忍耐像现在的莱顿市一样程度的痛苦。面包、小麦饼、马肉已经被吃个精光，就连狗、猫、老鼠和其他对人类有害的动物都被认为是奢侈品。为了保持牛奶的供给，人们仍旧保留了很少数量的奶牛的性命，但每天都有几头被杀，它们命悬一线，在饥饿的人群中艰难地支撑着生命。可怜的人们像饿死鬼一样每天挤在屠宰场，争夺任何可能掉下来的一丁点食物，发疯了一样地去舔舐流在地上的血，哄抢着去吞食剁碎的熟兽皮。

妇女儿童们每天挤在排水沟和粪堆周围，与同样饥饿的狗激烈地争抢那点可怜的食物。树叶也全部被拽光，地上的草只要没枯萎，也都成了人们的口粮。但杯水车薪，这些根本无法解决饥饿的困境。每天的死亡率都是惊人的！婴儿含着母亲因为饥荒而变得干瘪的乳房饿死，母亲们的尸体横在街道上，怀里抱着她们早已死去的孩子。

守夜者在巡视时经常能看到整家人的尸体——父亲、母亲、孩子们——一具尸体紧挨着另一具。如今一场名为"黑死病"的灾祸也来临了，它一般都与苦难与饥荒相连。现在看来，它似乎"仁慈"地减少了人们的痛苦。瘟疫白天在城市中蔓延，居民们的命运已被注定——就好像它镰刀下的草。大约6 000～8 000人在这次灾祸之前就已经崩溃了，然而人们毅然地支撑坚持着，男人与女人互相鼓励，每个人共同抵抗外敌——一个比鼠疫和饥荒更可怕的不幸。

莱顿陷入了绝望之中。然而，人们偶尔会听到顽固的地方官员发发牢骚，一具死尸被安放在市长先生的门前，作为一个无声的证人反对他的固执。甚至一群懦弱的人都威胁辱骂英勇的阿德里安·范·沃夫，此时到处都是欺骗。当他来到城镇中心一处三角地带时，一群人将他团团围住，许多重要的街道已经空无一人，街道的一端，矗立着圣潘克拉斯大教堂。

市长就站在那儿，一个身材高大、面容憔悴、仪表堂堂的人物，表情阴沉，眼神宁静而又威严。他挥舞着他的阔叶毡帽让场面安静下来，然后大声叫道，"你们要干什么，我的朋友们？你们为什么私下议论，我们不失誓言，并且要我将这座城市交给西班牙？这是比如今她所承受的痛苦更可怕的命运。我告诉你们，我曾发誓要保护这座城市，愿上帝给我力量实现我的誓言！我可以死，但是无论是你们还是敌人杀死了我，甚至是上帝结束了我的生命。对我而言，我自己的命运已经不再重要了，重要的是这座托付给我照顾的城市的命运。

"我知道，如果我们不解除这次灾难就会饿死，但是如果不光彩地活着，是唯一的出路，那么饥饿要比它更好。你们的威胁不会让我动摇。我的命已经在你们手上了。这是我的剑，你们可以将它插进我的胸膛，你们还可以分割了我的尸体。把我的尸体拿去安抚你们的饥饿吧，但是我希望，只要我还活着，绝不投降。"……

9月28日，一只鸽子飞到了这座城市，带来了一封博伊索特海军上将的来信。信中带来了鼓舞人心的消息，被派遣来的舰队现在已经位于在不远处的北大西洋上，居民们得到了保证，最迟在几天之后，他们期盼已久的救援舰队就会来到他们面前。

这场暴乱开始减弱。一场猛烈的赤道风暴，在10月1日和2日的夜晚，从西北方向吹来。在几个小时的吹拂之后，继而更猛烈地从西南方向吹来。北大西洋海域众多的海水，被堆积在荷兰的南部海岸，然后冲向陆地，海水在陆地上不羁地席卷了整个堤坝。在24个小时的航程中，北大西洋上的舰队，吃水超过两英尺，而不是九英寸……

舰队在广阔的水域中继续穿行前进。当他们靠近一些伸向大海中的浅滩时，舰船会紧急地冲向大海，由此产生的强大力量，能够推挤着使每一艘船只通过。

一场针对莱门的突围，连同博伊索特的进攻，都应该在黎明临时完成。夜幕降临，这是一个漆黑的夜晚，充满了对西班牙人、无敌舰队和莱顿的焦虑。奇怪的景象和声音，在不同的时刻迷惑着焦虑的哨兵。在死寂的黑夜中，长长的光束从堡垒中发射出来，匆匆地掠过黑色的水域。位于牛栏和勃艮第镇之间的正面墙壁，伴随着一声巨响，突然间崩塌了下来。惊恐的莱顿市民想着，西班牙人最终还是对他们发起了进攻。而西班牙人则以为这声巨响，预示着莱顿市民在进行一次绝望的突围。一切都是如此模糊而神秘。

一个焦虑的夜晚过后，黎明再次来临。海军上将准备进攻。一种死一般的沉静笼罩了堡垒内部，这会激发一种令人厌恶的疑虑。莱顿城真的在夜里被攻占了吗？大屠杀已经开始了吗？所有的这些无畏的努力难道都是徒劳的吗？

突然有人发现，一个人正在齐腰深的水里跋涉，从莱门淌水到舰队所在地。同时也有人看见，一个男孩在堡垒的顶部挥舞着他的帽子。经过片刻的迟疑，谜团被揭开，如此令人振奋。西班牙人在黑暗中惊慌失措地逃离。

他们占据的位置，仍然能够确保他们挫败这些英国爱国者的努力。但是，上帝之手解除了困扰莱顿的海潮和风暴，也同样让它的敌人们变得惊恐。

人们在夜里看到的光亮，是撤退的西班牙人在移动着灯笼。那个如今在堡垒挥舞着胜利信号的男孩，成为这一景象唯一的见证者。他对他得出的结论是如此确信，以至于在黎明时分，他自愿的独自一人登上了堡垒顶部。

莱顿的长官们害怕这是西班牙人的一个陷阱，久久不能相信这个事实。但很快，真相就变得非常明显了。从莱顿逃离的瓦尔迪兹，已经向博尔吉亚上校下令，率领他的所有部队从莱门撤退。

因此，在西班牙人撤退的同一时刻，一件非凡的事情在这个城市发生了！对西班牙人来说，墙壁倒塌的声音成为一种新鲜的警报。因为他们由此相信，莱顿的市民们在黑暗中一下子涌了出来，来帮助前进的援救舰队发起对他们的进攻。

现在所有的障碍都已移除，博伊索特的舰队经过莱门，于10月3日的清晨进入了莱顿城。莱顿得救了！

——J. L. 莫特利

Lesson 22   THE GLOVE AND THE LIONS
第二十二课　　手套与狮子

King Francis was a hearty king, and loved a royal sport; and one day, as his lions fought, sat looking on the court. The nobles filled the benches round, the ladies by their side; and amongst them sat the Count de Lorge, with one for whom he sighed: and truly it was a gallant thing to see that crowning show—valour and love, and a king above, and the royal beasts below.

Ramped and roared the lions, with horrid laughing jaws. They bit, they glared, gave blows like beams, a wind went with their paws. With wallowing might and stifled roar they rolled on one another, till all the pit with sand and mane was in a thunderous smother. The bloody foam above the bars came whizzing through the air; said Francis then, "Truth, gentlemen, we are better here than there!"

De Lorge love overheard the king—a beauteous lively dame, with smiling lips and sharp bright eyes, which always seemed the same. She thought, "The count, my lover, is as brave as brave can be: he surely would do wondrous things to show his love of me.—King, ladies, lovers, all look on; the occasion is divine! I'll drop my glove, to prove his love; great glory will be mine!"

She dropped her glove to prove his love, then looked at him and smiled: he bowed, and in a moment leaped among the lions wild. The leap was quick, return was quick; he had regained his place: then threw the glove—but not with love—right in the lady's face!

"In truth," cried Francis, "rightly done" and he rose from where he sat. "Not love," quoth he, "but vanity, sets love a task like that!"

—Leigh Hunt

Words

beauteous, *lovely*.
divine, *heavenly*.
gallant, *splendid*.
hearty, *jovial*.
moment, *instant*.
occasion, *opportunity*.
quoth, *said*.
ramped, *bounded*.

regained, *resumed*.
stifled, *smothered*.
thunderous, *noisy*.
valour, *bravery*.
vanity, *idle show*.
wallowing, *floundering*.
wondrous, *astonishing*.

DESPISED OLD AGE

I have lived long enough: my way of life
Is fallen into the sear, the yellow leaf;
And that which should accompany old age,
As honour, love, obedience, troops of friends,
I must not look to have; but in their stead,
Curses, not loud, but deep,—mouth-honour, breath,
Which the poor heart would fain deny, but dare not.

—Shakespeare

☆ ☆ ☆ ☆ ☆ ☆ ☆ ☆ ☆ ☆ ☆ ☆ ☆ ☆ ☆ ☆ ☆ ☆ ☆ ☆

弗朗西斯国王精力旺盛，喜欢一项高贵的运动。这天他又坐在看台上观看他的狮子们搏斗，贵族们围坐在四周，身旁是他们的夫人。其中坐着德洛奇伯爵。他叹息道：观看这种至高无上的表演真的是一件英勇的事情，充满了勇猛和爱。上面坐着国王，下面是高贵的猛兽。

狮子奔跑、咆哮，张开它们的血盆大口，啃咬着，怒视着对方，像电光一样互相厮打，爪下生风。它们有一种可怕的力量和异常低沉的咆哮，前仆后继地向前战斗，直到它们身上布满沙砾，鬃毛布满血泊。沾满血沫的棍棒在风中嗖嗖作响。国王说道：我们在这里观看，比在赛场里与狮子撕咬强太多了。

德洛奇伯爵深爱一位美丽活泼的夫人。她时刻都有一张微笑的嘴唇和一双明亮的眼睛。她想到：我的爱人德洛奇伯爵如此英勇，他一定会做出精彩的事情来表达对我的爱。她说道，国王，女士们，我的爱人。这一刻是神圣的，我将扔下我的手套来证明他对我的爱。这一刻，光荣将属于我！

继而她扔下手套，微笑着望向德洛奇伯爵。他鞠了一躬，一跃跳进狮子的赛场。他迅速一跃，同样迅速地回到原位。然后他不是充满爱意地，而是将手套扔到了这位夫人的脸上。国王从座位上站起来说道：做得实在太对了！不是爱，而是虚荣，让爱情变成了这样一项任务！

——李希·亨特

Lesson 23 THE POLAR WORLD (I)
第二十三课 极地世界（一）

Let us imagine ourselves elevated above the region of the North Pole to a height sufficient to enable us to take in at one view the whole Arctic Circle. What we should see immediately beneath us can now be certainly affirmed. It would be the open Polar Sea discovered by Dr. Hayes of Kane's Expedition, in 1853. The view adopted by most geographers has been found correct, and there rolls around the Pole a sea about twelve hundred miles in breadth, abounding in animal life, and kept free from ice during a great part of the year by the influence of equatorial waters, which reach it by way of Spitzbergen and Nova Zembla. But beyond this unexplored region we should see three distinct zones, forming what are called the Arctic Regions,—an icy barrier, treeless wastes, and vast forests.

The belt of ice which girdles the Polar Sea and the Pole itself has been the scene of many a deadly struggle between man and the frost-king, who reigns supreme in these inhospitable regions. To force a passage across or through this barrier has been the life-dream of many a heroic explorer; and hundreds of brave men, from the 17th century onwards, have perished in making the attempt. On September 6, 1909, the memorable announcement was made to the world by Commander Peary of the United States Navy that five months previously, on April 6th, he had "nailed the Stars and Stripes to the Pole." So intense is the cold within the whole Arctic Circle, and in the interior of Asia and America even beyond it, that, the average winter temperature ranges from 50° to 60°" below the freezing point of water, and during a great part of the year converts mercury into a solid body. But at the remote points to which man has penetrated in the northern ice-zone the spirit-thermometer has been known to fall as low as 90°, and even 100°, below the point at which water freezes! It may well be asked how man is able to bear these excessively low temperatures, which must seem appalling to an inhabitant of the temperate zone. But thick fur clothing; a hut small and low, where the warmth of a stove, or simply of an oil-lamp, is husbanded in a narrow space; above all, the wonderful power of the human constitution to adapt itself to every change of climate, go far to counteract the rigour of the cold.

The treeless zone, called "the barren-grounds," or simply "the barrens," extends southward from the ice-bound shores of the polar seas, and gradually merges into the forest-region, where it is encircled by a garland of evergreen. The want of trees in this region is caused not so much by its high northern latitude as by the cold sea-winds which sweep unchecked over the islands and the flat coast-lands of the Polar Ocean, and for miles and miles compel even the hardiest plant to crouch before the blast and creep along the ground. Nothing can be more melancholy than the aspect of the boundless morasses or arid wastes of the barrens of Siberia. Dingy mosses and gray lichens form the chief vegetation; and a few scanty grasses and dwarfish flowers that may have found a refuge in some more sheltered spot are not sufficient to relieve the dull monotony of the scene.

The Desket of Ice

In winter, when animal life has mostly retreated to the south, or sought a refuge in burrows and in caves, an awful silence, interrupted only by the hooting of a snow-owl or the yelping of a fox, reigns over this vast expanse; but in spring, when the brown earth reappears from under the melted snow, and the swamps begin to thaw, enormous flights of wild-birds return to the scene, and enliven it for a few months. An admirable instinct leads those winged legions from distant climes to the Arctic wildernesses, where, in the morasses and lakes, on the banks of the rivers, on the flat strands, and along the fish-teeming coasts, they find abundance of food; and where, at the same time, they can with greater security build their nests and rear their young. Some remain on the skirts of the forest-region; others, flying farther northward, lay their eggs upon the naked wastes.

Eagles and hawks follow the traces of the swimming- and strand-birds; troops of ptarmigans roam among the stunted bushes; and when the sun shines, the finch or the snow-bunting warbles his merry note.

While thus the warmth of summer attracts hosts of migratory birds to the Arctic wildernesses, shoals of salmon and sturgeons enter the rivers, in obedience to the instinct that forces them to quit the seas and to swim up the streams, for the purpose of depositing their spawn in the tranquil sweet waters of the river or lake. About this time, also, the reindeer leaves the forests, to feed on the herbs and lichens of the barrens; and to seek along the shores, fanned by the cool sea-breeze, some protection against the attacks of the stinging flies that arise in myriads from the swamps.

Thus during several months the barrens presents an animate scene, in which man also plays his part. The birds of the air, the fishes of the water, the beasts of the earth, are all obliged to pay their tribute to his various wants—to appease his hunger, to clothe his body, or to gratify his greed of gain.

But as soon as the first frosts of September announce the approach of winter, all animals, with but few exceptions, hasten to leave a region where the sources of life must soon fail. The geese, ducks, and swans return in dense flocks to the south; the strand-birds seek in some lower latitude a softer soil which allows their sharp beaks to seize a burrowing prey; the waterfowl forsake the bays and channels that will soon be blocked up with ice; the reindeer once more return to the forest; and in a short time nothing is left that can induce man to prolong his stay in the treeless plain. Soon a

The Forest Region of the North

thick mantle of snow covers the hardened earth, the frozen lake, the ice-bound river; and conceals them all—for seven, eight, nine months at a time—under its monotonous pall, except where the furious north-east wind sweeps it away and lays bare the naked rock.

This snow, which, after it has once fallen, persists until the long summer day has effectually thawed it, protects in an admirable manner the vegetation of the higher latitudes against the cold of the long winter season. Thanks to this protection, and to the influence of a sun which for three or four months together circles above the horizon, and in favourable localities calls forth the powers of vegetation in an incredibly short time, even Washington, Grinnell Land, and Spitzbergen are able to boast of flowers.

The Arctic forest-regions are of still greater extent than the vast treeless plains which they encircle. When we consider that they form an almost continuous belt, stretching across three fourths of the world, in a breadth of from one thousand to fourteen hundred miles, even the woods of the Amazon, which cover a surface fifteen times greater than that of the British Isles, shrink into comparative insignificance. Unlike the tropical forests, which are characterized by an endless variety of trees, these northern woods are almost entirely composed of cone-bearers, and one single kind of fir or pine often covers an immense extent of ground.

Another peculiarity of these forests is their apparent youth. This is sufficiently explained by the shortness of the summer, which, though able to bring forth new shoots, does not last long enough for the formation of wood. Hence the growth of trees become slower and slower the farther north they are found.

A third distinctive feature of the Arctic forests is their harmless character. There the traveller finds no poisonous plants; even thorns and prickles are rare. No venomous snake glides through the thicket, no crocodile lurks in the swamp. Even their beasts of prey—the bear, the lynx, the wolf—are less dangerous and blood-thirsty than the dreaded monsters of the torrid zone.

Words

abundance, *plenty*.
announce, *intimate*.
appease, *assuage*.

burrowing, *mining*.
converts, *transforms*.
counteract, *check*.

depositing, *placing*.

distinctive, *characteristic*.

effectually, *thoroughly*.

elevated, *raised*.

enormous, *vast*.

excessively, *extremely*.

geographers, *writers on geography*.

incredibly, *not to be believed*.

inhospitable, *unfriendly*.

insignificance, *unimportance*.

interrupted, *broken*.

latitude, *distance from the equator*.

localities, *districts*.

melancholy, *saddening*.

migratory, *wandering*.

morasses, *marshes*.

penetrated, *advanced*.

persists, *lasts*.

unexplored, *not searched*.

venomous, *poisonous*.

Questions

Who discovered the North Pole? Who discovered the sea that rolls around it? What is its breadth? Name the three zones of the Arctic regions. Of what has the belt of ice been the scene? How far has man penetrated into it? What is the average winter temperature within the Arctic Circle? How low has the thermometer been known to fall in the extreme north? How is man able to bear these low temperatures? What is the treeless zone called? By what is the want of trees there caused? What forms the chief vegetation there? What causes its awful silence in winter? When do the birds return? What has attracted them? What birds of prey follow the sea-fowl? With what do the rivers at the same time swarm? What leads the reindeer to the sea-shore? What leads man also into that region in summer? When do the animals again migrate southward? Of what use is the snow in these high latitudes? Why is the sun's influence so great there in summer? What is the extent of the Arctic forest regions? Compare their extent with that of the woods of the Amazon. Wherein do they differ in character from tropical woods? How is their apparent youth accounted for? What is meant by their harmless character?

让我们想象自己上升到高于北极地区以上，到达一个足以使我们观察到整个北极圈的高度。在紧挨着我们的下方，我们应该看到的东西，现在就可以确认了。我们看到的，一定是海斯博士在1853年凯恩的探险中发现的广阔的北极海。大多数地理学家所采纳的观点都在这次探险中被证实是正确的，在极地周围，环绕着一片大约1 200百英里宽的海域。这里动物资源丰富，并且因为受到经过斯匹次卑尔根岛和新地岛来到这里的赤道洋流的影响，这片海域在一年中的大多数时间中，都保持无冰的状态。然而，在这片未知的区域之外，我们可以看到三个不同的区域：冰冷的障碍，寸草不生的荒地和宽广的森林，它们构成了我们所谓的北极地区。

冰雪地带围绕着北极海和北极本身，在那里也存在着很多人类与在这片荒凉地区占据统治地位的丛林之王之间的可怕斗争。跨越过这一障碍，一直是许多英勇的探险家们平生的梦想。从17世纪开始，数以百计的勇士在此番尝试中牺牲性命。1909年9月6日，美国海军指挥官派利发表了令人难忘的公告，他说，在5个月之前，也就是4月6日，他曾"将美国的星条旗插在了北极点上"。在整个北极圈内，寒冷是如此的强烈，甚至都超过了在亚洲和美洲内部的极端严寒。在那里，冬季的平均温度比水的冰点还要低50～60度。而且，一年中的大部分时间里，水银都会转换成坚硬的固体。然而，在人类已经穿越的北极地带，酒精温度计的温度显示出，那里的温度比水的冰点还要低90度甚至100度！可能会有人问，人类是如何能够忍受这种极低的温度的，毕竟这种严寒对适宜居住在温带的人类来说过于可怕。但厚厚的皮衣，一个小而低的木屋，温暖的火炉，或者只是简单的油灯，都在一个如此狭小的空间里得到了使用。最重要的是，人类为适应气候变化而进行改良的巨大力量，远远超过了任何可怕的严寒。

寸草不生的地带，被称为"贫瘠的地面"或者更简单的"荒野"，从冰封的海岸向南一直延伸到北极海，并逐步与森林带融合，被常绿植物所形成的花环所包围。海洋风在这里肆虐着，席卷不知名的岛屿和北极海平地海岸，数英里的距离之内，它沿着地面蔓延，迫使即使最坚硬的岩石低头。这比极高的北纬度更需要树木的存在，没有什么能比西伯利亚无边无际的沼泽和干旱的荒漠更使人感到悲伤。昏暗的苔藓和灰色地衣形成了这里的主要植被，还有一些稀疏的草地和矮小的花朵，可能找到了一些地方作为自己的庇护，它们也缓解了这里景色的枯燥和单调。

在冬季，动物基本已经迁徙到了南方，或者在地洞或者洞穴里寻找庇护。这里可怕死寂的沉默，会被雪枭的呜呜呜叫或者狐狸的一声尖叫所打破。这时也只有它统治着这广阔的一切。但到了春天，在融化的雪地之下，棕色的地面重新出现，沼泽开始解冻，庞大的野生鸟群又重新出现在这里的景象之中，并会一直到好几个月之后都使这片地域保持生机。一种令人钦佩的本能，会带领这支飞翔的队伍从遥远的地方，飞回到北极的荒野之上。在这里，在沼泽和湖泊之上，在河岸上，沿着平缓的海岸线，它们会发现丰富的食物。与此同时，他们可以在这里安全地筑巢，培育它们的后代。有一些鸟类，依然停留在森林地带的边缘；另一些则向北飞得更远，在一片荒凉的荒原上产下它们的卵。

老鹰和秃鹫会跟踪这些鸟类。雷鸟的部队在低矮的灌木丛中漫步，当阳光照耀时，雀类和雪鸟的鸣叫声形成了愉快的音符。当夏天的温暖吸引了大量的候鸟飞到这片北极地区的荒地上，大量的鲑鱼和鳟鱼也会进入河流之中。在本能的驱使下，它们顺从地离开大海，向上游游去，为了能够进入宁静的河流或湖泊之中产卵。这时，在北方的森林地区，驯鹿也离开了森林，在荒漠里靠草本植物和地衣为生。它们也要沿着海岸，在凉爽的海风中，寻找能够抵御出现在沼泽上空，给它们以激烈攻击的飞鸟的庇护地。

因此在几个月前还是荒野的这里，现在也充满了生命力，在这其中，人类也发挥了他相应的作用。空中的飞鸟、水中的鱼、陆地上的野兽，所有的一切都必须向他多样的需求贡献出各种礼物——为了满足他的饥饿，为了给他的躯体穿上新衣，或者是为了满足他贪婪的欲望。

但是9月第一次的霜冻宣告了冬天的即将来临。所有的动物，除了少数个别的例外，都匆忙地离开了这片生命力很快就会衰减的地域。鹅、鸭和天鹅，穿着它们浓密的羽毛回到南方；陆行的鸟，在较低纬度的地带找寻到一些更柔软的土壤，在那里，它们用自己锋利的喙去猎捕土壤中的猎物。水禽离开了海湾和渠道，因为这里很快就会被冰阻塞；驯鹿也再次返回到了森林之中。在极短的时间之内，这里就什么都没有剩下。人类也因此没有任何原因，不离开这片寸草不生的荒原。很快，一层厚厚的雪覆盖了坚硬的地面。冰冻的湖泊，冰封的河流，隐藏起了所有的生物。大约七到九个月的时间里，在冰雪单调地笼罩下，只有愤怒的东北风清扫着积雪，露出下面赤裸裸的岩石。

这场雪一旦落下，持续的时间就非常长，直到下一个夏季将它完全解冻。这是一种令人钦佩的保护方式，在高纬度地区保护植被度过寒冷漫长的冬季。由于这种保护，还有三到四个月的时间内地平线上都会出现的太阳的照耀，植物在难以置信的极短的时间内又重新出现在这里。甚至在华盛顿，格林奈尔和斯匹次卑尔根岛都可以开出令人骄傲的花朵。

北极的森林地带，比它们包围住的荒芜的平原要广阔得多。当我们注意到，它形成了一个几乎横跨地球四分之三的连续地带，宽度从1 000～1 400英里不等。即使是占地面积达不列颠群岛十五倍之多的亚马孙森林，与它相比，也全然没有可比性。不同于以各种各样的树木为特色的热带森林，北极的森林完全由圆锥形的冷杉和松树构成，它们占据了这里极大的范围。

这片森林的另一个特点，就是它形成的时间明显较短。这一点可以得到充分的解释：这里的夏天极其短暂，虽然能够带来新的芽，但不能持续很长时间以足够树木的长成。因此，越向北走，树木的成长就会变得越发缓慢。

北极森林的第三个独特特点就是它无害的本质。旅行者不会在这里发现有毒的植物，即使是荆棘和刺在这也是十分罕见的。没有毒蛇穿过灌木丛，也没有鳄鱼潜伏在沼泽之中。甚至于这里捕食猎物的猛兽——熊、猞猁、狼——也没有热带地区那些可怕的怪物那样危险、嗜血。

Lesson 24　THE BELLS
第二十四课　钟　声

Hear the sledges with the bells—silver bells! What a world of merriment their melody foretells! How they tinkle, tinkle, tinkle, in the icy air of night! while the stars, that oversprinkle all the heavens, seem to twinkle with a crystalline delight; keeping time, time, time, in a sort of Runic rhyme, to the tintinnabulation that so musically wells from the bells, bells, bells, bells, bells, bells, from the jingling and the tinkling of the bells.

Hear the mellow wedding bells—golden bells! What a world of happiness their harmony foretells! Through the balmy air of night how they ring out their delight! From the molten-golden notes, and all in tune, what a liquid ditty floats to the turtle-dove that listens, while she gloats on the moon! Oh, from out the sounding cells what a gush of euphony voluminously wells! How it swells, how it dwells on the future! How it tells of the rapture that impels to the swinging and the ringing of the bells, bells, bells, of the bells, bells, bells, bells, bells, bells, bells—to the rhyming and the chiming of the bells!

Hear the loud alarum bells—brazen bells! What a tale of terror, now, their turbulency tells! In the startled ear of night how they scream out their affright! Too much horrified to speak, they can only shriek, shriek, out of tune; in a clamorous appealing to the mercy of the fire, in a mad expostulation with the deaf and frantic fire, leaping higher, higher, higher, with a resolute endeavour now—now to sit or never, by the side of the pale-faced moon. Oh, the bells, bells, bells! what a tale their terror tells of despair! How they clang, and clash, and roar! What a horror they outpour on the bosom of the palpitating air! Yet the ear it fully knows, by the twanging and the clanging, how the danger ebbs and flows: yet the ear distinctly tells, in the jangling and the wrangling, how the danger sinks and swells, by the sinking or the swelling in the anger of the bells, of the bells, of the bells, bells, bells, bells, bells, bells, bells—in the clamour and the clangour of the bells!

Hear the tolling of the bells—iron bells! What a world of solemn thought their monody compels! In the silence of the night how we shiver with affright at the melancholy menace of their tone; for every sound that floats from the rust within their throats is a groan. And the people—ah, the people—they that dwell up in the steeple all alone, and who, tolling, tolling, tolling, in that muffled monotone, feel a glory in so rolling on the human heart a stone—they are neither man nor woman—they are neither brute nor human—they are Ghouls! And their king it is who tolls; and he rolls, rolls, rolls, rolls a pæan from the bells! And his merry bosom swells with the pæan of the bells! And he dances and he yells; keeping time, time, time, in a sort of Runic rhyme, to the pæan of the bells—of the bells: keeping time, time, time, in a sort of

Runic rhyme, to the throbbing of the bells—of the bells, bells, bells—to the sobbing of the bells; keeping time, time, time, as he knells, knells, knells, in a happy Runic rhyme, to the rolling of the bells—of the bells, bells, bells—to the tolling of the bells, of the bells, bells, bells, bells, bells, bells, bells—to the moaning and the groaning of the bells.

—Edgar Allan Poe

Words

alarum, *warning*
clamorous, *vociferous.*
clangour, *harshness.*
crystalline, *clear sparkling.*
endeavor, *attempt.*
euphony, *pleasant sound.*
expostulation, *remonstrance.*
frantic, *furious.*
harmony, *musical concord.*
horrified, *terrified.*
mellow, *rich.*
melody, *sweet sound.*

menace, *threat.*
merriment, *rejoicing.*
monody, *lament.*
monotone, *unvaried sound.*
pæan, *song of triumph.*
palpitating, *throbbing.*
rapture, *delight.*
Tintinnabulation, *tinkling.*
turbulency, *tumult.*
voluminously, *copiously.*
wrangling, *jangling.*

　　你听那雪橇的银铃——那银色的小钟！它们悦耳的钟声预言了一个多么快活的世界！它们是如何叮叮锵锵，在夜晚冰冷的空气中！点缀于天幕之中的颗颗星际，仿佛都快活地眨着眼睛，眨着水晶般的眼睛；铃儿叮叮锵锵地和着拍子，和着一种北方神秘的旋律，和着那悠扬快活的叮叮锵锵，铃声流出那小钟般的银铃，叮锵、叮锵、叮锵、叮锵——铃声流出那叮叮锵锵，叮叮锵锵的银铃。

　　你听那柔和的婚礼钟声——听那金钟！它们和谐的钟声预示了一个多么幸福的世界！划破芬芳馥郁的夜空，如何奏鸣出喜乐融融！从那悠扬的金钟，和谐的铮铮锵锵，一支多么清新的曲调，飘向那只爱慕地凝望着月亮的斑鸠。她在倾听！哦，从那些钟楼，荡漾出那么多如此美妙动听的钟声！如此抑扬顿挫，如此悠扬峥嵘。飘向未来！如此颂扬，那欣欣愉愉乐乐融融，是那欢天喜地鸣响的钟声，叮咚、叮咚、叮咚！金钟奏响，叮咚、叮咚、叮咚！奏响这悠扬起伏贯珠扣玉的金钟！

　　你听那刺耳的警钟——听那铜钟！它们喧嚷的声音，在讲述一种怎样的惊恐！在夜晚惊惶的耳里，它们的声音那么凄厉！惊慌得已不成声调，只能悲鸣尖叫，多不和谐，吵吵嚷嚷嘟嘟嚷嚷向烈火乞讨哀怜，疯疯癫癫当当嚷嚷规劝又聋又狂的火焰，火越蹿越高，越蹿越高，以一种孤注一掷的心愿，以一种不屈不挠的努力，现在，现在，不然就休想，窜到那脸色吓得苍白的月亮身旁。哦，那警钟，警钟，警钟！在讲述一种怎样的惊恐和绝望！它们是怎样的当啷当啷当啷！它们把一种什么样的惊惶，倾泻进瑟瑟发抖的空气的胸膛！可那耳朵，它一清二楚，凭那钟声铿锵，凭那丁零当啷，那危险是如何此起彼伏，是的，那耳朵一听就明了，凭那钟声铿锵，凭那丁零当啷，那危险是如何此起彼伏，凭着那愤怒钟声的起起伏伏低低涌涌——那钟声——那吵吵嚷嚷当当嚷嚷的铜钟。

你听那悠悠丧钟——听那铁钟！一个多么肃穆的使节出自那哀婉的钟声之中！在那万籁俱寂的夜里，我们不寒而栗，当听到那悲伤忧郁的钟声！因为那声声奏鸣，发自生锈的喉咙，是声声呻吟，而那些——哦，那些人，那些住在尖塔之上的人，孤孤单单，他们把丧钟鸣奏，鸣奏，在沉闷单调的钟声里，感受到一种光荣在涌动，一块石头在人们心头，他们既不是男人也不是女人，他们既不是人类也不是野兽，他们是幽灵，正是他们的君王把丧钟鸣奏，他鸣奏，鸣奏，鸣奏，鸣奏，从钟里奏出一曲赞歌！他快活的胸膛起伏！随着丧钟的那曲赞歌！他叫嚷着高歌起舞，和着丧钟幽幽咽咽的节奏，和着一种北方神秘的节奏，和着那一曲赞歌，发自丧钟，和着丧钟幽幽咽咽的节奏，和着一种北方神秘的节奏，和着钟声的震动——钟声，钟声，钟声，呜呜咽咽抽抽噎噎的钟声——和着幽幽咽咽的节奏，当他鸣奏，鸣奏，鸣奏，以快活的北方节奏，和着钟声的荡荡悠悠，丧钟、丧钟、丧钟，和着钟声的荡荡悠悠，钟声荡荡悠悠，荡荡悠悠，丧钟、丧钟，和着呻吟哀号悠悠荡荡、荡荡悠悠的铁钟。

——埃德加·爱伦·坡

Lesson 25   THE POLAR WORLD (II)
第二十五课   极地世界（二）

Though nature generally wears a more stern and forbidding aspect on advancing towards the Pole, yet the high latitudes have many beauties of their own. Nothing can exceed the magnificence of an Arctic sunset, clothing the snow-clad mountains and the skies with all the glories of colour; or be more serenely beautiful than the clear star-lit night, illumined by the brilliant moon, which for days continually circles around the horizon, never setting until she has run her long course of brightness. The uniform whiteness of the landscape and the general transparency of the atmosphere add to the lustre of her beams, which serve to guide the natives in their nomadic life, and to lead them to their hunting-grounds.

A number of icebergs floating in the sea—a familiar scene in polar regions—is one of the most magnificent spectacles in nature. But the wonderful beauty of these crystal cliffs never appeal's to greater advantage than when clothed by the midnight sun with all the splendid colours of twilight. In the distance, they seem like masses of burnished metal or solid flame. Nearer at hand, they are like huge blocks of purest marble inlaid with pearl and opal gems. Thousands of sparkling little cascades leap into the sea from their sides, the water being discharged from lakes of melted snow and ice that repose in the quietude of their valleys.

But of all the magnificent spectacles that relieve the monotonous gloom of the Arctic winter, there is none to equal the magical beauty of the Aurora. Night covers the snow-clad earth; the stars glimmer feebly through the haze which so frequently dims their brilliancy in the high latitudes, when suddenly a broad and clear bow of light spans the horizon in the direction where it is traversed by the magnetic meridian. This bow sometimes remains for several hours, heaving or waving to and fro, before it sends forth streams of light toward the zenith. Sometimes these flashes proceed from the bow of light alone; at others they simultaneously shoot forth from many opposite parts of the horizon, and form a vast sea of fire, whose brilliant waves are continually changing their position. Finally they all unite in a magnificent crown or cupola of light, with the appearance of which the phenomenon attains its highest degree of splendour.

The brilliancy of the streams, which are commonly red at their base, green in the middle, and light yellow towards the zenith, increases, and at the same time they dart with greater vivacity athwart the skies. The colours are wonderfully transparent; the red approaching to a clear blood-red, the green to a pale emerald tint. On turning from the flaming firmament to the earth, this also is seen to glow with a magical light. The dark sun, black as jet, forms a striking contrast to the white snow plain or the distant ice mountain: all the outlines tremble as if they belonged to the unreal world of dreams. The imposing silence of the night heightens the charms of the magnificent spectacle.

But gradually the crown fades; the bow of light dissolves; the streams become shorter, less frequent, and less vivid; and finally the gloom of winter once more descends upon the northern desert.

In these desolate regions, which are winter-bound during the greater part of the year, man, elsewhere the lord of the Earth, plays but an insignificant part. He is generally a mere wanderer over its surface—a hunter, a fisherman, a herdsman. A few small settlements, separated by vast deserts, give proof of his having made some weak attempts to establish a footing.

In the absence of manufactures and agriculture, man is entirely dependent on the lower animals for the means of subsistence. They constitute his wealth, and occupy all his care. They yield him food and clothing, and materials for shelter and for fashioning his rude implements and weapons. The defence with which nature has furnished them against the rigours of the climate, forms the very attraction which exposes them to the attacks of man. The rich furs yielded by the bear, the fox, the sable, the ermine, the lynx, the sea-otter, the seal, and many other Arctic animals, are valuable articles of commerce; and are, indeed, the only means by which the nomads of Siberia and the Esquimaux of North America can procure the foreign articles they require. The pursuit of the whale, the walrus, and the dolphin, the shark-fisheries of Greenland, the cod-fisheries of Greenland and Norway, and the eider-down trade of Iceland, complete the list of the mercantile resources of these regions.

The most useful, however, of all the Arctic animals is the reindeer. Indeed it is as indispensable to the Laplander, the Siberian, and the Esquimaux, as the camel is to the Bedouin, or the mule to the Peruvian, or as the cocoa-nut palm—the tree of a hundred uses—is to the islanders of the Indian Ocean. Living and dead, he renders to the busy Lapp all the services which it requires three or four animals—the horse, the cow, and the sheep or the goat—to render to the inhabitants of temperate climes. He is tractable and easily tamed. He even saves his master the trouble of providing him with food. For the most remarkable circumstance about him is the unerring instinct with which he discovers his favourite moss, even when the snow covers it to the depth of several feet. As the camel is the "ship" of the ocean of sand, so assuredly is the reindeer the camel of the desert of snow!

The Antarctic regions are far more desolate than the Arctic. There no energetic hunters like the Esquimaux chase the seal or the walrus; no patient herdsmen like the Lapps follow their reindeer to the brink of the icy ocean: all is one dreary, cheerless waste, uninhabited and uninhabitable, except by migratory birds,—the petrel, the albatross, the penguin. No plant of any description is found on any part of the Antarctic continent; no land quadruped lives there; everywhere the snow-line descends to the water's edge.

Certainly the grandest feature which nature presents in these regions is the Parry mountain-chain, about 1700 miles south of New Zealand. The most conspicuous object of the chain is Mount Erebus, an active volcano, of which Sir James Ross—the greatest of Antarctic explorers—had the good fortune to witness a magnificent eruption in 1841. The enormous column of flame and smoke rising 2000 feet above the mouth of the crater, which is elevated 12,400 feet above

Mount Erebus

the level of the sea, together with the snow-white mountain-chain and the deep blue ocean, formed a magnificent scene. The South Pole was first reached on December 10, 1911, by a Norwegian expedition under Captain Amundsen, which was favoured in crossing the ice by exceptionally good weather. Little more than a month later it was also reached under the most adverse conditions by Captain Scott, who perished on the return journey.

Words

brilliancy, *brightness.*
burnished, *polished.*
column, *pillar.*
conspicuous, *prominent.*
continent, *a large portion of land.*
crystal, *glass-like.*
emerald, *green.*
energetic, *vigorous.*
firmament, *heavens.*
implements, *tools.*
imposing, *striking.*
indispensable, *essential.*

magnificence, *grandeur.*
mercantile, *commercial.*
phenomenon, *appearance.*
resources, *means.*
serenely, *calmly.*
simultaneously, *at one time.*
spectacles, *sights.*
subsistence, *sustenance.*
transparency, *clearness.*
unerring, *never-failing.*

Questions

What are the most striking aspects of nature in the Arctic regions? Where are icebergs seen to greatest advantage? Which is the most magnificent of Arctic phenomena? Where is it seen? How does it begin? What does the bow afterwards send forth? When does the phenomenon attain its highest splendour? Of what colours are the streams? What heightens the charms of the spectacle? What part does man play in those regions? On what is he solely dependent for sustenance? What animals yield valuable furs? Mention the other mercantile resources of the Arctic regions. What animal is most useful to man there? What is the most remarkable circumstance about the reindeer? What is the character of the Antarctic regions? What birds are seen there? Of what are these regions entirely destitute? What is their grandest feature? What is the highest summit of the chain called? After what? When was a grand eruption of it seen? By whom? Who discovered the South Pole?

☆ ☆

　　虽然越向极地走去，大自然一般会展现出它更严厉、可怕的面貌，然而，高纬度地区也拥有许多属于自己的美丽。没有什么能比北极的日落更壮观的了，它为积雪覆盖的山峦和天空披上了各种色彩的荣耀；也没有什么比这里纯净的群星闪烁的夜空更加宁静、美丽，明亮的月球照亮了这里，它一天天不断地围绕着地平线，直到它跑完自己漫长明亮的旅途，它才最终落下。景观统一的白色和大气的纯净透明，增添了极地的光亮，这也有助于帮助当地人过着他们的游牧生活，并引导他们走向自己的猎场。

　　众多冰山漂浮在海上——这是一种人们熟悉的两极地区的场景——也是大自然中一种最壮观的场面。但是，这些水晶一般的悬崖无比美丽，只有当午夜的太阳为它们披上黄昏的绚烂色彩时，才显示出它们最极端的魅力。在远处，它们看起来像一块块磨光的金属或固体火焰。站在近处，它们又像是巨大、纯粹的大理石石块，上面点缀着珍珠和淡白色的宝石。成千上万条闪闪发光的小瀑布从这些悬崖的边缘跃入大海，水从雪和冰的湖泊融化而来，在山谷的宁静安详之中静静流淌。

　　但是在所有能够弱化北极地区冬天的单调忧郁的壮观场面之中，没有一种能够与神奇的美丽极光相媲美。黑夜覆盖了白雪皑皑的大地，星星透过薄雾闪烁，雾气会如此频繁地使它们的辉煌在高纬度地区若隐若现。忽然间，一条广泛而清晰的弓箭形状的光线，从磁子午线的方向，跨越了地平线。这条弓一般的光线有时会持续几个小时，来回膨胀、挥舞，它发出的光在向顶峰蔓延。有时这些闪光从弓形光线的本身出现；有时，它们则同时从地平线上的许多不同地方喷出，形成了一个巨大的火海，其辉煌的海浪不断改变自身的位置。最后它们都集合在一处，形成一束华丽的王冠之光或冲天的光线，这一现象的出现预示着极光达到了它最大程度的辉煌。

　　通常光线在源头处展现红色，在中间是绿色，朝向天顶的顶点处则看起来是淡黄色。此时，光线的辉煌增加了，同时它们更活泼地在天空中狂奔。透明的颜色是如此绚烂，红色接近一种明亮的血红色，绿色则是苍白的翡翠色。我们的目光从燃烧的天空中转向地球，这里此时也同样散发出神奇的光亮。黯淡的太阳，像黑色的玉一样，与白雪皑皑的平原或遥远的冰山形成鲜明的对比，所有的轮廓，就像属于虚幻世界的梦想一样颤抖着。夜晚庄严的寂静为这宏伟的场面又平添了一分魅力。

但光冠逐渐消失；弓形的光线也慢慢溶解；光线越来越短，越来越少，也越发得不生动；最后，昏暗的冬天再一次降临到北方的沙漠里。

在这荒凉的地区，冬季占据了一年中大部分的时间，在地球上其他地方都作为主人出现的人类，在这里却成为无关紧要的一部分。一般来说，他只不过是一个在这片区域流浪的人——一个猎人、渔民、牧民。一些小的定居点，被广阔的沙漠分割开来，证明了他确实为了在这里立足，进行了一些微不足道的尝试。

因为在这里没有制造业和农业，人类完全依赖于更低等级的动物作为他们维持生命的手段。它们构成他们的财富，也得到他们所有的照料。它们为他们提供食品和服装以及用以遮蔽和装饰他们粗陋器具和武器的材料。大自然赋予了这些动物以抵御严酷气候的能力，这也就吸引了人类对它们的攻击。熊、狐狸、紫貂、貂、猞猁、海獭、北极的海豹，还有许多其他的极地动物，都为人类提供了充足的皮毛，这也成为极有价值的商品；事实上，它们也成为西伯利亚的游牧民族和北美的爱斯基摩人借以换取他们所需的外国商品的媒介。而对海象、鲸鱼、海豚、格陵兰的鲨鱼、格陵兰岛和挪威的鳕鱼以及冰岛的鸭绒，则构成了这些地区商业资源的完整列表。

然而，在所有动物中，最有价值的是北极驯鹿。的确，对于拉普兰人、西伯利亚人和爱斯基摩人来说，它是不可或缺的，就像骆驼对贝都因人，或骡子在秘鲁，或有一百种用途的椰子棕榈树对于印度洋岛民一样。不管是活着还是死去了，它为忙碌的拉普兰人提供了所有服务，而这些工作需要三到四种动物来替温带气候地区的居民完成，它们是马、牛、绵羊或山羊。驯鹿还很听话，容易驯服。它甚至为他的主人省掉了喂它食物的麻烦。驯鹿最显著的特点是凭借它准确无误的本能，发现它最喜爱的青苔，即使当雪将青苔覆盖到几英尺的深度。正如骆驼是沙漠海洋之中的"船只"一样，驯鹿也肯定是白雪沙漠中的骆驼！

南极地区远比北极地区更加荒凉。在那里，没有充满活力的猎人像爱斯基摩人一样追逐海豹或海象；也没有如拉普兰人一般耐心的牧民喜欢追随他们的驯鹿，一直来到冰冷的海洋边缘。这里是一片沉闷的、乏味的荒凉之地，杳无人迹，不，这里还有一些候鸟的痕迹——信天翁、海燕和企鹅。在南极大陆的任何地方，都没有丝毫关于植物的描述；没有陆生的四足动物定居在这里；在这里，四处的雪线都下降到水域的边缘。

当然，大自然赋予这一区域的最大特点是帕里山脉。它位于新西兰向南约1 700英里处。这一山脉最引人注目的事物便是一座活火山。最伟大的南极探险者杰姆斯·罗斯爵士，极其幸运地在1841年目睹了这一火山壮观的喷发。火焰和烟雾形成的巨大气柱，上升到位于海平面以上12 400英尺处的火山口上方2 000英尺，在雪白的山脉和深蓝色的海洋之中，形成如此壮观的场面。人类最初抵达南极是在1911年12月10日。当时，一支由队长阿蒙森率领的挪威探险队，在一个出其大好的天气里跨越了通往南极的冰川。不到一个月的时间之后，在最不利的条件下，斯科特队长也率队抵达了这里，而他在返程的路途中却牺牲了。

Lesson 26　THE BURNING OF MOSCOW
第二十六课　莫斯科的大火

A. D. 1812

When Napoleon first came within sight of Moscow, with its domes, and towers, and palaces, he gazed long and thoughtfully on that goal of his wishes. Murat was the first to enter the gates, with his splendid cavalry; but as he passed along the streets he was struck by the solitude that surrounded him. Nothing was heard but the heavy tramp of his squadrons: a deserted and abandoned city was the meagre prize for which such unparalleled efforts had been made.

As night drew its curtain over the splendid capital, Napoleon entered the gates, and immediately appointed Mortier governor. In his directions he commanded him to abstain from all pillage "For this," said he, "you shall be answerable with your life. Defend Moscow against all, whether friend or foe."

The bright moon rose over the mighty city, tipping with silver the domes of more than two hundred churches, and pouring a flood of light over a thousand palaces, and the dwellings of three hundred thousand inhabitants. The weary arm sank to rest; but there was to sleep for Mortier's eyes. Not the gorgeous and variegated palaces and their rich ornaments, nor the parks and gardens and Oriental magnificence that everywhere surrounded him, kept him wakeful, but the ominous forebodings that some dire calamity was hanging over the silent capital.

When he had entered it, scarcely a living soul met his gaze as he looked down the long streets; and when he broke open the buildings, he found salons, and parlours, and bed-rooms, all furnished and in order—but no occupants! This sudden abandonment of their homes betokened some secret purpose, yet to be fulfilled. The midnight moon was stealing over the city, when the cry of "Fire!" reached the ears of Mortier: the first light over Napoleon's faltering empire was kindled, and that most wondrous scene of modern times commenced—The Burning of Moscow.

Mortier, as governor of the city, immediately issued his orders, and was putting forth every exertion, when at daylight Napoleon hastened to him. Affecting to disbelieve the reports that the inhabitants were firing their own city, he put more rigid commands on Mortier to keep the soldiers from the work of destruction. The marshal simply pointed to some iron-covered houses that had not yet been opened, from every crevice of which smoke was issuing like steam from the sides of a pent-up volcano. Sad and thoughtful, Napoleon turned towards the Kremlin, the ancient palace of the Czars, whose huge structure rose high above the surrounding edifices.

In the morning, Mortier, by great exertions, was enabled to subdue the fire. But the

General View of Moscow

next night, Sept. 15, at midnight, the sentinels on watch upon the lofty Kremlin saw below them the flames bursting through the houses and palaces, and the cry "Fire! fire!" again passed through the city. The dread scene was now fairly opened. Fiery balloons were seen dropping from the air and alighting on the houses; dull explosions were heard on every side from the shut-up dwellings: the next moment light burst forth from them, and the flames were raging through the apartments.

All was uproar and confusion. The serene air and moonlight of the night before had given way to driving clouds, and a wild tempest, like the roar of the sea, swept over the city. Flames arose on every side, blazing and crackling in the storm; white clouds of smoke and sparks in an incessant shower went driving towards the Kremlin. The clouds themselves seemed turned into fire, rolling wrath over devoted Moscow. Mortier, crushed with the responsibility thrown upon his shoulders, moved with his Young Guard amid this desolation, blowing up the houses and facing the tempest and the flames—struggling nobly to arrest the conflagration.

He hastened from place to place amid the ruins, his face blackened with smoke, and his hair and eyebrows singed with the fierce heat. At length the day dawned, and Mortier, who had strained every nerve for thirty-six hours, entered a palace and dropped down from fatigue. The manly form and stalwart arm that had so often carried death into the ranks of the enemy, at length gave way, and the gloomy marshal lay and panted in utter exhaustion. The night of tempest was succeeded by a day of fiery storm; and when night again enveloped the city, it was one broad flame, waving to and fro in the blast!

The wind had increased to a perfect hurricane, and shifted from quarter to quarter, as if on purpose to swell the sea of fire and extinguish the last hope. The fire was approaching the Kremlin: already the roar of the flames, the crash of falling houses, and the crackling of burning timbers, were borne to the ears of the startled. Emperor. He arose and walked to and fro, stopping convulsively and gazing on the terrific scene. Murat and others of his marshals rushed into his presence, and on their knees besought him to flee; but he still clung to that haughty palace, as if it were his empire.

At length the shout, The Kremlin is on fire!" was heard above the roar of the conflagration, and Napoleon reluctantly consented to leave. He descended into the streets with his staff, and looked about for a way of egress, but the flames blocked every passage. At length they discovered a postern gate leading to the Moskwa, and passed through it; but they had entered still further into the danger.

As Napoleon cast his eye round the open space, girdled and arched with fire, smoke, and cinders, he saw one single street yet open, but all on fire. Into this he rushed, and amid the crash of falling houses and the raging of the flames, over burning ruins, through clouds of rolling smoke, and between walls of fire, he pressed on. At length, half suffocated, he emerged in safety from the blazing city, and took up his quarters in the imperial palace of Petrowsky, nearly three miles distant.

Mortier, relieved from his anxiety for the Emperor, redoubled his efforts to arrest the conflagration. His men cheerfully rushed into every danger. Breathing nothing but smoke and ashes—canopied by flame and smoke and cinders—surrounded by walls of fire that rocked to and fro, and fell with a crash amid the blazing ruins, carrying down with them roofs of red-hot iron—he struggled against an enemy that no boldness could awe or courage overcome.

Those brave troops had heard the tramp of thousands of cavalry sweeping to battle, without fear; but now they stood in still terror before the march of the conflagration, under whose burning footsteps was heard the incessant noise of falling houses and palaces and churches. The continuous roar of the raging hurricane, mingled with that of the flames, was more terrible than the thunder of artillery; and before this new foe, in the midst of this battle of the elements, the awe-struck army stood powerless and affrighted.

When night again descended on the city, it presented a spectacle the like of which had never been seen before, and which baffles all description. The streets were streets of fire; the heavens a canopy of fire; and the entire body of the city a mass of fire, fed by a hurricane that sped the blazing fragments in a constant stream through the air. Incessant explosions, from the blowing up of stores of oil and tar and spirits, shook the very foundations of the city, and sentvast volumes of smoke rolling furiously toward the sky. Huge sheets of canvas on fire came floating, like messengers of death, through the flames; the towers and domes of the churches and palaces, glowing with red-heat over the wild sea below, then tottering a moment on their bases, were hurled by the tempest into the common ruin.

Thousands of wretches, before unseen, were driven by the heat from the cellars and hovels, and streamed in an incessant throng along the streets. Children were seen carrying their parents, the strong the weak; while thousands more were staggering under loads of plunder which they had snatched from the flames. These, too, would frequently take fire in the falling shower, and the miserable creatures would be compelled to drop them and flee for their lives. Oh, it was a scene of woe and fear inconceivable and indescribable! A mighty and closely-packed city of houses and churches and palaces, wrapped from limit to limit in flames, which are fed by a whirling hurricane, is a sight this world has seldom seen.

But this was within the city. To Napoleon without, the spectacle was still more sublime and terrific. When the flames had overcome all obstacles, and had wrapped everything in their red mantle, that great city looked like a sea of rolling fire, swept by a tempest that drove it into billows. Huge domes and towers, throwing off sparks like blazing firebrands, now disappeared in their maddening flow, as they meshed and broke high over their tops, scattering their spray of fire against the clouds. The heavens themselves seemed to have caught the conflagration, and the angry masses that swept it rolled over a bosom of fire.

Columns of flame would rise and sink along the surface of this sea, and huge volumes of bleak smoke suddenly shoot into the air, as if volcanoes were working below. The black form of the Kremlin alone towered above the chaos—now wrapped in flame and smoke—again emerging into view—standing amid this scene of desolation and terror, like Virtue in the midst of a burning world, enveloped but unscathed by the devouring element. Napoleon stood and gazed on the scene in silent awe. Though nearly three miles distant, the windows and walls of his apartment were so hot that he could scarcely bear his hand against them. Said he, years afterwards,—

"It was the spectacle of a sea and billows of fire, a sky and clouds of flame; mountains of red rolling flames, like immense waves of the sea, alternately bursting forth and elevating themselves to the skies of flame above. Oh! it was the most grand, the most sublime, the most terrific sight the world ever beheld!"

—J. T. Headley

Words

abstain, *refrain*.
apartment, *room*.
baffles, *defies*.
betokened, *foretold*.
canopied, *over-arched*.
conflagration, *burning*.
convulsively, *spasmodically*.
devoted, *doomed*.
discovered, *found*.
elevating, *raising*.
enveloped, *enshrouded*.
exertion, *effort*.
explosions, *reports*.
faltering, *tottering*.
fatigue, *exhaustion*.
firebrands, *fagots*.
forebodings, *portents*.
hovels, *cellars*.

hurricane, *tempest*.
indescribable, *beyond the power of words*.
issuing, *emerging*.
occupants, *inhabitants*.
ominous, *inauspicious*.
pillage, *plunder*.
relieved, *delivered*.
reluctantly, *unwillingly*.
rigid, *strict*.
sentinels, *watchmen*.
solitude, *loneliness*.
staggering, *reeling*.
suffocated, *choked*.
surface, *bosom*.
unparalleled, *unequalled*.
unscathed, *unharmed*
volcano, *burning mountain*.

Questions

What struck Murat as strange when he entered Moscow? What directions did Napoleon give to Mortier? What kept the latter wakeful that night? From what did he infer some secret purpose, to be fulfilled? What cry reached him at midnight? What commands did Napoleon give him when he went to him at daylight? How did Mortier answer him? By what means was the fire spread the next night? What increased its fury? To what place did Napoleon cling? What danger had he to encounter before he escaped from the city? What means did Mortier adopt to try to arrest the progress of the fire? What was the aspect of the city on the third night? Who then thronged the streets? Where did they come from? From what point was the spectacle most sublime? What building alone towered above the chaos? What did Napoleon say of the scene, years afterwards?

公元1812年

当拿破仑第一次来到莫斯科，看到这里的穹顶、高塔和宫殿，他长时间若有所思地凝视着这里，这里成为他想要得到的目标。缪拉率领他杰出的骑兵团，首先进入了莫斯科的城门。但是当他走过街道，四周向他袭来的一阵荒凉，使他备受打击。在这里，除了他的骑兵队伍发出的沉重的脚步声之外，什么也听不到。他们在前所未有的努力之后，得到的可怜的奖赏，却是一座如此废弃的荒凉的城市。

夜幕在这座辉煌的都城拉开了帷幕，拿破仑踏入了城门，并即刻任命莫蒂埃为莫斯科的指挥官。从自己的立场出发，他吩咐放弃所有的掠夺，他说："你必须用你的生命，捍卫莫斯科的一切，无论它们是属于朋友还是敌人。"

在这个巨大的城市上空，明亮的月亮升了起来，给两百多座教堂的圆顶涂上了银色，在近千座宫殿和三十万座居民住宅上方倾注下一片光亮。莫蒂埃疲倦的手臂垂下，他的眼睛也渐渐倦怠。不管是华丽的宫殿还是它们丰富的装饰物，东方化的富丽堂皇的公园和花园，都不会阻止他入眠，但不祥之兆总萦绕在这座沉默的都城之中。

当他进入这座都城之时，他望向长长的街道上，看不到甚至一个活生生的生命；当他砸开一座建筑物的大门，他会发现洗漱间、会客室、卧室里所有的家具都在，但是没有任何人存在！这种对他们自己家园的突然放弃，暗示着某种神秘的目的，但现在还没有实现。午夜的月光照耀着整座都城，继而莫蒂埃听到了一声惊呼："着火了！"这似乎是拿破仑摇摇欲坠的帝国里点燃的第一束光亮，近代史上最奇妙的场景开始了——莫斯科的大火。

　　作为整个城市的指挥官，莫蒂埃立即发布了命令，即刻执行，并在白天时候急忙报告给拿破仑。大受震撼的拿破仑，由于不相信莫斯科的居民会放火烧掉自己的城市，向莫蒂埃发布了更多的命令，阻止法国士兵做出任何蓄意破坏的行为。元帅仅仅发现了一些铁制的房子，它们的大门还未打开。从它的每一个缝隙中都冒出了烟，就像火山一样从两侧喷发着蒸汽。悲痛的拿破仑沉思着回到克里姆林宫，这是沙皇的一个古代宫殿，它在周围的建筑物中高高耸立，鹤立鸡群。

　　虽然付出了极大的努力，但直到早晨，莫蒂埃还是没能制服这场大火。但是在第二天的晚上，也就是9月15日的午夜，在巍峨的克里姆林宫上方的哨所执勤观察的哨兵，看到了下方的城市中，火焰再次在每一处房屋和宫殿之中蔓延开来。"着火了！着火了！"的叫喊声再次响彻了这座城市。令人恐惧的场景如今已经开始了。人们看到火球从天空中降落在房屋上，沉闷的爆炸声就像从四面八方而来，下一刻突然一阵光爆发了过来，大火就这样席卷了所有房子。

　　这一切变得喧嚣和混乱，前一天晚上的莫斯科还是平静的，月光笼罩，而现在的莫斯科，就像被大海上的风暴所咆哮着席卷其中。在这场暴风雨中，火焰不停地燃烧，发出爆裂声，白烟和火花不停地朝着克里姆林宫奔涌而来。云朵本身似乎都变成了火，在陷入火海的莫斯科上空翻滚。莫蒂埃的肩膀上担负着责任，匆忙带领着他年轻的军队，在这片被炸毁的房屋和暴风雨般的火焰席卷的废墟上，豪迈地与这场大火作起了斗争。

　　他匆忙地在废墟中跑来跑去，他的脸被烟熏黑，他的头发和眉毛被热焰烧焦。最后天亮了，莫蒂埃的神经已经紧绷了36个小时，他走进一处宫殿，想从疲劳中稍微放松一下。他极具男子气概的身躯和坚定健壮的手臂，常常给敌人的军队带来死亡和失败，最后它们都放弃了，他终于在筋疲力尽下沉沉地睡去。骚乱的一晚之后，又是一天的狂风暴雨；当夜晚再次笼罩着这座城市，巨大的火焰来回挥舞，引起不断的爆炸！

　　风已经逐渐增强，最后变成了一股飓风不停地旋转移动，仿佛要膨胀成为一片火海，浇灭人们最后的希望。大火接近了克里姆林宫，在燃烧的火焰中，房屋崩溃般地倒塌，木头被烤成脆皮，都一一传进受到惊吓的人们的耳朵。拿破仑站了起来，向前走了几步，又颤抖着停了下来，盯着这可怕的场景。守卫缪拉和所有将军急忙赶到他的面前，跪下来，恳求他赶快逃离，可他仍然坚持留在这高贵的宫殿里，仿佛这里是属于他的帝国。

　　终于有人大喊道："克里姆林宫着火了！"拿破仑在火焰的咆哮中听到这一消息，才极不情愿地同意离开。他和他的守卫流落在街头，试图寻找一条出路，但似乎每一条通道都已经被火焰所阻塞。又向前走了一段路，他们发现了一个后门，这里能通往莫斯克瓦。众人穿过了这道门。但他们又离危险更近了一步。

拿破仑通过拱门之后，看到了一个到处都是火焰、烟雾和灰烬的开阔地区。他能看到一条通畅的街道，但街上全都着火了。他冲进这条街道，四周是正在崩塌的房屋，肆虐的火焰和燃烧的废墟。他穿越了翻滚烟雾形成的云团，在四周如墙壁一般高耸的火焰之间，继续前行。

最终，在近乎快要窒息的时候，他从燃烧的城市安全地逃了出来，并最终将营地重新建立在彼得罗夫斯基皇家宫殿，这里距离克里姆林宫有三英里远。

消除了对拿破仑皇帝的焦虑，莫蒂埃开始更加努力地扑救着大火。他的守卫也更拼命地进入了斗争。呼吸着烟和灰烬——到处都覆盖着火焰的浓烟和灰烬，每一米的城墙都在来回摇晃，最终在燃烧的废墟里轰然倒塌。一并掉下来的，还有屋顶上被烧成红色炽热的铁块。他挣扎着对抗着敌人，但似乎没有任何威严和勇气可以打败这场火焰。

那些勇敢的士兵，在面对成千上万的敌方骑兵时也从不害怕。但现在，他们站立在静静的恐惧中，面对着汹涌的火焰向他们逼近。在它蔓延的脚步下，人们听着房屋的倒塌，宫殿和教堂发出的轰鸣。不断咆哮的飓风，夹杂着火焰的肆虐，比火炮的轰鸣声更加可怕。在这个新的敌人面前，处于这场战斗之中，这支军队感到前所未有的无能为力和惊慌失措。

当夜晚再次降临在这座城市，人们看到了一种前所未见的、难以描述的景象。整个街道正在燃烧，树顶上的火好像和天空燃烧在了一起，飓风带着燃烧的碎片流动在空中。炸毁的石油和焦油不断引发爆炸，震动了整个城市的地面，巨大的浓烟滚滚地卷上了天空。一幅巨大的描绘火焰的画面在这座城市浮动，就像死亡的使者在火焰中向我们袭来。高塔、教堂和宫殿的圆顶，都像在闪闪发光，像是漂浮在大海之上摇摇欲坠的船舶，最后将被暴风雨卷席，而共同毁灭。

成千上万可怜的人，在其他人看到他们之前，被大火驱逐出了地窖或者小屋，一起涌上了街头，川流不息。父母带着他们的孩子们，强壮的人带着体弱的人，超过想象的成千上万的人被大火夺去了生命。这些幸免于难的人们也一样会遭遇大火焦灼的痛苦，不得不放弃了他们现在的生活，逃离这里。这是一种怎样的景象，充满难以形容的悲哀和恐惧！一座如此强大、建筑密集的城市，布满房屋、教堂和宫殿，如今它的每一寸土地却都被大火吞噬。这些大火已经达到了它的极致，飓风围绕着整座城市，这景象是全世界都不曾见过的。

但这都是在这座城市内部。对于位于城外的拿破仑来说，景象甚至更加庄严和可怕。当火焰已经包围了所有的一切，并将一切事物都置于它的红色斗篷之下，这座伟大的城市看起来就像一团火焰，被风暴和巨浪所扫荡。

巨大的穹顶和高塔，向外投掷着如燃烧着的火把一般的火花，发狂地在它们的顶部编织着火网，向周围的云朵散射着火苗，如今也消失在让人发狂的激烈火焰中。天空也像起了火，满怀愤怒地将胸中的火焰喷吐向大地。

火焰形成的高柱不断地在火海上方上升和下沉。大量黑色的烟雾突然向空中蔓延，就像下面的火山正在喷发。克里姆林宫黑色的框架独自耸立在这片混乱的废墟中，如今它已经包裹在一片火焰和浓烟中，再次消逝在人们的视线当中。在这一片荒凉和恐怖中，在燃烧的世界里，它被火焰笼罩着却毫发未损。拿破仑站在原地，沉默地凝视着这片场景。尽管位于接近三英里的距离之外，但是克里姆林宫燃烧着的窗户和墙壁，简直要灼伤他的手臂。多年以后，他说，"这是一片火海和巨浪的景象，遍布燃烧着的天空和云彩：红色的咆哮火焰如山峰一般，就像宽广海面上的波浪，交替着破裂或者上升至火焰上空的天际。哦！这是世界上最壮观、最庄严、最可怕的景象！"

——J. T. 海德里

Lesson 27
THE RETREAT OF THE
FRENCH ARMY FROM MOSCOW
第二十七课　　法国军队从莫斯科撤退

Magnificence of ruin! what has Time,

　　In all it ever gazed upon of war,

Of the wild rage of storm, or deadly clime,

　　Seen, with that battle's vengeance to compare?

　　How glorious shone the invaders' pomp afar!

Like pampered lions from the spoil they came:

　　The land before them silence and despair,

The land behind them massacre and flame.

Blood will have tenfold blood! What are they now?—A name.

Homeward by hundred thousands, column deep,

　　Broad square, loose squadron, rolling like the flood,

When mighty torrents from their channels leap,

　　Rushed through the land the haughty multitude,

　　Billow on endless billow: on through wood,

O'er rugged hill, down sunless, marshy vale,

　　The death-devoted moved, to clangour rude

Of drum and horn, and dissonant clash of mail,

Glancing disastrous light before that sunbeam pale.

Again they reached thee, Borodino! Still

　　Upon the loaded soil the carnage lay,

The human harvest, now stark, stiff, and chill;

　　Friend, foe, stretched thick together, clay to clay.

　　Iu vain the startled legions burst away—

The land was all one naked sepulchre:

　　The shrinking eye still glanced on grim Decay;

Still did the hoof and heel their passage tear

Through cloven helms and arms, and corses mouldering drear.

The field was as they left it; fosse and fort

　　Streaming with slaughter still, but desolate—

The cannon flung dismantled by its port:

Each knew the mound, the black ravine whose strait
   Was won and lost, and thronged with dead, till Fate
Had fixed upon the victor—half undone.
   There was the hill from which their eyes elate
Had seen the burst of Moscow's golden zone:
But Death was at their heels—they shuddered and rushed on.

The hour of vengeance strikes! Hark to the gale,
   As it bursts hollow through the rolling clouds,
That from the North in sullen grandeur sail
    Like floating Alps. Advancing darkness broods
    Upon the wild horizon; and the woods,
Now sinking into brambles, echo shrill,
   As the gust sweeps them; and those upper floods
Shoot on their leafless boughs the sleet-drops chill,
That on the hurrying crowds in freezing showers distil.

They reach the wilderness! The majesty
   Of solitude is spread before their gaze,—
Stern nakedness—dark earth and wrathful sky;
    If ruins were there, they long had ceased to blaze;
    If blood was shed, the ground no more betrays,
E'en by a skeleton, the crime of man:
    Behind them rolls the deep and drenching haze,
Wrapping their rear in night; before their van
The struggling daylight shows the unmeasured desert wan.

Still on they sweep, as if their hurrying march
   Could bear them from the rushing of His wheel
Whose chariot is the whirlwind. Heaven's clear arch
    At once is covered with a livid veil:
    In mixed and fighting heaps the deep clouds reel:
Upon the dense horizon hangs the sun,
    In sanguine light, an orb of burning steel:
The snows wheel down through twilight, thick and dun.
Now tremble, men of blood—the judgment has begun!

The trumpet of the northern winds has blown,
   And it is answered by the dying roar
Of armies on that boundless field o'erthrown.
    Now in the awful gusts the desert hoar
    Is tempested—a sea without a shore,

Lifting its feathery waves! The legions fly;—
    Volley on volley down the hailstones pour:
Blind, famished, frozen, mad, the wanderers die;
And, dying, hear the storm but wilder thunder by.

Such is the hand of Heaven! A human blow
    Had crushed them in the fight, or flung the chain
Round them where Moscow's stately towers were low;
    And all be stilled. But thou! thy battle-plain
    Was a whole empire: that devoted train
Must war from day to day with storm and gloom
    (Man following, like the wolves that rend the slain);
    Must lie from night to night as in a tomb;
Must fly, toil, bleed for home—yet never see that home!

—Croly

Words

brambles, *prickly shrubs*.	livid, *murky*.
carnage, *corpses*.	marshy, *fenny*.
clangour, *clamour*.	massacre, *butchery*.
clime, *climate*.	pampered, *gorged*.
disastrous, *destructive*.	ravine, *gorge*.
dismantled, *dismounted*.	sanguine, *blood-red*.
dissonant, *discordant*.	sepulchre, *burial-place*.
distil, *diffuse*.	stately, *commanding*.
drenching, *soaking*.	tempest, *agitated*.
fosse, *ditch*.	torrents, *currents*.
grandeur, *majesty*.	unmeasured, *immense*.
judgment, *doomsday*.	vengeance, *revenge*.

如此壮观的废墟！
在时间目睹过的所有战争之中，
无论是狂怒的风暴，还是致命的气候，
有什么，能跟这场复仇的战斗相比较？
辉煌，照耀着远方侵略者的盛况！
像骄纵的狮子掠夺着它们的战利品。

他们面前的大地，如此沉默和绝望，
他们身后的土地，布满屠杀和火焰。
血将有十倍的血来偿还！他们现在怎样？——只剩下名字。

几十万部队朝着家的方向前行，
宽阔的广场，松散的中队，就像滚滚洪水，
当洪流从沟渠中跃起，
匆匆地在傲慢的人群中涌过，
波涛无尽翻滚：越过森林，
通过崎岖的山路，沿着不见天日的沼泽河谷，
甘于牺牲的战士们前行着，铿锵有力，
鼓和号角的声响，还有刺耳的盔甲声，
一阵凶光，在灰暗的日光下匆匆掠过。

他们又来到了这里，波罗底诺！
在这片土地之上，仍发生着屠杀，
人们曾在这里收获，现在他们的尸体僵硬冰冷；
朋友，敌人，尸体厚厚的四处叠放，一具挨着一具。
受到惊吓的军团徒然地匆忙散开，
土地就像一座张开的坟墓：
战士们枯萎的眼睛仍然看着这残忍的衰变；
他们仍一步一步地向前行进，
身着劈开的头盔和武器，还有充血腐烂的阴郁。

这片土地就像他们离开时一样，
壕沟与堡垒，在屠杀后仍然荒凉，而更加绝望。
大炮的端口已被拆除，
每个人都知道坟堆，像是黑色的沟壑，
横亘在胜利和失败之间，挤满了死亡，
直到胜利者的命运已经确定——虽然事情的一半还没有结束。
在这里，他们的眼睛随着山脉缓缓升起，
看到了莫斯科金黄色火焰的爆发，
但是死亡就跟在他们后面——它们颤抖着冲了上来。

复仇的时刻来到了！听那巨大的声响，
它爆发在贯通的浮云之间，
阴沉壮阔地从北方袭来，
像漂浮的阿尔卑斯山，在黑暗中前进，
在宽广的地平线和森林之上前进，
现在陷入荆棘之中，发出尖锐的回响，
随着阵风横扫过这里，之上的洪水，
敲打着无叶的枝梢，带来了阵阵寒意，
在匆忙的人群之中，伴随着冰冷的雨水滴落。

他们来到了旷野之中，
宏伟的孤独感在他们面前蔓延，
蔓延到黑暗的地球，愤怒的天空；
如果这里有废墟，它们也早已不再闪耀；
如果有鲜血流出，大地上就不会再有更多的背叛，
尸骨嶙嶙，人类的罪行，
在他们身后，血淋淋的浓雾翻滚着，
夜晚缠绕在他们的身后，在他们的车前，
苦苦挣扎的曙光展现在广阔的沙漠上。

他们仍在前行，仿佛他们匆忙的行军，
能承受如旋风一般的战车，
战争的车轮匆匆向前翻滚。
清澈的天空，立即覆盖上了一层铅色的面纱，
深暗的云朵卷卷而来，
太阳悬挂在阴沉的地平线之上，
闪耀着血红色的光，像极了燃烧着的铁球，
雪在黄昏之中滚滚而来，厚重而暗淡。
现在，人类的鲜血颤抖着——审判已经开始了！

北方的风吹响了号角，
军队在无垠的大地中推行，
军队垂死的轰鸣声回答着它。
现在在可怕的灰白色的沙漠中，

一片无边的海正在涌起，
如羽毛一般的波浪涌起！军团飞了起来；
在凌空之下，冰雹倾盆而下：
前途暗淡，饥肠辘辘，瑟瑟发抖，几近疯狂，漫步在此的人们就这样死去；
奄奄一息之时，他们却听到了暴风雨和狂暴的雷鸣。

这是上帝之手对人类的一次打击，
将它们在一场战斗中粉碎，撕裂了链条，
在此周围，莫斯科雄伟的高塔也变得低矮；
一切平息。但你，战斗的平原，
是一个完整的帝国，专门训练人类，
必须一天一天处在战争的风暴和黑暗之中，
人跟随着，如狼一般，不停厮杀；
必须每晚都如处于坟墓里一般躺下；
必须为了自己的家乡，飞奔，辛劳，流血，却再也看不到自己的家乡！

——克罗利

Lesson 28 THE TEMPERATE REGIONS
第二十八课　温带地区

The North Temperate Zone is the work-shop of the world. In the Frigid and Torrid Zones nature is preeminent. She defeats human labour in the former, by her sterility; in the latter she makes it unnecessary, by her luxuriance. But the supremacy of Man is the leading characteristic of the temperate regions of the globe. They contain three-fourths of the whole human race. Within them civilization has been most highly developed; and there the great events of history have been enacted, both in ancient and in modern times.

This activity and movement are due in a great measure to the influences of climate. In temperate climes, says Guyot, "the alternations of heat and cold, the changes of the seasons, a fresher and more bracing air, incite man to a constant struggle, to forethought, and to the vigorous employment of all his faculties. A more economical nature yields nothing, except to the sweat of his brow; every gift on her part is a recompense for effort on his. Nature here, even while challenging man to the conflict, gives him the hope of victory; and if she does not show herself prodigal, she grants to his active and intelligent labour more than his necessities require. While she calls out his energy, she thus gives him ease and leisure, which permit him to cultivate all the lofty faculties of his higher nature. Here, physical nature is not a tyrant, but a useful helper: the active faculties, the understanding, and the reason, rule over the instincts and the passive faculties; the soul over the body; man over nature.

"In the frozen regions man also contends with nature, but it is with a niggardly and severe nature; it is a desperate struggle—a struggle for life. With difficulty, by force of toil, he succeeds in providing for himself a miserable support, which saves him from dying of hunger and hardship during the tedious winters of that climate. High culture is not possible under such unfavourable conditions."

The excessive heat of the Tropics, on the other hand, enfeebles man. It invites to repose and inaction. Not only in the vegetable world and in the lower animals is the power of life carried to its highest degree,—in tropical man, too, physical nature excels. There the life of the body overmasters that of the soul. The physical instincts eclipse the higher faculties; passion predominates over intellect and reason; the passive over the active faculties.

"A nature too rich, too prodigal of her gifts, does not compel man to wrest from her his daily bread by his daily toil. A regular climate, and the absence of a dormant season, render forethought of little use to him. Nothing invites him to that struggle of intelligence against nature which raises the powers of man to their highest pitch. Thus he never dreams of resisting physical nature: he is conquered by her; he submits to the yoke, and becomes again the animal man, in proportion as he abandons himself to external influences, forgetful of his high moral destination."

While a temperate climate is thus most favourable for developing man's intellectual vigor and physical strength, it is also most suitable for those animal and vegetable products which are best adapted to meet the wants of the great mass of mankind. Thus the ox and the sheep—the ruminants most useful to man—are natives of the Temperate Zone, and are diffused very widely and in vast numbers over it. From his home in Central Asia, the horse—the indispensable ally of man in every kind of industry, in war as in peace, in his pleasures as in his toils—has spread round and round the globe. The feathered tribes, too, exist in such abundance in these regions as to form in some countries a staple article of food.

Turning now to the vegetable kingdom, we find the corn-plants—the plants which are best adapted for the food of civilized man—scattered profusely over the Temperate Zone. It is only when man has settled down in a fixed abode,—when he has abandoned his nomadic life and become an agriculturist, attaching himself to a certain locality,—that it is possible for him to rear corn. Corn is not self-sustaining, self-diffusing, like the wild grass. Self-sown, it gradually dwindles away, and finally disappears. "It can only be reared permanently by being sown by man's own hand, and in ground which man's own hand has tilled."

Corn, therefore, a great German botanist has said, precedes all civilization. With it are connected rest, peace, and domestic happiness, of which the wandering savage knows nothing. In order to rear it, nations must take possession of certain lands; and when their existence is thus firmly established, improvements in manners and customs speedily follow. They are no longer inclined for bloody wars, but fight only to defend the fields from which they derive their support.

The Corn Field

Corn is the food most convenient and most suitable for man in a social state. It is only by the careful cultivation of it that a country becomes capable of permanently supporting a dense population. All other kinds of food are precarious, and cannot be stored up for any length of time: roots and fruits are soon exhausted; the produce of the chase is uncertain, and if hard pressed ceases to yield a supply. In some countries the pith of the sago-palm, the fruit of the bread-fruit tree, the root of the esculent fern, and similar food, supplied spontaneously by nature, serve to maintain a thinly scattered and easily satisfied population; but man in these rude circumstances is invariably found depraved in body and in mind, and hopelessly incapable of bettering his condition. But the cultivation of corn, while it furnishes him with a supply of food for the greater part of the year, imposes upon him certain labours and restraints which have a most beneficial influence upon his character and habits.

Such are the plants which form the characteristic vegetable product of temperate regions. Wheat, which will not thrive in hot climates, flourishes all over the Temperate Zone, at various ranges of elevation. Maize spreads over an immense geographical area in North America, as well as in Southern Europe. Barley is cultivated in those parts of Europe and Asia where the soil and climate are not adapted for wheat; while oats and rye extend far into the bleak North, and disappear only when we reach those desolate Arctic regions where man cannot exist in his social capacity. By such striking adaptations of different varieties of grain to gradations of climate and varieties of soil, does Providence furnish the food indispensable for the sustenance of the human race.

Again: what are the trees that are most useful to man in a high state of civilization? Unquestionably those yielding the largest supply of common timber. Now the chief fancy-wood trees—those which form part of man's luxuries—belong to the Tropics; but the pines and hard-wood trees—those which minister to man's necessities— belong distinctively to the Temperate Zone. The inhabitant of that zone must send to Honduras for mahogany, to Brazil for rosewood, to make his finer furniture; but the pine, the ash, the oak, the elm, the beech—the timber used in building his houses and work-shops, the wood used in fashioning his tools and carts and carriages, and in making his most complicated machinery—these he finds abundantly in his own woods. They are reared in the same climate, they breathe the same air as himself.

What is true of the vegetable world above the soil, is true also of the mineral world beneath it. All the metals most useful to man, both for domestic and for industrial purposes—iron, tin, copper, lead—are found in abundance within the temperate regions. Coal, too, without which the ores could not be profitably smelted or supplied in sufficient quantities, and which is the main-spring of all manufacturing industry, is most plentiful in the Temperate Zone.

But very marked differences occur within the Temperate Zone itself—the result of differences of climate and configuration. Central Asia, for example—indeed, the whole of Asia north of the line of the Caucasus, the Himalaya, and the Chinese Wall—consists of barren steppes, which now, as much as six centuries ago, are the home of barbarism and rapine. And why is this? Because its inland deserts are far removed from the influences of the sea; because lofty mountains give most of its land a northern aspect; because its rivers flow either into salt lakes with no outlet, or into a frozen ocean which completely shuts out commerce.

Look at Europe on the other hand. It is of all the continents the one which is most thoroughly broken up by inroads of the sea. Asia is four and a half times as large as Europe in superficial area; yet Europe has a coast-line five times as great as that of Asia. Excepting only the plains of Russia, no part of Europe is more than three hundred miles distant from the sea; while the number and the distribution of its navigable rivers bring the ocean within easy reach even of its remotest parts.

And what are the consequences of this? A glance at the map of Europe will tell us. It is evidently the continent most thickly covered with cities and towns; and with high-roads, canals, and railways, weaving the towns into a living and ever-busy net-work. There civilization has struck its roots deepest, and stretched its branches widest. There the arts and sciences have reached their highest development. There the great mechanical inventions which have knit the world into one vast inter-dependent society, have had their birth; and commerce, manufactures, and agriculture have been brought to the greatest perfection.

Europe has laid the whole world under contribution for the supply of her physical wants. In return, she has laid the whole world under obligation to her for more ethereal but not less real benefits. She has been the cradle of those free political institutions which have developed the self-control and the independence of man as a member of society. Her literature is the richest and most varied in the world. In Europe the Christian religion has been most widely diffused, and it has been the centre from which the message of peace has been sent to the farthest corners of the world.

What is true of Europe as a whole is preeminently true of Great Britain. There the circle of European—nay, of universal—civilization and industry has its centre. By her colonies she has diffused the influence of her spirit and the energy of her sons throughout the world, so that her greatest rivals in material and social progress are her own children.

This is a proud position for so small a land to hold. But insignificant as the British Isles appear on the map of the world, Britain is in no small degree indebted to climate, physical configuration, and geographical position for the greatness which she has achieved.

"The territory," says Emerson, "has a singular perfection. The climate is warmer by many degrees than it is entitled to be by latitude. Neither hot nor cold, there is no hour in the whole year when one cannot work. The temperature makes no exhaustive demands on human strength, but allows the attainment of the largest stature. In variety of surface it is a miniature of Europe, having plain, forest, marsh, river, sea-shore. From first to last it is a museum of anomalies. This foggy and rainy country furnishes the world with astronomical observations. Its short rivers do not afford water-power, but the land shakes under the thunder of its mills. There is no gold mine of any importance, but there is more gold in England than in all other countries. It is too far north for the culture of the vine, but the wines of all countries are in its docks; and oranges and pine-apples are as cheap in London as on the Mediterranean."

Words

adaptations, *adjustments*.
alternation, *succession*.
anomalies, *irregularities*.
barbarism, *savageness*.
beneficial, *improving*.
characteristic, *distinctive*.
complicated, *intricate*.
configuration, *form*.
convenient, *advantageous*.
destination, *destiny*.
development, *growth*.
distribution, *arrangement*.
employment, *use*.
esculent, *eatable*.
ethereal, *immaterial*.
exhausted, *consumed*.
exhaustive, *wearing out*.
faculties, *powers*.
indispensable, *necessary*.

insignificant, *unimportant*.
intelligent, *wise*.
luxuriance, *prolificness*.
miniature, *reduced copy*.
miserable, *wretched*.
niggardly, *penurious*.
obligation, *indebtedness*.
permanently, *lastingly*.
predominates, *has mastery*.
preeminent, *supreme*.
prodigal, *liberal*.
profusely, *abundantly*.
ruminants, *cud-chewers*.
smelted, *separated into metal and dross*.
spontaneously, *voluntarily*.
sterility, *barrenness*.
superficial, *surface*.
territory, *land*.
unfavourable, *adverse*.

Questions

What is the leading characteristic of the temperate regions? What proportion of the human race do they contain? To what is the activity of these regions in a great measure due? How does a temperate climate enable man to work? How does it compel him to work? What is the character of his struggle with nature in the frozen regions? What prevents labour in the Tropics? What renders it unnecessary? What animals are characteristic of the temperate regions? What plants? Why does corn precede all civilization? What is necessary to its permanent production? What are the chief corn-plants of the Temperate Zone? What trees are most abundant there? What minerals? By what are the differences that occur within the Temperate Zone produced? What is the character of Central Asia? How is this accounted for? What is remarkable in the configuration of Europe? What are the consequences of this? What country in Europe is preeminent in these respects? To what is Britain in some degree indebted for her proud position? What does Emerson say of the effects of its climate? Mention some of the anomalies which he points out.

北温带地区是世界的工厂。在寒带和热带，大自然的特征是如此显著。在寒带地区，她依靠她的贫瘠，打败了人类的劳动；而在热带地区，因为自然的富饶，她又让人类的劳动变得根本不必要。但地球上温带地区的主要特点却是人类的至高无上。这里存在着整个人类的四分之三。在这里，文明最为高度发达；而历史上所发生的伟大事件，无论是在古代还是在现代，也都多发生在这里。

从很大程度上，这里的活动和变化也受到气候的影响。在温带地区的气候中，盖约特说："冷热的交替，季节的变化，一种更清新、凉爽的空气，激励这里的人们进行不断的斗争，同时深谋远虑，也更积极地发挥他们的才能。这里的大自然更节俭，不会为人类创造任何收益，而只会让人们抛洒眉头的汗水；每一种人类的天赋，都是一种为弥补自然的不足而做出的努力。这里的大自然，即使在挑战着人类，也同样带给了他胜利的希望，即使它不主动提供物品，它也资助了人类主动的、智能化的劳动，而不是提供给他所需要的必需品。当它呼唤人类的能量，它就会让他变得轻松自在，这允许他培养了位于他之上的大自然所有崇高的能力。在这里，大自然并不是一个暴君，而是一个有用的帮助者，活跃的能力、理解和推理，统治了人类的本能和被动的能力；灵魂统治了身体，人统治了自然。"

"在寒冷的地区，人类还与自然相斗争，但那里的自然是如此的吝啬和恶劣，那是一种绝望的挣扎——为生活而挣扎。面临困难，迫于辛劳，他成功地为自己赢得了悲惨的支持，从而免于在单调的寒冬气候中死于饥饿和苦难。高度的文明，在这种不利的条件中是不可能存在的。"

另一方面，热带地区热量的过剩也削弱了人类的力量。它邀请人类休息和无为。这里不仅拥有蔬菜王国和低等动物生命的最高层次，热带地区的人类同样也进化得最为发达。在这里，人类的躯体控制着灵魂。人类生理的本能使他们更高层次的才能黯然失色，激情支配了智慧和理智，被动的能力超越了主动的能力。

"自然太丰富，太过于挥霍自己给人类的礼物，就不会迫使人类为了每天得到面包而辛苦劳作。一种规律的气候，没有休眠期，就不会让深思熟虑对人类有所用途。这样，就不会有什么事物能让人类用自己的智慧，同超越他们的能量相抗衡。因此，他们从来不会梦想着他们会摆脱掉这种自然，他们被大自然征服了，他们屈服于这种枷锁，而又一次变得像动物一样，他们将自己放逐于外部的影响之中，而遗忘了自己更高尚的道德目标。"

因此，温带地区的气候是最有利于发展人类的智力和生理强度的。它也同样最适宜于这里大自然所创造出的动物和植物，来满足人类的大量需求。因此牛和羊——对人类最有用的反刍动物在温带地区变得很常见，非常广泛地散布于此，数量巨大。以亚洲中部为故乡的马——不论是在战争中还是在和平时代，在人类的娱乐活动中还是在辛勤的劳作中，马是人类在任何事业中都不可缺少的盟友——已经遍布了全球。同样，那些长有羽毛的鸟类禽类族群，也丰富地存在于这些地区，同样成为一些国家人们的主要食品。

现在我们来到植物王国，我们会发现玉米——这是最适合于文明人类的一种食品——广泛地分布在温带地区。只有当人类在一个固定的住处安顿下来——当他放弃了他的游牧生活，成为一个农民，把自己固定在某个地方，那他才有可能来种植玉米。玉米通常是不能像野草一样自己生长、自己扩散、自己播种的，没有人类的培育，它会逐渐减少，最后消失不见。"它只能由人类的手亲自长期播种，并且是在人类已经耕种过的土地上。"

因此，一个伟大的德国植物学家说，玉米超越了之前所有的文明。它与休养、和平和家庭的幸福紧密相连，而流浪的野蛮人对此却一无所知。为了培育它，国家必须拥有一定的土地；而当它的存在因此变得稳定时，方法和风俗的改进就会快速跟上。他们不再倾向于血腥的战争，而只为了保卫从中可以获得粮食的土地而参与战斗。

在一个社会之中，玉米是对人类来说最方便、最适合的食物。只有通过人类对玉米的精心培育，一个国家才能永久地支撑密集的人口。所有其他种类的食物都是不稳定的，并且不能被长期储存，它们的根和果实很快就会枯竭；它们的产量也是不确定的，如果很难生产，就会停止供应。在一些国家，西谷椰子、面包树的果实，还有一些可食的植物的根部以及一些类似的食物，由大自然自发地供给人类，有助于保持稀疏的、容易满足的人口；但在这种粗鲁的环境中，人类的身体和头脑都如此发展滞后，他们也很难改善自身的状况。然而，玉米的种植，虽然能够向人类在一年中的更多时候提供更大部分的食物，却强加给他们一定的劳动和约束，这对他们的性格和习惯都有极其有益的影响。

这里也产生了一些具有温带地区特色的植物。不会在炎热气候中生长的小麦在整个温带气候中蓬勃繁殖，甚至可以生长在不同的海拔高度范围内。玉米广泛分布在北美以及欧洲南部。大麦种植在欧洲和亚洲那些气候和土壤条件都不适合种植小麦的地区；而燕麦和黑麦则延伸到荒凉的北方，只有当我们到达荒凉的北极地区时，在那里，人类不可能再拥有自己的社会能力，它们才会逐渐消失。根据气候的渐变和土壤的不同种类，通过这样让人类惊人地适应了不同品种的粮食，上帝向人类提供了他们生存所不可或缺的食物。

那么，在这样高度发达的文明之中，对人类最有用的树是什么？毫无疑问，是那些提供常见木材的最大供给的树木。现在主要的花式木材的树木——那些作为人类的奢侈品出现的树木——属于热带；但松树和硬木树——那些供应了人类必需品的树木——明显属于温带。这一区域的居民，必须将这些树木运到洪都拉斯或巴西，来打磨红木，做成更精细的家具；但是松树、白蜡树、橡树、榆树、白桦——

这些用于建造房子和商店的木材，这些用于制作工具和车辆的木材，这些用于制作最复杂的机械的木材——却大量生长在温带的森林中。这些树木，与这里的人类一样，在同样的气候之中培育，也呼吸着同样的空气。

土壤之上的植物世界的现象，也同样存在于土壤之下的矿物世界。所有对人类最有用的金属，家庭事务和工业都会用到的铁、锡、铜、铅，都在温带区域内大量发现。同样，煤也在温带地区最为丰富。如果没有这些矿石，冶炼就不能盈利或拥有足够的供应量，它同时也是所有制造业的主要原动力。

但在温带地区内部，也存在很明显的差异。这都是由气候和形态的差异造成的。例如，中亚地区——事实上，位于高加索、喜马拉雅和中国山脉北部的整个亚洲——由贫瘠的草原组成，而现在，像六个世纪之前一样，这里是野蛮人和掠夺者的故乡。而这是为什么呢？因为它的内陆沙漠远离大海的影响；因为高耸的山脉赋予了其大部分北方土地的特征；因为它的河流，要么流到没有出口的盐湖之中，要么流入到一片完全不可能从事商务活动的冰冻的海洋之中。

另一方面，我们来看看欧洲。在所有大洲之中，这是一块最彻底地被海洋的支流打破的陆地。亚洲的陆地面积是欧洲的4.5倍大；然而，欧洲的海岸线却是亚洲的五倍。除了俄罗斯的平原地区，欧洲的其他部分距离大海都不超过三百英里；在欧洲可通航河流的数量和分布情况，使即使位于它最偏远地区的人们都可以接触到海洋。

这样的结果是什么？在欧洲地图上的一瞥就会告诉我们答案。欧洲显然是一片最密集地覆盖了城市和乡镇的大陆；而高速公路、运河和铁路，将这里的城镇编织成一张鲜活而一直繁忙的网络。在那里，文明根深蒂固，枝繁叶茂。在那里，艺术和科学都得到了最高层次的发展。在那里，伟大机械的发明使整个世界变成了一个巨大的相互依赖的社会；商业、制造业、农业也都得到了最长足的进步和发展。

欧洲向全世界贡献了它所需的供应。作为回报，全世界都有责任向它提供更超脱但也同样真实的利益。它成为自由机制的摇篮，它培育了人类作为一个社会成员所需的自控力和独立性。这里拥有全世界最丰富、最多样的文学创作。在欧洲，基督教已得到了最广泛的扩散，而这里作为中心，向世界上甚至最遥远的角落也发出了自由的信息。

对于整个欧洲来说成立的现实，在大英帝国也是绝对成立的。这里，是整个欧洲文明和工业的中心。通过它的殖民地，它将她国家的精神和它子民的能量在全世界扩散开来。所以在物质进步和社会进步方面，它最大的竞争对手就是它自己的孩子。

这一片如此狭小的土地却拥有一种如此令人骄傲的地位。虽然当出现在世界地图上时，英伦三岛是如此微不足道。在很大程度上，英国实现的伟业受惠于自身的气候、自然形态和地理位置。

　　"英国的领土，"爱默生说，"有一个奇异的完美之处。这里的气候比该纬度应该有的温度要高出许多度。既不冷也不热，在整整一年的时间里，甚至没有一个小时，会妨碍一个人工作。这里的温度对人类工作的强度不会提出苛求，却允许人类获得最大的成就。在地表的多样性上，它是整个欧洲的一个缩影，这里有平原、森林、湿地、河流和海岸。从第一个到最后一个，简直就是一个奇异的博物馆。这个多雾多雨的国家给世界带来了各种景观。短小的河流提供不了水力，但这片土地却在磨坊之下震动。这里没有任何重要的金矿，但英国却拥有比其他国家都更多的黄金。这里与葡萄酒文化相距甚远，但所有国家的葡萄酒都堆积在英国的码头之上；橘子和菠萝在伦敦和在地中海一样便宜。"

Lesson 29   THE OVERLAND ROUTE
第二十九课　陆　路

(*To be read before a Map of the Eastern Hemisphere*)

Embarking at Southampton in one of the splendid steamers of the Peninsular and Oriental Company, we soon pass the Isle of Wight, and make for the open sea. The second day brings us in contact with the rough waters of the Bay of Biscay. The Spanish coast is probably sighted off Cape Finisterre; and here the Englishman begins to recall with patriotic pride the many triumphs achieved by his countrymen on the Peninsula and in the surrounding waters. Here, in 1805, Sir Robert Calder inflicted a partial defeat on Villeneuve, the French admiral; who, a few months later, was completely overthrown at Trafalgar. Corunna is not far off, where Moore so gallantly held the French at bay till he completed his plans for embarkation.

At the south-western angle of Portugal we are off Cape St. Vincent—a lone, romantic promontory, with some fractured rocks at its base standing out into the ocean, and having on its summit a fine light-house with a brilliant light revolving every two or three minutes. The cape was the scene of two great victories gained by the English fleet over that of Spain; in connection with the second of which it gave his title to one of England's foremost sailors. There the Spaniards were defeated by Sir George Rodney in 1780, and still more signally by Sir John Jervis (afterwards Earl St. Vincent) in 1793. It was on the latter occasion that Nelson, then bearing the rank of commodore, took one of the Spanish ships, the *San Nicolas*, by entering through its cabin windows! Seeing this, the captain of the *San Josef* discharged a volley on the captors. Nelson thereupon closed with the *San Josef* and boarded her from the deck of the *San Nicolas*.

Ere long we discern the promontory of Trafalgar stretching into the Atlantic—a spot hallowed by what, in the estimation of Englishmen, is certainly the most of all the events which have made this corner of Europe famous in ancient and in modern story.

On the south, the lonely headland of Cape Spartel rises from the African coast above the Atlantic waters; and to the east of it may be seen the white buildings of Tangier, a city of Phoenician origin, and of note in the times of the Romans. Seized in 1457 by the Portuguese, Tangier was by them ceded to England in 1662, along with Bombay, as part of the dower of Catherine of Braganza, when she became queen of Charles II. It proved so useless and so expensive a possession, however, owing to the constant attacks of the Moons, that it was very soon abandoned to them, and they at once set about repairing the costly works which the English had dismantled at their departure. In this region, according to ancient fable, the Hesperides—daughters of the evening star—had their famous gardens, whose golden apples Hercules ruthlessly carried off.

We are now fairly within the renowned strait which was regarded by the ancients with so much awe as the remote boundary of their world, beyond which all was mystery and fable. On our left are the green hills of Spain, swelling into lofty mountains not far from the shore, with here and there a white village or a picturesque watch-tower. By-and-by we get a glimpse of the mouldering and forlorn ramparts of Tarifa, the most thoroughly Moorish town in Spain, and the most southern in Europe. From this point the Vandals were driven across to Africa by the Goths in 417 A. D. At this point Tarif, a great Moorish general, after whom Tarifa is named, landed with his army in 711, when he came to conquer the Goths and establish the Moorish kingdom in Spain. Here, finally, Alfonzo XI. overthrew the Moors in a decisive action in 1340. Tarifa is a quaint old town, with its island fortress and lighthouse—fitting memento of the fierce struggles in which the inhabitants of the opposing shores engaged.

In a few hours we reach the grand fortress of Gibraltar, which keeps stern watch at the gates of the Mediterranean, and forms with the Rock of Ceuta, on the African side, the famous "Pillars of Hercules." Nothing could well be more imposing than the view of Gibraltar from the bay on its western side. Ranges of batteries rising from the shore, tier above tier, extend along its entire sea-front. At the northern extremity is the town. Every nook in the crags bristles with artillery. White barracks and gay villas, embowered in gardens and groves, occupy the midway ascent. Above all towers in rugged grandeur the summit of the Rock itself.

No less striking is the contrast which presents itself when we have doubled Europe Point, and look back to the eastern side of the Rock from the bosom of the Mediterranean. The scene which we have quitted was one of busy excitement and varied life. Now one long unbroken precipice, 1400 feet in height, towers above us. There are few signs of vegetation, and none of human habitation, save only the little village of white houses in Catalan Bay, which crouches at the foot of the Rock, as if in constant dread of being crushed by the overhanging masses.

Off Cape do Gata, the south-eastern headland of Spain—infamous to the mariner for the squalls that come suddenly down from its lofty crest—we get our last glimpse of the Peninsula, and of its brown, stern, and rugged mountains. As we skirt the African coast we discover the whereabouts of Algiers, now a French colony; then of Tunis, near which is the site of ancient Carthage, so long the rival of Rome for the supremacy of the world.

Our next stoppage is at Valetta, the port and capital of Malta, where the Knights of St. John triumphed so heroically over the infidel Turk in the sixteenth century. This, like Gibraltar, is now a British possession—one of the ocean towers which emphatically mark England's empire of the seas.

Our next port is Alexandria. The castle of Farillon, which serves as our land-mark in approaching the town, occupies the site of the famous Pharos of antiquity. A few miles eastward from it is Aboukir Bay, where Nelson annihilated the French fleet in 1798, and shut up Buonaparte's army in Egypt. Here the literally overland part of our route commences. From Alexandria we proceed by rail to Suez, taking Cairo on our way. Travellers hastening to India have to content themselves with a passing glimpse of Cleopatra's Needles and Pompey's Pillar at the first of these cities, and of the Pyramids in the vicinity of the last.

By the opening of the Suez Cana the only truly overland part of the Overland Route has been dispensed with, and steamers from Southampton reach India direct by way of the Mediterranean and the Red Sea. At first only private vessels, specially adapted to the dimensions of the canal, and carrying both merchandise and passengers, performed the voyage without break. The adoption of the same course by the mail steamers was only a question of time, and is now universal.

The Suez Canal is certainly one of the greatest triumphs of modern engineering. Yet it is only an improvement on a much earlier plan; for it is well known that in the fifth century before the Christian era, an indirect line of canal connected the two seas, the Mediterranean and the Red Sea. It began at about a mile and a half north of Suez, and struck in a north-westerly direction, availing itself of a series of natural hollows, to a point on the eastern branch of the Nile. By-and-by it became silted up; and after having been several times restored, it was finally filled with the never-resting sands in 767 A. D.

Upwards of ten centuries passed before any attempt was made to renew communication between the two seas. Then the idea occurred to the ingenious mind of Buonaparte; but as his engineers erroneously reported that there was a difference of level between the Mediterranean and the Red Sea to the extent of thirty feet, he suffered it to drop. In 1847 a scientific commission, appointed by England, France, and Austria, ascertained that the two seas had exactly the same mean level; and in 1854 Ferdinand de Lesseps, an ingenious and enterprising Frenchman, obtained permission from the Viceroy of Egypt to make a canal across the isthmus. It was not, however, until 1858 that de Lesseps found himself in a position to appeal to the public for support. A company was then formed, and the canal was proceeded with; a variety of ingenious machinery being invented by the French engineers to meet the exigencies of their novel and magnificent enterprise. On the 17th of November 1869 it was formally opened for navigation, in the presence of a host of illustrious personages, representing every European State.

"As we went along the Canal," says Dr. Carpenter, describing a visit to Egypt, "we passed between mounds or banks, higher than the ordinary level. These banks were composed of material which had been excavated from the Canal, and thrown up on either side. As we steamed along very slowly, I mounted the 'bridge' of the steamer, so as to be able to look over these banks; and there I saw the interminable barren waste on the Egyptian side covered with water, and on the eastern side a sandy desert extending to Palestine.

"One of the first features of interest Was a 'floating bridge,' thrown across the

Canal by steam, at a point which, I was told, was in the track of the caravans. Now here was a most curious conjuncture of modern and ancient civilisation. This caravan track is one of the most ancient of all roads, leading from Egypt into Palestine and Syria, on the very line along which Jacob's sons may have gone down into Egypt to buy corn; and there we found one of the appliances of modem civilisation, in the shape of this 'floating bridge,' consisting of a large Hat-bottomed boat which crosses and recrosses the Canal by means of chains wound and unwound upon large drums by a steam engine. This contact of ancient and modern civilisation is one of the most remarkable features in Egypt.

"But there was another noticeable feature. There are stations all along the Canal, at which the officers reside, as well as the men who keep watch over the Canal, and who are ready to give help if any vessel should run aground. At most of these stations I noticed that there was a garden, generally with a gay show of flowers, and great cultivation of edible vegetables. Now what was the meaning of this? How could these gardens be made out of this sand and mud? The secret is, that every one of these places is supplied with fresh water.

"That fresh water is brought all the way from the Nile; for there is no fresh water to be got between Port Said and Suez—nothing but brackish water, obtained by digging. A *fresh-water canal* was therefore cut from the Nile at Cairo to Ismalia, a sort of half-way house between Suez and Port Said. Pipes convey this water to the railway which runs from Cairo to Suez by way of Ismalia. By this means a supply of wholesome water is conveyed regularly to all parts of the Canal, and flowers of every kind can be grown, nothing being wanted for the soil in that sunny clime but water. At Ismalia the head engineer has a villa with the most beautiful plants of all kinds, those of tropical as well as of temperate climes growing luxuriantly in his garden."

Before the establishment of the Overland Route, Suez, though a place of considerable transit trade between Egypt and the East, was a small, ill-built, wretched-looking town. Since that time it has been much improved, and has become the residence of many merchants and agents. The country around it is desert, and provisions and water have to be brought from great distances.

Reembarking at Suez, we pass down the gulf of the same name, which is the western of the two arms at the head of the Red Sea. The Gulf of Suez is 190 miles in length; and near the head of it is believed by many to be the place at which the Israelites crossed the Red Sea in their exodus from Egypt. As, however, the gulf is known to have receded many miles from its ancient head, even since the Christian era, it is more probable that the scene of the passage is now in the sandy waste of the isthmus.

The eastern arm of the Red Sea is the Gulf of Akaba, which is 100 miles in length. On the triangular tongue of land between the two gulfs are the mountains of Horeb-Sinai, in whose midst there appeared to Moses " an angel of the Lord in a flame of fire in a bush;" and on whose "secret top" he received from God the " lively oracles " to give to the people.

Bird's Eye View of the Suez Canal

Half way down the Red Sea, the navigation of which is rendered difficult by sudden changes of wind and heavy gales, we reach Jedda, one of the most active sea-ports in Arabia. Here thousands of pilgrims land every year on their way to Mecca, the birth-place of Mohammed and the cradle of the Mussulman faith. Near the southern extremity of the sea, on the margin of a sandy plain on the Arabian coast, is Mocha, a fortified sea-port, from which thousands of tons of the finest coffee are annually exported. Passing through the Straits of Bab-elmandeb, we reach Aden, where the sign-board of "the Prince of Wales Hotel" reminds us that we are once more in a British possession. Like Gibraltar and Valetta, Aden is considered an impregnable fortress. Like Gibraltar, too, it stands on a rocky peninsula, connected with the mainland by a narrow isthmus. Its harbour is the best in Arabia; and the town abounds in mosques and Mohammedan remains, which testify to its former magnificence. From Aden we steam through the Gulf of Aden and across the Arabian Sea; and before many days pass we are at anchor in the spacious harbour of Bombay.

Words

abandoned, *given up*.

achieved, *obtained*.

annihilated, *reduced to nothing*.

availing, *taking advantage*.

dismantled, *destroyed*.

dispensed, *departed (from)*.

embarkation, *going aboard ship*.

embowered, *sheltered by trees*.

emphatically, *forcibly*.

enterprising, *adventurous*.

erroneously, *mistakenly*.

excitement, *activity*.

exigencies, *requirements*.

exodus, *journey out*.

expensive, *costly*.

fortified, *defended by forts*.

glimpse, *view*.

habitation, *dwelling*.

illustrious, *distinguished*.

imposing, *majestic*.

impregnable, *not to be taken*.

ingenious, *skilful*.

magnificence, *grandeur*.

memento, *memorial*.

memorable, *worthy of remembrance*.

mystery, *a profound secret*.

navigation, *ship-steering*.

picturesque, *striking*.

promontory, *headland.*   spacious, *roomy.*
residence, *place of abode.*   supremacy, *lordship.*
ruthlessly, *pitilessly.*   surrounding, *encompassing.*
signally, *decisively.*   triangular, *three-sided.*
silted, *filled with sand.*   vicinity, *neighbourhood.*

Questions

Where do the steamers in connection with the Overland Route sail from? Where is the Spanish coast sighted? What does an Englishman then recall? What battle-field is not far off? For what two events is Cape St. Vincent famous? Who was Earl St. Vincent? What feat did Nelson perform at the second battle of St. Vincent? What is, to an Englishman, the most hallowed spot in that corner of Europe? Why? What African city now comes in sight? Near what cape? When was Tangier ceded to England? Why was it abandoned? What fabled region is in the same neighbourhood? What strait is now entered? What town is by-and-by seen? What is remarkable in its position? With what historical events is it connected? What rock on the African shore is opposite Gibraltar? What do they together form? What is the appearance of Gibraltar from the bay? What contrast is presented by its eastern side? Where do we get our last glimpse of the Peninsula? What places of interest do we pass on the African coast? Where is our next top page? For what is Valetta famous? Where do we next proceed? What serves as our land mark in approaching the town? What battle was fought a few miles to the east? Name the places of interest passed between Southampton and Alexandria. How do we reach Suez? What city do we take in our way? What objects of interest are to be seen near Alexandria, and in the vicinity of Cairo? How are the Mediterranean and the Red Sea now connected? What effect is the canal likely to have on the Overland Route? What do you know of an ancient canal there? Who was the engineer of the modern canal? When was it opened? What effect has the Overland Route had on Suez? What interesting events took place near the head of the Red Sea? For what is Jedda interesting? What other Arab town do we pass? Where do we next stop? How are we reminded that it is a British possession? What is its character as a fortress? What remains maybe seen there? Name the places of interest between Alexandria and Bombay.

☆ ☆

（请参照东半球的地图阅读此文）

我们乘坐着由东方半岛公司生产的豪华蒸汽船自南安普顿港出发，很快，我们经过了怀特岛，然后向波涛汹涌的大海进发。第二天我们见识到了比斯开湾的汹涌浪涛。从船上远望向菲尼斯特雷岬角，那里便是西班牙海岸。而在船内，我们这些英国人开始回忆我们的同胞曾在这片半岛和波涛中所成就的伟业。在这里，1805

年，罗伯特·考尔德爵士挫败了法国的海军上将维尔纳夫，而这位上将在几个月之后，就在特拉法加被彻底打倒。克罗纳离这里也不远了，而正是在这里，摩尔在如此英勇地完成了登陆计划之后，荣享法兰西。

于葡萄牙的西南角向远处望，便可看见圣文森特角，这是一个浪漫的、孤立的海角，海角的基石上有一些断裂的石头，石滩向外延伸到海里，石滩的顶部有一处灯塔，灯塔上的明灯每隔两到三分钟就会旋转。而这个海角，是英国舰队两次大胜西班牙舰队的遗址所在。英格兰最著名的水手被授予其称号就与第二次战役有关。1780年，罗德尼爵士在那里挫败了西班牙人，而后，1793年，杰维斯爵士（后来是圣文森特伯爵）又一次重挫了西班牙人。后来，海军准将纳尔逊，从西班牙航船圣·尼古拉斯号的小窗子进入，驾驶着它出发了。看到这些，圣·约瑟夫号的船长鸣放出一连串的炮弹。于是纳尔逊接近了圣·约瑟夫号，并且从圣·尼古拉斯号的甲板上登上了它。

不久，我们就会见到向大西洋延伸的特拉法尔加海角，这里在英国人看来是一个非常神圣的地方。在这里发生过许多最值得纪念的事件，正是它们使得这个欧洲的小角落闻名于古今。

往南边，斯帕特尔角从位于大西洋的非洲海岸显现出来，在它的东边，你会看到丹吉尔的白色建筑，丹吉尔是腓尼基人的发源地，在罗马时代就非常知名。1457年，丹吉尔被葡萄牙人控制，最后，又于1662年同孟买一起臣服于英格兰，而这一切，都是作为布拉甘萨的凯瑟琳嫁给查尔斯二世的嫁妆。事实上，这后来被证明是无用且昂贵的陪嫁，因为非洲摩尔人连年的袭扰，这座城市很快就被英国遗弃给摩尔人，摩尔人随即开始修缮那些英国人离开时毁坏的工事。根据这一地区一则关于黄昏之星赫斯帕里得斯的古老寓言所讲，在他的金苹果园里，他的金苹果被大力士无情地摘走了。

我们现在恰好位于著名的海峡上，这里曾被祖先们所敬畏，他们认为这里是世界的尽头，在这以外，到处都是虚无缥缈的。在我们左边是西班牙葱绿的小山丘，渐向远方变成离岸不远的高大山岭，山岭上到处是白色的小村庄和别致的观景台。逐渐靠近之后，我们瞥见了崩塌的、被遗弃的塔里法壁垒阵，这座壁垒阵是西班牙最具摩尔风情的小镇，也是欧洲最南部的小镇。从那里开始，汪达尔人于公元417年被哥特人横追到了非洲。这时，一个伟大的摩尔将领塔里夫，率领军队于711年开赴这里，打败了哥特人，在西班牙建立了摩尔王国。塔利法这个城市就是以他的名字命名的。最后，阿方索四世于1340年在这里以决定性的胜利推翻了摩尔年代。塔利法是一座古色古香的老城，它的岛屿要塞和灯塔，都能使人想起那些激烈的战斗，而这些战斗牵连了对岸的居民。

几个小时后，我们抵达了直布罗陀的宏伟堡垒，这座堡垒由休达山组成，严格地监控着地中海的门户。在它面向非洲的部分，便是著名的赫丘利斯之柱。没有什么景象比从西海岸看到的直布罗陀海峡更宏伟，一排排山峦、高物从海岸上升起，层层叠叠，沿海岸线伸向远方，在北边的尽头便是城镇。峭壁的每一个角落都直立着大炮。白色的兵营和美丽的别墅坐落在花园里，被树叶遮蔽着，占据着半坡的位置。休达山崎岖的山峰矗立在这一切之上，异常壮丽。

当我们再次到达欧洲之角，而从地中海回望休达山时，它所呈现出的这种对比也同样引人注目。我们已经远离那些忙碌、多变而振奋人心的生活。现在，一处未破损的悬崖，足有1 400英尺高，高悬于我们头顶。这里几乎没有植物的迹象，也没有人类居住，只生存着那些曾居住在加泰罗尼亚海湾村庄的人。这些村庄卧在休达山的山脚之下，仿佛害怕被那些突出的大怪物压碎似的。

西班牙西南面的加塔角，因从高处突然袭来的暴风而对水手们来说异常声名狼藉。我们最后瞥了一眼这处半岛，望见了它那粗壮而崎岖的褐色山脉。当我们沿海岸边缘走过，我们看到了阿尔及尔的踪迹，它现在是法国殖民地。然后是突尼斯，在它附近便是古老的迦太基的遗址，在很长一段时间内，迦太基都在和罗马争夺世界霸权。

我们的下一站是马耳他的重要港口和首都瓦莱塔，圣约翰爵士曾经在16世纪在这里英勇地战胜了土耳其的异教徒。而这里同直布罗陀海峡一样是英国人的领地，是英国海上霸权的坚固城墙之一。

我们下一个停靠的港口是亚历山大港。法利兰城堡是接近这座城镇的地标和指引，在这里坐落着著名的古老灯塔。再向东几英里便是阿布基尔海湾，1798年，纳尔逊在这个海湾消灭了法国舰队，并且在埃及阻断了波拿巴的军队。由此，我们开始了陆地上的行程。从亚历山大港出发，我们乘坐火车向苏伊士进发，途中经过了开罗。游客们急速向印度前进，切不可忘记大饱眼福，在途中首先会经过克娄巴特拉方尖碑和庞贝柱，然后会看到附近的埃及金字塔。苏伊士运河开放后，我们此行真正的陆上行程便开始了。我们的蒸汽船从南安普顿港出发，经由地中海和红海终于到达了印度。最初只有私人船只游走于此条航线中，他们都是依据运河的规模特定的，装载着货物和乘客，顺利地完成了无故障的航行。现在该类船只已经相当普及应用了。

苏伊士运河的确是现代工程中的伟大胜利，然而，这个胜利仅仅是相对于早些时候一条河渠的改进。因为我们都知道，基督纪元前的第五个世纪，一条迂回的运河将地中海和红海连接起来。这条运河自苏伊士北边1.5英里开始，然后转向西北方向，在这个过程中产生了自然的凹陷，进而转向尼罗河东部的分支。日久天长，泥沙淤积，在经过几次修复之后，在公元767年，它最终被无休止的泥沙填满。

随后的10个世纪，两大海域都没有互相联系的可能。直到波拿巴独创性地想到了海域的互联，但是他的工程师错误地报告称，地中海和红海之间有30英尺的海平面差，所以波拿巴不得不放弃了互联的计划。在1847年，一个由英、法、奥地利派出的科学使团证实两大海域的海平面高度是相同的。随后在1854年，斐迪南·德·雷赛布，一位富有创新精神和开拓精神的法国人，被埃及总督授权在地峡之间开凿一条运河。然而，直到1858年，德·雷赛布才意识到他还需要呼吁公众的支持。随后，他成立了一家公司，运河工程得以继续，法国工程师发明了大量独具创意的机器，来满足这项浩大工程中独特而巨大的需求。1860年的11月17日，该运河正式通行用以航运，它以主人的姿态出现，迎接着代表欧洲各国的要人。

卡朋特博士这样形容一次到埃及的旅行，他说："当我们沿着运河前行的时候，我们在土丘和水岸当中经过，位置高于平均海拔，这些水岸由运河里的泥沙构成，这些泥沙由河底挖出，被堆放到河的两岸。当蒸汽船缓缓前进时，我登上了船桥以观看这些海岸的全貌，我看到了埃及那边无尽的贫瘠荒滩被水所覆盖，而在东边，一处沙漠一直延伸到巴勒斯坦。"

首先使我感兴趣的点源自于一座浮桥，这座浮桥被蒸汽船横抛在运河之中。这个地方，我从别人口中得知正好位于旧时的大篷车的轨道上。现在，这里是古今文明交汇的地方。这条大篷车道路是所有道路里最古老的，从埃及一直延伸到巴勒斯坦和叙利亚，雅各布的儿子正是通过这条路来到埃及买玉米。此外，我们还在这里发现了来自现代文明的电器工具，以浮桥的形态出现，由一艘船组成，这艘船的链条或缠绕或松散地搭在一座大鼓上。这种古今文明互联的特征是埃及最大的特点之一。

但是，这里还有另一个突出的特点。运河沿岸有很多站点，这些站点里居住着军官和那些监测运河状况的人以及那些随时准备救援搁浅船只的人。站在站点的桅杆旁可以看到一个花园，令人愉悦。这里面有很多花和培育良好的食用蔬菜。那这些东西意味着什么呢？它们是如何在泥沙中生长的呢？秘密就是，这里的每一个人都享有淡水供给。

这些淡水都是从尼罗河全程运来的，因为在塞得港和苏伊士之间除了打井挖掘出来的盐水以外是没有淡水的。因此，一条运送淡水的运河就从开罗的尼罗河挖到了伊斯梅里亚。伊斯梅里亚可以看作是苏伊士和塞得港之间的中转站，管道将淡水运到那些从开罗经由伊斯梅里亚到苏伊士的列车上去。通过这种供应方法，健康纯净的淡水被运送到运河沿岸的每一个地方，如此一来，各种花儿得以欣欣向荣。要知道，在阳光充足的气候下，没有什么是比淡水更稀缺的东西了。在伊斯梅里亚，总工程师有一栋别墅，那里长满了各式各样美丽的植物，既包括热带也包括温带的丰富物种。

在这条通道建立之前，苏伊士尽管是埃及和东方之间的贸易重地，但是仍旧是一个小小的、残破的、其貌不扬的小城镇。自运河建成以来，这座小镇的环境大为改善，逐渐变成了商贾云集、商铺林立的地方。它周围的地区满是沙漠，食品补给和水源必须从很远的地方运过来。

从苏伊士运河重新出发，我们经过同名的苏伊士海湾。这处海湾是红海前端两翼当中的西侧部分。苏伊士海湾共有190英里长，在其前端附近的位置在很多人看来是以色列人出逃埃及跨越红海的地方所在。然而，众所周知的是，随着海湾在原有基础上后退，甚至从基督纪元时期就是如此，因此，那些在古书上出现的场景很有可能已经埋在地峡的沙子里了。

红海的西翼便是阿克巴海湾，这处海湾有100英里长，在这两处海湾之间的便是摩西山。就是在这里，上帝的使者在圣光中出现在摩西面前，而摩西从中收到了上帝的圣谕并将它传递给人们。

由于突如其来的狂风在红海中继续航行，变得异常艰难。我们到达吉达，这里是阿拉伯最活跃的海港之一。每年都有成千上万的朝圣者经由此地前往麦加——穆罕默德的出生地以及伊斯兰教的发源地。在这片海域的最南端，在阿拉伯海岸一片沙滩平原的边缘，就是一处强化防御的港口穆哈，每年都有成千上万吨的上好咖啡从这里出口海外。而后穿过曼德海峡，我们到达亚丁，这里的王子酒店的招牌又一次提示我们，我们又一次来到英国的属地。像直布罗陀和瓦莱塔一样，亚丁被认为是不可攻取的堡垒。和直布罗陀一样，它建立在岩质的半岛上，由一道狭窄的地峡与大陆相连。这处港口是阿拉伯最好的港口，这里的城镇拥有大量清真寺和伊斯兰教遗址，这都是其宏伟往昔的标志。从亚丁出发，我们经过亚丁湾，穿过阿拉伯海，几天之后，我们终于可以在广阔的孟买港抛锚了。

Lesson 30   CAIRO AND THE PYRAMIDS
第三十课　开罗和金字塔

The best view of Cairo and its vicinity is obtained from the Citadel, which commands the whole city. It is thus described by Dean Stanley: "The town is a vast expanse of brown, broken only by occasional interludes of palms and sycamores, and by countless minarets. About half a dozen large buildings, mosques or palaces, also emerge. On each side rise shapeless mounds;—those on the east covered with tents, and, dimly seen beyond, the browner line of the desert; those on the west, the sites of Old Cairo, of the Roman fortress of Babylon, and of Fostat, where Amrou first pitched his tent, deserted since the time of Sal'adin. Beyond is the silver line of the Nile; and then, rising in three successive groups, above the delicate green plain which sweeps along nearly to the foot of the African hills, the Pyramids of Abu'sir, Saka'rah, and Ghi'zeh—these last being '*The Pyramids*', and the nearest. There is something very striking in their total disconnection with Cairo. They stand alone on the edge of that green vale which is Egypt. There is no intermingling, as in ancient and modern Rome. It is as if you looked out on Stonehenge from London, or as if the Colis'um stood far away in the depths of the Campagna. Cairo is not the ghost of the dead Egyptian empire, nor anything like it. Cairo itself leaves a deep feeling, that, whatever there was of greatness or wisdom in those remote ages and those gigantic monuments, is now the inheritance, not of the East, but of the West. The Nile, as it glides between the tombs of the Pharaohs and the city of the Caliphs, is indeed a boundary between two worlds."

The Pyramids stand at the edge of the desert, on the western side of the Nile, but an hour or two's distance from the city. After crossing the ferry, the stranger imagines them close at hand, though he has still a good long mile to traverse. A near view is generally disappointing; and it is not until the visitor begins to make comparisons, that the fact of their exceeding vastness comes home to the mind. The base of the Great Pyramid of Cheops is nearly 800

CAIRO FROF THE CITADEL. (LOOKING WEST)

feet square, covering a surface of eleven acres; and its height is 461 feet, being 117 feet higher than St. Paul's Cathedral. It is a common feat of travellers to ascend, with the aid of a couple of Arab guides, to the summit; which may be reached by an active man in about twenty minutes.

"The view from the top," says Stanley, "has the same vivid contrast of life and death which makes all wide views in Egypt striking—the desert and the green plain: only the view over the desert—the African desert—being much more extensive here than elsewhere, one gathers in better the notion of the wide, heaving ocean of sandy billows, which hovers on the edge of the Valley of the Nile. The white line of the minarets of Cairo is also a peculiar feature—peculiar, because it is strange to see a modern Egyptian city which is a grace instead of a deformity to the view. You see also the strip of desert running into the green plain on the east of the Nile, which marks Heliop'olis and Goshen."

It is said that six million tons of stone were used in the construction of the Great Pyramid, that of Che'ops, and that its erection occupied one hundred thousand men for twenty years! The mass is not solid, but contains a series of chambers, the entrance to which is on the north side. A long, close, and devious passage leads to the Queen's Chamber, 17 feet long by 12 high. From thence another long passage leads to the King's Chamber, 37 feet by 17, and 20 feet high. At one end of this apartment stands a sarcophagus of red granite, in which the monarch of the greatest kingdom of the Earth is supposed to have been laid.

The second Pyramid, that of Chephre'nes, is not much inferior in size to this one, its base being 684 feet, and its height 456; but it is not in such good preservation. Herodotus had asserted that it contained no chambers; but Belzoni effected an entrance to a chamber hewn out of the solid rock. In the sarcophagus he found the bones of an animal, probably the sacred bull of the Egyptians. The third large Pyramid contained a mummy; the remains of which, and of its cedar coffin, were deposited in the British Museum.

There can be no doubt that all of them were designed as receptacles for the dead. Around them lie scattered about, as far as the eye can reach, both up and down the bank of the river, and along the edge of the desert for miles beyond the ruined city of Memphis, numberless edifices and tumuli of a monumental character, some of which were once profusely embellished

THE SPHINXAND THE PYRAMID OF CHEPHRENES

with sculptures, and in which mummies have been found.

In front of the Pyramid of Chephrenes stands the great Sphinx,—the hugest marvel of sculpture which the world has ever seen. For centuries this colossal wonder lay almost submerged beneath the sand-drift of the desert. Caviglia undertook the laborious task of uncovering it; in the course of which he made some important discoveries, tending to show that there was anciently a temple on the area beneath the stony gaze of the colossal countenance, and an altar upon which sacrifices were offered. The features are Nubian, or rather ancient Egyptian, and their expression is strikingly calm and benignant.

"There was something," says Stanley, "stupendous in the sight of that enormous head—its vast projecting wig, its great ears, its open eyes, the red colour still visible on its cheeks, the immense projection of the lower part of its face. Yet what must it have been when on its head there was the royal helmet of Egypt, on its chin the royal beard; when the stone pavement by which man approached the Pyramids ran up between its paws; when immediately under its breast an altar stood, from which the smoke went up into the gigantic nostrils of that nose, now vanished from the face, never to be conceived again! All this is known with certainty from the remains which actually exist deep under the sand on which you stand, as you look up from a distance into the broken but still expressive features."—In regard to the Sphinx we may add, that so continuous is the drift of sand from the desert, that nearly all those portions of the figure which modern investigators have at different times laid bare have been again covered.

—Stanley

Words

apartment, *room*

benignant, *kind.*

construction, *erection.*

countenance, *face.*

deformity, *blemish.*

designed, *intended.*

devious, *winding.*

disconnection, *separation.*

embellished, *ornamented.*

expressive, *intelligent.*

extensive, *wide.*

imagines, *fancies.*

inheritance, *possession.*

interludes, *intervening spaces.*

intermingling, *mixing.*

occasional, *irregular.*

preservation, *keeping; entirety.*

receptacles, *depositories.*

submerged, *buried.*

successive, *in a series.*

surface, *area.*

vanished, *disappeared.*

Questions

Whence is the best view of Cairo and its vicinity obtained? What is the general aspect of the town? What is very striking in the situation of the Pyramids? What is the height of the Great Pyramid? What contrast does the view from the top of it present? How long was it in building? What does it contain? What were found in the chamber of the second Pyramid? For what purpose were the Pyramids designed? What is the Sphinx? Where does it stand?

　　开罗和它周边最美的风景都可以从俯瞰全城的大城堡看到，因此迪恩·斯坦利如此描述："整个城市都布满了棕褐色的残垣断壁和无边无际的尖塔，偶尔穿插一些棕榈树和悬铃木。还有众多高耸的楼房、清真寺、宫殿。城市的周围有许多不成样子的土丘，东边遍布帐篷，一直延伸至沙漠颜色更深的边缘；西边是开罗旧城，有古巴比伦的城堡，阿姆罗曾在这里首次驻扎，但从萨拉丁时代开始就变成了荒漠。这片地域一直延伸至一片碧绿的平原，直到非洲山脉的脚下。这里分布着阿布希尔、撒哈拉和盖茨的金字塔。令人震撼的是，它们与开罗毫无关联。它们孑立在一片丛林茂盛的深谷边缘，而这就是埃及。就像你在伦敦遥望巨石阵，或者站在坎帕尼亚深处遥望罗马斗兽场一样。开罗并非埃及王国的魂灵。开罗本身，不管是对遥远古代先哲的伟大智慧，还是对那些巨大的纪念碑，都存在深刻的情怀。它如今是西方，而非东方的继承者。在法老的陵墓和国王的城市之间蜿蜒的尼罗河，实质上隔开了两个世界。"

　　金字塔位于尼罗河西岸的沙漠边缘，距开罗市有一到两小时的距离。穿过渡口之后，旅行者会以为它近在眼前，但事实是他们还要穿越很远的距离。离近一点，人们一般会更加失望。但直到人们开始做出比较时，他们才真正意识到金字塔巨大无比的事实。胡夫王金字塔接近800平方英尺，占地11英亩。它高达461英尺，甚至比圣保罗大教堂高出117英尺。人们大多在几个阿拉伯向导的帮助下登顶，这需要花费一个身手矫健之人大约20分钟的时间。

　　斯坦利说过："站在金字塔顶部，可以看到壮丽广阔的埃及沙漠和绿洲，生命与死亡的对比是如此生动。在这里俯瞰整个非洲沙漠的景象，比在其他任何地方都更广阔，就像澎湃的沙漠巨浪，盘桓在尼罗河边缘的山谷周围。开罗市中的尖塔形成一条白色的线条，同样也是奇特的景象。因为能够看到繁荣的现代埃及，而不是残垣断壁。在尼罗河东岸，连绵的沙漠演变成绿色的平原。"

　　据说，建造胡夫王金字塔的过程用到了600吨石头，并花费了10万人20年的精力。它并非固若金汤，但却包含了一系列的房间，它们的入口多位于背面。一条漫长、蜿蜒的路通往王后的房间，长17英尺，高12英尺。另一条路通往国王的房间，长37英尺，宽17英尺，高20英尺。在这间房间的一端，立着一具红色花岗岩做的石棺。这个世界最伟大王国的君主应该曾经沉睡在这里。

第二大金字塔，卡夫拉金字塔，不如胡夫王金字塔那么大，占地684平方英尺，高456英尺。它没有胡夫王金字塔保存得那么好。希罗多德声称，这座金字塔没有任何房间。但贝尔颂尼在挖出一块坚硬石头后，发现了通往一个房间的入口。在石棺中，他发现了动物的尸骨，这也许是埃及人的圣牛。第三大金字塔里有一具木乃伊。它的残骸和它存放其中的雪松棺材，如今放置在大英博物馆。

毫无疑问，所有的金字塔都是为了逝去之人而设计的。它们漫布在尼罗河两岸，目光所及之处，沿着沙漠边缘横亘数公里，直到破败的孟菲斯市。在这里，曾经充满了装饰有各种雕塑的建筑物，它们曾那么富有纪念意义。

在卡夫拉金字塔之前，矗立着巨大的狮身人面像斯芬克斯。它是迄今为止世界上最大的大理石雕塑。几个世纪以来，这一巨大的奇迹都几乎淹没在沙漠之下。卡维基利亚负责挖掘它的复杂工程，在此过程中他有了一些重大发现：在这座巨大大理石雕塑之下，曾有一座古代庙宇和一座用于祭祀的圣坛。而它们显示出努比亚特色，而并非属于埃及。它们表现出一种令人震惊的宁静和和蔼。

斯坦利说："看到这个巨大的头颅时，确有一些惊人的东西，比如它巨大的突出的假发，巨大的耳朵，张开的眼睛，面颊上仍然可见的红色，它面部下方的巨大突起。在它头上顶着埃及国王的帽子，在它的下巴上有国王的胡须。它的爪子出现在通往金字塔的石路上。正位于它的胸膛下方，有一处神坛，神坛上的烟雾会直接升到它巨大的鼻孔里。而如今，鼻子却消失不见。人们确信，狮身人面像曾埋藏在它们如今站立的沙子之下，正如你在远方能看到的一样，它虽已残破，但仍表情丰富。"关于斯芬克斯，我们还要说，沙漠中的流沙会一直存在，所以这些现代研究者在不同时期挖掘发现的所有建筑，会再次被淹没。

——斯坦利

Lesson 31　FAMILY WORSHIP
第三十一课　家庭敬拜

The cheerful supper done, wi' serious face,
　　They round the ingle form a circle wide;
The sire turns o'er, wi' patriarchal grace,
　　The big ha'-Bible, once his father's pride:
　　His bonnet reverently is laid aside,
His lyart haffets wearin' thin and bare;
　　Those strains that once did sweet in Zion glide,
He wales a portion with judicious care;
And "Let us worship God," he says, wi' solemn air....

The priest-like father reads the sacred page,
　　How Abraham was the friend of God on high;
Or, Moses bade eternal warfare wage
　　With Amalek's ungracious progeny;
　　Or how the royal bard did groaning lie
Beneath the stroke of Heaven's avenging ire;
　　Or, Job's pathetic plaint and wailing cry;
Or rapt Isaiah's wild, seraphic fire;
Or other holy seers that tune the sacred lyre.

Perhaps the Christian volume is the theme,—
　　How guiltless blood for guilty man was shed;
How he who bore in heaven the second name
　　Had not on earth whereon to lay His head:
　　How his first followers and servants sped;
The precepts sage they wrote to many a land:
　　How he, who lone in Patinos banished,
Saw in the sun a mighty angel stand,
And heard great Babylon's doom pronounced by Heaven's command.

Then kneeling down to heaven's eternal King,
　　The saint, the father, and the husband prays:
Hope "springs exulting on triumphant wing,"
　　That thus they all shall meet in future days;
　　There ever bask in uncreated rays,
No more to sigh, or shed the bitter tear,
　　Together hymning their Creator's praise,

In such society, yet still more dear,
While circling time moves round in an eternal sphere.......

Then homeward all take off their several way;
    The youngling cottagers retire to rest:
The parent pair their secret homage pay,
    And proffer up to Heaven the warm request,
    That he who stills the raven's clamorous nest,
And decks the lily fair in flowery pride,
    Would, in the way His wisdom sees the best,
For them and for their little ones provide;
But chiefly in their hearts with grace divine preside.

—Robert Burns
FROM "THE COTTAR'S SATURDAY NIGHT."

Words

avenging, *retributive.*

circling, *revolting.*

clamorous, *noisy.*

followers, *disciples.*

guiltless, *sinless.*

haffets, *temples; sides of the head.*

homage, *devotion.*

hymning, *singing.*

ingle, *fire-place.*

judicious, *sagacious.*

lyart, *gray.*

pathetic, *touching.*

patriarchal, *paternal.*

precepts, *maxims.*

proffer, *offer.*

progeny, *children.*

pronounced, *proclaimed.*

provide, *furnish the means of life.*

reverently, *devoutly.*

seraphic, *angelic.*

triumphant, *exulting.*

ungracious, *unfriendly.*

wales, *selects.*

wearin, *turning.*

youngling, *very young.*

愉快的晚餐之后，他们表情严肃，

围坐在炉火边，坐成一圈；

男主人转过身来，带着父权的威严，

手中拿着圣经，带着他父亲的骄傲；

他的帽子被恭敬地放在一边，

他灰白色的额头瘦弱、赤裸；

额头上的皱纹，也曾在锡安山泛起，
在庄严的气氛中，他坚定地说道：
"让我们敬拜上帝。"

父亲像神父一样读着圣经上神圣的句子，
亚伯拉罕是如何成为上帝的朋友；
摩西命令臣民与亚玛力人无礼的后代，
进行永恒的战争；
或是皇家吟游诗人呻吟着躺在，
天堂的复仇怒火之中；
还有约伯可悲的感叹和哀号，
以赛亚全身美丽的熊熊大火；
或其他神圣的先知用竖琴奏出的旋律。

也许基督教的神卷正是他们敬拜的主题，
无罪之人的血是怎样为有罪之人而流；
上帝是怎样在天堂中拥有自己的第二个名字，
而在这人世间，他却没有；
他的追随者和仆人是如何前行；
他们为戒律圣人指明了许多土地：
他如何驱逐孤独的人，
看到一个全能的天使站在阳光下，
听到因天堂的指令而毁灭的巴比伦。

然后他们跪拜天堂的永恒之王，
圣人、父亲、丈夫祈祷着：
希望"圣泉插上胜利的翅膀"，
因此他们都将在未来的日子里见面；
在那里，他们将沐浴在永远不会消失的光线之中，
不会再有更多的叹息，或是流下辛酸的眼泪，
他们一起唱起圣歌，赞美造物主，
在这样的社会中，更为亲爱的是，
在一个循环的时间里环绕一颗永恒的星球……

然后他们各自走上回家的道路；
年轻人回到自己的茅舍休息，
家长对他们秘密的敬拜献上贡品，
并向天堂提出了温柔的请求，
照耀在乌鸦喧嚷的巢穴，
和百合花绚丽的骄傲之中，
在此过程中，他会得到最好的智慧，
为了他们自己和他们的孩子；
但重要的是，神圣的威严在他们心中就此驻扎。

——罗伯特·彭斯《佃户家的周六夜晚》

Lesson 32　THE VALLEY OF THE NILE
第三十二课　尼罗河流域

Egypt may be said to owe its very existence as a habitable country to the presence of the Nile. The course of that magnificent river has now been traced to great lakes lying across the Equator, more than two thousand miles south of Alexandria in a direct line. After receiving its two Abyssinian branches, at Khartoum and at Berber in Nubia, it pours the broad, deep volume of its waters through a flat, alluvial valley for fifteen hundred miles without being increased by any other tributary, and finally discharges itself by two principal channels and several minor outlets into the sea.

The whole of the cultivable soil of Egypt, with the exception of the oases of the desert, consists of the meadow-land on either bank of this noble river; and it varies in width from five to one hundred and fifty English miles. It has been renowned for its fertility from the earliest ages, and was long rightly regarded as the granary of the ancient world. Even at the present day its fruitfulness is without a parallel in any region of like extent.

This fruitfulness is consequent upon the periodic inundations of the river. Although there is little no rain in Egypt, there are continuous and heavy rains at the sources of the Nile. These begin to fall in March, and being supplemented by the melting of the mountain snows in the following months, occasion a perceptible rise in the river about the end of June. From this period to the close of September, the rise increases with a regularity almost certain and constant, at a rate of four inches a day.

When the flood is at the highest, the whole valley and delta of the Nile appear as a vast inland sea, dotted with towns and villages, and scattered mounds, barely emerging from the surface. At this season all communication has to be maintained by boats, save where, between places of importance, a few viaducts have been raised. Between September and December the river subsides, and the land is tilled; and by June the harvest has been reaped. But the cultivators of Egypt need not limit their labours to the production of a single crop: in lands advantageously situated as many

Alexandria

as three crops are annually raised by means of artificial irrigation, managed by water-wheels of the simplest construction; the crops being chiefly grain, cotton, and indigo.

Alexandria, the second town of Egypt, and its chief mercantile port, is but a desolate and wretched-looking city, not-withstanding the advantages it has of late years derived from its position in the route of the overland journey to India. The Turkish quarter is yet most filthy and unwholesome, and the mass of the inhabitants are to all appearance plunged in squalor and poverty. This town, which, from its fine harbour, has been termed "The key of Egypt," does not stand on the site of the famous city built by Alexander the Great, which, according to Pliny, was fifteen miles in circuit, and contained three hundred thousand inhabitants. The ancient city, which was burnt to ashes, with its world-renowned library, by the Kaliph Omar, in the year 640, stood to the south of the present Alexandria, on a site which is now covered for the space of six or seven miles in circuit with a confused mass of ruins. Here stands the famous. Pompey's Pillar; and hence it was that many of the spoils which enrich the public places and the museums of European cities were derived.

The English traveller in Egypt is generally willing to get away from Alexandria as soon as he can, and that for sanitary reasons. Cairo is distant some hundred miles, and the route thither lies either along the famous canal made by order of Mehemet Ali in 1819-20, or along the railway, which has brought the city of Saladin within a few hours of the coast.

On approaching Cairo by way of the Nile, the Pyramids are first seen from a point in the river, here about a mile in width, near the separation of the two great branches which form the delta of Lower Egypt, about ninety miles from their outlets at the coast. Standing on the western bank of the river, on a platform elevated some fifty feet above the surrounding level, they form most striking and suggestive objects, even when viewed from a great distance.

In the neighbourhood of the Pyramids are the ruins of Memphis, the ancient capital of Lower Egypt, and the residence of the Pharaohs at the time of the exodus of the Jews. "For miles," says Dean Stanley, "you walk through layers of bones and skulls and mummy swathings, extending from the sand, and deep down in shaft-like mummy-pits; and among these mummy-pits are vast galleries filled with mummies of ibises, in red jars, which are being gradually despoiled. Lastly, there are long galleries, only recently discovered, hewn in the rock, and opening from time to time—say every fifty yards—into high arched vaults, under each of which stands the most magnificent black marble sarcophagus that can be conceived—a chamber rather than a coffin—smooth, and sculptured within and without; grander by far than even the granite sarcophagi of the Theban kings—how much grander than any human sepulchres anywhere else; and all for the successive corpses of the bull Apis!"

Continuing a course against the stream, the traveller passes many interesting scenes,—the great corn tract of Faioum, pits packed with crocodile mummies, rock tombs excavated in the face of the mountains, magnificent ruins and scattered monuments, as at Dendera and Thebes. One hundred miles above Thebes he reaches the first cataract (of which there are seven in all), and the town of Assouan on the borders of Nubia.

The course of the Nile through the territory of Nubia presents considerable modifications in the scenery. For the most part the river is shut in by hills of granite and sandstone. The valley between these is arid, barren, sun-baked. It has the dull, leaden aspect of a desert. A few stunted palms are the only traces of vegetation that the eye can discover. Cultivation is nearly impossible, except here and there within a narrow strip of land on either side of the river. In some parts it is painfully carried on by means of irrigation—the water-wheels being worked by oxen, on whose labours those of the husbandman depend for success.

The traveller now finds himself beyond the domain of history; and though he constantly passes both town and temple in never-ending series, he knows of interest connected with them apart from that which usually attaches to the ruins of the past. He feels now that the Nile itself is the greatest marvel of his journey; which, although rolling along at the distance of eight hundred miles from the sea, has lost nothing of its volume or its majesty.

At this long distance from the coast of the Mediterranean he arrives at Ipsambul, or Abou-Simbel. Here, on the confines of the pathless and unpeopled desert, stands one of Egypt's most striking marvels—the Temple of the Sun, built by Rameses, whose gigantic statue sits there in the solitude, still unbroken, and revealed from head to foot. This statue is repeated four times: two are buried in the sand, and the third is overthrown and in fragments; but from the fourth still looks down the face of the greatest man of the old world, who flourished long before the rise of Greece and Rome—the first conqueror recorded in history—the glory of Egypt, the terror of Asia—the second founder of Thebes, which must have been to the world then what Rome was in the days of her empire.

"The chief thought," says Dean Stanley, "that strikes one at Ipsambul, and elsewhere, is the rapidity of transition in Egyptian worship from the sublime to the

THE NILE IN NUBIA

ridiculous. The gods alternate between the majesty of antediluvian angels and the grotesqueness of pre-Adamite monsters. By what strange contradiction could the same sculptors and worshippers have conceived the grave and awful forms of Ammon and Osiris, and the ludicrous images of gods in all shapes 'in the heavens and in the earth, and in the waters under the earth,' with heads of hawk, and crocodile, and jackal, and ape? What must have been the mind and muscle of a nation who could worship, as at Thebes, in the assemblage of hundreds of colossal Pashts—the sacred cats?

"And again: how extraordinary the contrast of the serenity and the savageness of the kings! Raineses, with his placid smile, grasping the shrieking captives by the hair, is the frontispiece of every temple; and Ammon, with a smile no less placid, is giving him the falchion to smite them. The whole impression is that gods and men alike belong to an age and world entirely passed away, when men were slow to move, slow to think; but that when they did move or think, their work was done with the force and violence of giants. One emblem there is of true monotheism—a thousand times repeated—always impressive and always beautiful—chiefly on the roof and cornice, like the cherubim in the Holy of Holies—the globe with its wide-spread wings of azure blue, of the all-embracing sky: 'Under the shadow of Thy wings shall be my refuge.'"

Beyond Ipsambul, the Nile comes floating, not through mountain passes, but through an absolute desert. The second cataract, by stopping the navigation, terminates the explorations of ordinary travellers; nor is there much beyond to tempt inquiry. In the dim distance two isolated mountains mark the route to Dongola, and they are often veiled in the clouds of sand driven upwards by the winds over the wide expanse of the desert.

Words

advantages, *benefits*.
alluvial, *deposited by water*.
antediluvian, *before the Deluge*.
approaching, *nearing*.
circuit, *circumference*.
colossal, *gigantic*.
communication, *intercourse*.
conceived, *imagined*.
confines, *boundaries*.
cultivators, *agriculturists*.
derived, *obtained*.
despoiled, *robbed*.
discharges, *empties*.
domain, *region*.

elevated, *raised*.
excavated, *hollowed out*.
existence, *being*.
explorations, *researches*.
falchion, *sword*.
frontispiece, *decoration in front*.
fruitfulness, *fertility*.
impressive, *affecting*.
inundations, *overflowing*.
irrigation, *artificial watering*.
isolated, *detached*.
ludicrous, *exciting laughter*.
marvel, *wonder*.
modifications, *changes*.

perceptible, *noticeable*.
recorded, *mentioned*.
regularity, *uniformity*.
renowned, *famous*.
sanitary, *affecting health*.
sculptured, *carved*.
serenity, *calmness*.
solitude, *loneliness*.

squalor, *foulness*.
suggestive, *stimulating thought*.
supplemented, *augmented*.
swathing, *grave-clothes*.
transition, *passage*.
tributary, *affluent*.
vegetation, *plant-growth*.

Questions

What makes Egypt a habitable country? How far has the course of the Nile been traced? What is the breadth of the cultivable Nile Valley? For what has that valley always been famous? Upon what is its fruitfulness consequent? When does the river begin to rise? What causes the inundation? When is it at its highest? When is the land tilled? When is the harvest reaped? How many crops are sometimes obtained in one year? What crops are chiefly grown? What is the capital of Lower Egypt? What is its character? Where are the ruins of the ancient city? When was it destroyed? What are the two modes of reaching Cairo? From what point are the Pyramids first seen? What was the ancient capital of Lower Egypt? Where are its ruins? What were recently discovered there? How far is the first cataract above Thebes? How many cataracts are there? What generally shuts in the Nile Valley in Nubia? What is the character of the country there? How is cultivation there carried on? What, above this, is the greatest marvel to be seen? What remarkable place stands eight hundred miles from the Mediterranean? What great temple is at Ipsambul? And what gigantic statue?

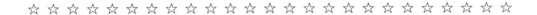

可以说埃及能以它独特的方式成为一个适宜居住的国家，都归功于尼罗河的存在。这条宏伟河流的流域，可以追溯到横跨赤道的巨大湖泊，位于在直线距离上距亚历山大港两千多英里的地方。在努比亚的喀土穆和柏柏尔融汇了来自阿比西尼亚的两条支流后，宽广的尼罗河水域将其极大的水量，从没有其他支流汇入的1 500英里的平坦的冲积平原上倾泻而来，最后从它两条主要的河道和其他一些较小的河口流入大海。

埃及所有可耕种的土地以及沙漠中的绿洲，都是由这条宏伟的河流两岸的草滩构成的，它们的宽度，从5英里到150英里不等。在早期的时候，尼罗河流域因为它的肥沃而闻名，并且在很长一段时间内，都因为它的盛产而备受尊重。甚至一直到现在，它的肥沃程度仍然是世界上其他地方所无法比拟的。

这样的肥沃是尼罗河定期泛滥的结果。虽然在埃及几乎没有降水，但是在尼罗河的源头地区有大量的持续降水。降水开始于每年的3月，在接下来的几个月中，由山上的积雪融水增补河水，在6月底水位有明显的上升。从这时到9月结束，水位几乎是每天规则性地上升四英寸。

当河流的水量达到最大时，整个尼罗河流域和三角洲就像一片巨大的内陆海洋，星罗棋布的村子和小镇勉强能露出水面。在这个季节，所有的通信维持都要依靠船只，除非在一些重要的地方会架一些高架桥。在9月~12月，河流平静下来，人们重新耕种，并在来年的6月丰收。但是埃及的耕种者们不会把他们的劳动力限制在只耕种一种农作物上，在一些便利的适宜耕种的土地上，人们都会通过人为灌溉种植农作物，用水车这种简单的工具来管理。这些农作物主要有粮食、棉花和一些染料作物。

亚历山大是埃及的第二大城市，也是埃及的主要贸易港口，但看起来却异常荒凉、破败，不像从前一样显现出它作为通往印度的陆地通道的优势。河畔的城镇是脏乱、贫困的，大量的居民也陷入脏乱和贫困之中。这个被称为埃及钥匙的齿形的小镇，不是位于由亚历山大大帝建立的这座著名城市的遗址上。据普林尼说，这座城市的一整圈有15英里，居住着30万人口。这座古老的城市，曾经和它闻名世界的图书馆一起在640年被烧为灰烬。它位于现在的亚历山大的南边，在一片脏乱的占地6~7英里的废墟上。这里矗立着著名的庞贝柱，大量丰富了欧洲的公共建筑和博物馆的战利品都来源于此。

在埃及的英国旅行者，通常会因为它的卫生问题而尽快离开亚历山大。亚历山大与开罗相距几百公里，连接两地的路线不是沿着由穆罕默德·阿里在1819年~1820年下令建造的著名的运河，就是沿着铁路。而这条铁路将从萨拉丁市到海岸线的路程控制在几个小时内。

途径尼罗河，快到达开罗的时候，人们在尼罗河上首先看到的便是金字塔。它大约有1英里宽，位于构成下埃及三角洲的两条主要分支的河流之间，距入海口90英里的地方。这些金字塔位于河流的西岸，在高于海平面50英尺的台子上矗立。即使是从很远的地方看，它们也如此宏伟壮观。

在金字塔的附近是孟菲斯的遗址，这里是下埃及的古老首都。在大批犹太人逃离埃及之后，这里成为法老的居住地。"有几英里，"迪恩·斯坦利说，"你都一直站在一层层堆叠的白骨和头盖骨之上，沿着沙子一直向下，在这些木乃伊坑中有大量埋着木乃伊的地道，最后是一些刚发现的从岩石中凿出来的地道。有许多埋在红色罐坛中的木乃伊已经逐渐被劫掠一空。最后，你会走到最近才发现的长廊里，凿在磐石之间，穿梭在古代和现代之间。它们有五十码高，最上方是拱顶，每一处都放置着最华丽的黑色大理石石棺，可以被看作是一个小房间，而不是一副棺材。它们表面光滑，里面和外面都刻有雕塑。它们甚至比底比斯国王的花岗岩石棺更加宏伟，更比其他地方任何人的坟墓更加壮观，甚至也比阿庇斯神所有的棺木更加富丽堂皇！"

继续逆流而行，旅行者们会经过许多有趣的地方，一大片玉米地，放满鳄鱼皮做的木乃伊的坑洼，在山坡表面的坟墓，宏伟的废墟和分散的纪念碑，就像是单德拉和底比斯。在底比斯上游100英里的地方，旅行者会到达第一大瀑布（总共有七大瀑布），还有努比亚边境上的阿斯旺。

在努比亚境内，尼罗河河道的景色展现出巨大的改变。河流的大部分都被花岗岩和砂岩的小山挡住，在这片区域之间的流域是干旱的、贫瘠的、阳光炽烤的，有着荒漠般阴暗沉闷的外貌。一些长势不好的棕榈树是这里唯一能看到的植物。除了在河流两岸这一块那一块的狭长土地里，要想在其他地方耕种几乎是不可能的。在一些地方灌溉是很费力的，水车要由牛来拉动，而这里的农民们恰恰就是依靠水牛的劳动力来成功劳作。

现在旅行者们发现自己超出了历史的局限，即使不断地路过小镇与高塔，他知道它们与过去的废墟之间有趣的联系。他认为在他的旅行中，尼罗河本身就是最大的奇迹，虽然它在离海洋800英里的地方流淌，也毫不丧失它的流量与魅力。

从地中海沿岸开始这段长途旅行，旅行者会到达阿布辛拜勒或者阿布辛贝。这里，在人迹罕至的荒漠的边缘，矗立着埃及最宏伟的奇迹——太阳神庙。由罗马人建造的这座巨大的雕塑从头到脚都显露在外，矗立在这荒僻的地方，至今仍然没有受到破坏。这座雕塑被重新修建了四次，前两次被埋在了沙子里，第三次分解成了碎片，第四次让我们又一次看到了古老世界中最伟大的创造。埃及在希腊与罗马建立之前繁荣了很长一段时间——历史记录中称它的国王为第一位征服者、埃及的光荣、亚洲的恐怖之人、底比斯的第二次发现者。在它存在的时期，一定是像罗马帝国一样伟大。

迪恩·斯坦利说："阿布辛拜勒和其他许多地方的人们，信仰的主要思想表现出埃及崇拜从崇高到荒谬的迅速转移。他们信仰的神明，在古老的神明和亚当之前怪诞的天使之间变化。是出于怎样奇怪的矛盾，这些雕塑家和信徒们才能创造出如亚扪和奥西里斯这样威严而可怕的雕塑？创造出所有在天堂、地球和地下水域之中神的滑稽形象？它们拥有鹰、鳄鱼、豺狼与猿的头。一个如底比斯一样的派士斯——名为"神圣的猫"的极其巨大的神——会拥有怎样的头脑和躯体？"

"如此平静又野蛮的国王有着多么惊人的对比！雷恩斯平静地微笑着，一把抓住俘虏的头发，他是每一座庙宇山墙上都会刻画的人；亚扪狰狞地微笑着，用他的刀击杀敌人。整体印象是神和人一样，属于一个完全逝去的时代和世界。那时，人的行动缓慢，思维也缓慢，但是，当人类有所行动或思维时，巨人的力量和暴力会完成他们所做的工作。那里的一个符号代表了真正的一神教——一千次的重复总是令人印象深刻，也永远充满魅力——这种符号多次被重复在屋顶上的檐口，比如在众神殿出现的小天使。天使蔚蓝色的翅膀展开，包住了整片天空，在它翅膀的阴影之中，将有我的避难所。"

流过阿布辛拜勒之后，尼罗河继续流动，不是通过山脉，而是通过一片无垠的沙漠。第二处大瀑布停止了航行，终止了普通旅客的探索，但仍诱惑人们去进行探查。在昏暗的距离内，两座孤立的山标记出通往栋古拉的路线，在这广阔无垠的沙漠中，它们通常隐藏在四处浮动的沙海之中。

Lesson 33
PANEGYRIC ON MARIE ANTOINETTE
第三十三课　玛丽·安托瓦内特的颂歌

It is now sixteen or seventeen years since I saw the Queen of France—then the Dauphiness—at Versailles; and surely never lighted on this orb, which she hardly seemed to touch, a more delightful vision. I saw her just above the horizon, decorating and cheering the elevated sphere she had just begun to move in—glittering like the morning star, full of life, and splendour, and joy.

Oh, what a revolution! and what a heart must I have, to contemplate without emotion that elevation, and that fall! Little did I dream, when she added titles of veneration to those of enthusiastic, distant, respectful love, that she should ever be obliged to carry the sharp antidote against disgrace concealed in that bosom; little did I dream that I should live to see such disasters fallen upon her in a nation of gallant men, in a nation of men of honour and of cavaliers. I thought ten thousand swords must have leaped from their scabbards to avenge even a look that threatened her with insult.

But the age of chivalry is gone. That of sophisters, economists, and calculators has succeeded; and the glory of Europe is extinguished for ever. Never, never more shall we behold that generous loyalty to rank and sex—that proud submission, that dignified obedience, that subordination of the heart—which kept alive, even in servitude itself, the spirit of an exalted freedom. The unbought grace of life, the cheap defence of nations, the nurse of manly sentiment and heroic enterprise is gone! It is gone,—that sensibility of principle, that chastity of honour, which felt a stain like a wound; which inspired courage whilst it mitigated ferocity; which ennobled whatever it touched; and under which vice itself lost half its evil, by losing all its grossness.

—Edmund Burke

Words

antidote, *corrective.*
cavaliers, *high-minded knights.*
chastity, *purity.*
contemplate, *regard.*
decorating, *adorning.*
disasters, *calamities.*
enterprise, *daring.*

enthusiastic, *impetuous.*
extinguished, *put out.*
ferocity, *fierceness.*
horizon, *where earth and sky meet.*
loyalty, *allegiance.*
mitigated, *alleviated.*
panegyric, *eulogy.*

revolution, *overturning*.   splendour, *magnificence*.
scabbards, *sheaths*.   subordination, *subjection*.
sensibility, *conscientiousness*.   titles, *claims*.
servitude, *bondage*.   veneration, *reverence*.
sophisters, *quibblers*.

　　我在凡尔赛见到法国王后和王太子妃距今已有十六七年了。阳光还没有照亮在这颗她似乎无法触碰的星球，那将是更令人愉快的景象。我看见她闪烁如晨星，在地平线上冉冉升起，欢呼着点缀了这个她刚刚开始步入的国度，充满活力、辉煌和快乐。

　　哦，这是一场革命！我要有怎样的魄力，不带有任何情绪地思考沉浮！我从未想到，她会崇拜那些热情的、遥远的、带有敬意的爱；她会被迫在心中深藏尖锐的武器来对抗隐藏的耻辱；我从未想到我会看到，在一个英勇的国度，在一个属于荣誉与骑士的国度，这样的灾难会降临在她身上。我原本以为，即使是对她无礼的一个眼神，都会引发骑士们无数的恶言飞跃出刀鞘来报复。

　　然而骑士的时代已然终结，诡辩者、经济学家和数学家的时代随即到来。欧洲的荣耀已永远消逝。我们永远不会再看到那种对地位和性别的忠诚，那种骄傲的谦恭、高贵的顺服和对心灵的归属——这种高贵的自由，甚至在奴隶心中都一直葆有活力。对生命的慈悲、对国家的守卫、对男子气概和英雄主义事业的维护，全部一去不返了。同时消逝的还有如伤口上的污点一般的、激情的感性和荣誉的纯净。所有这些都激励着勇气，瓦解着暴行，使它碰触到的都变得高贵，使恶行丧失它的罪恶和卑劣。

——埃德蒙·伯克

Lesson 34　CRUELTY TO ANIMALS
第三十四课　对动物的残忍行为

Man is the direct agent of a wide and continual distress to the lower animals; and the question is, "Can any method be devised for its alleviation?" On this subject that scriptural image is strikingly realized: "the whole [inferior] creation groaning and travailing together in pain" because of him. It signifies naught to the substantive amount of the suffering, whether it be prompted by the hardness of his heart, or only permitted through the heedlessness of his mind. In either way it holds true, not only that the arch-devourer Man stands preeminent over the fiercest children of the wilderness as an animal of prey, but that for his lordly and luxurious appetite, as well as for his service or merest curiosity and amusement, Nature must be ransacked throughout all her elements. Rather than forego the veriest gratifications of vanity, he will wring them from the anguish of wretched and ill-fated creatures; and whether for the indulgence of his barbaric sensuality or his barbaric splendour, he can stalk paramount over the sufferings of that prostrate creation which has been placed beneath his feet.

These sufferings are really felt. The beasts of the field are not so many automata without sensation, so constructed as to assume all the natural expressions of it. Nature hath not practised this universal deception upon our species. These poor animals just look, and tremble, and give forth the very indications of suffering that we do. Theirs is the distinct cry of pain. Theirs is the unequivocal physiognomy of pain. They put on the same aspect of terror on the demonstrations of a menaced blow. They exhibit the same distortions of agony after the infliction of it. The bruise, or the burn, or the fracture, or the deep incision, or the fierce encounter with one of equal or of superior strength, affects them similarly to ourselves. Their blood circulates as ours. They have pulsations in various parts of the body as we have. They sicken, and they grow feeble with age, and, finally, they die, just as we do.

They possess the same feelings; and, what exposes them to like sufferings from another quarter, they possess the same instincts with our own species. The lioness robbed of her whelps causes the wilderness to ring aloud with the proclamation of her wrongs; or the bird whose little household has been stolen fills and saddens all the grove with melodies of deepest pathos. All this is palpable even to the general and unlearned eye; and when the physiologist lays open the recesses of their system, by means of that scalpel under whose operation they just shrink and are convulsed as any living subject of our own species, there stands forth to view the same sentient apparatus, and furnished with the same conductors for the transmission of feeling from every minutest pore upon the surface.

Theirs is unmixed and unmitigated pain, the agonies of martyrdom without the alleviation of the hopes and the sentiments whereof men are capable. When they lay them down to die, their only fellowship is with suffering; for in the prison-house of their beset and bounded faculties, no relief can be afforded by communion with other interests or other things. The attention does not lighten their distress, as it does that of man, by carrying off his spirit from that existing pungency and pressure which might else be overwhelming. There is but room in their mysterious economy for one inmate; and that is, the absorbing sense of their own single and concentrated anguish. And so on that bed of torment whereon the wounded animal lingers and expires, there is an unexplored depth and intensity of suffering which the poor dumb animal itself cannot tell, and against which it can offer no remonstrance—an untold and unknown amount of wretchedness of which no articulate voice gives utterance.

—Thomas Chalmers

Words

alleviation, *mitigation*
articulate, *distinct*.
communion, *intercourse*.
concentrated, *self-contained*.
constructed, *put together*.
convulsed, *affected spasmodically*.
deception, *fraud*.
distortions, *writhings*.
gratification, *indulgence*.
heedlessness, *carelessness*.
instinct, *natural impulse*.
luxurious, *sensual*.
mysterious, *incomprehensible*.
paramount, *chief*.
physiognomy, *expression of face*.

preeminent, *supreme*.
proclamation, *publication*.
prompted, *suggested*.
prostrate, *down-trodden*.
pulsations, *throbbing*.
pungency, *sharpness*.
ransacked, *pillaged*.
remonstrance, *expostulation*.
scalpel, *dissecting knife*.
substantive, *actual*.
travailing, *labouring with pain*.
unequivocal, *unmistakable*.
unmitigated, *undiminished*.
wretchedness, *misery*.

☆ ☆

　　人类是低等动物各种持续伤痛的直接制造者。问题是：有没有什么方法能够减缓这种伤痛？在这个问题上，圣经手稿上的影像尤其真实："所有低等动物都在痛苦地呻吟着。"而这，正是因为人类。这对大量的苦难几乎意味着零，无论是由于人类内心的狠毒，还是意识的淡薄。不仅因为人类是高高在上将动物视作猎物的掠食者，也因为人类高傲、奢侈的欲望，同时还因为人类单纯的好奇心和快感，这两种情况都讲得通，大自然因此要彻底地经历人类的洗劫。不会放弃这种虚荣的满足感，而是沉浸其中，人类会从向这些可悲、不幸的生物倾泻愤怒的过程中享受它，或是在放纵自身野蛮的感官享受或残忍的壮丽场景时，高高在上地俯视被置于脚下的动物。

这些苦难，动物都感受得到。大地的猛兽不是毫无感知的器械，但也并非如此复杂得能够承担所有大自然的表达。大自然没有将这种普遍的诡计施加在人类身上。这些可怜的动物只能看着，颤抖着，发出苦难的哀鸣。而这并非痛苦地嚎叫，而是人类承受苦难的清晰表情。它们在承受痛苦的打击时与人类有同样的恐惧表现，它们在受伤之后也表现出同样的痛苦的扭曲。瘀伤、灼伤、骨折、深深的伤口，或是受到相同或更强力量的打击，对它们的影响与对人类的影响相同。它们像人类一样有血液的循环，一样在身体的各部位存在脉搏。它们生病，随着年龄变大而日渐虚弱，最后像人类一样逝去。

它们拥有相同的感受，也拥有像人类一样的本能，这使它们成为人类世界苦难的承受者。母狮会在伤害了自己的幼狮之后发出响彻的吼叫来宣称自己的错误，鸟会在自己的小窝遭洗劫之后用深深的悲怆声撼动整片树林，即使最无知的眼睛也能感知到这一切。当生理学家用手术刀解剖它们的身体，它们也会像人类一样畏缩、颤抖，它们拥有同人类一样有知觉的器官，也会像人类一样在表皮上最微小的毛孔之间传递感觉。

不存在单纯的、绝对的痛苦，希望与感觉不会减少，这时人类是可以感知到它们牺牲的痛苦。当人类放倒它们即将杀戮，人类这唯一的伙伴正遭受苦难。当它们被困到牢房中，任何内容的交流都不可能带来对它们的释放和宽容。即使对精神的麻痹也不会减轻已存在的刺激和压力会给它们带来的痛苦。在困住它们的牢房中挤满了动物，已经没有任何空间能够存留那深入骨髓的愤怒感受。在折磨动物的手术台上，它们受伤，直至死去。而它们对这种深深的、强烈的痛苦，没有任何抗议。它们不会用任何声音表达出这些未知的悲楚。

——托马斯·查默斯

Lesson 35   THE DELUGE
第三十五课　大洪水

Look for a moment on the catastrophe of the Deluge. And let not our attention be so engrossed by its dread and awful character, as to overlook all that preceded it, and see nothing but the flood and its devouring waters.

The waters rise till rivers swell into lakes, and lakes become seas, and the sea stretches out her arms along fertile plains to seize their flying population. Still the waters rise; and now, mingled with beasts that terror has tamed, men climb to the mountain-tops, with the flood roaring at their heels. Still the waters rise; and now each summit stands above them like a separate and sea-girt isle.

Still the waters rise; and, crowding closer on the narrow spaces of lessening hill-tops, men and beasts fight for standing-room. Still the thunders roar, and the lightnings flash, and the rains descend, and the waters rise, till the last survivor of the shrieking crowd is washed off, and the head of the highest Alp goes down beneath the wave.

Now the waters rise no more. God's servant has done his work. He rests from his labours; and, all land drowned, all life destroyed, an awful silence reigning and a shoreless ocean rolling. Death for once has nothing to do but ride in triumph on the top of some giant billow, which, meeting no coast, no continent, no Alp, no Andes against which to break, sweeps round and round the world.

We stand aghast at the scene; and as the corpses of gentle children and sweet infants float by, we exclaim, Hath God forgotten to be gracious? Hath he in anger shut up his tender mercies? No; assuredly not. Where, then, is his mercy?

Look here; behold this Ark, as, steered by an invisible hand, she comes dimly through the gloom. Lonely ship on a shoreless ocean, she carries mercy on board. She holds the costliest freight that ever sailed the sea. The germs of the Church are there—the children of the old world, and the fathers of the new.

Suddenly, amid the awful gloom, as she drifts over that dead and silent sea, a grating noise is heard. Her keel has grounded on the top of Ararat. The door is opened; and, beneath the sign of the olive branch, her tenants come forth from their baptismal burial, like life from the dead, or like souls which have passed from a state of nature into the light and the liberty of grace, or like the saints when they shall rise at the summons of the trumpet to behold a new heaven and a new earth, and see the sign which these "gray fathers" hailed encircling a head that was crowned with thorns.

—Thomas Guthrie

Words

assuredly, *certainly*.
baptismal, *consecrating*.
catastrophe, *calamity*.
corpses, *dead bodies*.
costliest, *richest*.
destroyed, *annihilated*.
encircling, *surrounding*.
engrossed, *absorbed*.
exclaim, *cry out*.

freight, *cargo*.
invisible, *unseen*.
lessening, *diminishing*.
preceded, *went before*.
shrieking, *screaming*.
summit, *peak*.
survivor, *one who outlives others*.
tenants, *occupants*.

☆ ☆

　　看一下大洪水的灾难。不要只将注意力集中在它可怕的特性上，俯瞰在它之前发生的一切，只看着洪水和它吞噬一切的水流。

　　水在上涨，河汹涌着变成了湖，湖变成了海，海继续蔓延，直到占据了肥沃的平原，驱散了平原之上的众多人口。水依旧在上涨，如今，混同那些被恐惧驯服的野兽，人类爬上了山顶，看着洪水在他们身后咆哮。水依旧在上涨。如今，每一座山峰都变得像是汪洋中孤立的小岛。

　　水依旧在上涨。因为山顶聚集的生物越来越多，人类和野兽开始争夺自己的领地。电闪雷鸣，水仍旧在一直上涨，直到山顶最后尖叫的人群被洪水冲走，至高的山峰也被洪水淹没。

　　如今，水不再上涨。上帝的仆人已经完成了使命，而观赏着自己的劳动成果。他淹没了所有土地，毁灭了所有生灵。可怕的寂静统治了世界，无边的海洋四处蔓延。此时，死亡站在巨浪之巅庆祝着它的胜利，它不会再见到海岸、陆地、阿尔卑斯、安第斯，而横行全世界。

　　我们惊骇地看着这幅场景。当看到可爱婴儿的尸体飘过，我们惊呼，上帝忘却了他的慈悲吗？他是否已经停止了他温柔的仁慈？不，肯定并非如此。那他的仁慈在哪里？

　　看那儿，看方舟！一只看得见的手正操纵着它，从昏暗中驶来一艘无边汪洋中唯一的船。船上载着仁慈和最昂贵的货物。教会的根源在此，旧世界的孩子，新世界的祖先。

　　忽然之间，当它在一片死亡和沉寂的海洋中漂流之时，一声东西磨碎的巨响传来。方舟的船底着陆在阿拉若山的山顶，门打开了，在橄榄枝的信号下，乘客从死亡的洗礼中出现，就像他们的生命来自死亡，像他们的灵魂从本性转变为慈悲的自由之光，像他们接受召唤，而来注视着一个新的天堂，一个新的世界，注视着这些新世界的祖先，欢呼着接受荆棘的王冠的加冕。

——托马斯·格思里

Lesson 36   WHAT IS WAR?
第三十六课　战争是什么

What is war? I believe that half the people that talk about war have not the slightest idea what it is. In a short sentence it may be summed up to be the combination and concentration of all the horrors, atrocities, crimes, and sufferings of which human nature on this globe is capable. But what is even a rumour of war? Is there anybody here who has anything in the funds, or who is the owner of any railway stock; or anybody who has a large stock of raw material or of manufactured goods? The funds have recently gone down 10 percent. I do not say that the fall is all on account of this danger of war, but a great proportion of it undoubtedly is. A fall of 10 percent, in the funds is nearly £80,000,000 sterling of value; and railway stock having gone down 20 percent, makes a difference of £60,000,000 in the value of the railway property of this country. Add the two—£140,000,000—and take the diminished prosperity and value of manufactures of all kinds during the last few months, and you will under-state the actual loss to the country now if you put it down at £200,000,000 sterling. But that is merely a rumour of war. That is war a long way off—the small cloud no bigger than a man's hand: what will it be if it come nearer and becomes a fact? And surely sane men ought to consider whether the case is a good one, the ground fair, the necessity clear, before they drag a nation of nearly thirty millions of people into a long and bloody struggle, for a decrepit and tottering empire, which all the nations in Europe cannot long sustain.

Well, if you go into war now, you will have more banners to decorate your cathedrals and churches. Englishmen will fight now as well as they ever did; and there is ample power to back them, if the country can be but sufficiently excited and deluded. You may raise up great generals. You may have another Wellington, and another Nelson too; for this country can grow men capable of every enterprise. Then there may be titles, and pensions, and marble monuments to eternize the men who have thus become great;—but what becomes of you and your country, and your children?

Speaking here, however, to such an audience—an audience probably, for its numbers, as intelligent and as influential as ever was assembled within the walls of any hall in this kingdom—I think I may put before you higher considerations even than those of property and the institutions of your country. I may remind you of duties more solemn, and of obligations more imperative. You profess to be a Christian nation. You make it your boast even—though boasting is somewhat out of place in such questions—you make it your boast that you are a Christian people, and that you draw your rule of doctrine and practice, as from a well pure and undefiled, from the lively oracles of God, and from the direct revelation of the Omnipotent. You have even conceived the magnificent project of illuminating the whole Earth, even to its remotest and darkest recesses, by the dissemination of the volume of the New Testament, in whose every page are written for ever the words of peace. Within the limits of this island alone, every Sabbath-day, 20,000, yes, far more than 20,000 temples are thrown open, in which devout men and women assemble to worship him who is the "Prince of Peace."

Is this a reality? or is your Christianity a romance, and your profession a dream? No; I am sure that your Christianity is not a romance, and I am equally sure that your profession is not a dream. It is because I believe this that I appeal to you with confidence, and that I have hope and faith in the future. I believe that we shall see, and at no very distant time, sound economic principles spreading much more widely amongst the people; a sense of justice growing up in a soil which hitherto has been deemed unfruitful; and—which will be better than all—the churches of the United Kingdom, the churches of Britain, awaking as it were from their slumbers, and girding up their loins to more glorious work, when they shall not only accept and believe in the prophecy, but labour earnestly for its fulfillment, that there shall come a time—a blessed time—a time which shall last for ever—when "nation shall not lift up sword against nation, neither shall they learn war any more."

—John Bright.

Words

atrocities, *cruelties*.
combination, *union*.
concentration, *essence*.
considerations, *motives*.
decrepit, *broken-down*.
deluded, *deceived*.
diminished, *lessened*.
dissemination, *distribution*.
eternize, *immortalize*.

obligations, *duties*.
revelation, *communication*.
romance, *fiction*.
sufficiently, *enough*.
illuminating, *enlightening*.
under-state, *under-rate*.
imperative, *binding*.
undoubtedly, *certainly*.

战争是什么？我相信谈论战争的人们中，会有一半人对战争甚至没有丝毫概念。可能一句很短的句子可以概括：战争是这个世界中，人类所有恐惧、残暴、罪行和苦难的结合和集中。但关于战争的传言是怎样的？如果战争中涉及一些占有资金的人，铁路股份的所有者，或者拥有原材料、制造业巨大股份的人？他所拥有的资金会跌10个百分点。我并非想说这种跌落是源于战争的危险，但毫无疑问，其中绝大部分肯定是源于此。一份资金跌落10个百分点，市值接近8千万英镑；铁路股份下降20%，意味着全国铁路资产减少了6千万英镑。另外两项价值1亿4千万英镑，在过去的两个月内就能摧毁全国所有制造业的繁荣。而如果你认为全国经济减少了2亿英镑，那么你就低估了实际的损失，但这些只是关于战争的传言。战争像一片比手掌还要小的云朵一样遥不可及，但如果它离我们越来越近或者成为现实，又会怎样？神志清醒的人自然能辨出它是好是坏，将一个国家接近3千万的人口置于漫长、血腥的争斗中，而整个欧洲都难以长期支撑这个日渐衰弱而摇摇欲坠的帝国。

诚然，如果你现在置身于战争之中，你会在教堂插上更多的旗帜。英国人会像他们曾经投身战争时一样去参与其中。如果国家能够煽动、蛊惑大众，也会有足够的力量来支撑他们。会有伟大的将军再次出现，他们是又一个惠灵顿，或者纳尔逊，因为这个国家可以在任何事业中成就伟人。会有更多的头衔、津贴、大理石纪念碑来永远铭刻这些伟人。但对你，对你的国家，你的子孙，战争会带来什么？

说到这，我想到我的听众中可能会有一部分人，在这个国家的任何一处，有相当的学识或权势。我将让你更加注意庄严的责任和必要的义务，而不是财富和贵国的制度。

你声称来自于一个基督教国家，你甚至以此自居，虽然这从某种程度上与战争的问题无关。你自居是基督教徒，所以你的信条和行为都来自于纯粹的上帝的神谕，来自于全能的上帝的直接指引。你甚至坚信开化全世界的伟大工程，即使是针对最偏远、阴暗的角落，即使它歧视每一页都写满了"和平"二字的《新约》。单单在这一个岛国，在每一个安息日，就会有2万座圣堂开放，虔诚的人们聚集在里面祭拜他们称之为"和平王子"的上帝。这是真的吗？或者，基督教只是一种浪漫的幻想，你的宣言也只是一个梦想？不，我相信绝对不是。因为我坚信，所以我自信地向你呼吁，并且对将来充满了希望与信念。我相信我们会看到，在不远的将来，稳固的经济原则会在人民之中广泛传播，公平的信条迄今为止还会在一直贫瘠的土地上滋长。另外，最好的是，英国的教堂会从沉睡中苏醒，全力以赴去实现更光荣的职责。它们不会再仅仅接受、信赖预言，而同时也努力实现这些预言，会有一个美好的时刻到来，而它也会成为永恒。在这一时刻，国家之间不会再剑拔弩张，同时，它们也不会再了解战争。

——约翰·布赖特

Lesson 37   COLONIAL LOYALTY
第三十七课　殖民地的忠诚

Our attachment to the Queen, our own Victoria, is mingled with a tenderness not inconsistent with the sterner sentiment, which it softens and embellishes without enervating. Let her legitimate authority as a constitutional monarch, let her reputation as a woman, be assailed, and notwithstanding the lamentation of Burke that the age of chivalry was past, thousands of swords would leap from their scabbards to avenge her. Ay, and they would be drawn as freely and wielded as vigorously and bravely in Canada or in Nova Scotia, as in England. Loyalty! love of British institutions!—they are ingrafted on our very nature; they are part and parcel of ourselves; and I can no more tear them from my heart (even if I would, and lacerate all its fibres) than I could sever a limb from my body.

And what are those institutions? A distinguished American statesman recently answered this question. He said: "The proudest Government that exists upon the face of the Earth is that of Great Britain. And the great Pitt, her proudest statesman, when he would tell of Britain's crowning glory, did not speak, as he might have done, of her wide-spread dominion, upon which the sun never sets. he did not speak of martial achievements, of glorious battle-fields, and of splendid naval conflicts. But he said, with swelling breast and kindling eye, that the poorest man of Great Britain in his cottage might bid defiance to all the force of the Crown. It might be frail, its roof might shake, the wind might blow through it, the storm might enter, the rain might enter; but the King of England could not enter it. In all his forces he dared not cross the threshold of that ruined tenement."

—Hon. W. Young

Words

achievements, *exploits.*
attachment, *affection (for).*
distinguished, *illustrious.*
dominion, *empire.*
embellishes, *adorns.*
inconsistent, *irrevocable.*

ingrafted, *rooted.*
lacerate, *mangle.*
lamentation, *complaint.*
recently, *lately.*
tenement, *habitation.*
vigorously, *powerfully.*

　　我们对维多利亚女王的依恋，与一种亲切感混杂在一起，并不受严厉情绪的影响而有所减轻和衰退。一旦她的合法权力不能成为宪法的王权，她女性的名声受到损害，即使伯克悲叹如今骑士的时代已经终结，还会有无数的人会拔剑而出为她复仇。他们会在加拿大或者新斯科舍自由挥洒，英勇战斗，就像在英格兰一样。忠诚！对不列颠制度的热爱！它们被深刻在我们的本性里，是我们重要的一部分，即使我们砍掉自己的四肢，也不会将它从心中剔除。虽然我能这样做，甚至能割开它的每一寸肌理。

　　而这是怎样的制度？一位显赫的美国政治家刚刚回答了这个问题。他说道："世界上最骄傲的政府存在于大不列颠。最优秀的伟大政治家皮特，不会称道不列颠至高无上的荣耀，虽然他能够这样做。他不会诉说祖国广阔的疆域，甚至一天中太阳时刻都可以照耀。他不会诉说祖国军事的成就，无论是在陆战战场上，还是在海军的战斗中。但他昂首挺胸，眼睛奕奕有神，他会诉说大不列颠最贫穷的人，会在他的茅舍里嘲笑王冠的力量。他的茅舍可能很脆弱，屋顶会动摇，狂风暴雨会钻进来。但英国国王不会进来。虽然他有至高的权力，但他却不敢跨进这样一间破败的屋子的门槛。"

——W·杨阁下

Lesson 38   JERUSALEM FROM THE MOUNT OF OLIVES
第三十八课　橄榄山上的耶路撒冷

Morning dawned; and I ascended to the terraced roof of a little tower on the western side of Olivet, rented by a friend to whom every spot in Jerusalem was familiar. Behind Olivet, in the east, the sky was all aglow with red light, which shot slanting across the hill-tops and projecting cliffs, and upon the walls and prominent buildings of the city, throwing them up in bold relief from the deeply-shaded glens. No time could have been more opportune, no spot better fitted for seeing and studying the general topography of the Holy City. The whole site was before us, distinct and full, like a vast and beautiful embossed picture.

At our feet, along the base of Olivet, was the Kidron, a deep and narrow glen, coming down from an undulating plateau on the right, and disappearing round the shoulder of the hill on the left; its banks terraced, and dotted here and there with little groves and single olive trees. Directly opposite us was Mount Moriah, its bare sides rising precipitously from the bottom of the Kidron to a height of some two hundred feet.

On its summit is a rectangular platform, about thirty acres in extent, and taking up fully one half of the eastern side of the city. It is encompassed and supported by a massive wall, in some places nearly eighty feet high and looking even higher where it impends over the ravine. This platform constitutes by far the most striking feature of the city. It is unique. There is nothing like it in the world. Its history, too, is wonderful. It has been a "holy place" for more than thirty centuries.

Its Cyclope'an walls were founded by Solomon. Upon it stood the Temple, in whose shrine the Glory of the Lord so often appeared, and in whose courts Christ so often taught. It is still to the Moslem "the Noble Sanctuary," and, next to Mecca, the most venerated sanctuary in the world.

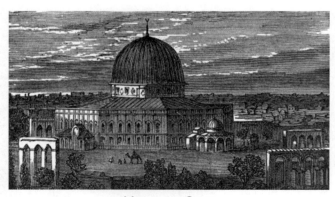
Mosque or Omar

The platform itself—simple, massive, and grand—is a striking object; but the buildings it contains greatly contribute to its beauty. In its centre, on a raised area of white marble, stands the Mosque of Omar, one of the most splendid mosques in the world, octagonal in form, encrusted with encaustic tiles of gorgeous colours, and surmounted by a graceful dome. From its area the ground slopes away to the encircling ramparts in gentle undulations of green turf, diversified with marble arcades, gilded cupolas, fountains, and prayer-niches;—all interspersed with venerable cypresses, olives, and palms.

At the southern end is a large group of stately buildings, including the Mosque el-Aksa, once the Church of the Virgin; and round the sides of the platform are cloisters, here and there covered with domes, and surmounted by tall minarets. The quiet seclusion of this sanctuary, the rich green of its grass and foliage, the dazzling whiteness of its pavements and fountains, the brilliant tints of the central mosque, and, above all, its sacred associations, make it one of the most charming and interesting spots on Earth.

Just behind Moriah the Tyrope'an Valley was distinctly marked by a deeply-shaded belt, running from north to south through the city. Beyond it rose Zion, higher and longer than Moriah; in front, a confused mass of terraced roofs, tier above tier; farther back were seen the white buildings of the Armenian Convent, like an immense factory; more to the right the new English Church; and in the back-ground, crowning the hill, the massive square keep of the Castle of David.

The southern section of Zion is now outside the city wall; and there a high minaret and cupola mark the Tomb of David. From it the hill sinks into the Valley of Hin'nom in steep terraced slopes, covered with vineyards, olives, and corn-fields. As I looked, a moving object in one of the fields riveted my attention. "Haste! give me the glass," I said. I turned it towards the spot. Yes, I was right;—a plough and yoke of oxen were there at work. Jeremiah's prophecy was being fulfilled before my eyes: *"Zion shall be ploughed like a field."*

Along the farther side of Zion runs the deep glen of Hinnom, which, turning eastward, sweeps round the southern end of the hill and joins the Kidron at Enrogel. These two ravines form the great physical boundaries and barriers of Jerusalem; they completely cut it off from the surrounding tableland; and they isolate the hills on which it stands, and those other hills, too, or hill-tops, which, as the Psalmist tells us, "are round about Jerusalem." These natural barriers also serve to confine the city within regular and definite limits—to prevent it from sending forth straggling suburbs and offshoots, as most other cities do; hence it was said, "Jerusalem is builded as a city *that is compact together.*"

A high battlemented wall encompasses the modern city. It runs for half a mile along the brow of the Kidron valley, facing Olivet, then turns at right angles and zigzags across Moriah, the Tyropean, and Zion, to the brow of Hinnom. The whole circuit is two miles and a half. The city was always fortified, and the walls and towers formed its most prominent features. Hence the language of the exulting Psalmist: "Walk about Zion, and go round about her: tell the towers thereof, mark ye well her bulwarks."

Jerusalem has no suburbs. There is no shading off of the city into the country—no long streets radiating from a centre, then straggling houses, and villas, and gardens, such as we are accustomed to see in English towns. The moment you pass the gates of Jerusalem you are in the country,—a country open, bare, without a single house, and almost desolate. Not a green spot is visible, and not a tree, save here and there a little clump of gnarled, dusky olives. Rounded hill-tops, and long reaches of plain, strown with heaps of gray limestone, extend from the walls far away to the north and to the south. There is no grandeur, beauty, or richness in the scenery. It is bleak and featureless.

Hence the sad disappointment felt by most travellers on approaching Jerusalem from the west and the south. They can only see the serrated line of gray Saracenic walls extending across a section of a bleak, rocky plateau. But when I stood that morning on the brow of Olivet, and looked down on the city, crowning those battlemented heights, encircled by those deep and dark ravines, and when the rising sun bathed in a flood of ruddy light the terraced roofs of the city, I involuntarily exclaimed,—*"Beautiful for situation, the joy of the whole, earth, is Mount Zion, the city of the great King!"*

—J. L. Porter

Words

accustomed, *used.*
battlemented, *fortified.*
confused, *irregular.*
dazzling, *overpowering.*
desolate, *deserted.*
diversified, *varied.*
encaustic, *enamelled.*
encompassed, *surrounded.*
exulting, *triumphant.*
familiar, *well known.*
interspersed, *mingled.*
involuntarily, *spontaneously.*

octagonal, *eight-sided.*
opportune, *convenient.*
precipitously, *steeply.*
prominent, *outstanding.*
radiating, *diverging.*
riveted, *enchained.*
serrated, *notched.*
straggling, *scattered.*
topography, *position of places.*
undulating, *rising and falling; irregular.*
unique, *unmatched.*
venerated, *revered.*

Questions

What is the best point for obtaining a general view of Jerusalem? Where is Mount Olivet? At what time did the writer ascend the tower on that mount? What glen lay at his feet? What Mount, on the other side of Kidron? Why is the platform on Moriah so deeply interesting? What great building stands upon it now? What valley separates Moriah from Zion? What divides Zion into two sections? Where is David's tomb? How is its position marked? What valley runs on the farther side of Zion? What effect have the valleys of Hinnom and Kidron on Jerusalem? Why are most travellers disappointed with the first view of Jerusalem?

☆ ☆

　　清晨来临时，我登上了橄榄山西侧一座小塔的屋顶，这所房子是向朋友租借来的，对他来说，耶路撒冷的每一个地方都是如此熟悉。在橄榄山的后面，东方的天空被阳光映得发红，红色的光线歪斜地穿过山顶和突出的悬崖，照在墙上和城市中的著名建筑上，将它们从山谷的荫蔽中释放出来。要想观看和学习整个圣城的一般地形，没有别的时间比此时更合适，也没有其他视角比这里更契合。呈现在我们面前的整个画面，清晰又丰富，就像一幅广阔壮丽的浮雕画。

　　在我们的脚下，在圣城与橄榄山山麓的交界处是汲沦溪，它流淌在幽深又狭窄的峡谷中，从起伏的高原右翼流下来，消失在半山腰的左翼；它的河岸是呈阶梯状分布的，到处都零零散散地布满了小稻草人和零星的橄榄树。正对着我们的是摩亚力山，它暴露在外面的边缘从汲沦溪底部陡然上升到离我们脚下200多米的高度。

　　在它的最顶端是一处长方形的平台，面积大概有30英亩，占据城市东部整整一半的地方。一堵厚重的巨大的墙壁围住这一平台，在某些地方它有将近80英尺那么高，在临近峡谷的地方看起来甚至更高。这一平台是迄今为止这一城市最显著的特色之所在，它独一无二，世界上没有什么和它相似。它的历史也同样奇妙，三个多世纪以来它一直都是圣殿的所在地。

　　所罗门发现了这里的巨石城墙。其上矗立着神庙，在此上帝的光辉经常出现，而在它的庭院之中经常进行基督教徒的布道仪式。它仍旧朝向穆斯林的至圣所，并且紧挨着世界上最受人尊敬的耶路撒冷的避难所——麦加。

　　这个平台本身简单厚重又宏伟，异常引人注目，而它之上的建筑物又为它平添了几分魅力。在它中心处的一块白色大理石上凸起的区域内，仁立着世界上最辉煌的清真寺之一——奥尔玛清真寺。这所清真寺从外形上看是八边形，镶以颜色华丽的琉璃瓦，并且有一个完美的圆屋顶构成拱顶。从清真寺所在地，土地一直倾斜向环绕在四周的城墙和柔和起伏的绿色草坪边缘。大理石拱廊、镀金的圆顶、喷泉和神龛让这儿的建筑风格显得异常多样，所有这些都穿插在古老的柏树、橄榄树和棕榈树之间。

　　在南部的尽头是一大片庄严宏伟的建筑，包括曾经的圣母玛利亚教堂，它现在是阿克萨清真寺。在平台的边缘周围是长长的回廊，回廊到处都覆盖着由很高的尖塔支撑起来形成的拱形顶。这处至圣所安静隐蔽的风格，这里植物和草坪的满眼的绿色，这里人行道和户外喷泉让人眼花缭乱的白色，中央清真寺灿烂的视角，尤其是这里神圣的宗教氛围，使它成为世界上最有魅力、最吸引世人的景点之一。

就在摩利亚山后面，泰罗波恩谷明显地被一个深深的阴影地带所标记，并从北到南贯穿整座城市，越过玫瑰花色的锡安山，比摩利亚山更高更远；在前面，混乱的平房顶呈梯田状排列，一层叠着一层，更远一点的后面是美国修道院的白色建筑，就像一所无边无际的工厂；再往右边一点是崭新的英国教堂，而在后面小山丘的顶部，厚重的方形广场守护着大卫之城。

锡安山的南部地区现在处于城墙之外，那里有高尖塔和圆屋顶标志着大卫之墓的所在地。从那里，小山丘在呈阶梯状的陡峭山坡上陷入了山谷，那山坡被葡萄园、橄榄树和玉米田覆盖着。当我望向那里，田野当中的一个移动的物体引起了我的注意。"快点！把望远镜递给我！"我说道。我把视线转向了那里。是的，我是对的——一头牛拉着犁在那里干着农活。耶米利的预言十分完整地呈现在我眼前："锡安山将被开垦成为一片田地。"

在锡安山的一侧延绵着深邃的欣嫩谷。它向东侧延伸，穿过锡安山的最南端，最后在隐罗与汲沦山合并成一脉。这两座藤蔓一样的山脉形成耶路撒冷巨大的物理边界和屏障壁垒；它们将耶路撒冷与周围的高原完全阻隔开来，同时也将这里的山丘和其他那些高山孤立出来。正如诗人告诉我们的一样："它们围绕着耶路撒冷。"这些天然的屏障，同时也可以把城市都归置在规则和明确的界限之内，这样可以防止耶路撒冷像其他城市那样，分散出许多零零落落的郊区和分支。因此有人说："耶路撒冷是一座如此紧凑建造的城市。"

一堵高高的有城垛的城墙包围着这座现代都市。它沿着汲沦谷的眉峰跨过了半英里，面对着橄榄山，然后向右转90度，呈之字形穿过摩利亚山后翼、泰罗波恩谷和锡安山，到达欣嫩谷的眉峰。整个线路长达两英里半。这座城市一直处于高度坚固的防御工事中，而且城墙和高塔都被建造成最突出的地标物。因此令人欢欣鼓舞的赞美诗里才会这样说道："在锡安山周围漫步，一直穿行于此：这里的高塔会向你标记出它的壁垒所在。"

耶路撒冷没有郊区。那儿没有由城市转向乡村的阴影地带，也没有从中央地带发出的长长的街道以及后方的房屋别墅和花园，就像我们在英国的城镇习惯看到的那样。在你踏入耶路撒冷的一瞬间，你就身处于一个这样的国家中——一个开放的，毫不遮掩的，没有独栋房屋的，几乎接近于荒凉的国家。你看不到一丝一毫绿色的景象，没有一棵树，除了偶尔有一小丛深色的橄榄树。圆形的山头，延绵数里的平原，到处都散落着灰色的岩石堆，从城墙处向遥远的北方和南方延伸。这里的风景没有庄严宏伟，没有魅力也不多姿多彩。它单调，毫无特色可言。

因此对从西方和南方来到此地的大多数旅行者来说，当他们接近耶路撒冷时，都会感到伤心和失望。他们看到的只有灰色的撒拉逊墙沿着一条锯齿线，一直延伸穿过黯淡、多山的高原。但那天早上，当我站在橄榄山上俯瞰这座城市，看到那些矗立的防御工事环绕着那些深邃的沟壑，当旭日将整座城市的屋顶和凉台沐浴在一片红色的光芒之中，我不由自主地惊呼："如此美丽的景象是属于全人类的幸福之景。锡安山，伟大国王的城市！"

——J. L. 波特

Lesson 39   THE SIEGE OF JERUSALEM
第三十九课　公元 70 年

A. D. 70

The aspect of Jerusalem had changed but little from that which it had worn at the time of the Crucifixion, when, thirty-five years later, the Roman eagles gathered round their prey. But during these years the Jews had been plunging deeper and deeper into sin and wretchedness. At last, goaded by outrage and insult, they had risen against their Roman masters; and the great Vespasian had been sent by Nero to tame their stubborn pride.

Galilee and Perea were subdued after some trouble and delay; and the conqueror, having drawn a circle of forts round Jerusalem, was at Caesarea, preparing for the last great blow, when he heard the news of Nero's death. The army in Palestine then proclaimed Vespasian emperor. He hastened to secure Alexandria, the second city in the empire; and having heard while there that the people of Rome were holding feasts in his own honour, he set out for Italy. So the siege of Jerusalem was left to his son Titus.

Mustering his forces at Caesarea, and dividing them into three bands, Titus marched for the doomed city. Arrived there, he fortified three camps—one on the north, one on the west, and one, garrisoned by the Tenth Legion, on the Mount of Olives. Upon this last the Jews made a sally as the soldiers were digging the trenches; but they were soon beaten down the hill.

While the trumpets were blowing at Caesarea, and the clang of the Roman march was shaking the land, murder, and outrage, and cruel terror filled all Jerusalem. Robbers, calling themselves Zealots, had flocked in from the country. Eleazar, at the head of one set of these, held the inner court of the Temple. John of Gischala, another leader of ruffians, occupying ground somewhat lower, poured constant showers of darts and stones into the holy house, often killing worshippers as they stood at the very altar. In this mad war, houses full of corn were burned, and misery of every kind was inflicted on the wretched people. In despair they called Simon of Gerasa to their aid, and thus there were three hostile factions within the walls.

The great feast of the Passover came, and the Temple was thrown open to the thousands who crowded from every comer of the land to offer up their yearly sacrifice. Mingling in disguise with the throng, with weapons under their clothes, John's party gained entrance into the sacred court, and soon drove out their foes. The poor worshippers, all trampled and bleeding, escaped as best they could. John remained master of the Temple; and the three factions were reduced to two.

Within the city there were above 23,000 fighting men—a strong body if united. There was, indeed, a temporary union, when they saw the Roman soldiers busily cutting down all the trees in the suburbs, rolling their trunks together, and to the top of the three great banks thus formed dragging the huge siege-engines of the time—rams, catapults, and balistas.

The siege opened in three places at once, towards the end of March, 70 A. D. The Roman missiles poured like hail upon the city; but none were so terrible as the stones, sometimes weighing a talent (125 pounds), which were cast from the east by the Tenth Legion. The Jews replied with some engines planted on the wall by Simon, flung torches at the Roman banks, and made an unavailing sally at the Tower of Hippicus.

Three towers of heavy timber, covered with thick iron plates,, were then erected by Titus. Rising higher than the walls, and carrying light engines, they were used to drive the Jews from their posts of defence. The falling of one of these at midnight with a loud crash spread alarm through the Roman camp; but it did not last long. At dawn the rams were swinging away, and pounding against the shaking wall, which on the fifteenth day of the siege yielded to Nico (the Conqueror), as the most ponderous of the Roman engines was called by the Jews. The legions, pouring through the breach, gained the first wall: nine days later, the second wall was levelled with the ground.

Then followed a pause of five days, after which the attack was renewed at John's Monument, and the Towner of Antonia. At the same time, Josephus, a noble Jew, from whose graphic history this sketch is drawn, went to the walls, as he had done before—as he did more than once again, to plead with his countrymen. But all in vain, for the Zealots were bent on holding out, and slew such of the people as they found trying to desert.

Famine had long before begun its deadly work. Mothers were already snatching the morsels from their children's lips. The robbers broke open every shut door in search of food, and tortured most horribly all who were thought to have a hidden store. Gaunt men, who had crept beyond the walls by night to gather a few wild herbs, were often robbed by these wretches of the handful of green leaves for which they had risked their lives. Yet, in spite of this, the starving people went out into the valleys in such numbers that the Romans caught them at the rate of five hundred a day, and crucified them before the walls, until there was no wood left to make another cross.

His serious losses made Titus resolve to hem in the city with a wall. It was built in the amazingly short time of three days! The attack was then directed against the Tower of Antonia, which stood at the north-west corner of the Temple, on a slippery rock, fifty cubits high. Four banks were raised. Some Roman soldiers, creeping in with their shields above their heads, loosened four of the foundation stones; and the wall, battered at all day, fell suddenly in the night.

But there was another wall inside. One Sabi'nus, a little dark Syrian soldier, led a forlorn hope of eleven men up to this in broad noon-day, gained the top, and put the Jews to flight; but tripping over a stone he was killed, as were three of his band. A night or two after, sixteen Romans stole up the wall, slew the guards, and blew a startling trumpet blast. The Jews fled. Titus and his men, swarming up the ruined wall, dashed at the entrance of the Temple. After ten hours' fighting, the Jews drove the Romans out of the Temple, but not from the Tower of Antonia.

After the Roman wall was built, the famine and the plague grew worse. Young men dropt dead in the streets. Piles of decaying corpses filled the lanes, and were thrown by thousands over the walls. No herbs were to be got now. Men, in the rage of hunger, gnawed their shoes, the leather of their shields, and even old wisps of hay. Robbers, with wolfish eyes, ransacked every dwelling, and, when one day they came clamouring for food to the house of the daughter of Eleazar, she set before them the roasted flesh of her own infant son! Brutal and rabid though they were, they fled from the house of that wretched mother.

At last the daily sacrifice ceased to be offered, and the war closed round the Temple. The cloisters were soon burned. Six days' battering had no effect on the great gates; fire alone could clear a path for the eagles. A clay was fixed for the grand assault; but on the evening before, the Romans having penetrated as far as the Holy House, a soldier, climbing on the shoulders of another, put a blazing torch to one of the golden windows of the north side. The building was soon a sheet of leaping flames; and Titus, who had always desired to save the Temple, came running from his tent, but the din of war and the crackling flames prevented his voice from being heard.

On over the smoking cloisters trampled the legions, fierce for plunder. The Jews sank in heaps of dead and dying around the altar, which dripped with their blood.

BAS–RELIEF ON THE ARCH
OF TITUS – *(From a Photograph)*

More fire was thrown upon the hinges of the gate; and then no human word or hand could save the house, where God himself had loved to dwell. Never did the stars of night look down on a more piteous scene. Sky and hill and town and valley were all reddened with one fearful hue. The roar of flames, the shouts of Romans, the shrieks of wounded Zealots, rose wild into the scorching air, and echoed among the mountains all around. But sadder far was the wail of broken hearts which burst from the streets below, when marble wall and roof of gold came crashing down, and the Temple was no more. Then, and only then, did the Jews let go the trust which had all along sustained them, that God would deliver his ancient people, smiting the Romans with some sudden blow.

The Upper City then became a last refuge for the despairing remnant of the garrison. Simon and John were there; but the arrogant tyrants were broken down to trembling cowards. And when, after eighteen days' work, banks were raised, and

---

the terrible ram began to sound anew on the ramparts, the panic-struck Jews fled like hunted foxes to hide in the caves of the hill. The eagles flew victorious to the summit of the citadel, while Jewish blood ran so deep down Zion that burning houses were quenched in the red stream!

The siege lasted 134 days, during which 1,100,000 Jews perished, and 97,000 were taken captive. Some were kept to grace the Roman triumph; some were sent to toil in the mines of Egypt; some fought in provincial theatres with gladiators and wild beasts; those under seventeen were sold as slaves. John was imprisoned for life; Simon, after being led in triumph, was slain at Rome.

It was a gay holiday, when the emperor and his son, crowned with laurel and clad in purple, passed in triumph through the crowded streets of Rome. Of the many rich spoils adorning the pageant none were gazed on with more curious eyes than the golden table, the candlestick with seven branching lamps, and the holy book of the Law, rescued from the flames of the Temple. It was the last page of a tragic story. The Jews—homeless ever since, yet always preserving an indestructible nationality—were scattered among the cities of Earth, to be the Shylocks of a day that is gone by, and the Rothschilds of our own happier age.

—W. F. Coller

Words

amazingly, *wonderfully.*
citadel, *fortress.*
clamouring, *shouting.*
despairing, *losing hope.*
disguise, *false dress.*
engines, *machines.*
foundation, *basement.*
garrisoned, *occupied.*
gladiators, *sword-fighters.*
indestructible, *imperishable.*
inflicted, *visited.*
levelled, *razed.*
loosened, *detached.*

missiles, *projectiles.*
nationality, *unity as a people.*
pageant, *spectacle.*
penetrated, *made way.*
piteous, *melancholy.*
plague, *disease.*
ponderous, *heavy.*
ransacked, *plundered.*
siege, *investment.*
temporary, *for a time.*
unavailing, *fruitless.*
weighing, *in weight.*
wretchedness, *misery.*

Questions.

Who was sent by Nero to subdue the rebellious Jews? Why did he leave Syria? To whom was the siege of Jerusalem left? How did he dispose his forces around the city? What different factions existed within the city? How were these reduced to two? When did the siege open? At how many point? How did the Romans drive the Jews from the walls? When was the first wall gained? When the second? Who went to the walls to plead with his countrymen? What led many of the Jews to desert the city? What plan did Titus adopt to hem them in more effectually? Against what tower was the attack then directed? How was it gained? To what extremities did the famine drive the besieged? What brought the siege to a sudden crisis? What became a last refuge for the garrison? In how many days was it reduced? How long did the siege last? How many Jews perished? How many were taken captive? What spoils were displayed in the Roman triumph?

☆ ☆ ☆ ☆ ☆ ☆ ☆ ☆ ☆ ☆ ☆ ☆ ☆ ☆ ☆ ☆ ☆ ☆ ☆ ☆

与耶稣被钉死在十字架上的时候相比，耶路撒冷的某些部分已经略有改变。三十五年后的今天，罗马的上空聚集着一群雄鹰围绕着它们的猎物。这些年来，犹太人已被贬低为越来越深的罪恶和悲惨的化身。最后，由于愤怒和侮辱的刺激，犹太人开始行动起来反抗罗马的领导者。尼禄派出伟大的维斯帕西安去压制犹太人顽固的骄傲。

在遇到了一些麻烦和延误之后，罗马人征服了加利利和佩雷亚。之后征服者维斯帕西安开始对耶路撒冷进行围城并在该赛利亚准备进行最后的进攻。就在这个时候，维斯帕西安听到了尼禄的死讯。随后，军队在巴基斯坦宣布维斯帕西安为皇帝。之后他快速前往帝国的第二大城市，安全的亚历山大。当听说罗马人在为他的荣誉举行盛宴时，他又动身去了意大利，因此，围攻耶路撒冷的事情就交给了他的儿子提图斯。

提图斯在该赛利亚召集了他的部队，并将其分为三队，他带领着这支队伍向着这座注定要毁灭的城市前进。到了那里，他建造了三大防御工事，一处在北面，一处在西面，一处在橄榄山由第十军团驻守。当士兵们正在最后一处防御工事修筑战壕时，犹太人进行了突袭，但很快他们就被打下了山。

当号鸣声在凯赛利亚响起时，罗马军队使得这片土地震动得叮当响。杀戮、暴行、残酷的恐怖充斥着整个耶路撒冷，这群从罗马蜂拥而来的强盗们不知羞耻地声称自己是狂热者。圣殿内的决战开始了，以利亚赛被安置在这些军队的最前面。一个恶棍的领袖基斯卡拉·约翰占领了一些南部更低处的阵地，他们把阵雨般不断倾泻于圣殿内的飞镖和石头投向站在圣坛上的信徒们。在这场疯狂的战争中，装满谷物的房子被烧毁，这些可怜的人们遭受了各种悲惨的境遇。他们在绝望中寻求西蒙杰拉什的援助，于是城墙中出现了三方的对立。

随着逾越节盛宴的到来，神庙被打开，成千上万的人从四面八方奔涌而来，奉献他们的年祭。将武器隐藏在衣服中混入人群的约翰的党羽进入了神圣的庭院，并很快赶走了敌人。这群可怜的信徒们啊，他们本可以很好地逃离所有的践踏和流血。约翰仍然是这座神殿的守护者，即便三个军队的派别已被减少到两个。

在这座城市中大约有23 000多名勇士，如果他们联合在一起，会组成一支强大的军队。事实上，这是一个临时的联盟。当他们看见罗马的士兵们不停地砍伐郊区的树木，他们便一起滚动砍下的树干，一时间他们将当代的巨大攻城引擎——撞木、弩炮、投石机拖到了三大堤岸的顶部。

这次围攻在三个地方同时进行，一直持续到公元70年3月的末期。罗马部队发射的炮弹，就像一泻而下的冰雹降落在这座城市。但最可怕的袭击，来自于东部的第十军团，他们的炮弹有时会重达125磅。犹太人认为，西蒙在墙上设置的一些投向罗马对岸的火炮引擎，对于希皮库斯塔的突围是徒劳无效的。

提图斯竖立起三架沉重的覆盖着厚厚铁板的木材高架。他们用高于城墙的木架来支撑轻便的攻击引擎，干扰着犹太人在城墙上的防御。其中一个高架，在某一午夜塌了下来，伴随着一声震裂的巨响，惊扰了整个罗马军队。黎明时分，城墙由于连续的撞击变得摇摆不定，在城墙内被围困了15天的犹太人最终向罗马最高统治者的尼科（征服者）投降。罗马军队通过这不间断的进攻攻破了第一座城门，9天之后，第二座城门也被夷为平地。

暂停了5天之后，罗马军队开始进攻被重建的约翰纪念碑和安东尼亚塔。与此同时，绘制出生动历史草图的高贵的犹太人约瑟夫斯，正准备着防御工作，就像他之前做这些工作一样，就像他不止一次这样做一样——约瑟夫斯一再地恳求他的同胞们能看清事实。但这一切都是徒劳的，狂热者们下定决心叛变并杀死了那些试图邀功的人。

饥荒早已经开始夺取人们的性命。母亲们从她们孩子的嘴里抢夺食物的碎屑；强盗们打开每一扇关闭的门去寻找食物，并可怕的折磨着所有被认为有秘密储存食物的人；一些憔悴难耐的男人，在夜间偷偷地爬到墙外去采集一些野菜，为了这几片可怜的菜叶他们常常冒着被劫的生命危险。然而尽管如此，罗马人仍以每天500个人的速度，抓捕着那些逃进山谷的饥饿人民，直到没有地方再立十字架，没有木头可以再做十字架来钉人为止。

犹太人严重的损失使得提图斯决定解决了城市的边缘问题。难以置信的是，这个问题的解决仅用了三天的时间！这次袭击针对的是坐落在圣殿西北角的湿滑岩石上，有50肘高度的安东尼亚塔。四大部队聚集在一起。突袭是在一天晚上进行的，一部分罗马士兵将他们的盾牌放置在头顶匍匐上前，松开了安东尼亚塔的四大基石，他们向着城墙攻击了一整天，庙里的城墙最终突然崩塌了。

在其中还有另外一面城墙。一个黑黑的叙利亚小士兵赛比勒斯，在白天带领着

11个人组成的敢死队，到达城墙的顶部与犹太人战斗。但他最终被石头绊倒而被杀死，其他三个分队的成员最后的结局也一样。两个晚上之后，16个罗马人偷偷爬上了墙，杀死了守卫，并吹响了号角。犹太人逃跑了。提图斯和他的士兵们翻过摧毁的城墙，冲向神庙的入口。十个小时的战斗后，犹太人将罗马人驱逐出圣殿，但仍没有赶出安东尼亚塔。

罗马墙建成以后，饥荒和瘟疫变得更严重了。大量的年轻人死于街头。腐烂的尸体堆满了整个街道，成千上万的尸体被扔掷到墙外。没有药物能拿来救治人们。饥饿使人们变得愤怒，开始撕咬自己的鞋子、盾牌的皮革、甚至一捆捆干草。强盗们的眼中发出贪婪的目光，洗劫着每一所住宅，当有一天他们在伊利亚赛家的女儿面前叫嚷着要食物的时候，伊利亚赛竟烤着她亲生的婴儿的肉招待他们！尽管他们野蛮又疯狂，但他们还是从那位可怜母亲的房子中离开了。

日复一日的牺牲终于结束了，战争使得神庙的四周被封闭起来，修道院也很快被烧毁了。六天的持续进攻，对这扇雄伟的大门没有造成什么严重的影响，大火倒是为罗马人开辟了一条道路。黏土本来是作为最大的进攻方式用来突击的，但在之前一天的傍晚时分，罗马人已经秘密潜入神庙之中。一个士兵爬到另一个士兵的肩膀上，将熊熊燃烧的火炬投掷到北侧的金色窗户上，这座神庙很快就染上了一片跳跃的火焰的色彩。提图斯从他的帐篷中跑过来想要保住神庙，但战争的喧闹声和火焰的噼啪声掩盖了他的声音。

在烟雾缭绕的修道院回廊内，充满了罗马军队无情的践踏和残忍的掠夺。无数被杀的犹太人被堆积在祭坛的周围，整个祭坛都浸满了他们的鲜血。越来越多的火把被投掷在门的铰链上面，没有人用实际行动去挽救这座上帝偏爱的房子。夜空中的星辰俯视着人间如此凄凉的景象。天空、山冈、城镇和山谷全都是一片可怕的红色色调。火焰的咆哮、罗马人的喊叫、受伤狂热者的尖叫声、野蛮的掠夺声，都在这灼热的空气中升起，回荡在四周的群山当中。但更可悲的是当大理石的墙壁和金色的屋顶轰然倒塌，神庙不复存在，随之破碎的是犹太人的心。一直以来，犹太人都相信上帝会拯救他古老的子民，会给罗马人突如其来的还击。

上城成为绝望的残余驻军最后的避难所。西蒙和约翰仍在坚守，然而傲慢的暴君却被打成了一个颤颤发抖的懦夫。18天的准备工作之后，城池已经高筑，西蒙和约翰做着最后的宣讲，可怕的进攻声在防御的城墙边重新响起，惊慌失措的犹太人像狐狸一样四处逃窜，想躲在山中洞穴里面。胜利的雄鹰飞翔到城堡的顶端，犹太人那深红色的鲜血流淌在要塞马萨达，房子里燃烧的大火也都被扑灭在红色的溪流中。

围攻持续了134天，在这期间110万犹太人丧生，97 000人被虏。一些人因为罗马人彰显的恩泽而逃过一劫，一些人被送往埃及的矿山去做苦力，一些人被送往各大地方的剧院与角斗士和猛兽进行斗争表演，那些17岁以下的孩子被卖为了奴隶。西蒙被处死，约翰死于罗马狱中。

这是个令人愉快的节日，当皇帝和他的儿子戴上桂冠，穿上紫色的长袍，走向那通往胜利的拥挤的罗马街道。比起那金表、七宝烛台和圣书，这些丰富战利品装饰的宴会，更让那些好奇的人们无法挪开眼神。神庙是这个悲惨故事的最后一页，犹太人从此无家可归，但它仍旧是一个坚不可摧的民族——散落在地球上的各大城市之间。终有一天夏洛克的时代将会过去，而属于犹太人的罗斯柴尔德家族的幸福时代终会来临。

——W.F·科勒

Lesson 40   LEBANON
第四十课　黎巴嫩

Lebanon stands in some respects alone and unrivalled among the mountains of the world. A most impressive signal of approach to the Holy Land is the first glimpse, off the shores of Cy'prus, of the ancient mountain rising from the eastern waters, its peaks wreathed with everlasting snows, and flushed with shifting hues of rose and purple in the clear evening sky. High up in its aerial solitude, pure and lustrous like a cloud steeped in sunshine, it stands for us as the emblem of that old oriental world which lies in its shadow;—Damascus, buried in its depths of ever-blooming verdure; Antioch, where the Oron'tes runs sparkling through its laurel groves to the sea; Baalbee, with its gray colossal relics—the Stonehenge of the desert; Tyre, discrowned and desolate, by the waters; and away in the south, the hills of Galilee with Jerusalem beyond, and the red peaks of the great and terrible wilderness which closes in this land of wonder.

From the time when the Jewish leader sighed to see "the good land beyond Jordan, that goodly mountain, even Lebanon," through those later days when Hebrew seers and poets looked up to its vineyards and forests, its purple slopes and its burnished silver diadem, and drew from them eternal types of truth and beauty, what a boundless wealth of sacred tradition and imagery has been treasured up in the venerable name of Lebanon!

This name, which is now confined to the eastern mountain chain, "Lib'anus" properly so called, is used in a wider sense by the inspired waiters, and includes the great parallel range of "Anti-Libanus," which in Hermon, its loftiest summit, attains a height of ten thousand feet. This mountain, towering in its magnificent elevation over the plain, is "the tower of Lebanon which looketh toward Damascus."

BEIROUT AND MOUNTAINS OF LEBANON

To the Jewish people, so proud of their national Temple and its associations with the golden age of their history, Lebanon, on this account alone, would be reverently endeared. From its quarries were hewn the massive blocks of stone which rose on Mori'ah without sound of axe or hammer, and many a giant tree had been felled by the Tyrian woodman in its forests to yield the precious wood so largely employed in the building. In the luxurious days of the later kings the mansions of the noble and the wealthy in Jerusalem were embellished with this costly wood—"ceiled with cedar, and painted with vermilion."

The height of this tree made it a symbol of pride; its stateliness and far-spreading branches, of extended empire: "The Assyrian was a cedar in Lebanon with fair branches, and with a shadowing shroud, and of an high stature; no tree in the garden of God was like unto him for beauty." With a deeper meaning, as an emblem of the spiritual progress of the believer, the psalmist says: "The righteous shall grow like a cedar in Lebanon."

The mountain region of Lebanon is a world in itself, peopled by ancient races, whose religious feuds have often carried devastation through its fairest valleys. The northern part of the range is occupied mainly by a Christian population, the Ma'ronites; the southern by the Drus'es, a brave, high-spirited people, whose religion is a mystery, and seems to be a kind of Moham'medanism, tinctured with the wild fanaticism of the East.

Situated on a lovely bay at the base of Lebanon is Bei'rout, suggesting to us what Tyre may have been like, in the days of its glory. The coast is dotted with villages, and the number of them scattered about the mountain is amazing. On approaching it from the sea, one is struck by the groups of white dwellings that gleam among the vineyards on its lower slopes, and higher up speckle the dark pine-groves,—multitudes of little hamlets clinging to its sides, or hanging like swallows' nests from its rocky eaves. Everywhere, as one makes his way through the storm-gashed ravines of the mountain, where cataracts leap and torrents twist and foam, each sudden turn of the road brings into view new villages, dropped about here and there in green retreats, and slumbering in their orchards and mulberry groves like nooks of Paradise shut out from the world.

From the highest point, which perhaps one has gained on a journey from Damascus and Baalbec to the Cedar Forest, the prospect is one of surpassing grandeur. All at once the mountains sink and fall away to a giddy depth beneath—a maze of furrowed ridges, surging, like the waves of a frozen sea, through a veil of warm blue vapour; old castles and convents perched on islanded heights; villages everywhere clustering on the terraced steeps; at your feet the venerable Cedar Wood dwindled to a thicket of shrubs; and away in the distance the hazy gleam of the Mediterranean waters. One is reminded of the paradise of that gorgeous dream of Coleridge:—

"There were gardens bright with sinuous rills,
    Where blossomed many an incense-bearing tree;
And here were forests ancient as the hills,
    Infolding sunny spots of greenery."

It is not for the multitude of its cedars that Lebanon is now renowned; but the spot where stand the last surviving relics of the forests that once clothed its sides

THE CEDAR GROVE

will always be a haunt of pilgrimage. The wood contains about three hundred cedars, of which fifty trees, twisted by the storms and scarred by the tempests of centuries, may challenge special admiration. On a mound in the centre stands the patriarch of the grove, nine feet in diameter, spreading his ponderous arms, each a tree in itself, over the heads of the many generations that have grown up below.

Nowhere, perhaps, is the wonderful union of mountain grandeur with beauty of site and richness of culture better seen than near the Christian village of Ehden, described in glowing terms by all who have visited it. It stands on the brink of a gorge nearly two thousand feet in depth, its houses of hewn stone scattered under the shade of walnut trees, every slope and terrace waving with cornfields and vineyards, and groves of mulberry and poplar. The chime of bells, so seldom heard in the East, awakens a peculiar emotion when ringing the hour of prayer in these Christian villages.

Stability, fragrance, fruitfulness, types of the highest graces that beautify and exalt the life of man, dwell in pure and endless companionship beneath the cedars of Lebanon.

—J. D. Burns

Words

associations, *connections*.
burnished, *polished*.
colossal, *huge*.
culture, *cultivation*.
devastation, *ruin*.
dwindled, *reduced*.
embellished, *ornamented*.
emblem, *token*.
emotion, *feeling*.
fanaticism, *religious frenzy*.

fragrance, *aroma*.
fruitfulness, *productiveness*.
impressive, *affecting*.
includes, *embraces*.
lustrous, *bright*.
luxurious, *voluptuous*.
magnificent, *grand*.
multitudes, *crowds*.
reminded, *put in mind*.
slumbering, *sleeping*.

stability, *steadfastness*.
surpassing, *excessive*.
surviving, *remaining*.

tinctured, *tinged*.
unrivalled, *peerless*.
wilderness, *desert*.

Questions

What relics of the old oriental world lie in the shadow of Lebanon? What is the highest peak of Anti-Lebanon? and its height? Why would Lebanon be reverently endeared to the Jewish people? Of what was the cedar tree the symbol? Who dwell in the northern and the southern parts of the Lebanon region respectively? By what is one struck on approaching Lebanon from the sea? How many trees does the Cedar Forest now contain? Describe the patriarch of the grove. Where is the village of Ehden situated? For what is it remarkable?

从某种程度上，黎巴嫩独自位于世界的山脉之中，无与伦比。第一眼瞥见的最令人印象深刻的信号，是在靠近圣地的地方。远离塞浦路斯的海岸，从东部海域上升起古老山脉，它的山峰永远环绕着白雪。玫瑰色和紫色的薄雾，在晴朗的夜空中晕眩开来。在高高的空中，黎巴嫩像纯洁、光辉的沐浴在阳光之中的云朵，它象征着这个处于它的阴影之中的古老的东方世界——大马士革，埋藏在四季翠绿的深处；在安提阿，奥伦特河通过它的月桂树林流向了波光粼粼的大海；巴力的灰色巨大的蜜蜂，像沙漠中的巨石阵一般；泰尔山被水域包围着，显得如此荒凉；在南部，加利利山和耶路撒冷，红峰和可怕的旷野，将神奇封锁在这片土地之内。

从犹太领袖叹着气看到"约旦以外的美丽大地，那巍峨的山峰存在在黎巴嫩"开始，从希伯来的先知和诗人望着它的葡萄园和森林开始，它紫色的斜坡和充满光泽的王冠点缀着它们永恒的真理与美丽。这是多么无限丰富的神圣传统和形象，它们早已珍藏在黎巴嫩的古老名字之中！

这个名字，目前仅局限于东部的山区，"lib'anus"是更准确的称呼，被受到鼓舞的朝圣者们用在更广泛的意义上，包括了位于对面赫尔蒙山的大范围区域。它最巍峨的顶峰达到一万英尺的高度，从平原地区升起的这座山，因为它的巍峨与壮丽，是"黎巴嫩之塔，俯瞰着大马士革。"

犹太人对于自己国家的圣殿，连同这与他们历史上的黄金时代的关联，感到如此骄傲。在这个方面，黎巴嫩会为虔诚的人们所钟爱。从采石场凿出的石头，不经过斧子或者锤子的打造，由摩利亚山的大石块中凿出。泰尔山的樵夫们为了得到主要用于建筑业中的珍贵木材，砍伐许多森林中的大树。在最后的君王统治的辉煌时代，在耶路撒冷的贵族和富人的豪宅之中，都装饰有这种昂贵的木材，"雪松做成的天花板，被涂成了朱红色"。

这种树木的高度，使它成为一种骄傲的象征；它的威严和远远伸展开的树枝象征着扩张的帝国，"亚述帝国是一棵成长于黎巴嫩的香柏树，拥有美丽的树枝，巨大的荫蔽和极高的高度；在上帝的花园中，没有什么树木比它更美了。"它象征着信徒精神的进步，有了这一层更深的意义，诗人说："正义如黎巴嫩的香柏树一般成长。"

黎巴嫩的山区本身就是一个世界。古老的种族居住在这里，他们的宗教纷争常常给他们最美丽的山谷带来破坏。山区的北部范围主要由信奉基督教的人口占据，他们被称作马龙族；南部的晶簇是一个勇敢的民族，意气风发，他们的宗教极其神秘，似乎是伊斯兰教的一种，带有东方的野蛮与狂热。

一个叫故乡的地方，位于黎巴嫩底部一个可爱的海湾之上。它提醒着我们，在它的光辉岁月中，泰尔山是什么样的。海岸零星布满了一些村庄，它们散布在山脉之中的数目是惊人的。从海洋之中接近它，一个人会被这样的景象深深震撼，白色的住宅群闪烁在其下的山坡上的葡萄园之间，在较高的地方，则散布着棕黑色的松树林——众多的小村庄紧贴着树林的两侧，或者像燕子的巢穴一般，悬挂在岩石的屋檐之下。当一个人通过风暴划过的沟壑时，这里瀑布飞跃着，山洪扭曲着，喷吐出泡沫，每条道路的突然转向，都将展现出一个新的村庄，在每一个地方在绿色中消退，最终沉睡在果园和桑树林之中，就像天堂的角落，与外面的世界完全隔绝开来。

从最高点出发，这也许是一次经过大马士革和巴勒贝克雪松森林的旅程，前景都将充满了伟大的壮丽景象。突然之间，山脉沉了下去，一直降到令人眩晕的低处。这里像极了一个布满沟渠的迷宫，汹涌澎湃，像冰封的海面涌起了波涛，透过了一层温暖的蓝色水蒸气；古老的城堡和修道院坐落在孤岛的高处；村庄到处聚集在梯田周围；在你的脚下，古老的雪松木已经缩小成了一丛灌木林；在远方朦胧的微光之中是地中海的水域。一个人会想到柯勒律治那华丽的梦的天堂：

花园里蜿蜒的小溪熠熠闪光，
树梢之上，繁花似锦；
英雄一样古老的森林与山脉，
在阳光洒满的地方充斥着绿色。

如今黎巴嫩变得著名，并不是因为它的柏树的壮观，但最后幸存的森林曾矗立的地方，会成为朝圣者经常出现的地方。森林中包含约300棵的香柏树，其中的50棵树，在几个世纪以来的风暴和飓风的扭曲中变得伤痕累累，它们可能会引发人们特别的钦佩。在一个土堆的中心，有小树林的元老，直径达9英尺。它笨重的臂膀伸展开来，都能形成一棵小树。在它们脚下，已经有许多世代的小树成长起来。

说到基督教的埃登村，正如看到过这里的人们热情洋溢地描述一样，也许没有任何其他地方，比它更能将山的雄伟奇妙与丰富美好的文化如此奇妙地连接在一起。它位于峡谷的边缘，这条峡谷深近2 000英尺，其间凿石砌成的房子分散在核桃树的树荫之下，每个斜坡和梯田都布满了玉米地和葡萄园，还有桑树林和白杨林。钟鸣声在东方很少能听到，当它在这些基督徒的村庄祷告的时刻，唤醒了一种特殊的感情。

稳定、芬芳、多产、美景和提升了人类生命的优雅，在纯洁和无尽的友谊的陪伴下，在黎巴嫩的香柏树下成长。

Lesson 41   GREAT OCEAN ROUTES
第四十一课   大洋航线

(To be read before a Map of the World)

Southampton, which is the station of most of the great ocean mails, is a quaint old English sea-port at the head of Southampton Water in Hants. Two passages lead from Southampton Water to the English Channel—the Solent and the Spithead; and between them lies the Isle of Wight. A northern branch of the Spithead is Portsmouth Harbour, the principal station of the English Navy.

The great ocean routes which have their starting-point at Southampton are—the Mediterranean, the West Indian, the Cape, East Indian, Australian, and China routes.

The principal vessels that follow the Mediterranean route are those in connection with the overland route to India. But by this route also communication is kept up with the whole of the Mediterranean coasts, and an extensive trade—chiefly in corn—is earned on between the Black Sea and the principal British ports.

The Cape and East Indian mail steamer, on leaving Southampton, makes direct for St. Vincent, one of the Cape Verd Islands, where there is a commodious harbour, a free port, and a coaling station. These islands are situated 320 miles west of Cape Verd, on the coast of Africa. They form a Portuguese possession. Cotton cloth and salt are their most valuable exports.

The next station on the Cape route is Ascension Island, 1800 miles south-east of St. Vincent. This small island, which is 8 miles long, by 6 broad at its western end, has belonged to England since 1815. At George Town, on its north-western coast, there is a fort with military quarters, surrounded by a few detached residences; and opposite the town there is an open roadstead. It is a convenient victualling station for the African squadron of the English Navy.

Eight hundred miles south-east of Ascension, the steamer reaches the interesting island of St. Helena, the scene of the captivity and death of Napoleon Buonaparte. The chief settlement in the island is James Town, on the north-western shore. The interior is an elevated table-land, 1500 feet above the sea-level. Near the centre of this plateau is Longwood, the residence of Napoleon from 1815 till 1821. He was buried on the island; but in 1840 his remains were removed to Paris. Indian steamers do not often call at St. Helena on the outward voyage, but it is a usual station in the homeward track.

After St. Helena, the steamer next stops at Cape Town; so called from the Cape of Good Hope, in the neighbourhood of which it stands. Cape of Good Hope Province, of which Cape Town is the capital, became a British possession in 1814. Prior to that time it belonged to Holland; and the town bears evident traces of its Dutch origin. It has canals in the principal streets; the houses are flat-roofed and painted or whitewashed, with terraces and gardens in front. It is situated on the south-western shore of Table Bay, under the shadow of Table Mount.

From Cape Town the steamer proceeds to Mauritius, a considerable island (36 miles long by 20 broad) in the Indian Ocean. The Dutch called the island Mauritius, after Prince Maurice, their Stadtholder, when they settled there in 1598. Abandoned by the Dutch in 1715, the French took possession of it, and called it the Isle of France. In 1810 it was taken by the British, and its possession was confirmed to them in 1814; but the companion island of Bourbon, which had been taken at the same time, was restored to the French. Port Louis, the capital of Mauritius, is a place of growing prosperity. It has over 50,000 inhabitants, and it is now in direct communication, not only with India, but with Aden and Australia.

The next station on the direct route is Point de Galle, a seaport at the southern extremity of the island of Ceylon. Here the Cape and Overland routes meet, as the steamers from Aden and Bombay also touch at Point de Galle. This port forms a kind of mail depot for the whole of the East, as branch mails proceed thence to Madras, Calcutta, Penang, Singapore, Australia, New Zealand, and Hong-Kong.

Ships returning to England from Australia generally prefer the Pacific and Cape Horn route to that by the Cape of Good Hope and the Atlantic. By this means vessels are able, both in going and returning, to take advantage of the westerly winds and currents which prevail in the neighbourhood of both of these stormy Capes.

After doubling Cape Horn, the homeward-bound ship makes for the Falkland Islands, which form a convenient British outpost in the southern seas. This group, consisting of two large and a host of small islands, is situated about 300 miles from the coast of Patagonia. The western of the two large islands is 90 miles, the eastern is 100 miles in length. Their population is sparse; but vegetation is luxuriant, and cattle abundant. Vessels frequenting these seas call at the Falkland Islands to procure provisions and fresh water. The direct route from the Falkland Islands to Southampton is by the Cape Verd Islands, where the homeward and outward routes meet. A vessel that has sailed from St. Vincent to Melbourne by the Cape of Good Hope, and has returned to St. Vincent by Cape Horn, has obviously sailed round the world.

The West Indian mail is carried direct from Southampton to St. Thomas, a small island belonging to Denmark, in the group called the Virgin Islands. The capital of St. Thomas is a free port, and one of the best trading places in the West Indies. It is built in the form of an amphitheatre around a spacious bay; hence its selection as a great mail station, and as the chief magazine and market for West Indian produce.

From St. Thomas the mail steamer proceeds to Kingston in Jamaica, which has also a fine harbour, available for the largest ships. Another route to Kingston is by the Bermudas, a group of nearly four hundred islands, about 600 miles from the coast of the United States. These islands—the "still vexed Bermoothes" of Shakespeare—are of great value to Britain as a naval station, one of them containing a land-locked harbour, which has few equals in the -world. The port referred to is also used as an arsenal and as a convict settlement; and it is the centre of important transit trade between the West Indies and the mainland of North America. There is regular steam communication from Bermuda to Halifax, New York, and St. Thomas.

From Kingston the mail route is continued to Colon, on the northern side of the Isthmus of Panama. Thence it proceeds by canal across the isthmus to Panama—a distance of 42 miles. Panama has thus been raised to a position of great importance among Pacific sea-ports. It is now the station for the mails between Great Britain and Peru and Chili. Steamers also ply between Panama and San Francisco in California.

The South American and Pacific route, starting from Liverpool, proceeds by way of Bordeaux, and calls at Lisbon, the capital of Portugal, which stands in the relation of parent state to the modern Brazilian Republic. From Lisbon the route proceeds in a south-westerly direction for upwards of 600 miles to the mountainous island of Madeira, which gives its name to a famous wine made from the grapes grown on the island.

Madeira is also a favourite resort of consumptive patients during the winter and spring months.

Madeira is a Portuguese island. The Canaries, those next visited, belong to Spain, and form a station at which all ships sailing between Spain and the East or West Indies regularly call. Conspicuous among them by its lofty snow-capped peak is Teneriffe, an extinct, or, at least, quiescent volcano, which rises 12,182 feet above the ocean.

Teneriffe

The Cape Verd Islands, already referred to in connection with the East Indian route, mark the next stage in the voyage. The steamer then crosses the Atlantic in a south-westerly direction, and makes no further pause till it reaches either Pernambuco or Bahia (for they are visited alternately by successive mails) on the north-eastern coast of Brazil. Thence it proceeds to Rio de Janeiro, the capital of the country, and the second city in commercial importance in South America. Rio, to which alternate steamers sail direct from Lisbon, is situated on the western shore of a vast bay or inlet, 17 miles in length, and 11 in extreme width, which is studded with islands, and forms one of the noblest harbours in the world. This harbour communicates with the Atlantic by a deep and narrow passage between two granite mountains. The entrance is so safe as to render the services of local pilots entirely unnecessary. Yet so commanding is the position of the fortresses at the mouth of the harbour, on its islands, and on the surrounding heights, that the ingress of a hostile fleet would be a work of the utmost difficulty.

From either side of that contracted entrance stretch away, as far as the eye can reach, lofty mountains, whose pointed summits and fantastic shapes recall the glories of Alpland. On the left, the Sugar-Loaf Mountain stands like a giant sentinel over the metropolis of Brazil. On the right another lofty range commences near the principal fortress, which commands the entrance of the bay, and, forming curtain-like ramparts, reaches away in picturesque headlands to the bold promontory well known to all South Atlantic navigators as Cape Frio. Far through the opening of the bay, and in some places towering even above the lofty coast-barrier, can be discovered the blue outline of the distant Organ Mountains, whose lofty pinnacles will at once suggest the origin of their name.

As far up the bay as the eye can reach, lovely little islands, verdant and palm-clad, may be seen rising out of its dark bosom; while the hills and lofty mountains which surround it on all sides, when gilded by the rays of the setting sun, form a fitting frame for such a picture. At night the lights of the city have a fine effect; and when the land-breeze begins to blow, the rich odour of the orange and other perfumed flowers is borne seaward along with it.

The aspect which Rio de Janeiro presents to the beholder bears no resemblance to the compact brick walls, the dingy roofs, the tall chimneys, and the generally level sites of Northern cities. Its surface is diversified by hills of irregular but picturesque shape, which shoot up in different directions, leaving between them flat intervals of greater or less extent. Along the bases of these hills, and up their sides, stand rows of buildings, whose whitened walls and red-tiled roofs are in happy contrast with the deep green foliage that always surrounds and often embowers them.

From Rio, the steamer continues its course to Monte Video, the capital of Uruguay, situated at the mouth of the La Plata. Monte Video has an excellent harbour, around which the city is built in crescent form. On the opposite side of the La Plata, farther up the estuary, is Buenos Ayres, the capital of the Argentine Republic, and the largest city of the southern hemisphere. The navigation of the La Plata is rendered difficult by its numerous rocks and sand-banks, and it is especially dangerous daring the prevalence of the tempestuous south-west winds called pamperos. Prior to 1885 passengers and mails for Buenos

RIO DE JANEIRO

Ayres were landed at Monte Video, but in that year a harbour, large enough to accommodate the mail steamers, was constructed at Buenos Ayres.

After leaving Buenos Ayres the steamer proceeds southward; and passing through the Strait of Magellan or weathering Cape Horn, makes for Valparaiso, the chief port of Chili. Four hundred miles westward, in the midst of the Pacific, is the island of Juan Fernandez, Alexander Selkirk's solitary residence which for four years suggested to Defoe his well-known story, "Robinson Crusoe." From Valparaiso, the steamer proceeds to Callao, the port of Lima, which is six miles inland, and with which it is connected by rail. Lima, the city founded by Pizarro to be the Spanish capital of his conquests, has the reputation of being the handsomest city in. South America—its cathedral and numerous churches, with their domes and spires, giving it a magnificent appearance. We have now crossed the line of the West Indian and Panama route already described, of which the traveller may, for variety's sake, avail himself on his homeward journey.

Words

abundant, *plentiful*.
amphitheatre, *circular space*.
arsenal, *store of war material*.
available, *suitable*.
captivity, *imprisonment*.
chimneys, *smoke vents*.
commercial, *mercantile*.
commodious, *roomy*.
communication, *intercourse*.
companion, *accompanying*.
consumptive, *afflicted with disease of the lungs*.
contracted, *narrow*.
convenient, *advantage*.
convict, *criminal*.
crescent *semicircular*.
detached, *standing alone*.
elevated, *raised*.
estuary, *river-mouth*.
extensive, *large*.
extremity, *termination*.
fantastic, *fanciful*.
harbour, *haven; port*.
intervals, *spaces*.

luxuriant, *rich; copious*.
magazine, *store-house*.
magnificent, *grand*.
metropolis, *chief city*.
mountainous, *rocky*.
neighbourhood, *vicinity*.
obviously, *evidently*.
perfume, *scented*.
picturesque, *striking*.
pinnacles, *pointed summits*.
plateau, *table-land*.
prevalence, *continuance*.
promontory, *headland*.
quiescent, *dormant*.
resemblance, *likeness*.
residences, *dwelling-houses*.
roadstead, *anchorage*.
spacious, *wide*.
squadron, *division*.
terraces, *raised platforms*.
unnecessary, *needless*.
verdant, *green*.
volcano, *burning mountain*.

（请参照世界地图阅读此文）

作为大多数大洋航线的一个站点，南安普顿是一处古雅的古英国港口，在汉普郡南安普顿水域的最前端。两个通道连接南安普顿水域和英吉利海峡——索伦特海峡和斯皮利特岛，在它们之间有怀特岛。后者的北面部分突出了朴次茅斯港，是英国海军的主要海站。

大洋航线的起点在南安普顿，而途径地中海、西印度、好望角、东印度、澳大利亚和中国。

地中海航线的主要通道，是那些与印度相连接的陆路。但通过这条路线，整个地中海海岸也被连接了起来。这里存在一种广泛的贸易——主要是玉米——在黑海和主要的英国港口之间发展。

好望角和东印度邮船，离开南安普顿，直接驶向耶德群岛之一的圣文森特。那里有一个宽阔的港口、一个自由港和一个装煤站。这些岛屿位于耶德群岛以西320英里，处于非洲海岸上。它们形成了一个葡萄牙族群，棉布和盐是它们最有价值的出口物品。

好望角路线上的下一站是阿森松岛，位于圣文森特东南1 800英里处。这个小岛有8英里长，它的最西端自1815年以来就属于英格兰。在其西北海岸的乔治城，有一个军事要塞，周围有几栋独立式住宅；相反方向的小镇上有一片开放的锚地。对于非洲海军中队和英国海军来说，这里是一个方便的储粮站。

向东南方向继续前行800英里，轮船会到达有趣的圣赫勒那岛上，这里是囚禁和处死拿破仑·波拿巴的地方。岛上的主要定居点在位于海岸西北部的詹姆斯镇。这片区域的内部是一片高原地带，位于海平面以上1 500英尺高的地方。在这个高原中心的附近，是拿破仑从1815年~1821年居住的地方洛伍德。他死后葬在这个岛上，但在1840年，他的遗体被迁到巴黎。去往印度的轮船不经常造访圣赫勒那岛，但在返航的途中，此处却是一个通常的停靠点。

离开圣赫勒那岛后，轮船下一处停靠的地方在开普敦；它是因位于它附近的好望角得名的。以开普敦为首府的好望角省在1814年为英国所占有。在此之前，它属于荷兰，所以这里的城镇拥有很明显的荷兰管辖的印记。它的主要街道都通有运河，房屋是平顶的，房屋外墙绘有彩绘或粉刷成为白色，在房屋的最前端有露台和花园。它坐落在桌湾的西南海岸，在桌山的阴影笼罩之下。

轮船从开普敦继续前行，到达毛里求斯。这是印度洋上一个相当大的岛屿（有36英里长，20英里宽）。因为莫里斯王子，荷兰人将这个岛屿命名为毛里求斯，因为1598年当他们定居那里时，莫里斯王子是他们的省长。荷兰人在1715年抛弃了这个岛，法国人占领了它，并将它改名为法国之岛。在1810年，它被英国占有，其拥有权于1814年得到证实；但英国同时占有的波旁岛就被归还给了法国。毛里求斯的首都路易港是一个日益繁荣的地方，它拥有超过50 000名居民，这里现在不仅可以与印度进行直接沟通，还有亚丁湾和澳大利亚。

这条航线上的下一站是德·加勒角，这是处于锡兰岛最南端的一个海港。好望角和陆路航线在这里相逢，因为从亚丁湾和孟买驶来的航船也可以到达德·加勒角。对于整个东方世界来说，这个港口是一个很好的站点，因为从这里分航的船只可以继续前行，到达马德拉斯、加尔各答、槟城、新加坡、澳大利亚、新西兰和中国香港。

相较于途经好望角和大西洋的航线，从澳大利亚返回英国的航船，一般更喜欢途经太平洋和合恩角的路线。在这条航线中，无论去程还是返程的船只，都可以利用在这两个海角附近盛行的西风和洋流。

两次折行于合恩角之后，返航的船驶向马尔维纳斯群岛，这里在南部海域形成了一个方便到达的英国前哨。这一组群岛由两个大岛和许多小岛组成，位于巴塔哥尼亚海岸线以外约300英里处。两个大岛之中位于西部的岛长90英里，东部的则长100英里。这里人口稀疏，但植被繁茂，牛群密布。频繁航行于此的船只会在马尔维纳斯群岛登陆，以补充供给和淡水。从马尔维纳斯群岛返回南安普顿的直接航线要途经佛得角群岛，这里是去程和返程的航线相遇的地方。途经好望角从圣文森特航行到墨尔本的船只，在返回圣文森特时会途经合恩角。显然，它已经完成了一次环球航行。

西印度的航线直接从南安普顿航行到圣托马斯，这是维尔京群岛之中的一个小岛，隶属于丹麦。圣托马斯的首府是一个自由港，也是西印度群岛之中最好的交易场所之一。在一片宽敞的海湾上，它形成了一个圆形剧场的形状，因此人们选择它作为一个较大的航站和西印度产品的一个重要推广地和市场。

从圣托马斯起航，邮船继续前行至牙买加的金斯敦，这里也是一个良好的港口，即使最大的船只也可以停泊。另一条可以抵达金斯顿的路线要途经百慕大群岛。这是由近四百个岛屿组成的群岛，距美国海岸约600英里。这些岛屿——莎士比亚笔下的"宁静的百慕斯"，是极富价值的英国海军基地，其中一个岛屿包含了一个内陆港口，在全世界都很难有相应的地方与之媲美。这些港口也被用作军械库和监狱，同时，它还是西印度群岛和北美大陆之间一个重要的进出口贸易中心。在百慕大和哈利法克斯、纽约、圣托马斯之间，有定期的航船来往。

从金斯敦开始，航线继续延伸到位于巴拿马地峡北面的科朗。从那里开始，航船沿运河穿越42英里的巴拿马地峡。因此，在太平洋的海港之中，巴拿马拥有极其重要的地位。它现在是大不列颠和秘鲁、智利之间的重要站点。轮船也在巴拿马和加利福尼亚的旧金山之间航行。

　　在冬季和春季，对于酷爱消费的人们来说，马德拉也是一个他们最喜欢的度假胜地。

　　马德拉是隶属于葡萄牙的一个小岛。航线的下一站加那利群岛，则隶属于西班牙。所有航行于西班牙和东印度、西印度群岛之间的船只都经常停靠在此。在这些白雪覆盖的高耸山峰之间，最引人注目的当属特内里费岛，一个已经停喷的，或者至少休眠的火山，它位于海平面之上12 182英尺高的地方。佛得角岛屿与东印度的路线相连，标志着旅程的下一个阶段。接下来轮船在大西洋中朝着西南方向航行，直到它到达巴西东北海岸的伯南布哥或者巴伊亚（不停航行于此的轮船会交替停靠在这两个地方）时，才会做下一次停靠。从那里出发，轮船继续航行到巴西的里约热内卢，它同时也是南美第二大重要的商业城市。从里斯本驶来的船只会直接交替停靠在里约热内卢。它位于一个巨大的海湾或者也可以说是河口的西岸，长17英里，最大宽度达11英里。这里的岛屿星罗棋布，形成了世界上最重要的港口之一。这个港口与大西洋，在深处由两个位于花岗岩山脉之间的狭窄通道相连。入口处如此安全，使当地海员的服务显得完全不必要。然而，港口深处、岛屿上方和周围高处的位置却如此难以航行，这些都让一个对此处不熟悉的船队在此航行变成一项极度困难的工作。

　　从两侧的入口延伸出去，在人们看得到的地方，巍峨的山脉都因其高耸的山峰和壮丽的形象，让人想起阿尔卑斯山的荣耀。在左侧，面包山像一名哨兵一样巍峨地屹立在巴西的大都市之上。右侧则是另一片高耸的山脉，俯视着海湾的入口处，形成如帘子一样的壁垒，一直延伸到一处风景如画的海角，这就是对所有航行在南大西洋上的航海家都很著名的弗里奥海角。从海湾的入口处向前行进很远之后，甚至在海岸上的巍峨山脉之上，人们可以看到遥远的奥干山脉的蓝色轮廓，其巍峨的顶峰将立刻显示出它的名字的起源。

　　在眼睛可以看到的海湾的最远处，有一些可爱的小岛屿，翠绿的棕榈树覆盖其上，这些小岛会一直延伸到深色的海洋深处；而山丘和高山环绕四周，当夕阳的光线将它们照耀成金黄色，人们眼前就会形成一幅拥有美好轮廓的画卷。城市的灯光有美好的作用，当陆地上吹来的风开始拂动，橙子和其他芳香鲜花的丰富气味也会一并吹向大海。

　　与一些北方的城市相比，里约热内卢呈现给旁观者的各个方面，似乎没有相似的紧凑的砖墙、昏暗的屋顶、高大的烟囱和一般高度的地表。它的表面因各种形状不规则但风景如画的山脉而变得多样，在这些山脉之间，留下一些范围或大或小的平坦盆地。沿着这些山脉的底部延伸，或向上攀爬，有成排的建筑矗立。这些房屋都绘有令人愉悦的白色墙壁和红色的屋顶，它们与环绕在周围的绿色树叶形成明显但鲜亮的对比。

　　从里约热内卢出发，航船继续它的航程，一直到蒙得维的亚。这是乌拉圭的首都，坐落在拉普拉塔河的河口。蒙得维的亚拥有一个优良的港口，城市在这个港口周围按新月的形状建成。在拉普拉塔河的另一侧，沿河口向上游行进更远，会到达阿根廷共和国的首都布宜诺斯艾利斯，它是南半球最大的城市。大量的岩石和沙质的河岸使在拉普拉塔河航行变得异常困难，而当名为派姆佩洛斯的西南风横行时，在这里航行则变得尤其危险。在1885年之前，要想到达布宜诺斯艾利斯的乘客和航船，都必须在蒙得维的亚停靠，但在那一年，布宜诺斯艾利斯建造起一个港口，足够容纳众多轮船。

　　离开布宜诺斯艾利斯之后，轮船继续向南前行。穿过麦哲伦海峡或者合恩角之后，船只会到达智利的一个主要港口瓦尔帕莱索。向西400英里处，在太平洋中央，有一个胡安费尔南德斯岛，在笛福著名的小说《鲁宾孙漂流记》中，亚历山大·塞尔扣克在此独居了4年。从瓦尔帕莱索出发，轮船开往利马的一个港口卡亚俄。它向内陆延伸六英里，由铁路连接。皮萨罗征服利马时，将它作为当时西班牙占据地区的首都，它作为最美丽的城市而享有美誉。南美洲的大教堂和众多的教堂，穹顶和尖塔，赋予了这座城市华丽的外表。我们已经穿过了之前描述过的西印度和巴拿马的航线，旅行者可能，因为不同的缘故，踏上自己回家的旅程。

Lesson 42
THE LLANOS OF SOUTH AMERICA
第四十二课　南美大草原

In South America the features of Nature are traced on a gigantic scale. Mountains, forests, rivers, plains, there appear in far more colossal dimensions than in our part of the world. Many a branch of the Amazon surpasses the Danube in size. In the boundless primitive forests of Guiana more than one Great Britain could find room. The Alps would seem but of moderate elevation if placed beside the towering Andes; and the plains of Northern Germany and Holland are utterly insignificant when compared with the lla'nos of Venezuela and New Grana'da, which cover a surface of more than 250,000 square miles.

Nothing can be more remarkable than the contrast which these immeasurable plains present at various seasons of the year—now parched by a long-continued drought, and now covered with the most luxuriant vegetation. When, day after day, the sun, rising and setting in a cloudless sky, pours his vertical rays upon the thirsty llanos, the calcined grass-plains present the monotonous aspect of an interminable waste. Like the ocean, their limits melt in the hazy distance with those of the horizon; but here the resemblance ceases, for no refreshing breeze wafts coolness over the desert to comfort the drooping spirits of the wanderer.

In the wintry solitudes of Siberia the skin of the reindeer affords protection to man against the extreme cold; but in these sultry plains there is no refuge from the burning sun above and the heat reflected from the glowing soil, save where, at vast intervals, small clumps of the Mauri'tia palm afford a scanty shade. The water-pools which nourished this beneficent tree have long since disappeared; and the marks of the previous rainy season, still visible on the tall reeds that spring from the marshy ground, serve only to mock the thirst of the exhausted traveller.

Yet even now the parched savanna has some refreshment to bestow, for the globular melon-cactus, which flourishes on the driest soil, and sometimes measures a foot in diameter, conceals a juicy pulp under its tough and prickly skin. Guided by an admirable instinct, the wary mule strikes off with his forefeet the long, sharp thorns of this remarkable plant, the emblem of good nature under a rough exterior, and then cautiously advances his lips to sip the refreshing juice.

As, in the Arctic regions, the intense cold during winter retards pulsation, or even suspends the operations of life, so in the llanos the long continuance of drought causes a similar stagnation in animated nature. The thinly scattered trees and shrubs do not, indeed, cast their foliage, but the grayish-yellow of their leaves announces that vegetation is suspended. Buried in the clay of the dried-up pools, the alligator and the water-boa lie plunged in a deep summer sleep, like the bear of the North in his long winter slumber; and many animals which, at other times, are found roaming over the llanos have left the parched plains and migrated to the forest or the river.

The large maneless puma, and the spotted jaguar, following their prey to less arid regions, are now no longer seen in their former hunting-grounds; and the Indian has also disappeared with the stag he pursued with his poisoned arrows. In Siberia, the reindeer and the migratory birds are scared away by cold; here, life is banished and suspended by an intolerable heat.

Sometimes the ravages of fire are added to complete the image of death on the parched savanna.

"We had not yet penetrated far into the plain," says Sir Robert Schomburgk, "when we saw to the south-east high columns of smoke ascending to the skies—the sure signs of a savanna fire; and at the same time the Indians anxiously pressed us to speed on, as the burning torrent would most likely roll in our direction.

"We could already distinguish the flames of the advancing column, already hear the bursting and crackling of the reeds, when, fortunately, the sharp eye of the Indians discovered some small eminences before us, only sparingly covered with a low vegetation, and to these we now careered as if Death himself were behind us. Half a minute later and I should not have lived to relate our adventures. With beating hearts we saw the sea of fire rolling its devouring billows towards us: the suffocating smoke, beating on our faces, forced us to turn our backs upon the advancing conflagration, and to await the dreadful decision with the resignation of helpless despair.

"And now we were in the midst of the blaze. Two arms of fire encircled the base of the little hillock on which we stood, and united before us in a waving mass, which, rolling onwards, travelled further and further from our gaze. The flames had devoured the short grass of the hillock, but had not found sufficient nourishment for our destruction. Soon the deafening noise of the conflagration ceased, and the dense black clouds in the distance were the only signs that the fire was still proceeding on its devastating path over the wide wastes of the savanna."

At length, after a long drought, when all nature seems about to expire from the want of moisture, various signs announce the approach of the rainy season. The sky, instead of its brilliant blue, assumes a leaden tint, from the vapours which are beginning to condense. Like distant mountain-chains, banks of clouds begin to rise over the horizon, and, forming in masses of increasing density, ascend higher and higher, until at length the sudden lightnings flash from their dark bosom, and with the loud crash of thunder the first rains burst in torrents over the thirsty land.

Scarcely have the showers had time to moisten the earth, when the dormant powers of vegetation begin to awaken with an almost miraculous rapidity. The dull, tawny surface of the parched savanna changes, as if by magic, into a carpet of the most lively green, enamelled with thousands of flowers of every colour.

And now, also, the animal life of the savanna awakens to the full enjoyment of existence. The horse and the ox rejoice in the grasses, under whose covert the jaguar frequently lurks to pounce upon them with his fatal spring. On the border of the swamps, the moist clay, slowly heaving, bursts asunder, and from the tomb in which he lay embedded rises a gigantic water-snake or huge crocodile.

The new-formed pools and lakes swarm with life, and a host of water-fowl,—ibises, cranes, flamingoes,—make their appearance to regale on the abundant banquet. A new creation of insects and other unbidden guests now seek the wretched hovels of the Indians. Worms and vermin of all names and forms emerge from the inundated plain; for the tropical rains have gradually converted the savanna, which erewhile exhibited a waste as dreary as that of the Sahara, into a boundless lake.

—Hartwig and Schomburgk

Words

admirable, *wonderful.*
announce, *intimate.*
banquet, *feast.*
cautiously, *carefully.*
density, *bulk thickness.*
devastating, *destroying.*
devouring, *ravaging.*
eminences, *elevations.*
exhausted, *worn-out.*
existence, *life.*
immeasurable, *immense.*

insignificant, *inconsiderable.*
interminable, *endless.*
inundated, *overflowed.*
migratory, *wandering.*
monotonous, *tiresome.*
nourished, *supported.*
penetrated, *made way.*
protection, *covering.*
rapidity, *speed celerity.*
stagnation, *deadness.*
surpasses, *excels exceeds.*

Questions

What is the characteristic feature of Nature in South America? What striking contrast do the llanos of South America present at different seasons? Wherein do they differ from the wintry solitudes of Siberia? What refreshment does the mule obtain in the savanna? What effect has the drought upon animated nature? What animals bury themselves for the season? What sometimes adds its ravages to complete the image of death? What is the best way to escape from it? What signs announce the approach of the rainy season? What is remarkable about the revival of vegetation? What animals return to the savanna? Into what have the tropical rains converted it?

南美洲的自然特性已被细致探查。山脉、森林、河流、平原，都比欧洲的要广阔得多。亚马孙河的流域超过多瑙河，圭亚那无边的原始森林要比整个大不列颠还宽广，如果阿尔卑斯山位于高耸的安第斯山附近，它也只是中等高度，北德和荷兰平原与委内瑞拉与新格兰纳达的大平原相比，完全小得多，因为后者横跨25万平方公里。

这片无边无际的平原在一年中的不同季节表现出的差别是最壮丽的，有时蔓延着持续的干旱，有时覆盖着繁茂的植被。在万里无云的天际，日复一日的日升日落，太阳在这片干渴的平原上洒落它的垂直射线，将草原烤成了单一无边的样貌。如同海洋一样，草原的尽头融合进远方朦胧的地平线。但还是有一点不同，这里没有新鲜凉爽的风吹拂，来安抚人们消沉的情绪。

在西伯利亚孤寂的冬天，驯鹿的皮毛会给人类提供抵御严寒的良策。但在这片干涸的平原上，在灼烧的烈日之下，人们很难找到避难所。热量从灼热的土壤反射上来。毛里塔尼亚棕榈树下的小小土块偶尔能提供一点稀有的树荫。而哺育这种仁慈之树的小水塘早已消失。人们依旧可以在沼泽地带高高的芦苇丛中，寻觅到上一次雨季的痕迹。但如今，它只会嘲笑筋疲力尽的旅行者的干渴。

但即使在这时，干涸的稀树草原也能提供一些新鲜，因为在最干燥的土壤之上，仙人球可以繁茂地生长。有时它的直径可达一英寸，在它坚硬多刺的肌肤之下，隐藏着鲜美多汁的果肉。机警的骡子有时会受天性的驱使，先用前蹄踢掉长长的尖刺，然后小心翼翼地凑上前去，用嘴唇吮吸这种坚硬外表下的新鲜果汁。

在北极地区，漫长的严寒会阻止生命的悸动，甚至将其暂停。同样，在这片大草原上的长期干旱中，生命也面临相同的停滞。虽然稀疏分布的树木和灌木没有落尽它们的叶子，但灰黄色的叶子依旧宣称了植被生命的暂停。短吻鳄和水蟒，就像北极熊冬眠一样，将自己深埋在干涸的池塘下，进入了长期的夏季休眠。其他许多动物逃离了干涸的区域，在大草原上徘徊，寻找森林或者河流。

巨大的没有鬃毛的美洲狮和布满斑点的美洲虎，离开它们之前捕猎的地方，而追逐猎物到了稍微湿润的地域。印第安人也同样带着他们有毒的箭追逐雄鹿而离去。在西伯利亚，驯鹿和候鸟因为严寒而消失，在这儿，生命则是因为难忍的酷暑消失或暂停。有时，在干涸的稀树草原上，烈火会使这种死亡的景象更加完整。

罗伯特·施姆博科爵士说："我们还没有深入到这片平原的内里。当我们看到东南方升入天际的烟雾时，那肯定是稀树草原上的大火。同时，印第安人会迫使我们加快速度前进，因为这片火势很有可能会朝着我们蔓延过来。

"我们已经认清了会向前蔓延的火势，已经听到了燃烧的芦苇的噼啪声。非常幸运，印第安人在我们前方找到了植被稀疏的高地。我们朝它进发，就像死神已经在我们身后。半分钟的停留可能就会夺走我的生命，而不能再继续这次探险。在我们剧烈的心跳声中，我们看到了大火张开它的血盆大口，正朝着我们烧来。令人窒息的烟雾拍打着我们的脸庞，逼迫我们背对着朝我们前进的火势。我们却只能听从于无望的绝望，做出可怕的决定。

　　"如今我们身处火焰的正中。我们站着的小山丘，已经被火焰包围。火海已经在我们的注视下连成一片，继续前行，越来越远。火焰吞噬掉了山丘上的所有草木，再也找不到能蔓延着烧到我们面前的植物。大火震耳欲聋的声响很快停止了。远处浓密的黑色烟雾，标志着火焰在这片稀树草原上继续前行。所过之地，留下一片狼藉的废墟。"

　　最后，在漫长的旱季之后，所有生物都似乎渴求着湿润。此时，不同的迹象表明雨季即将来临。天空不再是明朗的蓝色，而因为水气的开始聚集变成了铅灰色。像远方的山脉一样，成片的云朵开始在地平线聚集，越来越厚，越升越高，直到最后，突然间的闪电带来了这片干涸大地上的第一场大雨。

　　这场倾盆大雨还没来得及让整片大地湿润起来，各种植物的生命力就开始迅速苏醒。干涸的稀树草原像被施了魔法一样，原本干枯的黄褐色变成了最生机盎然的绿色，像一片绿色的毯子，上面点缀着众多花朵的不同色泽。

　　如今，稀树草原上的动物们也都快乐地复苏了。野马和野牛在草原上欢庆，而在草丛之下，美洲虎频繁地潜伏其中，准备用它致命的跳跃来扑倒它们。在沼泽的边缘，潮湿的黏土慢慢不再像旱季时一样是个整块，而巨大的水蛇和鳄鱼正是潜伏在里面。

　　刚刚形成的水塘和湖泊挤满了生命，有众多水禽：朱鹭、鹤、火烈鸟，都出现在这场盛宴中。如今，一大批昆虫和其他不速之客找寻着印第安人可怜的小屋。各种昆虫和鸟类出现在湿润的草原中，让之前还像撒哈拉一样沉闷的一片废墟变成了无边的湖泊。

Lesson 43　THE DEATH OF NAPOLEON AT ST. HELENA

第四十三课　拿破仑死于圣海伦娜

May 5, 1821.

Wild was the night, yet a wilder night
　Hung round the soldier's pillow;
In his bosom there raged a fiercer fight
　Than the fight on the wrathful billow.

A few fond mourners were kneeling by,—
　The few that his stern heart cherished;
They knew, by his glazed and unearthly eye,
　That life had nearly perished.

They knew, by his awful and kingly look,
　By the order hastily spoken,
That he dreamed of days when the nations shook,
　And the nations' hosts were broken.

He dreamed that the Frenchmen's sword still slew,
　Still triumphed the Frenchmen's "eagle;"
And the struggling Austrian fled anew,
　Like the hare before the beagle.

The bearded Russian he scourged again,
　The Prussian's camp was routed;
And again on the hills of haughty Spain
　His mighty armies shouted.

Over Egypt's sands, over Alpine snows,
　At the pyramids, at the mountain,
Where the wave of the lordly Danube flows,
　And by the Italian fountain;

On the snowy cliffs where mountain streams
　Dash by the Switzer's dwelling,

He led again, in his dying dreams,
    His hosts, the broad earth quelling.

Again Maren'go's field was won.
    And Jena's bloody battle;
Again the world was over-run,
    Made pale at his cannons' rattle.

He died at the close of that darksome day—
    A day that shall live in story:
In the rocky land they placed his clay,
    And "left him alone with his glory."

—M'LELLAN

Words

billow, *wave.*
cherished, *fostered; held dear.*
darksome, *dismal.*
haughty, *imperious.*
kneeling, *on bended knee.*

mourners, *sorrowers.*
quelling, *overpowering.*
scourged, *lashed, punished.*
triumphed, *prevailed.*
wrath full, *angry.*

☆ ☆ ☆ ☆ ☆ ☆ ☆ ☆ ☆ ☆ ☆ ☆ ☆ ☆ ☆ ☆ ☆ ☆ ☆ ☆

1821年5月5日

夜如此荒凉，一夜更甚一夜，
潜伏在战士们的枕边；
他胸中的怒火猛烈，
更甚于可怕的巨浪。

些许哀悼者长跪于此，
他们是他如此珍重的人；
他们知晓：他呆滞、神秘的眼睛，
暗示了他的生命几乎消亡。

他们明白，他威严、高贵的神情，

他急切地下发命令，
他梦想着政权撼动的时刻，
但国家的主人正在被摧毁。

他梦想着法国之剑所向披靡，
法国雄鹰仍可高歌凯旋；
反抗的奥地利人再次逃亡，
如猎犬追赶的野兔一般。

他再次惩治了大胡子的俄国人，
普鲁士人的阵地也由此震动；
在傲慢的西班牙的山顶，
他强大的军队再次高呼着胜利。

埃及的沙漠之上，阿尔卑斯山顶的积雪之上，
金字塔旁，山脉之巅，
宏伟的多瑙河流经之地，
意大利喷泉池旁边；

在白雪皑皑的山脉之下，
他猛冲向瑞士人的居住地。
在他奄奄一息之时，他再次梦想着，
他带领自己的军队，向广阔的大地进军。

他再次占领了马伦戈的土地，
耶拿战役如此血腥；
世界再次遭受蹂躏，
炮弹轰鸣，一片阴沉。

阴沉的一天结束，他也随之逝去——
这一天会被史册所铭刻；
他的尸骨埋葬之地，
只留下他的荣耀与他共眠。

——M. 莱伦

Lesson 44
HYMN BEFORE SUNRISE,
IN THE VALE OF CHAMOUNI
第四十四课　日出之前的赞歌，于沙莫尼山谷

Hast thou a charm to stay the morning star
In his steep course? So long he seems to pause
On thy bald, awful head, O sovereign Blanc!
The Arve and Arveiron at thy base
Rave ceaselessly; but thou, most awful form,
Risest from forth thy silent sea of pines,
How silently! Around thee, and above,
Deep is the air and dark, substantial, black,
An ebon mass: methinks thou piercest it
As with a wedge. But when I look again,
It is thine own calm home, thy crystal shrine,
Thy habitation from eternity.
O dread and silent mount! I gazed upon thee
Till thou, still present to the bodily sense,
Didst vanish from my thought; entranced in prayer
I worshipped the Invisible alone.

Yet, like some sweet beguiling melody,
So sweet we know not we are listening to it,
Thou the meanwhile wast blending with my though
Yea, with my life, and life's own secret joy;
Till the dilating soul, enrapt, transfused,
Into the mighty vision passing—there,
As in her natural form, swelled vast to heaven.

Awake, my soul! not only passive praise
Thou owest! not alone these swelling tears,
Mute thanks, and secret ecstasy! Awake,
Voice of sweet song! Awake, my heart! awake,
Green vales and icy cliffs! all join my hymn.

Thou first and chief, sole sovereign of the vale!
Oh, struggling with the darkness all the night,

And visited II night by troops of stars,
Or when they climb the sky, or when they sink,—
Companion of the morning star at dawn,
Thyself Earth's rosy star, and of the dawn

THE VALE OF CHAMOUNI

Co-herald, wake, O wake, and utter praise!
Who sank thy sunless pillars deep in earth?
Who filled thy countenance with rosy light?
Who made thee parent of perpetual streams?

And you, ye five wild torrents fiercely glad!
Who called you forth from night and utter death,
From dark and icy caverns called you forth,
Down those precipitous, black, jagged rocks,
For ever shattered, and the same for ever?
Who gave you your invulnerable life,
Your strength, your speed, your fury, and your joy,
Unceasing thunder, and eternal foam?
And who commanded, and the silence came,—
"Here let the billows stiffen and have rest"?

Ye ice-falls! ye that from the mountain's brow
Adown enormous ravines slope amain—
Torrents, methinks, that heard a mighty voice,
And stopped at once amid their maddest plunge!
Motionless torrents! silent cataracts!

Who made you glorious as the gates of heaven
Beneath the keen full moon? Who bade the sun
Clothe you with rainbows? Who, with living flowers
Of loveliest blue, spread garlands at your feet?—
God! let the torrents, like a shout of nations,
Answer! and let the ice plains echo, God!
God! sing, ye meadow streams, with gladsome voice!
Ye pine groves, with your soft and soul-like sounds!
And they, too, have a voice, yon piles of snow,
And in their perilous fall shall thunder, God!

Ye living flowers that skirt the eternal frost!
Ye wild goats sporting round the eagle's nest!
Ye eagles, playmates of the mountain storm!
Ye lightnings, the dread arrows of the clouds!
Ye signs and wonders of the elements!
Utter forth God! and fill the hills with praise!

—S. T. Coleridge

Words

beguiling, *fascinating*.
Cataracts, *waterfalls*.
ceaselessly, *constantly*.
companion, *associate*.
dilating, *expanding*.
entranced, *enraptured*.
eternal, *everlasting*.
invulnerable, *impregnable*.

precipitous, *steep*.
ravines, *gorges*.
shattered, *shivered*.
struggling, *contending*.
substantial, *solid*.
transfused, *translated*.
worshipped, *adored*.

你难道有什么魔法，能阻挡启明星，
凌空直上？它在你的赫赫秃顶旁，
似乎已滞留许久了，巍峨的勃朗峰！
阿尔沃与阿尔维隆，在你的脚底，
咆哮不休；而你，最威严的形象！
耸立着，拔起在静默的松树林之路，
静默无声！你的周遭和上方，

是深邃无尽的天宇，坚实，浓重，
如一块乌木；而你呢，把它刺穿了，
像一根楔子！我再度向天空仰望，
看出：它是你宁静的家园，是你
晶莹的圣殿，漫无边际的寓所！
庄严肃穆的崇峰！我向你注目，
直到你，虽然还在我的观感里留存，
却已从我的思维中消逝；我独自
潜心祈祷，参拜无形的上帝。

像陶冶情操的清妙乐曲，多美啊！
我们竟然没有意识到自己在倾听。
这期间，你恰似融入了我的思想，
我的生命，和生命神秘的欢乐；
直到灵魂陶醉了，充盈了，膨胀了，
蔚为壮阔的奇观，仿佛这灵魂
以它的本相，扩展着，磅礴于天空之间！

醒来吧，我的灵魂！你该献出的
不只是空乏的颂歌！不只是涌溢的
泪水，无言的感谢，隐秘的欢欣！
醒来吧，歌声！醒来吧，我的心，醒来！
绿谷，冰崖，都与我同声礼赞吧。

你，至高无上的，群山的唯一君主！
你彻夜不休，与黑暗决一胜负；
彻夜不休，有群星（在它们升起
或是沉落的途中）来将你探访；
哦，启明星的伴侣！你本身就是
大地的绚烂星辰，曙光的向导！
醒来吧，醒来，快倾诉你的颂词！
谁将你的幽冥柱石深埋在地底？
谁以绯红的彩霞渲染你的容颜？
谁让你养育了长流不息的川涧？

而你们，这五道急湍，欢快而猛烈！
是谁唤你们逃脱黑夜和覆灭，
唤你们奔出幽暗的冰凌的洞窟，
冲下那崎岖险峻的黑色山崖，
不断被捣碎，又始终安然无恙？
是谁给你们坚不可摧的生命，
给你们威力，速度，愤怒，欣喜，
不绝于耳的轰鸣，无尽的飞沫？
又是谁发号施令，让怒涛停滞，
水波不兴，迎来了一片沉寂？

你们，峭拔的冰川！你们从山顶
极速倾泻，沿巨壑延伸而下，
原先想必是急湍，猛听得一声
狂吼，狂躁的奔腾便戛然而止！
停滞的急湍！无声的飞瀑！
是谁把你们雕琢得这般绚烂，
像天国之门洒满月亮的清辉？
是谁让艳阳用霓虹装扮你们，
把鲜丽的蓝花铺撒在你们脚下？
上帝啊！让急湍回答吧，如万众齐呼！
让皎洁的冰原同声呼应吧，上帝！
绿野的清溪啊，请你们欣然吟唱！
松树林啊！请演奏曼妙的灵魂之曲！
山头的积雪也并非沉默无声，
雪崩的时候似惊雷滚滚，上帝啊！

你们，依偎着万年霜雪的鲜花！
你们，奔逐于鹰巢附近的山羊！
你们，与风雪雨雷结伴的山鹰！
你们，云霓的神箭——凌厉的电火！
你们，自然之力壮丽的信号和奇迹！
向上帝礼赞吧，让颂歌响遍群山！

——塞缪尔·泰勒·柯勒律治

Lesson 45　"WITH BRAINS, SIR"
第四十五课　"先生，用脑子"

"Pray, Mr. Opie, may I ask what you mix your colours with?" said a brisk dilettante student to the great painter. "With *Brains*, sir," was the gruff reply—and the right one. It did not give much of what we call information; it did not expound the principles and rules of art: but, if the inquirer had the commodity referred to, it would awaken him; it would set him a-going, a-thinking, and a-painting to good purpose. If he had not the wherewithal, as was likely enough, the less he had to do with colours and their mixture the better.

Many other artists, when asked such a question, would have either set about detailing the mechanical composition of such and such colours, in such and such proportions, compounded so and so; or perhaps they would have shown him how they laid them on: but even this would have left him at the critical point. Opie preferred going to the quick and the heart of the matter: "With Brains, sir."

Sir Joshua Reynolds was taken by a friend to see a picture. He was anxious to admire it, and he looked over it with a keen and careful but favourable eye. "Capital composition; correct drawing; the colour and tone excellent: but—but—it wants—it wants—*That*!" snapping his fingers; and wanting "that," though it had everything else, it was worth nothing.

Again: Etty, who was appointed teacher of the students of the Royal Academy, had been preceded by a clever, talkative, scientific expounder of æsthetics, who had delighted to tell the young men how everything was done—how to copy this, and how to express that. A student went up to the new master: "How should I do this, sir?" "Suppose you try."—Another: "What does this mean, Mr. Etty?" "Suppose you look." "But I have looked." "Suppose you look again."

And they did try, and they did look, and look again; and they saw and achieved what they never could have done, had the how or the what (supposing that possible, which it is not in its full and highest meaning) been told them, or done for them. In the one case, sight and action were immediate, exact, intense, and secure; in the other, mediate, feeble, and lost as soon as gained.

But what are "Brains"? what did Opie mean? And what is Sir Joshua's "That"? what is included in it? And what is the use or the need of trying and trying, of missing often before you hit, when you can be told at once and be done with it? or of looking, when you may be shown? Everything depends on the right answers to these questions.

What the painter needs, in addition to, and as the complement of, the other elements, is genius and sense; what the doctor needs, to crown and give worth and safety to his accomplishments, is sense and genius: in the first case, more of this than of that; in the second, more of that than of this. These are the "Brains" and the "That."

And what is genius? and what is sense? *Genius* is a peculiar in-born aptitude, or tendency, to any one calling or pursuit over all others......It was as natural, as inevitable, for Wilkie to develop himself into a painter, and into such a painter as we know him to have been, as it is for an acorn when planted to grow up an oak.

But genius, and nothing else, is not enough, even for a painter; he must likewise have sense; and what is sense? *Sense* drives, or ought to drive, the coach: sense regulates, combines, restrains, commands, all the rest—even the genius; and sense implies exactness and soundness, power and promptitude of mind.

But it may be asked, how are the brains to be strengthened the sense quickened, the genius awakened, the affections raised—the whole man turned to the best account? You must invigorate the containing and sustaining mind; you must strengthen him from within, as well as fill him from without; you must discipline, nourish, edify, relieve and refresh his entire nature; and how?

Encourage not merely book knowledge, but the personal pursuit of natural history, of field botany, of geology, of zoology. Give the young, fresh, unforgotten eye exercise and free scope upon the infinite diversity and combination of natural colonies, forms, substances, surfaces, weights, and sizes. Give young students everything, in a word, that will educate their eye and ear, their touch, taste, and smell, their sense of muscular resistance. Encourage them to make models, preparations, and collections of natural objects. Above all, try to get hold of their affections, and make them put their hearts into their work.

But one main help is to be found in study; and by this we do not mean the mere reading, but the digging into and through, the energizing upon and mastering, the best books. Taking up a book and reading a chapter of lively, manly sense, is like taking a game at cricket or a run to the top of a hill. Exertion quickens your pulse, expands your lungs, makes you blood warmer and redder, fills your mouth with the pure waters of relish, strengthens and supple your legs: and though on your way to the top you may encounter rocks and baffling debris, just as you will find in serious and honest books difficulties and puzzles, still you are rewarded at the top by a wide view. You see as from a tower the end of all. You see the clouds, the bright lights and the everlasting hills on the far horizon. You come down from the hill a happier, a better, and a hungrier man, and of a better mind.

But, as we said, you must eat the book—you must crush it, and cut it with your teeth and swallow it; just as you must walk up, and not be carried up the hill, much less imagine you are there, or look upon a picture of what you would see were you up, however accurately or artistically done: no—you yourself must do both. He who has obtained any amount of knowledge is not truly wise unless he appropriates and can use it for his need.

—J. Brown, M.D.

Words

accurately, *correctly*.

achieved, *accomplished*.

anxious, *desirous*.

appropriates, *assimilates*.

aptitude, *fitness*.

artistically, *tastefully*.

commodity, *article*.

complement, *what supplies a deficiency*.

debris, *rubbish*.

discipline, *train*.

diversity, *variety*.

energizing, *exercising the mind*.

 expound, *explain*.

imagine, *fancy*.

information, *knowledge*.

intense, *earnest*.

invigorate, *strengthen*.

mechanical, *physical*.

muscular, *physical*.

promptitude, *readiness*.

proportions, *quantities*.

regulates, *controls*.

relieve, *succour*.

restrains, *curbs*.

scientific, *theoretical*.

supples, *makes pliant*.

Questions

What question did the student ask Opie? What kind of student was he? What answer did Opie give him? What might many other artists have replied? What did Sir Joshua Reynolds say his friend's picture wanted? What did Etty reply to students who asked him how to do things, and what things meant? What did all these answers point to as necessary to the painter? What is Genius? What is the office of Sense? What must be done to awaken genius and quicken sense? To what is reading a chapter of lively, manly sense compared? How must a book be read, that it may do good? He who has obtained any amount of knowledge is not truly wise unless —?

　　"奥佩先生，请问，您是怎样混合您的色彩的？"一个年轻的业余学习者这样问一位著名画家。"先生，用脑子。"这是他得到的生硬的答复，而这也确是正确的答复。它没有给出相当的信息，也没有详细解释出艺术的原则和规矩。但如果问询者悟出了其中的价值，就能够被这句答复点醒。它能够为他的前行、思考和绘画设立目标。如果他悟不出此中道理，也就最好不要去碰色彩和颜料了。

　　其他许多艺术家，当被问及此问题时，可能会回答一些细节的、技巧性的这种那种颜色的组合，以这样那样的比例来混合颜料，等等。或者他们会告诉提问者如何把它们放在画布上。但即便如此，提问者还是没有得到最重要的答案。奥佩就更喜欢迅速地直达要点："先生，用脑子。"

一个朋友带约书亚·雷克雅维克爵士欣赏一幅画。他急于赞美它，所以用敏锐细致的眼神欣赏着它，并说道："极佳的作品，准确的绘画，色彩与色调也都很棒。但……但……它需要……需要……这个！"他打着响指说道。虽然这幅画什么都好，但却一文不值。

另一次，皇家艺术学院任命的教师艾迪也成为一位智慧、善言、严谨的艺术解说家。他很乐意告诉年轻人怎样做事：如何复制，如何表达。一个学生问他："我应该怎么做，先生？""假设你在尝试。""先生，这是什么意思？""假设你在观察。""但我已经观察了。""假设你再观察一遍。"

他们确实尝试了，也一遍又一遍地观察了。他们也得出了他们从未得到的成果，就像他们所问的"如何"和"什么"已经被告知或者完成。如果别人可能告诉他们或者替他们完成，他们得到的成果也并非是完全彻底的。在这种情况下，视觉和行动都是迅捷的、精准的、强烈的、可靠的。若非如此，便是简洁的、微弱的，一旦有所得便会有所失。

但究竟什么是"用脑子"？奥佩先生的意思是什么？约书亚先生所说的"这个"又包含了什么？当你能够立即知道答案或者完成任务时，却要不停地尝试又尝试，击中要点之前错过；能有人展示给你答案，你却还要观察。这些做法的用处是什么？这都取决于这些问题的正确答案。

除此之外，同时也作为其他要点的补充，一个画家还需要天赋和感觉。为了能实现、保证他的成就，一个医生也需要天赋和感觉。在第一个故事里，天赋比感觉重要。在第二个故事里，感觉比天赋重要。而它们也就是上面提到的"脑子"和"这个"。

那什么是天赋？什么又是感觉？天赋是一种特殊的与生俱来的能力，每一种工作或者追求都需要它。威尔奇成长为我们所知道的这样一名画家，所需的就是这种自然的、必然的能力，就像橡果会成长为一棵橡树。

但只有天赋，对一名画家而言又是不够的，他也必须同样具备感觉。那什么是感觉？感觉驱使或者应该驱使行为。它控制、联合、限制、指挥着其他所有能力，甚至包括天赋在内。它意味着准确、合理、力量和思维的敏捷。

但会有人问，如何能加强大脑、加快感觉、唤醒天赋、提升感觉？如何将人变得最好？必须振奋所有意识，必须加强意识中，甚至意识之外的所有一切，必须训练、滋养、启发、缓解、更新所有本性。但应怎样做？

不仅仅要学习书本上的知识，还应该有对自然历史、生物学、地理学、动物学的有所追求。给这些年轻、新鲜、过目不忘的学生们训练的机会，让他们学习自然、物质、地表、重量和尺寸的无穷多样性。总之，它们会训练他们的眼睛、耳朵、触觉、听觉、嗅觉，还有肌肉的持久感觉。鼓励他们制作标本、有所准备、收集自然物体。更重要的一点是尝试让他们控制自己的情感，全心全意地投入到自己的工作中。

最主要的帮助来自于学习。我们说的不仅仅是读书，而是彻底的通读、掌握最好的书籍。拿起一本书，阅读里面生动、人性的思想，就像打一局板球或者登到山顶。活动能够加快脉动，扩大肺活量，让血液更温润健康，让口腔吃什么都津津有味，让腿部变得更有力、更柔软。虽然在登顶的过程中会遇到岩石或碎片，就像在严肃、诚恳的书籍中，你会遇到一些困难和谜题。但你仍会在山顶拥有更广阔的视野，就像在塔尖一样俯瞰全城。你能看到云朵、亮光和远处地平线上延绵不绝的山脉。从山上下来，人就会变得更开心，更成功，更渴求知识，也拥有更优秀的思想。

就像我们所说，必须吃透书籍，必须咀嚼它、用牙磨碎它、咽下它。就像一个人必须自己走到山顶，而不是被人抬上去。不能想象着你已经在那儿了，或者看着一幅画觉得自己在那儿，无论这幅画儿有多栩栩如生，艺术造诣多高。不，必须自己做。那些有一定知识的人，直到能够为己所需的应用知识时，才能真正获得智慧。

——J. 布朗

Lesson 46   LIFE IN SAXON ENGLAND (I)
第四十六课   撒克森时期英国的生活（一）

When the sun rose on Old England, its faint red light stirred every sleeper from the sack of straw, which formed the only bed of the age. Springing from this rustling couch, and casting of the coarse sheeting and coverlets of skin, the subjects of King Alfred donned the day's dress. Men wore linen or woollen tunics, which reached to the knee; and, over these, long fur-lined cloaks, fastened with a brooch of ivory or gold. Strips of cloth or leather, bandaged cross-wise from the ankle to the knee over red and blue stockings; and black, pointed shoes, slit along the instep almost to the toes, and fastened with two thongs, completed the costume of an Anglo-Saxon gentleman. The ladies, wrapping a veil of silk or linen upon their delicate curls, laced a loose-flowing gown over a tight-sleeved bodice, and pinned the graceful folds of their mantles with golden butterflies and other tasteful trinkets.

The breakfast hour in Old England was nine o'clock. This meal consisted probably of bread, meat, and ale, but was a lighter repast than that taken when the hurry of the day lay behind. It was eaten often in the bower. Between breakfast and noon-meat at three lay the most active period of the day. Let me picture a few scenes in Old English life, as displayed in the chief occupations of the time.

Leaving the ladies of his household to linger among the roses and lilies of their gardens, or to ply their embroidering needles in some cool recess of the orchard, festooned with broad vine leaves and scented with the smell of apples, the earl or thane went out to the porch of his dwelling, and, sitting there upon a fixed throne, gave alms to a horde of beggars, or presided over the assembly of the local court.

Autumn brought delightful days to the royal and noble sportsmen of Old England. Galloping down from his home, perched, as were all great English houses, on the crest of a commanding hill, the earl, with all care or thought of work flung aside, dashed with his couples of deep-chested Welsh hounds into the glades of a neighbouring forest, already touched with the red and gold of September.

Gaily through the shadowy avenues rang the music of the horns, startling red deer and wild boars from their coverts in the brushwood. Away after the dogs, maddened by a fresh scent, goes the gallant hunt—past swine-herds with their goads, driving vast herds of pigs into the dales, where beech-mast and acorns lie thick upon the ground—past wood-cutters, hewing fuel for the castle fire, or munching their scanty meal of oaten bread about noon; nor is bridle drawn until the game, antlered or tusked, has rushed into the strong nets spread by attendants at some pass among the trees.

Hawking long held the place of our modem shooting. Even the grave and business-like Alfred devoted his pen to this enticing subject. And we can well understand the high spirits and merry talk of a hawking party, cantering over rustling leaves, all white and crisp with an October frost, on their way to the reedy mere, where they made sure of abundant game. On each rider's wrist sat a hooded falcon, caught young, perhaps in a dark pine-wood of Norway, and carefully trained by the falconer, who was no unimportant official in an Old English establishment.

Arrived at the water, the party broke into sets; and as the blue heron rose on his heavy wing, or a noisy splashing flight of ducks sprang from their watery rest, the hood was removed, and the game shown to the sharp-eyed bird, which, soaring loose into the air from the up-flung wrist, cleft his way in pursuit with rapid pinion, rose above the doomed quarry, and descending with a sudden swoop, struck fatal talons and yet more fatal beak into its back and head, and bore it dead to the ground. A sharp gallop over the broken surface had meantime brought the sportsman up in time to save the game, and restore the red-beaked victor to his hood and perch.

But hunting and hawking were the pastimes of the rich. While fat deer fell under the hunter's dart, and blue feathers strewed the banks of lake and river, the smith hammered red iron on his ringing anvil—the carpenter cut planks for the mead-bench or the bower-wall, or shaped cart-wheels and plough-handles for the labours of the farm—the shoemaker, who also tanned leather and fashioned harness, plied his busy knife and needle—the furrier prepared skins for the lining of stately robes—and in every cloister monks, deep in the mysteries of the furnace, the graving-tool, the paint-brush, and a score of similar instruments, manufactured the best bells, crucifixes, jewelry, and stained glass then to be found in the land.

The Old English farmers were rather graziers than tillers of the soil. Sheep for their wool, swine for their flesh, kine for their beef and hides, dotted the pastures and grubbed in the forests near every steading. But there was agriculture too. A picture of an Old English farm-house would present, though of course in ruder form, many features of its modem English successor. Amid fields, often bought for four sheep an acre, and scantily manured with marl after the old British fashion, stood a timbered house, flanked by a farm-yard full of ox-stalls and stocked with geese and fowl. A few bee-hives—the islands of the sugar-cane not being yet discovered—suggested a mead-cask always well filled, and a good supply of sweetmeats for the board; while an orchard, thick with laden boughs, supplied pears and apples, nuts and almonds, and in some districts figs and grapes.

From the illustrations of an Old English manuscript we know something of the year's farm-work. January saw the wheel of the iron plough drawn down the brown furrows by its four oxen, harnessed with twisted willow ropes or thongs of thick whale-skin. They dug their vineyards in February, their gardens in March. In April, when seed-time was past, they took their ease over horns of ale. May prepared for the shearing of the wool. June saw the sickles in the wheat: July 6 heard the axe among the trees. In August barley was mown with scythes. In September and October hounds and hawks engrossed every day of good weather. Round November fires farming implements were mended or renewed; and the whirling flail, beating the grain from its husk, beat also December chills from the swiftly-running blood. We find in the threshing scene a steward, who stands keeping count, by notches on a stick, of the full baskets of winnowed grain which are pouring into the granary.

Ships came from the Continent to Old England, laden with furs and silks, gems and gold, rich dresses, wine, oil, and ivory; bearing back, most probably, blood-horses, wool for the looms of Flanders, and in earlier times English slaves for the markets of Aix-la-Chapelle and Rome. The backward condition of trade may be judged from a law which enacted that no bargain should be made except in open court, in presence of the sheriff, the mass-priest, or the lord of the manor.

Merchants, travelling in bands for safety, and carrying their own tents, passed round the different country towns at certain times, when holiday was kept and village sports filled the green with noisy mirth. The wives and daughters of Old English cottages loved bright ribbons and showy trinkets, after the fashion of their sex. So while Gurth was wrestling on the grass, or grinning at the antics of the dancing bear, Githa was investing her long-hoarded silver pennies in some strings of coloured beads or an ivory comb.

Close to the merchant or pedler (if we give him the name which best expresses to modern ears the habit of his life) stood an attendant with a pair of scales, ready to weigh the money in case of any considerable sale. Slaves and cattle formed, in early times in England, a common medium of exchange. Whenever gold shone in the merchant's sack, it was chiefly the Byzan'tine gold *solidus*, shortly called Byzant', worth something more than nine of our shillings. Silver Byzants, worth two shillings, also passed current; and in earlier times Roman money, stamped with the heads of emperors, found its way into English purses.

By the English in olden times a journey was never undertaken for mere pleasure, for many perils beset the way. The rich went short journeys in heavy waggons, longer journeys on horseback—the ladies riding on side-saddles as at present. But most travelling was performed afoot. Horsemen carried spears, for defence against robbers or wild beasts; pedestrians held a stout oak staff, which did double work in aiding and in defending the traveller. The stirrup was of an odd triangular shape, the spur a simple spike. A cover wrapped the head, and a mantle the body, of the traveller. That they sometimes carried umbrellas we know; but these were probably very rare, being confined, like gloves, to the very highest class.

Ale-houses, in which too much time was spent, abounded in the towns; but in country districts inns were scarce. There were indeed places, like an Eastern caravansary, where travellers, carrying their own provisions, found a refuge from wind and rain by night within bare stone walls; the patched-up ruins, perhaps, of an old Roman villa or barrack, which afforded a cheerless shelter to the weary, dripping band. But the hospitality of the Old English folk, implanted both by custom and by law—not after the narrow modern fashion of entertaining friends, who give parties in return, but the welcoming to bed and board of all comers, known and unknown— caused the lack of inns to be scarcely felt, except in the wilder districts of the land.

No sooner did a stranger show his face at the iron-banded door of an Old English dwelling than water was brought to wash his hands and feet; and when he had deposited his arms with the keeper of the door, he took his place at the board among the family and friends of the host. For two nights no question pried into his business or his name; after that time the host became responsible for his character. There were few solitary wayfarers; for the very fact of being alone excited suspicion, and exposed the traveller to the risk of being arrested, or perhaps slain, as a thief.

Words

antics, *tricks*.
arrested, *seized*.
avenues, *alleys, groves*.
deposited, *left*.
displayed, *exhibited*.
engrossed, *monopolized*.
enticing, *attractive*.
exchange, *commerce*.
excited, *aroused*.
fashioned, *shaped*.
features, *aspects*.
festooned, *garlanded*.
harnessed, *yoked*.
hospitality, *kindness to guests*.
illustrations, *pictures*.

implanted, *instilled*.
implements, *tools*.
investing, *laying out*.
munching, *chewing*.
mysteries, *secrets*.
probably, *likely*.
provisions, *supplies of food*.
pursuit, *chase*.
quarry, *prey*.
responsible, *answerable*.
supplied, *furnished*.
timbered, *wooden*.
triangular, *three-cornered*.
unimportant, *insignificant*.

Questions

Of what did beds in Old England consist? How were the men dressed? How were the women? What was the busiest part of the day in Old England? In what did the ladies occupy themselves? In what sports did the rich take part? What held the place of modem shooting? What handicrafts did the workingmen follow? What were the farmers chiefly? Whence do we know something of the year's farm work? How did the steward keep count of the quantity of grain? What did ships bring from the Continent? What did they bear back? How did merchants travel? What formed common mediums of exchange? What were the means of travelling? Where did companies of travellers spend the night? What supplied the lack of inns?

当太阳在古英格兰升起的时候，它的微微红光将每一个沉睡的人唤醒，而它们都睡在作为那个年代唯一的床的麻布袋之中。国王艾尔菲尔德从嘎嘎作响的睡椅中

起身，在肌肤之上披上粗糙的被单和床罩一样的衣服，他就这样定义了那时的穿衣风格。男子穿着亚麻质或者是羊毛质的长过膝盖的束腰外衣，在这外面还有一层超过膝盖的衣服，有长长的戴着花纹的斗篷，并且用象牙质的或者金质的胸针来固定。布质的或者皮质的条纹从脚踝纵横交织到膝盖，绑在红色或蓝色的长裤外面。还有黑色的尖头皮鞋，它的长度从脚背基本到了脚趾，并且由两条皮带系紧。这样就完成了一个盎格鲁·撒克逊绅士的着装。而女士的衣着则是：在她们柔美的卷发上戴上一块丝质或者麻质的面纱，在紧致有袖的收身上衣外面加上一件用带子束紧的长外衣，然后把这些斗篷上华丽的褶皱用金色的蝴蝶胸针或者其他有品位的小挂件穿起。

在古英格兰，早餐时间是9点，这顿饭大概包含了面包、肉类和麦芽酒。相对于在接下来一天中紧张工作之间吃的饭，这只是随便吃的一顿饭。人们经常在树荫处进食早餐。早餐和下午3点的下午茶之间的这段时间是一天中最活跃的时期。现在我来描绘一下，一些在那个时代的重要行业中展现出来的古英格兰的生活场景。

男士们把女士们留在了屋子中做一些家务活，或者徘徊在他们花园中的玫瑰花和百合花之间，或者在一些凉爽的可供休息的果园里。在宽大的藤蔓拧成的花簇下，在弥漫在周围的苹果的香气之中，女士们会使用她们的绣花针做一些针线活。伯爵和绅士从他们的住处走到长廊，坐在属于他们的宝座上给一大群乞丐救济物，或者召开主持当地的集会。

秋天给那些古英格兰的皇室成员和高贵的运动员们一个美好的时机。英格兰的居民屋都是置于高处的，处于一座高山的最高点。伯爵们从他们的住所飞驰出来，摆脱了所有关于工作的心思和想法，和他们的威尔士猎犬一起走进邻近的森林之中。他们已经被金色和红色的九月所深深打动。

在朦朦胧胧的森林大道中，号角演奏出的音乐的声响在华丽地流淌。猎犬追赶着受到惊吓而从遮蔽它们的灌木丛里跑出来的红鹿和野猪。猎犬因新鲜的气味而发狂冲动，在它们身后，英勇的猎人也狂追不舍。他们穿过了围网，将大量的野猪群驱赶到了橡树果实十分稀少的山谷之中；他们用树木切割机为城堡中生火割下燃料，或者在中午时分用力咀嚼他们仅有的燕麦面包。直到这些长着鹿茸或者长牙的猎物冲进了被侍者撒在树丛之间、过道之中的强大的网中，才会有人勒紧缰绳停下这场追逐。

带着猎鹰打猎，长期以来都占据了我们现代狩猎中的一席之地。就连如商人一般谨慎的艾尔菲莱德也全身心地投入到了这一迷人的活动之中。我们很容易就能够理解，这样的聚会所带来的高昂的情绪和愉悦的会谈。在落叶上慢跑发出瑟瑟的响声。在十月的森林中，一切都是苍白和易碎的。一切都在流向长满芦苇的小湖，在那里，他们可以尽情游乐。每一个骑士的手腕上都站立着一只戴着头巾的猎鹰。或许在挪威一个黑暗的松制的屋子里，它曾经被一个驯鹰者认真地训练过。而这些驯鹰者，在古英格兰建立的过程中，并不是一些无足轻重的官员。

来到水边，这些骑士会分散成小队伍。蓝色的苍鹭挥动它们强壮的翅膀，或者有从已经被淹没的住所中逃出来的鸭子拍打着水面，发出嘈杂的声响。猎鹰开始飞翔，它们视力敏锐，能够将所有这些场景都尽收眼底。此时，它们已经被狩猎者的胳膊抬到了很高的空中。它们用强有力的翅膀罩出一片新的天地，在这些灾难临头的猎物上方盘旋，紧接着是一次突然的俯冲。猎鹰具有重创性的爪子刺入对方的背部和脑袋之中，最后将它们杀死在地面上。猎鹰在陈尸累累的地面上疾驰，同样给了参加猎杀的骑士们结束这场游戏的时间。此时，他们会将这些喙上沾满鲜血的胜利者，召回到自己的头巾和杆子上。

但是打猎和猎鹰比赛只不过是富人们的一种消遣方式。当健壮的鹿倒在猎人的飞镖下，或者蓝色的羽毛散落在了大量的湖泊和河流之中，铁匠们正在他明亮的铁毡上敲打红色的铁块。木工则切下了木片，用来做草地上的长椅或者供种植园使用，或者用来制作二轮马车的方向盘和农场里农民所用的手用犁。鞋匠忙碌地用他的刀子和针在晒制的皮革和制成的马具上工作。毛皮商正准备着制作成庄严肃穆的礼服内衬的皮料。而每个在修道院里的修道士，利用火炉、雕刻工具、油漆刷子以及一系列相同设备的神秘结合，制造出了最精美的钟、十字架、珠宝，和一些彩色玻璃。之后，它们都会呈现给人们。

古代英国的农民不是放牧者，也不是土地上的农夫。他们放羊，为了得到羊毛；养猪，为了得到猪肉；养牛，为了得到牛肉和牛皮。这样的农民分布在每一处牧场，占据了每一片农场附近的森林。但这里同样也存在农业。古英格兰的农场生活，虽然比他们后来的现代农民的生活要不开化得多，但也有许多方面是一致的。在田地里，每英亩经常会有四匹羊，因为那时缺乏肥料，人们不得不用古英格兰的方式，用泥灰来施肥。在这之间，矗立着一间木质结构的屋子，农场满院子都布满了牛棚和大量的鹅和鸡。几个蜂箱是糖分的孕育基地——当时还没有发现甘蔗，承装蜂蜜酒的酒桶总是装得满满的，它们为人们提供了大量的甜食。此时的果园里，树枝已经负载着大量的苹果和梨，还有坚果和杏仁，在其他一些地区，还有很多无花果和葡萄。

从古英格兰的一些手稿中，我们可以得知一些刻画当年农场工作的场景。一月份，由四头公牛所拉着的铁犁正在工作。它们驾驭着厚厚的鲸皮绳索或者皮带。人们会在二月开采他们的葡萄园，开采花园，则需要在三月。在四月，当播种的时候已经过去，他们就会悠闲地享用他们的麦芽酒。五月，人们开始为剪羊毛做准备了。六月，我们就可以看到人们在挥舞着镰刀割小麦。七月，我们可以听到斧头切割树木的声音。八月，人们会用镰刀割大麦。九月和十月是属于猎鹰和猎犬的好天气。人们在十一月对农具进行修补和更新。十二月，人们用疾走的连枷拨开了壳粒，这样就可以依靠劳动的热情来驱散冬天的严寒。我们在脱粒现场，会看到一个站立着的管家，手里拿着一个放满谷物的篮子，将它们倒入粮仓之中。

从欧洲大陆来到古英格兰的船，装满了皮草和丝绸、宝石和黄金、丰富的服装、酒、油、象牙回来了。它们很可能会载着汗血宝马、弗兰德斯的羊毛纺织机，还有在更早的时候来自远方的英国奴隶，回到欧洲大陆，这些都会在罗马找到市场。贸易的落后状况，可以从除了在公开法庭之外从不允许讨价还价等方面来判断。在公开法庭之上，会有警长、大众牧师或者庄园的领主在场。

为了安全，商人们以商队的形式出行，他们会携带着各自的帐篷。在某些时间，他们穿过了不同的乡村和小镇。这些地方因为庆祝节日或者举行运动会，而充斥着各式各样的嘈杂声和欢笑声。古英格兰的妇人们和女孩儿们非常喜爱明亮的绸缎和华丽的装饰品，这些都是属于女性的时尚。所以，当武士们在草地上进行摔跤比赛，或者用笑嘻嘻的滑稽动作跳着舞的时候，名叫吉萨的姑娘就会用她长期收集的钱币，购买很多彩色的珠子和一些字符串或者象牙梳子。

在商人或者小贩（我们这样称呼他们，是因为这样最能向现代人反映出当时他们的生活习惯）的旁边，站立着一个手拿天平的帮手，准备好来称重一笔大买卖的钱币。在早期的英格兰，奴隶和牲畜是产品交换的主要媒介。不管在商人们的麻布袋里，金子是怎样的闪光，那时主要流通的还是拜占庭的金币苏勒德斯，人们简单地把它叫作银币，它的价值是我们的先令的九倍之多。而另一种银币价值两个先令，同样也在当时流通。在早些时候，印着帝王头像的罗马货币也一样进入了英国人的钱包之中。

在古代的英国，人们不会仅仅为了愉悦身心而进行一趟旅程。因为太多的灾害影响了旅行。有钱的人会乘坐大卡车去到附近进行郊游，而在长途旅行之时，他们则会选择骑马——那时的女士坐在侧鞍。但是那时大多数的旅行是徒步进行的。骑士们携带长矛，用于防御强盗或者野兽。徒步远行的人们则会拿着一块结实短小的橡树块，用来完成协助和保护旅客的双重目的。那时的马镫拥有一种奇怪的三角形形状，马刺也相当简单。旅客的头部带上一个裹头，身上穿着一件斗篷。正如我们所知道的，他们有时也会带雨伞。但有些东西是非常少见的，像手套就仅限于非常高的阶层。

麦芽酒小屋在镇上随处可见，人们会在这里消磨很多时间。但是在乡村，旅舍是很少见的。正如东方的旅馆一样，这些地方事实上只是石头墙垒起来的一个空间。途经此处的旅客们带着自己的商品，可以在夜晚在那里找到能够免遭风雨的避难所。或许古罗马的别墅或者营房的遗址，能够给这些疲惫的商队提供一处荫蔽的乘凉之地。但是古代英国公民的热情好客，已经深入到了他们的法律和习惯之中。

不像后来拥挤的现代朋友圈的娱乐现象，现在的人们只会互相回报。而在那时，人们会欢迎任何人来借宿，不管这些人是熟悉还是不熟悉。这导致了在那时的英国，基本找不到任何旅馆，除了在大陆上某些更旷远的地方。

当一个陌生人出现在一个古英格兰人住处的金属门前时，他就会得到水来洗手和洗脚。当他将自己的装备行李卸下来交给主人，他就会以一种介于主人的家人或朋友一样的身份，进驻到这个家庭之中。两晚之间，主人不会问起关于他的行当或者名字的任何问题，在那之后主人就会承担起他的角色了。在那个时代，很少有孤独的旅客，因为当时的事实是，一个人单独出门会引起怀疑，并且会使这名旅客置于被捕的风险之中，或者有可能像贼一样被杀害。

Lesson 47　LIFE IN SAXON ENGLAND (II)
第四十七课　撒克森时期英国的生活（二）

The central picture in Old English life—the great event of the day—was *Noon-meaty* or dinner in the great hall. A little before three, the chief and all his household, with any stray guests who might have dropped in, met in the hall, which stood in the centre of its encircling bowers—the principal apartment of every Old English house. Clouds of wood-smoke, rolling up from a fire which blazed in the middle of the floor, blackened the carved and gilded rafters of the arched roof before it found its way out of the hole above, which did duty as a chimney.

Tapestries of purple dye, or glowing with variegated pictures of saints and heroes, hung, or, if the day was stormy, flapped upon the chinky walls. In palaces and in earls' mansions coloured tiles, wrought like Roman *tesserce* into a mosaic, formed a clean and pretty pavement; but the common flooring of the time was of clay, baked dry with the heat of winter evenings and summer noons. The only articles of furniture always in the hall were wooden benches; some of which, especially the *high settle* or seat of the chieftain, boasted cushions, or at least a rug.

While the hungry crowd, fresh from woodland and furrow, were lounging near the fire or hanging up their weapons on the pegs and hooks that jutted from the wall, a number of slaves, dragging in a long, flat, heavy board, placed it on movable legs, and spread on its upper half a handsome cloth. Then were arranged with other utensils for the meal some flattish dishes, baskets of ash-wood for holding bread, a scanty sprinkling of steel knives shaped like our modern razors, platters of wood, and bowls for the universal broth.

The ceremony of "laying the board," as the Old English phrased it, being completed, the work of demolition began. Great round cakes of bread—huge junks of boiled bacon—vast rolls of broiled eel—cups of milk—horns of ale—wedges of cheese—lumps of salt butter—and smoking piles of cabbages and beans, melted like magic from the board under the united attack of greasy fingers and grinding jaws. Kneeling slaves offered to the lord and his honoured guests long skewers or spits, on which steaks of beef or venison smoked and sputtered, ready for the hacking blade.

Poultry, too, and game of every variety, filled the spaces of the upper board; but, except naked bones, the crowd of *loaf-eaters*, as Old English domestics were suggestively called, saw little of these daintier kinds of food. Nor did they much care, if to their innumerable hunches of bread they could add enough pig to appease their hunger. Hounds, sitting eager-eyed by their masters, snapped with sudden jaws at scraps of fat flung to them, or retired into private life below the board with some sweet bone that fortune sent them.

With the washing of hands, performed for the honoured occupants of the high settle by officious slaves, the solid part of the banquet ended. The board was then dragged out of the hall; the loaf-eaters slunk away to have a nap in the byre, or sat drowsily in corners of the hall; and the drinking began. During the progress of the meal, Welsh ale had flowed freely in horns or vessels of twisted glass. Mead, and in very grand houses wine, now began to circle in goblets of gold and silver, or of wood inlaid with those precious metals.

Most of the Old English drinking-glasses had rounded bottoms, like our soda-water bottles, so that they could not stand upon the table—a little thing, which then as in later times suggested hard drinking and unceasing rounds. Two attendants, one to pour out the liquor, and the other to hand the cups, waited on the carousers, from whose company the homes of the household soon withdrew. The clinking of cups together, certain words of pledge, and a kiss, opened the revel.

In humbler houses, story-telling and songs, sung to the music of the harp by each guest in turn, formed the principal amusement of the drinking-bout. But in great halls, the music of the harp—which, under the poetic name of "glee-wood," was the national instrument—of fiddles played with bow or finger, of trumpets, pipes, flutes, and horns, filled the hot and smoky air with a clamour of sweet sounds. The solo of the ancient scop or maker, who struck his five-stringed harp in praise of old Teutonic heroes, was exchanged in later days for the performances of the glee-man, who played on many instruments, danced with violent and often comical gestures, tossed knives and balls into the air, and did other wondrous feats of jugglery.

Meantime the music and the mead did their work upon maddened brains: the revelry grew louder; riddles, which had flown thick around the board at first, gave place to banter, taunts, and fierce boasts of prowess; angry eyes gleamed defiance; and it was well if in the morning the household slaves had not to wash blood-stains from the pavement of the hall, or in the still night, when the drunken brawlers lay stupid on the floor, to drag a dead man from the red plash in which he lay.

From the reek and riot of the hall the ladies escaped to the bower, where they reigned supreme. There, in the earlier part of the day, they had arrayed themselves in their bright-coloured robes, plying tweezers and crisping-irons on their yellow hair, and often heightening the blush that Nature gave them with a shade of rouge. There, too, they used to scold and beat their female slaves, with a violence which said more for their strength of lung and muscle than for the gentleness of their womanhood.

When their needles were fairly set going upon those pieces of delicate embroidery, known and prized over all Europe as "English work," some gentlemen dropped in, perhaps harp in hand, to chat and play for their amusement, or to engage in games of hazard and skill, which seem to have resembled modem dice and chess. When in later days supper came into fashion, the round table of the bower was usually spread for *Evening-food*, as this meal was called. And not long afterwards, those bags of straw, from which they sprang at sunrise, received tor another night their human burden, worn out with the labours and the revels of the day.

Words

arranged, *laid out*.
arrayed, *decked*.
carousers, *revellers*.
central, *most important*.
chieftain, *lord*.
completed, *finished*.
defiance, *challenge*.
demolition, *consumption*.
gestures, *actions*.
heightening, *intensifying*.

honoured, *distinguished*.
longing, *loitering*.
officious, *over-obliging*.
principal, *chief*.
resembled, *been like*.
revelry, *festivity*.
suggestively, *significantly*.
unceasing, *incessant*.
utensils, *appliances*.
variegated, *checkered*.

Questions

What was the great event of the Old English day? When did it take place? Of what did the table consist? By whom was the board laid? Of what did the meal consist? What food did the domestics receive? With what did the solid part of the banquet end? What then began? What did they drink? What was peculiar about their drinking-glasses? Of what is this suggestive? By what performances was the banquet accompanied? In what did it often end? Where had the ladies meantime gone? How did they spend the evening?

☆ ☆

　　古英格兰生活的一个主要场景——一天中一件非常重大的事情——是在大厅之中享受午餐或者晚餐。3点之前，主人和他所有的家人，同时还包括来拜访的客人，到处于一栋圆环形房子中心位置的大厅来用餐——这样的房屋结构，也是古英格兰房屋的主要种类。烧木头所燃起的烟，从楼层中间的部位燃烧，而释放出来。拱形的屋顶上的镀金和雕刻的装饰，在这股烟雾从房顶的出口排放出去之前就被熏黑了。而这个房顶洞口的作用相当于一个烟囱。

　　染成紫色的挂毯，或者是泛着不同颜色的圣人或者英雄的图片，悬挂在沉重的墙壁之上。如果在狂风暴雨的天气之中，它们会拍打着墙壁。在宫殿或者伯爵的府邸之中，彩色的瓷砖都是嵌花式的，就像罗马的马赛克的走廊，形成了干净而清洁的地面。但在那个时代，一般情况下地板的材料是被冬天晚上和夏天下午的热量所烘干的泥。在大厅中唯一的家具是一些木制的长椅，尤其是那些靠背长椅或者家族长的凳子，会铺有一个垫子或至少一个毯子。

　　当那些饥饿的人群刚从林地或者田地回来，他们会躺在火炉旁边，或者将他们的工具悬挂在墙上的钉子上或者桩上。大量的奴隶正在用他们的腿拖着又长又沉的平面板子，腿的上半部分穿着一块漂亮的布。然后人们拿起一些为吃饭设计的器具，比如比较平的盘子，灰和木材制成的篮子可以用来装面包，钢刀的稀疏的制作方式比较像我们现在的剃须刀，木材料的盘子和碗是用来盛肉汤的。

当古代英国人所说的"入座"仪式结束之后，拆分食物的工作就开始了。大块的圆形面包、巨大的熏肉卷、许多鳗鱼卷、许多瓶牛奶、楔形的奶酪、非常多的咸黄油，还有大量的卷心菜和豆子，在人们油腻腻的手指和不停发出刺耳咀嚼声的下巴的联合攻击之下，神奇地被人们消化掉。跪着的奴隶会向他们的主人和他尊贵的客人献上叉子和盘子，上面装满了烟熏成的牛排或者鹿肉，它们已经用刀切成块，可以直接吃了。

各种各样的家禽肉，还有各种各样的游戏，也会不时出现在餐桌之上。但是除了干净的骨头，这些古英国人不怎么吃这样的食物。所以他们被有内涵意义地称呼为"吃面包的古英格兰人"。他们也不是特别关心在他们大量的面包之外，还可以增加一定量的猪肉来充饥。猎犬们睁着饥饿的眼睛坐在他们的主人旁边，主人会给它们一些残留在嘴角的碎肉，或者有时候，它们在餐桌之下也会得到一些私下的奖励，比如得到一些可口的骨头。

伴随着房中尊贵的主人和客人们一起在奴隶们的辅佐之下洗手，宴会的固有部分就结束了。宴会桌随后被拖出了大厅，吃面包的仆人们会偷偷去牛棚打个盹，或者懒洋洋地坐在大厅开始喝酒。在这顿饭进行期间，异型的玻璃杯子里面已经盛满了威尔士啤酒。当前在酒吧中流行的蜂蜜酒，在当时是一种只会出现在贵族家中的酒，被放在木质的或者是金属镶嵌的杯子里。

绝大多数的古英格兰酒杯的杯底是圆的，就像我们的苏打水瓶子一样，所以它们无法立在桌子上。这样的一个小物件，正如后来一样，让人想到带酒精的饮品和一轮一轮不停地喝酒。两个服务员，一个负责倒酒，另一个负责拿着杯子，在传送带旁边提供服务。在他们的工作中，家里的酒很快就空了。杯子碰撞到一起时发出的叮当声，举杯祝福的某些话语，一个吻，开启了这次狂欢的盛宴。

讲故事和演奏歌曲，每一个客人轮流和着木琴合唱，是那时候普通家庭里人们主要的娱乐方式。但在大厅里面，竖琴演奏出来的音乐——竖琴，拥有一个诗一样美丽的名字："欢乐的木头"，一种全国性的乐器——夹杂着小提琴、小号、管乐器、长笛和长号演奏出的音乐，让炎热且不清新的空气中顿时充满了甜蜜的欢呼声。古老歌曲的节奏还在演绎着对古代英雄的颂歌，到了后来演化成了能演奏多种乐器的舞蹈，演绎出疯狂且有时滑稽的动作，给人们带来欢乐。他们向天空中扔出球和刀子，做出一些杂耍动作或者其他的高难度动作。

与此同时，音乐需要与疯狂的表演相契合，人们狂欢的声音越来越大。谜语起初是活动中出现最多的部分，后来被嘲讽还有激进、高亢的自我演讲所代替。有些人愤怒的眼睛里闪烁着蔑视的眼神。如果在早晨或者晚上，家里的奴隶们不需要清洗一些大厅中走廊上的血迹。在宁静的夜晚，很多愚蠢的醉鬼经常会在他躺下的水池里拉过来一个死人。这些都是属于那个时代的场景。

女士们从臭气和暴乱弥漫着的大厅逃到了属于她们统治的区域。在那里，在早些时候，她们穿上华丽的浅色衣服，在她们金黄色的头发上夹上一些发卡，她们的脸上经常会泛起红晕，这是大自然赐予她们的胭脂的色彩。她们也经常责骂或者殴打她们的女性奴隶，这时她们显现出的浑身的力气，相比于她们女性的一面要体现得多得多。

当她们的针线在这些精致的刺绣之间穿梭之时，这些刺绣被全欧洲冠以美誉地称为"英国作品"。一些绅士也会参与其中，有的可能会做得非常好，当然有些人是为了得到愉悦，或者参与到正如当代的骰子和象棋一样的游戏之中，这在那时候是一种娱乐的方法。当后来吃晚饭变成一种潮流的时候，人们就经常选用树荫处的圆桌子来进食"夜晚食物"——当时的人们是这样称呼晚饭的。在不久之后，在阳光下装满稻草的袋子缓解了人们一天的劳累和负担，在人们一天的劳动和欢笑中慢慢变旧。

Lesson 48   THE RELIEF OF LUCKNOW
第四十八课　勒克瑙的救援

September 26th, 1857

Havelock had determined, when he started in the morning, to relieve the anxiously-waiting garrison that night, or not survive the attempt; and the soldiers, who at first were glad to obtain a moment's rest, became impatient at delay. They had fought their way for nearly a hundred miles to rescue their beleaguered comrades with their wives and children, and they could not rest till they thundered at the gates of their prison.

The garrison in the meantime were anxiously listening for their arrival. They had heard the heavy firing in the morning, and noticed that there was a great sensation in the city. Towards noon they could see the smoke of battle as it rolled upwards over the houses; and, a little later, people hurrying out of the city, carrying bundles of clothes on their heads, followed by large bodies of cavalry and infantry. Although the enemy kept up a steady fire upon them, they were too excited to pay much heed to it, but listened with beating hearts to the heavy cannonade as it wound hither and thither through the streets.

By four o'clock some officers on the look-out reported that they saw, far away, near a palace, a regiment of Europeans and a bullock battery. Soon after, the rattle of musketry was heard in the streets. While they stood listening, a rifle ball went whistling over their heads, and never before was the sound of a bullet so sweet to the ear. It was a voice from their friends, and whispered of deliverance. Five minutes later, and the Highlanders were seen storming through one of the principal streets; and although they dropped rapidly, under the fire from roofs, windows, and doors, there was no faltering.

Then the long restrained excitement burst forth in cheer upon cheer—"from every fort, trench, and battery—from behind sand-bags piled on shattered houses—from every post still held by a few gallant spirits, rose cheer on cheer." The thrilling shouts penetrated even to the hospital, and the wounded crept out into the sun, a ghastly throng, and sent up their feeble voices to swell the glad shout of welcome!

The conversation between Outram and Havelock was long and earnest. The former was at first firm in his opinion that they should remain in the palace-court and other sheltered places till morning, and Havelock as thoroughly determined to push on. He said that the garrison might even then be exposed to the final assault; and if it were not, that the enemy could concentrate such a force around them before morning that it would be almost impossible to advance. At length it was agreed to leave the wounded, the heavy guns, and a portion of the army behind, and with only two regiments, the

78th Highlanders and the Sikhs, to attempt to reach the Residency.

Outram had been wounded in the arm by a musket-ball early in the morning; but, though faint from loss of blood, he refused to leave the saddle, and even now would not dismount. Enduring as he was bold and chivalric, he resolved to accompany Havelock, and share with him the danger, and, if need be, death, in this last perilous advance to the relief of the garrison.

Everything being ready, these two gallant commander put themselves at the head of the slender column, and moved out of the place of shelter. As soon as they entered the street, the houses on either side shot forth flame; while, to prevent the rapid advance of the troops, and hold them longer under the muzzles of their muskets, the enemy had cut deep trenches across the street, and piled up barricades.

Passing under an archway that streamed with fire, the gallant Neill fell from his horse—dead. His enraged follower halted a moment to avenge his death; but the stern order of Havelock, "Forward!" arrested their useless attempt, and the column moved on. Each street as they entered it became an avenue of flame, through which it seemed impossible for anything living to pass. Every door and window was ablaze, while an incessant sheet of fire ran along the margin of the flat roofs, which were black with men.

At each angle batteries were placed, and as soon as the head of the column appeared in view the iron storm came drifting down the street, piling it with the dead. The rattling of grape-shot and musket-balls against the walls and on the pavement was like the pattering of hail on the roof of a house! From out those deep avenues the smoke arose as from the mouth of a volcano, while shouts and yells rending the air on every side made still more appalling the night, which had now set in.

Between those walls of fire, through that blinding rain of death, Havelock walked his horse composedly as if on parade, his calm, peculiar voice, now and then rising over the clangour of battle. That he escaped unhurt seems a miracle, for in the previous eleven hours he had lost nearly one-third of his entire force, while of the two other generals one was dead and the other wounded.

At length the gate of the Residency was reached. A little time was spent in removing the barricades, during which the bleeding column rested, while the moon looked coldly down on the ruins by which they were surrounded. When the passage was cleared, the soldiers, forgetting their weariness, gave three loud cheers, and rushed forward.

Cheers without and cheers within, cheers on every side, betokened the joy and excitement that prevailed, while over all arose the shrill pipes of the Highlanders. The "column of relief" and the garrison rushed into each other's arms, and then the officers passed from house to house to greet the women and children. The stern Highlanders snatched up the children and kissed them, with tears streaming down their faces, thanking God they were in time to save them.

—J. T. Headley

Words

appalling, *terrifying*.
arrested, *checked; prevented*.
avenue, *passage; alley*.
barricades , *barriers; defences*.
beleaguered, *besieged*.
cannonade, *firing of great guns*.
composedly, *collectedly*.
concentrate, *bring together*.
conversation, *conference*.
deliverance, *relief; rescue*.
determined, *resolved*.

excitement, *agitation*.
impatient, *fretful*.
incessant, *unbroken*.
peculiar, *sifigular*.
perilous, *dangerous*.
prevailed, *existed*.
refused, *declined*.
removing, *clearing away*.
restrained, *pent-up; repressed*.
sensation, *commotion*.
survive, *outlive*.

Questions

How far had Havelock's force fought its way to rescue the garrison of Lucknow? By what signs did the garrison know that relief was approaching? When did their excitement burst forth in cheers? What was Outram's opinion of what should be done? Why did Havelock differ from him? What was at last agreed upon? What general was shot in the advance? How had the rebels obstructed the passage through the streets? What proportion of his force did Havelock lose before he reached the Residency? What took place when the "column of relief" got inside?

☆ ☆ ☆ ☆ ☆ ☆ ☆ ☆ ☆ ☆ ☆ ☆ ☆ ☆ ☆ ☆ ☆ ☆ ☆ ☆

1857年9月26日

当哈夫洛克早上醒来时，他就决定了当天晚上去救援焦急等待的驻军，哪怕在这次尝试中丧命；他的士兵们之前高兴地得到了片刻的休息，现在因为行动的延迟而变得不耐烦了起来。他们几乎向前战斗了一百英里，去营救他们的同胞以及他们陷入困境之中的妻子和孩子们。直到他们猛烈地拍打着那里的监狱大门，他们都一直无法休息。

同时，驻军们也焦急地听到了他们抵达的声音。他们早上时候听到了熊熊燃烧的大火，并注意到在城市里有明显的骚乱。到了中午，他们看到战争的硝烟在房屋上方滚滚上升；晚一些时候，人们匆忙赶出城外，他们头上顶着一捆捆的衣服，接着是大型的骑兵和步兵部队赶来了。虽然敌人不停地向他们开火，他们已经过于兴奋，全然不去关注这些火力，而只伴随着自己的心跳声，倾听炮弹轰鸣着击打在街道上。

4点，一些驻扎在守卫处的官兵报告说，他们看到在远处一座宫殿附近，有一个欧洲人的兵团。不久之后，在街上就可以听到滑膛枪发出的咯咯声。他们站在那里听到一颗步枪发出的子弹呼啸着从他们的头顶飞过，在此之前，似乎从未有过一颗子弹的声音如此让人甜蜜。这是来自于他们朋友的声音和拯救的低沉声响。五分钟后，人们看到英国人奔涌到一条主要街道上；他们在从屋顶、窗户、大门喷涌出的火焰之中迅速跳下，没有人踟蹰着前行。

接着，长时间受到抑制的兴奋感爆发了出来，成为一片又一片的欢呼，从每一处堡垒、沟槽和炮台里，从每一处堆放在破败房子旁边的沙袋后面，从每一个仍然有一个勇敢的人坚守的位置，都发出了一声接着一声的欢呼。兴奋的欢呼声甚至穿透空气来到了医院里，伤员们爬了出来，到太阳底下，人群发出了微弱的声音，为这欢迎的欢呼声又增添一分力量！

欧南与哈夫洛克之间的谈话是漫长而严肃的。一开始，欧南还坚持他的观点，认为他们应该留在宫廷和其他的庇护场所直到天亮。而哈夫洛克则坚定地认为应该继续进攻。他说，驻军可能到那时就会受困于最后的攻击之中；如果不是这样，敌人就能够在早上之前集中力量攻打他们，到那时，就几乎不可能再前进了。最后，他们终于同意让伤员连同重型武器和后方军队的一部分留在这里，而只有两个兵团，第七十八高地团和锡克团，尝试前往驻地。

欧男的手臂在早晨早些时候已经被一颗火枪的子弹射中，但是，尽管因失血变得苍白，他仍拒绝离开马鞍，即使现在他也不下马。他一直是如此英勇的骑士。在这最后的前往救援驻军的危险之中，他决心要陪伴哈夫洛克，与他共同承担危险，如果需要，还会共同承担死亡。

一切都已经准备好，这两位勇敢的指挥官将自己置于长长的兵团的前部，并从他们栖身的地方搬出。当他们走到街上，从两边的房子里射出了火焰；同时，为防止他们军队的快速推进，并能够将他们置于自己的步枪枪口之下，敌人已经在街道对面挖出了一条深深的沟壑，还堆放起了路障。

穿过了一扇汹涌着大火的拱门之后，英勇的尼尔从马上摔下来牺牲了。他的追随者停止了一会儿，要为他的死报仇；但哈夫洛克命令道："前进！"这声命令阻止了敌人无用的尝试，军队继续向前移动。他们进入的每一条街道都变成了火焰的通道。似乎任何有生命的物体都不可能通过这样的街道。每一扇大门和窗户都闪着亮光，而火不断地沿着屋顶的边缘扫射，屋顶也因为人类的战斗而早已变成了黑色。

军团进驻到每一个角落，一旦部队的前排进入到敌人的视线之中，子弹就会像暴风雨一样袭来，在整个街道咆哮，带给他们死亡。霰弹和火枪子弹的呼啸声，拍击着墙壁和路面，就像冰雹敲打在屋顶上的声音一样！从这些深长的路径之中，烟雾就像从一个火山口里一样喷涌而出，而呼喊和尖叫撕裂了每一寸空气，让刚刚开始的夜晚变得更加可怕。

在这些火焰铸成的墙壁之间，哈夫洛克坚定地骑着他的马通过死亡的暴风骤雨，就像在游行。他平静、奇特的声音，不时在战斗的铿锵声中出现。他没有受伤，这似乎是一个奇迹，因为在过去的十一个小时里，他已经失去了他全部人员的近三分之一，而其他两个将军，一个牺牲了，另一个受了伤。

最后他们终于到达了驻地的城门。他们花了一点时间用来清除路障，在此期间，受伤的士兵们得到了休息。此时，月亮冷淡地俯视着包围住他们的废墟。当通道被清除干净，士兵们忘记了疲劳，发出了三声欢呼声，继续向前进军。

欢呼声一片接着一片，每一处的欢呼声都预示着人们的喜悦和激动，而在所有欢呼声中，出现了一声英国人尖锐的管弦乐声。救援部队和当地的驻军互相拥抱对方，然后士官们挨家挨户去慰问妇女和儿童。兴奋的英国人抱起他们的孩子，亲吻他们，泪水在他们的脸上流下来，感谢上帝让他们能够及时拯救了自己的同胞。

——J.T. 海德里

Lesson 49　THE BALACLAVA CHARGE
第四十九课　巴拉克拉瓦冲锋

October 25, 1854

After their repulse in the plain of Balaclava by the Highlanders, two deep,—"that thin red streak topped by a line of steel,"—and by the heavy brigade, the Russian cavalry retired. Their infantry at the same time fell back towards the head of the valley, leaving men in three of the redoubts they had taken, and abandoning the fourth. They had also placed some guns on the heights over their position on the left of the gorge. Their cavalry joined the reserves, and drew up in six solid divisions, in an oblique line, across the entrance to the gorge. Six battalions of infantry were placed behind them, and about thirty guns were drawn up along their line, while masses of infantry were also collected on the hills behind the redoubts on our right. Our cavalry had moved up to the ridge across the valley on our left, and had halted there, as the ground was broken in front.

And now occurred the melancholy catastrophe which fills us all with sorrow. It appears that the Quartermaster-General, Brigadier Airey, thinking that the light cavalry had not gone far enough in front when the enemy's horse had fled, gave an order in writing to Captain Nolan, 15th Hussars, to take to Lord Lucan, directing his lordship "to advance" his cavalry nearer to the enemy. A braver soldier than Captain Nolan the army did not possess. He rode off with the order to Lord Lucan. (He is now dead and gone: God forbid that I should cast a shade on the brightness of his honour, but I am bound to state what I am told occurred when he reached his lordship.)

When Lord Lucan received the order from Captain Nolan, and had read it, he asked, we are told, "Where are we to advance to?" Captain Nolan pointed with his finger to the line of the Russians, and said, "There are the enemy, and there are the guns, sir, before them; it is your duty to take them,"—or words to that effect. Lord Lucan, with reluctance, gave the order to Lord Cardigan to advance upon the guns, conceiving that his orders compelled him to do so. The noble earl, though he did not shrink, also saw the fearful odds against them. Don Quixote, in his tilt against the windmill, was not nearly so rash and reckless as the gallant fellows who prepared without a thought to rush on almost certain death.

It is a maxim of war, that "cavalry never act without a support;" that " infantry should be close at hand when cavalry carry guns, as the effect is only instantaneous;" and that it is necessary to have on the flank of a line of cavalry some squadrons in column, the attack on the flank being most dangerous. The only support our light cavalry had was the reserve of heavy cavalry at a great distance behind them, the infantry and guns being far in the rear. There were no squadrons in column at all, and there was a plain to charge over, before the enemy's guns could be reached, of a mile and a half in length!

At ten minutes past eleven our light cavalry brigade advanced. The whole brigade scarcely made one effective regiment, according to the numbers of continental armies, and yet it was more than we could spare. As they rushed towards the front, the Russians opened on them, from the guns in the redoubt on the right, with volleys of musketry and rifles. They swept proudly past, glittering in the morning sun in all the pride and splendour of war.

We could scarcely believe the evidence of our senses. Surely that handful of men are not going to charge an army in position? Alas! it was but too true. Their desperate valour knew no bounds, and far indeed was it removed from its so-called better part— discretion. They advanced in two lines, quickening their pace as they closed upon the enemy. A more fearful spectacle was never witnessed than by those who beheld these heroes rushing to the arms of Death.

At the distance of twelve hundred yards the whole line of the enemy belched forth from thirty iron mouths a flood of smoke and flame, through which hissed the deadly balls. Their flight was marked by instant gaps in our ranks, by dead men and horses, by steeds flying wounded or riderless across the plain. The first line is broken— it is joined by the second—they never halt, or check their speed an instant. With diminished ranks, thinned by those thirty guns, which the Russians had laid with the most deadly accuracy; with a halo of flashing steel above their heads, and with a cheer which was many a noble fellow's death-cry, they flew into the smoke of the batteries: but ere they were .lost from view the plain was strewed with their bodies, and with the carcasses of horses.

They were exposed to an oblique fire from the batteries on the hills on both sides, as well as to a direct fire of musketry. Through the clouds of smoke we could see their sabres flashing, as they rode up to the guns and dashed into their midst, cutting down the gunners where they stood. We saw them riding through the guns, as I have said: to our delight we saw them returning after breaking through a column of Russian infantry, and scattering it like chaff, when the flank fire of the battery on the hill swept them down, scattered and broken as they were. Wounded men and riderless horses flying towards us told the sad tale. Demi-gods could not have done what they had failed to do.

At the very moment when they were about to retreat, an enormous mass of Lancers was hurled on their flank. Colonel Shewell, of the 8th Hussars, saw the danger, and rode his few men straight at them, cutting his way through with fearful loss. The other regiments turned, and engaged in a desperate encounter. With courage too great almost for credence, they were breaking their way through the columns which enveloped them, when there took place an act of atrocity without parallel in the modern warfare of civilized nations.

The Russian gunners, when the storm of cavalry passed, returned to their guns.

They saw their own cavalry mingled with the troopers who had just ridden over them; and, to the eternol disgrace of the Russian name, the miscreants poured a murderous volley of grape and canister on the mass of struggling men and horses, mingling friend and foe in one common ruin!

It was as much as our heavy cavalry brigade could do to cover the retreat of the miserable remnants of the band of heroes as they returned to the place they had so lately quitted. At thirty-five minutes past eleven not a British soldier, except the dead and the dying, was left in front of those guns.

—W. H. Russell

Words

abandoning, *relinquishing.*
atrocity, *barbarity.*
battalions, *large companies.*
carcasses, *dead bodies.*
catastrophe, *disaster.*
cavalry, *horse soldiers.*
compelled, *obliged.*
delight, *joy.*
diminished, *reduced.*
effective, *efficient; complete.*
encounter, *conflict.*
enormous, *very great.*
evidence, *testimony.*

infantry, *foot soldiers.*
instantaneous, *momentary.*
miscreants, *wretches.*
oblique, *slanting.*
occurred, *happened.*
parallel, *match.*
redoubts, *outworks.*
reluctance, *unwillingness.*
remnants, *survivors.*
repulse, *defeat.*
spectacle, *sight.*
squadrons, *bodies troops.*

Questions

What position did the Russian cavalry take up after retiring? How many guns were drawn up along their line? What order did Airey send to Lucan? How did Nolan explain it? To whom did Lucan give the order to advance? What maxim of war was violated in this? What took place at the distance of twelve hundred yards from the enemy? Where did the light cavalry then make their way? To what were they exposed on their way back? Of what act of atrocity were the Russian gunners guilty?

1854年10月25日

在高地骑兵和英法联军的重装旅将俄国军队击退到巴拉克拉瓦平原之后，俄国骑兵团如两条细长、红色的钢铁线一样大举撤退。他们的步兵团也在同一时间退回到山谷处，他们在已经夺取的三个堡垒中还留有人手，而放弃了第四座堡垒。在峡谷左侧他们位置的高度，他们架起了枪支。他们进行充分准备的骑兵团分成六个小分队，沿着一条斜线一字排开，驻守在峡谷的入口处。六个步兵营被安排在他们之后，大约30个火力点已经准备好，瞄准了他们的驻守之处。而在我们右方，还有他们大量的步兵聚集在后面山上的堡垒之上。在我们左方，我们的骑兵已沿着山脊向上攀爬，而由于前方的路已经毁坏，他们不得不停在了那里。

眼前发生的灾难让我们所有人都充满了忧郁和悲伤。军需官将军布里格迪尔·艾瑞，因为认为当敌人骑马逃跑时，轻骑兵团在前方没有前进足够的距离，于是给诺兰上尉下达了书面命令，要他带着第十五轻骑兵团，向卢肯勋爵传达命令，要他指挥"推进"他的骑兵团进一步接近敌人。敌人那边是没有像诺兰上尉这样英勇的士兵的。他骑上马，带着命令前往卢肯勋爵那里。（他现在去世了：上帝肯定不会允许我诋毁他的名誉，但我必须陈述出当他到达之时我听到的信息。）

在卢肯勋爵收到诺兰上尉带来的命令，读过它之后，他问道："我们向哪里前进？"诺兰上尉手指向俄国人的阵线说："那边有敌人，还有他们的步枪，先生到他们面前去；这是您的职责，带领轻骑兵团冲向那里。"或诸如此类的话。卢肯勋爵极其不情愿地向卡迪根伯爵传达了命令，向着敌人的炮火前进，设想着自己的命令会强迫他这样做。高贵的伯爵，虽然没有丝毫的退缩，也想到了他们可能会遇到的可怕后果。这些想都不想就准备好冲向几乎必然的死亡的勇敢战士们，即使同与风车搏斗的堂吉诃德相比，也似乎显得轻率、鲁莽。

有一句关于战争的格言这样讲："骑兵从不会在没有支持的情况下采取行动，"而"当骑兵携带枪支冲上前去时，步兵应该近在咫尺，因为战争的影响是瞬时的。"在轻骑兵团的侧翼，我们有必要同时派出一个骑兵中队，因为对他们侧翼的攻击是最危险的。如今，对我们轻骑兵团的唯一支持来自于他们身后距离甚远的重骑兵团，而其中，步兵和火炮被远远地放在最后面。我们根本就没有派出骑兵中队出现在队列之中，而他们要冲锋向前的却是一片平原，在这之上，敌人的炮火可以达到的距离足足有一英里半长！

11点10分，我们的轻骑兵团开始进军。整个旅简直都不是一个有效的兵团，因为他们装备的标准武器的数量是如此有限，而就是这有限的武器也是我们极力节省下来的。当他们发起冲锋时，俄国人开始向他们开火，从右边的堡垒处、从山谷处频频发射出步枪和来复枪的子弹。他们勇敢地前进，早晨的阳光闪烁着战争的骄傲与辉煌。

我们简直不能相信自己的感觉。难道众战士们不是要冲锋去占领敌人的堡垒吗？唉！现在的战况太真实了。他们带着绝望的刚勇，毫无畏惧，但事实上，他们也被迫失去了他们应有的谨慎。他们排成两条战线前进，在敌人面前加快了步伐。比起现在我们所看到的这些英雄昂首冲向死亡的场景，世上不会再有更可怕的场景了。

在1097米的距离之外，敌人的战线，从30处火枪口发射出嘶嘶致命的火球，夹杂着浓烟和烈火。炮弹飞行过的地方，在我们的队伍中不停地制造出间隔，这些间隔属于已经战死的士兵和骏马。还有一些骏马疾驰着飞奔过平原，自身受了伤，或者马背上已经没有了骑兵。第一排战线断了——马上由第二排的士兵补上，他们从未停止或减速。我们的战线不断地被敌军的30处火力打击，而俄国人可以从这些火力点精确地打击敌人；钢球的光环在他们的头顶上方闪烁，许多高尚的战士因死亡而呼喊，他们冲进了炮弹的烟雾之中，最终他们都消失在了平原之中，战场上战士们的尸体和马的尸体四处横陈。

他们暴露于一片从山脉两侧袭来的倾斜的火力之中，而在他们正前方还有一排步枪的直接射击。透过炮火的烟雾，我们仍然可以看到他们的军刀在闪着光，他们骑马横刀冲到敌军中间，奋力砍杀。我们看见他们穿过枪炮，正如我所说：我们很高兴地看见他们在突破了一支俄国的步兵队之后成功返回，而当山上的侧面火力扫射下来之时，他们像谷壳一样分散在战场的四处。受伤的战士们和马背上已经没有骑手的骏马飞奔向我们，向我们诉说战场上悲壮的故事。即使是神明也无法挽救这场战局。

在他们正要撤退的时刻，一支大规模的骑兵队伍被安排到他们侧翼。第八骑兵团的休厄尔上校看到了危险，带领他的小股分队直接骑行到他们面前，伴随着可怕的损失切断了敌人前进的道路。另一个团转变方向，绝望地遭遇了敌军。凭借着几乎是面对牺牲的伟大勇气，他们从包围住他们的敌军中间突围了出来，而这种残暴凶恶的战斗方式，在文明国家的现代战争中是几乎无可匹敌的。

当如暴风骤雨一般来临的我方骑兵突围之后，重新拿起了他们的枪。他们看到自己的骑兵混杂在刚刚袭击过他们的我方骑兵中间，带着俄国的恶名，这些凶残的俄国枪手对战场上的士兵和战马进行了屠杀，他们的战友和敌人，因此一起走向了毁灭！

只有我们的重骑兵旅可以掩护这支英雄队伍的可悲的残部撤退到他们刚刚离开的地方。11点35分之时，在敌人的炮弹面前，英国士兵无一幸存。

——W. H. 罗素

Lesson 50
THE CHARGE OF THE LIGHT BRIGADE
第五十课　轻骑兵进击

Half a league, half a league,	半里格，半里格，
Half a league onward,	前进半里格的路，
All in the valley of Death	六百名骑兵，
Rode the Six Hundred.	全部进入了死亡之谷，
"Forward the Light Brigade!	"前进，轻骑队！
Charge for the guns," he said:	向炮位冲锋！"他命令；
Into the valley of Death	六百名轻骑兵
Rode the Six Hundred.	进入了死亡之谷。
"Forward the Light Brigade!"	"冲啊，轻骑队！"
Was there a man dismayed?	可有一人踌躇退后？
Not though the soldier knew	纵然士兵知道，
Some one had blundered:	有人判断错了；
Theirs not to make reply,	他们也无话可说，
Theirs not to reason why,	他们不问为什么，
Theirs but to do and die:	他们只知奉命这样做，
Into the valley of Death	六百名轻骑兵，
Rode the Six Hundred.	进入了死亡之谷。
Cannon to right of them,	炮在他们右边，
Cannon to left of them,	炮在他们左边，
Cannon in front of them,	炮在他们前边，
Volleyed and thundered;	发出阵阵雷鸣；
Stormed at with shot and shell,	炮弹碎片横飞，
Boldly they rode and well;	打不退他们整齐的骑队，
Into the jaws of Death,	进入死神的牙口，
Into the mouth of Hell,	进入地狱的范围，
Rode the Six Hundred.	六百名轻骑兵。

Flashed all their sabres bare,	他们抽出军刀一亮，
Flashed as they turned in air,	在空中闪闪发光，
Sabring the gunners there,	看见炮手就砍，
Charging an army, while	直向大军进犯，
All the world wondered:	全世界为之震惊；
Plunged in the battery smoke,	冲入炮火的硝烟，
Right through the line they broke:	捣入敌军的阵线，
Cossack and Russian	哥萨克人、俄罗斯人，
Reeled from the sabre stroke,	在军刀挥舞之间，
Shattered and sundered.	被打得支离破碎。
Then they rode back, but not—	然后他们策马归来，
Not the Six Hundred.	可不再是，可不再是六百人。

Cannon to right of them,	炮在他们右边，
Cannon to left of them,	炮在他们左边，
Cannon behind them,	炮在他们后边，
Volleyed and thundered:	发出阵阵雷鸣；
Stormed at with shot and shell,	炮弹碎片横飞，
While horse and hero fell,	英雄坠落马匹倒地，
They that had fought so well	奋战成功的骑兵队，
Came through the jaws of Death,	脱离了死亡的大嘴，
Back from the mouth of Hell,	从地狱门口回归，
All that was left of them—	那六百名中剩下的骑兵，
Left of Six Hundred.	那六百名中剩下的骑兵。

When can their glory fade?	他们的光荣会有消退的一天？
Oh! the wild charge they made!	啊，他们的那次冲锋好大胆！
All the world wondered.	全世界为之震惊，
Honour the charge they made!	赞美他们那次的冲锋！
Honour the Light Brigade,	赞美那一队轻骑兵，
Noble Six Hundred!	高贵的六百人！

—Alfred Tennyson	——艾尔弗雷德·丁尼生

Words

battery, *number of cannon.*
blundered, *made a mistake.*
dismayed, *alarmed.*
league, *measure of length.*
plunged, *swallowed.*
reply, *answer; objection.*
sabring, *cutting down.*

shattered, *broken.*
sundered, *separated.*
thundered, *roared.*
valley, *hollow.*
volleyed, *bellowed.*
wondered, *marveled.*

FRIENDS

Friend after friend departs;
Who hath not lost a friend?
There is no union here of hearts
That finds not here an end:
Were this frail world our final rest
Living or dying, none were blest.

Beyond the flight of time,
Beyond this vale of death,
There surely is some blessed clime
Where life is not a breath,
Nor life's affections transient fire,
Whose sparks fly upward and expire.

There is a world above,
Where parting is unknown;
A long eternity of love,
Formed for the good alone;
And Faith beholds the dying here
Translated to that glorious sphere.

—Jas. Montgomery

Lesson 51　THE DISCOVERY OF THE SEA ROUTE TO INDIA
第五十一课　通往印度海上航线的发现

The Map of the World, until the end of the fifteenth century, exhibited only one hemisphere, and even that was not completely explored. The general outlines of Europe and Asia were correctly laid down, with the exception of the north-east corner of the latter, which was still a blank. The shores of Africa which are washed by the Mediterranean and the Red Sea were well known, as was also the Atlantic coast as far down as Cape Nun. The remainder of the continent was a blank, which the geographers filled in at pleasure with dragons, serpents, and all manner of strange monsters.

It was not without an indefinable terror that European mariners spoke of the mysterious regions to the south, which lay beyond their ken. "He who would pass Cape Nun," said a current proverb, "will either return or not;" implying that if he had not the good sense to turn before he reached the cape, he would never have the chance of doing so afterwards. And so for long years the dreaded promontory stretched out into the waves, and all ships were careful to keep well to the north of it.

It was reserved for Portugal to tear aside the veil which hung over the greater part of Africa. Confined to a narrow strip of coast, and isolated from the Mediterranean by its position outside of the Strait of Gibraltar, it was natural that this little kingdom should turn its attention to the navigation of the Atlantic. Thanks to the wise provisions of various sovereigns, and to its admirable situation at the mouth of the greatest river in the Peninsula, Lisbon had, before the end of the fourteenth century, become an important seat of commerce.

A strong desire, however, possessed the Portuguese to find a new route to India. The Moors had familiarized them with the luxuries of the East; but when a religious crusade was declared against these dusky neighbours, that source of supply was cut off. At the same time that this want was felt, great improvements were being made in the art of navigation.

The phenomenon of the magnet had long been known, but it was only about this period that it became more than a scientific toy, and was rendered useful for practical purposes in the shape of the mariner's compass. Armed with this simple little instrument, the seaman could now steer his course even when the stars, which had hitherto been his only guides, were hidden—he ceased to be afraid of venturing out of sight of land.

The impulse which this invention gave to navigation was sudden and direct. "The compass twinkling on its card," it has been said, "was a beam from Heaven. Like

TABLE MOUNTAIN AND CAPE TOWN

a new revelation, the mysteries of an unknown world were unveiled, and the bold and noble were inspired to lead the way. Diaz doubles the Cape of Storms; Da Gama, finds his course to the East Indies; Columbus treads the Bahamas; and twelve years do not separate these discoveries."

Don Henry, " the Navigator," as he is usually called, the fifth son of King John of Portugal, enthusiastically promoted the exploration of Africa. Impressed with a strong conviction that the continent did not end at Cape Nun, as represented on the maps, he organized repeated voyages of discovery, and taking up his abode on the promontory of Sa'gres, in the south of Portugal, he watched the white specks of sail sink below and rise above the horizon, as they went and came on their adventurous mission.

The first expedition was despatched about 1415; and when Prince Henry died, in 1463, the farthest point explored was Cape Verd and the adjoining group of islands. For no less than fifty-two years that enlightened man had devoted almost the whole of his time, thoughts, and revenues to this work; and yet the only fruit within his lifetime was the discovery of about fifteen hundred miles of coast.

Gradually creeping on from headland to headland along the coast, the Portuguese, under Bartholomew Diaz, in 1486, seeking the land of Prester John, unconsciously doubled the southern extremity of Africa, and did not learn their success until they were returning disheartened, under the belief that their voyage had been a failure.

Landing in Table Bay, Diaz planted the banner of St. Philip, under the shadow of Table Mountain, where a large and flourishing city has since sprung up. In order that future explorers might not be deterred by the name of Cape of Storms, which Diaz had conferred on the promontory, King Emanuel changed it to Cape of Good Hope.

The circumnavigation of the continent and the direct voyage to India were not accomplished till ten years later. Vasco da Gama, sailing from Lisbon with six ships on 8th July 1497, on the 20th May of the following year arrived at Calicut on the coast of Malabar.

The problem of a new route to the East was now solved, and the Portuguese for a time entered on a brilliant career of conquest and commercial prosperity. In the short space of fifteen years they established their authority in India over the whole coast from Ormuz to Ceylon, from Cape Comorin to the Moluccas, and the entire commerce of the East was almost exclusively in their hands.

The foreign empire of Portugal was brilliant but brief. A single century saw its rise, culmination, and decline. Internal factions and revolts; the want of discipline; neglect of defences; a shameful system of rapine, by which individuals were enriched at the expense of the state; pride, selfishness, and avarice, were among the chief causes of its decay.

—J. H. Fyfe

Words

accomplished, *overtaken.*
completely, *entirely.*
conferred, *bestowed.*
culmination, *zenith.*
dispatched, *sent out.*
devoted, *dedicated.*
disheartened, *crestfallen.*
enlightened, *intelligent.*
enthusiastically, *zealously; earnestly.*
exclusively, *entirely.*
exhibited, *showed; displayed.*
explored, *examined.*
familiarized, *acquainted.*
improvements, *advances.*

impulse, *impetus.*
indefinable, *vague.*
individuals, *private persons.*
inspired, *encouraged.*
mysterious, *secret; hidden.*
organized, *planned.*
phenomenon, *circumstance.*
promontory, *headland.*
promoted, *forwarded.*
prosperity, *success.*
provisions, *measures.*
rapine, *plunder.*
remainder, *residue; rest.*
unconsciously, *unwittingly.*

Questions

What was the extent of the Map of the World, until the end of the fifteenth century? How far south were the Atlantic shores of Africa known? What country first explored the greater part of the African coast? Why was it natural for Portugal to turn its attention to the Atlantic? Who had familiarized the Portuguese with the luxuries of the East? What invention gave a great impulse to navigation? Who enthusiastically promoted the exploration of Africa? How much of the coast had been discovered when he died? Who was the first to double the Cape of Good Hope? When? What was its former name? Who discovered the passage to India round the Cape? When? How long did the foreign empire of Portugal last? What led to its fall?

直到15世纪末，世界地图仍然只展现出一个半球，甚至是这个半球也没有被彻底探索。除了亚洲的东北角仍然是一片空白，欧洲和亚洲的大体轮廓已经被正确地描绘出了。被地中海和红海冲刷的非洲海岸是众所周知的，从大西洋海岸一直向南到嫩角，大家也都很熟悉。大陆地区的其余部分仍是一片空白，地理学家们在这些地方随意填写龙、蛇和其他各种各样的奇异怪物。

欧洲的航海家们谈到神秘的南部地区时，确实是带着一丝莫名的恐惧的，这里显然超出了他们所了解的范围。当时的谚语说道："那个跨过了嫩角的人将再也不会回来。"这意味着如果一个人在到达这个海角之前不想好怎么返回，他在此之后就永远不会有机会这样做了。所以，多年来，这个可怕的海岬延伸到波涛之中，而所有的船只都小心翼翼地在它的北部航行。

披在非洲大部分区域上方的面纱留给葡萄牙人来揭开。被限制在一条海岸边的狭窄水道中，在直布罗陀海峡之外被地中海分离开来，这个小小的王国，很自然地开始关注起在大西洋上的航行。因为众多明智君王的规定，也因为其位于半岛上一条大河的河口处，里斯本在14世纪结束之前，就成为一个重要的贸易港口。

然而，一个强烈的欲望迫使葡萄牙人找到一条通往印度的全新路线。摩尔人已经熟悉了东方的奢侈品，但是，当宗教运动起来反对这些忧郁的邻国时，这些商品的供应源被切断了。同时，对航海技术必须进行很大的改进也成为人们的希望。

人类早已了解了磁的现象，但直到这一时期，它才不再只是一种科学的玩具，并被赋予了富有实效的实际用途，它被做成了航海人的指南针。有了这个简单的小仪器，即使作为目前为止唯一为指引他们的天空中的繁星隐藏了起来，船员们如今也能够找到航线。人类再也不害怕冒险离开陆地了。

这一发明带给航海的冲动是突然而直接的。"指南针闪烁的光芒，"有人说道，"是来自天堂的光束。它像一个新的启示，一个未知世界的奥秘完全被揭露出来，它激励着勇敢而高尚的人们走向前方的道路。迪亚兹在风暴角折回；德迦玛发现了通往东印度群岛的航线；哥伦布踏上了巴厘岛；十二年的时间并没有使这些发现脱离开来。"

唐·亨利拥有"航海家"的称号，是葡萄牙约翰国王的第五个儿子，他热情积极地促进对非洲的探索。他拥有一个强烈的信念：非洲大陆并没有像地图上所描绘的一样在嫩角结束。他不断组织发现之旅，并将自己的住所迁到了萨格里什海角。这个海角位于葡萄牙南部，在这里，他看着白色的帆在地平线的边际沉下去又升上来，正如他们带着他们冒险的使命离去又回来。

大约在1415年，第一次远征队伍被派遣了出去，而当1463年亨利王子去世时，探索的最远点到达了佛得角和附近成片的岛屿。这位开明的君王，几乎在不少于52年的时间里，将他的全部时间、思想和收入都投入到这项工作之中；然而在他的有生之年，他唯一的收获是他的探险队发现了约1 500英里的海岸。

沿着海岸线，经过一个海岬又一个海岬地逐渐前行，葡萄牙人于1486年，在巴塞洛缪·迪亚兹的带领之下，为了探寻约翰长老的土地，不知不觉地在非洲大陆的最南端前行又折回。直到他们沮丧地返回时，他们才意识到了自己的成功，在此之前，他们都已经相信了这次航行的失败。

在桌湾登陆之后，迪亚兹将圣菲利普的旗帜插在了桌山的阴影之中。由此，一个巨大、繁荣的城市出现了。为了使今后的探险家不再被"风暴角"这个名字吓倒，伊曼纽尔国王将迪亚兹确认的这个海岬更名为"好望角"。

直到十年之后，环绕非洲大陆和直接通向印度的航行还没有实现。1497年7月8日，达伽马率六艘船只从里斯本出发，在第二年的5月20日，他们到达了马拉巴尔海岸边的卡利卡特。

一条通往东方的新路线如今已经找到，有一段时间，葡萄牙人进入了一段辉煌的征服事业和商业的繁荣之中。在短短的十五年之内，沿着印度整个海岸，从霍尔木兹海峡到锡兰，从科摩林角到摩鹿加群岛，他们建立起了自己的权威，整个东方的贸易几乎全握在他们手中。

葡萄牙在境外建立的帝国是辉煌而短暂的。仅仅一个世纪的时间里，人类就见证了它的上升、高潮和衰败。内部的派系和叛乱、缺乏纪律、忽视防御、可耻的掠夺、个人变得富有起来而牺牲了国家的利益、傲慢、自私、贪婪、都是葡萄牙衰败的主要原因。

——J·H·法伊夫

Lesson 52   GREECE
第五十二课　希　腊

He who hath bent him o'er the dead,
Ere the first day of death is fled—
Before Decay's effacing fingers
Have swept the lines where beauty lingers
And marked the mild, angelic air,
The rapture of repose that's there—
The fixed, yet tender traits, that streak
The languor of the placid cheek;
　　And—but for that sad, shrouded eye,
That fires not, wins not, weeps not now;
And but for that chill, changeless brow,
　　Where cold obstruction's apathy
Appals the gazing mourner's heart,
As if to him it could impart
The doom he dreads, yet dwells upon;—
Yes, but for these, and these alone,
Some moments, ay, one treacherous hour,
He still might doubt the tyrant's power;
So fair, so calm, so softly sealed,
The first, last look, by Death revealed!

Such is the aspect of this shore.
'Tis Greece—but living Greece no more!
So coldly sweet, so deadly fair,
We start—for soul is wanting there.
Hers is the loveliness in death
That parts not quite with parting breath;
But beauty with that fearful bloom,
That hue which haunts it to the tomb—
Expression's last receding ray,
A. gilded halo hovering round decay—
The farewell beam of feeling passed away!
Spark of that flame, that flame of heavenly birth,
Which gleams, but warms no more its cherished earth!
Clime of the unforgotten brave!
Whose land from plain to mountain cave

Was freedom's home, or glory's grave!
Shrine of the mighty! can it be,
That this is all remains of thee?
Approach, thou craven, crouching slave:
   Say, is not this Thermop'ylæ?
These waters blue that round you lave,
   O servile offspring of the free—
Pronounce, what sea, what shore is this?—
The gulf, the rock of Sal'amis!
These scenes, their story not unknown.
Arise, and make again your own;
Snatch from the ashes of your sires
The embers of their former fires;
And he who in the strife expires,
Will add to theirs a name of fear
That Tyranny shall quake to hear,
And leave his sons a hope, a fame,
They, too, will rather die than shame:
For freedom's battle, once begun,
Bequeathed by bleeding sire to son,
Though baffled oft, is ever won.
Bear witness, Greece, thy living page;
Attest it, many a deathless age!
While kings, in dusty darkness hid,
Have left a nameless pyramid;
Thy heroes, though the general doom
Hath swept the column from their tomb,
A mightier monument command—
The mountains of their native land!
There points thy Muse to stranger's eye
The graves of those that cannot die!
'Twere long to tell, and sad to trace,
Each step from splendour to disgrace;
Enough—no foreign foe could quell
Thy soul, till from itself it fell;
Yes! self-abasement paved the way
To villain bonds and despot sway.

—Byron

Words

apathy, *indifference.*
attest, *bear witness.*
bequeathed, *transmitted.*
changeless, *immovable.*
craven, *cowardly.*
effacing, *expunging.*
embers, *brands; cinders.*
languor, *feebleness.*

loveliness, *beauty.*
pyramid, *monument.*
rapture, *transport.*
receding, *withdrawing.*
splendour, *magnificence.*
treacherous, *faithless.*
unforgotten, *undying.*

☆ ☆

那个专心看着死者的人，
在死亡的第一天逃离——
在他纤细的手指腐烂之前，
曾抚摸过美景逗留的地方，
喘息着温和、天使般的气息，
在那里惬意地休息——
有种坚定而温柔的特质，
在他平静脸上的疲倦中稍纵即逝；
只有忧伤笼罩了他的眼睛，
而没有愤怒、胜利和悲哀，
冷漠的敌人怀揣着同情，
凝视着哀悼者的心，
就像能够传递给他，
他害怕这命运，却又依赖于它；
他害怕厄运，但又依赖于它；
是的，只有这些，只有这些，
某些时刻，唉，一个危险的时刻，
他仍可能怀疑那暴君的政权；
如此美丽，如此平静，如此温柔地隐藏，
死亡看见的第一眼，也是最后一眼！

这是这片海岸的景象，

这是希腊，但再也不是充满生机的希腊！

如此冷峻的甜蜜，如此致命的美好，

我们来到这里——因为那里需要灵魂。

这里有死亡的可爱之处，

不与离别的气息安静地分离；

但这种可怕绽放的美丽，

为坟墓之上的空气着色——

最后一种表情逝去的光阴，

镀金的圆晕徘徊着，渐渐衰退——

在告别的感情之中逝去！

那神圣的生命火焰的火花，

闪烁着温暖，但再也不属于他珍爱的地球！

勇士难忘的地方！

那里的土地有平原和山区的洞穴，

那里是自由人的家乡，或荣耀者的坟墓！

它可能是勇士的神殿！

所有这些都能为你保留吗？

靠近那个懦弱、蜷缩着的奴隶，

说，这里是塞莫皮莱吗？

这些蓝色的水域，围绕着周围的熔岩，

自由的奴隶的后代——

说道，这是什么海，什么海岸？

海湾，萨拉米斯的岩石！

这些场景，他们的故事，都为人所知。

让这里成为属于你的故土；

抓住你祖先的灰烬，

他们之前祖先的余烬；

他在冲突结束之时，

会为他们的名字增添上一丝恐惧，

当暴君听到时，他会瑟瑟发抖，

为他的儿子留下希望和声名，

他们也一样，宁死而不屈，

自由的战斗一旦开始，

流血的先辈们会为子孙们留下，

虽然经常充满困惑，但却曾经留下胜利。
希腊，历史见证了你辉煌的时代；
许多不朽的英雄都为它证明！
当国王在满是灰尘的黑暗中隐藏，
伊拉韦留下了一座无名的金字塔；
你的英雄们，尽管总是遭遇厄运，
哈利会将他们的坟墓建造，
巨大的纪念碑矗立在此——
这就是他们故乡的山脉！
在那里，陌生人的眼前会出现，
那些不朽之人的坟墓！
会经历漫长的时间诉说，充满悲伤地寻觅，
从辉煌走向耻辱的每一步；
够了，没有外来的敌人可以平息，
你的灵魂，直到它自己消亡；
是的！自卑铺平了道路，
通向恶棍的军队和暴君的政权。

——拜伦

Lesson 53　THERMOPYLÆ
第五十三课　塞莫皮莱

[In the year 480 B.C., ten years after the Battle of Marathon, Xerxes, the son and successor of Dari'us, opened the Second Persian War by invading Greece in person, at the head of the greatest army the world has ever seen. Their numbers have been estimated at more than two millions of fighting men. This immense host, proceeding by the way of Thessaly, had arrived without opposition at the narrow defile of Thermopylæ, between the mountains and the sea, where the Spartan Leonidas was posted with three hundred of his countrymen and some Thespian allies—in all fewer than a thousand men.

The Spartans were forbidden by their laws ever to flee from an enemy; they had taken an oath never to desert their standards; and Leonidas and his countrymen, and their few allies, prepared to sell their lives as dearly as possible. Bravely meeting the attack of the Persian host, and retreating into the narrowest part of the pass as their numbers were thinned by the storm of

Pass of Thermopylæ, with Tombs of the Spartans

arrows, and by the living mass that was hurled upon them, they fought with the valour of desperation until every one of their number had fallen. A monument was afterwards erected on the spot, bearing the following inscription:—"Go, stranger, and tell at Lacedæmon that we died here in obedience to her laws."]

They fell devoted, but undying;
The very gale their name seemed sighing;
The waters murmured of their name,
The woods were peopled with their fame;
The silent pillar, lone and gray,
Claimed kindred with their sacred clay;
Their spirits wrapped the dusky mountain,

Their memory sparkled o'er the fountain;—
The meanest rill, the mightiest river,
Rolls mingling with their fame for ever.
Despite of every yoke she bears,
That land is glory's still, and theirs!

'Tis still a watch-word to the earth;—
When man would do a deed of worth,
He points to Greece, and turns to tread,
So sanctioned, on the tyrant's head;
He looks to her, and rushes on,
Where life is lost, or freedom won.

—Byron

Words

claimed, *demanded*.	memory, *remembrance*.
defile, *pass*.	mangling, *mixing*.
desperation, *despair*.	murmured, *babbled*.
devoted, *dedicated*.	opposition, *obstruction*.
estimated, *calculated*.	retreating, *retiring*.
forbidden, *prohibited*.	sanctioned, *approved*.
invading, *marching into*.	standards, *colours*.
kindred, *relationship*.	

☆ ☆

　　马拉松战役结束10年之后，也就是公元480年，大流士的儿子薛西斯，也是他的继承者，亲自征战希腊，开始了第二次希波战争。此时他率领的，是有史以来世界上最强大的军队，据估计，他拥有200多万战士。这支部队从通往色萨利之路开始，几乎所向披靡地抵达了位于山脉和大海之间的塞莫皮莱的狭窄栈道。斯巴达国王雷奥尼达率他的300名同胞和同盟者驻扎在此，但总共也不超过1千人。

　　斯巴达法律禁止战士在战场上逃跑，他们也发誓永远不会放弃自己的原则。雷奥尼达和他的同胞以及他们的同盟者，已经做好了牺牲生命的准备。在英勇地抵抗波斯军队之后，他们被迫撤退到栈道最狭窄的区域。他们在敌军刀箭和大石块的猛烈打击之下人数骤减，同时他们也在与塞莫皮莱的狭窄栈道斗争。每个斯巴达人都怀着绝望的英勇坠落到山崖之下，之后，人们在此地树立起一块纪念碑，刻有下列碑铭："陌生人，去吧，去告诉拉斯迪蒙，我们誓死服从他的法律。"

他们无畏地纵身一跃，却没有死去，
他们的名字似乎在狂风中叹息；
大海在呢喃他们的姓名，
森林也布满他们的名誉；
安静的柱子，孤独而苍白，
神圣的躯体，认领了光荣的血脉。
他们的精神包裹着阴郁的山峰，
他们的记忆在山泉之上闪耀；
最普通的溪流，最壮阔的江河，
都永远因他们的盛名而蓬勃。
虽然这块土地饱受踩蹦，
她的光荣仍在，一如这些勇士！

他们是这世上的一句格言：
当人们做一件值得去做的事情，
他会满怀敬意地提到希腊，
他会转身践踏暴君的头颅；
他会望向她，急于奔到，
生命消逝，但自由重生的地方。

——拜伦

Lesson 54   PAUL AT ATHENS
第五十四课　保罗在雅典

There was something, to such an one as Paul, that was spirit-stirring in the mighty array that he had to cope with at Athens. He was full of courage and of hope. In the cause of Christ he had gone on conquering, and would trust that, even here, he should conquer. He felt that it was enough, even if lie saved but one, to recompense the effort and the peril—that it was enough, if, by his faithfulness, he only delivered his own soul.

But his was a mind to look and aim at more than this. He felt the splendour of the triumph there would be in levelling the wisdom and the idolatry of Athens at the foot of the Cross. He burned to make Olym'pus bow its awful head, and cast down its coronet of gods, at His feet who dwelt in Zion; and the pæans of Bacchus and Apollo were, in his ear, but preludes to the swelling "song of Moses and of the Lamb."

Animated by such feelings, we may now regard Paul, in what must have been one of the most interesting moments of even his eventful life, preparing himself on the Hill of Mars to address an auditory of Athenians on behalf of Christianity. He would feel the imposing associations of the spot on which he stood, where, in the darkness of night, and under the canopy of heaven, justice had been administered in its most awful form, by diameters the most venerable. Accompanied as it was with the solemnities of religion, it was attended with an authority which public opinion assimilated rather with the decrees of conscience and of the gods than with the ordinary power of human tribunals.

He would look around on many an immortal trophy of architect and sculptor; where genius had triumphed, but triumphed only in the cause of that idolatry to which they had been dedicated, and for which they existed. And beyond the city, clinging around its temples, like its inhabitants to their enshrined idols, would open on his view that lovely country and the sublime ocean, and the serene heavens bending over them, and bearing that testimony to the Universal Creator which man and man's works withheld.

With all would Grecian glory be connected—the brightness of a day that was closing, and of a sun that had already set, where recollections of grandeur faded into sensations of melancholy. And he would gaze on a thronging auditory, the representatives, to his fancy, of all that had been, and of all that was; and think of the intellects with which he had to grapple, and of the hearts in whose very core he aimed to plant the barbed arrows of conviction.

There was that Multitude, so acute, so inquisitive, so polished, so athirst for novelty, and so impressible by eloquence; yet with whom a barbarian accent might break the charm of the most persuasive tongue; over whom their own oligarchy of orators would soon reassert their dominion, in spite of the invasion of a stranger; and with whom taste, feeling, and habit would throw up all their barriers against the eloquence of Christianity. There would be the Priest, astonished at an attempt so daring; and as the speaker's design opened on his mind, anxiously, and with alternate contempt and rage, measuring the strength of the Samson who thus grasped the pillars of his temples, threatening to whelm him, his altars, and his gods beneath their ruins. There would be the Stoic, in the coldness of his pride, looking sedately down, as on a child playing with children, to see what new game was afloat, and what trick or toy was now produced for wonderment. There the Epicurean, tasting, as it were, the preacher's doctrine, to see if it promised aught of merriment; just lending enough of idle attention not to lose amusement should it offer; and venting the full explosion of his ridicule on the resurrection of the dead.

There the Sophist, won, perhaps, into something of an approving and complacent smile by the dexterity of Paul's introduction; but finding, as he proceeded, that this was no mere show of art or war of words; and vibrating between the habitual love of entangling, bewildering, and insulting an opponent, and the repulsiveness which there always is to such men in the language of honest and zealous conviction. There the Slave, timidly crouching at a distance to catch what stray sounds the winds might waft to him, after they had reached his master's ears, of that doctrine, so strange and blessed, of man's fraternity. And there the young and noble Roman, who had come to Athens for education;—not to sit like a humble scholar at a master's feet, but, with all the pride of Rome upon his brow, to accept what artists, poets, and philosophers could offer as their homage to the lords of Earth.

If for a moment Paul was overwhelmed by the feeling,—in the circumstances, perfectly natural,—that he was the central object of such a scene and such an assemblage, there would rush upon his mind the majesty of Jehovah; and the words of the glorified Jesus; and the thunders that had struck himself to the earth on the road to Damascus; and the sense of former efforts, conflicts, and successes; and the approach of that judgment to come, whose righteousness and universality it was now his duty to announce.

Unappalled and collected, he began:—"Ye men of Athens, I perceive that in all things ye are too superstitious. For as I passed by, and beheld your devotions, I found an altar with this inscription. To the unknown God. Whom therefore ye ignorantly worship, him declare I unto you. God that made the world and all things therein, seeing that he is Lord of heaven and earth, dwelleth not in temples made with hands; neither is worshipped with men's hands, as though he needed any thing, seeing he giveth to all life, and breath, and all things; and hath made of one blood all nations of men for to dwell on all the face of the earth."

—W. J. Fox

Words

administered, *dispensed.*
animated, *inspired.*
announce, *proclaim.*
array, *display.*
assimilated, *identified.*
astonished, *surprised.*
auditory, *audience.*
barbarian, *foreign.*
complacent, *satisfied.*
conquering, *triumphing.*
coronet, *crown.*
enshrined, *consecrated.*

fraternity, *brotherhood.*
grapple, *struggle.*
homage, *tribute of praise.*
merriment, *amusement.*
recollections, *remembrances.*
recompense, *repay.*
sedately, *calmly.*
sensations, *pangs.*
superstitious, *idolatrous.*
trophy, *achievement.*
unappalled, *undismayed.*
universality, *comprehensiveness.*
vibrating, *oscillating.*

Questions

What feelings would encourage Paul to preach boldly at Athens? Where did he address the Athenians? What "imposing associations "would the place suggest to his mind? What would he see from that spot? What classes of people would be represented in his audience? By what would the Sophist be won at first? What was that introduction?

☆ ☆

对保罗这样的人，当他在雅典不得不应付强大的人群时，存在一些振奋人心的事情。他充满了勇气和希望。在基督教的事业中，他已经一直前进并征服。他相信即使在这里，他也一样会征服。他认为即使他只能拯救一个人的生命来报答他的努力和他所经历的危险，这也足够了。通过他的忠诚，他表达了自己的灵魂。

但他的意识和目标都比这更多。他觉得那里辉煌的胜利，将与雅典的十字山脚下的智慧和崇拜旗鼓相当。

他将使奥林匹斯山，在定居在锡安山的人们的脚下，垂下它可怕的头颅和它神灵的王冠。酒神与阿波罗在他的耳边，奏响了起伏的"摩西和羔羊之歌"。

被这种感情所激励，现在我们看到的这一刻，在保罗富有意义的一生之中，必然是最有趣的时刻。他正准备在火星山上，代表基督教徒对雅典的听众们进行一场演讲。他会感觉到他现在所站立的这雄伟的地方是如此令人振奋，在夜的黑暗之中和天堂的天幕之下，司法在这里用最威严、最值得尊敬的方式呈现。宗教的庄严肃穆也随之而来，伴随着被公众舆论同化了的权威，伴随着富有良知的众神的法令，而不是普通的人类法庭的力量。

他会环顾许多不朽的建筑师和雕塑家们的奖杯，在那里，他们的天才取得了胜利，但是这种胜利只存在于他们奉献于这种偶像崇拜的过程之中，也只存在于他们存在的时刻。城市周围环绕着庙宇，就像这里的居民环绕着他们供奉的偶像，将在他的眼前展现出可爱的国度和肃穆的海洋，而宁静的天空笼罩在它们上方，见证了人类的作品和人类的创造者呈现的世界。

希腊的荣耀将与这一切连接到一起——明亮的一天即将结束，太阳已经下山，此时，关于宏伟事件的回忆逐渐消散，变成了忧郁的感受。他将目光落在拥挤的听众和代表们之中，他很开心地看到一切原来的样子和现在的样子；他想到那些他必须与之搏斗的知识分子，在他们的心中，他将要种下信念的种子。

这些信众是如此急切，如此好奇，如此渴望新奇，即使拥有再好口才的人也无法满足他们；然而对于他们，一种野蛮的说辞就可以打破最有说服力的语言的魅力；他们自己关于寡头政治的演说很快就会重申他们的统治，即使有陌生人的入侵也无济于事；他们的品位、感觉和习惯，会将他们所有反对基督教的障碍掀翻。会有一位牧师令人惊讶地尝试这样大胆的行为，而传教者的说辞会开阔他的思想，焦急地交替着蔑视和愤怒，带着参孙抓住柱子的力量，威胁要在废墟之下淹没了他，他的祭坛，还有他的神灵。

他一定是一个禁欲主义者，在他的骄傲与冷漠之中，他平静地俯视这些信众。他看着孩子们在玩耍，看是否出现了什么新的游戏，还有什么魔术或玩具被创造出来供他们玩乐。而享乐主义者学习着牧师的信条，懒散地看它是否能够提供任何欢乐，对死者的复活发泄他的所有讽刺。

在那里，也许通过保罗的介绍之中的精妙之处，智者得到了令他满意的东西而微笑，但当继续进行，他发现这不仅仅是艺术的表演或词汇的战争，而他会摇摆不定，因为这演说充斥了纠缠、困惑和对对手的侮辱以及在诚实和热情的语言之中对这种人的厌恶。在那里，奴隶们胆怯地蹲在远处，听着飘荡流浪的风带给他们的声音，但主人们在这些声音中，听到了如此奇异而美好的信条，充满了人类的博爱。在那里，年轻、高贵的罗马人来到雅典接受教育；他们也不会如卑微的学者一样坐在主人的脚边，他们的额头写满了所有罗马人的骄傲，接受任何艺术家、诗人和哲学家可能传授给他们的知识。

在某个时刻，保罗沉醉于这种感觉之中，他是整个场景和所有这些信众的中心。他在这种情况下有这种感受也是很自然的。这时，耶和华的威严和荣耀的话会冲到他的思想之中，这给他飘飘然的思想有力一击，让他回到大地之上通向大马士革的道路之中。之前努力的感觉，冲突感和成就感以及这种审判的方式和他的公义，都在现在宣布了他的职责。

他大胆而镇定地开始了他的演讲："是的，希腊的人们，我坚信你们的所有一切都缘起于迷信。因为当我经过这里看到你们的奉献，我看到一座圣坛之上你们献给无名神明的手稿，因此你们盲目无知地崇拜的神明派我来到了这里。是上帝制造了这个世界和这里的所有东西，看，他是天堂和地球的主，住在神明建造的寺庙之中，崇拜他的信众也不是普通的人类，他不需要任何东西，是他将呼吸和一切赋予了所有的生命；是他创造了所有国家的人民，还有这些人民居住所需要的所有住所。"

——W. J. 福克斯

Lesson 55
EVIDENCES OF DESIGN IN CREATION
第五十五课　世界中设计的证据

When we observe a number of separate forces acting in union and harmony, we must believe that there has been a designing mind bringing them together and causing them to cooperate. When we see these agencies working in happiest association to produce innumerable effects of a beneficent character; when we find them consenting and consorting throughout thousands or myriads of years or geological ages,—the evidence is felt to be overwhelming beyond the power of human calculation.

"How often," asks Tillotson, "might a man, after he had jumbled a set of letters in a bag, fling them out upon the ground before they would fall into an exact poem, yea, or so much as make a good discourse in prose? And may not a little book be as easily made by chance as this great volume of the world?—How long might a man be sprinkling colours upon canvas, with a careless hand, before they would happen to make the exact picture of a man? And is a man easier made by chance than this picture?

" How long might twenty thousand blind men, which should be sent out from the several remote parts of England, wander up and down before they would all meet upon Salisbury Plain, and fall into rank and file in the exact order of an army? And yet this is much more easy to be imagined than that the innumerable blind parts of matter should rendezvous themselves into a world."

Every manual labourer may see something analogous to the art by which he earns his livelihood, operating among the natural objects by which he is surrounded.

The sailor may discover the peculiarities of his craft among marine animals. Thus, among the lower tribes, he has observed a jelly-fish—called by him the Portuguese man-of-war—setting up a sail which consists of a crest surmounting the bladder. He may notice, too, how the mussel and pinna anchor themselves by means of threads of a horny material. The tail of the fish, it is well known, acts as a scuttle, enabling its possessor to plough its way through the deep.

The web-foot of the swimmers is an example of what is called "feathering the oar:" when pushed forward, the web and toes collapse. The leg (usually so called) of the guillemot and of divers is compressed laterally, presenting a knife-edge before and behind, and thus gives less resistance in the fore and back stroke. It is worthy of being mentioned, as illustrating the same point, that the whale's tail collapses in the upward but expands in the downward stroke.

The shepherd knows how much care and watchfulness are necessary in order to protect his flocks from the wild beasts which attack them, and is thus led to admire the instincts of those animals, such as the deer, which set a watch to give a signal of danger. The hunter knows how much cunning he must exercise in order to come within reach of the wild animals pursued by him, and should not withhold a feeling of wonder when he observes how their instincts lead the brutes to show such dexterity in avoiding their natural enemies.

We find that those liable to be chased as prey, often take the colour of the ground on which they habitually feed. Riflemen are invariably dressed in the hue which is deemed least conspicuous, and which is best fitted for concealment; and is there not an equally clear proof of design furnished by the circumstance that fishes are often of the colour of the ground over which they swim, and that wild animals are not unfrequently of the colour of the covert in which they hide themselves? The red grouse and red deer are of the colour of the heath on which they feed; whereas the lapwing and curlew, themselves and their eggs, take the hue of the pasture among which they are usually found.

Speaking of the ptarmigan, the late Mr. Thompson says: "We hardly draw on the imagination by viewing its plumage as an exquisite miniature of the seasonal changes which the mountain summit undergoes;—a miniature drawn, too, by a Hand that never errs! In summer we look upon the beautiful mixture of gray, brown, and black, as resembling the three component parts of ordinary granite—feldspar, mica, and horn-blende—among the masses of which the ptarmigan usually resides. Late in autumn, when snows begin to fall about the lofty summits, and partially to cover the surface of the rocks, we find the bird pied with white; and in winter, when they present a perfect chrysolite, it is almost wholly of the same pure hue." Nor is it unworthy of being noted, that whitish or grayish colours, which are known to be the warmest, prevail in the covering of animals in the arctic regions.

The builder may easily perceive that the woody structure of plants and the bones of animals are constructed on architectural principles, being strengthened where weight has to be supported and pressure resisted, and becoming more slender where lightness is required. The form of the bole of a tree, and the manner in which it fixes itself into the ground, so as to be able to face the storms of a hundred winters, are said to have yielded some suggestions to the celebrated engineer, Smeaton, in the construction of the Eddystone Light-house. The architect of the Crystal Palace confessed that he derived some of the ideas embodied in that structure from observing the wonderful provision made for bearing up the very broad leaf of the beautiful lily, which has been brought within these few years from the marshes of Guiana to adorn our conservatories.

Every joint in the animal frame can be shown to be exactly suited to the function which it has to perform. In flesh-eating animals, where strength is the chief requisite in the lower jaw, there is a simple hinge-joint of great power; whereas in herbivorous species, which have to grind hard vegetable matter, the joint admits of free motion in all directions. Where motion in one direction is all that is required, we have a common joint, as in the fingers; where motion all round is necessary, we have, as at the shoulder and hip, the ball-and-socket joint, admitting of a rotatory motion round a ball.

In some parts of the animal frame, a single bone is all that is required, and more would injure the strength; in other parts, as in the fore-arm, a kind of rotatory motion is furnished by two bones, a radius and an ulna, so adjusted as to move to some extent round each other.

The tubes and pipes which conduct water and gas through all the streets and dwellings of a great city, are not such ingenious contrivances as the veins and arteries which convey the blood to and from every extremity of the frame. The means by which water is forced to rise in a pump are not so wonderful as those by which, proceeding on a different principle, fluid is made to mount in the plant to the most distant twig and leaf. We construct valves to allow fluids to pass in one direction, but to prevent them from flowing back in the opposite direction; but before man devised such agency they were already in his own veins; and it was upon noticing them that Harvey, proceeding, as he tells us, on the principle that they were there to serve a purpose, was led to the discovery of the circulation of the blood.

It is a circumstance of great significance, that parts of animals which, to superficial observers, might seem useless, or even inconvenient, have been found, in the progress of discovery, to serve most important ends in the economy of life. The hump of the camel might readily be regarded as a very unseemly encumbrance, and we find even the distinguished naturalist Buffon speaking of these humps, and of the callous pads on the legs of that animal, as marks of degradation and servitude. A little patient investigation, however, suffices to show that these parts of their frame, like every other, fit these useful creatures for the purposes served by them in the regions which they inhabit.

It has often been remarked, that the abundant supply of fluid laid up in the cells of one of the stomachs, is a beautiful provision for enabling the animal to endure a long continuance of thirst; and it can be shown that the enlargement of their feet, with their convex soles, allows them to tread easily on the loose, yielding sand of the desert; that the callosities or pads on their legs permit them to lie down and repose on scorching surfaces; and that their humps are supplies of superabundant nourishment provided for their long journeys, so that, when deprived of other food, their frames feed on this nutriment,—and it has been observed, that at the close of a long journey their humps have been much diminished in size.

Such facts as these go to prove that it is our own ignorance and presumption which lead us to complain of the inconveniences of nature; and that a little more knowledge, and, better still, a little more humility and patience, would lead us to discover and to acknowledge, that there are admirable wisdom and benevolence even in those parts of God's works which may seem to be useless, or even injurious.

—J. M. Cosh

Words

beneficent, *kind*.	herbivorous, *herb-eating*.
calculation, *estimate*.	investigation, *inqutry*.
callous, *hard*.	laterally, *from side to side*.
celebrated, *famous*.	miniature, *reduction*.
collapses, *contracts*.	peculiarities, *features*.
component, *constituent*.	principles, *rules*.
conspicuous, *prominent*.	pursued, *chased*.
contrivances, *devices*.	requisite, *essential*.
cooperate, *work together*.	rotatory, *revolving*.
dexterity, *cleverness*.	significance, *force*.
diminished, *reduced*.	sprinkling, *scattering*.
encumbrance, *burden*.	superabundant, *spare*.
exquisite, *beautiful*.	surmounting, *overtopping*.

Questions

What are the proofs of a designing mind in any work? By what comparisons does Tillotson enforce this? What remarkable adaptation is there in the leg of swimming birds? With what natural means of protection are animals chased as prey provided? What is remarkable in the case of the ptarmigan? Mention cases in which builders have taken their ideas from natural objects. Give instances of adaptation in the joints of the body. What led Harvey to discover the circulation of the blood? Give examples of parts of animals which seem useless, being really most useful contrivances. What Lesson is to be learned from this?

当我们看到很多单独的力量相结合并和谐共处，我们就必须相信其中蕴含一种设计的思想使它们聚集起来相互合作。当我们看到各种机制在快乐地协同工作，产生出数不清的美好效果；当我们认同它们延续数以万年的地质年代——造物主的存在是无法抗拒的，它远远超出了人类的能力。

提勒森问道："一个人将一套字母抛起，落在地面上，之后他能将这些字母准确地排列成一首诗或者是优美的散文，要花多久时间？一本小书，正如这个巨大的世界一样，可能偶然完成吗？一个人随意地用少量的颜料画在帆布上，多久才会有人偶然将它们构成精妙的图画呢？比起这张画，难道创造人类更容易吗？"

"两万个盲目的人们，从英格兰数个偏僻的地域出发，向四面八方徘徊后，要经过多久，才能全部在索尔斯堡平原集结？而他们像一支部队一样排列成行，编制出精确的规则，又要花多长时间呢？然而，很容易想象到，这个过程中无数个盲目、困难的过程在创造世界的过程中发生，是多么的困难。"

每一个手工劳动者，都可以在环绕着他们的自然物体中，发现一些类似的技巧，可以让他维持他的生计。

水手们可以从海洋动物身上发现他的船只的特性。因此，在这些较低等级的物种之中，他观察到了那些水母——战争中的葡萄牙人给了它们这样的称呼——它们在气囊上方装置有一个冠顶，并依靠它们开始航行。他也会注意到，那些蚌和小型船的锚，都是通过角质材料的穿线而完成的。众所周知，鱼的尾巴，作为一个气窗，能够给它的拥有者在深海之中指引出一条前行的道路。

用网缠住脚的潜水者是一个例子，向我们验证了"船桨"的原理。当向前推进时，这张网和脚趾都会下垂。海鸽的腿（人们总是这样称呼它）和潜水员的腿一样，前后都呈现出锋利的边缘，因此在向前和向后推行的时候，就会产生很少的阻力。同样值得一提的是，像上面说明的一样，鲸鱼的尾巴在向上游行时会下垂，而受到向下的冲击时则会展开。

牧羊人深知，在有野兽袭击它们而要保护他的羊群时，谨慎和警惕是多么重要。因此，他会特别欣赏动物的本能，就像鹿那样，会设置一个危险时刻会发出信号的装置。猎人深知他要想追捕到一只野生动物时，他必须多么狡猾；野兽在躲避自身的自然敌人时是如此灵巧，猎人们在看到这种行为展现出的它们的本能时，是不应该抑制自己的惊讶情绪的。

我们发现那些容易被当作猎物追逐的动物，往往会采纳它们习惯生存的地面的色彩。步兵总是穿着被认为是最不显眼的色调，而这最适合他们的隐蔽；鱼身上的颜色总是与它们所游过的地方一致，而野生动物也总是保持与自己藏起来的地方颜色一样，这些不也提供了同样清楚的证据来证明，环境提供给生物一些设计的方法吗？红色的鸡和红鹿的颜色与它们所生长的灌木丛的颜色一样；而田凫和杓鹬以及它们的蛋，与它们通常被发现的草原颜色也是一样的。

说到松鸡，已故的汤普森先生说："我们很难画出它羽毛里精妙的季节性变化，就像山峰经历的季节性变化一样；即使很少出错的画家，也很难画出如此精妙的画卷！在夏天，我们看到各种颜色美丽的混合：灰色、棕色、黑色，类似于普通的花岗岩的三个组成部分：长石、云母和角闪石组成的这片混乱之地，正是松鸡经常驻足的地方。深秋时节，当高耸的山峰上开始下雪，岩石的表面部分被积雪覆盖，我们发现松鸡会变成白色；而冬季，当山峰展现出一种完美的橄榄色，它又几乎换上了完全一样的颜色。"同样值得注意的一点是：白色或浅灰色是众所周知的最温暖的颜色，而在北极地区的动物身上，它们也是最普遍的色彩。

建筑师很容易察觉到，植物的木质结构和动物的骨骼构造，都是以建筑的原则来构建的。在这些结构内，需要支撑重量和抵制压力的地方都被加强，而需要轻便的地方则变得更苗条。一棵树的树干的形状和它自身安插到地面的方式，使它能够抵抗一百场冬天里的风暴。这些结构被一些著名的工程师所采纳，比如斯姆顿，在涡石灯塔建筑之中就用到了这样的结构。水晶宫的建筑师承认，从美丽的百合花异常宽大的叶子结构之中，他观察并衍生出了一些精彩的结构，并已经在这几年，应用到包括法属圭亚那的沼泽地和国内一些建筑物的建设之中。

在动物的骨骼中，每一个关节都已证明是完全适合它们所必须完成的功能的。在食肉动物体内，下颚是最需要力量的部位，因此在这里会存在具有超大力量的简单链条；而在食植性物种的体内，它们需要研磨较硬的植物物质，因此它们的关节就必须能够胜任向各个方向的运动。在所需的一切就是简单的向一个方向运动时，我们也拥有一个同样的关节，就像手指一样，当必须向四周运动时，就像在肩部和臀部，我们有球穴关节，它们可以进行圆球体的旋转运动。

在动物骨骼的某些部分，单骨是它们所需要的一切，更多的骨头会对力量有所伤害；在其他部分，比如前臂，旋转运动就是由桡骨和尺骨这两块骨头来共同完成的。它们会互相调整，因而能够围绕对方运动到一定的程度。

水管和管道，允许水流和气体通过一个伟大城市的所有街道和住宅，但它们与将血液输送到身体各个部位的静脉和动脉相比，则不是什么天才的设计了。水在泵中被迫上升的方法，与下面这一现象相比并不是那么精彩：从不同的原理出发，流体被提升到植物最边缘的枝叶处。我们构建了阀，以使液体通过一个方向，而防止它们朝相反的方向回流；但在人类设想出这样的构造之前，它们早已经存在在人类自身的血脉里；正如哈维告诉我们的，正是由于注意到了这一点，他才基于它们存在是有所作用的这一原则，发现了血液的循环。

这是一种十分重要的情况，对肤浅的观察者来说，动物身体的某些部分，似乎是无用的，甚至在发现的过程中，遵循生命的经济性原则，这些部分会给它们带来不便。骆驼的驼峰可能很容易被视为一种很不体面的累赘，我们发现，即使是著名的博物学家巴顿也这样评价这些驼峰。还有骆驼腿部下方坚硬的肉垫，也被认为是一种退化和舒服的产物。然而，一些耐心细致的调查就足以说明，这些身体的部分正如其他部分一样，对它们能够在它们居住的地区存活是十分有益和必要的。

人们常说，胃部细胞中丰富的分泌液是一种美丽的供给，保证了动物能够承受长期持续的口渴；它们巨大的脚掌以及凸起的脚底，让它们能够在松散、易滑落的沙漠中轻松行走；腿上的老茧或肉垫，允许它们在灼热的地表躺下；而它们的驼峰，则为它们的长途旅行提供了足够充分的营养，因此，当它们没有其他食物时，它们的身体内部也充满营养。而且，人们已经观察到，在一段漫长的旅程将要结束时，它们驼峰也会变小。

这样的事实进一步证明了，是我们自己的无知和假定，才使我们抱怨自然给我们带来的不便；再多一点点的知识，尤其是更好的知识，多一点点的谦卑和忍耐，就会引导我们去发现和承认，即使在上帝那些看似无用甚至有害的作品中，也有其独特的智慧和仁慈。

——J. M. 科什

Lesson 56   THE STORY OF HORATIUS
第五十六课　贺雷修斯的故事

A LEGEND OF ANCIENT ROME.

The early history of Rome, as recorded by Livy and other Latin writers, was probably compiled from legendary poems that had been transmitted from generation to generation, and often rehearsed at the banquets of the great. The historian Macaulay has aimed at reconstructing some of these poetic legends, which he has given to the world under the title of *Lays of Ancient Rome*. As a specimen of these beautiful and stirring poems, the "Story of Horatius" is here given.

It is stated by all the Latin historians, that, a few years after the expulsion of the Tarquins for their despotism and crimes, the neighbouring Etrua cans, to which nation they belonged, endeavoured to restore the tyrants to power, and came against Rome with an overwhelming force. The Romans, repulsed at first, fled across a wooden bridge over the Tiber, when the Roman Consul ordered the bridge to be destroyed, to prevent the enemy from entering the city. The continuation of the legend is supposed to be narrated by one of the Roman minstrels, at a period one hundred years later than the events recorded:—

> But the Consul's brow was sad.
>> And the Consul's speech was low,
> And darkly looked he at the wall,
>> And darkly at the foe.
> "Their van will be upon us
>> Before the bridge goes down;
> And if they once may win the bridge,
>> What hope to save the town?"
>
> Then out spake brave Horatius,
>> The captain of the gate:
> "To every man upon this Earth
>> Death cometh, soon or late;
> And how can man die better
>> Than facing fearful odds,
> For the ashes of his fathers,
>> And the temples of his gods!

"Hew down the bridge, Sir Consul,
    With all the speed ye may;
I, with two more to help me,
    Will hold the foe in play.
In you strait path a thousand
    May well be stopped by three;
Now, who will stand on either hand,
    And keep the bridge with me?"

Then out spake Spurius Lartius,—
    A Ramnian proud was he:
"Lo, I will stand at thy right hand,
    And keep the bridge with thee."
And out spake strong Hermiuius,—
    Of Titian blood was he:
"I will abide on thy left side,
    And keep the bridge with thee."

"Horatius," quoth the Consul,
    As thou say'st, so let it be."
And straight against that great array
    Forth went the dauntless three.

Meanwhile the Tuscan army,
    Right glorious to behold,
Came flashing back the noonday light,
Rank behind rank, like surges bright
    Of a broad sea of gold.
Four hundred trumpets sounded
    A peal of warlike glee,
As that great host, with measured tread,
And spears advanced, and ensigns spread,
Rolled slowly toward the bridge's head,
    Where stood the dauntless three.

The three stood calm and silent,
    And looked upon the foes,
And a great shout of laughter
    From all the vanguard rose:
And forth three chiefs came spurring
    Before that mighty mass;
To earth they sprang, their swords they drew,

And lifted high their shields, and flew
    To win the narrow pass.

But the scorn and laughter of the Etruscans were soon changed to wrath and curses,
for their chiefs were quickly laid low in the dust at the feet of the "dauntless three."

But now no sound of laughter
    Was heard among the foes.
A wild and wrathful clamour
    From all the vanguard rose.
Six spears' length from the entrance
    Halted that mighty mass,
And for a space no man came forth
    To win the narrow pass.

But hark! the cry is "Astur:"
    And lo! the ranks divide,
And the great lord of Luna
    Comes with his stately stride.
Upon his ample shoulders
    Clangs loud the fourfold shield,
And in his hand he shakes the brand
    Which none but he can wield.

The proud Astur advances with a smile of contempt for the three Romans, and
turns a look of scorn upon the flinching Tuscans.

Then, whirling up his broadsword.
    With both hands to the height,
He rushed against Horatius,
    And smote with all his might
With shield and blade Horatius
    Right deftly turned the blow.
The blow, though turned, came yet too nigh:
It missed his helm, but gashed his thigh:
The Tuscans raised a joyful cry
    To see the red blood flow.

He reeled, and on Herminius
    He leaned one breathing-space;
Then, like a wild-cat mad with wounds,
    Sprang right at Astur's face.
Through teeth and skull and helmet,

So fierce a thrust he sped,
　The good sword stood a handbreadth out
　　Behind the Tuscan's head!

And the great lord of Luna
　Fell at that deadly stroke,
As falls on Mount Alvernus
　A thunder-smitten oak.
Far o'er the crashing forest
　The giant arms lie spread;
And the pale augurs, muttering low,
　Gaze on the blasted head.

In the meantime the axes had been busily plied; and while the bridge was tottering to its fall, Lartius and Herminius regained the opposite bank in safety. Horatius remained facing the foe until the last timber had fallen, when, weighed down with armour as he was, he "plunged headlong in the tide."

No sound of joy or sorrow
　Was heard from either bank;
But friends and foes, in dumb surprise,
With parted lips and straining eyes,
　Stood gazing where he sank:
And when beneath the surges
　They saw his crest appear,
All Rome sent forth a rapturous cry,
And even the ranks of Tuscany
　Could scarce forbear to cheer.

But fiercely ran the current,
　Swollen high by months of rain:
And fast his blood was flowing;
　And he was sore in pain,
And heavy with his armour,
　And spent with changing blows:
And oft they thought him sinking,
　But still again he rose.

"Curse on him!" quoth false Sextus.
　Will not the villain drown?"
But for this stay, ere close of day
　We should have sacked the town! "—

"Heaven help him!" quoth Lars Porsena,
  "And bring him safe to shore;
For such a gallant feat of arms
  Was never seen before."

And now he feels the bottom;
  Now on dry earth he stands;
Now round him throng the fathers,
  To press his gory hands;
And now with shouts and clapping,
  And noise of weeping loud,
He enters through the river-gate,
  Borne by the joyous crowd.

    Then follows an account of the rewards which a grateful people bestowed upon the hero. The minstrel thus concludes the legend:—

When the good-man mends his armour,
  And trims his helmet's plume;
When the good-wife's shuttle merrily
  Goes flashing through the loom;
With weeping and with laughter
  Still is the story told,
How well Horatius kept the bridge
  In the brave days of old.

Words

augurs, *soothsayers*.
bestowed, *conferred*.
clamour, *shouting*.
compiled, *composed*.
concludes, *closes; ends*.
contempt, *disdain*.
continuation, *sequel*.
crashing, *shattering*.
dauntless, *courageous*.
deftly, *cleverly*.
despotism, *tyranny*.
divide, *open up*.
flinching, *yielding*.

gallant, *heroic*.
measured, *regular*.
overwhelming, *overpowering*.
rapturous, *joyous*.
reconstructing, *rebuilding*.
recorded, *narrated*.
rehearsed, *recited*.
sacked, *pillaged*.
strait, *narrow*.
surges, *waves*.
vanguard, *front*.
wrathful, *angry*.

一则古罗马的传说

正如李维和其他拉丁语的作家记录的一样，罗马早期的历史可能是由传说中的诗歌构成，代代相传，并经常在伟人的宴会中宣讲。历史学家麦考莱着眼于重构这些传说史诗，他以《古罗马方位》为标题向全世界展示了这些历史。作为这些美丽的、激动人心的诗歌中的一个样本，我们现在要展示给大家的，就是《贺雷修斯的故事》。

所有的拉丁历史学家都有记载，因为他的专制和暴行，塔克文国王被驱逐出罗马。而之后的几年中，他都一直停留在邻近的属于伊特鲁里亚人的联邦之内竭力恢复他暴君的权力，带领一支势不可挡的部队与罗马抗衡。最初罗马人将他们击退了。他们通过一座横跨台伯河的木桥逃脱了。罗马的执政官于是下令破坏这座桥梁，以防止敌人由此进入自己的城市之中。这一传说的过程应该在所记录的事件发生的100年之后，由一个罗马诗人叙述出来的：

> 但是执政官的眉宇间透露着伤心。
> 执政官的演讲也很低沉，
> 他的眼神黯淡地望着墙上，
> 黯淡地望向敌人。
> "他们的战车将抵达我们这里，
> 在木桥倒塌之前；
> 如果一旦由他们占领了木桥，
> 还有什么希望拯救罗马？"
>
> 这时勇敢的贺雷修斯说道，
> 他本是城门的守卫队长，
> "凡立身此大地者，
> 死亡终将到来。
> 与充满恐惧地死去相比，
> 怎样死去才真正高尚？
> 为了祖先的荣誉，
> 为了神明的庙宇。"
>
> "砍坏木桥，执政官先生，
> 用你最快的速度，

我和两个帮助我的人，
会将敌人打退。
在通往你领地的路上，
我们三人会抵挡一千个敌人；
现在，帮助我的人在哪里，
与我一起保住木桥？"

这时普利乌斯·拉提乌斯说道
他是一个自豪的罗马人，
"瞧，我会站在你的右边，
与你一起保住桥梁。"
接着健壮的贺米尼乌斯也说话了，
他有提香的血脉，
"我会守在你的左边，
与你一起保住桥梁。"

"贺雷修斯，"执政官说道，
"就像你说的，一切见机行事。"
接着这毫无畏惧的三个人，
排成一列勇往直前。

同时，伊特鲁里亚人的军队，
拥有如此的风光与荣耀，
在正午时分卷土重来，
一排紧接着一排，如汹涌的巨浪，
泛起在一片金色的海洋之上。
四百只号角响起，
部队中传出一阵好战的欢乐，
它们伟大的主人，大踏步地前进，
矛头指向前方，旗帜四处飘扬，
不断缓缓地向木桥的方向进军，
那里站着无畏的三个人。

三个人冷静而沉默地站着，

他们望着敌人，
从部队的前锋位置，
传出一阵大笑之声；
三个人鼓舞起了斗志，
在强大的敌人面前；
他们从地面上跳起，把他们的剑拔出，
高高地举起盾牌，一跃腾空，
他们要赢得这狭窄的通道。

但伊特鲁里亚人的蔑视和笑声很快就转变成了愤怒和诅咒，因为在这"无畏的三个人"面前，他们的首领都很快败下阵来。

但现在敌人之中，
再也没有了笑声。
一阵狂暴和愤怒的叫喊，
从所有的先锋部队中传来。
从入口处开始六只矛的距离之内，
这强大的部队就这样停滞不前，
没有一个人可以通过，
来赢得这狭窄的通道。

听！正在叫嚷的是阿斯图，
看！部队分成几排，
伟大的月亮神，
伴随着他庄严的步伐。
在他宽大的肩膀之上，
盔甲的铿锵声四处响起，
在他的手中，摇晃着盾牌，
这只有他能使用。

傲慢的阿斯图带着轻蔑的笑容望着这三个罗马人，并回头向着那些退缩的伊特鲁里亚人露出了轻蔑的神情。

然后，他举起长剑，

用双手高高地举起，
他冲向贺雷修斯，
用尽他所有的力量厮杀，
贺雷修斯用他的盾牌，
巧妙地抵住了打击。
尽管他回击了打击，但这打击还是太近了，
错过了他的头盔，但划伤了他的大腿。
这时贺雷修斯红色的血液在流淌，
伊特鲁里亚人发出一阵快乐的欢呼。

他朝着贺米尼乌斯打了个趔趄，
他靠在他身上，得到喘息的机会；
然后，像野猫一样因为受伤而变得狂躁，
他一跃而起，冲向阿图斯。
对着对方的牙齿、头骨和头盔，
他如此激烈地加速还击，
长剑刚好击打在对方的头部，
在距离其他伊特鲁里亚人一掌宽的位置！

伟大的月亮神，
看着那致命的抗击，
也照耀着阿尔沃纳斯山上，
一棵被雷电击倒的橡树。
在这片残败的森林之上，
伟大的部队四处驻扎；
淡淡的月光低声呢喃，
凝视着敌人受诅咒的头颅。

同时这三个人正忙着用他们的大斧子砍桥，而桥摇摇欲坠，拉提乌斯和贺米尼乌斯已经安全地回到了河的对岸。贺雷修斯仍然面对着敌人，直到木桥最后一根木料已经落下，他穿着满身重重的盔甲，一头扎进了河流之中。

台伯河的两岸，
没有任何欢乐或悲伤的声响，

但是，朋友和敌人都一样目瞪口呆，
他们张着嘴，使劲瞪着眼睛，
站在那里，望着他沉没的地方。
当在水波之下，
他们看到他随着波峰再次出现，
所有罗马人都发出狂喜的呼喊，
甚至在伊特鲁里亚人的行列之中，
也几乎忍不住地欢呼了起来。

但湍急的水流继续前行，
因为雨季来临，河水陡涨，
他的血液也如此快速地流动；
他浑身疼痛，
穿着沉重的盔甲，
不断承受水流的打击，
人们总是认为他会沉下去，
但每次，都能看到他再次从水中升起。

"诅咒他！"对方的将领塞克斯图斯说道，
这个恶人难道不会被淹死？"
如果没有他们的阻击，
我们应该在一天就可以洗劫了这个城镇！
"上帝帮助他！"拉斯波塞那说，
"把他安全带回到岸上；
我从来没有见过，
这样一个勇敢的武士。"

现在他能感觉到脚下的土地；
现在他站在干燥的土壤之上；
现在他周围的父老乡亲，
握住他血淋淋的双手；
在一片呼喊声之中，
当然还有响亮的哭声之中，
他进入河闸之中，

在欢乐的人群内走动。

接下来，就是一个感恩的民族赋予了这个英雄以奖励。因此吟游诗人这样结束了这段传说：

当男人们修补盔甲，
用羽毛装饰他的头盔；
当妇女们快乐地穿行在，
闪烁着光芒的织机之间；
哭泣和欢笑，
仍然讲述着这个故事，
贺雷修斯如何保住了木桥，
在古罗马时代属于英雄的一天。

Lesson 57　ROMAN GIRL'S SONG
第五十七课　罗马女孩之歌

Rome, Rome! thou art no more As thou hast been! On thy seven hills of yore Thou satst a queen.	罗马，罗马， 你不再像你过去那样！ 往昔，你在七座高山之上， 加冕了一位王后。
Thou hadst thy triumphs then Purpling the street; Leaders and sceptred men Bowed at thy feet	那时你拥有胜利， 它曾布满所有街道。 所有领袖和权贵之人， 都向它俯首称臣。
They that thy mantle wore, As gods were seen— Rome, Rome! thou art no more As thou hast been!	你那时曾披着斗篷， 像神明们一般。 罗马，罗马， 你不再像你过去那样！
Rome! thine imperial brow Never shall rise: What hast thou left thee now?— Thou hast thy skies!	罗马！你帝王般的神情， 永远不会再出现： 你将它留在了哪里？ 在你曾拥有的天空！
Blue, deeply blue, they are, Gloriously bright! Veiling thy wastes afar With coloured light.	深蓝色的天空， 因荣光而充满光亮！ 幻灭多彩的霞光， 遮住了远方的大海。
Thou hast the sunset's glow, Rome, for thy dower, Flushing tall cypress-bough, Temple and tower!	你有落日一般的光辉， 罗马，因你的天赋， 摇曳着如柏树枝干一般的， 庙宇和尖塔。

And all sweet sounds are thine,
    Lovely to hear;
While night o'er tomb and shrine
    Rests darkly clear.

所有甜蜜的声音都属于你，
如此动听悦耳；
当夜幕降临坟墓与圣坛，
黑暗是如此接近。

    Many a solemn hymn,
    By starlight sung,
Sweeps through the arches dim.
    Thy wrecks among.

这是多么庄严的颂歌，
由星空来吟诵，
你的残骸徘徊于此，
在昏暗的穹顶之间。

    Many a flute's low swell
    On thy soft air
Lingers, and loves to dwell
    With summer there.

这是长笛低沉的乐声，
在温柔的空气中回荡，
它徘徊居住在此，
伴着夏日依旧停留。

Thou hast the South's rich gift
    Of sudden song,
A charmed fountain, swift,
    Joyous, and strong.

你拥有南方的丰富财富，
如一首骤然的乐章，
如一眼迷人的深泉，
迅疾，欢乐，生命旺盛。

Thou hast fair forms that move
    With queenly tread;
Thou hast proud fanes above
    Thy mighty dead.

你有如女王一般的脚步，
有如此美好的形体。
在强大的亡灵之上，
你拥有骄傲的神殿。

    Yet wears thy Tiber's shore
    A mournful mien;—
Rome, Rome! thou art no more
    As thou hast been!

你台伯河的河岸，
拥有悲恸的表情。
罗马，罗马，你不再
像你过去那样！

—Felicia Hemans

——费利西亚·赫门兹

Words

charmed, *bewitched.*
dower, *portion.*
fanes, *temples.*
flushing, *suffusing.*
imperial, *sovereign.*
lingers, *loiters.*
mantle, *garment.*

mien, *aspect.*
shrine, *altar.*
solemn, *religious.*
triumphs, *exultations.*
veiling, *covering.*

Lesson 58
REGULUS BEFORE
THE ROMAN SENATE
第五十八课　雷古拉斯在罗马元老院前

[In the year 263 before Christ the First Punic War began; and, after it had continued eight years with varied success, the Romans sent the Consul Regulus, at the head of a large army, to carry the war into Africa. On the passage across the Mediterranean, the Carthaginian fleet, bearing not less than one hundred and fifty thousand men, was met and defeated; but in the following year, in a battle on land, the Romans were defeated with great loss, and Regulus himself, being taken prisoner, was thrown into a dungeon. Five years later, the Carthaginians were in turn defeated in Sicily, with a loss of twenty thousand men, and the capture of more than a hundred of their elephants, which they had trained to fight in the ranks.

It was then that the Carthaginians sent an embassy to Rome with proposals of peace. Regulus was taken from his dungeon to accompany the embassy, the Carthaginians trusting that, weary of his long captivity, he would urge the Senate to accept the proffered terms; but the inflexible Roman persuaded the Senate to reject the proposals and continue the war, assuring his countrymen that the resources of Carthage were nearly exhausted. Bound by his oath to return if peace were not concluded, he voluntarily went back, in spite of the prayers and entreaties of his friends, to meet the fate which awaited him. It is generally stated that after his return to Carthage he was tortured to death by the exasperated Carthaginians. Thus he spoke to the Senate:—]

<blockquote>
Urge me no more; your prayers are vain,
 And even the tears ye shed:
When I can lead to home again
 The bands that once I led;
When I can raise your legions slain
 On swarthy Libya's fatal plain,
 To vengeance from the dead,
Then will I seek once more a home,
And lift a freeman's voice in Rome!

Accursed moment! when I woke
 From faintness all but death,
And felt the coward conqueror's yoke
</blockquote>

Like venomed serpent's wreath
Round every limb!—if lip and eye
Betrayed no sign of agony,
    Inly I cursed ray breath:
Wherefore, of all that fought, was I
The only wretch that could not die?

To darkness and to chains consigned,
    The captive's fighting doom,
I recked not;—could they chain the mind,
    Or plunge the soul in gloom?
And there they left me, dark and lone,
Till darkness had familiar grown;
    Then from that living tomb
They led me forth, I thought, to die;—
Oh! in that thought was ecstasy!

But no! kind Heaven had yet in store
    For me, a conquered slave,
A joy I thought to feel no more,
    Or feel but in the grave.
They deemed, perchance, my haughtier mood
Was quelled by chains and solitude;
    That he who once was brave—
Was I not brave?—had now become
Estranged from honour, as from Rome.

They bade me to my country bear
    The offers these have borne;
They would have trained my lips to swear
    Which never yet have sworn.
Silent their base commands I heard;
At length I pledged a Roman's word,
    Unshrinking, to return.
I go, prepared to meet the worst;
But I shall gall proud Carthage first.

They sue for peace;—I bid you spurn
    The gilded bait they bear;
I bid you still, with aspect stern,
    War, ceaseless war, declare.
Fools as they were, could not mine eye,

Through their dissembled calmness, spy
    The struggles of despair?
Else had they sent this wasted frame
To bribe you to your country's shame?

Your land—I must not call it mine;
    No country has the slave;
His father's name he must resign,
    And even his father's grave—
But this not now—beneath her lies
Proud Carthage and her destinies;
    Her empire o'er the wave
Is yours; she knows it well, and you
Shall know, and make her feel it too.—

Ay, bend your brows, ye ministers
    Of coward hearts, on me;
Ye know no longer it is hers,
    The empire of the sea;
Ye know her fleets are far and few,
Her bands a mercenary crew;
    And Rome, the bold and free,
Shall trample on her prostrate towers.
Despite your weak and wasted powers!

One path alone remains for me—
    My vows were heard on high;
Thy triumphs, Rome, I shall not see,
    For I return to die.
Then tell me not of hope or life;
I have in Rome no chaste, fond wife,
    No smiling progeny;
One word concentres for the slave,
Wife, children, country, all—the grave.

—Dale

Words

captivity, *imprisonment.*
capture, *seizure.*
concentres, *embraces.*

consigned, *committed.*
continued, *lasted.*
defeated, *overthrown.*

destinies, *fate.*
dissembled, *feigned.*
ecstasy, *rapture.*
embassy, *deputation.*
entreaties, *importunities.*
exasperated, *infuriated.*
exhausted, *worn out.*
inflexible, *stubborn.*

mercenary, *hireling.*
perchance, *perhaps.*
pledged, *plighted.*
progeny, *offspring.*
resources, *means.*
swarthy, *dark.*
venomed, *poisonous.*

☆ ☆ ☆ ☆ ☆ ☆ ☆ ☆ ☆ ☆ ☆ ☆ ☆ ☆ ☆ ☆ ☆ ☆ ☆ ☆

【在公元前263年，第一次布匿战争开始，持续八年多的成功之后，罗马人派执政官雷古拉斯，在一支大部队之前把战争引入到非洲。在通过地中海的过程中，他们遭遇并打败了一支不少于15万人的迦太基舰队，但在之后一年的陆地战斗之中，罗马人遭受了巨大的损失而失败，雷古拉斯本人也被停虏，投进了地牢之中。五年后，迦太基人反过来在西西里岛被打败，损失了两万人，他们一百多只的大象也被捕获，而这些大象是他们训练有素的战斗队伍。

就在那时，迦太基人派出了一位使节前往罗马，提出和平的建议。雷古拉斯从他的地牢被释放出来，被要求去陪伴这位使节。迦太基人相信，疲于长期的囚禁，雷古拉斯将敦促罗马的元老院接受他们提出的建议，但这个丝毫不圆滑的罗马人，却说服元老院否决了这一建议，并继续进行战争。他向他的同胞们提出迦太基的资源已近枯竭，他曾立下誓言，如果和平没有达成，他将自愿返回迦太基，尽管他的朋友们都在祈祷和恳求他，他仍然要去面对等待着他的命运。人们普遍接受的说法是，当他返回迦太基之后，他被愤怒的迦太基人折磨致死。下面是他对罗马元老院说的话：】

不要再要求我了；你们的祈祷是徒劳的，
即使你们流下眼泪，
我可以带着我的军团，
再次回到祖国；
当我可以带领你们的军团杀敌，
在黝黑的利比亚平原，
从死亡中复活，
我会再一次找到我的家，
在罗马发出自由的声音！

该死的时刻！当我醒来时
从昏睡但不是死亡中醒来，
发现胆小的征服者的战车，
像放了毒蛇的花环，
碾压着每一具肢体！如果嘴唇和眼睛，
不会流露出痛苦，
那么我就会诅咒呼吸：
难道，在所有的战斗之中，
只有我不会死亡吗？

我将回到黑暗和枷锁之中，
一名俘虏战斗的厄运，
我不在乎，难道他们能囚禁我的思想，
或让我的灵魂变得忧郁？
他们将我留在黑暗和孤独之中，
直到我怕已经熟悉了天黑；
然后从活的坟墓里，
他们放出了我，我却想着去死；
哦！这个想法让我狂喜！

但不！仁慈的上帝已经储存了
为我，一个被征服的奴隶，储存了
我已经不想再感受的快乐，
但却能在坟墓中感受。
他们认为，也许我的傲慢情绪，
会被锁链和孤独磨平；
我曾是那么勇敢，
我不勇敢吗？现在已经
——与荣誉，与罗马疏离。

他们让我的祖国承担，
他们所需的一切；
他们会训练我的嘴唇发誓，
但它从未发下过誓言。

我听到他们沉默的命令；
最后我说出了一个罗马的字符，
坚定地返回。
我准备去迎接最坏的命运；
但我将首先吓破骄傲的迦太基人的胆子。

他们要求和平，我请求你们踢开，
他们带来的镀金的诱饵；
我请求你们保持坚定，带着严峻的面容，
宣布战争，不断的战争。
他们像傻瓜一样，逃不出我的眼睛，
通过他们隐藏的冷静，
间谍在进行绝望的挣扎。
他们将用这没用的议和，
来贿赂你们，这是对你的国家的耻辱。

你们的土地——我不能说是我的土地；
没有任何一个联邦拥有奴隶；
他必须卸去他父亲的名字，
连同他父亲的坟墓——
但现在——在她的谎言之中，
骄傲的迦太基，她的命运；
她的帝国处于波浪之中，
她属于你们；她非常了解这一点，
你们也要知道，并让她也感觉到。

唉，阁下，弯曲你们的眉毛，
那些对我胆怯的情绪；
你们知道不再是她的，
大海的帝国；
你们知道她的舰队遥远而稀少，
她拥有的是唯利是图的船员；
而罗马，大胆而自由，
将会踏上她的浮屠宝塔。
尽管你们拥有薄弱而无助的力量！

在我面前，只剩下一条路可走——

我的高声誓言会有人听到；
罗马，你的胜利，我却不能看见，
因为回去之后，我会死去。
不要向我诉说希望或生命；
我在罗马没有纯洁美好的妻子，
也没有微笑成长的后代；
在我所受的奴役中只存在一个词，
不是"妻子、孩子、国家、所有人"，而是"坟墓"。

——戴尔

Lesson 59　THE SAHARA
第五十九课　撒哈拉沙漠

The Sahara may be likened to a vast ocean separating the negro kingdoms of equatorial Africa from the more civilized states of the north; and the numerous oases with which it is studded are like so many islands in the midst of the desert waste. This waste, however, though destitute of everything helpful to human life and comfort, does not consist solely of barren sands. There is a vast extent of dry, stunted herbage, on which the camel can pasture; and thus a passage across the desert is rendered practicable, by routes which would be impossible were the Sahara what it is often represented as being—one wide sandy plain.

In the desert, a route through the sand is always chosen in preference to any other; because in the sandy tracts springs are most likely to be found, and because the sand presents a soft dry bed on which the traveller can repose after the fatigues of the day. It is this preference of the natives which has led Europeans to suppose that the whole of the Sahara is a sandy waste. The character of the desert is very much the reverse of this, there being hundreds of miles of hard, firm soil, while hundreds more are a mixture of stony fragments and pebbles.

Travelling on sand, there is of course no visible road, as the fierce winds that frequently recur soon obliterate all trace of footsteps. The guides, therefore, find their way by land-marks, which they carefully renew when necessary. These are often the most trifling objects, such as a tuft of herbage, a single plant, or the summit of a swell in the soil. In places where the plain is one void and arid flat, even such objects are wanting, and their place is supplied by heaps of stones or cairns, piled at great distances. Sometimes the route extends for ten or twelve days over a plain affording not a single drop of moisture!

OASES

Along nearly the whole length of the northern shores of the continent there extends a fertile belt of land, called by the natives the Tell, the cultivation of which yields the means of life to the populations of the coast. In the neighbourhood of this fertile belt there are numerous oases extending into the interior; while others, fortunately for the purposes of commerce and civilization, exist within practicable distances across the whole desert.

Farther eastward, near the limits of the Sahara, a line of oases extends from its northern to its southern boundary. One of these, the Great Oasis of Thebes, is one hundred and twenty miles in length. It is watered by a pleasant stream, with groves of palm and acacia on its banks.

The oases invariably lie in the lowest levels of the soil, and doubtless owe their existence to the moisture which naturally gravitates towards such localities. Mast of these isolated spots, even though hundreds of miles apart, enjoy a constant supply of water, and are favourable to the cultivation of the date palm and other fruit-trees, as well as of various kinds of vegetables.

The date palm supplies a large proportion of the food of the dwellers in the desert. The tree is thirty-three years in coming to maturity; after which it will bear fruit for seventy years more, the annual crop of each tree averaging from three to four hundred pounds weight. Not only man, but all the animals of the desert can feed on the date. The fruit is easily preserved by packing it closely in woollen bags; and when thus compressed into solid masses it may be kept for several years. Sometimes a tree is tapped for the sake of its sap, which is much relished as a beverage, and which, when allowed to ferment, forms a drink resembling cider. A single tree will yield fourteen or fifteen quarts a day for two years, but will die if the drain be continued longer.

Every part of the date palm is turned to profitable account. The wood is used for building, and for every kind of carpenter-work; the fibre is twisted into ropes; baskets are made of the branches; and sheep are fattened with the pounded stones of the fruit.

The population of the desert is necessarily sparse and scanty, in proportion to its enormous area. It consists of various tribes of two distinct nations;—the Berbers, made up of descendants of the ancient Lib'yans, of the Romans, and of the Van'dals; and the Arabs, originally invaders, who yet retain, in no small degree, their original characteristics.

The Berbers are the settled inhabitants of the oases, where the men cultivate the ground, and the women manage the manufactures. They maintain amicable relations with their nomadic brethren, to whom they are in the habit of confiding the care of such cattle as they possess, and of whose property they undertake the custody during the wanderings of the owners. The oasis generally contains a village (*ksar*), which is built of stone, and, together

An Oasis in The Desert

with the gardens, is walled in. Nothing is grown but what will produce food of some kind, and the utmost use is made of every foot of land and drop of water.At the same time, provision is made for defence, and sentinels are kept continually on the watch for an enemy.

Outside the walls are the *marabets*, or sepulchres of the dead; upon which are lavished far more expense and taste than on the abodes of the living. Near each tomb rises a little sepulchral chapel, executed in a finished style of architecture, by the most skilful artisans that can be procured. These buildings are universally held sacred; and even the foe who would slaughter the living and make a prey of their property, leaves the resting-places of the dead inviolate.

THE ARABS

The life of the desert nomads, even when free from war and brigandage, is one of pedestal variety and excitement. They spend the winter and the spring in the wilderness, where, at these seasons, there are both water and pasture; but they remain in one spot only for a few days, striking their tents and migrating to another as soon as the pasture is consumed.

As summer approaches, they resort to the oases where their property is kept; here they load their camels with merchandise, and journey northward. They arrive in the *Tell* just at harvest time, when the price of com is low. Here they pass the summer in barter and commerce, exchanging their woollen goods and dates for raw wool, sheep, &c.

At the close of the summer they set off southward again, arriving at the oases in October, just as the dates are ripe. Their assistance is now valuable in gathering in the crops, which occupies them a month; and another month is spent in bartering their raw wool and other late purchases for a portion of the dates which they have helped to gather, and for manufactured garments made by the women. These they deposit in their magazines, and then withdraw again to the desert, with their flocks and herds.

CARAVANS

There are two classes of caravans, either of which a traveller may join. The first, and most expeditious, is the *gafa'la*, or merchants' caravans, which start with some degree of regularity from certain depots in the northern oases, and whose departures are always made known beforehand. The camel-drivers regulate the speed of the journey, generally travelling from twenty to twenty-five miles a day, save in regions infested by robbers, where they will occasionally double that rate of speed. In case of attack, every one defends himself and his property as he best can; and the timid are seen rushing towards the centre, to escape being cut off as stragglers.

The second kind of caravan is the *ne'ja*, which consists of a whole tribe in migration, and which travels much more slowly. They can with them, not their

CARAVAN CROSSING THE DESERT

merchandise merely, but all their cattle, tents, and household stuff, together with their women, children, domestic animals, and poultry.

They move along at an easy rate, and the journey is pleasant enough so long as no enemy appears; but should they meet the bands of a hostile tribe while thus encumbered, it may chance to go hard with them. The battle which ensues is one in which quarter is neither asked nor given, the Arabs being much more bitter in their warfare against each other than in their encounters with Europeans. Sunset is the signal for the cessation of the strife, and the defeated party is allowed to make off in the night. In these conflicts prisoners are never made, the conquerors preferring the heads of their victims to any ransom that could be offered.

From Morocco six caravans traverse the Sahara every year, when from two thousand to three thousand camels are loaded with European produce, and start for the distant countries of the interior. Some of these caravans penetrate as far into Soudan as Timbuctu. They bring thence gold dust, buffalo-skins, ivory, senna, alkali, rhinoceros-horns, indigo, diamonds, perfumes, gums, and other articles of commerce. On reaching the banks of the Niger, the Moors deposit their merchandise on a hill. They then retire, and the negroes advance and criticise the goods. After an examination of three days, they generally come to terms, and the business is done.

Words

amicable, *friendly*.
assistance, *help*.
bartering, *exchanging*.
brigandage, *plunder*.
civilized, *cultivated*.
compressed, *squeezed*.
consumed, *exhausted*.
cultivate, *till*.
custody, *guardianship*.

destitute, *devoid*.
encounters, *conflicts*.
encumbered, *embarrassed*.
enormous, *vast*.
expeditious, *rapid*.
fertile, *productive*.
invariably, *uniformly*.
inviolate, *uninsured*.
lavished, *squandered*.

magazines, *store-houses*.
maturity, *ripeness*.
merchandise, *goods*.
migration, *travelling*.
neighbourhood, *vicinity*.
obliterate, *efface*.
occasionally, *sometimes*.
perpetual, *constant*.

practicable, *performable*.
preference, *choice; liking*.
profitable, *lucrative*.
relished, *enjoyed*.
reverse, *opposite*.
sepulchers, *tombs*.
supplied, *filled up*.

Questions

What mistake is frequently made regarding the nature of the Sahara? What has led to this mistake? How do the guides find their way across the desert?

What is the *Tell*? Where do the oases usually lie? With what does the date palm supply the dwellers in the desert? To what two nations do these inhabitants belong? Who are the Berbers? Where do they live? What is the *ksar*? What are the *marabets*?

What part of the year do the Arabs spend in the wilderness? For what purpose do they leave it?

What are the two classes of caravans called? Which travels the more quickly? To what danger are they exposed? What is characteristic of Arab warfare? How many caravans cross the Sahara from Marocco every year? How far do they penetrate? What do they bear thence?

☆ ☆ ☆ ☆ ☆ ☆ ☆ ☆ ☆ ☆ ☆ ☆ ☆ ☆ ☆ ☆ ☆ ☆ ☆ ☆

　　我们可以把撒哈拉沙漠比作一片巨大的海洋，它将赤道非洲的黑人王国与北部更文明的国家分隔开来。在它其中镶嵌的众多绿洲，像许多在沙漠荒原中的零星岛屿。然而，这片荒原，虽然缺少一切有利于人类生活和舒适的事物，却不完全由贫瘠的沙子组成。这里有众多干燥、发育不良的植被，骆驼可以在上面吃草；因此一段穿越沙漠的旅途是可行的，而通过撒哈拉沙漠的路线却是不可能的，它经常被描述为一片宽阔的沙质平原。

　　在沙漠中，人们总是偏好于选择通过沙地的路线，因为沙子就像一张柔软干燥的大床，旅行者在一天的疲劳之后可以在此之上休息。这是一种偏好，因为在沙地的广阔地带，当地人总是能发现泉水，这使得欧洲人把整个撒哈拉沙漠认定是一片沙漠的荒原。沙漠的特点刚好是相反的，有数百英里坚硬、固定的土壤，而更多的则是多石的混合碎片和鹅卵石。

　　在沙地上旅行，当然没有可见的道路，因为经常反复吹拂的激烈的大风，会很快将所有脚印吹得无影无踪。因此，向导会根据路标找到他们前行的路。当然，他们会在必要时更新这些路标。他们往往会选择最微不足道的物体，比如一簇草<u>丛</u>、一株单一的植物或土壤上高耸的土堆。当平原是一片干燥平坦的荒地时，甚至这样的物体也找不到，他们会找到一大堆石头或者将石头推成一堆，之间有很长一段距离的间隔。有时他们的行程会在沙漠平原上持续10～12天，整个旅程中没有一滴水。

绿　洲

在这片大陆的几乎整个北部海岸，延伸有一片肥沃的土地，当地人称其为"沙漠里的绿洲"。这里栽种的植物为整个海岸的人口提供了生活必需品。在这片肥沃地带的周围，许多块绿洲延伸进入内陆地区；而其他的绿洲，幸运地出于商业和文明的目的，在整个沙漠之中存在于人们可以达到的距离之内。

在更远东部的撒哈拉的边缘附近，一片绿洲从它北部到南部的边界一直延伸。其中之一的底比斯大绿洲足足有120英里长。它由一条欢愉的河流浇灌，它的两岸布满了棕榈树和橡胶树。

绿洲总是位于土地的最低水平线上，毫无疑问，这样的低地自然能吸引水分，这也是它们存在的原因。这些孤立的绿洲，虽然相隔数百英里，却都享受着持续的水源。这有利于培养枣椰树和其他果树以及各类蔬菜。

枣椰树提供了沙漠中居民食物的相当一大部分。这种树33年才会成熟；在它成熟之后的70年之中，它会结出果实，每棵树平均每年产出300～400磅的果实。不仅是人类，沙漠中的所有动物都可以以椰枣为食。它的果实很容易保存，可以将它们紧紧包在羊毛袋里，当被压缩成坚实的一团时，就可以保存它们好多年了。有时为了得到它的汁液，人们也会轻轻拍打树干，它的滋味就像饮料，当发酵之后，会形成一种类似于苹果汁的饮品。在两年的时间内，一棵树每天会产出14～15夸脱的汁液，但如果被继续榨汁很久，枣椰树就会死去。

枣椰树的每一个部分都有用。它的木材用于建筑以及各种木工活；它的纤维可以扭曲成绳索，它的树枝可以做成篮子；它的果实可以碾压成饼状来喂养羊群。

与沙漠巨大的面积相比，沙漠之中的人口必然是稀疏的。它由两个不同国家的不同部落组成——柏柏尔人，由古老的利比亚人、罗马人、汪达尔人的后代组成；还有最初的入侵者阿拉伯人，至今仍在很大程度上保留了他们最初的特征。

柏柏尔人是绿洲地区定居的居民，在那里，男性负责耕种土地，而女性管理生产。他们与游牧民族的同胞保持友好的关系。他们习惯将自己拥有的牛群托付给这些游牧民族；而当这些人四处漫游的时候，他们会为这些游牧民族监护他们的财产。绿洲通常包含一个村（在当地语言中称为"ksar"）。它们由石头建造，加上花园，都围在一堵墙内部。这里的人们不会耕种任何不能生出食物的植物。人们最大限度地利用每一寸土地和每一滴水。同时，人们会为防御备下粮食，哨兵不断地在哨所提防着敌人。

城墙外分布着死者的坟墓"marabet"，建造这些坟墓，比建造活人的住所挥霍了多得多的费用和艺术品位。每个墓附近都矗立着阴森森的教堂，它们践行了一种终结的建筑风格，它们由最熟练的工匠完成。人们普遍认为这些建筑是神圣的，甚至是那些在这里大肆屠杀活人、掠夺他们财产的敌人，也不会侵犯死者的栖息之地。

阿 拉 伯 人

沙漠里游牧民族的生活，即使在没有战争和抢掠行为的时候，也充满了多样性和兴奋感。他们在冬天和春天游荡在旷野之中，在那里的这两个季节里，水和青草都存在；但他们只会在一个地方停留几天，当青草被消耗殆尽，他们就会收拾起帐篷迁移到另一个地方。

随着夏天的临近，他们会到他们保存财产的绿洲去；在这里，他们用骆驼运送商品，向北行进。正当收获的时候，他们会抵达一片叫戴尔的绿洲，这个时候羊毛的价格很低。在这里，通过易货和商业，他们度过了夏天，他们与当地人交换他们的羊毛制品和椰枣，以换取羊毛原料和羊，等等。

夏季结束时他们再次向南出发，在10月到达绿洲，这时椰枣刚刚成熟。他们为当地居民收割粮食提供的帮助，在这时显得特别珍贵。这会花掉他们一个月的时间。接下来的一个月，他们在这里用羊毛原料和其他商品来交换一部分他们帮助收成的椰枣以及女性制作出来的衣服。他们将这些东西存放在仓库之中，然后赶着他们的羊群和牛群再次向沙漠中行进。

商　　队

商队有两种类型，旅行者都可能加入其中。第一种是最迅速的一种，叫作gafa'la或商人的商队。某种程度上他们会带有一定的规律性，他们从位于北部绿洲的某个仓库出发。他们的离开，总会让其他人预先知道。赶骆驼的人会调节旅行的速度，一般每天前进20～25英里，除非在强盗出没的地区，他们偶尔会将速度调整到两倍。为了防止受到攻击，每个人都极尽所能地维护自己及财产；胆小的人会奔到商队中心，为了避免自己掉队而与其他人隔离开。

第二种商队叫作neja，是由一个不断迁徙的整体部落组成，他们的旅行要慢得多。他们不仅仅可以带着他们的商品，还有他们所有的牛群、帐篷和家里的东西，连同他们的女人、孩子、家畜和家禽也一起上路。

他们以一种轻松的速度前行，只要没有敌人出现，他们的旅程就很愉快。但如果他们遇到一队敌对部落而因此受到阻碍，他们的前行就会变得很困难。在随之而来的战斗中，不会出现安营扎寨。阿拉伯人之间的战争，比起他们与欧洲人的战争要激烈得多。日落是冲突停止的信号，被打败的一方在晚上可以离开。在这些冲突之中，从来不会出现囚犯，征服者喜欢用受害者的人头来交换任何赎金。

从摩洛哥出发，每年会有六支商队穿越过撒哈拉沙漠。这其中，2 000~3 000只骆驼会运载着欧洲生产的商品，从遥远的国家出发，一直到达非洲的内陆国家。其中一些商队穿越沙漠到达遥远的苏丹或丁布各都。他们将金粉、水牛皮、象牙、番泻叶、碱、犀牛角、靛蓝、钻石、香水、橡胶和其他的商品带到那里。到达尼日尔的河岸之后，摩尔人将商品存放在一座小山上。然后他们撤回去，当地的黑人走上前去并评判这些商品。经过三天的检验之后，他们通常会达成协议，生意就这样做成了。

Lesson 60   THE LIGHT-HOUSE
第六十课   灯   塔

The rocky ledge runs far into the sea,
　　And on its outer point, some miles away.
The light-house lifts its massive masonry,—
　　A pillar of fire by night, of cloud by day.

Even at this distance I can see the tides,
　　Upheaving, break unheard along its base;—
A speechless wrath, that rises and subsides
　　In the white lip and tremor of the face.

And as the evening darkens, lo! how bright,
　　Through the deep purple of the twilight air,
Beams forth the sudden radiance of its light,
　　With strange, unearthly splendour in its glare.

Not one alone;—from each projecting cape
　　And perilous reef along the ocean's verge,
Starts into life a dim, gigantic shape,
　　Holding its lantern o'er the restless surge.

And the great ships sail outward and return.
　　Bending and bowing, o'er the billowy swells;
And ever joyful, as they see it burn,
　　They wave their silent welcomes and farewells.

They come forth from the darkness, and their sails
　　Gleam for a moment only in the blaze;
And eager faces, as the light unveils,
　　Gaze at the tower, and vanish while they gaze.

The mariner remembers when a child,
　　On his first voyage, he saw it fade and sink;
And, when returning from adventures wild,
　　He saw it rise again o'er ocean's brink.

Steadfast, serene, immovable, the same

Year after year, through all the silent night,
Burns on for evermore that quenchless flame,
  Shines on that inextinguishable light!

It sees the ocean to its bosom clasp
  The rocks and sea-sand with the kiss of peace;—
It sees the wild winds lift it in their grasp,
  And hold it up, and shake it like a fleece.

The startled waves leap over it; the storm
  Smites it with all the scourges of the rain;
And steadily against its solid form
  Press the great shoulders of the hurricane.

The sea-bird wheeling round it, with the din
  Of wings and winds and solitary cries,
Blinded and maddened by the light within,
  Dashes himself against the glare, and dies.

A new Prome'theus, chained upon the rock,
  Still grasping in his hand the fire of Jove,
It does not hear the cry, nor heed the shock,
  But hails the mariner with words of love.

"Sail on!" it says, "sail on, ye stately ships;
  And with your floating bridge the ocean span;
Be mine to guard this light from all eclipse,—
  Be yours to bring man nearer unto man!"

—Longfellow

Words

adventures, *enterprises*.
billowy, *surging*.
eclipse , *obscuration*.
gigantic, *colossal*.
grasping, *holding*.
hurricane, *tempest*.
immovable, *steadfast*.
maddened, *irritated*.
massive, *bulky*.
perilous, *dangerous*.

projecting, *outstanding*.
quenchless, *inextinguishable*.
radiance, *brightness*.
solitary, *lonely*.
speechless, *voiceless*.
subsides, *falls*.
tremor, *quivering from fear*.
upheaving, *swelling*.
vanish, *disappear*.

一长条岩石远远窜入大海，
在它的尽头——已是好几里之外，
灯塔昂然耸立起魁梧的石身，
夜间是一柱火，白天是一柱云彩。

即使那么远，我也能望见海潮的上涨，
冲击着塔座，然而听不到声响，
恰似无言的怒气，升腾又消退；
在苍白的唇边，痉挛的脸上。

当暝色渐深渐浓，看！多么明亮。
透过天边暗紫的残霞暮霭，
灯塔蓦然吐射出灿灿的光辉，
闪耀着尘世之间罕见的夺目光亮。

不只它一个，每一处突出的涯角，
海岸近旁每一处险要的礁岩，
都有一尊朦胧的巨影亮起来，
高举明灯俯视不息的波涛。

汹涌狂澜上颠簸俯仰的航船，
每当望见天亮了，都不胜喜悦；
在远航的返航途中，默默无言地，
向它打招呼，表示欢迎与别离。

航船从黑暗中出现，一片片帆蓬，
只在它的亮光下闪露了片刻。
那亮光照见一张张焦灼的脸庞，
向它凝视着，又在黑暗中隐没。

水手望见它，回忆起他的童年。
第一次远航，遥望它消失不见；
经历了艰危惊险从异域归来。
又见它赫然浮现在远处的天边。

坚定，从容沉着，岿然不动，
一年又一年，度过了多少漫漫长夜，
它那炽烈的光辉永不消损，
它那高烧的巨火永不熄灭！

它看见滚滚洋流似和平之吻，
把卵石沙砾推挤到它的怀抱；
它看见狂风，攥紧它，将它顶起，
拔举它，摇撼他，仿佛它软若羊毛。

惊涛骇浪从它的身躯上越过，
暴风抽打它，把骤雨当作钢鞭；
紧紧压住它坚不可摧的躯体的，
是那十二级飓风的双肩。

海鸟绕着它旋转，风声，振翅声，
凄寂的鸣声，响成了嘈杂的一片。
亮光闪花了眼睛，发了狂似地，
向火光冲去，葬身于一团烈焰之中。

像另一个普罗米修斯，绑在岩石之上，
手里仍然紧握着约夫的火炬，
不理会周遭的喧嚣，和周遭的冲击，
向水手说出安详慈爱的话语。

他说："继续航行吧，壮丽的船队！
架起你们跨越大海的桥身；
有我守护这光亮，不让它消逝。
由你们带着人类去靠近人类！"

——朗费罗

Lesson 61
THE LAST FIGHT IN THE COLISÆUM

第六十一课　　竞技场最后的战斗

A. D. 404

The grandest and most renowned of all the ancient amphitheatres is the Colisea'um at Rome. It was built by Vespa'sian and his son Titus, the conquerors of Jerusalem, in a valley in the midst of the seven hills of Rome. The captive Jews were forced to labour at it; and the materials—granite outside, and a softer stone within—are so solid, and so admirably built, that still, at the end of eighteen centuries, it has scarcely even become a ruin, but remains one of the greatest wonders of Rome.

Five acres of ground were enclosed within the oval of its outer wail, which, outside, rises perpendicularly in tiers of arches one above another. Within, the galleries of seats projected forwards, each tier coining out far beyond the one above it; so that between the lowest and the outer wall there was room for a great variety of chambers, passages, and vaults around the central space, called the arena.

Altogether, when full, this huge building held no fewer than 87,000 spectators!

THE COLISÆUM

It had no roof; but when there was rain, or if the sun was too hot, the sailors in the porticos unfurled awnings that ran along upon ropes, and formed a covering of silk and gold tissue over the whole. Purple was the favourite colour for this veil; because, when the sun shone through it, it cast such beautiful rosy tints on the snowy arena and the white purple-edged togas of the Roman citizens.

When the emperor had seated himself and given the signal, the sports began. Sometimes a rope-dancing elephant would begin the entertainment, by mounting even to the summit of the building and descending by a cord. Or a lion came forth with a jewelled crown on his head, a diamond necklace round his neck, his mane plaited with gold, and his claws gilded, and played a hundred pretty gentle antics with a little hare that danced fearlessly within his grasp.

Sometimes water was let into the arena, a ship sailed in, and falling to pieces in the midst, sent a crowd of strange animals swimming in all directions. Sometimes the ground opened, and trees came growing up through it, bearing golden fruit. Or the beautiful old tale of Orpheus was acted: these trees would follow the harp and song of the musician; but—to make the whole part complete—it was in no mere play, but in real earnest, that the Orpheus of the piece fell a prey to live bears.

For the Coliæum had not been built for such harmless spectacles as those first

Interior of the Coliæum

described. The fierce Romans wanted to be excited and to feel themselves strongly stirred; and, presently, the doors of the pits and dens around the arena were thrown open, and absolutely savage beasts were let loose upon one another—rhinoceroses and tigers, bulls and lions, leopards and wild boars— while the people watched with ferocious curiosity to see the various kinds of attack and defence, their ears at the same time being delighted, instead of horror-struck, by the roars and howls of the noble creatures whose courage was thus misused.

Wild beasts tearing each other to pieces might, one would think, satisfy any taste for horror; but the spectators needed even nobler game to be set before their favourite monsters;—men were brought forward to confront them. Some of these were, at first, in full armour, and fought hard, generally with success. Or hunters came, almost unarmed, and gained the victory by swiftness and dexterity, throwing a piece of cloth over a lion's head, or disconcerting him by putting their fist down his throat.

But it was not only skill, but death, that the Romans loved to see; and condemned criminals and deserters were reserved to feast the lions, and to entertain the populace with their various kinds of death. Among those condemned was many a Christian martyr, who witnessed a good confession before the savage-eyed multitude around the arena, and " met the lion's gory mane" with a calm resolution and a hopeful joy that the lookers-on could not understand. To see a Christian die, with upward gaze, and hymns of joy on his tongue, was the most strange and unaccountable sight the Coliæum could offer; and it was therefore the choicest, and reserved for the last of the spectacles in which the brute creation had a part.

The carcasses were dragged off with hooks, the blood-stained sand was covered with a fresh clean layer, perfume was wafted in stronger clouds, and a procession came forward—tall, well-made men, in the prime of their strength. Some carried a sword and a lasso, others a trident and a net; some were in light armour, others in the full, heavy equipment of a soldier; some on horseback, some in chariots, some on foot. They marched in, and made their obeisance to the emperor; and with one voice their greeting sounded through the building: "Hail, Cæsar; those about to die salute thee!" They were the gladiators—the swordsmen trained to fight to the death to amuse the populace.

Fights of all sorts took place,—the light-armed soldier and the netsman—the lasso and the javelin—the two heavy-armed warriors,—all combinations of single combat, and sometimes a general melee. When a gladiator wounded his adversary, he shouted to the spectators, "He has it!" and looked up to know whether he should kill or spare. When the people held up their thumbs, the conquered was left to recover, if he could; if they turned them down, he was to die: and if he showed any reluctance to present his

THE DYING GLADIATOR.

throat for the death-blow, there was a scornful shout, "Receive the steel!" Many of us must have seen casts of that most touching statue of the wounded glad'iator, that called forth from Byron these noble lines of indignant pity:—

"I see before me the gladiator lie:
 He leans upon his hand; his manly brow
Consents to death, but conquers agony;
 And his drooped head sinks gradually low;
 And through his side the last drops, ebbing slow
From the red gash, fall heavy, one by one,
 Like the first of a thunder-shower; and now
The arena swims around him—he is gone,
Ere ceased the inhuman shout which hailed the wretch
   who won.

"He heard it, but he heeded not; his eyes
 Were with his heart, and that was far away:
He recked not of the life he lost, nor prize;

But where his rude hut by the Danube lay—
There were his young barbarians all at play,
There was their Dacian mother—he their sire,
Butchered to make a Roman holiday.—
All this rushed with his blood.—Shall he expire,
And unavenged?—Arise, ye Goths, and glut your ire!"

Christianity, however, worked its way upwards, and at last was professed by the emperor on his throne. Persecution came to an end, and no more martyrs fed the beasts in the Colisæum. The Christian emperors endeavoured to prevent any more shows where cruelty and death formed the chief interest, and no truly religious person could endure the spectacle; but custom and love of excitement prevailed even against the emperor. They went on for fully a hundred years after Rome had, in name, become a Christian city, and the same customs prevailed wherever there was an amphitheatre or pleasure-loving people.

Meantime the enemies of Rome were coming nearer and nearer. Al'aric, the great chief of the Goths, led his forces into Italy, and threatened the city itself. Hono'rius, the emperor, was a cowardly, almost idiotic boy; but his brave general, Stil'icho, assembled his forces, met the Goths at Pollen'tia (about twenty-five miles from where Turin now stands), and gave them a complete defeat, on Easter-day of the year 403. He pursued them to the mountains, and for that time saved Rome.

In the joy of victory, the Roman Senate invited the conqueror and his ward Honorius to enter the city in triumph, at the opening of the new year, with the white steeds, purple robes, and vermilion cheeks with which, of old, victorious generals were welcomed at Rome. The churches were visited instead of the Temple of Jupiter, and there was no murder of the captives; but Roman bloodthirstiness was not yet allayed, and, after the procession had been completed, the Colisæum shows commenced, innocently at first, with races on foot, on horseback, and in chariots; then followed a grand hunt of beasts turned loose in the arena; and next a sword-dance. But after the sword-dance came the arraying of swordsmen, with no blunted weapons, but with sharp spears and swords—a gladiator combat in full earnest. The people, enchanted, applauded with shouts of ecstasy this gratification of their savage tastes.

Suddenly, however, there was an interruption. A rude, roughly-robed man, bareheaded and barefooted, had sprung into the arena, and, waving back the gladiators, began to call aloud upon the people to cease from the shedding of innocent blood, and not to requite God's mercy, in turning away the sword of the enemy, by encouraging murder. Shouts, howls, cries, broke in upon his words; this was no place for preachings—the old customs of Rome should be observed—"Back, old man!"— "On, gladiators!"

The gladiators thrust aside the meddler, and rushed to the attack. He still stood between, holding them apart, striving in vain to be heard. "Sedition! sedition!"— "Down with him!"—was the cry; and the prefect in authority himself added his voice.

The gladiators, enraged at interference with their vocation, cut him down. Stones, or whatever came to hand, rained upon him from the furious people, and he perished in the midst of the arena! He lay dead; and then the people began to reflect upon what had been done.

His dress showed that he was one of the hermits who had vowed themselves to a life of prayer and self-denial, and who were greatly reverenced, even by the most thoughtless. The few who had previously seen him, told that he had come from the wilds of Asia on pilgrimage, to visit the shrines and keep his Christmas at Rome. They knew that he was a holy man—no more: it is not even certain what his name was. But his spirit had been stirred by the sight of thousands flocking to see men slaughter one another, and in his simple-hearted zeal he had resolved to stop the cruelty, or die.

He had died, but not in vain. His work was done. The shock of such a death before their eyes turned the hearts of the people; they saw the wickedness and cruelty to which they had blindly surrendered themselves; and since the day when the hermit died in the Colisæum, there has never been another fight of gladiators. Not merely at Rome, but in every province of the empire, the custom was utterly abolished; and one habitual crime at least was wiped from the earth by the self-devotion of one humble, obscure, and nameless man.

—A Book of Golden Deeds

Words

abolished, *destroyed.*
absolutely, *positively.*
admirably, *excellently.*
agony, *suffering.*
amphitheatres, *circuses.*
awnings, *canopies.*
bloodthirstiness, *desire for slaughter.*
carcasses, *dead bodies.*
condemned, *sentenced to death.*
confront, *encounter.*
descending, *going down.*
dexterity, *cleverness.*
disconcerting, *confusing.*
ecstasy, *rapture.*
enchanted, *delighted.*
endeavoured, *attempted.*
entertainment, *amusement.*
equipment, *outfit.*
excitement, *sensation.*

galleries, *tiers.*
inhuman, *merciless.*
innocently, *harmlessly.*
leopards, *spotted animals.*
melee (ma-la), *confused light.*
obeisance, *reference.*
perpendicularly, *vertically.*
populace, *the common people.*
porticos, *porches.*
previously, *formerly.*
procession, *pageant.*
reluctance, *unwillingness.*
renowned, *famous.*
requite, *repay.*
resolution, *firmness.*
reverenced, *venerated.*
rhinoceroses, *thick-skinned animals.*
spectacles, *exhibitions.*
surrendered, *yielded.*

threatened, *menaced.*
unaccountable, *inexplicable.*
unavenged, *without retaliation.*

vermilion, *bright red.*
vocation, *profession.*

Questions

Which was the grandest of the ancient amphitheatres? By whom was it built? What space does it cover? What number of spectators did it hold? Who gave the signal for the sports to begin? What was the nature of the opening sports? By what were the more harmless spectacles succeeded? What followed the fight of beasts with beasts? What was considered the choicest spectacle of this kind? Who then marched in, and greeted the emperor? How did the spectators indicate whether they wished a vanquished gladiator to be killed or spared? What put an end to these displays? When were they revived at Rome? Who suddenly interrupted the sports? What was his fate? What effect had his death?

公元404年

古建筑中最伟大最著名的露天剧场是古罗马竞技场。这是由耶路撒冷的征服者维斯帕先和他的儿子提多在罗马祁山的山谷中修筑的。被俘虏的犹太人被迫在这里劳作。它外部的材料是花岗岩，内部是一种稍柔软的石料。这些石头是如此稳固，这是多么令人钦佩的建造。不过，18世纪末，它几乎沦为废墟，但即使这样，它仍然是古罗马最伟大的奇迹之一。

占地五亩的竞技场封闭在椭圆形的围墙之内。而这之外，在拱门一层的垂直处，石块一个叠一个地向上升起。在内部，座椅的长廊向前延伸，每一层突出的建筑都远远超出了上面一层，所以在最低处和外壁之间，还有各种各样的空地留给众多房间和通道，并围绕着中心空间的竞技场。

总共计算起来，装满人时，这幢巨大的建筑能够容纳不少于8.7万名观众！它没有屋顶，但当下雨时或如果太阳灼热，地面门廊的帐幔沿着绳索展开，会形成一个丝绸和金子编织成的帐幔。紫色是这面纱最喜欢的颜色，因为当阳光照耀它，它就将在耀眼的竞技场上美丽的玫瑰色彩和白色紫色的外袍，展现在罗马公民眼前。

当皇帝入坐在这里并给出信号时，竞技就会开始。有时一个走钢索的大象开始这场表演，它会沿着一根绳子走到竞技场里的至高点，然后再重新向下走。或者，一头狮子出场，它的头上带着一个镶满宝石的皇冠，颈间有一条钻石项链，它的鬃毛梳理得整齐，它的爪子镀着金。狮子与一只小野兔一起，温柔地表演着各种杂技。在它的带领之下，小兔子毫无畏惧地跳着舞。

有时人们会放水进入竞技场，一艘船在水面航行，然后在水面中央摔得粉碎。一群稀奇的动物朝着四面八方游散。有时竞技场开放，树木会在此成长起来，长满金色的果实。关于俄耳甫斯的美丽传说也会在这里实现：这些树将应着竖琴音乐家的歌曲起舞，但使整个故事变得完整的，是俄耳甫斯最终变成一只熊的猎物，而这不是出现在戏剧中，而是残忍的现实。

建造罗马竞技场的最初目的，并非像先前描述的那样残忍。罗马人想变得兴奋，觉得自己受到了强烈刺激；此时，竞技场四周的深坑和窝点的大门会打开，特别凶残的野兽会一只接着一只地被解锁放出——犀牛和老虎，牛和狮子、豹、野猪。人们怀着强烈的好奇心，观看各种动物之间的攻击和防守。同时，因为这些高贵的动物，他们的耳朵也变得兴奋起来——人类的勇气就这样被滥用，他们咆哮和怒吼，而没有丝毫的恐惧。

有人会摄像野兽将对方撕成碎片的场景，这可能会满足人们对恐怖的任何品味，但是观众们需要更加高贵的游戏呈现在他们面前。他们最喜欢的怪物便是人类。壮士们被带到他们面前。最初，有些人全副武装，努力争斗，他们一般都会成功。或者有时，猎人几乎手无寸铁地上场，并迅速、灵巧地取得胜利，在狮子的头上扔一块布，或用他们的拳头将它的喉咙打碎，来彻底打败这头野兽。

但罗马人真正喜欢看的不仅仅是技能，而是死亡。死刑犯和逃兵的性命被留下来成为狮子的盛宴，并用各种方式的死亡娱乐大众。在这些应受谴责的表演中，会有许多基督徒的受难者，在围坐在竞技场周围的群众野蛮的注视中，带着平静的决心和充满希望的兴奋，在狮子的鬃毛之中战斗，这是所有观众根本无法理解的。一个基督徒向上凝视着，口中仍快乐地唱着赞美诗，他这样死去，是罗马竞技场可以提供给观众的最奇怪、最不可理喻的景象。因此这一场景，一般被选择性地保留到这种野蛮创作的最后一部分。

钩子拖着尸体，血迹斑斑的沙子覆盖着一层新鲜干净的血液，一阵香气飘来，一群高个、壮实的男人怀着对自己力量的自豪感，列队走上竞技场。一些人拿着一把剑和套索，有的人拿着三叉戟和网；有的人轻装上阵，其他人全副武装；有的骑着战马，有的驾着战车，一些人则是步行。他们在竞技场中游行，并向皇帝敬礼，高呼的声音响彻整个竞技场："万岁，凯撒；这些将要死去的勇士向你致敬！"他们是角斗士，他们为了娱乐大众而受到训练，直到战斗至死。

各种各样的战斗在这里呈现，轻武装的士兵和拿着套索的勇士，两个全副武装的战士，所有单独的作战相结合。有时则是一场混战。当角斗士让他的对手受了伤，他会向观众喊道，"轮到他了！"，并抬头看着观众，问大家是否应该杀了他还是留着他的性命。当人们举起大拇指，征服者就会尽他所能给被征服者一条活路；如果他们将手指朝下，失败者就会一命呜呼。如果他不愿刺向失败者的喉咙，将他的生命终结，观众就会轻蔑地喊道："收了他的武器！"我们大多数人一定见过许多感人的雕塑刻画受伤的角斗士。拜伦曾怀着愤慨的惋惜之情写下这些高贵的诗句：

> "我看到一个角斗士倒在我的面前，
> 他一手撑在地上，他威武的脸
> 显得视死如归，而把痛苦熬住，
> 他垂着的头渐渐地，渐渐地倒下去，
> 从他肋下鲜红的巨大创口，最后的血液
> 缓缓地溢出，重重地一滴滴地往下滴落，
> 像大雷雨的最初时刻，那大大的雨滴，
> 然后整个角斗场在他的周围摇晃，他死了，
> 但灭绝人性的人们，还在呼喊着，向那战胜的家伙叫好！"

> "他听见了，但他并不理会；他的眼神
> 随着他的心脏，已然飘然远去：
> 他并不为他逝去的生命而懊恼，也不是为了荣誉；
> 但是，在他多瑙河河畔粗陋的小屋里，
> 他年轻的亲人们都在那里玩耍，
> 还有他在达契亚的母亲。
> 他们的陛下，将屠杀作为罗马的假日。
> 所有这一切都冲斥着他的血液。
> 他岂能就这样死去，还没有报仇雪恨？
> 起来，哥特人，带着你的愤怒，起来！"

然而，基督教正蒸蒸日上地发展。最后由皇帝以他的王冠为它公开正名。迫害就此结束，也没有更多的烈士被杀戮来喂野兽。基督教的皇帝试图阻止任何以残忍和死亡为形式的表演来满足群众的乐趣。没有任何真正的宗教人士能够忍受这种场面，但习俗和狂热占了上风，甚至敢于反对皇帝。在罗马名义上成为基督教城市之后，他们又将这种杀戮活动持续了整整一百年。而同样的习俗，在拥有圆形剧场或者愉悦的以此为乐的观众的地方，也一样大行其道。

同时罗马的敌人也越靠越近。伟大的哥特人首领阿拉里克，带领他的军队进入了意大利，威胁着罗马这座城市。皇帝江东是一个懦弱，几乎白痴的男孩，但他勇

敢的将军斯提里克组装他的部队力量，在波兰提亚遭遇了哥特人的部队（距如今的都灵约25英里处），并完胜了他们。这是在公元403年的复活节这一天。他将他们驱逐到山上，并由此保住了罗马。

在胜利的喜悦中，罗马元老院邀请征服者和他的部队，在新年伊始凯旋地进入城市。白色的战马、紫色长袍、朱砂色的脸颊，胜利的将军们在罗马受到了夹道欢迎。他们访问了教堂，而不是木星殿。俘虏的性命被保留了下来。但嗜血的罗马人并没有由此结束他们的狂欢。游行结束之后，竞技场的节目才真正开始。最初的节目还很单纯，赤脚的人进行跑步比赛，还有马术比赛和战车比赛。接下来是释放野兽到竞技场里被猎杀，继而是剑术表演。进行剑术表演的战士，手持着的不是钝化的武器，而是锋利的长矛和剑——这是一场严肃完整的角斗士战斗。着了迷的人群兴奋地鼓掌呼喊，因为这表演满足了他们野蛮的口味。

然而，表演突然被中断。一个粗鲁的、衣衫褴褛的人，光着头，赤着脚，冲进了竞技场里。他挥舞着双臂，开始大声呼喊，来阻止竞技场里无辜的流血游戏。人们呼喊，嚎叫、叫嚷着，打段了他的话；这不是说教的地方——罗马的旧传统再次应验，人们喊着："退回去，老男人！""继续战斗！角斗士！"

角斗士们用力推开这个管闲事的人，冲向前继续互相攻击。他仍然站在他们中间，试图把他们分开，努力让他们听自己说话，但这都是徒劳的。"煽动叛乱！骚乱！""打倒他！"人们呼喊道。因在战斗中受到了干涉，被激怒的角斗士们，举起武器向他砍去。石头，或者手中能拿到的任何东西，从愤怒的人群中，像雨点一样砸在了他的身上。他就这样在竞技场中央死去了！他死了，躺在那里；然后人们开始反思刚刚自己做了什么。

他的穿着表明他是一个修道士，他可能曾经发誓自己会献身于祈祷和自我克制的生活中。他也曾被最轻率的人们跪拜，以前很少有人见过他，听说他来自亚洲的荒野朝圣之旅，他参拜过圣地，想在罗马推行他的教义。他们知道他是一个高尚的人。除此之外，对他的了解没有更多，人们甚至不确定他的名字是什么。但当他看到数千人奔涌而来，观赏人与人之间的相互屠杀，他的精神已经被激发。他怀着单纯的热情，决心停止这种掠杀或死亡。

他已经死了，但不是徒然的，他的工作完成了。这样的死亡的冲击，在人们眼前改变了他们的态度，他们看到自己盲目屈服于的邪恶和残忍。自从这个修道士死亡的那一天起，就再也没有过一场角斗士的战斗。不仅仅是在罗马，而在帝国的每一个省份，这种习俗得以完全废除。一个卑微、无名、大家都记不得名字的人的奉献，至少从这个地球上抹去了一种人们习以为常的犯罪。

——选自《嘉言懿行宝典》

Lesson 62
THE DESTRUCTION OF POMPEII
第六十二课　庞贝的毁灭

Once upon a time there stood a town in Italy, at the foot of Mount Vesu'vius, which was to Rome what Brighton or Hastings is to London—a fashionable watering-place. There Roman gentlemen and members of the Senate built villas, to which they were in the habit of retiring from the fatigues of business or the broils of politics.

The outsides of all the houses were adorned with frescoes, and every shop glittered with all the colours of the rainbow. At the end of each street there was a charming fountain, and any one who sat down beside it to cool himself had a delightful view of the Mediterranean, then as beautiful, as blue and sunny as it is now.

Atrium of a House in Pompeii

On a fine day, crowds might have been seen lounging here; some sauntering up and down in gala dresses of purple, while slaves passed to and fro bearing on their heads splendid vases; others sat on marble benches, shaded from the sun by awnings, and having before them tables covered with wine, and fruit, and flowers. Every house in that town was a little palace, and every palace was like a temple, or one of our great public buildings.

Any one who thinks a mansion in Belgravia the height of splendour, would have been astonished, had he lived in those days, to find how completely the abodes of those Roman lords outshone "the stately homes of England." On entering the former, the visitor passed through a vestibule decorated with rows of pillars, and then found himself in the *a'trium*, in which the household gods kept guard over the owner's treasure, which was placed in a safe, or strong-box, secured with brass or iron bands. In this apartment guests were received with imposing ceremony; and there the patron heard the complaints, supplications, and adulations of his great band of clients or dependants, who lived on his smiles and bounty, but chiefly on the latter. Issuing thence, the visitor found himself in the *tabli'num* an apartment paved with mosaic and decorated with paintings, in which were kept the family papers and archives. The house contained also (dining and supper rooms, and a number of sleeping rooms hung with the softest of Syrian cloths;—cabinets filled with rare jewels and antiquities, and sometimes a fine collection of paintings;—and last of all, a pillared *per'istyle*, opening out upon the garden. There the finest fruit hung temptingly in the rich light of a golden sky; and fountains, which flung their waters aloft in every imaginable form and device, cooled the air and discoursed sweet music to the ear. From behind each shrub there peeped a statue, or the bust of some great man, carved from the purest white marble, and placed in charming contrast with bouquets of rare flowers springing from stone vases. On the gate, or in mosaic on the pavement within, there was always the image of a dog, and beneath it the inscription, *Cave canem*—that is, "Beware of the dog!"

The frescoes on the walls represented scenes in the Greek legends, such as "The Seizure of Euro'pa," "The Battle of the Amazons," &c.; many of which are still to be seen in the museum at Naples. The pillars in the peristyle of which we have just spoken were encircled with garlands of flowers, which were renewed every morning. The tables of citron-wood were inlaid with silver ar'abesques; the couches were of bronze, gilt and jewelled, and were furnished with thick cushions, and tapestry embroidered with marvellous skill.

"Beware of the dog!"

When the master gave a dinner party, the guests reclined upon these cushions, washed their hands in silver basins, and dried them with napkins fringed with purple; and having made a libation on the altar of Bacchus, ate oysters brought from the shores of Britain, kids which were carved to the sound of music, and fruits served up on ice in the hottest days of summer. While the cup-bearers filled their golden cups with the rarest and most delicate wines in the world, other attendants crowned them with flowers wet with dew, and dancers executed the most graceful movements, and singers accompanied by the lyre poured forth an ode of Hor'ace or of Anac'reon.

After the banquet, a shower of scented water, thrown from invisible pipes, spread perfume over the apartment; and everything around, even the oil, and the lamps, and the jets of the fountain, shed forth the most grateful odour; and suddenly from the mosaic of the floor tables of rich dainties, of which we have at the present day no idea, arose, as if by magic, to stimulate the palled appetites of the revellers into fresh activity. When these had disappeared, other tables succeeded them, upon which senators, and consuls, and proconsuls gambled away provinces and empires by the throw of dice; and last of all, the tapestry was suddenly raised, and young girls, lightly

THE FORUM OF POMPELL

attired, wreathed with flowers, and bearing lyres in their hands, issued forth, and charmed sight and hearing by the graceful mazes of the dance.

One day, when festivities such as these were in full activity, Vesuvius sent up a tall and very black column of smoke, something like a pine-tree; and suddenly, in broad noonday, darkness black as pitch came over the scene! There was a frightful din of cries, groans, and imprecations, mingled confusedly together. The brother lost his sister, the husband his wife, the mother her child; for the darkness became so dense that nothing could be seen but the flashes which every now and then darted forth from the summit of the neighbouring mountain. The earth trembled, the houses shook and began to fall, and the sea rolled back from the land as if terrified; the air became thick with dust; and then, amidst tremendous and awful noise, a shower of stones, scoriæ, and pumice fell upon the town, and blotted it out for ever!

The inhabitants died just as the catastrophe found them—guests in their banquet-halls, brides in their chambers, soldiers at their post, prisoners in their dungeons, thieves in their theft, maidens at the mirror, slaves at the fountain, traders in their shops, students at their books. Some attempted flight, guided by blind people, who had walked so long in darkness that no thicker shadows could ever come upon them; but of these many were struck down on the way. When, a few days afterwards, people came from the surrounding country to the place, they found naught but a black, level, smoking plain, sloping to the sea, and covered thickly with ashes! Down, down beneath, thousands and thousands were sleeping "the sleep that knows on waking," with all their little pomps, and vanities, and frivolities, and pleasures, and luxuries, buried with them.

This took place on the 23rd of August, 79 A. D.; and the name of the town thus suddenly overwhelmed was Pompeii (*Pompa'ee*). Sixteen hundred and seventeen years afterwards, curious persons began to dig and excavate on the spot, and they found the city very much as it was when overwhelmed. The houses were standing, the paintings were fresh, and the skeletons stood in the very positions and the very places in which death had overtaken their owners so long ago!

The marks left by the cups of the tipplers still remained on the counters; the prisoners still wore their fetters, the belles their chains and bracelets; the miser held his hand on his hoarded coin; and the priests were lurking in the hollow images of their gods, from which they uttered responses and deceived the worshippers. There were the altars, with the blood dry and crusted upon them; the stables in which the victims of the sacrifice were kept; and the hall of mysteries, in which were symbolic paintings.

The researches are still going on, new wonders are every day coming to light, and we soon shall have almost as perfect an idea of a Roman town in the first century of the Christian era as if we had walked the streets and gossiped with the idle loungers at the fountains. Pompeii is the ghost of an extinct civilization rising up before us.

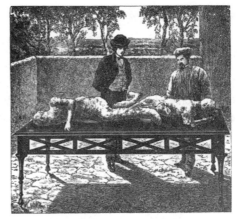

Casts of Bodies Discovered in the Ruins of Pompeii
(In the Museum at Sap Us.)

—Illustrated Magazine of Art

Words

adulations, *flatteries*.
antiquities, *curiosities*.
appetites, *desires*.
archives, *records*.
belles, *ladies*.
bonquets, *bunches*.
catastrophe, *calamity*.
delicate, *choice*.
delightful, *charming*.
discoursed, *gave forth*.
dungeons, *cells*.
embroidered, *sewed*.
excavate, *hollow out*.
fashionable, *much frequented*.
fatigues, *toils*.
festivities, *entertainments*.
frivolities, *frolics*.

garlands, *wreaths*.
gossiped, *tattled*.
grateful, *pleasant*.
imprecations, *curses*.
luxuries, *indulgences*.
mansion, *large house*.
mysteries, *secret rites*.
responses, *answers*.
sauntering, *strolling*.
stimulate, *excite*.
symbolic, *emblematic*.
tapestry, *needle-work*.
temptingly, *attractively*.
terrified, *frightened*.
tremendous, *horrible*.
vestibule, *entrance-hall*.

Questions

In what relation did Pompeii stand to Rome? How were its inhabitants chiefly occupied? What was the *atrium* in a Pompeian house? Describe the *tablinum*. What was the *peristyle*? How was it decorated? Describe a Pompeian dinner party. When did the eruption which buried the city take place? How were the inhabitants occupied at the time? When did the work of excavation begin? In what condition was the city found?

☆ ☆

从前在意大利有一座小镇，坐落在维苏威火山的山脚下，对于罗马来说，这座小镇拥有布莱顿或黑斯廷斯在伦敦的地位。这是一座时尚的水城。在这里，罗马的绅士们、参议院的成员们修建别墅，他们在隐退之后，可以从行业的疲劳或政治的争吵之中解脱出来，到这里来选择定居。

所有房子的外部都装饰着壁画，而每家店铺都闪烁着彩虹的所有颜色。在每条街道的尽头都有一处迷人的喷泉，当人们坐在它的旁边，想让自己畅享一丝清凉，都会看到地中海令人愉快的景色。那时的地中海，也如今天一样，是美丽的，蓝色的，撒满了阳光。

在晴朗的一天，会有很多人躺在这里；一些人穿着紫色的晚会礼服四处漫步，而奴隶们头顶着色彩斑斓的花瓶，走来走去；其他人会坐在房子中庭之中的大理石长凳上，这里有遮挡太阳的遮阳棚，在他们面前的桌子上摆满了酒、水果和花卉。在这个镇上的每一座房子都像一座小宫殿，而每座宫殿就像一座寺庙，或者像我们今天的一座巨大的公共建筑。如果有人认为贝尔塔莱维亚区的大厦就代表了壮丽的极限，那么如果他生活在那个时代，当他看到这些罗马贵族的房子是如何使"英国的豪华住宅"相形见绌的时候，他一定会大吃一惊。从房子的前门进入之后，客人们通过一个装饰有一排立柱的门厅，然后在中厅里，客人会发现主人的财宝都被放置在一个安全、坚固的用铜或铁条加固的大箱子之中。在这样的房子之中，客人会接受隆重仪式的招待；主人也会听到来自于他一众客人的赞美、祈祷和阿谀奉承。这些客人靠他的微笑和慷慨活着，但主要是依靠后者。从这里继续前行，客人们发现自己站在一个到处都镶嵌有装饰画的书房之中，其中保存有这个家庭的文件和档案。房子里还有一间客厅、一间餐厅和一些卧室。卧室里都挂着柔软的叙利亚布，里面的橱柜之上都装饰着珍贵的宝石和文物，有时还有图画的收藏品；房子的最后面，是一片带有立柱的花园。在这个花园里，最美好的果实迷人地悬挂在金色天空的光亮之下；喷泉，用几乎每一种人类可以想象出的形式和设备喷洒出水流，将凉爽的空气和甜美的音乐带到人们面前。在每一丛灌木的后方都矗立着一尊雕像，或者是某些著名人物的半身像，它们都用纯白色的大理石雕刻而成。一些罕见的鲜花，从石头花瓶中呈现在人们眼前，与这些白色的雕塑形成了迷人的对比。在门上或在走廊的镶嵌装饰之中，总会有一只狗的形象，而它下面会有一行题词，写着"当心狗！"

墙上的壁画展现了希腊神话中的场景，比如欧罗巴的捕获、亚马孙的战斗，等等；它们之中有很多仍然可以在那不勒斯博物馆看到。柱廊的列柱上装饰有花环，是由每天早晨采来的鲜花做成的。香橼木的桌子都镶嵌着银质的蔓藤花纹；沙发是由铜、镀金和宝石做成的，并配有厚厚的垫子，挂着绝妙的技艺刺绣而成的毯子。

当主人设宴时，客人坐卧在这些垫子上，在银盆之中洗手，并用配有紫色边穗的手帕将手擦干。他们在巴克斯的祭坛之上饮酒，吃着来自英国海岸的牡蛎，孩子们演奏出各种乐器的声响，在夏天最热的日子里，仆人们用优美的动作呈上冰块用以降温。在竖琴的伴奏之下，歌手们演奏着贺拉斯颂或阿克那里翁的颂歌。

宴会之后，不知从什么地方的管道喷出一阵带有香味的水，使整个房子里弥散着香气；周围的一切，甚至包括油、灯，还有喷泉的喷嘴儿，都散发出来最令人愉悦的气味；从地板上的镶嵌处，有一张摆满了丰富美食的桌子突然升起来，就像被施了魔法一样。而今天的我们，对这些美食几乎不会有任何概念，它们会刺激人们的食欲。接下来就进入品尝新鲜食物的狂欢活动之中。当这些桌子都撤下去之后，其他的桌子接着出现，在这之上，参议员、执政官还有总督们，通过投掷骰子，可能会输掉一个省份甚至一个帝国；最后，绣幔突然升起，一群年轻的女孩，身着薄衣，头戴鲜花，手中拿着竖琴，轻轻地翩翩起舞，并用优雅幻妙的舞蹈，吸引着观众们的视觉和听觉。

一天，当这样的庆典正全面喜庆地展开，维苏威火山喷射出一股高耸、黑色的烟雾，就像一颗巨大的松树。突然，正午时分陷入了一片黑暗之中，如沥青一般的黑暗席卷而来！一阵喧嚣、可怕的叫喊声、呻吟声和诅咒声，都混乱地交织在一起。兄弟失去了他的妹妹，丈夫失去了他的妻子，母亲失去了她的孩子。一切都笼罩在密布的黑暗之中，没有人能看到任何东西，只有源源不断从附近高山的山顶滚滚而来的火球。大地在颤抖，房子开始摇动，直至倒塌，海洋也像受到惊吓一样开始向大地反扑；空气变得厚重，充满粉尘；然后，在最巨大、可怕的声音之中，一阵由石头、岩浆、浮石形成的滚滚洪流，倾泻在这座城镇之上，并将它永远地淹没了！

这里的居民们死去了，都保持着这场灾难发生时候他们的样子——客人们都还在他们的宴会厅里，新娘在她们的房间中，士兵在他们的岗哨上，囚犯在他们的地牢中，小偷正在偷窃东西，少女在照着镜子，奴隶们在喷泉旁边，商人在商店里，学生正看着他们的书。一些人曾试图逃走，但他们眼前却一片茫然，在那么长时间深深的黑暗之中，不会再有更厚重的阴影降临到他们面前；有许多人在逃亡的路上就被岩浆淹没了。几天之后，人们从周围的地方来到这里，他们眼前看到的只有一片黑色的、平坦的、冒着烟的平原，向大海倾斜着，上面覆盖着厚厚的灰烬！它的下面，在很深的下面，有成千上万的人沉睡着，"在他们醒着的时候沉睡过去，"他们所有的浮华和虚荣、轻浮和欢乐，还有奢侈的生活，都与他们一起埋葬。

这发生在公元79年的8月23日；而这个被突然淹没的小镇的名字是庞贝（或者庞培）。1617年以后，好奇的人们开始挖掘这里。瞧！他们发现的城市的样子和它被淹没的时候一模一样。房子仍矗立在那里，图画仍然鲜亮，人们的尸体仍然像很久以前，这场灾难突然夺去他们主人性命的时候一样，站立在原地！

桌子上仍然留下了杯子的痕迹；囚犯仍然戴着脚镣、锁链和手铐；守财奴仍然手里紧握着他收集来的硬币；祭司仍跪拜在他们神明的神圣图像之下，从这些神明那里他们得到回应，欺骗他们的信众。这里还有祭坛，上面还覆盖着已经干涸的血液；马厩里仍然存放着祭祀用的贡品；大厅里还存留有一些神秘的符号画。

对这里的研究仍在继续，新的奇迹每天都会见诸天日，我们很快就对一座处于一世纪基督教时代的罗马城镇拥有几乎完美的见解，就好像我们走过那里的街道，闲散地在喷泉旁边的躺椅上闲聊一样。庞贝古城就像一个代表着已经灭绝的文明的幽灵，出现在我们面前。

——选自《艺术画报》

Lesson 63　THE SOUTH-WEST MONSOON IN CEYLON
第六十三课　锡兰的西南季风

May is signalized by the great event of the change of the monsoon, and all the grand phenomena which accompany its approach. It is difficult for one who has not resided in the tropics to comprehend the feeling of enjoyment which accompanies these periodical commotions of the atmosphere. In Europe they would be fraught with annoyance, but in Ceylon they are welcomed with a relish proportionate to the monotony they dispel.

Long before the wished-for period arrives, the verdure produced by the previous rains becomes almost obliterated by the burning droughts of March and April. The deciduous trees shed their foliage, the plants cease to put forth fresh leaves, and all vegetable life languishes under the unwholesome heat. The grass withers on the baked and cloven earth, and red dust settles on the branches and thirsty brushwood.

The insects, deprived of their accustomed food, disappear under ground, or hide beneath the decaying bark; the water-beetles bury themselves in the hardened mud of the pools; and the snails retire into the crevices of the rocks or the hollows among the roots of the trees. Butterflies are no longer seen hovering over the flowers; the birds appear fewer and less joyous; and the wild animals and crocodiles, driven by the drought from their accustomed retreats, wander through the jungle, or even venture to approach the village wells in search of water. Man equally languishes under the general exhaustion, ordinary exertion becomes distasteful, and the Singalese, although inured to the climate, move with lassitude and reluctance.

Meanwhile the air becomes loaded to saturation with aqueous vapour, drawn up by the augmented force of evaporation acting vigorously over land and sea: the sky, instead of its brilliant blue, assumes the sullen tint of lead; and not a breath disturbs the motionless rest of the clouds that hang on the lower range of the hills. At length, generally about the middle of the month, but frequently earlier, the sultry suspense is broken by the arrival of the wished-for change. The sun has by this time nearly attained his greatest northern declination, and created a torrid heat throughout the lands of Southern Asia and the peninsula of India.

The air, lightened by its high temperature and such watery vapour as it may contain, rises into loftier regions, and is replaced by in-draughts from the neighbouring sea; and thus a tendency is gradually given to the formation of a current bringing up from the south the warm humid air of the equator. The wind, therefore, which reaches Ceylon comes laden with moisture, taken up in its passage across the great Indian Ocean. As the monsoon draws near, the days become more overcast and hot, banks of clouds rise over the ocean to the west, and in the twilight the eye is attracted by the peculiar whiteness of the sea-birds that sweep along the strand to seize the objects flung on shore by the rising surf.

At last the sudden lightnings flash among the hills and sheet among the clouds that overhang the sea, and with a crash of thunder the monsoon bursts over the thirsty land, not in showers or partial torrents, but in a wide deluge, that in the course of a few hours overtops the river banks and spreads in inundations over every level plain. The rain at these periods excites the astonishment of a European. It descends in almost continuous streams, so close and dense that the level ground, unable to absorb it sufficiently fast, is covered with one uniform sheet of water; and down the sides of declivities it rushes in a volume that wears channels in the surface. For hours together, the noise of the torrent, as it beats upon the trees and bursts upon the roofs, flowing thence in rivulets along the ground, occasions an uproar that drowns the ordinary voice, and renders sleep impossible.

This violence, however, seldom lasts more than an hour or two, and gradually abates after intermittent paroxysms, and a serenely clear sky supervenes. For some days heavy showers continue to fall at intervals in the forenoon; and the evenings which follow are embellished by sunsets of the most gorgeous splendour, lighting the fragments of clouds that survive the recent storm.

The extreme heat of the previous month becomes modified in June; the winds continue steadily to blow from the southwest, and frequent showers, accompanied by lightning and thunder, serve still further to diffuse coolness throughout the atmosphere and verdure over the earth. So instantaneous is the response of nature to the influence of returning moisture, that in a single day, and almost between sunset and dawn, the green hue of reviving vegetation begins to tint the saturated ground.

In ponds from which, but a week before, the wind blew clouds of sandy dust, the peasantry may now be seen catching the reanimated fish; and tank-shells and water-beetles revive and wander over the submerged sedges. The electricity of the air stimulates the vegetation of the trees; and scarcely a week elapses before the plants are covered with the larvae of butterflies, the forest is murmuring with the hum of insects, and the air is harmonious with the voice of birds.

—J. Emerson Tennent

Words

aqueous, *watery*.
augmented, *increased*.
crevices, *fissures*.
declivities, *slopes*.
exhaustion, *weariness*.
instantaneous, *immediate*.

intermittent, *at intervals*.
inundations, *floods*.
languishes, *droops*.
larvae, *new-hatched young*.
lassitude, *lafiguor*.
modified, *lessened*.

moisture, *dampness*.

monotony, *sameness*.

obliterated, *effaced*.

paroxysms, *fits*.

phenomena, *appearances*.

saturation, *fulness*.

signalized, *distinguished*.

stimulates, *excites*.

submerged, *immersed*.

suspense, *delay*.

temperature, *degree of heat*.

vegetation, *plant life*.

Questions

What is the monsoon? When does its change occur in Ceylon? How are the commotions of the atmosphere which accompany the change regarded? In what state is vegetable nature before it arrives? What effect has the drought upon the animal creation? What are the first indications of the approaching change? Whence does the wind derive its moisture? By what is the arrival of the monsoon accompanied? What is remarkable about the rain? How soon do its effects appear in nature?

AMBITION CLAD IN HUMILITY.

'Tis a common proof

That lowliness is young Ambition's ladder,

Whereto the climber upward turns his face;

But, when he once attains the utmost round,

He then unto the ladder turns his back,

Looks in the clouds, scorning the base degrees,

By which he did ascend.

—Shakespeare

5月以季风的变化这一重大事件作为标志。随季风而来的，还有众多壮观现象。一个不居住在热带的人很难理解这种大气的间歇性运动所带来的巨大喜悦感受。在欧洲，人们常充满烦恼，但在锡兰，人们会特别欢欣地迎接这种单调气候的终结。

在这期盼已久的时刻到来之前，以往雨水带来的碧绿色彩已经几乎被三四月灼人的干旱抹去了。落叶林落下叶子，植被停止长出新叶，所有植物都在这恼人的热量之下枯萎。在干燥、裂开的土地上，草也都凋零了，热火在树枝和干渴的草丛定居了下来。

没有了熟悉的食物，昆虫也从地面消失了，或者藏匿于腐烂的树皮之下。甲壳虫藏身于池塘已坚硬的淤泥之下。蜗牛则躲在岩石的裂缝或树根之间的空洞里。人们再也见不到蝴蝶在花朵间徘徊，鸟也没有之前那么欢快了。野兽和鳄鱼，在它们习惯的聚居地受到干旱侵扰之后，被迫在丛林里游荡，甚至会冒险到人类村落的井里去寻找水源。人类在普遍的困倦之下也变得憔悴，原本普通的动作也变得让人讨厌。虽然习惯了这种气候，但锡兰人还是很厌烦地忍耐着。

同时，空气变得湿润得充满了水蒸气，在陆地和海洋之上开始产生强有力的蒸发作用。天空不再是它明亮的蓝色，而呈现出阴郁的铅色；什么也不会搅乱静止在较低山脉之上的云层。最后，一般大约在本月中旬，但有时频繁提前，人们期盼已久的气候变化终于打破了闷热。此时，太阳几乎达到了它最大的北方偏角，并在整个亚洲南部地区和印度半岛营造出一种酷热的气候。

空气受到高温和水蒸气的作用，上升到更高的地区，取而代之的是从附近海域吹来的气流。因此，这里逐渐形成了来自于南方赤道的温暖潮湿的空气。到达锡兰的风饱含水分，因为此前它穿越了广阔的印度洋。当季风临近，天变得更加阴沉和闷热。黄昏时候，大批海鸟为了抓住海浪抛出的鱼虾而掠过海面。这一奇特景观大大地吸引了人们的目光。

最后，突然的闪电在山丘之间咆哮，云朵悬在海面上，雷声鼎沸之后，季风爆发在这片焦渴的土地上，不是瓢泼大雨或湍急奔流，而是以洪水之势，在几个小时的过程中，高于河岸，蔓延泛滥过的每一片平原。此时，这样的大雨也惊醒了欧洲。它几乎连续降落，在平原地带如此密集地降落。大地无法足够快地吸收这些水分而形成一条水渠，而沿着下坡，水渠在土壤表面冲刷出了一条水道。一连几个小时，洪流的噪声沿着地面流淌的溪流，在树木和屋顶之上劈啪作响。整个场面现出一片哗然，淹没了普通的声音，使睡眠变得不可能。

然而，这种狂风暴雨很少持续超过一到两个小时，并在间歇性的发作中逐渐消退。此时，一片宁静晴朗的天空会意外出现。几天时间之内，几场瓢泼大雨会继续在中午之前的时间间隔出现，而接下来的夜晚则装饰有最华丽的日落，照亮大雨留下的云朵的碎片。

上个月的极端闷热，在6月得到了改观；风持续从西南方向吹来，还有频繁的阵雨伴随着电闪雷鸣，这些都进一步在大气中扩散了新鲜凉爽的空气。所以，自然对水分回升带来影响的反应是如此瞬间完成的。在一天之内，几乎在黄昏和黎明之间，植被恢复的绿色色调开始使地面的色彩饱和。

风带着沙尘吹散云朵，在一个星期之前还很萧条的池塘中，现在可以看到农民们又在捕捉那些恢复活力的鱼。贝壳和水甲虫也复原了，在水下的莎草中漫步。空气中的电刺激的着树木，一个星期还没有结束，植物就都覆盖上了蝴蝶的幼虫，森林遍布昆虫的嗡嗡声，空气与鸟鸣也和谐统一。

——J·艾默生·坦南特

Lesson 64　THE SEVEN AGES OF MAN
第六十四课　人生七阶

All the world's a stage,
And all the men and women merely players:
They have their exits and their entrances;
And one man in his time plays many parts,
His acts being seven ages. At first the infant,
Mewling and puking in the nurse's arms.
And then the whining school-boy, with his satchel
And shining morning face, creeping like snail
Unwillingly to school. And then the lover,
Sighing like furnace, with a woful ballad
Made to his mistress' eyebrow. Then a soldier,
Full of strange oaths, and bearded like the pard;
Jealous in honour, sudden and quick in quarrel,
Seeking the bubble reputation
Even in the cannon's mouth. And then the justice,
In fair round belly with good capon lined,
With eyes severe and beard of formal cut,
Full of wise saws and modern instances;
And so he plays his part. The sixth age shifts
Into the lean and slippered pantaloon,
With spectacles on nose and pouch on side,
His youthful hose, well saved, a world too wide
For his shrunk shank; and his big manly voice,
Turning again toward childish treble, pipes
And whistles in his sound. Last scene of all,
That ends this strange eventful history,
Is second childishness, and mere oblivion;
Sans teeth, sans eyes, sans taste, sans everything.

—Shakespeare—As You Like It.

Words

bubble, *empty*.
entrances, *in-comings*.

eventful, *changeful*.
exits, *out-goings*.

instances, *examples*.
jealous, *watchful*.
mewling, *squalling*.
oblivion, *forgetfulness*.
reputation, *fame*.
satchel, *school-bag*.

shrunk, *shriveled*.
spectacles, *glasses*.
unwillingly, *reluctantly*.
whining, *peevish*.
woful, *melancholy*.

☆ ☆ ☆ ☆ ☆ ☆ ☆ ☆ ☆ ☆ ☆ ☆ ☆ ☆ ☆ ☆ ☆ ☆ ☆ ☆

全世界是一个大舞台，所有的男男女女不过是一些演员；
他们都有下场的时候，也有上场的时候。
一个人的一生中扮演着好几个角色，他的表演可以分为七个时期。
最初是婴儿，在保姆的怀中啼哭呕吐。
然后是背着书包、满面红光的学童，
像蜗牛一样慢腾腾地拖着脚步，不情愿地呜咽着去学堂。
然后是情人，像炉灶一样叹着气，
写了一首悲哀的诗歌赞美他恋人的眉毛。
然后是一个军人，满口发着古怪的誓，胡须长得像豹子一样，
爱惜着名誉，动不动就要打架，在炮口上寻求着泡沫一样的声名。
然后是法官，胖胖圆圆的肚子塞满了阉鸡，凛然的眼光，
整洁的胡须，满嘴都是格言和老生常谈；他这样扮演他的一个角色。
第六个时期变成了精瘦的穿着拖鞋的年迈老叟，
鼻子上架着眼镜，腰边悬着钱袋；
他年轻时候节省下来的长裤子套在他皱瘪的小腿上显得宽大异常；
他那朗朗的男子的口音又变成了孩子似的尖声，像是吹着风笛和哨子。
终结着这段古怪多事的历史的最后一场，
是孩提时代的再现，全然的遗忘，
没有牙齿，没有眼睛，没有口味，没有一切。

——莎士比亚《皆大欢喜》

Lesson 65   LIFE IN NORMAN ENGLAND
第六十五课　诺曼时代的英国生活

The tall frowning keep and solid walls of the great stone castles, in which the Norman barons lived, betokened an age of violence and suspicion. Beauty gave way to the needs of safety. Girdled with its green and slimy ditch, round the inner edge of which ran a parapeted wall pierced along the top with shot-holes, stood the buildings, spreading often over many acres.

If an enemy managed to cross the moat and force the gateway, in spite of a portcullis crashing from above, and melted lead pouring in burning streams from the perforated top of the rounded arch, but little of his work was yet done; for the keep lifted its huge angular block of masonry within the inner bailey or court-yard, and from the narrow chinks in its ten-foot wall rained a sharp incessant shower of arrows, sweeping all approaches to the high and narrow stair, by which alone access could be had to its interior.

These loop-holes were the only windows, except in the topmost story, where the chieftain, like a vulture in his rocky nest, watched all the surrounding country. The day of splendid oriels had not yet come in castle architecture.

Thus a baron in his keep could defy, and often did defy, the king upon his throne. Under his roof, eating daily at his board, lived a throng of armed retainers; and around his castle lay farms tilled by martial franklins, who at his call laid aside their implements of husbandry, took up the sword and spear, which they could wield with equal skill, and marched beneath his banner to the war.

With robe ungirt and head uncovered each tenant had done homage and sworn an oath of fealty, placing his joined hands between those of the sitting baron, and humbly saying as he knelt, "I become your man from this day forward, of life and limb and of earthly worship; and unto you I shall be true and faithful, and bear to you faith for the tenements that I claim to hold of you, saving the faith that I owe unto our sovereign lord the king." A kiss from the baron completed the ceremony.

The furniture of a Norman keep was not unlike that of an English house. There was richer ornament—more elaborate carving. A *faldestol*, the original of our arm-chair, spread its drapery and cushions for the chieftain in his lounging moods. His bed now boasted curtains and a roof, although, like the English lord, he still lay only upon straw. Chimneys tunnelled the thick walls, and the cupboards glittered with glass and silver. Horn lanterns and the old spiked candlesticks lit up his evening hours, when the chess-board arrayed its clumsy men, carved out of walrus-tusk, then commonly called whale's-bone. But the baron had an unpleasant trick of breaking the chessboard on his opponent's head, when he found himself checkmated; which somewhat marred said opponent's enjoyment of the game. Dice of horn and bone emptied many a purse

PREPARING
FOR THE CHASR

in Norman England. Tables and draughts were also sometimes played.

Dances and music whiled away the long winter nights; and on summer evenings the castle court-yards resounded with the noise of foot-ball, *kayles* (a sort of ninepins), wrestling, boxing, leaping, and the fierce joys of the bull-bait. But out of doors, when no fighting was on hand, the hound, the hawk, and the lance attracted the best energies and skill of the Norman gentleman.

Rousing the forest-game with dogs, they shot at it with barbed and feathered arrows. A field of ripening corn never turned the chase aside: it was one privilege of a feudal baron to ride as ho pleased over his tenants' crops, and another to quarter his insolent hunting-train in the farm-houses which pleased him best! The elaborate details of *woodcraft* became an important part of a noble boy's education; for the numerous bugle calls and the scientific dissection of a dead stag took many seasons to learn.

After the Conquest, to kill a deer or own a hawk came more than ever to be regarded as the special privilege of the aristocracy. The hawk, daintily dressed, as befitted the companion of nobility, with his head wrapped in an embroidered hood, and a peal of silver bells tinkling from his rough legs, sat in state, bound with leathern jesses to the wrist, which was protected by a thick glove. The ladies and the clergy loved him. By many a mere the abbots ambled on their ponies over the swampy soil, and sweet shrill voices cheered the long-winged hawk, as he darted off in pursuit of the soaring quarry.

The author of "Ivanhoe," and kindred pens, have made the tournament a picture familiar to all readers of romance. It therefore needs no long description here. It was held in honour of some great event—a coronation, wedding, or victory. Having practised well during squirehood at the quintain, the knight, clad in full armour, with visor barred and the colours of his lady on crest and scarf, rode into the lists, for which some level green was chosen and surrounded with a palisade.

For days before, his shield had been hanging in a neighbouring church, as a sign of his intention to compete in this great game of chivalry. If any stain lay on his knighthood, a lady, by touching the suspended shield with a wand, could debar him from a share in the jousting. And if, when he had entered the lists, he was rude to a lady, or broke in any way the etiquette of the tilt-yard, he was beaten from the lists with the ash wood lances of the knights.

The simple joust was the shock of two knights, who galloped with levelled spears at each other, aiming at breast of head, with the object either of unhorsing the antagonist, or, if he sat his charger well, of splintering the lance upon his helmet or his shield. The mellay hurled together, at the dropping of the prince's baton, two parties of knights, who hacked away at each other with axe and mace and sword, often gashing limbs and breaking bones in the wild excitement of the fray. Bright eyes glanced from the surrounding galleries upon the brutal sport; and when the victor, with broken plume, and dusty, battered, red-splashed armour, dragged his weary or wounded limbs to the footstool of the beauty who presided as Queen over the festival, her white hands decorated him with the meed of his achievements.

The Normans probably dined at nine in the morning. When they rose they took a light meal; and ate something also after their day's work, immediately before going to bed. Goose and garlic formed a favourite dish. Their cookery was more elaborate, and, in comparison, more delicate, than the preparations for an English feed; but the character for temperance, which they brought with them from the Continent, soon vanished.

The poorer classes hardly ever ate flesh, living principally on bread, butter, and cheese;—a social fact which seems to underlie that usage of our tongue by which the living animals in field or stall bore English names—ox, sheep, calf, pig, deer; while their flesh, promoted to Norman dishes, rejoiced in names of French origin—beef, mutton, veal, pork, venison. Round cakes, piously marked with a cross, piled the tables, on which pastry of various kinds also appeared. In good houses cups of glass held the wine, which was borne from the cellar below in jugs.

Squatted around the door or on the stair leading to the Norman dining-hall, which was often on an upper floor, was a crowd of beggars or lickers, who grew so insolent in the days of Rufus, that ushers, armed with rods, were posted outside to beat back the noisy throng, who thought little of snatching the dishes as the cooks carried them to table!

The juggler, who under the Normans filled the place of the English gleeman, tumbled, sang, and balanced knives in the hall; or out in the bailey of an afternoon displayed the acquirements of his trained monkey or bear. The fool, too, clad in coloured patch-work, cracked his ribald jokes and shook his cap and bells at the elbow of roaring barons, when the board was spread and the circles of the wine began.

While knights hunted in the greenwood or tilted in the lists and jugglers tumbled in the noisy hall, the monk in the quiet Scriptorium compiled chronicles of passing events, copied valuable manuscripts, and painted rich borders and brilliant initials on every page. These illuminations form a valuable set of materials for our pictures of life in the Middle Ages.

Monasteries served many useful purposes at the time of which I write. Besides their manifest value as centres of study and literary work, they gave alms to the poor, a supper and a bed to travellers; their tenants were better off and better treated than the tenants of the nobles; the monks could store grain, grow apples, and cultivate their flower-beds with little risk of injury from war, because they had spiritual thunders at their call, which awed even the most reckless of the soldiery into a respect for sacred property.

Splendid structures those monasteries generally were, since that vivid taste for architecture which the Norman possessed in a high degree, and which could not find room for its display in the naked strength of the solid keep, lavished its entire energy and grace upon buildings lying in the safe shadow of the Cross. Nor was architectural taste the only reason for their magnificence. Since they were nearly all erected as offerings to Heaven, the religion of the age impelled the pious builders to spare no cost in decorating the exterior with fret-work and sculpture of Caen stone, the interior with gilded cornices and windows of painted glass.

As schools, too, the monasteries did no trifling service to society in the Middle Ages. In addition to their influence as great centres of learning, English law had enjoined every mass-priest to keep a school in his parish church, where all the young committed to his care might be instructed. This custom continued long after the Norman Conquest. In the Trinity College Psalter we have a picture of a Norman school, where the pupils sit in a circular row around the master as he lectures to them from a long roll of manuscript. Two writers sit by the desk, busy with copies resembling that which the teacher holds.

The youth of the middle classes, destined for the cloister or the merchant's stall, chiefly thronged these schools. The aristocracy cared little for book-learning. Very few indeed of the barons could read or write. But all could ride, fence, tilt, play, and carve extremely well; for to these accomplishments many years of pagehood and squirehood were given.

The only Norman coin we have is the silver penny. Round halfpence and farthings were probably issued. As in Old English days, the gold was foreign. In the reign of the Conqueror, and for some time afterwards, tax-collectors and merchants reckoned money after the English fashion.

—W. F. Collier

Words

aristocracy, *nobility*.
betokened, *indicated*.
chronicles, *annals*.
committed, *intrusted*.
cornices, *mouldings*.
decorated, *adorned*.

destined, *intended*.
dissection, *cutting up*.
elaborate, *minute*.
excitement, *commotion*.
exterior, *outside*.
familiar, *well known*.

fealty, *allegiance*.
husbandry, *agriculture*.
illuminations, *illustrations*.
lavished, *squandered*.
managed, *contrived*.
manifest, *evident*.
manuscripts, *writings*.
meed, *reward*.
mere, *lake*.
palisade, *fence*.
perforated, *pierced*.
privilege, *right*.
reckless, *heedless*.

reckoned, *calculated*.
rejoiced, *gloried*.
resounded, *echoed*.
retainers, *adherents*.
ribald, *vulgar*.
scientific, *systematic*.
snatching, *seizing*.
suspended, *up-hung*.
temperance, *abstinence*.
tenements, *lands and houses*.
tournament, *tilt*.
vanished, *disappeared*.

Questions

What did the structure of Norman castles betoken? Flow were they protected from attacks? What was the oath of fealty? How was a Norman keep furnished? In what out-door sports did the Normans engage? On what occasions were tournaments held? What was the difference between a joust and a *mellay*? What social fact underlies the distinction between *ox*, *sheep*, &c., and *beef*, *mutton*, &c.? Who were the jugglers? What useful purposes did monasteries serve in those times? What is the difference in architecture between the castles and the monasteries? How is this to be explained? What classes of society were taught in the schools of the Middle Ages? Why not the aristocracy? What is the only Norman coin we have? How was money reckoned after the Norman Conquest?

诺曼时代的男爵们都住在被多个堡垒和坚实的墙壁所包围起来的城堡之中，这些都能反应出当时那个时代的暴力和疑心现象，优美让步于安全的需要。城堡被绿色粘滑的沟渠所围绕，城堡边缘部分带有栏杆的墙体顶端，常常有射击口，而城堡中心则矗立着男爵门的楼宇，常常可以蔓延数英亩。

如果敌人要想设法越过护城河并闯入城门，尽管铁闸门会从上方掉下来，融进其中的铅水也会从其上圆形拱顶之中的孔里滚烫地奔涌而下，但是这些只是城堡内部人们防御措施的一点点；城内的人还会举起城壁上或者院子内的巨大石头，在城堡狭窄而且粗糙的高10英尺的墙上面，下起密密麻麻的箭雨，它们将撒满一切可以登上那些堡垒又高又狭窄的台阶，而这些台阶，是通往城堡内部的唯一途径。

这些漏洞就是所谓的窗户，除了首领所在的最高的地方，那样子就像一只在用石头筑成的巢穴里的秃鹫，观察着各个环绕其周围的城邦。那时华丽的窗户风格并没有在城堡建筑里面出现。

因此男爵在他的领地里可以公然藐视坐拥王位的国王，而这些男爵们确实也是这样做的。在他的屋檐下，在他自己的餐桌上进食，在有武装的侍卫身边生活；在他城堡的周围都是一些有钱的地主耕种的田地。他们听从他的命令，来到这里进行耕作，他们可以同样地挥舞着枪和矛，并且在竖着他的旗帜的队伍中行军参加战争。

穿着不受束缚的长袍，头顶也不戴着帽子，每一个佃户都将进行宣誓和祷告，来展示他们的忠诚。男爵坐在他们面前，他们伸出自己的双手，并且跪着说一些谦卑的话："我从此成为您的仆人。我的生命肢体以及我全部的尊重都将奉献给您，我会对您保持真诚和忠诚。我会感恩像神一样的国王带给我的一切。"最后男爵的一吻将结束这个仪式。

诺曼人的家具同英格兰人的没有什么不同。他们的家具有着更奢华的装饰品——更为精致的雕刻品。当这些贵族闲暇慵懒之时，一个跪拜台，我们现在的扶手椅的最初样貌，会为他们伸展开自己的帐幔和布垫。我们如今的床因为有帘子和床顶而变得更加华丽了，但是在当时，英格兰的贵族们依然还是只能睡在稻草之上。烟囱建造在坚实的墙上，四处都闪耀着玻璃和银质的光泽。灯和尖尖的蜡烛点亮了他们的夜晚时光，人们笨拙地将海象的牙齿制成的象棋排列在一起，在那时，海象牙一般被叫作"鲸的骨骼"。但是感觉自己即将失败时，伯爵就会有一个不怎么优雅的伎俩，比如将棋桌掀翻，砸到对手的头上。如果一些东西被损坏了，这就是对手的过错。角质和骨质的骰子，基本清光了许多诺曼时代英国人的钱包。桌游和汇票有时也会成为他们的消遣工具。

舞蹈和音乐可以消磨冬天漫长的夜晚，而在夏天的晚上，城堡的庭院里，会回响着球场传来的嘈杂声。这里进行着Kayles（一种九柱球系的木柱）、摔跤、拳击、跳远比赛，或者是刺激的斗牛游戏。但是在屋外，最近没有什么战争的话，猎犬、鹰还有长矛，能最大地吸引诺曼时代绅士们的能量和技术。

和自己的猎犬在森林中游玩，他们会射出带有刺和羽毛的箭头。一片成熟的玉米地是游玩的最佳场所，在那个时代，封建社会的爵士们在地主的田地上快乐地游玩骑行是他们的一个特权。其他的时候，他们的霸道心理让他们选择在最使他满意的农屋里住下。精细的木工技术成为让孩子走向绅士教育的一个重要部分，而对大量的号角吹奏的练习和对一只公鹿尸体的科学解剖需要更长的时间去学习。

在完成这些之后，能够杀死一头鹿或者拥有一只属于自己的鹰，才能真正算得上拥有了贵族般的特权。贵族们的鹰穿着都十分讲究，它的头上都会戴一个刺绣的头巾，粗糙双腿上的铃铛发出叮叮的响声。它的坐姿十分端庄，在鹰爪处绑着被一个厚厚套子保护着的皮质脚带。女士和神职人员都爱戴这样的贵族。当修道院的院长骑着他步履缓慢的小马，途经沼泽的泥塘经过此地时，当他追逐着他翱翔的猎物疾驰而去之时，会发出一声尖叫来呼唤他长翅的鹰。

《劫后英雄传》的作者通过他的笔，给那些渴望浪漫的读者们一次亲身体验的机会。因此，这里就不需要更长的描述了。为了纪念一些重大的事件，人们会举行加冕典礼、婚礼或胜利宴会。在乡绅的领地里，骑士们练好打靶的本领，他们全副武装，头上戴着遮阳板，而他们的夫人则戴着帽子和围巾。骑士们在队列中骑行，在这中间，人们挑出一些平坦的绿地，并在周围围上一圈栅栏。

几天之前，骑士们的护盾被挂在一个邻近的教堂，作为这些人参加这个伟大的骑士游戏的象征。如果某一个人的骑士身份有任何污点的话，一位女士会用一根权杖，碰触一下他挂在空中的盾牌，如此一来，他就无权再参加这次比武。而当一个人已经进入到比武的名单之中，他如果对一位女士粗鲁或打破了任何比武场的礼仪，他也会被骑士的灰木枪剔除出这次比武的名单。

在简单的枪术比赛之中，两名骑士向着对方互相飞奔，用长矛刺向对方的帽檐。如果其中一方能够将对方击落下马，或者一方能够在自己的战马上保持不动，而将自己的长矛刺中了对方的头盔或者盾牌，他就胜利了。人们会欢呼着向他们扔下礼物，其中夹杂着王子的权杖。两方的骑士用自己的斧子、狼牙棒或者剑，砍向自己的对手。通常在这种斗争的兴奋之中，会有一方的四肢被砍下，或者骨头被砍断。在这场野蛮的运动之中，骑士们明亮的眼睛扫视了一眼周围的观众席；当胜利者的羽毛已经被折断，尘土飞扬，破旧的盔甲染满了鲜血，拖着疲惫、受伤的躯体，走向作为这一节日的王后的女主持的脚凳时，她雪白的手会为他的成就再添加一分装饰。

诺曼时代的人们，大概在早上9点吃饭。当他们起床时，他们会稍微吃些东西；一天的工作之后，在上床睡觉之前，他们也会吃些东西。鹅肉和大蒜做成了一道当时人们最喜欢的菜。与一顿英国饭菜相比，他们的烹饪更复杂，也更加精致；但他们从欧洲大陆带来的脾气和性格很快就消失了。

贫穷的阶层几乎不吃肉，主要靠面包、黄油和奶酪为食，这是一种社会事实，似乎为我们给这些在农场里或者畜栏中的动物们冠以属于它们的英文名字奠定了基础——牛、羊、猪、鹿；而当它们的肉出现在诺曼人的食物之中时，在法国这个最初食用这些食物的地方，它们被称为——牛肉、羊肉、猪肉、鹿肉。人们虔诚地标记有一个十字叉的圆饼，作为桌上的糕点，也以各种形式出现在各地。在富裕一点的家庭里，玻璃杯中都盛满了葡萄酒，这是从地窖下面的酒壶里被倒上来的。

一群乞丐或要饭的人会蹲在门外，或在通往位于上一层的餐厅的楼梯之上。这些鲁弗斯时代的乞丐是如此无礼。因此，一些手里拿着木棍的守卫站在屋子外面。当厨师端着盘子走到餐桌旁上菜，而这些嘈杂的乞丐抢食一点零星的菜品时，守卫们将他们打散！

玩杂耍的人在诺曼时代填满了英国游吟诗人的诗篇。他们打滚、唱歌，在大厅里耍着刀子；或者在下午时分，在城堡之外，展示他们训练有素的猴子或熊。同时，当观众的坐席已经准备好，人们开始喝酒的时候，头戴彩色补丁帽子的小丑会讲着一些语言粗俗的笑话，在不停大笑的男爵面前摇着他的帽子和钟。

当骑士们在绿林中打猎或者列队进行比武，而玩杂耍的人在嘈杂的大厅中表演时，和尚们则在安静的写字间里将过去的事件编译成编年史，复制成珍贵的手稿，并在每一页上都画上丰富的边线和辉煌的字母。这些手稿成为了我们了解中世纪生活的极有价值的图片材料。

在我描述的那个时代，修道院担负起了众多有价值的功能。除了作为研究和文化的中心，他们还向穷人进行施舍，为旅行者提供晚餐和住处；他们的佃户们，比起贵族们的佃户，得到了许多更好的待遇；僧侣们可以储存粮食，种植苹果，培育他们的小小花坛，而免受战争的伤害，因为他们的职业包含了一种精神的诉求，这使即使最鲁莽的士兵们也产生了对这份神圣职业的尊重。

这些寺院一般都拥有极其壮观的建筑，因为诺曼人对建筑拥有很高水准的品位，因此他们不允许自己的建筑物被赤裸裸的展示为坚硬的堡垒，而是将他们的全部技巧和优雅，都运用在十字架安全阴影之下的建筑物之中。当然，他们的品位也不是这些宏伟建筑产生的唯一原因。因为几乎他们所有的建筑物，都是竖立向天堂的祭祀物。那个时代的宗教也推动了这些虔诚的建设者，不遗余力地将这些建筑的外观用回纹细工来装饰，用卡昂石来雕塑，而这些建筑物的内饰，则装饰有镀金的飞檐和彩绘的玻璃窗。

同时，作为学校，中世纪的寺院并没有琐碎的社会服务。除了作为很大的学习中心之外，英国的法律规定每一个大祭司都应该在他的教区拥有一所教会学校，在那里，所有受到他关心的年轻人都能够得到指导。这一习俗在诺曼征服之后维持了很长一段时间。在圣三一学院诗篇里，我们了解了一所诺曼时代学校的场景。在那里，学生们围坐成圆形的一排，牧师手中拿着长卷的手稿，对他们讲课。两个作家会坐在桌子旁边，忙着记录下老师讲授的一切。

中产阶级的青年人，注定了将来会在修道院或商人的摊位上供职，他们是这些学校里的主要学习者。贵族很少关心学习。事实上，很少有贵族能读书或写字。但所有贵族都能骑马、击剑、战斗或者玩耍，并且他们能极好地进行雕刻；这些成就早已确定了他们今后多年的听差身份和随从身份。

我们了解的唯一的诺曼时代的硬币是银便士硬币。圆形的半便士和法新（四分之一便士）在当时流通。在古代英国，黄金是外国的钱币。在征服者的统治之下，很久之后，税吏和商人才将钱币认定为英国的习俗。

——W. F. 科利尔

Lesson 66　SIR ROGER DE COVERLET

第六十六课　罗杰·德·克里夫爵士

Having often received an invitation from my friend Sir Roger de Coverley to pass away a month with him in the country, I last week accompanied him thither, and am settled with him for some time at his country house, where I intend to form several of my ensuing speculations. Sir Roger, who is very well acquainted with my humour, lets me rise and go to bed when I please, dine at his own table or in my chamber as I think fit, sit still and say nothing without bidding me be merry......

I am the more at ease in Sir Roger's family, because it consists of sober and staid persons; for as the knight is the best master in the world, he seldom changes his servants; and as he is beloved by all about him, his servants never care for leaving him: by this means his domestics are all in years, and grown old with their master. You would take his *valet-de-chambre* for his brother, his butler is gray-headed, his groom is one of the gravest men that I have ever seen, and his coachman has the looks of a privy councillor......

I could not but observe with a great deal of pleasure the joy that appeared in the countenances of these ancient domestics, upon my friend's arrival at his country seat. Some of them could not refrain from tears at the sight of their old master; every one of them pressed forward to do something for him, and seemed discouraged if they were not employed.

At the same time, the good old knight, with a mixture of the father and the master of the family, tempered the inquiries after his own affairs with several kind questions relating to themselves. His humanity and good nature engage everybody to him, o that when he is pleasant upon any of them, all his family are in good humour, and none so much so as the person whom he diverts himself with; on the contrary, if he coughs, or betrays any infirmity of old age, it is easy for a stander-by to observe a secret concern in the looks of all his servants......

My chief companion, when Sir Roger is diverting himself in the woods on the fields, is a very venerable man, who is ever with Sir Roger, and has lived at his house in the nature of a chaplain above thirty years. This gentleman is a person of good sense and some learning, of a very regular life and obliging conversation. He heartily loves Sir Roger, and knows that he is very much in the old knight's esteem, so that he lives in the family rather as a relation than as a dependant......

My friend Sir Roger has often told me, with a great deal of mirth, that at his first coming to his estate he found three parts of his house altogether useless: that the best room in it had the reputation of being haunted, and by that means was locked up; that noises had been heard in his long gallery, so that he could not get a servant to enter it after eight o'clock at night; that the door of one of his chambers was nailed up, because there went a story in the family that a butler had formerly hanged himself in it; and that his mother, who lived to a great age, had shut up half the rooms in the house, in which either her husband, a son, or a daughter had died.

The knight, seeing his habitation reduced to so small a compass, and himself in a manner shut out of his own house, upon the death of his mother ordered all the apartments to be flung open, and exorcised by his chaplain, who lay in every room, one after another, and by that means dissipated the fears which had so long reigned in the family......

My friend Sir Roger, being a good Churchman, has beautified the inside of his church with several texts of his own choosing. He has likewise given a handsome pulpit-cloth, and railed in the communion table at his own expense. He has often told me, that at his coming to his estate he found his parishioners very irregular; and that in order to make them kneel and join in the responses, he gave every one of them a hassock and a Common Prayer Book, and at the same time employed an itinerant singing-master to instruct them rightly in the tunes of the psalms, upon which they now very much value themselves.

As Sir Roger is landlord to the whole congregation, he keeps them in very good order, and will suffer nobody in it to sleep besides himself; for if by chance he has been surprised into a short nap at sermon, upon recovering out of it he stands up and looks about him, and if he sees anybody else nodding, he either wakes them himself, or sends his servant to them.

Several other of the old knight's particularities break out upon these occasions. Sometimes he will be lengthening out a verse in the singing-psalms, half a minute after the rest of the congregation have done with it; sometimes, when he is pleased with the matter of his devotion, he pronounces Amen three or four times to the same prayer; and sometimes he stands up when everybody else is kneeling, to count the congregation, or see if any of his tenants are missing.

I was yesterday very much surprised to hear my old friend in the midst of the service, calling out to one John Matthews to mind what he was about, and not disturb the congregation. This John Matthews, it seems, is remarkable for being an idle fellow, and at that time was kicking his heels for his diversion. The authority of the knight, though exerted in that odd manner which accompanies him in all circumstances of life, has a very good effect upon the parish, who are not polite enough to see anything ridiculous in his behaviour; besides that the general good sense and worthiness of his character make his friends observe these little singularities as foils that rather set off than blemish his good qualities.

As soon as the sermon is finished, nobody presumes to stir till Sir Roger is gone out of the church. The knight walks down from his seat in the chancel between a double row of his tenants, that stand bowing to him on each side; and he every now and then inquires how such an one's wife, or mother, or son, or father does, whom he does not see at church; which is understood as a secret reprimand to the person that is absent.

The chaplain has often told me that, upon a catechising day, when Sir Roger has been pleased with a boy that answers well, he has ordered a Bible to be given him next day for his encouragement; and sometimes accompanies it with a flitch of bacon to his mother. Sir Roger has likewise added £5 a year to the clerk's place; and, that he may encourage the young fellows to make themselves perfect in the Church service, has promised, upon the death of the present incumbent, who is very old, to bestow it according to merit.

—Joseph Addison

Words

ancient, *old-fashioned.*
beautified, *ornamented.*
chambers, *apartments.*
coffeepots, *dimensions.*
countenances, *faces.*
devotion, *prayer.*
discouraged, *disappointed.*
dissipated, *dispelled.*
diversion, *amusement.*
domestics, *servants.*
ensuing, *following.*
habitation, *dwelling.*
hassock, *kneeling-stool.*
humanity, *kindness.*
incumbent, *holder.*
infirmity, *weakness.*
inquires, *asks.*

invitation, *request.*
itinerant, *travelling.*
obliging, *courteous.*
observe, *remark.*
particularities, *oddities.*
polite, *polished.*
pronounces, *repeats.*
reprimand, *reproof.*
reputation, *character.*
responses, *answers.*
ridiculous, *absurd.*
speculations, *meditations.*
surprised, *thrown unexpectedly.*
tempered, *mingled.*
venerable, *reverend.*

☆ ☆

　　之前我就经常接到我的朋友罗杰·德·克里夫爵士的邀请，到他在乡间的家与他共住一个月。上周我到那里去陪他，我打算在他乡下的家里完成几个问题的思索。罗杰爵士十分了解我的秉性，允许我随自己意愿起床或入睡，自己选择和他共餐或停留在我自己的房间，我可以静静地坐着，什么也不说，只要我快乐……

　　我呆在罗杰爵士家里感到特别舒服，因为这里都是冷静和稳重的人。作为一位爵士，他是世界上最好的主人，他很少更换他的仆人；他身边的人也都很爱戴他，他的仆人们从来没有想过要离开他。我的意思是，他的佣人都是常年在此工作，并且与他们的主人一起变老。你会认为他的贴身男仆是他的兄弟，他的管家如此老练沉稳，他的男仆是我曾经见过的最严肃认真的人，而他的车夫就像枢密官一样沉稳……

当我的朋友返回到他这个乡下的家时，我能非常愉快地看到，这些老仆人脸上浮现出的快乐的神情。他们中有些人在看到他们年迈的主人时，甚至无法克制住自己的眼泪。他们每个人都急于为他做点什么，如果他们没有什么事情做，他们看上去会特别沮丧。

与此同时，这位善良的老爵士，既是一位父亲，又是一个大家庭的主人，在解决好自己的事情之后，他还要调解许多关乎到家庭中所有人的问题。他会把他善良的本性用到身边所有人身上，当他自己很愉快时，他家里所有的人也都会特别开心，尤其是那个得到他关注的人；相反，如果他咳嗽，或透露出任何年老体弱的痕迹，一个旁观者就特别容易看到，在他所有仆人的神情中都会有一丝不经意的关切……

我最重要的一个朋友，一位非常令人尊敬的人，当罗杰爵士在田野树林中漫步时都会陪伴着他。三十多年以来，他一直以牧师的身份住在罗杰爵士的家里。这位先生拥有良好的修养和丰富学识，生活很规律，常与人促膝长谈。他由衷地爱着罗杰爵士，并且深知他作为爵士的尊严住在他家里，他们之间是一种朋友的关系，而不是一种依赖的关系……

我的朋友罗杰爵士经常欣喜地告诉我，在他第一次到达他的庄园时，他发现他家的三处是完全无用的。据说这里最好的房间有鬼魂萦绕，因此它们被锁了起来；在他的长廊里能一直听到这个声音，让他不得不禁止仆人晚上8点钟之后再进去那里；有一个房间的大门被钉了起来，因为家里流传着一个故事，一个管家曾在里面自缢而亡；而他的母亲活到极大的年纪，关闭了这里一半的房间，因为她的丈夫、一个儿子和一个女儿死在这些房间里了。

罗杰爵士看到他的居所如此缩减，他本身也被关在了自己的房子之外，在他的母亲去世时，他便下令打开所有的房间，让他的牧师在每一个房间驱鬼。他由此消除了长久以来笼罩在整个家庭的恐惧……

我的朋友罗杰爵士也是一位很好的牧师，他自掏腰包用一些文本装饰了教堂内部。同时，他还买了一块漂亮的讲坛布，并用自己的钱给祭坛安上了栏杆。他经常告诉我，进入这栋房子时，他发现这个教区极不寻常；为了让这里的教徒跪下并有所反应，他分发给他们一人一个跪垫和一本祈祷书，并同时雇了一位巡回演唱大师教导他们正确的圣歌曲调。经过这些努力，他们如今已经非常重视自身价值了。

罗杰爵士是整个教会的总领，他保持着他们非常良好的秩序，并且让大家在布道时都不会无精打采。如果他偶然在布道时小憩，当他醒来，他会站起来向四周望望；如果他看到有其他人在低着头睡觉，他要么自己唤醒他，或者让他的仆人去叫醒他。

老爵士的其他一些个性会打破这些场合的沉静。有时，在会众们唱完圣歌之后半分钟，他才唱完最后一节圣歌；有时，当他因为他的奉献而感到愉快时，他会对着同一个祷告者不停地说三到四次阿门；有时，大家都跪下的时候，他会站起来数数会众的人数，要么看看他的会众有没有缺席的。

我的老朋友在昨天的布道之中，在不打扰到其他会众的情况下，叫出约翰·马休斯问问他的心事。我听说此事非常惊讶。这位约翰·马休斯因是一个游手好闲的家伙而著称，当时正踢着自己的脚来分散注意力。爵士的权威虽然以奇怪的方式呈现在他生命的所有情形之中，但对教区有很好的影响，即使教区中的人们看到他可笑的行为时并不是那么礼貌。此外，他性格中的大多数优点，也使他的朋友们将这些小的奇怪的缺点看作是陪衬，而绝不会玷污了他的美好品质。

一旦布道结束，没有人敢在罗杰爵士离开教堂之前离开。爵士从他圣坛旁的座位上站起身，走过他的两排会众之间的小道，他们会在两旁向他鞠躬。他时不时地询问，没有到场的这个人的妻子，或母亲，或孩子，或是他的父亲，最近这个人怎么样；大家理解，这是对缺席之人的隐秘的训斥。

当地的牧师经常告诉我，当罗杰爵士满意地得到一个男孩的回答时，他会在第二天下令给他一本圣经作为给他的鼓励，有时还伴有给他母亲的一块熏肉。同样，罗杰爵士也为神职人员增加了一年5磅的薪水，以此鼓励这些年轻人更好地在教会服务，并承诺在现任郊区牧师逝世之后更好地奉献于神职事业。

——约瑟夫·艾迪生

Lesson 67
OLD ENGLISH AND NORMAN-FRENCH
第六十七课　古英语与诺曼法语

The proud Norman was not successful in imposing his own tongue upon the subjugated nation, when the fatal day of Hastings placed the British realm in the hands of his race. In vain was Norman-French spoken from throne, pulpit, and judgment-seat; in vain did the Norman nobles long disdain to learn the language of the enslaved English. For a time the two tongues lived side by side, though in very different conditions: the one, the language of the master, at court and in the castles of the soldiers who had become noble lords and powerful barons; the other, the language of the conquered, spoken only in the lowly huts of the subjugated people.

The Norman altered and increased the latter, but he could not extirpate it. To defend his conquest, he took possession of the country; and, master of the soil, he erected fortresses and castles, and attempted to introduce new terms. The universe and the firmament, the planets, comets, and meteors, the atmosphere and the seasons, all were impressed with the seal of the conqueror. Hills became mountains, and dales valleys; streams were called rivers, and brooks rivulets; waterfalls changed into cascades, and woods into forests.

The deer, the ox, the calf, the swine, and the sheep appeared on his sumptuous table as venison, beef veal, pork, and mutton. Salmon, sturgeon, lamprey, and trout became known as delicacies; serpents and lizards, squirrels, falcons and herons, cocks and pigeons, stallions and mules, were added to the animal kingdom.

Earls and lords were placed in rank below his dukes and marquises. New titles and dignities, of viscount, baron, and baronet, squire and master, were created; and the mayor presided over the English aldermen and sheriff; the chancellor and the peer, the ambassador and the chamberlain, the general and the admiral headed the list of officers of the government.

The king alone retained his name, but the state and the court became French: the administration was carried on according to the constitution; treaties were concluded by the ministers in their cabinet, and submitted for approval to the sovereign; the privy council was consulted on the affairs of the empire, and loyal subjects sent representatives to parliament. Here the members debated on matters of grave importance, on peace and war, ordered the army and the navy, disposed of the national treasury, contracted debts, and had their sessions and their parties.

At brilliant feasts and splendid tournaments collected the flower of chivalry; magnificent balls, where beauty and delicious music enchanted the assembled nobles, gave new splendour to society, polished the manners and excited the admiration of the ancient inhabitants; who, charmed by such elegance, recognised in their conquerors persons of superior intelligence, admired them, and endeavoured to imitate their fashions.

But the dominion of the Norman did not extend to the home of the Englishman; it stopped at the threshold of his house: there, around the fireside in his kitchen and the hearth in his room, he met his beloved kindred; the bride, the wife, and the husband, sons and daughters, brothers and sisters, tied to each other by love, friendship, and kind feelings, knew nothing dearer than their own sweet home.

The Englishman's flocks, still grazing in his fields and meadows, gave him milk and butter, meat and wool; the herdsman watched them in spring and summer; the ploughman drew his furrows, and used his harrows, and, in harvest, the cart and the flail; the reaper plied his scythe, piled up sheaves and hauled his wheat, oats, and rye to the barn. The waggoner drove his wain, with its wheels, felloes, spokes, and nave; and his team bent heavily under their yoke.

In his trade by land and sea, he still sold and bought; in the store or the shop, the market or the street, he cheapened his goods and had all his dealings, as pedler or weaver, baker or cooper, saddler, miller, or tanner. He lent or borrowed, trusted his neighbour, and with skill and care throve and grew wealthy. Later, when he longed once more for freedom, his warriors took their weapons, their axes, swords, and spears, or their dreaded bow and arrow. They leaped without stirrup into the saddle, and killed with dart and gavelock. At other times they launched their boats and ships, which were still pure English from keel to deck and from the helm or the rudder to the top of the mast, afloat and ashore, with sail or with oar.

As his fathers had done before him in the land of his birth, the Englishman would not merely eat, drink, and sleep, or spend his time in playing the harp and the fiddle, but by walking, riding, fishing, and hunting, he kept young and healthy; while his lady with her children were busy teaching or learning how to read and to write, to sing and to draw. Even needle-work was not forgotten, as their writers say that "by this they shone most in the world."The wisdom of later ages was not known then, but they had their home-spun sayings, which by all mankind are yet looked upon as true wisdom, as: God helps them that help themselves; Lost time is never found again; When sorrow is asleep, wake it not!

Thus the two languages, now contending and then mingling with each other, continued for nearly four hundred years side by side in the British kingdom; the Norman-French, an exotic plant, deprived of its native soil and heat, flourishing for a time, but gradually withering and fading away; the language of the subject, like an indigenous tree, trimmed by the rough storm, grafted in many a branch by an unskilful hand, but still giving shade with its wide-spreading foliage, and bearing flowers and fruit in abundance.

The Normans had conquered the land and the race, but they struggled in vain against the language. It conquered them in its turn, and, by its spirit, converted them into Englishmen. In vain did they haughtily refuse to learn a word of that despised tongue, and indignantly asked, in the words of the minister of Henry III., "Am I an Englishman, that I should know these characters and these laws?" In vain it was that William and his successors filled bishopric and abbey with the most learned and best educated men of France, and deposed English dignitaries, like Wulstan, Bishop of Worcester, because he was an "idiot who did not know the French tongue, and could not aid in the king's council."

Neither sufferings nor death itself, apparently, could teach those haughty Normans the necessity of learning the language of their new home. When in the year 1080 some Northumbrians presented to Vaulcher (Walchere), Bishop and Lord of Durham (Dunholme), an humble and submissive request, the proud prelate required, in answer to their request, that they should pay four hundred pounds of silver. Their astonished but determined spokesman asked for leave to consult with his associates, but, knowing the bishop's entire ignorance of English, he said to his friends: " Short red, gôd rèd; Slee ye se bisceop!" and immediately they fell upon the bishop and slew him and one hundred men of French and Flemish blood!......

Thus we see that conquest cannot exterminate a language, nor drive it from its native soil. The Normans, with all their power and strength, lords of the land, masters of the people, and with every advantage on their side, could not destroy a highly cultivated, ancient and national tongue, like the English. It rose against them and conquered them in its turn......

The Normans could, as conquerors, seat their Norman-French on the throne and on the judge's bench, at the dais of the noble and in the refectory of the monk; but they found the door of manor and of cottage jealously guarded. Their number, moreover, was too small to allow them to spread all over the kingdom. The few Norman soldiers and their families, immured in castles, and too haughty to associate with the despised English, anxiously preserved their connection with France, where many still possessed estates, and held on intercourse but with their own countrymen.

The Norman-French tongue was, therefore, neither carried to all parts of the kingdom, nor supported by the aid of intellectual superiority. The Old English speech, on the other hand, had been carefully guarded and preserved by the people; it had never lost its hold upon their affections; persecution and the necessity of concealment had made it but all the dearer to the suffering race. It now made its way, slowly and almost imperceptibly, but with unerring and unceasing perseverance, from rank to rank, until it finally reached the very court from which it had been so ignominiously driven, and seated itself once more upon the throne of England!

—De Vere

Words

administration, *executive*.
approval, *safiction*.

contending, *struggling*.
contracted, *incurred*.

deposed, *degraded.*
dignitaries, *men of rank.*
dominion, *rule.*
dreaded, *feared.*
enchanted, *fascinated.*
exotic, *foreign.*
exterminate, *cast out.*
extirpate, *up-root.*
felloes, *rims.*
firmament, *heavens.*
forgotten, *overlooked.*
ignominiously, *shamefully.*
imperceptibly, *unnoticed.*
imposing, *forcing.*

increased, *enlarged.*
indigenous, *native.*
indignantly, *angrily.*
intellectual, *mental.*
nave, *centre-block.*
persecution, *oppression.*
perseverance, *persistence.*
refectory, *dining-hall.*
rudder, *blade of the helm.*
subjugated, *subdued.*
submissive, *humble.*
sumptuous, *luxurious.*
wain, *waggon.*

Questions

What means did the Normans take to impose their language upon the English? With what result? Mention things and classes of things bearing Norman names. Where did the dominion of the Norman not extend? Mention classes of things bearing native English names. How long did the two languages exist side by side? What is the story of Walchere of Durham? What prevented the spread of Norman-French all over the kingdom? What was the result of the struggle between the two languages?

　　当黑斯廷斯将英语王国置于他的种族的管辖之下时，骄傲的诺曼人在它已经征服的国家推行它自身的语言这一点上是不成功的。即使从帝王、神坛，到审判台的公职人员都讲诺曼法语；即使诺曼贵族很长时间都鄙视学习已经成为奴役地位的英语；这些都是徒劳无功的。这两种语言并存了一段时间，尽管它们处于不同的情况之下，其中一种是统治者的语言，用在法庭上，也用在已然成为高贵的君主和有权力的爵士的士兵们的城堡之中；另一种是被征服的民族的语言，只在卑微的小屋里由被征服的人们说起。

　　诺曼法语改变并且加强了后者，但却不能灭绝它。为了捍卫他的战利品，他占据了这个国家，并掌握了土壤的控制权。他建造了堡垒和城堡，并尝试去介绍新的术语。宇宙和天空、星球、彗星、流星、大气层和季节，这些都伴随着征服者的封印而给人们留下了深刻印象。丘陵"hill"变成了山脉"mountain"，河谷"dale"被称作山谷"valley"；溪流"stream"被称为河流"river"，小溪"brook"被称作

小河 "rivulet"; 瀑布 "waterfall" 被称作 "cascade", 树林 "woods" 变成了森林 "forest"。

鹿肉 "deer"、牛肉 "ox"、小牛肉 "calf"、猪肉 "swine" 和羊肉 "sheep", 像鹿肉 "venison"、牛肉 "beefveal"、猪肉 "pork" 和羊肉 "mutton" 一样, 出现在他奢侈的餐桌上; 鱼 "salmon"、鲟鱼 "sturgeon"、七鳃鳗 "lamprey", 和鳟鱼 "trout" 都被称为美食; 蛇 "serpent"、蜥蜴 "lizard"、松鼠 "squirrel"、猎鹰 "falcon" 和苍鹭 "heron"、公鸡 "cock" 和鸽子 "pigeon"、马 "stallion" 和骡子 "mule", 都被加入到动物王国的词汇之中。

伯爵 "earl" 和领主 "lord" 在排名之中, 被放置在低于公爵 "duke" 和世袭贵族 "marquise" 的位置。关于男爵 "viscount"、子爵 "baron"、准男爵 "baronet"、乡绅 "squire" 和教士 "master", 他们创造出了一些新的头衔; 而市长 "mayor" 拥有高于英国的市议员 "aldermen" 和治安官 "sheriff" 的权力; 财政大臣 "chancellor" 和他的同行们, 大使 "ambassador" 和国王侍从 "chamberlain", 将军 "general" 和海军上将 "admiral", 则出现在政府办公人员名单的前列。

只有国王还保留了他的名字 "king", 但是国家 "state" 和法院 "court" 都变成由诺曼法语来表达; 行政管理 "administration" 根据宪法 "constitution" 来实施; 条约 "treaty" 由部长 "minister" 在内阁 "cabinet" 里制定, 他们要服从君王 "sovereign" 的同意; 枢密院委员会 "privycouncil" 对帝国的事务进行咨询, 忠诚的臣民 "subject" 会作为代表被派到议会 "parliament" 之中; 在这里, 议会成员们争论死亡、和平 "peace" 和战争 "war" 的价值, 并向海军 "navy" 和陆军 "army" 发出指令, 他们处理国库财产和债务, 并且有自己的会议 "session" 和派别 "party"。

在盛大的晚宴 "feast" 和辉煌的比赛 "tournament" 中, 英国人为骑士收集鲜花; 华丽的舞会 "ball"、优美动听的音乐 "music" 让聚集在此的贵族们, 像是被施了魔法一样沉迷于此。这一切都给这个社会增添了新的辉煌, 让这里古老居民的行为变得更加得体, 也激发了他们的崇敬之情。这些古老的居民为如此的高雅所着迷, 开始承认征服他们的人拥有高人一等的智力, 并欣赏他们, 尽力去模仿他们的举止。

但是诺曼人的主权并没有延伸到英国人的家里, 而在他家的入口处 "threshold" 停止了。那里, 在他厨房里的炉边 "fireside", 在他房间里的灶边 "hearth", 他会遇到他心爱的家庭、新娘 "bride"、妻子 "wife"、丈夫 "husband"、儿子 "son" 和女儿 "daughter"、兄弟 "brother" 姐妹 "sister"。爱 "love" 连接着这里的每一个人, 他们彼此充满友情和美好的感情, 觉得什么都比不上自己甜蜜的家庭更加珍贵。

英国人的牧群依旧在他的田地和草地里散养，提供给他们牛奶"milk"和黄油"butter"、肉"meat"和羊毛"wool"；牧人"herdsman"在春天和夏天看守它们；农夫"ploughman"仍旧使用铁耙手推车"furrow"犁田，在收获之时则使用手推车"cart"和连枷车"flail"；收割的人们"reaper"不断挥舞着镰刀"scythe"，将他的小麦"wheat"、燕麦"oat"、黑麦"rye"堆成一垛，堆积到仓库"barn"里。车夫"wagoner"驾驶着他的运货马车"wain"，车上有轮子"wheel"、外轮"felloes"、辐条"nave"和车轮中心；拉车的牲口在车架"yoke"的束缚下弯低着身子。

在陆地和海上贸易之中，英国人仍旧出售"sell"和购买"buy"商品；在商店或店铺中，在市场或街道上，他使他的货物减价并达成他所有的交易，这些人包括小贩"pedler"或织布师"weaver"，面包师"baker"或制桶工人"cooper"，马具师傅"saddler"，磨坊主"miller"，还有皮匠"tanner"。他向他信任的邻居借出"lend"或借入"borrow"东西。后来，当他再一次渴望自由，他会再次拿起自己的武器，斧子"axe"、剑"sword"和矛"spear"，或他们可怕的弓"bow"和箭"arrow"。他们不带镫筋"stirrup"地跳到马鞍"saddle"上，并用飞镖"dart"和投枪"gavelock"杀死敌人。在其他的时候，他们驶出他们的船只，这仍然是纯正的英国船，拥有龙骨"keel"和甲板"deck"、舵"helm"或者"rudder"和顶部的桅杆"mast"，在海上、岸上，靠帆"sail"或桨"oar"航行。

就像他们的父辈在他们出生的地方曾经做过的一样，英国人不仅要吃"eat"、喝"drink"、睡觉"sleep"，或弹奏着竖琴"harp"和小提琴"fiddle"来度过时间，他们也要散步"walk"、骑马"ride"、钓鱼"fish"，打猎"hunt"，他们保持着年轻和健康；而他们的太太们和孩子们则忙于教育"teach"或学习"learn"，学会如何读"read"和写"write"、唱歌"sing"和绘画"draw"。连刺绣"needle-work"的工作也没有被遗忘，正如他们的作家说的，"这是世界上最闪耀的智慧。"他们有自己的至理名言，当时还不起眼，但全人类都将其视为真正的智慧，那就是：上帝帮助那些自助之人"God helps them that help themselves"；逝去的时间一去不复返"Lost time is never found again"；新旧事别重提"When sorrow is asleep, wakeitnot"！

因此，这两种语言一会儿互相争斗，一会儿又互相融合进了对方之中，持续了近四百年的时间，在不列颠王国并存；诺曼法语像一株外来植物，脱离了它原本的乡土和热量，繁荣了一段时间，但渐渐地萎缩和消失；主体的语言英语，像一株本土的树种，被狂暴的风暴削减，被一只笨拙的手嫁接了许多分枝，但仍由其宽广的树叶给予当地人荫蔽，生出了丰富的花朵和水果。

诺曼人征服了这片土地和这里的民族，但他们仍徒然地与这里的语言相斗争。它却反过来征服了他们，并且用它的精神，将诺曼人都转化成了英国人。他们傲慢地拒绝学这种语言的任何一个单词，也是徒劳的。他们愤怒地问亨利三世的一个部长："我是一个英国人吗？我应该知道这些特征和这些法律吗？"威廉主教和他的继任者们将最有学问的人和最博学的人充斥到法国的修道院里，并废黜了一些英国政要，比如伍斯特的主教伍尔斯坦，因为他是一个"不懂法语的白痴，在国王的议会里不会有所帮助"。这一切都是徒劳无功的。

显然，痛苦和死亡本身，都不能教会傲慢的诺曼人学习他们新家园语言的必要性。在1080年，一些诺森博兰郡人对达勒姆（现在的达诺姆）的主教和勋爵，提出了一个谦卑的、恭顺的请求。按照请求，这位骄傲的教士回答他们的要求道，他们需要支付四百英镑的银子。他们惊讶但却仍旧坚定的发言人，要求离开一下与他的同胞们商量，但得知这位主教对英语一无所知的情况之后，他对他的朋友说："该死的主教！"他们立刻发起进攻，杀死了这位主教以及100个法国人和佛兰德人！

因此我们看到，征服不能消灭一种语言，也不能把它从本土驱逐出去。诺曼人拥有他们所有的力量，征了土地，管理着当地的人民，占据了所有优势，却不可能破坏一种高度发展的、古老的、属于一个国家的语言，比如英语。反过来，这种语言会征服他们……

作为征服者，诺曼人可以将他们的诺曼法语放在王位的宝座之上，或者审判席之上，放在贵族的圣坛之上和僧侣们的食堂之中；但他们发现英国人的庄园和小屋的大门都被小心地守护着。此外，他们的人数也太少了，不可能遍布整个王国。少数诺曼士兵和他们的家庭居住在城堡之中，如此傲慢，不愿意与他们鄙视的英语有所关联，焦急地保留他们与法语的联系，他们之中的很多人在法国仍保有领地，并仅仅与自己的同胞交往。

因此，诺曼法语不但没有推行到这个王国的所有地方，也没有受到知识分子的支持。另一方面，古老的英语一直被人们小心翼翼地守护和保存着，它一直没有失去他们的感情，迫害和隐藏的必要性使这个受压迫的民族觉得它更亲切。如今，它找到了自己的方式，慢慢地，几乎是不知不觉地，但准确无误并持续不变地，一点一滴地，直到最后，它又返回到了它曾经充满屈辱地被驱逐的那片殿堂，并再次坐在属于自己的英格兰的宝座之上！

——德·维尔

Lesson 68   VENICE
第六十八课　威尼斯

When Attila, King of the Huns, devastated Italy in the middle of the fifth century, the citizens of Aquileia, Padua, and other towns on the Adriatic, fled from the invader.

At the head of the gulf are about a hundred little islands, formed of mud and sand swept down by the rivers which drain the plains of Northern Italy. These islands are surrounded by shallow water, and protected from the waves by long bars of sand, between which by various narrow channels vessels pass out and in. Upon these islands the Veneti driven from the mainland established themselves, and there founded a city in the midst of the waters.

In their new home they missed the vines and the olives which clad their native slopes, as well as the bees and the cattle which they used to tend. The waste of wild sea-moor on which they now dwelt offered only a few patches of soil fit for cultivation, and these yielded but a scanty crop of stunted vegetables. The only supplies which Nature furnished were the fish which swarmed in the waters, and the salt which encrusted the beds of the lagoons.

A more miserable, hopeless plight than that of the inhabitants of these little islands, it would be hard to conceive; and yet out of their slender resources they built up Venice! The sandbanks which they contested with the sea-fowl became the site of a great and wealthy city; and their fish and salt formed the original basis of a world-wide commerce. Their progress, however, was slow and laborious. Seventy years after the settlement was formed, they were still obliged to toil hard for a bare Subsistence.

Some distinctions of rank—a tradition of their former condition—were maintained amongst them, but all were reduced to an equality of poverty. Fish was the common, almost the only, food of all classes. None could boast a better dwelling than a rude hut of mud and osiers. Their only treasure consisted of salt, which they transported to the mainland, receiving in exchange various articles of food and clothing; and, not less important, wood for boat-building. The security in which they pursued these humble occupations was, however, envied by Italians who were groaning under the tyranny and rapine of the barbarians, and the island-colony received accessions of population.

The Venetians, who could scarcely stir from one spot to another except by water, became the most expert of seamen. Their vessels not only threaded the tortuous courses of the rivers and of the Adriatic; and, gaining confidence, pushed out into the Mediterranean, and opened up a trade with Greece and Constantinople. Thus Venice became the port of Italy and Germany, and the means of communication between them and the seat of the Roman Empire in the East.

Every year the ships of the Republic grew larger and more numerous. In the fourteenth century it had afloat a fleet of three thousand merchantmen; but of these

THE GRAND CANAL VENICE

some were only of ten tons burden, while few exceeded one hundred tons. Fishing-boats were probably included in the estimate. In addition, there were about forty war-galleys, carrying eleven thousand men; which were kept cruising in different directions, for the protection of Venetian commerce.

The largest of the galleys was the famous *Bucentaur*, which, with its exterior of scarlet and gold, its long bank of burnished oars, its deck and seats inlaid with precious woods, its gorgeous canopy and throne, rivalled the magnificence of Cleopatras barge. It was in this splendid vessel that the Doge went annually in state to celebrate the marriage of Venice with the Adriatic, by dropping a ring into its waters; thus symbolizing the fact that a people whose habitations might be assigned either to earth or to water, were equally at home on both.

With an extensive commerce the Venetians combined several manufactures. They not only prepared immense quantities of salt, and cured fish but found in their sands the material of that exquisite glass, so pure, and yet so rich in hue, with which their name is still associated. The furnaces from which this beautiful product emanated were congregated, as they still are, in the island of Mura'no.

There were also brass and iron foundries; and the armourers of Venice were widely celebrated for the strength and beauty of their weapons, breastplates, helmets, and bucklers. The weaving of cloth-of-gold was another important industry. This costly and gorgeous material was in great demand in the Courts of France and Germany. Charlemagne himself was rarely seen without a robe of Venetian pattern and texture.

It was thus that Venice grew rich. The mud huts gradually gave place to palaces, and the peasants were transformed into haughty nobles. "The Venetians are grown so proud," says an old traveller in the fifteenth century, "that when one has a son, the saying goes, 'A lord is born into the world!'" In the beginning of the same century it was reckoned that there were at least a thousand nobles in the city, whose yearly incomes ranged from 4,000 to 70,000 ducats, and that at a time when 3,000 ducats bought a palace.

At the end of the twelfth century the population was 70,000, exclusive of persons in holy orders. Two hundred years later it had increased nearly fourfold.

Venice was then, as now, a city intersected by innumerable water highways, bordered by marble mansions mingled with tenements of wood, studded with churches, and having public squares confined on three sides by houses, while on the remaining side a quay overlooked the sea. The streets bustled with traffic. Gondolas skimmed rapidly along the canals. The merchants assembled on the Rialto, and the money-changers spread their tables under the shadow of the Campanile.

The Bank of Venice—the first institution of the kind ever established—the credit of which was guaranteed by the State, attested at once the wisdom and the commercial enterprise of the City of the Waters. In the shops, every article of use, luxury, or ornament, could be obtained. Contractors of all kinds and of different nations resorted thither, and the ships of every flag loaded and unloaded at the quays.

Tue Bridge or the Rialto

The rivalry of Genoa forms a large element in the history of Venice. The two republics were deadly and relentless enemies. Whenever their ships met there was a fight; and in a narrow sea like the Mediterranean, where in some cases they frequented the same ports, they met very often.

In 1261 a rupture with the Byzantine government at Constantinople led to the exclusion of the Venetians from the trade of the Black Sea. Genoa for a time was in the ascendant. A desperate war ensued, which at the end of four years terminated in the triumph of the Venetians, whose maritime and commercial supremacy was thus indicated. The object of the struggle—the trade of the Black Sea—was, however, lost to the victors as well as to the vanquished; for the Turks intervened and imposed their paralyzing influence on the commerce and industry of those parts. Within the Mediterranean, Venice remained without a rival. The blow which proved fatal to her influence came from without, and was as unexpected as it was inevitable. It was the discovery of a sea passage to India, which set aside the old caravan routes, of which Venice formed, as it were, the European centre.

—J. H. Fyfe.

Words

accessions, *additions.*
attested, *evidenced.*
celebrate, *solemnize.*
channels, *passages.*
conceive, *imagine.*
confidence, *assurance.*
Cruising, *sailing to and fro.*
desperate, *furious.*
devastated, *laid waste.*
emanated, *issued.*
encrusted, *coated.*
enterprise, *daring.*
established, *settled.*
estimate, *calculation.*
exclusive, *excepting.*
exquisite, *beautiful.*
frequented, *visited.*

inevitable, *unavoidable.*
intersected, *cut up.*
intervened, *interposed.*
mainland, *continent.*
maritime, *naval.*
original, *primary.*
pattern, *design.*
rapine, *plunder.*
relentless, *implacable.*
stunted, *dwarfed.*
subsistence, *living.*
symbolizing, *typifying.*
tenements, *houses.*
texture, *fabrication.*
tortuous, *winding.*
transformed, *changed.*

Questions

When and by whom was Venice founded? What was the common food of the first settlers? What article did they export? What made them so expert as seamen? With what distant places did they ere long open up a trade? What was the largest of the Venetian galleys called? On what occasion was it used? In what manufactures did the Venetians excel? What was the population of Venice at the end of the twelfth and the fourteenth centuries respectively? What has Venice for streets? and what for carriages? Where did the merchants assemble? and the moneychangers? What republic was a great rival of Venice? What gave Genoa the ascendency for a time? What deprived both of the object of their struggle? What blow at last proved fatal to Venice?

当匈奴的国王阿蒂拉，在5世纪中期侵占了意大利时，帕多瓦、阿奎拉和亚得里亚海其他城镇的居民们，逃离了侵略者。

在海湾的开端之处，有大约100个小岛屿，由灌溉了意大利北部平原的河流冲刷下来的泥沙堆积而成。这些岛屿周围被浅水围绕，在波浪之间由长长的砂砾形成的地带保护，在此之间，船只通过各种狭窄的水道进进出出。在这些岛屿上，从大陆被驱逐出来的威尼蒂人，在水域之中建立起了一座属于自己的城市。

在他们的新家园里，他们不再种植他们原本故乡的葡萄和橄榄，也不再像过去一样畜养蜜蜂和牛群。在野生沼泽的废墟之上，他们定居在仅有的几块适合耕种的土地之上，仅仅产出了数量很少且发育不良的蔬菜。大自然提供的唯一补给品就是在水上跳跃的鱼和镶嵌在湖床之上的盐。

比这些小小岛屿上的居民们的更悲惨、绝望的处境，将是很难想象的；然而，以他们匮乏的资源为基础，他们建立了威尼斯！他们从海鸟那里争抢过来的沙洲，成为一个伟大的、富有的城市；他们的鱼和盐形成了全球贸易的原始基础。然而，他们的进步是如此缓慢而费力。在他们定居在此70年之后，仅仅为了能在此生存，他们仍然不得不辛苦劳作。

在他们当中，等级的区别——这是一种之前的传统状态——也被保留了下来，但他们都被削弱到一种相同的贫困。对于所有阶层的人来说，鱼是常见的，也几乎是唯一的食品。没有人能拥有一个比由泥浆和柳枝做成的简陋的小屋更好的房屋。他们将唯一的珍宝包括盐，运到内地，作为交换，得到各种食物和衣服；还有，同样重要的，用来造船的木材。然而，他们从事这些卑微的职业而得到的安全，受到了在野蛮人的专制统治和掠夺之下痛苦呻吟的意大利人的嫉妒，因此，岛上的人口得到了持续的增长。

除了通过水路，威尼斯人很难从一个地方到另一个地方，因此他们成为最专业的航海专家。他们的船只不仅在亚得里亚海曲折蜿蜒的河流中航行；并且在他们获得信心之后，推到了地中海上，打开了与希腊和君士坦丁堡贸易的大门。因此，威尼斯成为意大利和德国的港口以及与东方的罗马帝国相联系的必经之地。

每一年，共和国的船舶变得更大、更多。在14世纪，三万商人的舰队漂浮在海上；其中有些船只能承担10吨的负重，而很少有船能负重超过100吨。渔船可能也包括在这个估计的数字之内。此外，大约有40只大战船载着11 000人；它们向着不同的方向航行，为威尼斯人的贸易提供保护。

最大的舰船是著名的礼舟，它拥有红色与金色的外观，长长的放满富有光泽的桨的船侧，镶嵌着珍贵木材的甲板和座椅以及华丽的冠层和宝座，甚至超越了克利奥帕特拉的驳船的辉煌。就是在这华丽的船上，总督每年都会参与庆祝威尼斯与亚得里亚海的结合。威尼斯将一只水环融入了它的水域之中，也因此标志着一个事实，那就是，这里居民的住处可以在陆地上，也可以在水域之中，两者都是相同的。

因为存在广泛的贸易，威尼斯人发展了多种制造业。他们不仅准备了大量的盐，腌制了鱼，同时也在沙滩上发现了精致的玻璃的材料，它是那么纯洁，又拥有如此丰富的色调，它的名字也同样与此相关。这种美丽的产品被锻造出来的熔炉，正如它们一样，如今存在在穆拉诺岛之上。

这里还有黄铜厂和钢铁厂，威尼斯的武器制造者们，大肆宣扬着他们的武器、护胸甲、头盔、铠甲和盾牌的力量与精致。黄金编织是另一个重要的产业。在法国和德国的宫廷里，对这种昂贵而华丽的材料存在巨大的需求。查理曼大帝本人，很少不穿着带有威尼斯图案和纹理的长袍出现。

正是因此，威尼斯变得富裕了起来。泥屋逐渐被宫殿所代替，农民也逐渐转化为了傲慢的贵族。"威尼斯人变得如此骄傲，"一个在15世纪去威尼斯旅行的人说道，"当一个人新生了一个儿子，按照当地的俗话说，'这个世界上又多了一个贵族！'"同样是在15世纪的开始之时，人们普遍认为在这个城市里，至少有1 000个贵族，他们的年收入介于4 000～70 000块钱，而当时，人们花3 000块钱，就可以买一座宫殿。

在12世纪末期，这里的人口达到了7万，他们全都属于贵族阶层。二百年后，它又增加了近四倍。

当时的威尼斯是这样一座城市，正如现在一样，无数的水路交织在一起，毗邻的大理石大厦与木质房屋混杂在一起，城市中布满了教堂，并有一些三面都被房屋环绕的公共广场，而在另一侧，码头俯视着大海。街道上交通忙乱。贡多拉迅速地沿着运河行驶其间。商人聚集在桥上，货币兑换商在钟楼的阴影下摆满他们的工作桌。

威尼斯银行是这一类机构中第一家成立的，它的信用是由国家保证的，这一点再一次证明水城威尼斯的智慧和商业企图心。人们可以在商店中买到任何一种必需品、奢侈品或者装饰品。来自不同国家的各种承包人聚集在此，飘扬着各国旗帜的船舶在这里的码头上装货、卸货。

与热那亚的竞争为威尼斯的历史画上了浓墨重彩的一笔。这两个共和国是一对无情的宿敌。每当他们的船只相遇，就会有一场战争，在一片狭窄的海域，比如地中海，在某些情况下他们会经常光顾同一个港口，由此便会频繁相遇。

在1261年，与拜占庭政府及君士坦丁堡的关系破裂，将威尼斯人排挤出了黑海的贸易。热那亚有一段时间处于上升期。一场绝望的战争接踵而至，最终在四年之后，威尼斯人的胜利宣告了这场战争的结束，其海上霸主和商业霸主的地位也从而得到了彰显。然而，斗争的主要目标——黑海贸易——由胜利者和失败者共同享有，因为土耳其人干预进来，并将他们的影响强加给了战争的两方。在地中海之内，威尼斯仍然没有竞争对手。之后，对它有巨大影响并产生致命打击的事件是如此难以预料，却又不可避免。一条通往印度的海上通道的发现，取消了原本以威尼斯作为欧洲中心的陆上航线。

——J. H. 法伊夫

Lesson 69
THE CIRCULATION OF WATER
第六十九课　水循环

The simplest form of the circulation of matter is that which is presented by the watery vapour contained in the atmosphere. From this vapour the dews and rains are formed which refresh the scorched plant and fertilize the earth. The depth of dew which falls we cannot estimate. On summer evenings it appears in hazy mists, and collects on leaf and twig in sparkling pearls; but at early dawn it vanishes again unmeasured—partly sucked in by plant and soil, and partly dispelled by the youngest sunbeams. But the yearly rain-fall is easily noted. In Britain it averages about thirty inches in depth; and in Western Europe generally, it is seldom less than twenty inches. Among the Cumberland mountains, in some places a fall of two hundred inches a year is not uncommon; while among the hills near Calcutta, as much as five hundred and fifty inches sometime falls within six months.

Now, as the whole of the watery vapour in the air, were it to fall at once in the form of rain, would not cover the entire surface of the Earth to a depth of more than five inches, how repeated must the rise and fall of this watery vapour be! To keep the air always duly moist, and yet to maintain the constant and necessary descent of dew and rain, the invisible rush of water upwards must be both great and constant. The ascent of water in this invisible form is often immediate and obvious, depending solely upon physical causes; but it is often also indirect, and being the result of physiological or of chemical causes, is less generally perceptible. Thus:—

1. Water circulates abundantly between earth and air through the agency of purely *physical* causes. We see this when a summer shower falling upon our paved streets is speedily licked up again by the balmy winds, and wafted towards the region of clouds, ready for a new fall. But this form of circulation takes place on the greatest scale from the surface of the sea in equatorial regions, heated through the influence of the sun's rays. Thence streams of vapour are continually mounting upwards with the currents of ascending air; and with these they travel north and south, till colder climates precipitate them in dew, rain, or snow. Returned to the arctic or the temperate seas by many running streams, these precipitated waters are carried back again to the equator by those great sea-rivers which mysteriously traverse all oceans; and, when there, are ready to rise again to repeat the same revolution. How often, since time began, may the waters which cover the whole Earth have thus traversed air and sea, taking part in the endless movements of inanimate nature!

2. Again: *physiological* causes, though in a less degree than the physical, are still very largely influential in causing this watery circulation. Thus the dew and rain which

fall sink in part into the soil, and are thence drunk in by the roots of growing plants. But these plants spread out their green leaves into the dry air, and from numberless pores are continually exhaling watery vapour in an invisible form. From the leafy surface of a single acre in crop, it is calculated that from three to five millions of pounds of water are yearly exhaled in the form of vapour, in Britain; while, on an average, not more than two and a half millions fall in rain. Whether the surplus thus given off be derived from dews or from springs, it is plain that this evaporation from the leaves of plants is one of the most important forms which the circulation of water assumes.

Animals take into their stomachs another portion of the same water, and, as a necessary function of life, are continually returning it into the air from their lungs and their insensibly reeking hides. About two pounds a day are thus discharged into the air by a full-grown man; and larger animals probably give off more, in proportion to their size. Multiply this quantity by the number of animals which occupy the land surface of the globe, and the sum will show that this also is a form of watery circulation which, though less in absolute amount than the others I have mentioned, is yet of much importance in the economy of nature.

3. But water circulates also, in consequence of unceasing *chemical* operations, in a way which, if less obvious to the uninstructed, is, if possible, more beautiful and more interesting than the mere physical methods above described. The main substance of plants—their woody fibre—consists in large proportion of water. The same is true of the starch and sugar which are consumed by an animal. When the plant dies and decomposes in the air, the water is again set free from its woody stem. When the animal digests the starch and sugar, the water which these contain is discharged from its lungs and skin. Thus the living plant works up water into its growing substance, which water the decaying plant and the breathing animal again set free; and thus a chemical circulation continually goes on, by which the same water is caused again and again to revolve. Within a single hour it may be in the form of starch in my hand, be discharged as watery vapour from my lungs, and be again absorbed by the thirsty leaf to add to the substance of a new plant!

—James F. W. Johnston

Words

absorbed, *drunk in.*
abundantly, *plentifully.*
circulation, *rotation.*
consumed, *swallowed.*
decomposes, *separates into elements.*
discharged, *expelled.*
dispelled, *dissipated.*

economy, *system.*
equatorial, *near the equator.*
estimate, *calculate.*
evaporation, *dispersion in vapour.*
exhaling, *breathing out.*
function, *duty.*
inanimate, *lifeless.*

influential, *operative*.

maintain, *uphold*.

mentioned, *named*.

mysteriously, *strangely*.

obvious, *evident*.

occupy, *inhabit*.

perceptible, *apparent*.

precipitate, *throw down*.

proportion, *degree*.

repeated, *frequent*.

revolve, *circulate*.

scorched, *withered*.

uncommon, *unusual*.

Questions

What proves the frequency with which the rise and fall of watery vapour must take place? To what three causes is the ascent of water into the atmosphere due? Give an example of the circulation of water due to purely physical causes. Show how physiological causes operate. Give an example of the chemical operations which cause water to circulate.

最简单的物质循环的形式，由大气中包含的水蒸气表现出来。露水和雨水都由这些水蒸气形成，它们能够使干旱的植物变得新鲜，也使土壤更加肥沃。露水下沉的深度是我们无法估计的，在夏天的夜晚，它们聚集在朦胧的雾气中和叶子、树枝上，如晶莹剔透的珍珠一般；但黎明来临时，它们又会再次消失得无影无踪：一部分由土壤和植物吸收，另一部分由清晨的阳光消除。但是人们却很容易注意到每年的降雨量。在英国，年平均的降雨量约30英寸深；而在西欧，一般的年降雨量均不小于20英寸。在坎伯兰山脉中的一些地方，甚至年均200英寸的降雨量也并不少见；而在加尔各答附近的山上，六个月内的降雨量就多达550英寸。

现在，所有悬浮在空气中的水蒸气，如果一旦以雨水的方式降落，它们不足以覆盖整个地球表面深于5英寸。由此可知，这种水蒸气的上升和下降是何等频繁地重复着！为了始终保持空气中的适当湿度，而保持恒定和必要的露水和雨水量，无形的向上蒸发的水汽量就必须是巨大而恒定的。这种看不见的水的上升往往是直接和明显的，它完全取决于物理原因；但它也往往是间接的，这却是由于生物或化学原因，而人们通常较少察觉到这些原因。因此：

（1）在地球和空气之间的丰富的水循环，以纯粹的物理原因为媒介。我们可以看到这一点，在夏天，落在我们街道的瓢泼大雨会很快被温暖的风取代，飘向有云朵的区域，准备好一场新的降水。而这种形式的水循环，最大规模地出现在赤道地区的海洋表面，因为这一区域由于太阳光线的影响而变热。那里的蒸汽流，伴随着上升的空气气流不断向上攀升；和气流一起，它们向北部和南部旅行，直到寒冷的气候将它们冷结为露水、雨或雪。由众多奔涌的水流带到极地或温带海洋之后，这些冷结后的水蒸气，由那些神秘穿行于海洋中的巨大水系，再次带回到赤道地区。在这里，它们做好了准备，再一次重复同样的水循环的变革。从这场变革的最初，这些覆盖了整个地球的水流，就极其频繁地穿梭于空气和海洋之间，成为自然界无休止的运动的一部分！

（2）生物的原因虽然比物理原因的影响力要小，仍然在很大程度上造成了水循环。因此，雨露中的一部分落入土壤中，由正在生长的植物的根系所吸收。而这些植物的绿色叶子伸展到干燥的空气中，并无形地从无数的孔隙中不断呼出水汽。据计算，在英国，从仅仅一英亩的农作物的叶子表面，每年就会有300~500万磅水以蒸汽的形式呼出到大气中，然而，平均说来，其中不超过250万磅的水是降雨。无论蒸发出的蒸气中那些多余的部分是来自于露水还是泉水，从植物的叶子中蒸发出来的水蒸气都显然是水循环最重要的形式之一。

动物将另一部分水吸入它们的肚子中，而作为一种必要的生命功能，它们不断通过肺部或不知不觉中散发水汽的皮毛，将这些水汽返回到空气中。一个成人每天将大约两磅水汽排放到空气中；更大的动物可能会释放得更多，这与它们的形体大小成正比。将这个数字与占领地球陆地表面的动物的数量相乘，乘积的总数表明这也是一种水循环的重要形式。虽然这比我所提到的前几种水循环的绝对量要小，但在自然经济中它也相当重要。

（3）但是，水循环也同样归因于不断的化学运动。对不了解它的人们来说，它并不那么明显，但如果可能的话，它比之前描述过的纯粹的物理原因要更加美丽、更加有趣。植物的实质，也就是它们的木质纤维，绝大比例上是由水构成的。动物消耗的淀粉和糖同样也是如此。当植物死去，在空气中分解，水汽会再次从它们木质的茎中释放出来。当动物消化淀粉和糖，它们包含的水会由动物的肺和皮肤排出。因此，存活的植物将水注入它们的生长物质，而腐烂的植物和动物的呼吸会再次将它们释放出来；因此，水的化学循环持续下去，同样的，水就这样反复旋转。在短短的一小时里，它或是以淀粉的形式出现在我手上，或者从我的肺部以水蒸气的形式呼出到空气中，继而又一次被干渴的叶片吸收，添加到一个新的植物物质里！

——杰姆斯·F. W. 庄士敦

Lesson 70   GINEVRA
第七十课　吉内乌拉

If thou shouldst ever come to Modena,
Stop at a palace near the Reggio Gate,
Dwelt in of old by one of the Orsini.
Its noble gardens, terrace above terrace,
And numerous fountains, statues, cypresses,
Will long detain thee; but before thou go,
Enter the house—prythee, forget it not—
And look a while upon a picture there.

'Tis of a lady in her earliest youth;—
She sits inclining forward as to speak,
Her lips half open, and her finger up,
As though she said, "Beware! her vest of gold,
Broidered with flowers, and clasped from head to foot—
An emerald stone in every golden clasp;
And on her brow, fairer than alabaster,
A coronet of pearls. But then her face,
So lovely, yet so arch, so full of mirth.
The overflowings of an innocent heart—
It haunts me still, though many a year has fled,
Like some wild melody!—Alone it hangs.
Over a mouldering heir-loom, its companion,
An oaken chest half eaten by the worm.

She was an only child; from infancy,
The joy, the pride, of an indulgent sire.
Her mother dying of the gift she gave,
That precious gift, what else remained to him?
The young Ginevra was his all in life;
Still as she grew, for ever in his sight.
She was all gentleness, all gaiety,
Her pranks the favourite theme of every tongue.
But now the day was come, the day, the hour;
And in the lustre of her youth, she gave,
Her hand, with her heart in it, to Francesco.

Great was the joy; but at the bridal feast,
When all sat down, the bride was wanting there—
Nor was she to be found! Her father cried.
"'Tis but to make a trial of our love!"
And filled his glass to all; but his hand shook,
And soon from guest to guest the panic spread.
'Twas but that instant she had left Francesco,
Laughing and looking back, and flying still,
Her ivory tooth imprinted on his finger.
But now, alas! she was not to be found;
Nor from that hour could anything be guessed,
But that she was not! Weary of his life,
Francesco flew to Venice, and forthwith
Flung it away in battle with the Turk.
Orsini lived; and long mightst thou have seen
An old man wandering as in quest of something,
Something he could not find—he knew not what.
When he was gone, the house remained a while
Silent and tenantless, then went to strangers.

Full fifty years were past, and all forgot,
When on an idle day, a day of search,
'Mid the old lumber in the gallery,
That mouldering chest was noticed; and 'twas said,
By one as young, as thoughtless, as Ginevra,
"Why not remove it from its lurking-place?"
'Twas done as soon as said; but on the way,
It burst—it fell; and lo, a skeleton!
And here and there a pearl, an emerald-stone,
A golden clasp, clasping a shred of gold.
All else had perished—save a nuptial ring,
And a small seal, her mother's legacy,
Engraven with a name, the name of both—
"Ginevra." There, then, had she found a grave!
Within that chest had she concealed herself,
Fluttering with joy, the happiest of the happy;
When a spring-lock, that lay in ambush there,
Fastened her down—for ever!

—Rogers

Words

ambush, *concealment*.
bridal, *wedding*.
cypresses, *evergreens*.
detain, *occupy*.
fluttering, *thrilling*.
gaiety, *sprightliness*.
gentleness, *tenderness*.
heir-loom, *family relic*.
imprinted, *indented*.
inclining, *bending*.
indulgent, *kind*.

innocent, *guileless*.
legacy, *bequest*.
lustre, *brilliancy*.
mouldering, *crumbling*.
nuptial, *marriage*.
overflowings, *outpourings*.
quest, *search*.
tenantless, *uninhabited*.
terrace, *platform*.
theme, *subject*.

Questions

To what family did Ginevra belong? Why was she very precious to her father? How was her marriage interrupted? What was her fate? When was it discovered? What became of Francesco? What is the starting point of the poem?

> 如果您有幸到过摩德纳，
> 你会停留在宫殿的门前，
> 奥尔西尼人，曾经定居于此，
> 座座宏伟的庭院，步步拾级的台阶，
> 无数的喷泉如乐，雕塑也千姿百态，
> 您定会在此流连忘返，但离去之前，
> 走进房子，别忘记，
> 凝视一幅那里的画卷。
>
> 画中一位正值曼妙年纪的女子，
> 她正倚栏而坐，仿佛有话诉说。
> 她的芳唇微张，手指微翘，
> 仿佛说着："当心！她的绣花金衣。"
> 她头戴珍珠花冠，浑身散发出光彩，

她的前额光洁如脂，远胜汉白美玉，
然而她的脸庞，
如此活泼漂亮，如此快乐洋溢，
展现着她的纯洁心灵，
多年已然逝去，却仍萦绕在我心间，
仍似狂热的旋律。这幅画独悬于此，
此间家传的宝物壁立，
一台橡木的衣柜，一半已遭虫噬。

她是家中的独生女，
被视作掌上明珠，因其自豪欢喜，
她的母亲去世之后，女儿就成了生命的礼物，
如此珍贵的礼物，唯一留给她的父亲。
少女吉内乌拉，是她父亲生命的意义；
他守望着女儿的成长，片刻不曾远离，
她得到他全部的温柔和关爱，
她赢得了所有的赞美。
如今这一天就要到来，那时那刻，
在她最好的年华，
她将自己的手，与爱，交给弗朗西斯。
婚宴即将开始，众人充斥着欢愉，
嘉宾已然落座，新郎翘首期盼着——
却无人寻得新娘痕迹！她的父亲惊呼，
"或许是她在考验新郎的爱意！"
父亲满脸笑意，双手却微微颤抖，
很快惊慌情绪就在宾客之间散遍，
可能她离开了弗朗西斯，
笑着回忆过往云烟，
她艳红的吻还曾印留在他的指间，
但如今，哎，却无人寻得她的足迹；
这一刻，谁也猜不透结局，
她再也找不到了！不顾自己的生命，
弗朗西斯逃离到威尼斯城，
随波逐流加入了对抗土耳其人的战斗。

你可能会见到，
一位老人踟蹰蹒跚，见人便问，
他的女儿去了哪里。
当他终有一天逝去，华庭变得
沉寂而落寞，随后便变更了主人。

五十年就这样过去，往事随云拂去。
一日闲来无聊，有人到画廊里寻趣，
在这些旧物之间，突然看到了，
那台腐朽的柜具，有人便说，
这人年轻、鲁莽，说道：这像吉内乌拉，
为何不将它搬离这个地方，占据了如此空间，
说话即刻搬起柜子，途中，
柜体崩裂坠落，呀！一具尸体！
满地落满了明珠灿玉，
一枚黄金别针，上面镶着翡翠宝石，
他物都已经朽烂，只有一枚戒指，
这是一方小小的印章，是她母亲的遗物，
上面镶刻着母女二人的名字——
"吉内乌拉"，她自掘坟墓于此，
因其幸福至极，带着欢愉藏于此柜之中，
谁料弹簧锁无意锁上，夺了她的性命，
因此永远地使她香消玉殒。

——罗杰斯

Lesson 71　THE DIGNITY OF LABOUR
第七十一课　劳动的尊严

The dignity of labour! Consider its achievements! Dismayed by no difficulty, shrinking from no exertion, exhausted by no struggle, over eager for renewed efforts in its persevering promotion of human happiness, "clamorous Labour knocks with its hundred hands at the golden gate of the morning," obtaining each day, through succeeding centuries, fresh benefactions for the world!

Labour clears the forest, and drains the morass, and makes the wilderness rejoice and blossom as the rose. Labour drives the plough, and scatters the seed, and reaps the harvest, and grinds the corn, and converts it into bread, the staff of life. Labour, tending the pastures and sweeping the waters, as well as cultivating the soil, provides with daily sustenance the thousand millions of the family of man.

Labour moulds the brick, and splits the slate, and quarries the stone, and shapes the column, and rears, not only the humble cottage, but the gorgeous palace, the tapering spire, and the stately dome.

Labour, diving deep into the solid earth, brings up its long-hidden stores of coal, to feed ten thousand furnaces, and in millions of habitations to defy the winter's cold. Labour explores the rich veins of deeply-buried rocks, extracting the gold, the silver, the copper, and the tin. Labour smelts the iron, and moulds it into a thousand shapes for use and ornament,—from the massive pillar to the tiniest needle, from the ponderous anchor to the wire-gauze, from the mighty fly-wheel of the steam-engine to the polished purse-ring or the glittering bead.

Labour hews down the gnarled oak, and shapes the timber, and builds the ship, and guides it over the deep, plunging through the billows and wrestling with the tempest, to bear to our shores the produce of every clime. Labour brings us Indian rice and American cotton; African ivory and Greenland oil; fruits from the sunny South and furs from the frozen North; tea from the East and sugar from the West;—carrying, in exchange, to every hind the products of British industry and British skill. Labour, by the universally spread ramifications of trade, distributes its own treasures from country to country, from city to city, from house to house, conveying to the doors of all, the necessaries and luxuries of life; and, by the pulsations of an untrammelled commerce, maintaining healthy life in the great social system.

Labour, fusing opaque particles of rock, produces transparent glass, which it moulds and polishes, and combines so wondrously, that sight is restored to the blind; while worlds, before invisible from distance, are brought so near as to be weighed and measured with unerring exactness; and atoms, which had escaped all detection from their minuteness, reveal a world of wonder and beauty in themselves.

Labour, possessing a secret far more important than the philosopher's stone, transmutes the most worthless substances into the most precious; and, placing in the crucible of its potent chemistry the putrid refuse of the sea and the land, extracts fragrant essences, and healing medicines, and materials of priceless importance in the arts.

Labour, laughing at difficulties, spans majestic rivers, carries viaducts over marshy swamps, suspends aerial bridges above deep ravines, pierces the solid mountain with its dark, undeviating tunnel, blasting rocks and filling hollows; and, while linking together with its iron but loving grasp all nations of the Earth, verifies, in a literal sense, the ancient prophecy: "Every valley shall be exalted, and every mountain and hill shall be made low."

Labour draws forth its delicate iron thread, and, stretching it from city to city, from province to province, through mountains and beneath the sea, realizes more than fancy ever fabled, while it constructs a chariot on which speech may outstrip the wind, compete with the lightning, and fly as rapidly as thought itself.

Labour seizes the thoughts of genius, the discoveries of science, the admonitions of piety, and with its magic types impressing the vacant page, renders it pregnant with life and power, perpetuating truth to distant ages, and diffusing it to all mankind.

Labour sits enthroned in palaces of crystal, whose high arched roofs proudly sparkle in the sunshine which delighteth to honour it, and whose ample courts are crowded with the trophies of its victories in every country and in every age.

Labour, a mighty magician, walks forth into a region uninhabited and waste; he looks earnestly at the scene, so quiet in its desolation; then, waving his wonder-working wand, those dreary valleys smile with golden harvests; those barren mountain-slopes are clothed with foliage; the furnace blazes; the anvil rings; the busy wheels whirl round; the town appears,—the mart of Commerce, the hall of Science, the temple of Religion, rear high their lofty fronts; a forest of masts, gay with varied pennons, rises from the harbour; the quays are crowded with commercial spoils,—the peaceful spoils which enrich both him who receives and him who yields. Representatives of far-off regions make it their resort; Science enlists the elements of earth and heaven in its service; Art, awaking, clothes its strength with beauty; Literature, new born, redoubles and perpetuates its praise; Civilization smiles; liberty is glad; Humanity rejoices; Piety exults,—for the voice of industry and gladness is heard on every hand. And who, contemplating such achievements, will deny that there is dignity in Labour!

—Newman Hall

Words

achievements, *accomplishments*.
admonitions, *warnings*.
benefactions, *good deeds*.

compete, *strive*.
contemplating, *pondering*.
desolation, *destitution*.

detection, *discovery*.
dignity, *nobleness*.
dismayed, *daunted*.
distributes, *dispenses*.
exertion, *labour*.
gorgeous, *splendid*.
perpetuating, *continuing*.
ponderous, *weighty*.

pulsations, *beats*.
ramifications, *branches*.
representatives, *emissaries*.
sustenance, *nourishment*.
transmutes, *changes*.
untrammelled, *free*.
verifies, *fulfils*.
viaducts, *road-ways*.

☆ ☆ ☆ ☆ ☆ ☆ ☆ ☆ ☆ ☆ ☆ ☆ ☆ ☆ ☆ ☆ ☆ ☆ ☆ ☆

劳动的尊严！遇到困难的时候，不沮丧，不退缩，奋斗的时候不疲惫，渴望通过努力坚持促进人类的幸福。"吵闹的劳动就像一百只手敲响了早晨的金门。"取得进步的每一天，都会经过百年的时间，奉献给崭新的世界！

劳动可以开辟森林、排干泥沼，就像盛开的玫瑰花给荒野带来欢乐。劳动可以驱动耕犁、撒播种子、收割庄稼、研磨玉米，并将其转换成纤维，作为生命的食材。劳动可以收拾牧场、清扫水域以及培育土壤，每天为成千上万的家庭提供粮食。

劳动能够塑造砖块、劈裂石板、开采石头，使它们变成圆柱状，并将其竖立，不仅能够建成简陋的小屋和华丽的宫殿，还可以呈现出锥形的尖顶和庄严的圆顶。

通过劳动，人类可以深深地潜入到坚硬的地下，挖掘长期隐藏并储存在里面的煤炭，从而放入十几万个火炉，使数百万的住所能够抵抗冬天的寒冷。通过劳动，人类探测到了深埋在岩石中的丰富的矿脉，开采出了金、银、铜和锡。通过劳动，人类冶炼出铁，再塑造成各种形状的用品和装饰物，包括巨大的柱子和微小的针，沉重的锚和线丝做的纱网，强大的蒸汽引擎的抛光环和闪闪发光的珠子。

通过劳动，人类砍伐下来粗糙的橡树，并利用木材的形状建造了在巨浪中颠簸的船，操纵它与暴风雨进行搏斗，忍受每一种气候所创造的恶劣环境，载着我们驶向海岸。劳动带给我们印度的大米和美国的棉花，非洲的象牙和格陵兰的石油，从阳光明媚的南方带来水果，从冰天雪地的北方带来毛皮，带来东方的茶和西方的糖，作为交换，也给这些地方带去英国的每一种工业产品和生产技能。劳动通过贸易的普遍蔓延，从国家到国家，从城市到城市，从家庭到家庭，在所有地方传播生活的必需品和奢侈品。劳动通过毫无限制的商业脉动，在一个巨大的社会系统中维持健康的生活。

通过劳动，人类融合了岩石的不透明粒子，生产出透明的玻璃，将它锻造和抛光，结合得如此美妙，使盲人的视力得到恢复；人们之前在遥远距离之外看不到的世界，现在可以准确无误地被测量；原子，因其自身的渺小而可以朝向四面八方扩散，现在通过精密的检测，它们揭示出了众多物质的神奇和美妙。

劳动拥有一个秘密，比魔法石还神奇得多。它会使毫无价值的物质蜕变成为最珍贵的东西；它可以用强大的化学力量提炼出海洋和陆地中的腐烂物，将它们放置在熔炉中，继而提取出芬芳的精华液、治疗用的药物和无价艺术品的原料。

劳动嘲笑困难，跨越雄伟的河流，将高架桥横跨于湿地和沼泽之上，在峡谷上空悬浮起空中的桥梁，刺破深山和沟壑，挖掘出坚固的隧道，爆破岩石和填充凹陷；坚韧不拔和满含爱意的劳动，也将地球上的所有国家连接到一起，在字面上验证了一句古老的预言："一切山洼都要抬高，一切山峰都要削平。"

劳动绘制出一段精致的铁路线，它能够贯穿从一个地方到另一个地方的路程，穿山越海，实现了以往的许多幻想和虚构故事，建造了一架可能超过风和闪电，甚至和思想一样迅速飞驰的战车。

劳动能够抓住天才的思想、科学的发现和虔诚的训诫，并用它独特的魔力使人印象深刻，从而充满了生机与力量，将真理一直延续到漫长的将来，扩散到全人类之中。

劳动为王者建造了水晶宫殿，其高高耸起的屋顶傲然闪耀在阳光之下，在每个国家的每个时代，它宽广的庭院都斩获了众多胜利的战利品。

劳动像一个伟大的魔术师，来到一片无人居住的荒野，他认真地观察了这片安静荒凉的土地；然后，他挥舞着他那能够创造奇迹的魔杖，让凄凉的山谷充满丰收的金色；让贫瘠的山坡都落满树叶；让火炉充满火焰；让铁环繁忙地运转；贸易的集市、科学的展厅、宗教的寺庙，都展现在大家面前；帆樯林立，港口的船只上都飘荡着不同的旗帜，码头上堆满了贸易商品——这些都是和平的战利品和劳动带来的收益。遥远的地区有自己的度假村；科学用它的角度诠释了天地；被唤醒的艺术为劳动的力量披上了美丽的外衣；新生的文学使对劳动的赞赏加倍并得以延续；文明微笑着，自由也因此愉悦；人类的欢呼雀跃和虔诚的狂喜——所有来自各个行业人们的喜悦声音充满了每个角落。因此，考虑到这些成就，有谁还会否认劳动的尊严！

——纽曼·霍尔

Lesson 72
THE PROBLEM OF CREATION
第七十二课　宇宙的问题

If we look out upon the starry heavens by which we are surrounded, we find them diversified in every possible way. Our own mighty Stellar System takes upon itself the form of a flat disk, which may be compared to a mighty ring breaking into two distinct divisions, severed from each other, the interior with stars less densely populous than upon the exterior. But take the telescope and go beyond this; and here you find, coming out from the depths of space, universes of every possible shape and fashion; some of them assuming a globular form, and, when we apply the highest possible penetrating power of the telescope, breaking into ten thousand brilliant stars, all crushed and condensed into one luminous, bright, and magnificent centre.

But look yet farther. Away yonder, in the distance, you behold a faint, hazy, nebulous ring of light, the interior almost entirely dark, but the exterior ring-shaped, and exhibiting to the eye, under the most powerful telescope, the fact that it may be resolved entirely into stars, producing a universe somewhat analogous to the one we inhabit. Go yet deeper into space, and there you will behold another universe—voluminous scrolls of light, glittering with beauty, flashing with splendour, and sweeping a curve of most extraordinary form and of most tremendous outlines.

Thus we may pass from planet to planet, from sun to sun, from system to system. We may reach beyond the limits of this mighty stellar cluster with which we are allied. We may find other island universes sweeping through space. The great unfinished problem still remains—Whence came this universe? Have all these stars which glitter in the heavens been shining from all eternity? Has our globe been rolling around the sun for countless ages? Whence, whence this magnificent architecture, whose architraves rise in splendour before us in every direction? Is it all the work of chance? I answer, No. It is not the work of chance.

Who shall reveal to us the true cosmogony of the universe by which we are surrounded? Is it the work of an Omnipotent Architect? If so, who is this August Being? Go with me tonight, in imagination, and stand with old Paul, the great apostle, upon Mars Hill, and there look around you as he did. Here rises that magnificent building, the Parthenon, sacred to Minerva, the goddess of wisdom. There towers her colossal statue, rising in its majesty above the city of which she was the guardian—the first object to catch the rays of the rising, and the last to be kissed by the rays of the setting, sun. There are the temples of all the gods; and there are the shrines of every divinity.

And yet I tell you these gods and these divinities, though created under the inspiring fire of poetic fancy and Greek imagination, never reared this stupendous structure by which we are surrounded. The Olympic Jove never built these heavens. The wisdom of Minerva never organized these magnificent systems. I say with St. Paul,—"The God that made the world and all things therein, seeing that he is Lord of heaven and earth, dwelleth not in temples made with hands."

No; here is the temple of our Divinity. Around us and above us rise Sun and System, Cluster and Universe. And I doubt not that in every region of this vast Empire of God, hymns of praise and anthems of glory are rising and reverberating from Sun to Sun and from System to System—heard by Omnipotence alone across immensity and through eternity!

—O. M. Mitchell

Words

analogous, *similar*.
anthems, *sacred songs*.
diversified, *varied*.
eternity, *infinitude of time*.
extraordinary, *remarkable*.
globular, *spherical*.
guardian, *protector*.
immensity, *infinitude of space*.
magnificent, *splendid*.

nebulous, *cloudy*.
penetrating, *piercing*.
reveal, *unfold*.
reverberating, *resounding*.
stupendous, *tremendous*.
surrounded, *encompassed*.
universes, *world-system*.
voluminous, *ample*.

☆ ☆

　　如果我们抬头仰望环绕着我们的星辰灿烂的寰宇，就会发现它们都是以不同的方式呈现的。我们拥有强大的恒星系统，它以一个扁平的圆盘形式存在，这与一个被割裂成两个不同部分的强大的圆环十分相似，它们相互脱离，密度大的在里面，密度小的在外面。但是如果你拿起望远镜向更远方眺望，在这里，在太空深处，你会发现宇宙中的每一种形状。它们中所拥有像是圆球的形状，并且，当我们运用穿透力极强的望远镜遥望一颗熠熠生辉的恒星，所有这些星星都会被击碎，凝结成一个闪烁的、明亮的、华丽的中心。

　　但是再看得远一些。在远处，你可以看到一个微弱的、朦胧的、模糊的光环，内部几乎是完全黑暗的，但是它外部的环形，在目光下却闪烁出强烈的光。事实上，你可以认定它是恒星，产生了一个就像我们的栖息地一样的宇宙。进入太空中的更深处，在那里你会看见另一个宇宙的浩瀚卷光，闪烁着美丽，闪耀着光辉，形成了非同寻常的卷曲的线条和巨大的轮廓。

因此，我们可以从一个星球穿越到另一个星球，从日出到日落，从一个系统到另一个系统。我们超越了这个强大的极限恒星的集群，而正是因为它，我们才被联系到了一起。我们发现了其他岛屿遍布了整个宇宙空间。这个巨大的未解决的问题仍然存在——宇宙是从何处来的？是否所有这些在天空中闪闪发光的恒星的光芒都是永恒的光辉？我们的地球绕着太阳转动，究竟经过了多少个岁月？这个在我们面前朝向四面八方辉煌上升的宏伟体系从何而来？所有这些都是偶然间实现的吗？我的回答是，不，这绝非偶然。

谁能向我们揭示包围我们的宇宙的真正起源？这是一个无所不能的建筑师的杰作吗？如果是这样，那谁又是这位令人敬畏的人呢？今晚你可以和我一起，在想象中和伟大的信徒保罗站在一起，站在火星山上，像他那样环顾四周。这里矗立着帕特农神庙、圣米勒娃像和智慧女神像这样的宏伟建筑。它巨大的雕像竖立在此，它守护着宏伟壮丽的城市——在第一缕光线上升的时候感受着太阳的亲吻。这里有属于所有神灵的庙宇，还有一个具有神性的圣坛。

然而我告诉你们，这些神和神灵，虽然在鼓舞人心的火焰之下创建了诗意的幻想和属于希腊的想象，却永远不会培养出这些将我们包围的巨大框架。奥林匹克的宙斯从来没有建造过这片宇宙。圣米勒娃的智慧也从不会组织起这些华丽的体系。我对圣保罗先生说："上帝创造了世界和其中所有的东西，天地的主就仰卧在世界之中，而不是居住在神明建造起来的寺庙中。"不，这里是我们神的宫殿。太阳和银河系在我们头顶升起，群集的行星和宇宙环绕在我们周围。我对此毫不怀疑，在这个属于上帝的庞大帝国的每个区域之中，荣耀的圣歌和光辉的赞美诗缓缓升起，从日出到日落，从一个体系向另一个体系，悠然回荡——只有万能的上帝一个人能够穿越浩瀚、通过永恒听得到！

——O. M. 米切尔

Lesson 73   EDUCATION AND THE STATE
第七十三课　教育与国家

I believe, sir, that it is the right and the duty of the State to provide means of education for the common people. This proposition seems to me to be implied in every definition that has ever yet been given of the functions of a Government. About the extent of those functions there has been much difference of opinion among ingenious men. There are some who hold that it is the business of a Government to meddle with every part of the system of human life: to regulate trade by bounties and prohibitions, to regulate expenditure by sumptuary laws, to regulate literature by a censorship, to regulate religion by an inquisition. Others go to the opposite extreme, and assign to Government a very narrow sphere of action. But the very narrowest sphere that ever was assigned to governments by any school of political philosophy is quite wide enough for my purpose. On one point all the disputants are agreed. They unanimously acknowledge that it is the duty of every Government to take order for giving security to the persons and property of the members of the community.

This being admitted, can it be denied that the education of the common people is a most effectual means of securing our persons and our property? Let Adam Smith answer that question for me. He has expressly told us that a distinction is to be made, particularly in a commercial and highly civilized society, between the education of the rich and the education of the poor. The education of the poor, he says, is a matter which deeply concerns the commonwealth. Just as the magistrate ought to interfere for the purpose of preventing the leprosy from spreading among the people, he ought to interfere for the purpose of stopping the progress of the moral distempers which are inseparable from ignorance. Nor can this duty be neglected without danger to the public peace. If you leave the multitude uninstructed, there is serious risk that their animosities may produce the most dreadful disorders.

The most dreadful disorders! Those are Adam Smith's own words; and prophetic words they were. Scarcely had he given this warning to our rulers when his prediction was fulfilled in a manner never to be forgotten. I speak of the riots of 1780. I do not know that I could find in all history a stronger proof of the proposition, that the ignorance of the common people makes the property, the limbs, the lives of all classes insecure. Without the shadow of a grievance, at the summons of a madman, a hundred thousand people rise in insurrection. During a whole week there is anarchy in the greatest and wealthiest of European cities. The Parliament is besieged. Your predecessor sits trembling in his chair, and expects every moment to see the door beaten in by the ruffians whose roar he hears all round the house. The peers are pulled out of their coaches. The bishops in their lawn are forced to fly over the tiles. The chapels of foreign ambassadors, buildings made sacred by the law of nations, are destroyed. The house of the Chief Justice is demolished. The little children of the Prime Minister are taken out of their beds and laid in their night clothes on the table of the Horse Guards,—the only safe asylum from the fury of the rabble. The prisons are opened. Highwaymen, housebreakers, murderers, come forth to swell the mob by which they have been set free. Thirty-six fires are blazing at once in London. The Government is paralyzed; the very foundations of the Empire are shaken.

Then came the retribution. Count up all the wretches who were shot, who were hanged, who were crushed, who drank themselves to death at the rivers of gin which ran down Holborn Hill; and you will find that battles have been lost and won with a smaller sacrifice of life. And what was the cause of this calamity—a calamity which, in the history of London, ranks with the Great Plague and the Great Fire? The cause was the ignorance of a population which had been suffered, in the neighbourhood of palaces, theatres, temples, to grow up as rude and stupid as any tribe of tattooed cannibals in New Zealand—I might say, as any drove of beasts in Smithfield Market.

The instance is striking; but it is not solitary. To the same cause are to be ascribed the riots of Nottingham, the sack of Bristol, all the outrages of Lud, and Swing, and Rebecca;—beautiful and costly machinery broken to pieces in Yorkshire, barns and hay-stacks blazing in Kent, fences and buildings pulled down in Wales. Could such things have been done in a country in which the mind of the labourer had been opened by education; in which he had been taught to find pleasure in the exercise of his intellect, taught to revere his Maker, taught to respect legitimate authority, and taught at the same time to seek the redress of real wrongs by peaceful and constitutional means?

This, then, is my argument:—It is the duty of Government to protect our persons and property from danger; the gross ignorance of the common people is a principal cause of danger to our persons and property: therefore it is the duty of the Government to take care that the common people shall not be grossly ignorant.

And what is the alternative? It is universally allowed that, by some means, Government must protect our persons and property. If you take away education, what means do you leave? You leave means such as only necessity can justify—means which inflict a fearful amount of pain, not only on the guilty, but on the innocent who are connected with the guilty. You leave guns and bayonets, stocks and whipping-posts, tread-mills, solitary cells, penal colonies, gibbets. See, then, how the case stands. Here is an end which, as we all agree, governments are bound to attain. There are only two ways of attaining it. One of those ways is by making men better, and wiser, and happier. The other way is by making them infamous and miserable. Can it be doubted which we ought to prefer?

—Lord Macaulay

Words

alternative, *other course*.
anarchy, *lawlessness*.
argument, *line of reasoning*.
bayonets, *short swords*.
calamity, *disaster*.
commonwealth, *state*.
constitutional, *statutory*.
demolished, *destroyed*.
disputants, *controversialists*.
distinction, *difference*.
expenditure, *outlay*.
functions, *duties*.
grievance, *ground of complaint*.
infamous, *disgraceful*.

inflict, *impose*.
inseparable, *indissoluble*.
insurrection, *rebellion*.
legitimate, *lawful*.
particularly, *especially*.
philosophy, *science*.
predecessor, *precursor*.
prediction, *prophecy*.
prohibitions, *restrictions*.
proposition, *statement*.
retribution, *punishment*.
sumptuary, *restricting expenditure*.
tattooed, *skin-dyed*.

Questions

On what point has there been much difference of opinion among ingenious men?—About the extent of the functions of Government.

What differences are pointed out?—Some have held that Government should meddle with every department of human life; others have assigned to Government a very narrow sphere of action.

On what are all parties agreed?—That it is the duty of Government to take order for the security of life and property.

What is a most effectual means of accomplishing this?—Education.

What does Adam Smith say leaving the multitude uninstructed is likely to produce?—The most dreadful disorders.

What striking example of such disorders is given?—The riots in London in 1780.

Mention some particulars of the excesses perpetrated by the mob.—Peers were pulled out of their coaches; bishops had to fly over the tiles; the chapels of foreign ambassadors were destroyed; the house of the Chief Justice was demolished; the prisons were opened, and the prisoners swelled the mob; thirty-six fires were blazing in London at once.

What was the true cause of that calamity?—The ignorance of the people, who, in the neighbourhood of palaces, had been allowed to grow up as rude as savages and brutes.

What other instances are mentioned?—The Machinery riots of the Luddites in Nottingham and Yorkshire, in 1811-16; the Reform riots in Bristol in 1831; the agricultural outrages in Kent in 1830-33; the Rebecca riots in Wales in 1843.

What would have made these things impossible?—Opening the minds of the labourers by education; &c., &c.

Sum up the argument.—Government should protect life and property; the ignorance of the people endangers life and property: therefore Government should take means to remove the ignorance of the people.

What is the alternative?—Education, or physical force—guns and bayonets, &c.

What are the consequences of each plan?—Education makes men better, wiser, and happier; physical force makes them infamous and miserable.

Notes

The answers to the Questions on the above Lesson are given in full, as the argument may be somewhat difficult for young scholars to follow. They will also serve to show how the main points in a lesson may be gathered up by means of a few leading questions.

　　先生，我相信国家有权力和义务向普通民众提供教育手段。在我看来，这个建议在针对政府职责的每个定义中都得到了暗示。但要在多大程度上履行这些职责，足智多谋的人们对此存在太多观点上的不同。有些人认为，政府的职责就是关心人们生活的方方面面：通过奖励和禁令管理交易，通过禁奢法管理开支，通过审查制度管理文化，通过宗教法庭管理宗教问题。而有些人则持完全相反的态度，他们将政府的行为限制在一个非常狭窄的圈子里。但是对于我来说，即使是所有政治哲学的分支限制的政府行动的最狭窄的圈子，也是相当广泛的。针对一个观点，所有的争执者是持相同意见的。他们一致承认，每一个政府都有责任有秩序地保护国家成员的人身和财产安全。

　　承认了这一点，就不能否认，对于普通群众的教育，是保护我们人身和财产安全的最有效手段。亚当·史密斯可以为我回答这个问题。他明确地告诉我们，在富人的教育和穷人的教育之间有一个区别，尤其是在一个商业国家和高度文明的社会。他说，穷人的教育是一个与国民整体息息相关的问题。正如地方行政长官应该为阻止麻风在人群中传播而有所干预一样，他应该有所行动来阻止与无知密不可分的道德缺陷的蔓延。政府不忽视这些责任，公共安全才是没有危险的。如果大量群众不受教育，国家就会存在紧迫的危险，他们的仇恨可能会产生最可怕的混乱。

　　最可怕的混乱！这是亚当·史密斯的原话，并且让它们也成为了预言。他仅仅是在当他的预言以一种难以被忘怀的方式成真时，才向我们的统治者发出这些警告。我说的是1780年的暴动。我不知道能否在所有人类历史中，找到比这更能证明这个观点的有力证据，那就是：普通群众的无知使得所有阶层的财产、健康、生命都变得毫无保障。没有任何抱怨作为前兆，在一个疯子的召唤下，成千上万的人们发动了起义。整整一周的时间里，欧洲最大、最富有的城市出现了混乱，议会被起义者围困，前任执政者颤抖着坐在椅子上，预料着每一刻都会看见暴徒敲开大门，在屋子的每一处，他都能听到他们的叫喊声。他的同事们被迫离开了他们的住所。主教不得不在草坪上和砖块上爬行。外国大使的教堂，国家法律保护的神圣建筑，都被一一摧毁。首席法官的房屋也被拆毁了。首相的孩子还穿着睡衣，就从他们床上被带到了皇家骑兵卫队的桌子上——这仅仅是为躲避乌合之众暴怒的安全避难所。监狱开放了，拦路强盗、入室抢劫者、谋杀犯即将被这些起义的民众释放。三十六处大火立刻在伦敦熊熊燃烧。政府变得麻痹，帝国的根基也在颤抖。

接下来的是惩罚。这次暴乱中有众多不幸的人被射死，被绞死，被碾死，或是喝了从哈波山留下的河水而死去，你将发现战争无论输赢，都带来了生命的牺牲。灾难发生的原因是什么——伦敦历史中的这样一次灾难，如同大瘟疫和大火灾一样严重的灾难，它的原因是什么？其原因是人们的无知，他们的周围布满了宫殿、剧院、好人、寺庙，但他们却像新西兰的纹身食人部落一般粗鲁愚蠢——我也许会说，正如一群野兽出现在史密斯菲尔的市场上一般。

这个例子非常特别，但又并不孤立。诺丁汉的暴乱、布里斯托的洗劫，所有路德、施威、丽贝卡的愤怒——约克郡精致、昂贵的机械被毁为碎片，肯特的仓库和草堆付之一炬，威尔士的篱笆和建筑被一一拆毁。在一个这样的国家，如果工人的思想都因为教育而变得开化，如果工人已经学会在他智力的训练中找寻快乐，已经学会尊敬他的上帝，学会尊重合理的权威，并且同时学会通过和平与宪法的方式去纠正真正的错误，这样的事情会发生吗？

因此，我的观点是保护我们的人身和财产安全是政府的责任，普通群众的极端无知是导致我们人身和财产危险的主要原因，因此，确保人们不会变得非常无知，正是政府的责任所在。

还有什么是替换物吗？政府必须保护我们的人身和财产安全，是所有人公认的。如果排除教育这个方法，你还有什么方法？你选择的方法必然会使人们遭受大量可怕的痛苦，不仅仅使罪犯遭受痛苦，甚至和罪犯有关的无辜的人们也一样。你选择了枪和刺刀、树枝和鞭子、踩踏、禁闭室、刑罚和绞刑架。然后，让我们看看事情会变成什么样子。正如我们都料想到的，最后的结果一定是政府来接手。而政府只能通过两种方式来接手这件事情，一种是通过使人们变得更好，更明智，更幸福；另一种是通过使他们变得臭名昭著、穷困不堪。我们应该选择哪一种，还值得怀疑吗？

——麦考利勋爵

Lesson 74　ENGLISH SELF-ESTEEM
第七十四课　英国的自尊

And now I will grapple with the noble Lord [Palmerston] on the ground which he selected for himself, in the most triumphant portion of his speech, by his reference to those emphatic words, Civis Romanus sum. He vaunted, amidst the cheers of his supporters, that under his administration an Englishman should be throughout the world what the citizen of Rome had been. What then, sir, was a Roman citizen? He was the member of a privileged caste; he belonged to a conquering race,—to a nation that held all others bound down by the strong arm of power. For him there was to be an exceptional system of law; for him principles were to be asserted, and by him rights were to be enjoyed, that were denied to the rest of the world.

Is such, then, the view of the noble lord, as to the relation that is to subsist between England and other countries? Does he make the claim for us, that we are to be uplifted on a platform high above the standing-ground of all other nations? It is, indeed, too clear, not only from the expressions, but from the whole spirit of the speech of the noble Viscount, that too much of this notion is lurking in his mind; that he adopts in part that vain conception, that we, forsooth, have a mission to be the censors of vice and folly, of abuse and imperfection among the other countries of the world; that we are to be the universal schoolmasters; and that all those who hesitate to rccognize our office can be governed only by prejudice or personal animosity, and should have the blind war of diplomacy forthwith declared against them......

Sir, the English people, whom we are here to represent, are indeed a great and noble people; but it adds nothing to their greatness or their nobleness, that, when we assemble in this place, we should trumpet forth our virtues in elaborate panegyrics, and designate those who may not be wholly of our mind as a knot of foreign conspirators. Now, the policy of the noble lord tends to encourage and confirm in us that which is our besetting fault and weakness, both as a nation and as individuals. Let an Englishman travel where he will as a private person, he is found in general to be upright, high-minded, brave, liberal, and true: but with all this, foreigners are too often sensible of something that galls them in his presence; and I apprehend it is because he has too great a tendency to self-esteem—too little disposition to regard the feelings, the habits, and the ideas of others.

I doubt not that use will be made of our present debate to work upon this peculiar weakness of the English mind. The people will be told that those who oppose the motion are governed by personal motives, have no regard for public principle, no enlarged ideas of national policy. You will take your case before a favourable jury, and you think to gain your verdict; but, sir, let the House of Commons be warned—let it warn itself—against all illusions. There is in this case also a course of appeal. There is an appeal, such as one honourable and learned member has already made, from the one House of Parliament to the other. There is a further appeal from this House of Parliament to the people of England. But, lastly, there is also an appeal from the people of England to the general sentiment of the civilized world; and I, for my part, am of opinion that England will stand shorn of a chief part of her glory and her pride, if she shall be found to have separated herself, through the policy she pursues abroad, from the moral support which the general and fixed convictions of mankind afford— if the day shall come in which she may continue to excite the wonder and the fear of other nations, but in which she shall have no part in their affections and their regard.

—William Ewart Gladstone

Words

administration, *government*.
animosity, *antipathy*.
besetting, *habitual*.
caste, race; *order*.
civilized, *cultivated*.
conception, *notion*.
conspirators, *plotters*.
convictions, *beliefs*.
designate, *characterize*.
disposition, *inclination*.
emphatic, *forcible*.
exceptional, *special*.
expressions, *words*.

favourable, *partial*.
foreigners, *strangers*.
illusions, *deceptions*.
imperfection, *fault*.
panegyrics, *eulogies*.
personal, *selfish*.
privileged, *favoured*.
recognize, *acknowledge*.
separated, *withdrawn*.
subsist, *continue*.
tendency, *proneness*.
triumphant, *exulting*.
vaunted, *boasted*.

☆ ☆

　　现在我将以高贵的帕莫斯顿爵士为自己辩护的语句为基础，来分析他的话。这是一次大获全胜的演讲，他在其中引用并强调了罗马公民。在他支持者的欢呼声中，他自夸道，在他的管理下，一个英国人可以像当初的罗马公民一样，在全世界都可自由穿行。那么先生，一个罗马公民是怎样的？他是一个享有特权的种姓制度的成员之一；他属于一个胜利的民族，属于一个使用强硬手段使所有人都臣服于自己的国家。对于他来说，存在一种特殊的法律系统；他主张自己的原则，享受自己的权利，然而世界上的其他人却无权享受。

　　如此看来，关于维持英国和其他国家的关系，高贵的帕莫斯顿爵士持有怎样的观点？他是否持这种观点，我们应该意气昂扬地立足在比所有其他国家都要高的一个平台上？实际上，不论从语言的表达上，还是从爵士演讲的情绪上，都可以非常清楚地看出这些理念大都潜伏在他的意识里。他采纳了这种虚荣设想的一部分：我们有着监察邪恶和愚蠢行为的使命，监察世界上其他国家出现的缺陷的使命；我们是全球的领袖；所有那些迟疑于认定我们地位的人，都应该受到歧视和敌意的对待，同时应该立即发布外交战争声明向他们宣战。

先生，我们在这里展示的英国人的确是一个崇高、伟大的民族，不过我们这样做，却不会给他们的伟大或高贵添彩。当我们聚集在这个地方，我们应该用精心的赞美来颂扬我们的美德，并指出那些可能不完全与我们同心的阴谋叛乱者。现在，帕莫斯顿爵士的宣称却是在鼓励我们，并使我们确信，不管是作为一个国家或是个人，这都是我们的缺陷和弱点。如果一个英国人作为个人到各地去旅行，别人一般会认为他是诚实的、高尚的、勇敢的、自由的，真实的，但这一切，通常会让外国人在有英国人出现的时候，因为他会羞辱到他们而特别敏感。据我的理解，这是因为英国人有太强烈的自尊的倾向——太少去顾及别人的习惯、情感和思想。

我不怀疑我们目前的辩论会对这特殊的英国人的思维弱点有所影响。人们将了解到那些反对运动是由个人动机驱使的，而与公共原则毫无关联，也不该扩大到国家政策的层面。你会将你的案件交给一个有利于你的陪审团，并认为自己会赢得你的判决，但是，先生，下议院会受到提醒——它自己就会提醒自己来反对这所有的幻想。在这个案件中，也有一个上诉的过程。正如一位尊贵的、有学识的成员已经上诉的那样，会有一次上诉，从一个议会进行到另一个，还有进一步的从国会到英国人民的上诉。但是最后，还会有一种上诉，从英国人民到文明世界，而站在我个人的角度，我认为英格兰将被剥夺她的荣耀和骄傲，如果她要通过她追求的外交政策，通过道义上的支持，通过一般的和固定的信念使自己与其他国家分离——如果这一天会到来，她将继续激发起其他国家的惊讶和恐惧，而再也不会拥有他们的关心和情感。

——威廉·尤尔特·格莱斯顿

Lesson 75　PLEASURES OF KNOWLEDGE
第七十五课　知识的快乐

"Not to know at large of things remote
From use, obscure and subtle, but to know
That which before us lies in daily life,
Is the prime wisdom."

—Milton

It is noble to seek Truth, and it is beautiful to find it. It is the ancient feeling of the human heart, that knowledge is better than riches; and it is deeply and *sacredly true*. To mark the course of human passions as they have flowed on in the ages that are past; to see why nations have risen, and why they have fallen; to speak of heat, and light, and the winds; to know what man has discovered in the heavens above and in the earth beneath; to hear the chemist unfold the marvellous properties that the Creator has locked up in a speck of earth; to be told that there are worlds so distant from our own, that the quickness of light, travelling since the world's creation, has never yet reached us;—it is worth while in the days of our youth to strive hard for this great discipline.

To wander in the creations of poetry, and grow warm again with that eloquence which swayed the democracies of the Old World; to go up with great reasoners to the First Cause of all, and to perceive, in the midst of all this dissolution and decay and cruel separation, that there is one thing unchangeable, indestructible, and everlasting;—it is surely worthwhile to pass sleepless nights for this; to give up for it laborious days; to spurn for it present pleasures; to endure for it afflicting poverty; to wade for it through darkness, and sorrow, and contempt, as the great spirits of the world have done in all ages and in all times.

I appeal to the experience of every man who is in the habit of exercising his mind vigorously and well, whether there is not a satisfaction in it, which tells him he has been acting up to one of the great objects of his existence? The end of nature has been answered: his faculties have done that which they were created to do—not languidly occupied upon trifles, not enervated by sensual gratification, but exercised in that toil which is so congenial to their nature, and so worthy of their strength.

A life of knowledge is not often a life of injury and crime. Whom does suck a man oppress? with whose happiness does he interfere? whom does his ambition destroy? and whom does his fraud deceive? In the pursuit of science he injures no man, and in the acquisition he does good to all.

A man who dedicates his life to knowledge, becomes habituated to pleasure which carries with it no reproach: and there is one security that he will never love that pleasure which is paid for by anguish of heart—his pleasures are all cheap, all dignified, and all innocent; and, as far as any human being can expect permanence in this changing scene, he has secured a happiness which no malignity of fortune can ever take away, but which must cleave to him while he lives, ameliorating every good, and diminishing every evil of his existence......

I solemnly declare, that, but for the love of knowledge, I should consider the life of the meanest hedger and ditcher as preferable to that of the greatest and richest man in existence; for the fire of our minds is like the fire which the Persians burn on the mountains—it flames night and day, and is immortal, and not to be quenched! Upon something it must act and feed—upon the pure spirit of knowledge, or upon the foul dregs of polluting passions.

Therefore, when I say, in conducting your understanding, love knowledge with a great love, with a vehement love, with a love coeval with life, what do I say but love innocence; love virtue; love purity of conduct; love that which, if you are rich and great, will sanctify the providence which has made you so, and make men call it justice; love that which, if you are poor, will render your poverty respectable, and make the proudest feel it unjust to laugh at the meanness of your fortunes; love that which will comfort you, adorn you, and never quit you—which will open to you the kingdom of thought, and all the boundless regions of conception, as an asylum against the cruelty, the injustice, and the pain that may be your lot in the outer world—that which will make your motives habitually great and honourable, and light up in an instant a thousand noble disdains at the very thought of meanness and of fraud?

Therefore, if any young man have embarked his life in the pursuit of Knowledge, let him go on without doubting or fearing the event: let him not be intimidated by the cheerless beginnings of Knowledge, by the darkness from which she springs, by the difficulties which hover around her, by the wretched habitations in which she dwells, by the want and sorrow which sometimes journey in her train; but let him ever follow her as the Angel that guards him, and as the Genius of his life. She will bring him out at last into the light of day, and exhibit him to the world comprehensive in acquirements, fertile in resources, rich in imagination, strong in reasoning, prudent and powerful above his fellows in all the relations and in all the offices of life.

—Sydney Smith

Words

acquisition, *attainment*.
ameliorating, *making better*.
ancient, *primitive*.
asylum, *refuge*.
coeval, *of the same age*.

comprehensive, *capacious*.
contempt, *neglect*.
democracies, *republics*.
dignified, *elevated*.
discovered, *found out*.

dissolution, *destruction*.
eloquence, *oratory*.
enervated, *weakened*.
expedience, *knowledge gained by
  practice*.
fertile, *fruitful; ready*.
habituated, *accustomed*.

indestructible, *everlasting*.
intimidated, *frightened*.
languidly, *feebly*.
marvellous, *wonderful*.
permanence, *durability*.
quenched, *extinguished*.
vehement, *powerful*.

☆ ☆

> 在使用中，不了解遥远的事物，
> 它们隐蔽而微妙，但知道
> 日常生活中它们就在我们面前，
> 这就是原本的智慧。
>
> ——弥尔顿

寻求真理是高贵的，发现它则是美好的。知识比财富更好，这是人类心中古老的感受，而这一感受拥有深刻、神圣的真实性。正如过去一样，知识标记了人类进步的进程，它探究为什么一些国家强大了，为什么它们又衰败了；它描绘热、光和风；它了解人类在天空中和地表下发现了什么；它看化学家展现了造物主锁定在土壤之上的奇妙特性；它听说存在一些如此遥远的地方，甚至从世界的创造之初就一直存在的光的旅行也从来没有到达过；所有这些，都值得我们在青年时代为了伟大的真理而努力。

人们可以在诗歌创作中徘徊，在动摇了旧世界统治的雄辩中再次感受温暖，追寻上帝这一所有生命的第一推动力，感知所有物质的溶解和分离，感知现实残酷的衰败。其中，有一件事是一成不变的、坚不可摧的、经久不衰的，它肯定值得人们在许多个不眠的夜晚为它劳神费力，为它摒弃现在的快乐，为它忍受贫苦的困扰，为它涉过黑暗、悲伤和蔑视，正如世界上众多伟人在所有时代做的那样。

我呼吁每一个习惯严格地、更好地锻炼自己思维的人，无论他是否满足于现状，都尝试告诉自己要一直努力实现自己最伟大的目标。自然的结局已然明了：他的能力已经完成了造物主创造他时要他做的，而不是懒洋洋地沉浸于琐事，也不是因感官满足而变得衰弱，而是辛苦地从事如此适合他们本性，如此值得他们奉献力量的事情。

一个有知识的人，往往不是一个会伤害别人或充满罪恶的人。谁会受人欺压？快乐会干扰谁？他的雄心会伤害谁？他的欺诈会欺骗谁？在对科学的追求中，撒谎不会伤害到任何人，而在对科学的收获中，这会对所有人有利。

一个毕生致力于知识的人会习惯于愉悦，而不受他人的责备侵扰。还有一点可以肯定，他永远不会爱上那种以心灵的痛苦为代价的娱乐方式，他的所有乐趣都是容易得来的、有尊严的、纯净的，而只要任何人可以期待这一情况的变化，他就肯定会拥有任何邪恶财富都带不走的幸福，但这种幸福必然会在他的生命中忠于他，改善他生活中的众多方面，减少他的一切灾祸……

我郑重声明，除了对知识的热爱，我还认为，最卑贱的种树园丁和挖沟工匠的生活，也优于那些最伟大、最富有的人的生活，因为我们的头脑中的火焰，就像波斯人在山上放的火一样——它日夜不休地燃烧，是不朽的而不灭的！它必须以某种事物为养料，或是热爱知识的纯粹精神，或是肮脏激情的污浊残渣。

因此，为了增强你的理解，你必须用伟大而强烈的爱、与时俱进的爱去热爱知识。按我说的做，去热爱美德，热爱行为的纯洁。如果你富裕而又伟大，热爱让你变得如此的神的眷顾和人们都承认的正义；如果你很贫穷，热爱那些会使你的贫穷受人尊敬，会使嘲笑你财富匮乏的傲慢之人感到不公平的事物，热爱会安慰你、美化你、永不放弃你的事物——这将在你面前打开思想的王国，打开所有无穷的概念，作为一种反对广泛存在于你周围世界中残酷、不公和痛苦的庇护。热爱会将你的目标变得一直伟大和光荣的事物，热爱会在一瞬间让人高贵地不屑于卑鄙和欺诈的事物。

因此，如果任何年轻人已经开始他追求知识的生活，就让他毫无疑问和担心地继续走下去吧，让他不要害怕开始时候对知识的缺乏，也不要害怕知识缘起的黑暗、徘徊在她周围的困难和知识存在之处的悲惨，在培养她的过程中时常出现的欲望和悲伤，而要让他跟随着知识，正如天使守护着他和他生命中的天赋。知识会最终为他带来光明，并将一个这样的他展现在世界面前，拥有全面的才华，丰厚的资源，丰富的想象力，强大的推理能力，比他生命中所有的同伴都更谨慎、更强大。

——西德尼·史密斯

Lesson 76
THE BRITISH CONSTITUTIONAL SYSTEM OF CANADA
第七十六课　加拿大的英国宪法制度

I take the British constitutional system as the great original system upon which are founded the institutions of all free States. I take it as one of a family born of Christian civilization. I take it as combining in itself permanence and liberty; liberty in its best form—not in theory alone, but in practice; liberty which is enjoyed in fact by all the people of Canada, of every origin and of every creed.

Can any one pretend to say that a chapter of accidents which we can trace for eight hundred years, and which some antiquaries may even trace for a much longer period, will account for the permanence of these institutions? If you say that they have not in themselves the elements of permanence which preserve the foundations of a free State from one generation to another—how do you account for their continued and prosperous existence? How do you account for it, that of all the ancient constitutions of Europe this alone remains; and remains not only with all its ancient outlines, but with great modern improvements,—improvements, however, made in harmony with the design of its first architects? Here is a form of government that has lasted, with modifications to suit the spirit of successive ages, for a period of eight hundred years. How is it that I account for the permanence of its institutions? By asserting that, in their outline plan, they combine all the good of material importance that has ever been discovered.

The wisdom of the middle ages, and the political writers of the present time, have all laid down one maxim of government,—That no unmixed form of government can satisfy the wants of a free and intelligent people; that an unmixed democracy, for instance, must result in anarchy or military despotism: but that the form of government which combines in itself an inviolable monarchy, popular representation, and the incitements of an aristocracy—a working aristocracy—an aristocracy that takes its share of toil and danger in the day of battle, of care and anxiety in the time of peace—an aristocracy of talent open to any of the people who make themselves worthy to enter it—that three-fold combination in the system of government is the highest conception of political science.

Let us see if the British form, apart from any details of its practice, combines in itself these three qualities. The leading principle of the British system is, that the head of the State is inviolable. It is necessary to the stability of any State that there should be an inviolable authority or tribunal; and under the British system this is recognized in the maxim that "the King can do no wrong." Having placed the principle of inviolability in the Crown, and the principle of privilege in the Peerage, the founders of the State took care at the same time that the peerage should not stagnate into a small and exclusive caste. They left the House of Lords open to any of the people who might distinguish themselves in war or in peace, although they might be the children of paupers (and some have been ennobled who were unable to tell who their parents were), to enter in and take their place on an equality with the proudest there, who trace back their descent for centuries.

It was for the people of Canada, with the precedent of England and the example of the American republic before them, to decide which should be the prevailing character of their government,—British constitutional, or republican constitutional. For my part, I prefer the British constitutional government, because it is the best; and I reject the republican constitutional government, because it is not the best. We are now witnessing a great epoch in the world's history; and the events daily transpiring around us should teach us not to rely too much upon our present position of secure independence, but rather to apprehend and be prepared for attempts against our liberties, and against that system of government which, I am convinced, is heartily cherished by the inhabitants of this province.

—Hon. T. D. M. Gee

Words

anarchy, *confusion.*
antiquaries, *students of antiquity.*
apprehend, *anticipate.*
architects, *designers.*
aristocracy, *government by nobles.*
combining, *uniting.*
conception, *ideal.*
democracy, *government by the people.*
distinguish, *make famous.*
elements, *principles.*
ennobled, *raised to the peerage.*
exclusive, *select.*

importance, *value.*
incitements, *attractions.*
inviolable, *sacred.*
original, *primary.*
permanence, *durability.*
prevailing, *predominant.*
privilege, *immunity.*
prosperous, *flourishing.*
recognized, *acknowledged.*
transpiring, *happening.*
tribunal, *authority.*

☆ ☆

我认为英国宪政制度是一项伟大的原创体系，在此之上创建了所有自由国家的机构。我认为它源自于基督教的文明。我认为它自身结合了持久性和自由性；不是在理论上，而是在实践中享受自由，这是自由的最好形式。事实上，在加拿大，无论出身和信条，所有人都享有这种自由。

有没有人能够假装说，八百年之前的任何事件，或者一些我们可以追溯到更长时间之前的什么古物，能够解释这些制度的长久性？如果你说，这些制度本身并不拥有能够一代又一代地永久保护一个自由国家的基础元素——那你怎么解释它们的持续、繁荣的存在？而在所有古代欧洲的宪法里，现在只剩下这个制度；而这个制度不只保留了它所有古老的大纲，同时也获得了伟大的现代的改进——虽然改进了，但却与它最初的设计是和谐一致的。这些，你又要如何解释呢？这是一种持续的政府形式，并通过修改来适应之后的时代精神，而这之后的时间跨度为八百年。我要如何解释这一制度的持久性？我可以断言，它们已经在其基本框架之中，把所有前人发现的最基本的要点都结合到了一起。

中世纪的智者和现代社会的政治写手们，都已经为政府定下了一个准则，那就是不混合的政府形式，不可能满足一个自由、智慧的民族的要求，例如，一种不混合的民主形式一定会引发无政府主义的混乱或者军事专制。但是，如果这种政府形式自身将神圣、不可侵犯的君主制政体，对普通民众的代表以及一种贵族政治的刺激这三者结合在一起——其中的贵族政治，在战争年代分担了辛劳和战斗的危险，在和平时期分担了人们的关心和焦虑，而它也是属于人才的贵族政治，它对任何能够证明自己值得进入它的人都保持开放——那么这种在政府机构中三者的结合，就是政治科学的最高理念。

让我们看看英国的政府形式，除了它实践的细节，是否在其本身结合了这三种品质。加载在英国制度的原则是国家的君主是神圣的，对于任何一个国家的稳定，拥有一个神圣的权威或法庭都是必要的。在英国的政治体系之中，就有这样一条信条："国王是不会犯任何错误的。"在确立了王位神圣不可侵犯的原则以及贵族的特权原则之后，国家的创始者们同时也非常留意，使贵族不能受限于一个很小的甚至唯一的种姓之中。他们将上议院的大门向任何可能在战争或和平时期表现出自己杰出特性的人们开放，尽管他们可能是贫民的孩子（甚至一些有爵位的人都无法说清谁是自己的父母），他们也可以进入贵族阶层之中并找到自己的一席之地，在那里与那些可以将自己的血统追溯到几个世纪之前的最骄傲的人们平起平坐。

有英国和美国共和国的例子在前，加拿大人民要来决定他们的政府应该拥有怎样的主要特征，是依据英国的宪法，还是共和制的宪法。在我看来，我喜欢英国的宪政，因为它是最好的；我反对共和宪政，因为这不是最好的。我们现在看到的是世界历史上的一个伟大事件；每天发生在我们周围的事情，教会了我们不要过分依赖于我们当前所处的安全独立的地位，而是要理解和做好准备，因为会有人尝试对抗我们的自由，同时，他们也会对抗现在的这种政治体系，而我相信，加拿大的居民们十分珍视这种政治体系。

——T. D. M. 吉阁下

Lesson 77
THE SCHOOLMASTER AND THE CONQUEROR
第七十七课　教师与征服者

There is nothing with which the adversaries of improvement are more wont to make themselves merry than with what is termed "*the march of intellect*;" and I confess that I think, as far as the phrase goes, they are in the right. It is a very absurd, because a very incorrect, expression. It is little calculated to describe the operation in question. It does not suggest an image at all resembling the proceedings of the true friends of mankind. It much more resembles the progress of the enemy of all improvement. The conqueror moves in a march. He stalks onward with "the pride, pomp, and circumstance of glorious war"—banners flying, shouts rending the air, guns thundering, and martial music pealing, to drown the shrieks of the wounded, and the lamentations for the slain.

Not thus the schoolmaster, in his peaceful vocation. He meditates and prepares in secret the plans which are to bless mankind; he slowly gathers around him those who are to further their execution; lie quietly, though firmly, advances in his humble path, labouring steadily, but calmly, till he has opened to the light all the recesses of ignorance, and torn up by the roots the weeds of vice. His is a progress not to be compared with anything like a march; but it leads to a far more brilliant triumph, and to laurels more imperishable than the destroyer of his species, the scourge of the world, ever won.

Such men—men deserving the glorious title of teachers of mankind—I have found, labouring conscientiously, though perhaps obscurely, in their blessed vocation, wherever I have gone. I have found them, and shared their fellowship, among the daring, the ambitious, the ardent, the indomitably active French; I have found them among the persevering, resolute, industrious Swiss; I have found them among the laborious, the warm-hearted, the enthusiastic Germans; I have found them among the high-minded Italians; and in our own country, thank Heaven, they everywhere abound, and their number is every day increasing.

Their calling is high and holy; their fame is the property of nations; their renown will fill the Earth in after ages, in proportion as it sounds not far off in their own times. Each one of those great teachers of the world, possessing his soul in patience, performs his appointed work; awaits in faith the fulfilment of the promises; and, resting from his labours, bequeaths his memory to the generation whom his works have blessed, and sleeps under the humble but not inglorious epitaph, commemorating "one in whom mankind lost a friend, and no man got rid of an enemy."

—Lord Brougham (1778—1868)

Words

adversaries, *enemies.*
bequeaths, *bands down.*
calculated, *fitted.*
commemorating, *celebrating.*
conscientiously, *faithfully.*
enthusiastic, *ardent.*
epitaph, *inscription on a tomb-stone.*
fulfilment, *performance.*
imperishable, *undying.*
incorrect, *inaccurate.*

indomitably, *invincibly.*
industrious, *laborious.*
lamentations, *wailings.*
obscurely, *humbly.*
persevering, *persistent.*
property, *possession.*
shrieks, *cries.*
vocation, *calling*

☆ ☆

投身战争的人们，因为被称为"智慧的行军"而变得最为快乐。我得承认，这个说法是有一定道理的。但这是一个因为错误而变得非常荒谬的表达。它的描述在受到质疑之前，没有经过任何深思熟虑。它丝毫没有阐释出所有那些对人类有益的进步。相反，它描绘了所有进步的敌人。征服者持续前进，他们带着"骄傲、虚荣、光荣战争的氛围"；昂首阔步地前进，旗帜飘扬着，他们的叫喊声不绝于耳，枪声的轰鸣、军乐的喧嚣，淹没了受伤者的尖叫声和被杀害者的哀鸣。

因此，与征服者的行军相比，教师安定的使命有所不同。他沉思着，并密谋着保护人类的计划；他慢慢地将那些能够进一步执行这一计划的人们聚集在他的周围；他静静地躺着，但却异常坚决，他冷静地在崎岖的路上前进，一直努力着，直到他将无知的凹槽打通，并将恶行的杂草连根拔起。他的这种历程并不是一种可以与行军相比的进步，但与之前人类的破坏者和祸害相比，他却会带来一种更辉煌的胜利和更不朽的荣誉。

无论走到哪里，我都发现，这些值得拥有人类教师这个光荣称号的人，在他们幸福的职业中异常认真地工作着，虽然这也许不明显。我发现了他们，并分享了他们的友谊。他们存在于勇敢的、雄心勃勃的、热情的、顽强而活跃的法国人中间；存在于不屈不挠的、坚定的、勤劳的瑞士人中间；存在于勤奋的、友善的、热情的德国人中间；存在于高尚的意大利人中间；在我们自己的国家，谢天谢地，他们也比比皆是，而他们的数量每天都在增加。

他们的职业高尚而神圣；他们的声誉是国家的财富；他们的名声虽然在他们自己的时代并不响亮，但在将来会誉满全球。每一位世界上伟大的教师都耐心地倾诉自己的灵魂，完成自己的工作；充满信仰地履行他的承诺；从他的工作中得以休息之后，他把记忆留给了这份工作祝福了的一代人，最终在谦逊而并不耀眼的墓志铭之下长眠，墓志铭这样纪念他："人类失去了一个朋友，而不是摆脱了一个敌人。"

——布鲁厄姆勋爵

Lesson 78
BRITISH COLONIAL AND NAVAL POWER
第七十八课　英国殖民和海军的力量

The sagacity of England is in nothing more clearly shown than in the foresight with which she has provided against the emergency of war. Let it come when it may, it will not find her unprepared. So thickly are her colonies and naval stations scattered over the face of the Earth, that her war-ships can speedily reach every commercial centre on the globe.

There is that great centre of commerce, the Mediterranean Sea. It was a great centre long ago, when the Phoenician traversed it, and, passing through the Pillars of Hercules, sped on his way to the distant and then savage Britain. It was a great centre when Rome and Carthage wrestled in a death-grapple for its possession. But at the present day England is as much at home on the Mediterranean as if it were one of her own Canadian lakes.

Nor is it simply the number of the British colonies, or the evenness with which they are distributed, that challenges our admiration. The positions which these colonies occupy, and their natural military strength, are quite as important facts. There is not a sea or a gulf in the world, which has any real commercial importance, but England has a stronghold on its shores. And wherever the continents tending southward come to points, around which the commerce of nations must sweep, there is a British settlement; and the cross of St. George salutes you as you are wafted by. There is hardly a little desolate, rocky island or peninsula, formed apparently by Nature for a fortress, and nothing else, but the British flag floats securely over it.

These are literal facts. Take, for example, the great Overland Route from Europe to Asia. Despite its name, its real highway is on the waters of the Mediterranean and Red Seas. It has three gates—three only. England holds the key to every one of these gates. Count them—Gibraltar, Malta, Aden. But she commands the entrance to the Red Sea, not by one, but by several strongholds. Midway in the narrow strait is the black, bare rock of Perim, sterile, precipitous, a perfect counterpart of Gibraltar; and on either side, between it and the mainland, are the ship-channels which connect the Red Sea with the great Indian Ocean. This England holds.

A little farther out is the peninsula of Aden, another Gibraltar, as rocky, as sterile, and as precipitous, connected with the mainland by a narrow strait, and having a harbour safe in all winds, and a central coal depot. This England bought in 1839. And to complete her security, she has purchased from some petty sultan the neighbouring islands of Socotra and Kouri, giving, as it were, a retaining fee, so that, though she does not need them herself, no rival power may ever possess them.

As we sail a little farther on, we come to the Chinese Sea. What a beaten track of commerce is this! What wealth of comfort and luxury is wafted over it by every breeze! The teas of China! The silks of Farther India! The spices of the East! The ships of every clime and nation swarm on its waters! The stately barques of England, France, and Holland! The swift ships of America! And mingled with them, in picturesque confusion, the clumsy junk of the Chinaman, and the slender, darting canoe of the Malaysian islanders.

At the lower end of the China Sea, where it narrows into Malacca Strait, England holds the little island of Singapore—a spot of no use to her whatever, except as a commercial depot, but of inestimable value for that; a spot which, under her fostering care, is growing up to take its place among the great emporiums of the world. Half way up the sea she holds the island of Labuan, whose chief worth is this, that beneath its surface and that of the neighbouring mainland there lie inexhaustible treasures of coal, which are likely to yield wealth and power to the hand that controls them. At the upper end of the sea she holds Hong-Kong, a hot, unhealthy island, but an invaluable base from which to threaten and control the neighbouring waters.

Even in the broad, and as yet comparatively untracked Pacific, she is making silent advances towards dominion. The vast continent of Australia, which she has secured, forms its south-western boundary. And pushed out six hundred miles eastward from this lies New Zealand, like a strong outpost, its shores so scooped and torn by the waves that it must be a very paradise of commodious bays and safe havens for the mariner. The soil, too, is of extraordinary fertility; and the climate, though humid, deals kindly with the Englishman's constitution. Nor is this all; for, advanced from it, north and south, like picket stations, are Norfolk Isle, and the Auckland group, both of which have good harbours. And it requires no prophet's eye to see that, when England needs posts farther eastward, she will find them among the green coral islets that stud the Pacific.

Turn now your steps homeward, and pause a moment at the Bermudas, those beautiful isles, with their fresh verdure—green gems in the ocean, with air soft and balmy as Eden's was! They have their home uses too. They furnish arrow-root for the sick, and ample supplies of vegetables earlier than sterner climates will yield them. Is this all that can be said? Reflect a little more deeply. These islands possess a great military and naval depot; and a splendid harbour, land-locked, strongly fortified, and difficult of access to strangers;—and all within a few days' sail of the chief ports of the Atlantic shores of the New World. England therefore retains them as a station on the road to her West Indian possessions; and should America go to war with her, she would use it as a base for 'offensive 'operations, where she might gather and whence she might hurl upon any' unprotected port all her gigantic naval and military power.

—Atlantic Monthly

Words

apparently, *evidently*.
beautiful, *lovely*.
challenges, *claims*.
commercial, *mercantile*.
commodious, *roomy*.
comparatively, *relatively*.
constitution, *physical*.
despite, *in spite of frame*.
distributed, *disposed*.
emergency, *unforeseen occasion*.
emporiums, *depots*.
fostering, *cherishing*.
furnish, *supply*.

inestimable, *priceless*.
inexhaustible, *unlimited*.
offensive, *making the attack*.
operations, *works*.
picturesque, *striking*.
precipitous, *steep*.
sagacity, *wisdom*.
security, *safety*.
settlement, *colony*.
splendid, *magnificent*.
traversed, *crossed*.
unprotected, *unguarded*.

Questions

How do Britain's colonies strengthen her naval power? On what commanding positions has she strongholds? What are the three gates of the Overland Route? Who holds the keys to them? How does Britain command the China Sea?

How the Pacific? What do the Bermudas enable her to control?

　没有什么比预见到紧急战争将要到来，并为其做好准备，更能清楚地显露出英格兰的精明了。当战争到来时，人们会发现英格兰早已做好准备。所以她的殖民地和海军站点广泛地分散在世界各地，它的战舰可以迅速地到达地球上的每一个商业中心。

　这里是一个伟大的商业中心，地中海。在很久之前，腓尼基人横越过地中海，并穿过赫拉克勒斯之柱，加速赶往遥远又荒凉的英格兰。那时，这里就是一个伟大的中心。当罗马和迦太基为了占有这里而斗争和厮杀，这里就是一个伟大的中心。但是，如今，就像加拿大的湖泊一样，英格兰也可以认定地中海是自己的家。

　也不仅仅是殖民地的数量或者它们分布的均匀性，引发了我们对它的钦佩。这些殖民地自然拥有的军事实力，都相当重要。在世界上，没有一片海洋或一个海湾有任何真正的商业重要性，但英格兰在其海岸线上拥有自己的据点。无论大陆向南延伸向哪里，只要国际商务会围绕这个地方辐射开来，这里都会成为英国的定居点。当你乘船路过，圣乔治的十字架都会向你致敬。世界上很少存在一个荒凉、多石的岛屿或者群岛，由大自然形成一个天然的堡垒，但英国的国旗会轻盈、安全地在这里飘扬。

这些都是明显的事实，从欧洲到亚洲的伟大的陆上路线就是一个例子。尽管它的名字是陆上路线，它真正的公路却是处于地中海水域和海床之上。它有三扇大门——只有三扇，而英格兰拥有每一扇大门的钥匙。数数看——直布罗陀、马耳他、亚丁湾。它控制红海的入口处，且不仅一个，而是几个据点。在狭窄的海峡中，黑色的中途岛，丕林岛赤裸、贫瘠、陡峭的岩石，都与直布罗陀形成完美的对应；而在它与大陆之间的两侧，是连接红海与伟大的印度洋的船舶通道。这些地方都被英格兰所占据。

稍远一点的地方是亚丁湾，另一个是直布罗陀海峡，一样贫瘠、陡峭，通过一个狭窄的海峡与大陆相连，并有一个安全避风港和一个贮煤场。这里是英格兰在1839年占领的。为了彻底的安全，它已经从小苏丹购买了一些邻近的岛屿，如索科特拉岛和库里，并一定程度地给予了一些占领费用，虽然它自身并不需要这样做，因为根本没有竞争对手有可能会拥有它们。

随着我们的航行进行得再远一点，我们来到了中国海。这里的商业是多么因循守旧！财富和豪华的舒适在这里是多么轻而易举！中国的茶！远一点的印度丝绸！东方的香料！每个地域和民族的船只都集聚在这片水域之上！英国、法国和荷兰庄严的轻舟！美国的快捷战舰船！在这风景如画的混杂之中，夹杂着一群朴拙的中国人和乘着疾飞的独木舟的马来西亚群岛的居民。

在中国海的最南端，水域逐渐变得狭窄，这里就是马六甲海峡。英格兰占领了新加坡的小岛——这个地方对英格兰来说，除了作为一个商业门户拥有不可估量的价值之外，没有什么其他用处；然而，在它的培养关怀下，新加坡正逐渐在世界上最进步的商场中获得一席之地。海面上方，它也同样占领了纳闽岛，其主要价值在于该岛的表面和邻近大陆之下隐藏着取之不尽、用之不竭的宝藏，这会为控制该岛的势力创造出巨大的财富和权力。在大海一端尽头的上方，她占领着香港。这是一个炎热而普通的小岛，但以此为基地，英格兰可以威胁和控制邻近的水域。

即使在广阔的太平洋上，英格兰也不露痕迹地沉默着走向统治。它已获得澳大利亚辽阔的大陆，并形成其西南部边界。从这里向东延伸600英里是新西兰，就像一个强大的前哨，新西兰的海岸和波浪将形成一个宽广的海湾天堂，为水手提供一个安全的避风港。这里的土壤也非常肥沃；这里虽然气候潮湿，但与英国人的宪法相得益彰，共处得秩序井然。这还不是全部；因为，从这里再向前走，不管是朝向北部还是南部，像哨站一般的诺福克岛和奥克兰群岛都拥有良好的港口。不需要先知的眼睛，人们就会看到，当英格兰需要更往东一点的站点，它会发现太平洋蜿蜒在绿色的珊瑚岛之间。

　　现在你可以踏上归途，在百慕大群岛停顿片刻，与它们的新鲜翠绿融合——这一颗在海洋中的绿色宝石，就像空气宜人的伊甸园！它们有自己的用途，它们为病人提供康复机会和充足的蔬菜来应对气候的变化。深刻思考一下，你会发现这些岛屿都是优良的军事和海军基地，它们有壮丽的海港与陆地相连，堡垒森严，陌生人难以进入。在几天之内，大西洋海岸的新世界都变成了英格兰主要的港口。因此，英国将它们保留下来，作为通往它在西印度群岛上领地的道路上的一个站点；如果美国向她开战，它会将这里作为基地而采取进攻行动，在那里，它可以聚集起她所有巨大的海军和军事力量，并从那里向任何未设防的港口进攻。

——选自《大西洋月刊》

Lesson 79　KING JOHN
第七十九课　约翰王

(ABRIDGED FROM SHAKESPEARE'S PLAY)
PERSONS REPRESENTED

King John. King.

Hubert de Burgh, *Chamberlain to the* Cardinal Pandulph, the *Pope's legate.*

Arthur, *son of Geffrey, late Duke of Bretagne, the elder brother of King John.*

CONSTANCE, *mother to Arthur.*

Earl of Salisbury.

Sir Robert Faulconbrido&.

Bigot, Earl of Norfolk.

Earl of Pembroke.

Prince Henry, *son of King John, afterwards Henry III.*

PART I.

King John invades France, to chastise Philip for espousing the cause of Prince Arthur, the rightful heir to the English throne. In a battle before Angiers, Arthur is taken prisoner. Hubert, chamberlain to King John, is appointed Arthur's keeper, with instructions to find some means of depriving the young prince of life.

Scene—King John's tent before Angiers.

K. John. Come hither, Hubert. O my gentle Hubert,
We owe thee much;......
Give me thy hand. I had a thing to say,—
But I will tit it with some better time.
In good sooth, Hubert, I am almost ashamed
To say what good respect I have of thee.
Hub. I am much bounden to your majesty.
K. John. Good friend, thou hast no cause to say so yet,
But thou shalt have: and creep time ne'er so slow,
Yet it shall come for me to do thee good.
I had a thing to say—but let it go:
The sun is in the heaven, and the proud day,
Attended with the pleasures of the world,
Is all too wanton, and too full of gawds,

To give me audience:—If the midnight bell
Did, with his iron tongue and brazen mouth,
Sound one unto the drowsy race of night;
If this same were a churchyard where we stand,
And thou possessed with a thousand wrongs;
Or if that surly spirit, melancholy,
Had baked thy blood, and made it heavy-thick,
(Which, else, runs tickling up and down the veins,
Making that idiot, laughter, keep men's eyes
And strain their cheeks to idle merriment,
A passion hateful to my purposes;)
Or if that thou couldst see me without eyes,
Hear me without thine ears, and make reply
Without a tongue, using conceit alone,
Without eyes, ears, and harmful sound of words;—
Then, in despite of brooded watchful day,
I would into thy bosom pour my thoughts:
But, ah, I will not:—yet I love thee well;
And, by my troth, I think thou lovest me well.

    Hub. So well, that what you bid me undertake,
Though that my death were adjunct to my act,
Indeed, I'd do't.

    K. John. Do not I know thou wouldst?
Good Hubert, Hubert, Hubert, throw thine eye
On yon young boy: I'll tell thee what, my friend,
He is a very serpent in my way;
And, wheresoe'er this foot of mine doth tread,
He lies before me: dost thou understand me?
Thou art his keeper.

    Hub.   And I will keep him so,
That he shall not offend your majesty.

    K. John.   Death.

    Hub. My lord?

    K. John.   A grave.

    Hub.   He shall not live.

    K. John.   Enough.
I could be merry now: Hubert, I love thee.
Well, I'll not say what I intend for thee:
Remember......

Constance, mother to Prince Arthur, is overwhelmed with grief at the capture of her son.

Scene—The French King's tent.

Pand. Lady, you utter madness, and not sorrow.
Const. Thou art not holy, to belie me so;
I am not mad: this hair I tear is mine;
My name is Constance; I was Geffrey's wife;
Young Arthur is my son, and he is lost:
I am not mad;—I would, in sooth, I were
For then, 'tis like I should forget myself:
O, if I could, what grief should I forget!—
Preach some philosophy to make me mad......
If I were mad, I should forget my son:
I am not mad; too well, too well I feel
The different plague of each calamity.
  K. Phi. Bind up those tresses.—O what love I note
In the fair multitude of these her hairs!
When but by chance a silver drop hath fallen,
Even to that drop ten thousand wiry friends
Do glue themselves in sociable grief,
Like true, inseparable, faithful lovers,
Sticking together in calamity.—
          Bind up your hairs.
  Const. Yes, that I will; and wherefore will I do it?
I tore them from their bonds; and cried aloud,
"O that these hands could so 'redeem my son,
As they have given these hairs their liberty!"
But now I envy at their liberty,
And will again commit them to their bonds,
Because my poor child is a prisoner.—
And, father cardinal, I have heard you say,
That we shall see and know our friends in heaven:
If that be true, I shall see my boy again;
For since the birth of Cain, the first male child,
To him that did but yesterday 'suspire,
There was not such a gracious creature born.
But now will canker sorrow eat my bud,
And chase the native beauty from his cheek,
And he will look as hollow as a ghost;
As dim and meagre as an ague's fit;
And so he'll die; and, rising so again,
When I shall meet him in the court of heaven
I shall not know him: therefore never, never

Must I behold my pretty Arthur more.

    Pand. You hold too 'heinous a respect of grief.

    Const. He talks to me that never had a son.

    King Phi. You are as fond of grief as of your child.

    Const. Grief fills the room up of my absent child,

Lies in his bed, walks up and down with me;

Puts on his pretty looks, repeats his words,

Remembers me of all his gracious parts,

Stuffs out his 'vacant garments with his form;

Then have I reason to be fond of grief.—

Fare you well: had you such a loss as I,

I could give better comfort than you do.—

I will not keep this form upon my head, (Tearing it off.

When there is such 'disorder in my wit.—

O Lord! my boy, my Arthur, my fair son!

My life, my joy, my food, my all the world!

My widow-comfort, and my sorrows' cure! [Exit.

    K. Phi. I fear some 'outrage, and I'll follow her. [Exit.

Arthur, having been sent to England, is imprisoned in Northampton Castle. (Historically this is not true. Arthur was first sent to Falaise, then to Rouen; but Shakespeare's arrangement of the play requires the scene to be laid in England.)

    Scene—*A Room in Northampton Castle.*

    Enter Hubert, *and two* Attendants.

Hub. Heat me these irons hot; and, look thou stand

Within the arras: when I strike my foot

Upon the bosom of the ground, rush forth,

And bind the boy, which you shall find with me,

Fast to the chair: be 'heedful: hence, and watch.

    1st Attend. I hope your 'warrant will bear out the deed.

    Hub. Uncleanly 'scruples! Fear not you: look to't.

                          [Exeunt Attendant&.

Young lad, come forth; I have to say with you.

Enter Arthur,

    Arth. Good morrow, Hubert.

    Hub.   Good morrow, little prince.

    Arth. As little prince (having so great a title

To be more prince) as may be.—You are sad.

    Hub. Indeed, I have been merrier.

    Arth.   Mercy on me!

Methinks nobody should be sad but I:

Yet, I remember, when I was in France,
Young gentlemen would be as sad as night,
Only for wantonness. By my Christendom,
So I were out of prison, and kept sheep,
I should be as merry as the day is long;
And so I would be here, but that I doubt
My uncle practices more harm to me:
He is afraid of me, and I of him.
Is it my fault that I was Geffrey's son?
No, indeed, is't not; and I would, in sooth,
I were your son, so you would love me, Hubert.

    Hub. [*Aside*] If I talk to him, with his innocent prate
He will awake my mercy, which lies dead:
Therefore I will be sudden and 'dispatch.

    Arth. Are you sick, Hubert? you look pale to-day:
In sooth, I would you were a little sick,
That I might sit all night and watch with you:
I warrant I love you more than you do me.

    Hub. [*Aside*] His Words do take possession of my bosom. Read here, young
Arthur.   [*Showing a paper.*

               [*Aside*] How now, foolish rheum!
Turning dispiteous torture out of door!
I must be brief, lest resolution drop
Out at mine eyes, in tender 'womanish tears.—
Can you not read it? is it not fair writ?

    Arth. Too fairly, Hubert, for so foul effect:
Must you with hot irons burn out both mine eyes?

    Hub. Young boy, I must.

    Arth.   And will you?

    Hub.   And I will.

    Arth. Have you the heart? When your head did but ache, I knit my handkerchief
about your brows,
(The best I had—a princess wrought it for me,)
And I did never ask it you again:
And with my hand at midnight held your head;
And, like the 'watchful minutes to the hour,
Still and anon cheered up the heavy time;
Saying, What luck you? and, Where lies your grief?
Or, What good love may I perform for you?
Many a poor man's son would have lain still,
And ne'er have spoke a loving word to you;
But you at your sick service had a prince.

Nay, you may think my love was crafty love,
And call it 'cunning: do, an if you will:
If Heaven be pleased that you must use me ill,
Why then you must—Will you put out mine eyes?
These eyes, that never did, nor never shall,
So much as frown on you?
    Hub.   I have sworn to do it;
And with hot irons must I burn them out.
Arth. Ah, none but in this iron age would do it!
The iron of itself, though heat red-hot,
Approaching near these eyes, would drink my tears,
And quench his fiery indignation
Even in the matter of mine 'innocence:
Nay, after that, consume away in rust,
But for containing fire to harm mine eye.
Are you more stubborn-hard than hammered iron?
An if an angel should have come to me,
And told me, Hubert should put out mine eyes,
I would not have believed him,—no tongue but Hubert's.
    Hub. Come forth.   [*Stamps*

      Re-enter Attendants, with cords, irons, d. c.

Do as I bid you.
    Arth. O, save me, Hubert, save me! my eyes are out,
Even with the fierce looks of these bloody men.
    Hub. Give me the iron, I say, and bind him here.
    Arth. Alas! what need you be so boisterous-rough?
I will not 'struggle, I will stand stone-still.
For pity, Hubert, let me not be bound!
Nay, hear me, Hubert! drive these men away,
And I will sit as quiet as a lamb;
I will not stir, nor wince, nor speak a word,
Nor look upon the iron angrily:
Thrust but these men away, and I'll forgive you,
Whatever torment you do put me to.
    Hub. Go, stand within; let me alone with him.
    1st Attend. I am best pleased to be from such a deed.
                       [*Exeunt Attendants.*
    Arth. Alas! I then have chid away my friend!
He hath a stern look, but a gentle heart:
Let him come back, that his 'compassion may
Give life to yours.

Hub.   Come, boy, prepare yourself.

Arth. Is there no remedy?

   Hub.   None, but to lose your eyes.

   Arth. O Hubert, were there but a mote in yours,
A grain, a dust, a gnat, a wandering hair,
Any 'annoyance in that precious sense!
Then, feeling what small things are boisterous there,
Your vile intent must needs seem horrible.

   Hub. Is this your promise? go to, hold your tongue.

   Arth. Hubert, the 'utterance of a brace of tongues
Must needs want pleading for a pair of eyes:
Let me not hold my tongue; let me not, Hubert;—
Or, Hubert, if you will, cut out my tongue,
So I may keep mine eyes. O, spare mine eyes;
Though to no use but still to look on you!—
Lo, by my troth, the 'instrument is cold,
And would not harm me!

   Hub.   I can heat it, boy.

Arth. No, in good sooth; the fire is dead with grief,
Being create for comfort, to be used
In undeserved extremes. See else yourself;
There is no malice in this burning coal;
The breath of heaven hath blown his spirit out,
And strewed repentant ashes on his head.

   Hub. But with my breath I can revive it, boy.

   Arth. And if you do, you will but make it blush
And glow with shame of your 'proceedings, Hubert:
Nay, it perchance will sparkle in your eyes;
And, like a dog that is compelled to fight,
Snatch at his master that doth tarre him on.
All things, that you should use to do me wrong,
Deny their office: only you do lack
That mercy which fierce fire and iron extends,
Creatures of note for mercy-lacking uses.

   Hub. Well, see to live; I will not touch thine eyes
For all the treasure that thine uncle owes:
Yet am I sworn, and I did purpose, boy,
With this same very iron to burn them out.

   Arth. O, now you look like Hubert! all this while
You were 'disguised.

   Hub.   Peace: no more. Adieu.
Your uncle must not know but you are dead:

I'll fill these dogged spies with false reports.
And, pretty child, sleep doubtless and secure,
That Hubert, for the wealth of all the world,
Will not offend thee.
    Arth.   O Heaven!—I thank you, Hubert.
    Hub. Silence; no more: go closely in with me.
Much danger do I undergo for thee.
                      [*Exeunt*

Words

annoyance, *cause of pain.*
approaching, *advancing.*
ashamed, *abashed.*
attended, *followed.*
audience, *hearing.*
boisterous, *violent.*
calamity, *affliction.*
compassion, *pity.*
cunning, *deceit.*
disguised, *masked.*
disorder, *derangement.*
dispatch, *make haste.*
heedful, *careful.*
heinous, *serious.*
indignation, *wrath.*
innocence, *blamelessness.*
instrument, *implement.*
intend, *purpose.*
meagre, *emaciated.*
melancholy, *sadness.*
merriment, *mirth.*
offend, *injure.*
outrage, *injury.*

philosophy, *abstraction.*
plague, *stroke; trial.*
practices, *works.*
proceedings, *doings.*
redeem, *recover.*
remedy, *relief; cure.*
repentant, *penitent.*
respect, *regard.*
scruples, *doubts.*
serpent, *viper.*
struggle, *contend.*
suspire, *breathe.*
torture, *torment.*
undergo, *incur.*
undertake, *perform.*
undeserved, *unmerited.*
utterance, *speaking.*
vacant, *empty.*
wantonness, *playfulness.*
warrant, *commission.*
watchful, *attentive.*
womanish, *effeminate.*

PART II

King John, alarmed at the disaffection of his nobles and people, repent of his conduct towards Prince Arthur, and accuses Hubert of tempting him to accede to the murder.

Scene.—*A Room of State in the Palace.*

Enter a Messenger.

K. John. A fearful eve thou hast; where is that blood
That I have seen inhabit in those cheeks?
So foul a sky clears not without a storm:
Pour down thy weather: how goes all in France?

Mess. From France to England.—Never such a power
For any foreign preparation
Was levied in the body of a land!
The copy of your speed is learned by them;
For when you should be told they do prepare,
The tidings come that they are all arrived.

K. John. O, where hath our intelligence been drunk?
Where hath it slept? Where is my mother's care,
That such an army could be drawn in France,
And she not hear of it?

Mess. My liege, her ear
Is stopped with dust; the first of April died
Your noble mother: and, as I hear, my lord,
The Lady Constance in a frenzy died
Three days before: but this from rumour's tongue
I idly heard; if true, or false, I know not.

K. John. Withhold thy speed, dreadful occasion!
O, make a league with me, till I have pleased
My 'discontented peers!   [*Exit Messenger.*
My mother dead!

Enter Hubert.

Hub. My lord, they say five moons were seen to-night;
Four fixed, and the fifth did whirl about
The other four, in wondrous motion.

K. John. Five moons!

Hub. Old men and beldams, in the streets,
Do 'prophesy upon it dangerously:
Young Arthur's death is common in their mouths:
And when they talk of him, they shake their heads,
And whisper one another in the ear;
And he that speaks doth gripe the hearer's wrist;
Whilst he that hears makes fearful action,
With wrinkled brows, with nods, with rolling eyes.
I saw a smith stand with his hammer, thus,
The whilst his iron did on the anvil cool,
With open mouth swallowing a tailor's news;

Who, with his shears and measure in his hand,
Standing on slippers (which his nimble haste
Had falsely thrust upon contrary feet),
Told of a many thousand warlike French
That were embattailled and ranked in Kent:
Another lean unwashed 'artificer
Cuts off his tale, and talks of Arthur's death.

   K. John. Why seek'st thou to possess me with these fears?
Why urgest thou so oft young Arthur's death?
Thy hand hath murdered him: I had mighty cause
To wish him dead, but thou hadst none to kill him.

   Hub. Had none, my lord! why, did you not 'provoke me?

   K. John. It is the curse of kings to be attended
By slaves, that take their humours for a warrant
To break within the bloody house of life;
And, on the winking of authority,
To understand a law; to know the meaning
Of dangerous majesty, when, perchance, it frowns
More upon humour than 'advised respect.

   Hub. Here is your hand and seal for what I did.

   K. John. O, when the last account 'twixt heaven and earth
Is to be made, then shall this hand and seal
Witness against us to damnation!
How oft the sight of means to do ill deeds
Makes deeds ill done! Hadst not thou been by,
A fellow by the hand of Nature marked,
Quoted and signed to do a deed of shame,
This murder had not come into my mind:
But, taking note of thy 'abhorred aspect',
Finding thee fit for bloody villany,
Apt, liable to be employed in danger,
I faintly broke with thee of Arthur's death;
And thou, to be 'endeared to a king,
Made it no conscience to destroy a prince.

   Hub. My lord,—

   K. John. Hadst thou but shook thy head, or made a pause,
When I spake darkly what I purposed;
Or turned an eye of doubt upon my face,
And bid me tell my tale in express Words;
Deep shame had struck me dumb, made me break off,
And those thy fears might have wrought fears in me:
But thou didst understand me by my signs,

And didst in signs again parley with sin;
Yea, without stop, didst let thy heart consent,
And 'consequently thy rude hand to act
The deed, which both our tongues held vile to name.—
Out of my sight, and never see me more!
My nobles leave me; and my state is braved,
Even at my gates, with ranks of foreign powers:
Nay, in the body of this fleshly land,
This kingdom, this confine of blood and breath,
Hostility and civil tumult reigns
Between my conscience and my cousin's death.
    Hub. Arm you against your other enemies,
I'll make a peace betwixt your soul and you.
Young Arthur is alive: this hand of mine
Is yet a maiden and an innocent hand,
Not painted with the crimson spots of blood.
Within this bosom never entered yet
The dreadful motion of a murderous thought;
And you have 'slandered Nature in my form,
Which, howsoever rude exteriorly
Is yet the cover of a fairer mind
Than to be butcher of an innocent child.
    K. John. Doth Arthur live? O, haste thee to the peers,
Throw this report on their incensed rage,
And make them tame to their obedience!
Forgive the 'comment that my passion made
Upon thy feature; for my rage was blind,
And foul imaginary eyes of blood
Presented thee more hideous than thou art.
O, answer not, but to my closet bring
The angry lords, with all 'expedient haste.
I conjure thee but slowly; run more fast.   [Exeunt.

Arthur, disguised as a sailor boy, tries to escape. He leaps from the castle wall, and is killed.

Scene.—*The Castle walls*

    Arth. The wall is high; and yet will I leap down:—
Good ground, be pitiful, and hurt me not!—
There's few, or none, do know me; if they did,
This ship-boy's semblance hath disguised me quite.
I am afraid; and yet I'll venture it.

If I get down, and do not break my limbs,
I'll find a thousand shifts to get away:
As good to die and go, as die and stay.—[Leaps down.
O me! my uncle's spirit is in these stones:—
Heaven take my soul, and England keep my bones! [Dies.

Pembroke, Salisbury, Bigot, and Faulconbridge enter, and discover his dead body on the ground.

Enter Hubert.

   Hub. Lords, I am hot with haste in seeking you:
Arthur doth live; the king hath sent for you.
   Sal. [Pointing to the body] O, he is bold, and blushes not
       at death.—
'Avaunt, thou hateful villain, get thee gone!
   Hub. I am no villain.
   Sal.   Must I rob the law? [Drawing his sword,
   Faul. Your sword is bright, sir; put it up again.
   Sal. Not till I sheathe it in a murderer's skin.
   Hub. Stand back, Lord Salisbury, stand back, I say;
In truth, I think my sword's as sharp as yours:
I would not have you, lord, forget yourself,
Nor tempt the danger of my true defence;
Lest I, by marking of your rage, forget
Your worth, your greatness and 'nobility.
   Big. Out, dunghill! darest thou brave a nobleman?
   Hub. Not for my life; but yet I dare defend
My innocent life against an emperor.
   Sal. Thou art a murderer.
   Hub.   Do not prove me so;
Yet, I am none: whose tongue soe'er speaks false,
Not truly speaks; who speaks not truly, lies.
Pem, Cut him to pieces!
   Faul.   Keep the peace, I say.
   Sal. Stand by, or I shall gall you, Faulconbridge.
   Faul. If thou but frown on me, or stir thy foot,
Or teach thy hasty spleen to do me shame,
I'll strike thee dead. Put up thy sword betime.
   Big. What wilt thou do, 'renowned Faulconbridge?
Second a villain and a murderer!
   Hub. Lord Bigot, I am none.
   Big.   Who killed this prince?

Hub. "'Tis not an hour since I left him well;
I honoured him, I loved him; and will weep
My date of life out for his sweet life's loss.

Sal. Trust not those cunning waters of his eyes,
For villany is not without such rheum;
And he, long traded in it, makes it seem
Like rivers of remorse and innocency.
Away, with me, all you whose souls abhor
The uncleanly savours of a slaughter-house;
For I am stilled with the smell of sin.

Big. Away, toward Bury, to the Dauphin there!
Pern. There, tell the king, he may inquire us out.
                          [Exeunt Lords.

Faul. Here's a good world!—Knew you of this fair work?
Beyond the 'infinite and boundless reach
Of mercy, if thou didst this deed of death,
Art thou doomed, Hubert.

Hub.   Do but hear me, sir.

Faul. Ha! I'll tell thee what;
Thou art stained as black—nay, nothing so black
As thou shalt be, if thou didst kill the child.

Hub. Upon my soul—

Faul.   If thou didst but consent
To this most cruel act, do but despair;
And, if thou want'st a cord, the smallest thread
That ever spider twisted from her womb
Will serve to strangle thee; a rush will be
A beam to hang thee on: or wouldst thou drown thyself.
Put but a little water in a spoon,
And it shall be as all the ocean,
Enough to stifle such a villain up.—
I do suspect thee very 'grievously.

Hub. I left him well.

Faul.   Go, bear him in thine arms.—
I am amazed, methinks; and lose my way
Among the thorns and dangers of this world.—
How easy dost thou take all England up
From forth this morsel of dead royalty,
The life, the right and truth of all this realm,
Is fled to heaven; and England now is left
To tug and scamble, and to part by the teeth
The unowed interest of proud-swelling state.

Now, for the bare-picked bone of majesty,
Doth dogged War bristle his angry crest,
And snarleth in the gentle eyes of Peace:
Now powers from home, and discontents at home,
Meet in one line; and vast 'confusion waits
(As doth a raven on a sick-fallen beast)
The imminent decay of wrested pomp.
Now happy he whose cloak and cincture can
Hold out this tempest—Bear away that child,
And follow me with speed; I'll to the king:
A thousand businesses are brief in hand,
And Heaven itself doth frown upon the land.   [Exeunt

The Dauphin, aided by the disaffected nobles of England, gives battle to John at St. Edmund's-Bury. The king's troops are repulsed, and John is conveyed to Swinstead Abbey, sick of a fever. There the King dies.

Scene.—*Swinstead Abbey.*
Enter Bigot and Attendants, *who bring in* King John *in a chair.*

K. John. Ay, marry, now my soul hath elbow-room;
It would not out at windows, nor at doors.
There is so hot a summer in my bosom,
That all my bowels crumble up to dust:
I am a scribbled form, drawn with a pen
Upon a 'parchment, and against this fire
Do I shrink up.
　　P. Henry.　　　　How fares your majesty?
　　K. John. Poisoned—ill fare;—dead, forsook, cast off;
And none of you will bid the Winter come,
To thrust his icy fingers in my maw;
Nor let my kingdom's rivers take their course
Through my burned bosom, nor entreat the North
To make his bleak winds kiss my parched lips,
And comfort me with cold. I do not ask you much,
I beg cold comfort; and you are so strait,
And so ungrateful, you deny me that.
　　P. Henry. O that there were some virtue in my tears.
That might relieve you!
　　K. John.　　　　The salt in them is hot.
Within me is a hell; and there the poison
Is, as a fiend, confined to tyrannize
On unreprievable condemned blood.

Enter Faulconbridge.

Faul. O, I am scalded with my violent motion,
And spleen of speed to see your majesty!

K. John. O cousin, thou art come to set mine eye:
The tackle of my heart is cracked and burned;
And all the shrouds, wherewith my life should sail,
Are turned to one thread, one little hair:
My heart hath one poor string to stay it by,
Which holds but till thy news be uttered;
And then all this thou seest is but a clod,
And module of 'confounded royalty.

Faul. The Dauphin is preparing hitherward;
Where Heaven lie knows how we shall answer him:
For, in a night, the best part of my power,
As I upon advantage did remove,
Were in the Washes all unwarily
Devoured by the unexpected flood. [The King dies

Sal. You breathe these dead news in as dead an ear.—
My liege! my lord! but now a king, now thus!

P. Henry. Even so must I run on, and even so stop.
What surety of the world, what hope, what stay,
When this was now a king, and now is clay?—
At Worcester must his body be interred,
For so he willed it.

Faul.   Thither shall it then.
And happily may your sweet self put on
The lineal state and glory of the land!
To whom, with all submission, on my knee
I do bequeath my faithful services
And true subjection everlastingly.

Sal. And the like tender of our love we make,
To rest without a spot for evermore.

P. Henry. I have a kind soul, that would give you thanks,
And knows not how to do it, but with tears.

Faul. O let us pay the time but needful woe,
Since it hath been beforehand with our griefs.—
This England never did, (nor never shall,)
Lie at the proud foot of a conqueror,
But when it first did help to wound itself.
Now these her princes are come home again,
Come the three corners of the world in arms,

And we shall shock them! Nought shall make us rue,
If England to itself do rest but true.

[*Exeunt*

Words

abhorred, *hated.*

advised, *intentional.*

artificer, *workman.*

avaunt, *begone.*

businesses, *affairs.*

comment, *criticism.*

confounded, *baffled.*

confusion, *tumult.*

consequently, *therefore.*

devoured, *swallowed up.*

discontented, *dissatisfied.*

endeared, *made a favourite.*

expedient, *prompt.*

grievously, *painfully.*

honoured, *revered.*

hostility, *war.*

humours, *whims.*

imminent, *threatening.*

incensed, *infuriated.*

infinite, *boundless.*

inhabit, *dwell.*

intelligence, *information.*

nobility, *rank.*

parchment, *scroll.*

preparation, *equipment.*

prophesy, *predict.*

provoke, *incite.*

remorse, *regret.*

renowned, *illustrious.*

savours, *odours.*

scamble, *struggle.*

semblance, *disguise.*

slandered, *defamed.*

strangle, *suffocate.*

unreprievable, *not to be respited.*

（莎士比亚戏剧节选）
剧中人物

约翰王：国王

赫伯特·德·勃格：潘杜尔夫主教的管家，罗马教皇的使节

亚瑟：约翰王的哥哥布列塔尼公爵杰弗里之子

康斯丹丝：亚瑟之母

萨立斯伯雷伯爵

罗伯特·福康勃立琪爵士

俾高特，诺福克伯爵

彭勃洛克伯爵

亨利亲王：约翰王之子，之后的亨利三世

第 一 部

约翰王入侵法国，讨伐拥护亚瑟王子的腓力普王，而亚瑟王子是英国王位的合法继承人。在安吉尔斯战役前的一场战斗中，亚瑟被俘。约翰王的随从赫伯特被指派为亚瑟王子的监护者。他得到指示，要想方设法剥夺这个年轻王子的生命。

约翰王在昂热前的营帐

约翰王　过来，赫伯特。啊，我的好赫伯特，我受你的好处太多啦；在这肉体的围墙之内，有一个灵魂是把你当作他的债主的，他预备用加倍的利息报偿你的忠心。我的好朋友，你的发自衷诚的誓言，深深地铭刻在我的胸头。把你的手给我。我有一件事要说，可是等适当的时候再说吧。苍天在上，赫伯特，我简直不好意思说我是多么看重你。

赫伯特　我的一切都是陛下的恩赐。

约翰王　好朋友，你现在还没有理由说这样的话，可是有一天你将会有充分的理由这样说。不论时间爬行得多么迂缓，总有一天我要大大地照顾你。我有一件事情要说，可是让它去吧。太阳高悬在天空，骄傲的白昼耽于世间的欢娱，正在嬉戏酣游，不会听我的说话。要是午夜的寒钟启动它的铜唇铁舌，向昏睡的深宵发出一响嘹亮的鸣声；要是我们所站的这一块土地是一块墓地；要是你的心头藏着一千种的冤屈，或者那阴沉的忧郁凝结了你的血液，使它停止轻快的跳动，使你的脸上收敛了笑容，而那痴愚无聊的笑容，对于我是可憎而不相宜的；或者，要是你能够不用眼睛看我，不用耳朵听我，不用舌头回答我，除了用心灵的冥会传达我们的思想以外，全然不凭借眼睛、耳朵和有害的言语的力量，那么，即使在众目昭彰的白昼，我也要向你的心中倾吐我的衷肠；可是，啊！我不愿。然而我是很喜欢你的；凭良心说，我想你对我也很忠爱。

赫伯特　苍天在上，陛下无论吩咐我干什么事，即使因此而不免一死，我也决不推辞。

约翰王　我难道不知道你会这样吗？好赫伯特！赫伯特，赫伯特，转过你的眼去，瞧瞧那个孩子。我告诉你，我的朋友，他是挡在我路上的一条蛇；无论我的脚踏到什么地方，他总是横卧在我的前面。你懂得我的意思吗？你是他的监守人。

赫伯特　我一定尽力监守他，不让他得罪陛下。

约翰王　死。

赫伯特　陛下？

约翰王　一个坟墓。

赫伯特　他不会留着活命。

约翰王　够了。我现在可以快乐起来了。赫伯特，我喜欢你。好，我不愿说我将要给你怎样的重赏。记着吧。……

亚瑟的母亲康斯丹丝，因为她儿子的被捕而伤心欲绝，无法自拔。

法国国王营帐

潘杜尔夫夫人　你的话全然是疯狂，不是悲哀。

康斯丹丝　你是一位神圣的教士，不该这样冤枉我，我没有疯。我扯下的这绺头发是我的，我的名字叫作康斯丹丝，我是吉弗雷的妻子，小亚瑟是我的儿子，他已经失去了！我没有疯；我巴不得祈祷上天，让我真的疯了！因为那时候我多半会忘了我自己。啊！要是我能够忘了我自己，我将要忘记多少悲哀！教诲我一些使我疯狂的哲理，主教，你将因此而被封为圣徒，因为我现在还没有疯，还有悲哀的感觉，我的理智会劝告我怎样可以解除这些悲哀，教我或是自杀，或是上吊。假如我疯了，我就会忘记我的儿子，或是疯狂地把一个布片缝成的娃娃当作是他。我没有疯。每一次灾祸的不同的痛苦，我都感觉得太清楚、太清楚了。

腓力普王　把你的头发束起来。啊！在她这一根根美好的头发之间，存在着怎样的友爱！只要偶然有一颗银色的泪点落在它们上面，一万缕亲密的金丝就会胶合在一起，表示它们共同的悲哀。正像忠实而不可分的恋人们一样，在患难之中也不相遗弃。把你的头发束起来。

康斯丹丝　是的，我要把它们束起来。为什么我要把它们束起来呢？当我扯去它们的束缚的时候，我曾经高声呼喊："啊！但愿我这一双手也能够救出我的儿子，正像它们使这些头发得到自由一样！"可是现在我却妒恨它们的自由，我要把它们重新束缚起来，因为我那可怜的孩子是一个囚人。主教神父，我曾经听见你说，我们将要在天堂里会见我们的亲友。假如那句话是真的，那么我将会重新看见我的儿子，因为自从第一个男孩子该隐的诞生起，直到在昨天夭亡的小儿为止，世上从来不曾生下过这样一个美好的人物。可是现在悲哀的蛀虫将要侵蚀我的娇蕊，逐去他脸上天然的美丽。他将要形销骨立，像一个幽魂或是一个患虐病的人；他将要这样死去。当他从坟墓中起来，我在天堂里会见他的时候，我再也不会认识他，所以我永远、永远不能再看见我的可爱的亚瑟了！

潘杜尔夫　你把悲哀过分重视了。

康斯丹丝　从来不曾生过儿子的人，才会向我说这样的话。

腓力普王　你喜欢悲哀，就像喜欢你的孩子一样。

康斯丹丝　悲哀代替了不在我眼前的我的孩子的地位，它躺在他的床上，陪着我到东到西，装扮出他的美妙的神情，复述他的言语，提醒我他一切可爱的美点，使我看见他的遗蜕的衣服，就像看见他的形体一样，所以我是有理由喜欢悲哀的。

再会吧，要是你们也遭到像我这样的损失，我可以用更动听的言语安慰你们。我不愿梳理我头上的乱发，因为我的脑海里是这样紊乱混杂。主啊！我的孩子，我的亚瑟，我的可爱的儿！我的生命，我的欢乐，我的粮食，我的整个的世界！我的寡居的安慰，我的销愁的药饵！

腓力普王　我怕她会干出些什么意外的事情来，我要跟上去瞧瞧她。

被派往英国的亚瑟，被囚禁关押在诺桑普敦城堡之中。

赫伯特及二侍从上。

赫伯特　把这两块铁烧红了，站在这帏幕的后面；听见我一跺脚，你们就出来，把那孩子缚紧在椅上，不得有误。去，留心着吧。

侍从甲　我希望您确实得到了指令，叫我们这样干。

赫伯特　卑劣的猜疑！你放心吧，瞧我好了。孩子，出来；我有话跟你说。

亚瑟上。

亚瑟　早安，赫伯特。

赫伯特　早安，小王子。

亚瑟　我这王子确实很小，因为我的名分本来应该使我大得多的。怎么？你看来不大高兴。

赫伯特　喂，我今天确实没有平常那么高兴。

亚瑟　嗳哟！我想除了我以外，谁也不应该不快乐的。可是我记得我在法国的时候，少年的公子哥儿们往往只为了游荡过度的缘故，变得像黑夜一般忧郁。凭着我的基督徒身份起誓，要是我出了监狱做一个牧羊人，我一定会一天到晚快快乐乐地不知道有什么忧愁。我在这里本来也可以很开心，可是我疑心我的叔父会加害于我，他怕我，我也怕他。我是吉弗雷的儿子，这难道是我的过失吗？不，不是的，我但愿上天使我成为您的儿子，要是您愿意疼我的话，赫伯特。

赫伯特　要是我跟他谈下去，他这种天真的饶舌将会唤醒我的已死的怜悯，所以我必须把事情赶快办好。

亚瑟　您不舒服吗，赫伯特？您今天的脸色不大好看。真的，我希望您稍微有点儿不舒服，那么我就可以终夜坐在您床边陪伴您了。我敢说我爱您是胜过您爱我的。

赫伯特　他的话已经打动我的心。读一读这儿写着的字句吧，小亚瑟。怎么，愚蠢的眼泪！你要把无情的酷刑撵出去吗？我必须赶快动手，免得我的决心化成温柔的妇人之泪，从我的眼睛里滚了下来——你不能读吗？它不是写得很清楚吗？

亚瑟　像这样邪恶的主意，赫伯特，是不该写得这样清楚的。您必须用烧热的铁把我的两只眼睛一起烫瞎吗？

赫伯特　孩子，我必须这样做。

亚瑟　您真会这样做吗？

赫伯特　真会。

亚瑟　您能这样忍心吗？当您不过有点儿头痛的时候，我就把我的手帕替您扎住额角，那是我所有的一块最好的手帕，一位公主亲手织成送我的，我也从不曾问您要过；半夜里我还用我的手捧住您的头，像不息的分钟用它嘀嗒的声音安慰那沉重的时辰一样，我不停地问着您，"您要些什么？""您什么地方难受？"或是"我可以帮您做些什么事？"许多穷人家的儿子是会独自睡觉，不来向您说一句好话的，可是您却有一个王子侍候您的疾病。啊，您也许以为我的爱出于假意，说它是狡猾的做作，那也随您的便吧。要是您必须虐待我是上天的意旨，那么我只好悉听您的处置。您要烫瞎我的眼睛吗？这一双从来不曾、也永远不会向您怒视的眼睛？

赫伯特　我已经发誓这样干了，我必须用热铁烫瞎你的眼睛。

亚瑟　啊！只有这顽铁时代的人才会干这样的事！铁块它自己虽然烧得通红，当它接近我的眼睛的时候，也会吸下我的眼泪，让这些无罪的水珠浇熄它的怒焰；而且它将要生锈而腐烂，只是因为它曾经容纳着谋害我的眼睛的烈火。难道您比锤打的顽铁还要冷酷无情吗？要是一位天使下来告诉我，赫伯特将要烫瞎我的眼睛，我也绝不会相信他，只有赫伯特亲口所说的话才会使我相信。

赫伯特　出来！

二侍从持绳、烙铁等重上。

赫伯特　照我吩咐你们的做吧。

亚瑟　啊！救救我，赫伯特，救救我！这两个恶汉的凶暴的面貌，已经把我的眼睛吓得睁不开了。

赫伯特　喂，把那烙铁给我，把他绑在这儿。

亚瑟　唉！你们何必这样凶暴呢？我又不会挣扎，我会像石头一般站住不动。看在上天的面上，赫伯特，不要绑我！不，听我说，赫伯特，把这两个人赶出去，我就会像一头羔羊似的安静坐下，我会一动不动，不躲避，也不说一句话，也不向这块铁怒目而视。只要您把这两个人撵走，无论您给我怎样的酷刑，我都可以宽恕您。

赫伯特　去，站在里边，让我一个人处置他。

侍从甲　我巴不得不参加这种事情。

亚瑟　唉！那么我倒把我的朋友赶走了，他的面貌虽然凶恶，他的心肠却是善良的。叫他回来吧，也许他的恻隐之心可以唤醒您的同情。

赫伯特　来，孩子，准备吧。

亚瑟　没有挽回的余地了吗？

赫伯特　没有，你必须失去你的眼睛。

亚瑟　天啊！要是您的眼睛里有了一粒微尘、一点粉屑、一颗泥沙、一只小小的飞虫、一根飘荡的游丝，妨碍了您那宝贵的视觉，您就会感到这些微细的东西也会给人怎样的难堪，那么像您现在这一种罪恶的决意，应该显得多么残酷。

赫伯特　这就是你给我的允许吗？得了，你的舌头不要再动了。

亚瑟　为一双眼睛请命，是需要两条舌头同时说话的。不要叫我停住我的舌头，不要，赫伯特！或者您要是愿意的话，赫伯特，割下我的舌头，让我保全我的眼睛吧。啊！饶赦我的眼睛，即使它们除了对您瞧看以外，一点没有别的用处。瞧！不骗您，那刑具也冷了，不愿意伤害我。

赫伯特　我可以把它烧热的，孩子。

亚瑟　不，真的，那炉中的火也已经因为悲哀而死去了。上天造下它来本来为要给人温暖，你们却利用它做非刑的工具。不信的话，您自己瞧吧，这块燃烧的煤毫无恶意，上天的气息已经吹灭它的活力，把忏悔的冷灰撒在它的头上了。

赫伯特　可是我可以用我的气息把它重新吹旺，孩子。

亚瑟　要是您把它吹旺了，赫伯特，您不过使它对您的行为感觉羞愧而胀得满脸通红。也许它的火星会跳进您的眼里，正像一头不愿争斗的狗，反咬那促使它上去的主人一样。一切您所用来伤害我的工具，都拒绝执行它们的工作。凶猛的火和冷酷的铁，谁都知道它们是残忍无情的东西，也会大发慈悲，只有您才没有一点怜悯之心。

赫伯特　好，做一个亮眼的人活着吧。即使你的叔父把他所有的钱财一起给我，我也不愿碰一碰你的眼睛。尽管我已经发过誓，孩子，的确预备用这烙铁烫瞎它们。

亚瑟　啊！现在您才像个赫伯特，刚才那一会儿您都是喝醉的。

赫伯特　静些！别说了，再会。你的叔父必须知道你已经死去，我要用虚伪的消息告诉这些追踪的密探。可爱的孩子，安安稳稳地睡吧，整个世界的财富，都不能使赫伯特加害于你。

亚瑟　天啊！我谢谢您，赫伯特。

赫伯特　住口！别说了，悄悄地跟我进去。我为你担着莫大的风险呢！

第二部

惊于英国贵族和人民的不满，约翰王对自己针对亚瑟王子展开的行动感到了悔恨，开始抱怨赫伯特怂恿他进行的杀戮。

一使者上。

约翰王　你的眼睛里充满着恐怖，你脸上的血色到哪儿去了？这样阴沉的天空是必须等一场暴风雨来把它廓清的；把你的暴风雨倾吐出来吧。法国人怎么样啦？

使者　法国人到英国来啦。从来不曾有一个国家为了侵伐邻邦的缘故，征集过这样一支雄厚的军力。他们已经学会了您的敏捷的行军，因为您还没有听见他们在准备动手，已经传来了他们全军抵境的消息。

约翰王　啊！我们这方面的探子都在什么地方喝醉了？他们到哪儿睡觉去了？我的母亲管些什么事，这样一支军队在法国调集，她却没有听到消息？

使者　陛下，她的耳朵已经为黄土所掩塞了，太后是在四月一日驾崩的。我还听人说，陛下，康斯丹丝夫人就在太后去世的三天以前发疯而死；可是这是我偶然听到的流言，不知道是真是假。

约翰王　停止你的快步吧，惊人的变故！啊！让我和你作一次妥协，等我先平息了我的不平的贵族们的怒气。什么！母后死了！

赫伯特　重上。

赫伯特　陛下，他们说昨晚有五个月亮同时出现，四个停着不动，还有一个围绕着那四个飞快地旋转。

约翰王　五个月亮！

赫伯特　老头儿和老婆子们都在街道上对这种怪现象发出危险的预言。小亚瑟的死是他们纷纷谈论的题目；当他们讲起他的时候，他们摇着头，彼此低声说话。那说话的人紧紧握住听话的人的手腕，那听话的人一会儿皱皱眉，一会儿点点头，一会儿滚动着眼珠，做出种种惊骇的姿态。我看见一个铁匠提着锤这样站着不动，他的铁已经在砧上冷了，他却张开了嘴恨不得把一个裁缝所说的消息一口吞咽下去。那裁缝手里拿着剪刀尺子，脚上跷着一双拖鞋，因为一时匆忙，把它们左右反穿了，他说起好几千善战的法国人已经在肯特安营立寨，这时候旁边就有一个瘦瘦的肮脏的工匠打断他的话头，提到亚瑟的死。

约翰王　为什么你要用这种恐惧充塞我的心头？为什么你老是开口闭口地提到小亚瑟的死？他是死在你手里的；我有极大的理由希望他死，可是你没有杀死他的理由。

赫伯特　没有，陛下！您没有指使我吗？

约翰王　国王们最不幸的事，就是他们的身边追随着一群逢迎取媚的奴才，把他们一时的喜怒当作了神圣的谕旨，狐假虎威地杀戮无辜的生命。这些佞臣们往往会在君王的默许之下曲解法律，窥承主上的意志，虽然也许那只是未经熟虑的一时的愤怒。

赫伯特　这是您亲笔写下的敕令，亲手盖下的御印，指示我怎样行动。

约翰王 啊！当上天和人世举行最后清算的时候，这笔迹和这铃记将要成为使我沦于永劫的铁证。看见了罪恶的工具，多么容易使人造成罪恶！假如那时你不在我的身旁，一个天造地设的适宜于干这种卑鄙的恶事的家伙，这一个谋杀的念头就不会在我的脑中发生，可是我因为注意到你的凶恶的面貌，觉得你可以担当这一件流血的暴行，特别适宜执行这样危险的使命，所以我才向你略微吐露杀死亚瑟的意思，而你因为取媚一个国王的缘故，居然也就恬不为意地伤害了一个王子的生命。

赫伯特 陛下——

约翰王 当我隐隐约约提到我心里所蓄的念头的时候，你只要摇一摇头，或者略示踌躇，或者用怀疑的眼光瞧着我，好像要叫我说得明白一些似的，那么深心的羞愧就会使我说不出话来，我就会中止我的话头，也许你的恐惧会引起我自己心中的恐惧。可是你却从我的暗示中间懂得我的意思，并且用暗示跟我进行罪恶的谈判，毫不犹豫地接受我的委托，用你那粗暴的手干下了那为我们两人所不敢形诸唇舌的卑劣的行为。离开我的眼前，再也不要看见我！我的贵族们抛弃了我，外国的军队已经威胁到我的国门之前，在我这肉体的躯壳之内，战争和骚乱也在破坏这血液与呼吸之王国的平和，我的天良因为我杀死我的侄儿，正在向我兴起问罪之师。

赫伯特 准备抵抗您那其余的敌人吧，我可以替您和您的灵魂缔结和平。小亚瑟并没有死，我这手还是纯洁而无罪的，不曾染上一点殷红的血迹。在我这胸膛之内，从来不曾进入过杀人行凶的恶念。您单凭着我的外貌，已经冤枉了好人，虽然我的形状生得这般丑恶，可是它却包藏着一颗善良的心，断不会举起屠刀，杀害一个无辜的小孩儿。

约翰王 亚瑟还没有死吗？啊！你赶快到那些贵族们的地方去，把这消息告诉他们，让他们平息怒火，重尽他们顺服的人臣之道。原谅我在一时气愤之中对你的面貌做了错误的批评；因为我的恼怒是盲目的，在想象之中，我的谬误的眼睛看你满身血迹，因此把你看得比你实际的本人更为可憎。啊！不要回答；快去把那些愤怒的贵族们带到我的密室里来，一分钟也不要耽搁。我吩咐你得太慢了；你快飞步前去。

亚瑟 城墙很高，可是我决心跳下去。善良的大地啊，求你大发慈悲，不要伤害我！不会有什么人认识我；即使有人认识，穿着这一身船童的服装，也可以遮掩我的真相。我很害怕；可是我要冒险一试。要是我下去了，没有跌坏我的肢体，我一定要千方百计离开这地方，即使走了也不免一死，总比留着等死好些。嗳哟！这些石头上也有我叔父的精神，上天收去我的灵魂，英国保藏我的尸骨！

彭勃洛克、萨立斯伯雷、俾高特及福康勃立琪上，在地上发现了亚瑟的尸体。

赫伯特上。

赫伯特 列位大人，我正在忙着各处寻找你们哩。亚瑟没有死，国王叫你们去。

萨立斯伯雷　啊！他好大胆，当着死人的面前还会厚脸撒谎。滚开，你这可恨的恶人！去！

赫伯特　我不是恶人。

萨立斯伯雷　我必须僭夺法律的威权吗？

庶子　您的剑是很亮的，大人，把它收起来吧。

萨立斯伯雷　等我把它插到一个杀人犯的胸膛里去再说。

赫伯特　退后一步，萨立斯伯雷大人，退后一步。苍天在上，我想我的剑是跟您的剑同样锋利的。我希望您不要忘记您自己，也不要强迫我采取正当的防卫，那对于您是一件危险的事，因为我在您的盛怒之下，也许会忘记您的高贵尊荣的身份和地位。

俾高特　呸，下贱的东西！你敢向贵人挑战吗？

赫伯特　那我怎么敢？可是即使在一个皇帝的面前，我也敢保卫我的无罪的生命。

萨立斯伯雷　你是一个杀人的凶手。

赫伯特　不要用您自己的生命证实您的话，我不是杀人的凶手。谁说着和事实相反的话，他就是说谎。

彭勃洛克　把他碎尸万段！

庶子　我说，你们还是不要争吵吧。

萨立斯伯雷　站开，否则莫怪我的剑不生眼睛碰坏了你，福康勃立琪。

庶子　你还是去向魔鬼的身上碰吧，萨立斯伯雷。要是你向我蹙一蹙眉，抬一抬脚，或是逞着你的暴躁的脾气，给我一点儿侮辱，我就当场结果你的生命。赶快收好你的剑，否则我要把你和你那炙肉的铁刺一起剁个稀烂，让你以为魔鬼从地狱里出来了。

俾高特　你预备怎样呢，声名卓著的福康勃立琪？帮助一个恶人和凶手吗？

赫伯特　俾高特大人，我不是什么恶人凶手。

俾高特　谁杀死这位王子的？

赫伯特　我在不满一小时以前离开他，他还是好好的。我尊敬他，我爱他，为了他可爱的生命的夭亡，我要在哭泣中消耗我的残生。

萨立斯伯雷　不要相信他眼睛里这种狡猾的泪水，奸徒们是不会缺少这样的急泪的；他玩惯了这一套把戏，所以能够做得好像真是出于一颗深情而无罪的心中的滔滔的泪河一样。跟我去吧，你们这些从灵魂里痛恨屠场中的血腥气的人们，我已经为罪恶的臭气所窒息了。

俾高特　向伯雷出发，到法国太子那里去！

彭勃洛克　告诉国王，他可以到那里去打听我们的下落。

庶子　好一个世界！你知道这件好事是谁干的吗？假如果然是你把他杀死的，赫伯特，你的灵魂就要被打下地狱，即使上帝的最博大为怀的悲悯也不能使你超生了。

赫伯特　听我说，大人。

庶子　嘿！我告诉你吧，你要永坠地狱，什么都比不上你的黑暗，你比魔王路锡福还要罪加一等。你将要成为地狱里最丑的恶鬼，要是你果然杀死了这个孩子。

赫伯特　凭着我的灵魂起誓——

庶子　即使你对于这件无比残酷的行为不过表示了你的同意，你也没有得救的希望了。要是你缺少一根绳子，从蜘蛛肚子里抽出来的最细的蛛丝也可以把你绞死；一根灯芯草可以作为吊死你的梁木；要是你愿意投水的话，只要在汤匙里略微放一点水，就可以抵得过整个的大洋，把你这样一个恶人活活溺死。我对于你这个人很有点不放心呢。

赫伯特　要是我曾经布下阴谋，或是起意劫夺这美丽的躯壳里的温柔的生命，愿地狱里所有的酷刑都不足以惩罚我的罪恶。我离开他的时候，他还是好好的。

庶子　去，把他抱起来。我简直发呆了，在这遍地荆棘的多难的人世之上，我已经迷失我的路程。你把整个英国多么轻易地举了起来！全国的生命、公道和正义已经从这死了的王裔的躯壳里飞到天上去了。英国现在所剩下的，只有一个强大繁荣的国家的无主的权益，供有力者的争持攫夺。为了王权这一根啃剩的肉骨，蛮横的战争已经耸起它的愤怒的羽毛，当着和平的温柔的眼前大肆咆哮，外侮和内患同时并发，广大的混乱正在等候着霸占的威权的迅速崩溃，正像一只饿鸦注视着濒死的病兽一般。能够束紧腰带，拉住衣襟，冲过这场暴风雨的人是有福的。把这孩子抱着，赶快跟我见国王去。要干的事情多着呢，上天也在向这国土蹙紧它的眉头。

俾高特率侍从等进入，约翰王坐在椅中。

约翰王　哦，现在我的灵魂可以有一点儿回旋的余地了。它不愿从窗子里或是从门户里出去。在我的胸头是这样一个炎热的盛夏，把我的脏腑都一起炙成了灰。我是一张写在羊皮纸上的文书，受着这样烈火的烘焙，全身都皱缩而焦枯了。

亨利亲王　陛下御体觉得怎样？

约翰王　毒侵骨髓，病入膏肓，死了，被舍弃，被遗忘了。你们也没有一个人肯去叫冬天来，把他冰冷的手指探进我的喉中，或是让我的国内的江河流过我的火热的胸口，或是请求北方的寒风吻一吻我的焦躁的嘴唇，用寒冷给我一些安慰。我对你们并没有多大的要求，我只恳求一些寒冷的安慰，你们却这样吝啬无情，连这一点也拒绝了我。

亨利亲王　啊！但愿我的眼泪也有几分力量，能够解除您的痛苦。

约翰王　你眼泪中的盐质也是热的。在我的身体之内是一座地狱，那毒药就是狱中的魔鬼，对那不可救赎的罪恶的血液横加凌虐。

庶子上。

庶子　啊！我满心焦灼，恨不得插翅飞到陛下的跟前。

约翰王　啊，侄儿！你是来闭我的眼睛的。像一艘在生命海中航行的船只，我的心灵的缆索已经碎裂焚毁，只留着仅余的一线，维系着这残破的船身。等你向我报告过你的消息以后，它就要漂荡到不可知的地方去了。你所看见的眼前的我，那时候将要变成一堆朽骨，毁灭尽了它的君主的庄严。

庶子　法国太子正在准备向这儿进攻，天知道我们有些什么力量可以对付他。因为当我向有利的地形移动我的军队，在经过林肯沼地的时候，一夜之间一阵突然冲来的潮水把我大部分的人马都卷去了。

萨立斯伯雷　你把这些致命的消息送进了一只失去生命的耳中。我的陛下！我的主上！刚才还是一个堂堂的国王，现在已经变成这么一副模样。

亨利亲王　我也必须像他一样前进，像他一样停止我的行程。昔为君王，今为泥土，这世上还有什么保障，什么希望，什么凭借？

庶子　那么就在那里安葬吧。愿殿下继承先王的遗统，肩负祖国的光荣，永享无穷的洪福！我用最卑恭的诚意跪在您的足前，向您掬献我的不变的忠勤和永远的臣服。

萨立斯伯雷　我们也敬向殿下呈献同样的忠诚，永远不让它沾上丝毫污点。

亨利亲王　我有一个仁爱的灵魂，要向你们表示它的感谢，可是除了流泪以外，不知道还有什么其他的方式。

庶子　啊！让我们仅仅把应有的悲伤付给这时代吧，因为它早就收受过我们的哀痛了。我们的英格兰从来不曾，也永远不会屈服在一个征服者的骄傲的足前，除非它先用自己的手把自己伤害。现在它的这些儿子们已经回到祖国的怀抱里，尽管全世界都是我们的敌人，向我们三面进攻，我们也可以击退他们。只要英格兰对它自己尽忠，天大的灾祸都不能震撼我们的心胸。